JESUS THE MESSIAH

JESUS
THE MESSIAH

AN ABRIDGED EDITION
OF
THE LIFE AND TIMES OF JESUS THE MESSIAH

BY

ALFRED EDERSHEIM

Wm. B. Eerdmans Publishing Company
Grand Rapids, Michigan

This edition published by
special arrangement with
LONGMANS, GREEN & COMPANY
New York and London

ISBN 0-8028-8131-9

Reprinted, May 1985

PHOTOLITHOPRINTED BY EERDMANS PRINTING COMPANY
GRAND RAPIDS, MICHIGAN, UNITED STATES OF AMERICA

PREFACE

WHEN the author of the *Life and Times of Jesus the Messiah* was taken away in the spring of this year from the labours and studies which he loved, he had already had under consideration the expediency of publishing an abridged edition of his larger work, such as should throw it open to a wider circle of readers. That abridgment has now been carried out, it is hoped, upon the lines which he would have desired.

Those who have attempted any such task will be aware how difficult it is to execute satisfactorily. When a replica is made of a great picture, its scale may be diminished without serious loss. The proportions are preserved; the contents are the same; it is only that they are indicated rather more slightly than before. The reduction takes place evenly over the whole surface. It is otherwise with a great literary work. Here reduction involves omission; and omission at once alters the proportions. It is not only that the logical connection is broken and that new links have to be supplied: the difficulties arising from this cause are perhaps less than might be supposed: but the whole texture of the work is disturbed. A style which was natural upon one scale, has to be adapted to another; and that by an external process which lacks the ease and freedom of first composition. Dr. Edersheim's work was planned emphatically upon a large scale. It had a certain breadth and richness of colouring which helped to carry off its profusion of detail. When the details were curtailed, this too had to be toned down. What could be done by omitting a phrase here, and a sentence there, has been done ; and upon this much anxious care and thought have been expended.

As to the matter of the omissions, this was to some extent prescribed by the nature of the case. The broad framework of narrative was of course indispensable ; and along with this every effort has been made to save as much of the illustrative accessories as the size of the volume permitted. It is, however, greatly to be regretted that so much should have been lost which constituted the peculiar and unrivalled excellence of the larger book. Our generation has seen a number of attempts—some in their way of great merit—to reproduce the externals and surroundings of the Life and Ministry of Christ. But it will, I think, be admitted by the general consent of scholars that in this respect Dr. Edersheim surpassed his predecessors. No one else has possessed such a profound and masterly knowledge of the whole Jewish background to the picture presented in the Gospels—not merely of the archæology, which is something, but of the essential characteristics of Jewish thought and feeling, which is far more. It was inevitable that heavy sacrifices should be made here. All-important as these details are to the student, the ordinary reader would be simply oppressed and overpowered by them. For such readers the abridged edition is intended ; but it is hoped that not a few may be encouraged to go on to the abundant stores of the larger book.

I am fain to believe that a more catholic spirit is growing than prevailed a short time ago, when the first thing a critic did was to ascertain to what school or party a book belonged, and then to praise or condemn it accordingly. This has been too much the case with those who aspired to be in the forefront of opinion. To label a book ' critical' or ' uncritical' was enough to determine its fate quite apart from its solid value. Dr. Edersheim's book—full as it was of information on the very points on which a scholar would desire it—was not one which could be called exactly ' critical.' It did not, for instance, presuppose any theory as to the origin and composition of the Gospels. It was not that the author was indifferent upon the subject: he had himself made independent studies upon it, which with time might have been matured and published : but he deliberately postponed the critical process until after his book was written. It was quite as well that it should be so ; as well to start with an absence of theory, as e.g. that Keim—to take the case of a very able and conscientious writer—should start from a theory which is pretty certainly untenable. We are learning by degrees to leave first principles in suspense until we know better what are the facts which have to be accounted for.

A high authority has said that whoever thinks himself capable of rewriting the story of the Gospels does not understand them. And this is indeed, in a sense, most true. The Gospels have filled for eighteen centuries a place which nothing else will ever fill. But that does not exclude the attempts which have been and are being made so to present the substance of their story as to set it in full relation at once to its own times and to ours. This has not yet been done finally. And if it ever should be done it will, I believe, be allowed that few have contributed more towards the culmination and crown of many efforts than he of whom all that is mortal now rests in peace by the waters of the Mediterranean. With serious purpose,

and after long and arduous preparation, he had put his
hand to a work which it was granted to him to prosecute
far, but not to finish—for the *Life and Times* was to have
been followed by a *Life of St. Paul*.   He who

Doth not need
Either man's work or His own gifts

gently took the pen from his grasp.   And the present
gleaning from the greatest of its many products is a tribute
of filial piety.   My own share in the work has been quite
subordinate : but as I have gone over the ground after the
preliminary abridgment had been made, and as I have
been freely consulted in cases of doubt, I gladly accept the
responsibility which falls to me.   Nor can I bring these
few words of preface to a close without acknowledging
the valuable assistance we have received from Mr. Norton
Longman, whom the author always regarded as among
the best and most trusted of his friends.

W. SANDAY.

OXFORD : *Oct.* 3, 1889.

CONTENTS

———◆◇◆———

JESUS THE MESSIAH

JESUS THE MESSIAH

---◆◇◆---

CHAPTER I

THE ANNUNCIATION OF ST. JOHN THE BAPTIST.

(St. Luke i. 5-25.)

IT was the time of the Morning Sacrifice.[1] As the massive
Temple gates slowly swung on their hinges, a threefold
blast from the silver trumpets of the Priests seemed to
waken the City to the life of another day.

Already the dawn, for which the Priest on the highest
pinnacle of the Temple had watched, to give the signal for
beginning the services of the day, had shot its brightness
far away to Hebron and beyond. Within the courts below
all had long been busy. At some time previously, unknown to those who waited for the morning, the superintending Priest had summoned to their sacred functions
those who had 'washed,' according to the ordinance.
There must have been each day about fifty priests on duty.
Such of them as were ready now divided into two parties,
to make inspection of the Temple courts by torchlight.
Presently they met, and trooped to the well-known Hall
of Hewn Polished Stones. The ministry for the day was
there apportioned. To prevent the disputes of carnal zeal,
the 'lot' was to assign to each his function. Four times

---

[1] For a description of the details of that service, see 'The Temple
and its Services,' &c.

was it resorted to: twice before, and twice after the
Temple gates were opened.   The first act of their ministry
had to be done in the grey dawn, by the fitful red light
that glowed on the altar of burnt-offering, ere the priests
had stirred it into fresh flame.   It was scarcely daybreak,
when a second time they met for the 'lot,' which designated those who were to take part in the sacrifice itself,
and who were to trim the golden candlestick, and make
ready the altar of incense within the Holy Place.   And
now nothing remained before the admission of worshippers
but to bring out the lamb, once again to make sure of its
fitness for sacrifice, to water it from a golden bowl, and
then to lay it in mystic fashion—as tradition described the
binding of Isaac—on the north side of the altar, with its
face to the west.

All, priests and laity, were present as the Priest,
standing on the east side of the altar, from a golden bowl
sprinkled with sacrificial blood two sides of the altar, below
the red line which marked the difference between ordinary
sacrifices and those that were to be wholly consumed.
While the sacrifice was prepared for the altar, the priests,
whose lot it was, had made ready all within the Holy
Place, where the most solemn part of the day's service was
to take place—that of offering the incense, which symbolised Israel's accepted prayers.   Again was the lot (the
third) cast to indicate him, who was to be honoured with
this highest mediatorial act.   Only once in a lifetime
might any one enjoy that privilege.   It was fitting that,
as the custom was, such lot should be preceded by prayer
and confession of their faith on the part of the assembled
priests.

It was the first week in October 748 A.U.C., that is, in
the sixth year before our present era, when 'the course of
Abia'—the eighth in the original arrangement of the
weekly service—was on duty in the Temple.

In the group ranged that autumn morning around the
superintending Priest was one, on whom at least sixty
winters had fallen.   But never during these many years
had he been honoured with the office of incensing.   Yet

the venerable figure of Zacharias must have been well known in the Temple. For each course was twice a year on ministry, and, unlike the Levites, the priests were not disqualified by age, but only by infirmity. In many respects he seemed different from those around. His home was not in either of the great priest-centres—the Ophel-quarter in Jerusalem, nor in Jericho—but in some small town in those uplands, south of Jerusalem : the historic 'hill-country of Judæa.' And yet he might have claimed distinction. To be a priest, and married to the daughter of a priest, was supposed to convey twofold honour. That he was surrounded by relatives and friends, and that he was well known and respected throughout his district, appears incidentally from the narrative.[a] For Zacharias and Elisabeth, his wife, were truly 'righteous,' in the sense of walking 'blamelessly,' alike in those commandments which were specially binding on Israel, and in those statutes that were of universal bearing on mankind.

[a] St. Luke i. 58, 59, 61, 65, 66

Yet Elisabeth was childless. For many a year this must have been the burden of Zacharias' prayer ; the burden also of reproach, which Elisabeth seemed always to carry with her.

On that bright autumn morning in the Temple, however, no such thoughts would disturb Zacharias. The lot had marked him for incensing, and every thought must have centred on what was before him. First, he had to choose two of his special friends or relatives, to assist in his sacred service. Their duties were comparatively simple. One reverently removed what had been left on the altar from the previous evening's service; then, worshipping, retired backwards. The second assistant now advanced, and, having spread to the utmost verge of the golden altar the live coals taken from that of burnt-offering, worshipped and retired. Meanwhile the sound of the 'organ,' heard to the most distant parts of the Temple, and, according to tradition, far beyond its precincts, had summoned priests, Levites, and people to prepare for whatever service or duty was before them. But the celebrant Priest, bearing

the golden censer, stood alone within the Holy Place, lit
by the sheen of the seven-branched candlestick. Before
him, somewhat farther away, towards the heavy Veil that
hung before the Holy of Holies, was the golden altar of
incense, on which the red coals glowed. To his right (the
left of the altar—that is, on the north side) was the table
of shewbread ; to his left, on the right or south side of the
altar, was the golden candlestick. And still he waited, as
instructed to do, till a special signal indicated that the
moment had come to spread the incense on the altar, as
near as possible to the Holy of Holies. Priests and people
had reverently withdrawn from the neighbourhood of the
altar, and were prostrate before the Lord, offering unspoken
worship. Zacharias waited, until he saw the incense kind-
ling. Then he also would have ' bowed down in worship,'
and reverently withdrawn, had not a wondrous sight
arrested his steps.

On the right (or south) side of the altar, between it
and the golden candlestick, stood what he could not but
recognise as an Angelic form. Never, indeed, had even
tradition reported such a vision to an ordinary Priest in
the act of incensing. The two supernatural apparitions
recorded—one of an Angel each year of the Pontificate of
Simon the Just ; the other in that blasphemous account of
the vision of the Almighty by Ishmael, the son of Elisha,
and of the conversation which then ensued—had both been
vouchsafed to High-Priests, and on the Day of Atonement.
Still, there was always uneasiness among the people as any
mortal approached the immediate Presence of God, and
every delay in his return seemed ominous. No wonder,
then, that Zacharias ' was troubled, and fear fell on
him.'

It was from this state of semi-consciousness that the
Angel first wakened Zacharias with the remembrance of
life-long prayers and hopes, which had now passed into
the background of his being, and then suddenly startled
him by the promise of their realisation. But that Child of
so many prayers, who was to bear the significant name of
John (Jehochanan, or Jochanan), 'the Lord is gracious,'

was to be the source of joy and gladness to a far wider circle than that of the family. The Child was to be great before the Lord; not only an ordinary, but a life-Nazarite,[1] as Samson and Samuel of old had been. Like them, he was not to consecrate himself, but from the inception of life wholly to belong to God, for His work. And, greater than either of these representatives of the symbolical import of Nazarism, he would combine the twofold meaning of their mission—outward and inward might in God, only in a higher and more spiritual sense. For this life-work he would be filled with the Holy Ghost, from the moment life woke within him. Then, as another Samson, would he, in the strength of God, lift the axe to each tree to be felled, and, like another Samuel, turn many of the children of Israel to the Lord their God. Nay, combining these two missions, as did Elijah on Mount Carmel, he should, in accordance with prophecy,[a] precede the Messianic manifestation, and, not indeed in the person or form, but in the spirit and power of Elijah, accomplish the typical meaning of his mission. Thus would this new Elijah ' make ready for the Lord a people prepared.'

^a Mal. iii. 1

If the apparition of the Angel, in that place, and at that time, had overwhelmed the aged priest, the words which he heard must have filled him with such bewilderment, that for the moment he scarcely realised their meaning. One idea alone, which had struck its roots so long in his consciousness, stood out: A son. And so it was the obvious doubt, that would suggest itself, which first fell from his lips, as he asked for some pledge or confirmation of what he had heard.

He that would not speak the praises of God, but asked a sign, received it. His dumbness was a sign—though the sign, as it were the dumb child of the prayer of unbelief, was its punishment also. And yet a sign in another sense also—a sign to the waiting multitude in the Temple; a sign to Elisabeth; to all who knew Zacharias in the

---

[1] On the different classes of Nazarites, see 'The Temple, &c.,' pp. 322–331.

hill-country; and to the Priest himself, during those nine months of retirement and inward solitude; a sign also that would kindle into fiery flame in the day when God should loosen his tongue.

A period of unusual length had passed, since the signal for incensing had been given. The prayers of the people had been offered, and their anxious gaze was directed towards the Holy Place. At last Zacharias emerged to take his stand on the top of the steps which led from the Porch to the Court of the Priests, waiting to lead in the priestly benediction[a] that preceded the daily meat-offering and the chant of the Psalms of praise, accompanied with joyous sound of music, as the drink-offering was poured out. But already the sign of Zacharias was to be a sign to all the people. The pieces of the sacrifices had been ranged in due order on the altar of burnt-offering; the Priests stood on the steps to the porch, and the people were in waiting. Zacharias essayed to speak the words of benediction, unconscious that the stroke had fallen. But the people knew it by his silence, that he had seen a vision in the Temple. Yet as he stood helpless, trying by signs to indicate it to the awestruck assembly, he remained dumb.

[a] Numb. vi. 24-26

Wondering, they had dispersed, people and Priests—some to Ophel, some to Jericho, some to their quiet dwellings in the country. But God fulfilled the word which He had spoken by His Angel.

CHAPTER II.

THE ANNUNCIATION OF JESUS THE MESSIAH, AND THE BIRTH OF HIS FORERUNNER.

(St. Matt. i.; St. Luke i. 26-80.)

THE Galilee of the time of Jesus was not only of the richest fertility, cultivated to the utmost, and thickly covered with populous towns and villages, but the centre of every known industry, and the busy road of the world's commerce.

Nor was it otherwise in Nazareth. The great caravan-route which led from Acco on the sea to Damascus divided at its commencement into three roads, one of which passed through Nazareth. Men of all nations, busy with another life than that of Israel, would appear in its streets ; and through them thoughts, associations, and hopes connected with the great outside world be stirred. But, on the other hand, Nazareth was also one of the great centres of Jewish Temple-life. The Priesthood was divided into twenty-four ' courses,' each of which, in turn, ministered in the Temple. The Priests of the ' course ' which was to be on duty always gathered in certain towns, whence they went up in company to Jerusalem, while those of their number who were unable to go spent the week in fasting and prayer. Now Nazareth was one of these Priest-centres. Thus, to take the wider view, a double symbolic significance attached to Nazareth, since through it passed alike those who carried on the traffic of the world, and those who ministered in the Temple.

We may take it, that the people of Nazareth were like those of other little towns similarly circumstanced : with all the peculiarities of the impulsive, straight-spoken, hot-blooded, brave, intensely national Galileans; with the deeper feelings and almost instinctive habits of thought and life, which were the outcome of long centuries of Old Testament training; but also with the petty interests and jealousies of such places, and with all the ceremonialism and punctilious self-assertion of Orientals. The cast of Judaism prevalent in Nazareth would, of course, be the same as in Galilee generally. We know, that there were marked divergences from the observances in that strong-hold of Rabbinism, Judæa—indicating greater simplicity and freedom from the constant intrusion of traditional ordinances. The purity of betrothal in Galilee was less likely to be sullied, and weddings were more simple than in Judæa—without the dubious institution of groomsmen, or ' friends of the bridegroom. [a]

ᵃ St. John iii. 29

The bride was chosen, not as in Judæa, where money was too often the motive, but as in Jerusalem, with chief regard to ' a fair degree ; ' and widows were (as in Jerusalem) more tenderly cared for.

Whatever view may be taken of the genealogies in the Gospels according to St. Matthew and St. Luke, there can be no question that both Joseph and Mary were of the royal lineage of David.   Most probably the two were nearly related, while Mary could also claim kinship with the Priesthood, being, no doubt on her mother's side, a ' blood-relative ' of Elisabeth, the Priest-wife of Zacharias.[a]   Even this seems to imply that Mary's family must shortly before have held higher rank, for only with such did custom sanction any alliance on the part of Priests.   But at the time of their betrothal, alike Joseph and Mary were extremely poor, as appears—not indeed from his being a carpenter, since a trade was regarded as almost a religious duty—but from the offering at the presentation of Jesus in the Temple.[b]   Accordingly, their betrothal must have been of the simplest, and the dowry settled the smallest possible.[1]   From that moment Mary was the betrothed wife of Joseph ; their relationship as sacred as if they had already been wedded.   Any breach of it would be treated as adultery ; nor could the bond be dissolved except, as after marriage, by regular divorce.   Yet months might intervene between the betrothal and marriage.

Five months of Elisabeth's sacred retirement had passed, when a strange messenger brought its first tidings to her kinswoman in far-off Galilee.   It was not in the solemn grandeur of the Temple, between the golden altar of incense and the seven-branched candlestick, that the Angel Gabriel now appeared, but in the privacy of a humble home at Nazareth.   And, although the awe of the Supernatural must unconsciously have fallen upon her, it was not so much the sudden appearance of the mysterious

[a] St. Luke i. 36

[b] St. Luke ii. 24

---

[1] Comp. 'Sketches of Jewish Social Life in the Days of Christ,' pp. 143–149. Also the article on ' Marriage ' in *Cassell's* Bible-Educator, vol. iv. pp. 267–270.

stranger in her retirement that startled the maiden, as the
words of his greeting, implying unthought blessing. The
'Peace to thee' was, indeed, the well-known salutation,
while the words 'The Lord is with thee' might waken
remembrance of the Angelic call to great deliverance
^{a Judg. vi.} in the past.^a But this designation of 'highly
¹² favoured' came upon her with bewildering sur-
prise, perhaps not so much from its contrast to the humbleness of her estate, as from the self-unconscious humility of
her heart. Accordingly, it is this story of special 'favour,'
or grace, which the Angel traces in rapid outline, from
the conception of the Virgin-Mother to the distinctive,
Divinely-given Name, symbolic of the meaning of His
coming; His absolute greatness; His acknowledgment as
the Son of God; and the fulfilment in Him of the great
Davidic hope, with its never-ceasing royalty, and its bound-
less Kingdom.

In all this, however marvellous, there could be nothing
strange to those who cherished in their hearts Israel's
great hope. Nor was there anything strange even in the
naming of the yet unconceived Child. It sounds like a
saying current among the people of old, this of the Rabbis,
concerning the six whose names were given before their
birth: Isaac, Ishmael, Moses, Solomon, Josiah, and 'the
Name of the Messiah, Whom may the Holy One, blessed
be His Name, bring quickly, in our days!'

Thus, on the supposition of the readiness of her believing heart there would have been nothing that needed
further light than the *how* of her own connection with the
glorious announcement. And the words, which she spake,
were not of trembling doubt, but rather those of enquiry,
for the further guidance of a willing self-surrender. And
now the Angel unfolded yet further promise of Divine
favour, and so deepened her humility. For the idea of
the activity of the Holy Ghost in all great events was
quite familiar to Israel at the time, even though the Indi-
viduation of the Holy Ghost may not have been fully
apprehended. Only, they expected such influences to rest
exclusively upon those who were either mighty, or rich, or

wise. And of this twofold manifestation of miraculous 'favour'—that she, and as a Virgin, should be its sub-ject—Gabriel, 'the might of God,' gave this unasked sign, in what had happened to her kinswoman Elisabeth.

The sign was at the same time a direction. The first, but also the ever-deepening desire in the heart of Mary, when the Angel left her, must have been to be away from Nazareth, and for the relief of opening her heart to a woman, in all things like-minded, who perhaps might speak blessed words to her. It is only what we would have expected, that ' with haste' she should have resorted to her kinswoman.

It could have been no ordinary welcome that would greet the Virgin-Mother. Elisabeth must have learnt from her husband the destiny of their son, and hence the near Advent of the Messiah. But she could not have known either when, or of whom He would be born. When, by a sign not quite strange to Jewish expectancy, she recognised in her near kinswoman the Mother of her Lord, her salutation was that of a mother to a mother—the mother of the 'preparer' to the mother of Him for Whom he would prepare.

Three months had passed, and now the Virgin-Mother must return to Nazareth. Soon Elisabeth's neighbours and kinsfolk would gather with sympathetic joy around a home which, as they thought, had experienced unexpected mercy. But Mary must not be exposed to the publicity of such meetings. However conscious of what had led to her condition, it must have been as the first sharp pang of the sword which was to pierce her soul, when she told it all to her betrothed. For only a direct Divine communi-cation could have chased all questioning from his heart, and given him that assurance, which was needful in the future history of the Messiah. Brief as the narrative is, we can read in the ' thoughts' of Joseph the anxious con-tending of feelings, the scarcely established, and yet delayed, resolve to ' put her away,' which could only be done by regular divorce; this one determination only standing out clearly, that, if it must be, her letter of divorce shall be handed to her privately, only in the presence of two witnesses. The humble *T'saddiq* of Nazareth would not willingly make of her ' a public exhibition of shame.'

The assurance, which Joseph could scarcely dare to hope for, was miraculously conveyed to him in a dream-vision. All would now be clear; even the terms in which he was addressed (' thou son of David '), so utterly unusual in ordinary circumstances, would prepare him for the Angel's message. The naming of the unborn Messiah would accord with popular notions ; the symbolism of such a name was deeply rooted in Jewish belief; while the explanation of *Jehoshua* or *Jeshua* (*Jesus*), as He Who would save His people (primarily, as he would understand it, Israel) from their sins, described at least one generally expected aspect of His Mission.

The fact that such an announcement came to him in a dream, would dispose Joseph all the more readily to receive it. ' A good dream ' was one of the three things popularly regarded as marks of God's favour. Thus Divinely set at rest, Joseph could no longer hesitate. The highest duty towards the Virgin-Mother and the unborn Jesus demanded an immediate marriage, which would afford not only outward, but moral protection to both.

Meanwhile the long-looked-for event had taken place in the home of Zacharias. No domestic solemnity was so important or so joyous as that in which, by circumcision, the child had, as it were, laid upon it the yoke of the Law, with all of duty and privilege which this implied. It was, so tradition has it, as if the father had acted sacrificially as High-Priest, offering his child to God in gratitude and love ; and it symbolised this deeper moral truth, that man must by his own act complete what God had first instituted. We can scarcely be mistaken in supposing, that then, as now, a benediction was spoken before circumcision, and that the ceremony closed with the usual grace over the cup of wine, when the child received his name in a prayer, that probably did not much differ from this at present in use : ' Our God, and the God of our fathers, raise up this child to his father and mother, and let his name be called in Israel Zacharias, the son of Zacharias.' The prayer closed with the hope that the child might grow up, and successfully 'attain to the Torah, the marriage-baldachino, and good works.'

Of all this Zacharias was, though a deeply interested, yet a deaf and dumb [1] witness. This only had he noticed, that, in the benediction in which the child's name was inserted, the mother had interrupted the prayer. Without explaining her reason, she insisted that his name should not be that of his aged father, as in the peculiar circumstances might have been expected, but John (*Jochanan*). A reference to the father only deepened the general astonishment, when he also gave the same name. But this was not the sole cause for marvel. For, forthwith the tongue of the dumb was loosed, and he, who could not utter the name of the child, now burst into praise of the name of the Lord. His last words had been those of unbelief, his first were those of praise; his last words had been a question of doubt, his first were a hymn of assurance. This hymn of the Priest closely follows, and, if the expression be allowable, spiritualises a great part of the most ancient Jewish prayer : the so-called Eighteen Benedictions. Opening with the common form of blessing, his hymn struck, one by one, the deepest chords of that prayer.

But far and wide, as these marvellous tidings spread throughout the hill-country of Judæa, fear fell on all—the fear also of a nameless hope : ' What then shall this Child be ? For the Hand of the Lord also was with Him !'

---

[1] From St. Luke i. 62 we gather that Zacharias was what the Rabbis understood by a Hebrew term signifying one deaf as well as dumb. Accordingly, he was communicated with by signs.

CHAPTER III.

THE NATIVITY OF JESUS THE MESSIAH.

(St. Matt. i. 25; St. Luke ii. 1-20.)

To Bethlehem as the birthplace of Messiah, not only Old
Testament prediction,[a] but the testimony of Rabbinic teaching, unhesitatingly pointed. Yet nothing could be imagined more directly contrary to Jewish
thoughts— and hence nothing less likely to suggest itself
to Jewish invention—than the circumstances which, according to the Gospel-narrative, brought about the birth of the
Messiah in Bethlehem. A counting of the people, or Census; and that Census taken at the bidding of a heathen
Emperor, and executed by one so universally hated as
Herod, would represent the *ne plus ultra* of all that was
most repugnant to Jewish feeling.

a Micah v. 2

That the Emperor Augustus made registers of the
Roman Empire, and of subject and tributary states, is
now generally admitted. This registration—for the purpose
of future taxation—would also embrace Palestine. Even if
no actual order to that effect had been issued during the
life-time of Herod, we can understand that he would deem
it most expedient, in view of the probable excitement which
a heathen census would cause in Palestine, to take steps
for making a registration rather according to the Jewish
than the Roman manner.

According to the Roman law, all country-people were
to be registered in their ' own city '—meaning thereby the
town to which the village or place, where they were born,
was attached. In so doing, the ' house and lineage ' of
each were marked. According to the Jewish mode of
registration, the people would have been enrolled according to *tribes, families* or clans, and the *house* of their fathers.
But as the ten tribes had not returned to Palestine, this
could only take place to a very limited extent, while it

would be easy for each to be registered in 'his own city.'
In the case of Joseph and Mary, whose descent from David
was not only known, but where, for the sake of the unborn
Messiah, it was most important that this should be distinctly noted, it was natural that, in accordance with
Jewish law, they should have gone to Bethlehem.   Perhaps
also, for many reasons which will readily suggest themselves, Joseph and Mary might be glad to leave Nazareth,
and seek, if possible, a home in Bethlehem.   Indeed, so
strong was this feeling, that it afterwards required special
Divine direction to induce Joseph to relinquish this chosen
ᵃ St. Matt.   place of residence, and to return into Galilee.ᵃ
ii. 22   In these circumstances, Mary, now the 'wife' of
Joseph, though standing to him only in the actual relation-
ᵇ St. Luke ii.   ship of 'betrothed,' ᵇ would, of course, accompany
5.   her husband to Bethlehem.

The short winter's day was probably closing in, as the
two travellers from Nazareth, bringing with them the
few necessaries of a poor Eastern household, neared their
journey's end.   Only in the East would the most absolute
simplicity be possible, and yet neither it, nor the poverty
from which it sprang, necessarily imply even the slightest
taint of social inferiority.   The way had been long and
weary—at the very least, three days' journey from Galilee.
Most probably it would have been by that route so commonly followed, from a desire to avoid Samaria, along the
eastern banks of the Jordan, and by the fords near
Jericho.

The little town of Bethlehem was crowded with those
who had come from all the outlying district to register
their names.   The very inn was filled, and the only avail-
able space was where ordinarily the cattle were stabled.
Bearing in mind the simple habits of the East, this scarcely
implies what it would in the West; and perhaps the
seclusion and privacy from the noisy, chattering crowd,
which thronged the khan, would be all the more welcome.
Scanty as these particulars are, even thus much is gathered
rather by inference than from the narrative itself.   Thus
early in this history does the absence of details, which

increases as we proceed, remind us, that the Gospels were not intended to furnish a biography of Jesus, nor even the materials for it; but had only this twofold object: that those who read them 'might believe that Jesus is the Christ, the Son of God,' and that believing they ' might have life

^aSt. John through His Name.' ^a The Christian heart and
xx. 31; imagination, indeed, long to be able to localise
comp.
St. Luke i. 4 the scene and linger with fond reverence over that Cave, which is now covered by 'the Church of the Nativity.' It seems likely that this, to which the most venerable tradition points, was the sacred spot of the world's greatest event. But certainty we have not. As to all that passed in the seclusion of that ' stable ' the Gospel-narrative is silent. This only is told, that then and there the Virgin-Mother ' brought forth her first-born Son, and wrapped him in swaddling clothes, and laid him in a manger.'

But as we pass from the sacred gloom of the cave out into the night, its loneliness is peopled, and its silence made vocal from heaven. Jewish tradition may here prove both illustrative and helpful. That the Messiah was to be born in Bethlehem, was a settled conviction. Equally so was the belief, that He was to be revealed from *Migdal Eder*, ' the tower of the flock.' This *Migdal Eder* was not the watch-tower for the ordinary flocks which pastured on the barren sheep-ground beyond Bethlehem, but lay close to the town, on the road to Jerusalem. A passage in the Mishnah leads to the conclusion, that the flocks, which pastured there, were destined for Temple-sacrifices, and, accordingly, that the shepherds, who watched over them, were not ordinary shepherds. The latter were under the ban of Rabbinism, on account of their necessary isolation from religious ordinances, and their manner of life, which rendered strict legal observance unlikely, if not absolutely impossible. The same Mishnic passage also leads us to infer, that these flocks lay out all the year round, since they are spoken of as in the fields thirty days before the Passover—that is, in the month of February, when in Palestine the average rainfall is nearly greatest.

It was, then, on that 'wintry night' of the 25th of December, that shepherds watched the flocks destined for sacrificial services, in the very place consecrated by tradition as that where the Messiah was to be first revealed. Of a sudden came the long-delayed, unthought-of announcement: an Angel stood before their dazzled eyes, while the outstreaming glory of the Lord seemed to enwrap them, as in a mantle of light. Surprise, awe, fear would be hushed into calm and expectancy, as from the Angel they heard that what they saw boded not judgment, but ushered in to waiting Israel the great joy of those good tidings which he brought: that the long-promised Saviour, Messiah, Lord, was born in the City of David, and that they themselves might go and see, and recognise Him by the humbleness of the circumstances surrounding His Nativity.

It was as if attendant angels had only waited the signal. As, when the sacrifice was laid on the altar the Temple-music burst forth in three sections, each marked by the blast of the Priests' silver trumpets, so, when the Herald-Angel had spoken, a multitude of heaven's host stood forth to hymn the good tidings he had brought. What they sang was but the reflex of what had been announced :—

> Glory to God in the highest—
> And upon earth peace—
> Among men good pleasure !

Only once before had the words of Angels' hymn fallen upon mortals' ears, when, to Isaiah's rapt vision, Heaven's high Temple had opened, and the glory of Jehovah swept its courts, almost breaking down the trembling posts that bore its boundary gates. Now the same glory enwrapt the shepherds on Bethlehem's plains. Then the Angels' hymn had heralded the announcement of the Kingdom coming; now that of the King come. Then it had been the *Tris-Hagion* of prophetic anticipation; now that of Evangelic fulfilment.

The hymn had ceased ; the light faded out of the sky ; and the shepherds were alone. But the Angelic message remained with them; and the sign, which was to guide them to the Infant Christ, lighted their rapid way up the terraced height to where, at the entering of Bethlehem, the lamp swinging over the hostelry directed them to the strangers of the house of David, who had come from Nazareth. There they found, perhaps not what they had expected, but as they had been told. The holy group only consisted of the Virgin-Mother, the carpenter of Nazareth, and the Babe laid in the manger. What further passed we know not, save that having seen it for themselves the shepherds told what had been spoken to them about this Child, to all around—in the ' stable,' in the fields, probably also in the Temple, to which they would bring their flocks, thereby preparing the minds of a Simeon, of an Anna, and of all them that looked for salvation in Israel.

CHAPTER IV.

THE PURIFICATION OF THE VIRGIN AND THE PRESENTATION IN THE TEMPLE.

(St. Luke ii. 21–38.)

FOREMOST amongst those who, wondering, had heard what the shepherds told, was she whom most it concerned: the Mother of Jesus.

At the very outset of this history, and increasingly in its course, the question meets us, how, if the Angelic message to the Virgin was a reality, and her motherhood so supernatural, she could have been apparently so ignorant of what was to come—nay, so often have even misunderstood it? Might we not have expected, that the Virgin-Mother from the inception of this Child's life would have realised that He was truly the Son of God? The question, like so many others, requires only to be clearly stated, to find its emphatic answer. For, had it been so, His history, His human life, of which every step is of such importance to mankind, would not have been possible. Apart from

C

all thoughts of the deeper necessity, both as regarded His Mission and the salvation of the world, of a true human development of gradual consciousness and personal life, Christ could not, in any real sense, have been subject to His Parents, if they had fully understood that He was Divine; nor could He, in that case, have been watched, as He 'grew in wisdom and in favour with God and men.' Such knowledge would have broken the bond of His Humanity to ours, by severing that which bound Him as a child to His mother. We could not have become His brethren, had He not been truly the Virgin's Son. The mystery of the Incarnation would have been needless and fruitless, had His Humanity not been subject to all its right and ordinary conditions. In short, one, and that the distinctive New Testament, element in our salvation would have been taken away. At the beginning of His life He would have anticipated the lessons of its end— nay, not those of His Death only, but of His Resurrection and Ascension, and of the coming of the Holy Ghost.

In all this we have only considered the earthward, not the heavenward, aspect of His life. The latter, though very real, lies beyond our present horizon. Not so the question as to the development of the Virgin-Mother's spiritual knowledge. Assuming her to have occupied the standpoint of Jewish Messianic expectancy, and remember- ing also that she was so 'highly favoured' of God, still there was not as yet anything, nor could there be for many years, to lead her beyond what might be called the utmost height of Jewish belief. On the contrary, there was much connected with His true Humanity to keep her back.

Thus it was, that every event connected with the Messianic manifestation of Jesus would come to the Virgin-Mother as a new surprise. Each event, as it took place, stood isolated in her mind, as something quite by itself. She knew the beginning, and she knew the end; but she knew not the path which led from the one to the other; and each step in it was a new revelation. And it was natural and well that it should be so. For, thus only could she truly, because self-unconsciously, as a Jewish woman and mother, fulfil all the requirements of the Law, alike as regarded herself and her Child.

The first of these was Circumcision, representing voluntary subjection to the conditions of the Law, and acceptance of the obligations, but also of the privileges, of the Covenant between God and Abraham and his seed. The ceremony took place, as in all ordinary circumstances, on the eighth day, when the Child received the Angel-given name *Jeshua* (Jesus). Two other legal ordinances still remained to be observed. The firstborn son of every household was, according to the Law, to be 'redeemed' of the priest at the price of five shekels of the Sanctuary.[a] The earliest period of presentation was thirty-one days after birth, so as to make the legal month quite complete. The child must have been the firstborn of his mother; neither father nor mother must be of Levitic descent; and the child must be free from all such bodily blemishes as would have disqualified him for the priesthood—or, as it was expressed: 'the firstborn for the priesthood.' It was a thing much dreaded, that the child should die before his redemption; but if his father died in the interval, the child had to redeem himself when of age. The value of the 'redemption-money' would amount to about ten or twelve shillings. The redemption could be made from any priest, and attendance in the Temple was not requisite. It was otherwise with 'the purification' of the mother.[b] The Rabbinic law fixed this at forty-one days after the birth of a son, and eighty-one after that of a daughter, so as to make the Biblical terms quite complete. But it might take place any time later—notably, when attendance on any of the great feasts brought a family to Jerusalem. Indeed, the woman was not required to be personally present at all, when her offering was provided for—say, by the representatives of the laity, who daily took part in the services for the various districts from which they came. But mothers who were within convenient distance of the Temple, and especially the more earnest among them, would naturally attend personally in

[a] Numb. xviii. 16

[b] Lev. xii.

the Temple; and in such cases, when practicable, the redemption of the firstborn, and the purification of his mother, would be combined. Such was undoubtedly the case with the Virgin-Mother and her Son.

For this twofold purpose the Holy Family went up to the Temple, when the prescribed days were completed. The ceremony at the redemption of a firstborn son was, no doubt, more simple than that at present in use. It consisted of the formal presentation of the child to the priest, accompanied by two short 'benedictions'—the one for the law of redemption, the other for the gift of a firstborn son, after which the redemption-money was paid.

As regards the rite at the purification of the mother, the scantiness of information has led to serious misstatements. Any comparison with our modern 'churching' of women is inapplicable, since the latter consists of thanksgiving, and the former primarily of a sin-offering for the Levitical defilement symbolically attaching to the beginning of life, and a burnt-offering, that marked the restoration of communion with God. Besides, as already stated, the sacrifice for purification might be brought in the absence of the mother. The service simply consisted of the statutory sacrifice. This was what, in ecclesiastical language, was termed an offering, 'ascending and descending,' that is: according to the means of the offerer. The sin-offering was, in all cases, a turtle-dove or a young pigeon. But, while the more wealthy brought a lamb for a burnt-offering, the poor might substitute for it a turtle-dove, or a young pigeon. The Temple-price of the meat- and drink-offerings was fixed once a month; and special officials instructed the intending offerers, and provided them with what was needed. There was also a special 'superintendent of turtle-doves and pigeons,' required for certain purifications. In the Court of the Women there were thirteen trumpet-shaped chests for pecuniary contributions, called 'trumpets.'[1] Into the third of these they who brought the poor's offering, like

[1] Comp. St. Matt. vi. 2. See 'The Temple and its Services,' &c., pp. 26, 27.

the Virgin-Mother, were to drop the price of the sacrifices which were needed for their purification. As we infer, the superintending priest must have been stationed here, alike to inform the offerer of the price of the turtle-doves, and to see that all was in order. For the offerer of the poor's offering would not require to deal directly with the sacrificing priest. At a certain time in the day this third chest was opened, and half of its contents applied to burnt-, the other half to sin-offerings. Thus sacrifices were provided for a corresponding number of those who were to be purified, without either shaming the poor, needlessly disclosing the character of impurity, or causing unnecessary bustle and work. Though this mode of procedure could, of course, not be obligatory, it would, no doubt, be that generally followed.

We can now, in imagination, follow the Virgin-Mother in the Temple. Her Child had been given up to the Lord, and received back from Him. She had entered the Court of the Women, probably by the ' Gate of the Women,' on the north side, and deposited the price of her sacrifices in Trumpet No. 3, which was close to the raised dais or gallery where the women worshipped, apart from the men. And now the sound of the organ, which announced throughout the vast Temple-buildings that the incense was about to be kindled on the Golden Altar, summoned those who were to be purified. The chief of the ministrant lay-representatives of Israel on duty (the so-called ' station-men ') ranged those, who presented themselves before the Lord as offerers of special sacrifices, within the wickets on either side the great Nicanor Gate, at the top of the fifteen steps which led up from the Court of the Women to that of Israel. The purification-service, with such unspoken prayer and praise as would be the outcome of a grateful heart, was soon ended, and they who had shared in it were Levitically clean. Now all stain was removed, and, as the Law put it, they might again partake of sacred offerings.

It has been observed, that by the side of every humiliation connected with the Humanity of the Messiah, the glory of His Divinity was also made to shine forth. The coincidences are manifestly undesigned on the part of the Evangelic writers, and hence all the more striking. And so, when now the Mother of Jesus in her humbleness could only bring the 'poor's offering,' the witness to the greatness of Him Whom she had borne was not wanting.

The 'parents' of Jesus had brought Him into the Temple for presentation and redemption, when they were met by one, whose venerable figure must have been well known in the city and the Sanctuary. Simeon combined the three characteristics of Old Testament piety: 'justice,' as regarded his relation and bearing to God and man; 'fear of God,' in opposition to the boastful self-righteousness of Pharisaism; and, above all, longing expectancy of the near fulfilment of the great promises, and that in their spiritual import as 'the Consolation of Israel.' And now it was as had been promised him. Coming 'in the Spirit' into the Temple, just as His parents were bringing the Infant Jesus, he took Him into his arms, and burst into thanksgiving. God had fulfilled His word. He was not to see death, till he had seen the Lord's Christ. Now did his Lord 'dismiss' him 'in peace'—release him from work and watch—since he had actually seen that salvation, so long preparing for a waiting weary world: a glorious light, Whose rising would light up heathen darkness, and be the outshining glory around Israel's mission.

But his unexpected appearance, the more unexpected deed and words, and that most unexpected and un-Judaic form in which what was said of the Infant Christ was presented to their minds, filled the hearts of His parents with wonderment. And it was as if their silent wonderment had been an unspoken question, to which the answer now came in words of blessing from the aged watcher. But now it was the personal, or rather the Judaic, aspect which, in broken utterances, was set before the Virgin-Mother—as if the whole history of the Christ upon earth were passing in rapid vision before Simeon. That Infant was to be a stone of decision; a foundation and corner-stone,[a] for fall or for uprising; a sign spoken

a Is. viii. 14 against; the sword of deep personal sorrow would pierce the Mother's heart; and so to the terrible end, when the veil of externalism which had so long covered the hearts of Israel's leaders would be rent, and the deep evil of their thoughts laid bare.

Nor was Simeon's the only hymn of praise on that day. A special interest attaches to her who responded in praise to God for the pledge she saw of the near redemption. A kind of mystery seems to invest this Anna. A widow, whose early desolateness had been followed by a long life of solitary mourning; one of those in whose home the tribal genealogy had been preserved. We infer from this, and from the fact that it was that of a tribe which had not returned to Palestine, that hers was a family of some distinction. Curiously enough, the tribe of Asher alone is celebrated in tradition for the beauty of its women, and their fitness to be wedded to High-Priest or King.

These many years had Anna spent in the Sanctuary, and spent in fasting and prayer—yet not of that self-righteous, self-satisfied kind which was of the essence of popular religion. Nor yet were 'fasting and prayer' to her the all-in-all of religion, sufficient in themselves; sufficient also before God. The seemingly hopeless exile of her own tribe, the political state of Judæa, the condition—social, moral, and religious—of her own Jerusalem, all kindled in her, as in those who were like-minded, deep, earnest longing for the time of promised 'redemption.' No place so suited to such an one as the Temple, with its services; no occupation so befitting as 'fasting and prayer.' And there were others, perhaps many such, in Jerusalem. Though Rabbinic tradition ignored them, they were the salt which preserved the mass from festering corruption. To her, as the representative of such, was it granted as prophetess to recognise Him, Whose Advent had been the burden of Simeon's praise.

CHAPTER V.

THE VISIT AND HOMAGE OF THE MAGI, AND THE FLIGHT INTO EGYPT.

(St. Matt. ii. 1–18.)

THE story of the homage to the infant Saviour by the *Magi* is told by St. Matthew, in language of which the brevity constitutes the chief difficulty.   Even their designation is not free from ambiguity.   The term *Magi* is used in the LXX., by Philo, Josephus, and by profane writers, alike in an evil and, so to speak, in a good sense—in the former case as implying the practice of magical arts ;[a] in the latter, as referring to those Eastern (specially Chaldee) priest-sages, whose researches, in great measure as yet mysterious and unknown to us, seem to have embraced much deep knowledge, though not untinged with superstition.   It is to these latter, that the Magi spoken of by St. Matthew must have belonged. Their number—to which, however, no importance attaches—cannot be ascertained.   Various suggestions have been made as to the country of ' the East,' whence they came.   The oldest opinion traces the Magi—though partially on insufficient grounds—to Arabia.   And there is this in favour of it, that not only the closest intercourse existed between Palestine and Arabia, but that from about 120 B.C. to the sixth century of our era, the kings of Yemen professed the Jewish faith.

Shortly after the Presentation of the Infant Saviour in the Temple, certain Magi from the East arrived in Jerusalem with strange tidings.   They had seen at its ' rising ' a sidereal appearance, which they regarded as betokening the birth of the Messiah-King of the Jews, in the sense which at the time attached to that designation.   Accordingly, they had come to Jerusalem to pay homage to Him, probably not because they imagined He must be born

a So also in Acts viii. 9 ; xiii. 6, 8

in the Jewish capital, but because they would naturally expect there to obtain authentic information, 'where' He might be found. In their simplicity, the Magi addressed themselves in the first place to the official head of the nation. But their inquiry produced on King Herod, and in the capital, a far different impression from the feeling of the Magi. Unscrupulously cruel as Herod had always proved, even the slightest suspicion of danger to his rule —the bare possibility of the Advent of One, Who had such claims upon the allegiance of Israel, and Who, if acknowledged, would evoke the most intense movement on their part—must have struck terror to his heart. Nor is it difficult to understand that the whole city should, although on different grounds, have shared the 'trouble' of the king. They knew only too well the character of Herod, and what the consequences would be to them, or to any one who might be suspected, however unjustly, of sympathy with any claimant to the royal throne of David.

Herod took immediate measures, characterised by his usual cunning. He called together all the High-Priests— past and present—and all the learned Rabbis, and, without committing himself as to whether the Messiah was already born, or only expected, simply propounded to them the question of His birthplace. At the same time he took care diligently to inquire the precise time, when the sidereal appearance had first attracted the attention of the Magi.[a] So long as any one lived, who was born in Bethlehem between the earliest appearance of this 'star' and the time of the arrival of the Magi, he was not safe. The subsequent conduct of Herod [b] shows that the Magi must have told him, that their first observation of the phenomenon had taken place two years before their arrival in Jerusalem.

The assembled authorities of Israel could only return one answer to the question submitted by Herod. As shown by the rendering of the *Targum Jonathan*, the prediction in Micah v. 2 was at the time universally understood as pointing to Bethlehem, as the birthplace of the Messiah. That such was the general expectation, appears from the

a St. Matt. ii. 7

b v. 16

Talmud, where, in an imaginary conversation between an Arab and a Jew, Bethlehem is authoritatively named as Messiah's birthplace. St. Matthew reproduces the prophetic utterance of Micah, exactly as such quotations were popularly made at that time. It will be remembered that, Hebrew being a dead language so far as the people were concerned, the Holy Scriptures were always translated into the popular dialect, the person so doing being designated *Methurgeman* (*dragoman*) or interpreter. These renderings, which at the time of St. Matthew were not yet allowed to be written down, formed the precedent for, if not the basis of, our later *Targum*.

The further conduct of Herod was in keeping with his plans. He sent for the Magi—for various reasons, secretly. After ascertaining the precise time when they had first observed the ' star,' he directed them to Bethlehem, with the request to inform him when they had found the Child; on pretence that he was equally desirous with them to pay Him homage. As they left Jerusalem for the goal of their pilgrimage, to their surprise and joy, the ' star,' [1] which had attracted their attention at its ' rising,' and which, as seems implied in the narrative, they had not seen of late, once more appeared on the horizon, and seemed to move before them, till ' it stood over where the young child was '—that is, of course, over Bethlehem, not over any special house in it. And, since in ancient times such extraordinary ' guidance ' by a ' star ' was matter of belief and expectancy, the Magi would,

---

[1] Astronomically speaking there can be no doubt that the most remarkable conjunction of planets—that of Jupiter and Saturn in the constellation Pisces, which occurs only once in 800 years—took place no less than three times in the year 747 A.U.C., or two years before the birth of Christ (in May, Oct., and Dec.). In the year following Mars joined this conjunction. Kepler, who was led to the discovery by observing a similar conjunction in 1603-4, also noticed that when the three planets came into conjunction a new, extraordinarily brilliant star was visible between Jupiter and Saturn, and he suggested that a similar star had appeared under the same circumstances in the conjunction preceding the Nativity. It has been astronomically ascertained that such a sidereal apparition would be visible to those who left Jerusalem, and that it would point—almost seem to go before—in the direction of and stand over Bethlehem.

from their standpoint, regard it as the fullest confirmation
that they had been rightly directed to Bethlehem—and
'they rejoiced with exceeding great joy.' It could not be
difficult to learn in Bethlehem, where the Infant, around
Whose Birth marvels had gathered, might be found. It
appears that the temporary shelter of the 'stable' had
been exchanged by the Holy Family for the more permanent abode of a 'house;'ᵃ and there the
Magi found the Infant-Saviour with His Mother.

ᵇ v. 11

Only two things are recorded of this visit of the Magi
to Bethlehem: their homage, and their offerings. Viewed
as gifts, the incense and the myrrh would, indeed, have
been strangely inappropriate. But their offerings were
evidently intended as specimens of the products of their
country, and their presentation was, even as in our own
days, expressive of the homage of their country to the
new-found King. In this sense, then, the Magi may
truly be regarded as the representatives of the Gentile
World; their homage as the first and typical acknowledgment of Christ by those who hitherto had been 'far off;'
and their offerings as symbolic of the world's tribute. The
ancient Church has traced in the gold the emblem of
His Royalty; in the myrrh, of His Humanity, and that in
the fullest evidence of it, in His burying; and in the incense, that of His Divinity.

It could not be, that these Magi should become the instruments of Herod's murderous designs; nor yet that
the Infant-Saviour should fall a victim to the tyrant.
Warned of God in a dream, the 'wise men' returned 'into
their own country another way;' and, warned by the Angel
of the Lord in a dream, the Holy Family sought temporary
shelter in Egypt. Baffled in the hope of attaining his
object through the Magi, the reckless tyrant sought to
secure it by an indiscriminate slaughter of all the children in Bethlehem and its immediate neighbourhood, from
two years and under. True, considering the population of
Bethlehem, their number could only have been small—
probably twenty at most. But the deed was none the less
atrocious; and these infants may justly be regarded as

the ' protomartyrs,' the first witnesses, of Christ, ' the blossom of martyrdom ' (' flores martyrum,' as *Prudentius* calls them).

But of two passages in his own Old Testament Scriptures the Evangelist sees a fulfilment in these events. The flight into Egypt is to him the fulfilment of this expression by Hosea, 'Out of Egypt have I called My ^a Son.' ^a In the murder of ' the Innocents,' he sees ^b the fulfilment of Rachel's lament ^b over her children, the men of Benjamin, when the exiles to Babylon met in Ramah,^c and there was bitter wailing at the prospect of parting for hopeless captivity, and yet bitterer lament, as they who might have encumbered the onward march were pitilessly slaughtered. Those who have attentively followed the course of Jewish thinking, and marked how the ancient Synagogue, and that rightly, read the Old Testament in its unity, as ever pointing to the Messiah as the fulfilment of Israel's history, will not wonder at, but fully accord with St. Matthew's retrospective view.

a Hos. xi. 1
b Jer. xxxi. 15
c Jer. xl. 1

CHAPTER VI.

THE CHILD-LIFE IN NAZARETH.

(St. Matt. ii. 19–23; St. Luke ii. 39, 40.)

THE stay of the Holy Family in Egypt must have been of brief duration. The cup of Herod's misdeeds, but also of his misery, was full. During the whole latter part of his life, the dread of a rival to the throne had haunted him, and he had sacrificed thousands, among them those nearest and dearest to him, to lay that ghost. And still the tyrant was not at rest. A more terrible scene is not presented in history than that of the closing days of Herod.[1] Tormented by nameless fears; even making attempts on

[1] For an account of the personal history of Herod see 'Life and Times,' bk. ii., chaps. ii. and ix., and app. iv.

his own life; the delirium of tyranny, the passion for blood, drove him to the verge of madness. The most loathsome disease had fastened on his body, and his sufferings were at times agonising. By the advice of his physicians, he had himself carried to the baths of Callirhoe (east of the Jordan), trying all remedies with the determination of one who will do hard battle for life. It was in vain. He knew that his hour was come, and had himself conveyed back to his palace under the palm-trees of Jericho.

The last days of Herod were stained by fresh murders. The execution of Antipater—the false accuser and real murderer of his half-brothers Alexander and Aristobulus —preceded the death of his father by but five days. The latter occurred from seven to fourteen days before the Passover, which in 750 took place on April 12.

Herod had reigned thirty-seven years—thirty-four since his conquest of Jerusalem. Soon the rule for which he had so long plotted, striven, and stained himself with untold crimes, passed from his descendants. A century more, and his whole race had been swept away.

Herod had three times changed his testament.[1] But a few days before his death he made yet another disposition, by which Archelaus, the elder brother of Antipas, was appointed king; Antipas tetrarch of Galilee and Peræa; and Philip tetrarch of the territory east of the Jordan. Although the Emperor seems to have authorised him to appoint his successor, Herod wisely made his disposition dependent on the approval of Augustus. But the latter was not by any means to be taken for granted. Archelaus had, indeed, been immediately proclaimed King by the army; but he prudently declined the title, till it had been confirmed by the Emperor.

Augustus decided, however, to do this, though with certain slight modifications, of which the most important was that Archelaus should bear the title of *Ethnarch*, which, if he deserved it, would by-and-by be exchanged

---

[1] Herod had married no less than ten times. See his genealogical table.

for that of King. His dominions were to be Judæa, Idumæa, and Samaria, with a revenue of 600 talents (about 230,000*l*. to 240,000*l*.). It is needless to follow the fortunes of the new Ethnarch. His brief reign ceased in the year 6 of our era, when the Emperor banished him, on account of his crimes, to Gaul.

It must have been soon after the accession of Archelaus, but before tidings of it had actually reached Joseph in Egypt, that the Holy Family returned to Palestine. The first intention of Joseph seems to have been to settle in Bethlehem, where he had lived since the birth of Jesus. Obvious reasons would incline him to choose this, and, if possible, to avoid Nazareth as the place of his residence. But when, on reaching Palestine, he learned who the successor of Herod was, and also, no doubt, in what manner he had inaugurated his reign, common prudence would have dictated the withdrawal of the Infant-Saviour from the dominions of Archelaus. It needed Divine direction to determine his return to Nazareth.

Of the many years spent in Nazareth, during which Jesus passed from infancy to manhood, the Evangelic narrative has left us but briefest notice. Of His childhood : that ' He grew and waxed strong in spirit, filled with wisdom, and the grace of God was upon him ; ' [a] of His youth : besides the account of His questioning the Rabbis in the Temple, the year before He attained Jewish majority—that ' He was subject to His Parents,' and that ' He increased in wisdom and stature, and in favour with God and man.' Considering what loving care watched over Jewish child-life, tenderly marking by not fewer than eight designations the various stages of its development,[1] and the deep interest naturally attaching to the early life of the Messiah, that silence, in contrast to the almost blasphemous absurdities of the Apocryphal Gospels, teaches us once more, that the Gospels furnish a history of the Saviour, not a biography of Jesus of Nazareth.

[a] St. Luke ii. 40

[1] See ' Sketches of Jewish Social Life,' pp. 103, 104, and ' Life and Times,' vol. i. pp. 226–234.

CHAPTER VII.

IN THE HOUSE OF HIS HEAVENLY, AND IN THE HOME OF
HIS EARTHLY FATHER—THE TEMPLE OF JERUSALEM—
THE RETIREMENT AT NAZARETH.

(St. Luke ii. 41–52.)

ONCE only is the silence which lies on the history of
Christ's early life broken. It is to record what took place
on His first visit to the Temple.

In strict law, personal observance of the ordinances,
and hence attendance on the feasts at Jerusalem, devolved
on a youth only when he was of age, that is, at thirteen
years. Then he became what was called 'a son of the
Commandment,' or 'of the Torah.' But, as a matter of
fact, the legal age was in this respect anticipated by two
years, or at least by one. It was in accordance with this
custom that, on the first Pascha after Jesus had passed
His twelfth year, His Parents took Him with them in the
'company' of the Nazarenes to Jerusalem. The text
seems to indicate, that it was their wont to go up to the
Temple; and we mark that, although women were not
bound to make such personal appearance, Mary gladly
availed herself of what seems to have been the direction
of Hillel (followed also by other religious women, mentioned in Rabbinic writings), to go up to the solemn
services of the Sanctuary. Politically, times had changed.
Archelaus was banished, and Judæa, Samaria, and Idumæa
were now incorporated into the Roman province of Syria,
under its Governor, or Legate, P. Sulpicius Quirinius. The
special administration of that part of Palestine was, however, entrusted to a Procurator, whose ordinary residence
was at Cæsarea.

It was, as we reckon it, in spring A.D. 9, that Jesus for
the first time went up to the Paschal Feast in Jerusalem.
A brief calm had fallen upon the land. The census and

taxing, with the consequent rising of the Nationalists with
Ezekias at their head, which had marked the accession of
Herod, misnamed the Great, were alike past. There was
nothing to provoke active resistance, and the party of the
Zealots, as the Nationalists were afterwards called, although
still existing, and striking deeper root in the hearts of the
people, was, for the time, rather 'the philosophical party '—
their minds busy with an ideal, which their hands were not
yet preparing to make a reality. And so, when, according to
ancient wont,[a] the festive company from Nazareth,
soon swelled by other bands, went up to Jerusalem, chanting by the way those 'Psalms of
Ascent'[b] to the accompaniment of the flute,
they might implicitly yield themselves to the spiritual
thoughts kindled by such words.

[a] Ps. xlii. 4;
Is. xxx. 29
[b] A.V.
'Degrees';
Ps. cxx.-
cxxxiv.

When the pilgrims' feet stood within the gates of
Jerusalem, there could have been no difficulty in finding
hospitality, however crowded the City may have been on
such occasions—the more so when we remember the extreme simplicity of Eastern manners and wants, and the
abundance of provisions which the many sacrifices of the
season would supply. Glorious as a view of Jerusalem
must have seemed to a child coming to it for the first time
from the retirement of a Galilean village, we must bear in
mind, that He Who now looked upon it was not an ordinary Child. But the one all-engrossing thought would be
of the Temple. As the pilgrim ascended the Mount, crested
by that symmetrically proportioned building, which could
hold within its gigantic girdle not fewer than 210,000
persons, his wonder might well increase at every step.
The Mount itself seemed like an island, abruptly rising
from out deep valleys, surrounded by a sea of walls,
palaces, streets, and houses, and crowned by a mass of
snowy marble and glittering gold, rising terrace upon
terrace. Altogether it measured a square of about 1,000
feet. At its north-western angle, and connected with it,
frowned the Castle of Antonia, held by the Roman garrison.[1]

----

[1] For a full description reference must be made to 'The Temple,
its Ministry and Services, &c.'

In some part of this Temple, 'sitting in the midst of the Doctors, both hearing them and asking them questions,' we must look for the Child Jesus on the third and the two following days of the Feast on which He first visited the Sanctuary. Only on the two first days of the Feast of Passover was personal attendance in the Temple necessary. With the third day commenced the so-called half-holidays, when it was lawful to return to one's home—a provision of which, no doubt, many availed themselves. For the Passover had been eaten, the festive sacrifice (or *Chagigah*) offered, and the first ripe barley reaped and brought to the Temple, and waved as the Omer of first flour before the Lord. Hence, in view of the well-known Rabbinic provision, the expression in the Gospel-narrative concerning the 'Parents' of Jesus, 'when they had fulfilled the days,'[a] cannot necessarily imply that Joseph and the Mother of Jesus had remained in Jerusalem during the whole Paschal week. We read in the Talmud that the members of the Temple-Sanhedrin, who on ordinary days sat as a Court of Appeal from the close of the Morning to the time of the Evening Sacrifice, were wont on Sabbaths and feast-days to come out upon 'the Terrace' of the Temple, and there to teach. In such popular instruction the utmost latitude of questioning would be given. It is in this audience, which sat on the ground, surrounding and mingling with the Doctors—and hence during, not after the Feast—that we must seek the Child Jesus.

The presence and questioning of a Child of that age did not necessarily imply anything so extraordinary, as to convey the idea of supernaturalness to those Doctors or others in the audience. Jewish tradition gives other instances of precocious and strangely advanced students. Besides, scientific theological learning would not be necessary to take part in such popular discussions. If we may judge from later arrangements, not only in Babylon, but in Palestine, there were two kinds of public lectures, and two kinds of students. The first, or more scientific lectures, implied considerable preparation on the part of the lecturing

a St. Luke ii. 43

D

Rabbis, and at least some Talmudic knowledge on the part
of the attendants.   On the other hand, there were Students
of the Court, who during ordinary lectures sat separated
from the regular students by a kind of hedge, outside, as
it were in the Court, some of whom seem to have been
ignorant even of the Bible.   The lectures addressed to
such a general audience would, of course, be of a very
different character.

But if there was nothing so unprecedented as to render
His Presence and questioning marvellous, yet all who
heard Him ' were amazed ' at His ' combinative insight '
and ' discerning answers.'   Judging by what we know of
such discussions, we infer that His questioning may have
been connected with the Paschal solemnities.   Or perhaps
He would lead up by His questions to their deeper meaning, as it was to be unfolded, when Himself was offered up,
' the Lamb of God, Which taketh away the sin of the
world.'

Other questions also almost force themselves on the
mind—most notably this : whether on the occasion of this
His first visit to the Temple, the Virgin-Mother had told her
Son the history of His Infancy, and of what had happened
when, for the first time, He had been brought to the
Temple.   It would almost seem so, if we might judge from
the contrast between the Virgin-Mother's complaint about
the search of His father and of her, and His own emphatic
appeal to the business of His Father.   But most sur-
prising—truly wonderful it must have seemed to Joseph,
and even to the Mother of Jesus, that the meek, quiet
Child should have been found in such company, and so
engaged.   The reply of Jesus to the expostulation of them
who had sought Him ' sorrowing ' these three days, sets
clearly these three things before us.   He had been so
entirely absorbed by the awakening thought of His Being
and Mission, however kindled, as to be not only neglectful,
but forgetful of all around.   Secondly : we may venture to
say, that He now realised that this was emphatically His
Father's House.   And, thirdly : so far as we can judge, it
was then and there that, for the first time, He felt the

strong and irresistible impulse—that Divine necessity of
His Being—to be ' about His Father's business.'

A further, though to us it seems a downward step, was
the quiet, immediate, unquestioning return of Jesus to
Nazareth with His Parents, and His willing submission to
them while there. It was not self-exinanition but self-
submission, all the more glorious in proportion to the
greatness of that Self. This constant contrast before her
eyes only deepened in the heart of Mary the ever-present
impression of ' all those matters, of which she was the
most cognisant.

With His return to Nazareth began Jesus' life of
youth and early manhood, with all of inward and outward
development, of heavenly and earthly approbation which it
carried.[a] Whether or not He went to Jerusalem
on recurring Feasts, we know not, and need not
inquire. Other influences were at their silent work to weld
His inward and outward development, and to determine the
manner of His later Manifesting of Himself. We assume
that the school-education of Jesus must have ceased soon
after His return to Nazareth.

a St. Luke ii.
52

Jewish home-life, especially in the country, was of
the simplest. Only the Sabbath and festivals, whether
domestic or public, brought what of the best lay within
reach. The same simplicity would prevail in dress and
manners. We cannot here discuss the vexed question
whether ' the brothers and sisters ' of Jesus were such in
the real sense, or step-brothers and sisters, or else cousins,
though it seems to us as if the primary meaning of the
terms would scarcely have been called in question, but for
a theory of false asceticism, and an undervaluing
of the sanctity of the married estate.[b] But,
whatever the precise relationship between Jesus
and these ' brothers and sisters,' it must, on any
theory, have been of the closest, and exercised
its influence upon Him.

b Comp. St.
Matt. i. 24 ;
St. Luke ii.
7 ; St. Matt.
xii. 46 ; xiii.
55, 56 ; St.
Mark iii. 31 ;
vi. 3 ; Acts i.
14 ; 1 Cor. ix.
5 ; Gal. i. 19

Passing over Joses or Joseph, of whose history we know next to nothing, we would venture to infer
from the Epistle of St. James, that his religious views had

originally been cast in the mould of Shammai. Of His cousin Simon [1] we know that he had belonged to the Nationalist party, since he is expressly so designated (*Zelotes*,[a] *Cananœan*[b]). Lastly, there are in the Epistle of St. Jude, one undoubted and another probable reference to two of those (Pseudepi-graphic) Apocalyptic books, which at that time marked one deeply interesting phase of the Messianic out-look of Israel.[c] We have thus within the nar-row circle of Christ's Family-Life—not to speak of any intercourse with the sons of Zebedee, who probably were also His cousins—the three most hopeful and pure Jewish tendencies, brought into constant contact with Jesus: in Pharisaism, the teaching of Shammai; then, the Nationalist ideal; and, finally, the hope of a glorious Messianic future. To these there should probably be added at least knowledge of the lonely preparation of His kinsman John, who, though certainly not an Essene, had, from the necessity of his calling, much in his outward bearing that was akin to them.

a St. Luke vi. 15; Acts i. 13
b St. Mark iii. 18

c St. Jude vv. 14, 15 to the book of Enoch, and v. 9 probably to the Assum. of Moses

From what are, necessarily, only suggestions, we turn again to what is certain in connection with His Family-Life and its influences. From St. Mark vi. 3, we may infer with great probability, though not with absolute cer-tainty,[d] that He had adopted the trade of Joseph. Among the Jews the contempt for manual labour, which was one of the characteristics of heathenism, did not exist. On the contrary, it was deemed a religious duty, frequently and most earnestly insisted upon, to learn some trade, provided it did not minister to luxury, nor tend to lead away from personal observance of the Law. There was not such separation between rich and poor as with us, and while wealth might confer social distinction, the absence of it in no way implied social inferiority.

d Comp. St. Matt. xiii. 55; St. John vi. 42

The reverence towards parents, as a duty higher than any of outward observance, and the love of brethren, which

---

[1] I regard this Simon (Zelotes) as the son of Clopas (brother of Joseph, the Virgin's husband) and of Mary.

Jesus had learned in His home, form, so to speak, the natural basis of many of His teachings. They give us also an insight into the family-life of Nazareth. Even the games of children, as well as festive gatherings of families, find their record in the words and the life of Christ. This also is characteristic of His past. And so are His deep sympathy with all sorrow and suffering, and His love for the family circle, as evidenced in the home of Lazarus. That He spoke Hebrew, and used and quoted the Scriptures in the original, has been shown,[1] although, no doubt, He understood Greek, possibly also Latin.

Thus, Christ in His home-life and surroundings, as well as by the prevailing ideas with which He was brought into contact, was in sympathy with all the highest tendencies of His people and time. Beyond this, into the mystery of His inner converse with God, the unfolding of His spiritual receptiveness, and the increasing communication from above, we dare not enter. It is best to remain content with the simple account of the Evangelic narrative: ' Jesus increased in favour with God and man.'

CHAPTER VIII.

A VOICE IN THE WILDERNESS.

(St. Matt. iii. 1–12; St. Mark i. 2–8; St. Luke iii. 1–18.)

A SILENCE, even more complete than that concerning the early life of Jesus, rests on the thirty years and more, which intervened between the birth and the open forth-showing of John in his character as Forerunner of the Messiah. Only his outward and inward development, and his being ' in the deserts,' are briefly indicated.[a]

[a] St. Luke i. 80

At last that solemn silence was broken by an appearance, a proclamation, a rite, and a ministry as startling as that of Elijah had been. In many respects, indeed, the two messengers and their times bore singular

[1] See ' Life and Times, &c.,' vol. i. p. 234.

likeness. John came suddenly out of the wilderness of Judæa, as Elijah from the wilds of Gilead; John bore the same strange ascetic appearance as his predecessor; the message of John was the counterpart of that of Elijah; his baptism that of Elijah's novel rite on Mount Carmel. And, as if to make complete the parallelism, even the more minute details surrounding the life of Elijah found their counterpart in that of John.

Palestine, the ancient kingdom of Herod, was now divided into four parts: Judæa being under the direct administration of Rome, two other tetrarchies under the rule of Herod's sons (Herod Antipas and Philip), while the small principality of Abilene was governed by Lysanias.

Herod Antipas, whose rule extended over forty-three years, reigned over Galilee and Peræa—the districts which were respectively the principal sphere of the Ministry of Jesus and of John the Baptist. Like his brother Archelaus, Herod Antipas possessed in an even aggravated form most of the vices, without any of the greater qualities, of his father. Of deeper religious feelings or convictions he was entirely destitute, though his conscience occasionally misgave, if it did not restrain, him. The inherent weakness of his character left him in the absolute control of his wife, to the final ruin of his fortunes. He was covetous, avaricious, luxurious, and utterly dissipated; suspicious, and with a good deal of that fox-cunning which, especially in the East, often forms the sum total of state-craft. Like his father, he indulged a taste for building—always taking care to propitiate Rome by dedicating all to the Emperor.

A happier account can be given of Philip, the son of Herod the Great and Cleopatra of Jerusalem. He was a moderate and just ruler, and his reign of thirty-seven years contrasted favourably with that of his kinsmen. The land was quiet and prosperous, and the people contented and happy.

As regards the Roman rule, matters had greatly changed for the worse since the mild sway of Augustus.

When Tiberius succeeded to the Empire, and Judæa was a province, merciless harshness characterised the administration of Palestine; while the Emperor himself was bitterly hostile to Judaism and the Jews, and that although, personally, openly careless of all religion.

St. Luke significantly joins together, as the highest religious authority in the land, the names of Annas and Caiaphas. The former had been appointed by Quirinius. After holding the Pontificate for nine years, he was deposed, and succeeded by others, of whom the fourth was his son-in-law Caiaphas, in whom the Procurator at last found a sufficiently submissive instrument of Roman tyranny. The character of the High-Priests during the whole of that period is described in the Talmud in terrible language. And although there is no evidence that ' the house of Annas ' was guilty of the same sins as some of their successors, they are included in the woes pronounced on the corrupt leaders of the priesthood, whom the Sanctuary is represented as bidding depart from the sacred precincts, which their presence defiled.

Such a combination of political and religious distress, surely, constituted the time of Israel's utmost need. As yet no attempt had been made by the people to right themselves by armed force. In these circumstances, the cry that the Kingdom of Heaven was near at hand, and the call to preparation for it, must have awakened echoes throughout the land, and startled the most careless and unbelieving. It was, according to St. Luke's exact statement, in the fifteenth year of the reign of Tiberius Cæsar —reckoning, as provincials would do, from his co-regency with Augustus (which commenced two years before his sole reign)—in the year 26 A.D. According to our former computation, Jesus would then be in His thirtieth year. The scene of John's first public appearance was in ' the wilderness of Judæa,' that is, the wild, desolate district around the mouth of the Jordan. We know not whether John baptized in this place, nor yet how long he continued there; but we are expressly told that his stay was not confined to that locality.[a] Soon afterwards

a St. Luke
iii. 3

we find him at Bethany ^a (A.V. Bethabara), which is farther

ᵃ St. John i. 28 up the stream. The outward appearance and the habits of the Messenger corresponded to the character and object of his Mission. Neither his dress nor his food was that of the Essenes ; and the former, at least, like that of Elijah,^b whose mission he was now

ᵇ 2 Kings i. 8 to ' fulfil.'

This was evidenced alike by what he preached, and by the new symbolic rite, from which he derived the name of ' Baptist.' The grand burden of his message was : the announcement of the approach of ' the Kingdom of Heaven,' and the needed preparation of his hearers for that Kingdom. The latter he sought, positively, by admonition, and, negatively, by warnings, while he directed all to the Coming One, in Whom that Kingdom would become, so to speak, individualised.

Concerning this ' Kingdom of Heaven,' which was the great message of John, and the great work of Christ Himself, we may here say, that it is the whole Old Testament sublimated, and the whole New Testament realised. This rule of heaven and Kingship of Jehovah was the very substance of the Old Testament; the object of the calling and mission of Israel ; the meaning of all its ordinances, whether civil or religious; the underlying idea of all its institutions. It explained alike the history of the people, the dealings of God with them, and the prospects opened up by the prophets. It constituted alike the real contrast between Israel and the nations of antiquity, and Israel's real title to distinction.

A review of many passages on the subject shows that, in the Jewish mind, the expression ' Kingdom of Heaven ' referred, not so much to any particular period, as in general to *the Rule of God*—as acknowledged, manifested, and eventually perfected. Very often it is the equivalent for personal acknowledgment of God : the taking upon oneself of the ' yoke ' of ' the Kingdom,' or of the commandments—the former preceding and conditioning the latter.

As we pass from the Jewish ideas of the time to the

teaching of the New Testament, we feel that while there is complete change of spirit, the form in which the idea of the Kingdom of Heaven is presented is substantially similar.

John came to call Israel to submit to the Reign of God, about to be manifested in Christ. Hence, on the one hand, he called them to repentance—a 'change of mind'— with all that this implied; and, on the other, pointed them to the Christ, in the exaltation of His Person and Office. Thus the symbolic action by which this preaching was accompanied might be designated 'the baptism of repentance.'

For what John preached, that he also symbolised by a rite which, though not in itself, yet in its application, was wholly new. Hitherto the Law had it, that those who had contracted Levitical defilement were to immerse before offering sacrifice. Again, it was prescribed that such Gentiles as became 'proselytes of righteousness,' or 'proselytes of the Covenant,' were to be admitted to full participation in the privileges of Israel by the threefold rites of circumcision, baptism, and sacrifice—the immersion being, as it were, the acknowledgment and symbolic removal of moral defilement, corresponding to that of Levitical uncleanness. But never before had it been proposed that Israel should undergo a 'baptism of repentance,' although there are indications of a deeper insight into the meaning of Levitical baptisms. Was it intended that the hearers of John should give this as evidence of their repentance, that like persons defiled they sought purification, and like strangers they sought admission among the people who took on themselves the Rule of God? These two ideas would, indeed, have made it truly a 'baptism of repentance.' But it seems difficult to suppose that the people would have been prepared for such admissions; or, at least, that there should have been no record of the mode in which a change so deeply spiritual was brought about. May it not rather have been that as, when the first Covenant was made, Moses was directed to prepare Israel by symbolic baptism of their persons [a] and their

[a] Comp. Gen. xxxv. 2

garments,[a] so the initiation of the new Covenant, by which

Ex. xix. 10, 14 the people were to enter into the Kingdom of God, was preceded by another general symbolic baptism of those who would be the true Israel, and receive, or take on themselves, the Law from God?

CHAPTER IX.

THE BAPTISM OF JESUS.

(St. Matt. iii. 13–17; St. Mark i. 7–11; St. Luke iii. 21–23; St. John i. 32–34.)

THE more we think of it, the better do we seem to understand how that 'Voice crying in the wilderness: Repent! for the Kingdom of Heaven is at hand,' awakened echoes throughout the land, and brought from city, village, and hamlet strangest hearers. For once, every distinction was levelled. Pharisee and Sadducee, outcast publican and semi-heathen soldier, met here as on common ground. Their bond of union was the common 'hope of Israel'— the only hope that remained: that of 'the Kingdom.'

That Kingdom had been the last word of the Old Testament. As the thoughtful Israelite, whether Eastern or Western, viewed even the central part of his worship in sacrifices, and remembered that his own Scriptures had spoken of them in terms which pointed to something beyond their offering,[1] he must have felt that 'the blood of bulls and of goats, and the ashes of an heifer sprinkling the unclean,' could only 'sanctify to the purifying of the flesh;' that, indeed, the whole body of ceremonial and ritual ordinances 'could not make him that did the service perfect as pertaining to the conscience.' They were only 'the shadow of good things to come;' of 'a new' and 'better covenant, established upon better promises.'[b] It

b Heb. ix. 13, 9; x. 1; viii. 6, 13 was otherwise with the thought of the Kingdom. Each successive link in the chain of prophecy,

---

[1] Comp. 1 Sam. xv. 22; Ps. xl. 6–8; li. 7, 17; Is. i. 11–13; Jer. vii. 22, 23; Amos v. 21, 22; Ecclus. vii. 9; xxxiv. 18, 19; xxxv. 1, 7.

even the wild fantasies of Apocalyptic literature, bound
Israel anew to this hope.

This great expectancy would be strung to utmost tension during the pressure of outward circumstances more
hopeless than any hitherto experienced. And now the cry
had been suddenly raised : 'The Kingdom of Heaven is
at hand!' It was heard in the wilderness of Judæa,
within a few hours' distance from Jerusalem. No wonder
Pharisee and Sadducee flocked to the spot. They would
not see anything in the messenger that could have given
their expectations a rude shock. His was not a call to
armed resistance, but to repentance, such as all knew and
felt must precede the Kingdom. The hope which he held
out was not of earthly possessions, but of purity. His
appearance would command respect, and his character was
in accordance with his appearance. Not rich nor yet
Pharisaic garb with wide fringes, bound with many-coloured
or even priestly girdle, but the old prophet's poor raiment
and a leathern girdle. Not a luxurious life, but one
of meanest fare. ' Not a reed shaken by the wind,' but
unbendingly firm in deep and settled conviction. For
himself he sought nothing; for them he had only one
absorbing thought: The Kingdom was at hand, the King
was coming—let them prepare !

Such entire absorption in his mission, which leaves us
in ignorance of even the details of his later activity, must
have given force to his message. And still the voice,
everywhere proclaiming the same message, travelled up-
ward, along the winding Jordan which cleft the land
of promise. It was probably the autumn of the year
779 (A.U.C.), which, it may be noted, was a Sabbatic
year. Released from business and agriculture, the multitudes flocked around him as he passed on his Mission.
He had reached what seems to have been the most
northern point of his Mission-journey, *Beth-Abara* ('the
house of passage,' or 'of shipping')—according to the
ancient reading, Bethany ('the house of shipping')—one
 ᵃ St. John i. of the fords across the Jordan into Peræa. Here
28   he baptized.ᵃ But long before John had reached

that spot, tidings of his word and work must have come even into the retirement of Jesus' home-life.

From earliest ages it has been a question why Jesus went to be baptized. We need not seek for any ulterior motive. The one question with Him was, as He afterwards put it: 'The Baptism of John, whence was it? from heaven, or of men?' (St. Matt. xxi. 25). That question once answered, there could be no longer doubt nor hesitation. He went not from any other motive than that it *was of God*. The Baptism of Christ was the last act of His private life ; and, emerging from its waters in prayer, He learned, when His business was to commence, and how it would be done.

Alone the two met—probably for the first time in their lives. Over that which passed between them Holy Scripture has laid the veil of reverent silence, save as regards the beginning and the outcome of their meeting, which it was necessary for us to know. When Jesus came, John knew Him not. And even when he knew Him, that was not enough. For so great a witness as that which John was to bear, a present and visible demonstration from heaven was to be given.

We can understand how what he knew of Jesus, and what he now saw and heard, must have overwhelmed John with the sense of Christ's transcendentally higher dignity, and led him to hesitate about, if not to refuse, administering to Him the rite of Baptism. Not because it was 'the baptism of repentance,' but because he stood in the presence of Him 'the latchet of Whose shoes' he was 'not worthy to loose.' And yet in so 'forbidding' Him, and even suggesting his own baptism by Jesus, John forgot and misunderstood his mission. John himself was never to be baptized ; he only held open the door of the new Kingdom ; himself entered it not, and he that was least in that Kingdom was greater than he. Jesus overcame his reluctance by falling back upon the simple and clear principle which had brought Him to Jordan: 'It becometh us to fulfil all righteousness.' Thus putting aside, without argument, the objection of the Baptist, He followed the Hand that pointed Him to the open door of 'the Kingdom.'

Jesus stepped out of the baptismal waters ' praying.'[a] One prayer, the only one which He taught His disciples, recurs to our minds.

* St. Luke iii. 21

As the prayer of Jesus winged heavenwards, His solemn response to the call of the Kingdom—' Here am I; ' ' Lo, I come to do Thy Will '—the answer came, which at the same time was also the predicted sign to the Baptist. Heaven seemed cleft, and, in bodily shape like a dove, the Holy Ghost descended on Jesus, remaining on Him. Here, at these waters, was the Kingdom into which Jesus had entered in the fulfilment of all righteousness; and from them He emerged as its Heaven-designated, Heaven-qualified, and Heaven-proclaimed King. As such He had received the fulness of the Spirit for His Messianic work. As such also the voice from Heaven proclaimed it, to Him and to John : ' Thou art (' this is ') My Beloved Son, in Whom I am well pleased.' The ratification of the great Davidic promise, the announcement of the fulfilment of its predictive import in Psalm ii., was God's solemn declaration of Jesus as the Messiah, His public proclamation of it, and the beginning of Jesus' Messianic work. And so the Baptist understood it, when he ' bare record ' that He was ' the Son of God.' [b]

b St. John i. 34

CHAPTER X.

THE TEMPTATION OF JESUS.

(St. Matt. iv. 1–11 ; St. Mark i. 12, 13; St. Luke iv. 1–13.)

THE proclamation and inauguration of the ' Kingdom of Heaven ' at such a time, and under such circumstances, was one of the great antitheses of history. A similar, even greater antithesis, was the commencement of the Ministry of Christ. From the Jordan to the wilderness with its wild beasts ; from the devout acknowledgment of the

Baptist, the consecration and filial prayer of Jesus, the descent of the Holy Spirit, and the heard testimony of Heaven, to the utter forsakenness, the felt want and weakness of Jesus, and the assaults of the Devil—no contrast more startling could be conceived.

And yet that at His consecration to the Kingship of the Kingdom, Jesus should have become clearly conscious of all that it implied in a world of sin; that the Divine method by which that Kingdom should be established, should have been clearly brought out, and its reality tested; and that the King, as Representative and Founder of the Kingdom, should have encountered and defeated the representative, founder, and holder of the opposite power, ' the prince of this world '—these are thoughts which must arise in every one who believes in any Mission of the Christ. We can understand how a Life and Work such as that of Jesus would commence with ' the Temptation,' but none other than His. Judaism never conceived such an idea; because it never conceived a Messiah like Jesus. The patriarchs indeed had been tried and proved; so had Moses, and all the heroes of faith in Israel. And Rabbinic legend, enlarging upon the Biblical narratives, has much to tell of the original envy of the Angels; of the assaults of Satan upon Abraham, when about to offer up Isaac; of attempted resistance by the Angels to Israel's reception of the Law; and of the final vain endeavour of Satan to take away the soul of Moses. Foolish, and even blasphemous, as some of these legends are, thus much at least clearly stands out, that spiritual trials must precede spiritual elevation. In their own language: ' The Holy One, blessed be His Name, does not elevate a man to dignity till He has first tried and searched him; and if he stands in temptation, then He raises him to dignity.'

But so far from any idea obtaining that Satan was to assault the Messiah, in a well-known passage the Arch-enemy is represented as overwhelmed and falling on his face at sight of Him, and owning his complete defeat.

Thus, though such ideas were, indeed, present to the Jewish mind, they were so in a sense opposite to the

Gospel narratives. But if the narrative cannot be traced to Rabbinic legend, the question may be raised if it be not an adaptation of an Old Testament narrative, such as the account of the forty days' fast of Moses on the mount, or of Elijah in the wilderness? Viewing the Old Testament in its unity, and the Messiah as the apex in the column of its history, we admit—or rather, we must expect—throughout points of correspondence between Moses, Elijah, and the Messiah. In fact, these may be described as marking the three stages in the history of the Covenant. Moses was its giver, Elijah its restorer, the Messiah its renewer and perfecter. And as such they all had, in a sense, a similar outward consecration for their work. But that neither Moses nor Elijah was assailed by the Devil, constitutes not the only, though a vital, difference between the fast of Moses and Elijah, and that of Jesus. Moses fasted in the middle, Elijah at the end, Jesus at the beginning of His ministry. Moses fasted in the Presence of God; Elijah alone; Jesus assaulted by the Devil. Moses had been called up by God; Elijah had gone forth in the bitterness of his own spirit; Jesus was driven by the Spirit. Moses failed after his forty days' fast, when in indignation he cast the Tables of the Law from him; Elijah failed before his forty days' fast; Jesus was assailed for forty days and endured the trial. Moses was angry against Israel; Elijah despaired of Israel; Jesus overcame for Israel.

Before proceeding further, a most difficult and solemn question arises: In what respect could Jesus Christ, the Perfect Sinless Man, the Son of God, have been tempted of the Devil? That He was so tempted is of the very essence of this narrative, confirmed throughout His after-life, and laid down as a fundamental principle in the teaching and faith of the Church.[a] On the other hand, temptation without the inward correspondence of existent sin is not only unthinkable, so far as man is concerned,[b] but temptation without the possibility of sin seems unreal—a kind of Docetism.[1]

a Heb. iv. 15

b St. James i. 14

---

[1] The heresy which represents the Body of Christ as only apparent, not real.

Yet the very passage of Holy Scripture in which Christ's equality with us as regards all temptation is expressed, also emphatically excepts from it this one particular, *sin*,[a] not only in the sense that Christ actually did not sin, nor merely in this, that 'our concupiscence'[b] had no part in His temptations, but emphatically in this also, that the notion of sin has to be wholly excluded from our thoughts of Christ's temptations.

[a] Heb. iv. 15
[b] St. James i. 14

To obtain, if we can, a clearer understanding of this subject, two points must be kept in view. Christ's was real, though unfallen Human Nature; and Christ's Human was in inseparable union with His Divine Nature. Jesus voluntarily took upon Himself human nature with all its infirmities and weaknesses—but without the moral taint of the Fall: without sin. It was human nature, in itself capable of sinning, but not having sinned. The position of the first Adam was that of being capable of not sinning, not that of being incapable of sinning. The first Adam would have been 'perfected'—or passed from the capability of not sinning to the incapability of sinning—by obedience. That 'obedience'—or absolute submission to the Will of God—was the grand outstanding characteristic of Christ's work; but it was so, because He was not only the Unsinning, Unfallen Man, but also the Son of God. To sum up: The Second Adam, morally unfallen, though voluntarily subject to all the conditions of our Nature, was, with a peccable Human Nature, absolutely impeccable as being also the Son of God—a peccable Nature, yet an impeccable Person: the God-Man, 'tempted in regard to all (things) in like manner (as we), without (excepting) sin.'

A few sentences are here required in explanation of seeming differences in the Evangelical narration of the event. The historical part of St. John's Gospel begins after the Temptation—that is, with the actual Ministry of Christ. If St. Mark only summarises in his own brief manner, he supplies the twofold notice that Jesus was 'driven' into the wilderness, 'and was with the wild beasts,' which is in fullest internal agreement with the

* Scapegoat.

detailed narratives of St. Matthew and St. Luke. The only noteworthy difference between these two is that St. Matthew places the Temple-temptation before that of the world-kingdom, while St. Luke inverts this order, probably because his narrative was primarily intended for Gentile readers, to whose mind this might present itself as to them the true gradation of temptation. To St. Matthew we owe the notice, that after the Temptation 'Angels came and ministered' unto Jesus; to St. Luke, that the Tempter only 'departed from Him for a season.'

During the whole forty days of Christ's stay in the wilderness His temptation continued, though it only attained its high-point at the last, when, after the long fast, He felt the weariness and weakness of hunger. As fasting occupies but a very subordinate place in the teaching of Jesus, and as, so far as we know, He exercised on no other occasion such ascetic practices, we are left to infer internal, as well as external, necessity for it in the present instance. The former is easily understood in His pre-occupation; the latter must have had for its object to reduce Him to utmost outward weakness, by the depression of all the vital powers. We regard it as a psychological fact that, under such circumstances, of all mental faculties the memory alone is active, indeed almost preternaturally active. During the preceding thirty-nine days the plan, or rather the future, of the Work to which He had been consecrated, must have been always before Him. It is impossible that He hesitated for a moment as to the means by which He was to establish the Kingdom of God. The unchangeable convictions which He had already attained must have stood out before Him : that His Father's business was the Kingdom of God ; that He was furnished to it, not by outward weapons, but by the abiding Presence of the Spirit; above all, that absolute submission to the Will of God was the way to it, nay, itself the Kingdom of God. It will be observed that it was on these very points that the final attack of the Enemy was directed in the utmost weakness of Jesus. But, on the other hand, the Tempter could not have failed to assault Him with considerations

E

Man of Sorrows what a name, for the Son of God who came, ruined sinners to reclaim.

50   *JESUS THE MESSIAH*

which He must have felt to be true. How could He hope, alone, and with such principles, to stand against Israel? He knew their views and feelings; and as, day by day, the sense of utter loneliness and forsakenness increasingly gathered around Him, in His increasing faintness and weakness, the seeming hopelessness of such a task as He had undertaken must have grown upon Him with almost overwhelming power. Alternately, the temptation to despair, presumption, or the cutting short of the contest in some decisive manner, must have presented itself to His mind, or rather have been presented to it, by the Tempter.

And this was, indeed, the essence of His last three great temptations; which, as the whole contest, resolved themselves into the one question of absolute submission to the Will of God. If He submitted to it, it must be suffering—suffering to the bitter end; to the extinction of life, in the agonies of the Cross; denounced, betrayed, rejected by His people. And when thus beaten about by temptation, His powers reduced to the lowest ebb of faintness, all the more vividly would memory hold out the facts so well known: the scene lately enacted by the banks of Jordan, and the two great expectations of His own people, that the Messiah was to head Israel from the Sanctuary of the Temple, and that all kingdoms of the world were to become subject to Him.

He is weary with the contest, faint with hunger, alone in that wilderness. He must, He will absolutely submit to the Will of God. But can this be the Will of God? One word of power, and the scene would be changed. By His Will the Son of God, as the Tempter suggests—not, however, calling thereby in question His Sonship, but rather proceeding on its admitted reality—can change the stones into bread. He can do miracles—put an end to present want and question, and, as visibly the possessor of absolute miraculous power, the goal is reached! But this would really have been to change the idea of Old Testament miracle into the heathen conception of magic, which was absolute power inherent in an individual, without moral purpose. The moral purpose—the grand moral purpose in all that was of God—was absolute submission to the Will of God. His Spirit had driven Him into that wilderness. His circumstances were God-appointed, and where He so appoints them, He will support us in them, even as in the failure of bread, He supported Israel by the manna.[a] Jesus does more than not succumb: He conquers. The Scriptural reference to a better life upon the Word of God marks more than the end of the contest; it marks the conquest of Satan. He emerges on the other side triumphant, with this expression of His assured conviction of the sufficiency of God.

[a] Deut. viii. 3

It cannot be despair—and He cannot take up His Kingdom alone, in the exercise of mere power. If it be not despair of God, let it be presumption!

The Spirit of God had driven Jesus into the wilderness; the spirit of the Devil now carried Him to Jerusalem. Jesus stands on the lofty pinnacle of the Tower, or of the Temple-porch, presumably that on which every day a Priest was stationed to watch, as the pale morning light passed over the hills of Judæa far off to Hebron, to announce it as the signal for offering the morning sacrifice. In the next temptation Jesus stands on the watch-post which the white-robed Priest has just quitted. Fast the morning light is spreading over the land. In the Priests' Court below Him the morning-sacrifice has been offered. The massive Temple-gates are slowly opening, and the blast of the Priests' silver trumpets is summoning Israel to begin a new day by appearing before their Lord. Now then let Him descend, Heaven-borne, into the midst of Priests and people. What shouts of acclamation would greet His appearance! What homage of worship would be His! The goal can at once be reached, and that at the head of believing Israel.

Jesus is surveying the scene. By His side is the Tempter. The goal might indeed thus be reached; but not the Divine goal, nor in God's way—and, as so often, Scripture itself explained and guarded the Divine promise by a preceding Divine command. And thus once more

Jesus not only is not overcome, but He overcomes by absolute submission to the Will of God.

To submit to the Will of God! But is not this to acknowledge His authority, and the order and disposition which He has made of all things? Once more the scene changes. They have turned their backs upon Jerusalem and the Temple. Behind are also all popular prejudices, narrow nationalism, and limitations. They no longer breathe the stifled air, thick with the perfume of incense. They have taken their flight into God's wide world. There they stand on the top of some very high mountain. Before Him from out the cloud-land at the edge of the horizon the world, in all its glory, beauty, strength, majesty, lies unveiled. Its work, its might, its greatness, its art, its thought, emerge into clear view. It is a world quite other than that which the retiring Son of the retired Nazareth-home had ever seen, that opens its enlarging wonders. But passingly sublime as it must have appeared to the Perfect Man, the God-Man—and to Him far more than to us from His infinitely deeper appreciation of, and wider sympathy with the good, the true, and the beautiful—He had already overcome. It was, indeed, not ' worship,' but homage which the Evil One claimed from Jesus, and that on the apparently rational ground that, in its present state, all this world ' was delivered ' unto him, and he exercised the power of giving it to whom he would. But in this very fact lay the answer to the suggestion. High above this moving scene of glory and beauty arched the deep blue of God's heaven, and brighter than the sun, which poured its light over the sheen and dazzle beneath, stood out the fact: 'I must be about My Father's business;' above the din of far-off sounds rose the voice : ' Thy Kingdom come ! ' Was not all this the Devil's to have and to give, because it was not the Father's Kingdom, to which Jesus had consecrated Himself? To destroy all this : to destroy the works of the Devil, to abolish his kingdom, to set man free from his dominion, was the very object of Christ's Mission. On the ruins of the past shall the new arise. It is to become the Kingdom of God ; and Christ's consecration to it is to be the corner-stone of its new Temple. Those scenes are to be transformed into one of higher worship; those sounds to merge into a melody of praise. An endless train, unnumbered multitudes from afar, are to bring their gifts, to pour their wealth, to con-secrate their wisdom, to dedicate their beauty—to lay it all in lowly worship as humble offering at His feet. And so Satan's greatest becomes to Christ his coarsest temptation, which He casts from Him; and the words: ' Thou shalt worship the Lord thy God, and Him only shalt thou serve,' which now receive their highest fulfilment, mark not only Satan's defeat and Christ's triumph, but the principle of His Kingdom—of all victory and all triumph.

Foiled, defeated, the Enemy has spread his dark pinions towards that far-off world of his, and covered it with their shadow. The sun no longer glows with melting heat; the mists have gathered on the edge of the horizon, and en-wrapped the scene which has faded from view. And in the cool and shade that followed have the Angels come and ministered to His wants, both bodily and mental. He would not yield to Jewish dream; He did not pass from despair to presumption; and lo, after the contest, with no reward as its object, all is His. He would not have Satan's vassals as His legions, and all Heaven's hosts are at His command.

They had been overcome, these three temptations against submission to the Will of God, present, personal, and specifically Messianic. Yet all His life long there were echoes of them: of the first, in the suggestion of His brethren to show Himself[a]; of the second, in the popular attempt to make Him a king, and per-haps also in what constituted the final idea of Judas Iscariot; of the third, as being most plainly Satanic, in the question of Pilate: ' Art Thou then a king?'

a St. John vii. 3–5

CHAPTER XI.

THE DEPUTATION FROM JERUSALEM—THE THREE SECTS OF
THE PHARISEES, SADDUCEES, AND ESSENES.

(St. John i. 19-24.)

APART from the carnal form which it had taken, there is something sublime in the continuance and intensity of the Jewish expectation of the Messiah. It outlived not only the delay of long centuries, but the persecutions and scattering of the people ; it continued under the disappointment of the Maccabees, the rule of a Herod, the administration of a corrupt and contemptible Priesthood, and, finally, the government of Rome as represented by a Pilate ; nay, it grew in intensity almost in proportion as it seemed unlikely of realisation. These are facts which show that the doctrine of the Kingdom, as the sum and substance of Old Testament teaching, was the very heart of Jewish religious life; while, at the same time, they evidence a moral elevation which placed abstract religious conviction far beyond the reach of passing events, and clung to it with a tenacity which nothing could loosen.

Tidings of what these many months had occurred by the banks of the Jordan must have early reached Jerusalem, and ultimately stirred to the depths its religious society, whatever its preoccupation with ritual questions or political matters. For it was not an ordinary movement, nor in connection with any of the existing parties, religious or political. An extraordinary preacher, of extraordinary appearance and habits, not aiming, like others, after renewed zeal in legal observances, or increased Levitical purity, but preaching repentance and moral renovation in preparation for the coming Kingdom, and sealing this novel doctrine with an equally novel rite, had drawn from town and country multitudes of all classes—inquirers, penitents, and novices. The great and burning question seemed, what the real character and meaning of it was? or rather, whence did it issue, and whither did it tend? The religious leaders of the people proposed to answer this by instituting an inquiry through a trustworthy deputation.

That the interview referred to occurred *after* the Baptism of Jesus, appears from the whole context. Similarly, the statement that the deputation which came to John was 'sent from Jerusalem' by 'the Jews' implies that it proceeded from authority, even if it did not bear more than a semi-official character. For, although the expression '*Jews*' in the fourth Gospel generally conveys the idea of contrast to the disciples of Christ (*e.g.* St. John vii. 15), yet it refers to the people in their corporate capacity, that is, as represented by their constituted religious authorities.[a] On the other hand, it seems a legitimate inference that, considering their own tendencies, and the political dangers connected with such a step, the Sanhedrin of Jerusalem would not have come to the formal resolution of sending a regular deputation on such an inquiry. Moreover, a measure like this would have been entirely outside their recognised mode of procedure. It is quite true that judgment upon false prophets and religious seducers lay with it; but the Baptist had not as yet said or done anything to lay him open to such an accusation. If, nevertheless, it seems most probable that 'the Priests and Levites' came from the Sanhedrin, we are led to the conclusion that theirs was an informal mission, rather privately arranged than publicly determined upon.

And with this the character of the deputies agrees. 'Priests and Levites'—the colleagues of John the Priest —would be selected for such an errand, rather than leading Rabbinic authorities. The presence of the latter would, indeed, have given to the movement an importance, if not a sanction, which the Sanhedrin could not have wished. Finally, it seems quite natural that such an informal inquiry, set on foot most probably by the Sanhedrists, should have been entrusted exclusively to the Pharisaic party.

[a] Comp. St. John v. 15, 16; ix. 18, 22; xviii. 12, 31

It would in no way have interested the Sadducees; and
ᵃ St. Matt. what members of that party had seen of John ᵃ
iii. 7, &c. must have convinced them that his views and
aims lay entirely beyond their horizon.

The two great parties of Pharisees and Sadducees [1]
mark, not sects, but mental directions, such as in their
principles are natural and universal, and, indeed, appear
in connection with all metaphysical questions. The latter
originally represented a reaction from the Pharisees—the
moderate men, who sympathised with the later tendencies
of the Maccabees.

Without entering on the principles and supposed practices of ' the fraternity ' or ' association ' of Pharisees,
which was comparatively small, numbering only about
6,000 members, the following particulars may be of interest. The object of the association was twofold: to
observe in the strictest manner, and according to traditional law, all the ordinances concerning Levitical purity,
and to be extremely punctilious in all connected with
religious dues (tithes and all other dues). A person might
undertake only the second, without the first of these obligations. But he could not undertake the vow of Levitical
purity without also taking the obligation of all religious
dues. If he undertook both vows he was a *Chabher*, or
Associate. Here there were four degrees, marking an
ascending scale of Levitical purity, or separation from all
that was profane. In opposition to these was the *Am ha-
arets*, or ' country people ' (the people which knew not, or
cared not for the law, and were regarded as ' cursed ').

The two great obligations of the ' official ' Pharisee, or
' Associate '—that in regard to tithing ᵇ and that
ᵇ St. Luke
xi. 42 ; xviii. in regard to Levitical purity—are pointedly re-
12 ; St. Matt.
xxiii. 23 ferred to by Christ.ᶜ In both cases they are associ-
ᶜ St. Luke ated with a want of corresponding inward reality,
xi. 39, 41 ;
St. Matt. and with hypocrisy. But the sayings of some
xxiii. 25, 26 of the Rabbis in regard to Pharisaism and the

---

[1] For further particulars as to the origin and peculiar views and
practices of these Parties see ' Life and Times, &c.,' Book i. ch. viii.,
and Book iii. ch. ii.

professional Pharisee are more withering than any in the
New Testament. Such an expression as 'the plague of
Pharisaism' is not uncommon; and a silly pietist, a clever
sinner, and a female Pharisee, are ranked among 'the
troubles of life.' The Sadducees had, indeed, some reason
for the taunt, that 'the Pharisees would by-and-by subject
the globe of the sun itself to their purifications,' the more
so that their assertions of purity were sometimes conjoined
with Epicurean maxims, betokening a very different state
of mind, such as, 'Make haste to eat and drink, for the
world which we quit resembles a wedding feast.'

But it would be unjust to identify Pharisaism, as a
religious direction, with such embodiments of it, or even
with the official 'fraternity.' While it may be granted
that the tendency and logical sequence of their views and
practices were such, their system, as opposed to Saddu-
ceeism, had very serious bearings: dogmatic, ritual, and
legal.

The fundamental *dogmatic* differences between the
Pharisees and Sadducees concerned: the rule of faith and
practice; the 'after death;' the existence of angels and
spirits; and free will and predestination. In regard to
the first of these points, the Sadducees did not lay down
the principle of absolute rejection of all traditions as such,
but they were opposed to traditionalism as represented
and carried out by the Pharisees. When put down by
sheer weight of authority, they would probably carry the
controversy further, and retort on their opponents by an
appeal to Scripture as against their traditions, perhaps
ultimately even by an attack on traditionalism; but always
as represented by the Pharisees. A careful examination
of the statements of Josephus on this subject will show
that they convey no more than this. That there was
sufficient ground for Sadducean opposition to Pharisaic
traditionalism, alike in principle and in practice, will
appear from the following quotation, to which we add,
by way of explanation, that the wearing of phylacteries
was deemed by that party of Scriptural obligation, and
that the phylactery for the head was to consist (according

to tradition) of four compartments. 'Against the words
of the Scribes is more punishable than against the words
of Scripture. He who says, No phylacteries, so as to
transgress the words of Scripture, is not guilty (free) ; [he
who says] five compartments—to add to the words of
the Scribes—he is guilty.'

The second doctrinal difference between Pharisees and
Sadducees concerned the 'after death.' According to the
New Testament,[a] the Sadducees denied the resurrection of the dead, while Josephus, going
further, imputes to them denial of reward or
punishment after death, and even the doctrine
that the soul perishes with the body. The latter
statement may be dismissed as among those inferences
which theological controversialists are too fond of imputing to their opponents. But it is otherwise in regard
to their denial of the resurrection of the dead. Not only
Josephus, but the New Testament and Rabbinic writings,
attest this. The Mishnah expressly states that the
formula ' from age to age,' or rather ' from world to world,'
had been introduced as a protest against the opposite
theory; while the Talmud, which records disputations
between Gamaliel and the Sadducees on the subject of
the resurrection, expressly imputes the denial of this
doctrine to the ' Scribes of the Sadducees.' In fairness
it is perhaps only right to add that in the discussion
the Sadducees seem only to have actually denied that
there was proof for this doctrine in the Pentateuch, and
that they ultimately professed themselves convinced by
the reasoning of Rabbi Gamaliel. Whether or not their
opposition to the doctrine of the resurrection in the first
instance was prompted by rationalistic views, which they
endeavoured to support by an appeal to the letter of
the Pentateuch, as the source of traditionalism, it deserves
notice that in His controversy with the Sadducees Christ
appealed to the Pentateuch in proof of His teaching.

Connected with this was the equally rationalistic
opposition to belief in Angels and Spirits.[b]
Remembering what the Jewish Angelology was,

[a] St. Matt.
xxii. 23, and
parallel pas-
sages ; Acts
iv. 1, 2 ;
xxiii. 8

[b] Acts xxiii. 8

one can scarcely wonder that in controversy the Sadducees should have been led to the opposite extreme.

The last dogmatic difference between the two ' sects' concerned the problem of man's free will and God's pre-ordination, or rather their compatibility. The difference seems to have been this : that the Pharisees accentuated God's pre-ordination, the Sadducees man's free will; and that, while the Pharisees admitted only a partial influence of the human element on what happened, or the co-opera-tion of the human with the Divine, the Sadducees denied all absolute pre-ordination, and made man's choice of evil or good, with its consequences of misery or happiness, to depend entirely on the exercise of free will and self-determination.

The other differences between the Pharisees and Sadducees can be easily and briefly summed up. They concern ceremonial, ritual, and juridical questions. In regard to the first, the opposition of the Sadducees to the excessive scruples of the Pharisees on the subject of Levitical defilements led to frequent controversy.

Even greater importance attached to differences on ritual questions, although the controversy here was purely theoretical. For the Sadducees, when in office, always conformed to the prevailing Pharisaic practices. But the Sadducean objection to pouring the water of libation upon the altar on the Feast of Tabernacles, led to riot and bloody reprisals on the only occasion on which it seems to have been carried into practice.[1] There were also many other minor differences which need not here be discussed.

Among the divergences on juridical questions it may be mentioned that the Sadducees only allowed marriage with the ' betrothed,' and not with the actually espoused widow of a deceased childless brother.[2] Josephus, indeed,

---

[1] For details about the observances on this festival, I must refer to ' The Temple, its Ministry and Services.'

[2] The Sadducees in the Gospel argue on the Pharisaic theory, apparently for the twofold object of casting ridicule on the doctrine of the resurrection, and on the Pharisaic practice of marriage with the *espoused* wife of a deceased brother.

charges the Sadducees with extreme severity in criminal matters; but this must refer to the fact that the ingenuity or punctiliousness of the Pharisees would afford to most offenders a loophole of escape. On the other hand, such of the diverging juridical principles of the Sadducees as are attested on trustworthy authority, seem more in accordance with justice than those of the Pharisees.

With the exception of dogmatic differences, the controversy between the two parties turned on questions of 'canon-law.' Josephus tells us that the Pharisees commanded the masses, and especially the female world, while the Sadducees attached to their ranks only a minority, and that belonging to the highest class. The leading priests in Jerusalem formed, of course, part of that highest class of society; and from the New Testament and Josephus we learn that the High-Priestly families belonged to the Sadducean party.[a] But not a few of the Pharisaic leaders were actually priests, while the Pharisaic ordinances make more than ample recognition of the privileges and rights of the Priesthood. Even as regards the deputation to the Baptist of 'Priests and Levites' from Jerusalem, we are expressly told that they 'were of the Pharisees.'[b]

[a] Acts v. 17

[b] St. John i. 24

The name Pharisees, '*Perushim*,' 'separated ones,' was not taken by the party itself, but given to it by their opponents. From 1 Macc. ii. 42; vii. 13; 2 Macc. xiv. 6 it appears that originally they had taken the sacred name of *Chasidim*, or 'the pious.'[c] This, no doubt, on the ground that they were truly those who, according to the directions of Ezra,[d] had separated themselves 'from the filthiness of the heathen' (all heathen defilement) by carrying out the traditional ordinances.[1] The derivation of the name 'Sadducee' has always been in dispute. But the inference is at hand, that, while the 'Pharisees' would arrogate to themselves the Scriptural name of *Chasidim*, or 'the pious,' their opponents would retort that they were satisfied to be *Tsaddiqim*, or 'righteous.' Thus the

[c] Ps. xxx. 4; xxxi. 23; xxxvii. 28

[d] vi. 21; ix. 1; x. 11; Neh. ix. 2

---

[1] Comp. generally, 'Sketches of Jewish Social Life,' pp. 230, 231.

name of *Tsaddiqim* would become that of the party opposing the Pharisees, that is, of the *Sadducees*.

There remains yet another party, mention of which could not be omitted in any description of those times. But while the Pharisees and Sadducees were parties *within* the Synagogue, the Essenes[1] were, although strict Jews, yet separatists, and, alike in doctrine, worship, and practice, *outside* the Jewish body ecclesiastic. Their numbers amounted to only about 4,000. They are not mentioned in the New Testament, and only very indirectly referred to in Rabbinic writings. Their entire separation from all who did not belong to their sect, the terrible oaths by which they bound themselves to secrecy about their doctrines, and which would prevent any free religious discussion, as well as the character of what is known of their views, would account for the scanty notices about them.

On one point, at least, our brief inquiry can leave no doubt. The Essenes could never have been drawn either to the person or the preaching of John the Baptist. Similarly, the Sadducees would, after they knew its real character and goal, turn contemptuously from a movement which would awaken no sympathy in them, and could only become of interest when it threatened to endanger their class by awakening popular enthusiasm, and so rousing the suspicions of the Romans. To the Pharisees there were questions of dogmatic, ritual, and even national importance involved, which made the barest possibility of what John announced a question of moment. And, although we judge that the report which the earliest Pharisaic hearers of John[a] brought to Jerusalem —no doubt, detailed and accurate—and which led to the despatch of the deputation, would entirely predispose them against the Baptist, yet it behoved them, as leaders of public opinion, to take such cognisance of it, as would not only finally determine their own relation to the movement, but enable them effectually to direct that of others also.

* St. Matt. iii. 7

---

[1] For a fuller account of the Essenes see 'Life and Times,' vol. i. pp. 324-334.

CHAPTER XII.

THE TWOFOLD TESTIMONY OF JOHN—THE FIRST SABBATH OF JESUS' MINISTRY—THE FIRST SUNDAY—THE FIRST DISCIPLES.

(St. John i. 15–51.)

THE forty days, which had passed since Jesus had come to him, must have been to the Baptist a time of unfolding understanding, and of ripened decision.   On first meeting Jesus by the banks of Jordan, he had felt the seeming incongruity of baptizing One of Whom he had rather need to be baptized.   Yet what he needed was not to be baptized, but to learn that it became the Christ to fulfil all righteousness.   This was the first lesson.   The next and completing one came when after the Baptism the heavens opened, the Spirit descended, and the Divine Voice of Testimony pointed to, and explained the promised

ª St. John i. sign.[a]   It told him that the work which he had
33 begun in the obedience of faith had reached fulfilment.

He had entered upon it not only without illusions, but with such entire self-forgetfulness as only deepest conviction of the reality of what he announced could have wrought.   As we gather the elements of that conviction, we find them chiefly in the Book of Isaiah.   His speech and its imagery, and especially the burden of his message, were taken from those prophecies.

In his announcement of the Kingdom, in his call to inward repentance, even in his symbolic Baptism, one Great Personality always stood out before the mind of John.   All else was absorbed in that great fact: he was only the voice of one that cried, ' Prepare ye the way! '

And now, on the last of those forty days, simultaneously, as it would seem, with the final great Temptation of Jesus, which must have summed up all that had preceded it in the previous days, came the hour of John's temptation by the deputation from Jerusalem. Very gently it came to him, not like the storm-blast which swept over the Master. Yet a very real temptation it was, this provoking to the assumption of successively lower grades of self-assertion, where only entire self-abnegation was the rightful feeling. And greatest temptation it was when, after the first victory, came the not unnatural challenge of his authority for what he said and did. This was the question which must at all times, from the beginning of his work to the hour of his death, have pressed most closely upon him, since it touched not only his conscience, but the very ground of his mission, nay, of his life. For what was the meaning of that question which the disciples of John brought to Jesus: 'Art Thou He that should come, or do we look for another?' other than doubt of his own warrant and authority for what he had said and done? But in that first time of his trial at Bethabara he overcame—the first temptation by the humility of his intense sincerity, the second by the simplicity of his own experimental conviction; the first by what he had seen, the second by what he had heard concerning the Christ at the banks of Jordan.

Yet, as we view it, the questions of the Pharisaic deputation seem but natural. After his previous emphatic disclaimer at the beginning of his preaching (St. Luke iii. 15), of which they in Jerusalem could scarcely have been ignorant, the suggestion of his Messiahship—not indeed expressly made, but sufficiently implied to elicit what the language of the fourth Gospel shows to have been the most energetic denial—could scarcely have been more than tentative. It was otherwise with their question whether he were 'Elijah.' Yet, bearing in mind what we know of the Jewish expectations of Elijah, this also could scarcely have been meant in its full literality—but rather as ground for the further question after the goal and warrant of his mission. Hence also John's disavowing of such claims is not satisfactorily accounted for by the common explanation, that he denied being Elijah in the sense of not being what the Jews expected of the Forerunner of the Messiah :

the real, identical Elijah of the days of Ahab; or else, that he denied being such in the sense of the peculiar Jewish hopes attaching to his reappearance in 'the last days.' There is much deeper truth in the disclaimer of the Baptist. It was, indeed, true that, as foretold in the *St. Luke i. 17* Angelic announcement,[a] he was sent 'in the spirit and power of Elias,' that is, with the same object and the same qualifications. Similarly, it is true what, in His mournful retrospect of the result of John's mission, and in the prospect of His own end, the Saviour said of him: 'Elias is indeed come.' But 'the spirit and power' of the Elijah of the New Testament, which was to accomplish the inward restoration through penitent reception of the Kingdom of God in its reality, could only accomplish that object if 'they received it'—if 'they knew him.' And as in his own view, so also in very fact the Baptist, though Divinely such, was *not* really Elijah *to Israel.* This is the meaning of the words of Jesus: 'And *St. Matt. xi. 14* if ye will receive it, this is Elias, which was for to come.'[b]

More natural still seems the third question of the Pharisees, whether the Baptist were 'that prophet.' The reference here is undoubtedly to Deut. xviii. 15, 18. Not that the reappearance of Moses as lawgiver was expected. But the prediction taken in connection with the pro- *Jer. xxxi. 31 &c.* mise[c] of a 'new covenant' with a 'new law' written in the hearts of the people was expected to take place in Messianic days, and by the instrumentality of 'that prophet.'

Whatever views the Jewish embassy might have entertained concerning the abrogation, renewal, or renovation of the Law in Messianic times, the Baptist repelled the suggestion of his being 'that prophet' with the same energy as those of his being either the Christ or Elijah. We mark increased intensity and directness in the testi- *St. John i. 22-28* mony which he now bears to the Christ before the Jerusalem deputies.[d]

And the reward of his overcoming temptation was at hand. On the very day of the Baptist's temptation Jesus had left the wilderness. On the morrow after it, 'John seeth Jesus coming unto him, and saith, Behold, the Lamb of God, Which taketh away the sin of the world!' We cannot doubt, that the thought here present to the mind of John was the description of 'The Servant of Jehovah,' as set forth in Is. liii. It must always have been Messianically understood;[a] it formed the groundwork of Messianic thought to the New Testament writers[b]—nor did the Synagogue read it otherwise, till the necessities of controversy diverted its application, not indeed from the times, but from the Person of the Messiah. But we can understand how, during those forty days, this greatest height of Isaiah's conception of the Messiah was the one outstanding fact before his view. And what he believed, that he spake, when again, and unexpectedly, he saw Jesus.

Yet, while regarding his words as an appeal to the prophecy of Isaiah, two other references must not be excluded from them : those to the Paschal Lamb, and to the Daily Sacrifice. These are, if not directly pointed to, yet implied. For the Paschal Lamb was, in a sense, the basis of all the sacrifices of the Old Testament, not only from its saving import to Israel, but as that which really made them 'the Church,' and people of God. Hence the institution of the Paschal Lamb was, so to speak, only enlarged and applied in the daily sacrifice of a Lamb, in which this twofold idea of redemption and fellowship was exhibited. Lastly, the prophecy of Isaiah liii. was but the complete realisation of these two ideas in the Messiah. Neither could the Paschal Lamb with its completion in the Daily Sacrifice be properly viewed without this prophecy of Isaiah, nor yet that prophecy properly understood without its reference to its two great types. Jewish comment explains how the morning and evening sacrifices were intended to atone, the one for the sins of the night, the other for those of the day, so as ever to leave Israel guiltless before God ; and it expressly ascribes to them the efficacy of a *Paraclete*—that being the word used. And

[a] Is. lii. 13-liii.

[b] Comp. St. Matt. viii. 17 ; St. Luke xxii. 37; Acts viii. 32; 1 Pet. ii. 22

F

both the school of Shammai and that of Hillel insisted on the symbolic import of the Lamb of the Daily Sacrifice in regard to the forgiveness of sin. In view of such clear testimony from the time of Christ, less positiveness of assertion might, not unreasonably, be expected from those who declare that the sacrifices bore no reference to the forgiveness of sins, just as, in the face of the application made by the Baptist and other New Testament writers, more exegetical modesty seems called for on the part of those who deny the Messianic references in Isaiah.

It was, as we have reason to believe, the early morning of a Sabbath. John stood, with the two of his disciples who most shared his thoughts and feelings. One of them we know to have been Andrew (v. 40); the other, un-named one, could have been no other than John himself, the beloved disciple. They had heard what their teacher had on the previous day said of Jesus. And now that Figure once more appeared in view. The Baptist is not teaching now, but learning, as the intensity and penetration of his gaze calls from him the now worshipful repetition of what, on the previous day, he had explained and enforced. There was no leave-taking on the part of these two—perhaps they meant not to leave John. It needed no direction of John, no call from Jesus. But as they went, in the dawn of their rising faith, He turned Him. It was not because He discerned it not that He put to them the question, ' What seek ye ? ' which elicited a reply so simple, so real, as to carry its own evidence. He is still to them the Rabbi—the most honoured title they can find —yet marking still the strictly Jewish view, as well as their own standpoint of ' *What* seek ye ? ' There is strict correspondence to their view in the words of Jesus. Their very Hebraism of ' Rabbi ' is met by the equally Hebraic ' Come and see ; '[1] their unspoken, but half-conscious longing by what the invitation implied.

[1] The precise date of the origin of this designation is not quite clear. When Jesus is so addressed it is in the sense of 'my Teacher.' Nor can there be any reasonable doubt that thus it was generally current in and before the time noted in the Gospels. The expression ' Come

It was but early morning—ten o'clock.[1]   The form of
the narrative and its very words convey, that the two, not
learners now but teachers, had gone, each to search for his
brother—Andrew for Simon Peter, and John for James.
Here already, at the outset of this history, the haste of
energy characteristic of the sons of Jona[2] outdistanced the
St. John i. 41   more quiet intenseness of John : [a] 'He (Andrew)
first findeth his own brother.'   But Andrew and
John equally brought the same announcement, still
markedly Hebraic in its form : ' We have found the
Messias.'   This, then, was the outcome to them of that
day—He was the Messiah; and this the goal which their
longing had reached, ' We have found Him.'

And still this day of first marvellous discovery had not
closed.   It could scarcely have been but that Andrew had
told Jesus of his brother, and even asked leave to bring
him.   The searching glance of the Saviour now read in
Peter's inmost character his future call and work : ' Thou
art Simon, the son of John—thou shalt be called Cephas,
which is interpreted (Grecianised) Peter.'

It was Sunday morning, the first of Christ's Mission-
work, the first of His Preaching.   He was purposing to return to Galilee.   The first Jerusalem-visit must be prepared
for by them all ; and he would not go there till the right
time—for the Paschal Feast.   It was probably a distance of
about twenty miles from Bethany (Bethabara) to Cana.   By
the way, two other disciples were to be gained—this time
not brought but called, where and in what precise circumstances we know not.   But the notice that Philip was a

and see' is among the most common Rabbinic formulas, although
generally connected with the acquisition of special and important information.

[1] The common supposition is, that the time must be computed
according to the Jewish method, in which case the tenth hour would
represent 4 P.M.   But remembering that the Jewish day ended with
sunset, it could, in that case, have been scarcely marked that ' they
abode with Him that day.'   The correct interpretation would therefore
point in this, as in other passages of St. John, to the Asiatic numeration
of hours, corresponding to our own.   Comp. *J. B. McLellan's* New
Testament, pp. 740-742.

[2] Note : According to the best text, John, and not *Jona*, as below.

fellow-townsman of Andrew and Peter seems to imply some instrumentality on their part. Similarly we gather that afterwards Philip was somewhat in advance of the rest, when he found his acquaintance Nathanael, and engaged in conversation with him just as Jesus and the others came up. But here also we mark, as another characteristic trait of John, that he, and his brother with him, seem to have clung close to the Person of Christ, just as did Mary afterwards in the house of her brother. It was this intense exclusiveness of fellowship with Jesus which traced on his mind that fullest picture of the God-Man, which his narrative reflects.

The call to Philip from the lips of the Saviour met with immediate responsive obedience. Yet though no special obstacles had to be overcome and hence no special narrative was called for, it must have implied much of learning, to judge from what he did and from what he said to Nathanael. In Nathanael's conquest by Christ there is something special implied, of which the Lord's words give significant hints. *Nathanael* (Theodore, 'the gift of God') had, as we often read of Rabbis, rested for prayer, meditation, or study, in the shadow of that widespreading tree so common in Palestine, the fig-tree. The approaching Passover-season, perhaps mingling with thoughts of John's announcement by the banks of Jordan, would naturally suggest the great deliverance of Israel in the age to come. Such a verse as that with which the meditation for the New Moon of Nisan, the Passover-month, closes—'Happy is he that hath the God of Jacob for his help'[a]—would recur, and so lead back the mind to the suggestive symbol of Jacob's vision, and its realisation in 'the age to come.'

Ps. cxlvi. 5

These are, of course, only suppositions; but it might well be that Philip had found him while still busy with such thoughts. It must have seemed a startling answer to his thoughts, this announcement, made with the freshness of new conviction: 'We have found Him of Whom Moses in the Law, and the Prophets, did write.' But this addition about the Man of Nazareth, the son of

Joseph, would appear a terrible anti-climax. It was so different from anything that he had associated either with the great hope of Israel, or with the Nazareth of his own neighbourhood, that his exclamation, without implying any special imputation on the little town, seems only natural. There was but one answer to this—that which Philip made, which Jesus had made to Andrew and John: 'Come and see.' And as he went with him evidences irrefragable multiplied at every step. As he neared Jesus, he heard Him speak to the disciples words concerning him, which recalled, truly and actually, what had passed in his soul. And to his astonished question came such answer that he could not but burst into immediate and full acknowledgment: 'Thou art the Son of God,' Who hast read my inmost being; 'Thou art the King of Israel,' Who dost meet its longing and hope.

Thus Nathanael, 'the God-given'—or, as we know him in after-history, Bartholomew, 'the son of Telamyon'—was on that first Sunday added to the disciples.

CHAPTER XIII.

THE MARRIAGE-FEAST IN CANA OF GALILEE.

(St. John ii. 1–12.)

WE are now to enter on the Ministry of 'The Son of Man,' first and chiefly in its contrast to the preparatory call of the Baptist, with the asceticism symbolic of it. We behold Him now as freely mingling with humanity, entering into its family life, sanctioning and hallowing all by His Presence and blessing; then as transforming the 'water of legal purification' into the wine of the new dispensation; and, lastly, as having absolute power as the 'Son of Man,' being also 'the Son of God' and 'the King of Israel.'

It must be borne in mind that marriage conveyed to the Jews much higher thoughts than merely those of festivity and merriment. The pious fasted before it, confessing their sins. It was regarded almost as a Sacrament. Entrance into the married state was thought to carry the forgiveness of sins. It almost seems as if the relationship of Husband and Bride between Jehovah and His people, so frequently insisted upon, not only in the Bible, but in Rabbinic writings, had always been standing out in the background.

A special formality, that of ' betrothal,' preceded the actual marriage by a period varying in length, but not exceeding a twelvemonth in the case of a maiden. At the betrothal, the bridegroom, personally or by deputy, handed to the bride a piece of money or a letter, it being expressly stated in each case that the man thereby espoused the woman. A legal document fixed the dowry which each brought, the mutual obligations, and all other legal points.

On the evening of the actual marriage, the bride was led from her paternal home to that of her husband. First came the merry sounds of music; then they who distributed among the people wine and oil, and nuts among the children; next the bride, covered with the bridal veil, her long hair flowing, surrounded by her companions, and led by ' the friends of the bridegroom,' and ' the children of the bride-chamber.' All around were in festive array; some carried torches, or lamps on poles; those nearest had myrtle-branches and chaplets of flowers. Every one rose to salute the procession, or join it; and it was deemed almost a religious duty to break into praise of the beauty, the modesty, or the virtues of the bride. Arrived at her new home, she was led to her husband. Some such formula as: ' Take her according to the Law of Moses and of Israel,' would be spoken, and bride and bridegroom crowned with garlands. Then a formal legal instrument was signed, which set forth that the bridegroom undertook to work for her, to honour, keep, and care for her, as is the manner of the men of Israel; that he promised to give his maiden-wife at least two hundred *Zuz* [1] (or more as might be),[2] and to increase her own dowry (which, in the

---

[1] If the *Zuz* be reckoned at 7*d.*, about 5*l.* 16*s.* 8*d.*

[2] This, of course, represents only the *minimum*. In the case of a Priest's daughter the ordinary legal minimum was doubled.

case of a poor orphan, the authorities supplied) by at least one-half, and that he also undertook to lay it out for her to the best advantage, all his own possessions being guarantee for it. Then, after the prescribed washing of hands and benediction, the marriage-supper began—the cup being filled, and the solemn prayer of bridal benediction spoken over it. And so the feast lasted—it might be more than one day, till at last 'the friends of the bridegroom' led the bridal pair to the bridal-chamber and bed. Here it ought to be specially noticed, as a striking evidence that the writer of the fourth Gospel was not only a Hebrew, but intimately acquainted with the varying customs prevailing in Galilee and in Judæa, that at the marriage of Cana no 'friend of the bridegroom' or 'groomsman' is mentioned, while he *is* referred to in St. John iii. 29, where the words are spoken outside the boundaries of Galilee. For among the simpler Galileans the practice of having 'friends of the bridegroom' did not obtain, though all the invited guests bore the general name of 'children of the bride-chamber.'[a]

ᵃ Comp. St. Matt. ix. 15

It was the marriage in Cana of Galilee. All connected with the account of it is strictly Jewish—the feast, the guests, the invitation of the stranger Rabbi, and its acceptance by Jesus. We are not able to fix with certainty the site of the little town of Cana. But if we adopt the most probable identification of it with the modern pleasant village of *Kefr Kenna*, a few miles north-east of Nazareth, on the road to the Lake of Galilee, we picture it to ourselves as on the slope of a hill, its houses rising terrace upon terrace. As we approach the little town we come upon a fountain of excellent water, around which clustered the village gardens and orchards that produced in great abundance the best pomegranates in Palestine. Here was the home of Nathanael-Bartholomew, and it seems not unlikely, that with him Jesus had passed the time intervening between His arrival and 'the marriage,' to which His Mother had come—the omission of all mention of Joseph leading to the supposition, that he had died before that time. There is not any difficulty in understanding that on His arrival

Jesus would hear of this ' marriage,' of the presence of His Mother in what seems to have been the house of a friend, if not a relative; that He and His disciples would be bidden to the feast; and that He resolved not only to comply with the request, but to use it as a leave-taking from home and friends—similar, though also far other, than that of Elisha, when he entered on his mission.

As we pass through the court of that house in Cana, and reach the covered gallery which opens on the various rooms—in this instance, particularly, on the great reception room—all is festively adorned. In the gallery the servants move about, and there the ' water-pots ' are ranged, ' after the manner of the Jews,' for purification—for the washing not only of hands before and after eating, but also of the vessels used.[a] ' Purification ' was one of the main points in Rabbinic sanctity, and the mass of the people would have regarded neglect of the ordinances of purification as betokening either gross ignorance or daring impiety.

[a] Comp. St. Mark vii. 1-4

At any rate, such would not be exhibited on an occasion like the present; and outside the reception-room, as St. John relates, six of those stone pots, of which we know from Rabbinic writings, were ranged. It seems likely that each of these pots might have held from 17 to $25\frac{1}{2}$ gallons. For such an occasion the family would produce or borrow the largest and handsomest stone-vessels that could be procured, and it seems to have been the practice to set apart some of these vessels exclusively for the use of the bride and of the more distinguished guests, while the rest were used by the general company.

Entering the spacious, lofty dining-room, which would be brilliantly lighted with lamps and candlesticks, the guests are disposed round tables on couches, soft with cushions or covered with tapestry, or seated on chairs. The bridal blessing has been spoken, and the bridal cup emptied. The feast is proceeding—not the common meal, which was generally taken about even, according to the Rabbinic saying, that he who postponed it beyond that hour was as if he swallowed a stone—but a festive evening meal. And now there must have been a painful pause, or something like it, when the mother of Jesus whispered to Him that 'the wine failed.' There could, perhaps, be the less cause for reticence on this point towards her Son, not merely because this failure may have arisen from the accession of guests in the persons of Jesus and His disciples, for whom no provision had been originally made, but because the gift of wine or oil on such occasions was regarded as a meritorious work of charity.

But all this still leaves the main incidents in the narrative untouched. How are we to understand the implied request of the Mother of Jesus, how His reply, and what was the meaning of the miracle? Although we have no absolute certainty of it, we have the strongest internal reasons for believing that Jesus had done no miracles these thirty years in the home at Nazareth, but lived the life of quiet submission and obedient waiting. That was the then part of His Work.

And so when Mary told Him of the want that had arisen, it was simply in absolute confidence in her Son, probably without any conscious expectancy of a miracle on His part. Yet not without a touch of maternal self-consciousness, almost pride, that He, Whom she could trust to do anything that was needed, was her Son, Whom she could solicit in the friendly family whose guests they were—and that what He did would be done if not for her sake, yet at her request. It was a true earth-view to take of their relationship: the outcome of His misunderstood meekness. And therefore it was that as on the first misunderstanding in the Temple, He had said: 'Wist ye not that I must be about My Father's business?' so now: 'Woman, what have I to do with thee?' With that 'business' earthly relationship, however tender, had no connection.

And Mary did not, and yet she did, understand Him, when she turned to the servants with the direction, implicitly to follow His behests. What happened is well known: how, in the excess of their zeal, they filled the water-pots to the brim—an accidental circumstance, yet useful, as showing that there could be neither delusion nor collusion; how,

probably in the drawing of it, the water became best wine
—' the conscious water saw its God, and blushed;' then
the coarse proverbial joke of what was probably the master
of ceremonies and purveyor of the feast, intended, of course,
not literally to apply to the present company, and yet in its
accidentalness an evidence of the reality of the miracle.
After this the narrative abruptly closes with a retrospective
remark on the part of him who relates it : ' And His disciples
believed on Him.'

CHAPTER XIV.

THE CLEANSING OF THE TEMPLE.

(St. John ii. 13–25.)

IMMEDIATELY after the marriage of Cana, Mary and the
' brethren of Jesus ' went with Him, or followed Him, to
Capernaum, which henceforth became ' His own
city ' [a] during His stay by the Lake of Galilee.

ᵃSt. Matt. iv.
13 ; ix. 1 ;
St. Mark ii. 1

It seems most probable that the *Tell Hûm* of
modern exploration marks the site of the ancient *Capernaum, Kephar Nachum,* or *Tanchumin.* At the time it could
have been of only recent origin, since its Synagogue had but
lately been reared, through the friendly liberality of the
true and faithful Centurion.[b] But already its
importance was such, that it had become the

ᵇ St. Matt.
viii. 5, &c.

station of a garrison, and of one of the principal custom-
houses. Its soft sweet air, the fertility of the country—
notably of the plain of Gennesaret close by ; and the
fertilising proximity of a spring which, from its teeming
with fish like that of the Nile, was popularly regarded as
springing from the river of Egypt—this and more must
have made Capernaum one of the most delightful places in
these ' Gardens of Princes,' as the Rabbis interpreted the
word ' Gennesaret,' by the ' cither-shaped lake ' of that
name. The town lay quite up on its north-western shore,
only two miles from where the Jordan falls into the lake.
Close by the shore stood the Synagogue, built of white
limestone on dark basalt foundation. All the houses of the

town are gone: the good Centurion's house, that of Mat-
thew the publican,[a] that of Simon Peter,[b] the temporary home which first sheltered the Master and His loved ones. All are unrecognisable —a confused mass of ruins—save only that white Synagogue in which He taught. From its ruins we can still measure its dimensions, and trace its fallen pillars; nay, we discover over the lintel of its entrance the device of a pot of manna, which may have lent its form to His teaching there.[c]

And this, then, is Capernaum—the first and the chief home of Jesus, when He had entered on His active work. But, on this occasion, He 'continued there not many days.' For, already, 'the Jews' Passover was at hand,' and He must needs keep that feast in Jerusalem. If our former computations are right this Passover must have taken place in the spring (about April) of the year 27 A.D. A month before the feast bridges and roads were put in repair, and sepulchres whitened, to prevent accidental pollution to the pilgrims. Then, some would select this out of the three great annual feasts for the tithing of their flocks and herds, which, in such case, had to be done two weeks before the Passover; while others would fix on it as the time for going up to Jerusalem before the feast 'to purify them-selves'[d]—that is, to undergo the prescribed purification in any case of Levitical defilement. But what must have appealed to every one in the land was the appear-ance of the 'money-changers' who opened their stalls in every country-town on the 15th of Adar (just a month before the feast). They were, no doubt, regularly accre-dited and duly authorised. For all Jews and proselytes —women, slaves, and minors excepted—had to pay the annual Temple-tribute of half a shekel, according to the 'sacred' standard, equal to about 1s. 2d. of our money. From this tax, many of the Priests—to the chagrin of the Rabbis—claimed exemption.

This Temple-tribute had to be paid in exact half-shekels of the Sanctuary, or ordinary Galilean shekels. When it is remembered that, besides strictly Palestinian silver and

[a] St. Mark ii. 15; comp. iii. 20, 31

[b] St. Matt. viii. 14

[c] St. John vi. 49, 59

[d] St. John xi. 55.

especially copper coin, Persian, Tyrian, Syrian, Egyptian, Grecian, and Roman money circulated in the country, it will be understood what work these ' money-changers ' must have had. From the 15th to the 25th Adar they had stalls in every country-town. On the latter date, which must therefore be considered as marking the first arrivals of festive pilgrims in the city, the stalls in the country were closed, and the money-changers henceforth sat within the precincts of the Temple. All who refused to pay the Temple-tribute, except Priests, were liable to distraint of their goods. The money-changers made a statutory fixed charge of from $1\frac{1}{2}d.$ to $2d.$ on every half-shekel. In some cases, however, double this amount was charged.

It is a reasonable inference that many of the foreign Jews arriving in Jerusalem would take the opportunity of changing at these tables their foreign money, and for this, of course, fresh charges would be made. For there was a great deal to be bought within the Temple-area, needful for the feast (in the way of sacrifices and their adjuncts), or for purification. We can picture to ourselves the scene around the table of an Eastern money-changer—the weighing of the coins, deductions for loss of weight, arguing, disputing, bargaining—and we can realise the terrible truthfulness of our Lord's charge that they had made the Father's House a mart and place of traffic. But even so the business of the Temple money-changers would not be exhausted. Through their hands would pass probably all business matters connected with the Sanctuary. Some idea of the vast accumulation of wealth in the Temple-treasury may be formed from the circumstance that, despite many previous spoliations, the value of the gold and silver which Crassus [a] carried from the Temple-treasury amounted to the enormous sum of about two and a half millions sterling.

[a] 54–53 B.C.

The noisy and incongruous business of an Eastern money-lender was not the only one carried on within the sacred Temple-enclosure. A person bringing a sacrifice might not only learn, but actually obtain, in the Temple from its officials what was required for the meat- and drink-offering. The prices were fixed by tariff every month, and on payment of the stated amount the offerer received one of four counterfoils, which respectively indicated, and, on handing it to the proper official, procured the prescribed complement of his sacrifice.[1] The Priests and Levites in charge of this made up their accounts every evening, and these (thoughn ecessary) transactions must have left a considerable margin of profit to the treasury. This would soon lead to another line of traffic. Offerers might, of course, bring their sacrificial animals with them, and we know that on the Mount of Olives there were four shops, specially for the sale of pigeons and other things requisite for sacrificial purposes. But then, when an animal was brought, it had to be examined as to its Levitical fitness by persons regularly qualified and appointed. Disputes might here arise, due to the ignorance of the purchaser or the greed of the examiner. But all trouble and difficulty would be avoided by a regular market within the Temple-enclosure, where sacrificial animals could be purchased, having presumably been duly inspected, and all fees paid before being offered for sale. It needs no comment to show how utterly the Temple would be profaned by such traffic, and to what scenes it might lead.

These Temple-Bazaars,[2] the property, and one of the principal sources of income, of the family of Annas, were the scene of the purification of the Temple by Jesus ; and in the private *locale* attached to these very Bazaars, where the Sanhedrin held its meetings at the time, the final condemnation of Jesus may have been planned, if not actually pronounced. We can now also understand why the Temple officials, to whom these Bazaars belonged, only challenged the authority of Christ in thus purging the Temple : the unpopularity of the whole traffic, if not their consciences, prevented their proceeding to actual violence. Nor do we any longer wonder that no resistance was offered by the people to the action of Jesus, and that even the remon-

[1] Comp. 'The Temple and its Services, &c.' pp. 118, 119.
[2] See Vol. i. pp. 370–72 of the larger work.

strances of the priests were not direct, but in the form of a perplexing question.

Many of those present must have known Jesus. The zeal of His early disciples, who, on their first recognition of Him, proclaimed the new-found Messiah, could not have given place to absolute silence. The many Galilean pilgrims in the Temple could not but have spread the tidings, and the report must soon have passed from one to the other in the Temple-courts, as He first entered their sacred enclosure. They would follow Him, and watch what He did. Nor were they disappointed. He inaugurated His Mission by fulfilling the prediction concerning Him Who was to be Israel's refiner and purifier (Mal. iii. 1-3). Scarce had He entered the Temple-porch, and trod the Court of the Gentiles, than He drove thence what profanely defiled it. There was not a hand lifted, not a word spoken to arrest Him as He made the scourge of small cords, and with it drove out of the Temple both the sheep and the oxen ; not a word said nor a hand raised as He poured into their receptacles the changers' money and overthrew their tables. His Presence awed them, His words awakened even their consciences; they knew only too well how true His denunciations were. And behind Him was gathered the wondering multitude, with whom such bold and Messianic vindication of Temple sanctity would gain Him respect, approbation and admiration, and which, at any rate, secured His safety.

For when ' the Jews,' by which here, as in so many other places, we are to understand the rulers of the people —in this instance, the Temple officials—did gather courage to come forward, they ventured not to lay hands on Him. Still more strangely, they did not even reprove Him for what He had done, as if it had been wrong or improper. With infinite cunning, as appealing to the multitude, they only asked for ' a sign ' which would warrant such assumption of authority. But this question of challenge marked two things : the essential opposition between the Jewish authorities and Jesus, and the manner in which they would carry on the contest, which was henceforth to be waged between Him and the rulers of the people.

And Jesus foresaw, or rather saw it all. As for ' the sign,' then and ever again sought by an ' evil and adulterous generation '—evil in their thoughts and ways, and adulterous to the God of Israel—He had then, as afterwards,[a] only one ' sign ' to give : ' Destroy this Temple, and in three days I will raise it up.' Thus He met their challenge for a sign by the challenge of a sign : Crucify Him, and He would rise again ; let them suppress the Christ, He would triumph.

a St. Matt.
xii. 38–40

CHAPTER XV.

JESUS AND NICODEMUS.

(St. John iii. 1–21.)

THE Feast of the Passover commenced on the 15th Nisan, dating it, of course, from the preceding evening. On the evening of the 13th Nisan, with which the 14th, or ' preparation-day,' commenced, the head of each household would, with lighted candle and in solemn silence, search out all leaven in his house, prefacing his search with solemn thanksgiving and appeal to God, and closing it by an equally solemn declaration that he had accomplished it, so far as within his knowledge, and disavowing responsibility for what lay beyond it. And as the worshippers went to the Temple, they would see prominently exposed, on a bench in one of the porches, two desecrated cakes of some thankoffering, indicating that it was still lawful to eat of that which was leavened. At ten, or at latest eleven o'clock, one of those cakes was removed, and then they knew that it was no longer lawful to eat of it. At twelve o'clock the second cake was removed, and this was the signal for solemnly burning all the leaven that had been gathered.

The ' cleansing of the Temple ' undoubtedly preceded the actual festive Paschal week.[b] To those who were in Jerusalem it was a week such as had never been before, a week when ' they saw the signs which

b St. John ii. 23

He did,' and when, stirred by a strange impulse, 'they believed in His Name' as the Messiah.

Among the observers who were struck by these signs was Nicodemus, one of the Pharisees and a member of the Jerusalem Sanhedrin. And, as we gather from his mode of expression, not he only, but others with him. From the Gospel-history we know him to have been cautious by nature and education, and timid of character, and we cannot wonder that he should have wished to shroud this his first visit in the utmost possible secrecy. It was a most compromising step for a Sanhedrist to take. With that first bold purgation of the Temple a deadly feud between Jesus and the Jewish authorities had begun, of which the sequel could not be doubtful.

Nevertheless, Nicodemus came. And as Jesus was not depressed by the resistance of the authorities, nor by the 'milk-faith' of the multitude (as Luther calls it), so He was not elated by the possibility of making such a convert as a member of the Great Sanhedrin.

The report of what passed reads, more than almost any other in the Gospels, like notes taken at the time by one who was present. We can almost put it again into the form of brief notes, by heading what each said in this manner, *Nicodemus*:—or, *Jesus*. They are only the outlines of the conversation, giving in each case the really important gist, and leaving abrupt gaps between, as would be the manner in such notes. Yet they are quite sufficient to tell us all that is important for us to know. We can scarcely doubt that it was the narrator, John, who was the witness that took the notes. His own reflections upon it, or rather his after-look upon it, in the light of later facts, and under the teaching of the Holy Ghost, is described in the verses with which the writer follows his account of what had passed between Jesus and Nicodemus (St. John iii. 16–21). In the same manner he winds up with similar reflections (ib. vv. 31–36) the reported conversation between the Baptist and his disciples. In neither case are the verses to which we refer part of what either Jesus or John said at the time, but what, in view of it,

John says in name of, and to the Church of the New Testament.

If from St. John xix. 27 we might infer that St. John had ' a home' in Jerusalem itself, the scene about to be described would have taken place under the roof of him who has given us its record. Up in the simply furnished *Aliyah*—the guest-chamber on the roof—the lamp was still burning. There was no need for Nicodemus to pass through the house, for an outside stair led to the upper room. It was night, when Jewish superstition would keep men at home; a wild, gusty spring night, when loiterers would not be in the streets; and no one would see him as at that hour he ascended the outside steps that led up to the *Aliyah*. His errand was soon told: one sentence, that which admitted the Divine Teachership of Jesus, implied all the questions he could wish to ask. It was all about ' the Kingdom of God,' so connected with that Teacher come from God, that Nicodemus would inquire.

And Jesus took him straight to whence alone that ' Kingdom' could be seen. ' Except a man be born from above,[1] he cannot see the Kingdom of God.' Judaism could understand a new relationship towards God and man, and even the forgiveness of sins. But it had no conception of a moral renovation, a spiritual birth, as the initial condition for reformation, far less as that for seeing the Kingdom of God. And it was because it had no idea of such ' birth from above,' of its reality or even possibility, that Judaism could not be the Kingdom of God.

All this sounded quite strange and unintelligible to Nicodemus. He could understand how a man might *become* other, and so ultimately *be* other; but how a man should first *be* other in order to *become* other—more than that, needed to be ' born from above,' in order to ' see the Kingdom of God '—passed alike his experience and his Jewish learning. Only one possibility of *being* occurred

---

[1] Notwithstanding the high authority of Professor *Westcott*, I must still hold that this and not ' anew,' is the right rendering. The word ἄνωθεν has always the meaning ' above' in the fourth Gospel (ch. iii. 3, 7, 31; xix. 11, 23); and otherwise also St. John always speaks of ' a birth' from God (St. John i. 13; 1 John ii. 29; iii. 9; iv. 7; v. 1, 4, 18).

to him : that given him in his natural disposition, or, as a
Jew would have put it, in his original innocency when he
first entered the world.   And this he thought aloud.[a]

But there was another world of being than that
of which Nicodemus thought.   That world was
the 'Kingdom of God' in its essential contrariety to the
kingdom of this world, whether in the general sense of
that expression, or even in the special Judaistic sense
attaching to the 'Kingdom' of the Messiah.   But that
'Kingdom' was spiritual, and here a man must *be* in order
to *become*.   How was he to attain that new being ?   The
Baptist had pointed it out in its negative aspect of repentance and putting away the old by his Baptism of water ;
and as regarded its positive aspect he had pointed to Him
Who was to baptize with the Holy Ghost and with fire.
This was the gate of *being*, through which a man must
enter into the Kingdom, which was of the Messiah, because it was of God and the Messiah was of God, and in
that sense 'the Teacher come from God'—that is, being
sent of God, He taught of God by bringing to God.   But
as to the mystery of this *being* in order to *become*—hark !
did he hear the sound of the wind as it swept past the
Aliyah ?   He heard its voice ; but he neither knew whence
it came, nor whither it went.   So was every one that was
born of the Spirit.   You might hear the voice of the Spirit
Who originated the new being, but the origination of that
new being, or its further development into all that it might
and would become, lay beyond man's observation.

Nicodemus now understood in some measure what
entrance into the Kingdom meant ; but he wanted to
know the *how* of these things before he believed them.
But to that spring of being no one could ascend but He
that had come down from heaven, the only true Teacher
come from God.   Or did Nicodemus think of another
Teacher — hitherto their only Teacher, Moses — whom
Jewish tradition generally believed to have ascended into
the very heavens, in order to bring the teaching unto
them ?   Let the history of Moses, then, teach them !   They
had heard what Moses had taught them ; they had seen

'the earthly things' of God—and, in view and hearing of it all, they had not believed but murmured and rebelled. Then came the judgment of the fiery serpents, and, in answer to repentant prayer, the symbol of new *being*, a life restored from death, as they looked on their no longer living but dead death lifted up before them. A symbol this, showing forth two elements : negatively, the putting away of the past in their dead death (the serpent no longer living, but a brazen serpent) ; and positively, in their look of faith and hope. Before this symbol, as has been said, tradition has stood dumb. It could only suggest one meaning, and draw from it one lesson. The meaning which tradition attached to it was that Israel lifted up their eyes, not merely to the serpent, but rather to their Father in heaven, and had regard to His mercy. This, as St. John afterwards shows (ver. 16), was a true but insufficient interpretation. And the lesson which tradition drew from it was that this symbol taught the dead would live again ; for, as it is argued, 'behold, if God made it that, through the similitude of the serpent which brought death, the dying should be restored to life, how much more shall He, Who is Life, restore the dead to life ? ' And here lies the true interpretation of what Jesus taught. If the uplifted serpent, as symbol, brought life to the believing look which was fixed upon the giving, pardoning love of God, then, in the truest sense, shall the uplifted Son of Man give true life to everyone that believeth, looking up in Him to the giving and forgiving love of God, which His Son came to bring, to declare, and to manifest. ' For as Moses lifted up the serpent in the wilderness, so must the Son of Man be lifted up, that whosoever believeth should in Him have eternal life.'

And so the record of this interview abruptly closes. Of Nicodemus we shall hear again in the sequel, not needlessly, nor yet to complete a biography, were it even that of Jesus ; but as is necessary for the understanding of this

^{a St. John iii. 16-21} History. What follows^a are not the words of Christ, but of St. John. In them, looking back many years afterwards in the light of completed events,

the Apostle takes his stand, as becomes the circumstances, where Jesus had ended His teaching of Nicodemus—under the Cross.

And to all time and to all men sounds, like the Voice of the Teacher come from God, this eternal Gospel-message: ' God so loved the world, that He gave His only-begotten Son, that whosoever believeth in Him should not perish, but have everlasting life.'

CHAPTER XVI.

IN JUDÆA AND THROUGH SAMARIA.

(St. John iv. 1–4.)

FROM the city Jesus retired with His disciples to 'the country,' which formed the province of Judæa.   There He
ª St. John iv. 2   taught, and His disciples baptized.[a]   The number of those who professed adhesion to the expected new Kingdom, and were consequently baptized, was as large, in that locality, as had submitted to the preaching and Baptism of John—perhaps even larger.   An exaggerated report was carried to the Pharisaic authorities:
ᵇ St. John iv. 1   ' Jesus maketh and baptizeth more disciples than John.'[b]   From which, at least, we infer that the opposition of the leaders of the party to the Baptist was now settled, and that it extended to Jesus ; and also, what careful watch they kept over the new movement.

But what seems at first sight strange is the twofold circumstance that Jesus should for a time have established Himself in such apparently close proximity to the Baptist, and that on this occasion, and on this only, He should have allowed His disciples to administer the rite of Baptism.   The latter must not be confounded with Christian Baptism, which was only introduced after the death of
ᶜ Rom. iv. 3   Christ,[c] or, to speak more accurately, after the outpouring of the Holy Ghost.   The administration of the same rite by John and by the disciples of Jesus seems not only unnecessary, but it might give rise to mis-

conception on the part of enemies, and misunderstanding or jealousy on the part of weak disciples.

Such was actually the case when, on one occasion, a discussion arose ' on the part of John's disciples with a

ᵃ St. John iii. 25 Jew,' [1] on the subject of purification.ᵃ We know not the special point in dispute. But what really interests us is, that somehow this Jewish objector must have connected what he said with a reference to the Baptism of Jesus' disciples. For, immediately afterwards, the disciples of John, in their zeal for the honour of their master, brought him tidings of what to them seemed interference with the work of the Baptist, and almost presumption on the part of Jesus. While fully alive to their error, we cannot but honour and sympathize with this loving care for their master. Never before had such deep earnestness and self-abnegation as his been witnessed. In the high-day of his power, when all men wondered whether he would announce himself as the Christ, or, at least, as His Forerunner, or as one of the great Prophets, John had disclaimed everything for himself, and pointed to Another! And, as if this had not been enough, the multitudes which had formerly come to John now flocked around Jesus; nay, He had even usurped the one distinctive function still left to their master. It was evident that, hated and watched by the Pharisees, watched also by the ruthless jealousy of a Herod, overlooked if not supplanted by Jesus, the mission of their master was nearing its close. It had been a life and work of suffering and self-denial; it was about to end in loneliness and sorrow. They said nothing expressly to complain of Him to Whom John had borne witness, but they told of what He did, and how all men came to Him.

The answer which the Baptist made may be said to mark the high-point of his life and witness. In the silence, which was now gathering around him, he heard but One Voice, that of the Bridegroom. For it he had waited and worked. And now that it had come, he was content: his ' joy was now fulfilled.' ' He must increase, but I must decrease.' It was the right and good order.

---

[1] This, and not ' the Jews,' is the better reading.

That these were his last words, publicly spoken and recorded, may, however, explain to us why on this exceptional occasion Jesus sanctioned the administration by His disciples of the Baptism of John. Far divergent as their paths had been, this practical sanction on the part of Jesus of John's Baptism, when the Baptist was about to be forsaken, betrayed and murdered, was Christ's highest testimony to him. Jesus adopted his Baptism ere its waters for ever ceased to flow, and thus He blessed and consecrated them.

Leaving for the present the Baptist, we follow the footsteps of the Master. St. John alone tells of the early Judæan ministry and the journey through Samaria, which preceded the Galilean work.

The shorter road from Judæa to Galilee led through Samaria; and this was the one generally taken by the Galileans on their way to the capital. On the other hand, the Judæans seem chiefly to have made a *détour* through Peræa, in order to avoid hostile and impure Samaria. The expression, ' He must needs go through Samaria,' probably refers to the advisability in the circumstances of taking the most direct road, since such prejudices in regard to Samaria would not influence the conduct of Jesus. Great as these undoubtedly were, they have been unduly exaggerated by modern writers, misled by one-sided quotations from Rabbinic works.

The Biblical history of that part of Palestine which bore the name of Samaria need not here be repeated.[a] Before the final deportation of Israel by Shalmaneser, or rather Sargon, the ' Samaria ' to which his operations extended must have considerably shrunk in dimensions. It is difficult to suppose that the original deportation was so complete as to leave behind no traces of the original Israelitish inhabitants.[b] Their number would probably be swelled by fugitives from Assyria, and by Jewish settlers in the troublous times that followed. Afterwards they were largely increased by apostates and rebels against the order of things established by Ezra and Nehemiah.

[a] Comp. 1 Kings xiii. 32 ; xvi. 24 &c. ; Tiglath-pileser, 2 Kings xv. 29 ; Shalmaneser, xvii. 3–5 ; xviii. 9–11 ; Sargon, xvii. 6, &c.

[b] Comp. 2 Chron. xxxiv. 6, 9 ; Jer. xli. 5 ; Amos v. 3

The first foreign colonists of Samaria brought their peculiar forms of idolatry with them.[a] But the Providential judgments by which they were visited led to the introduction of a spurious Judaism, consisting of a mixture of their former superstitions with Jewish doctrines and rites.[b] Although this state of matters resembled that which had obtained in the original kingdom of Israel, perhaps just because of this, Ezra and Nehemiah, when reconstructing the Jewish commonwealth, insisted on a strict separation between those who had returned from Babylon and the Samaritans, resisting equally their offers of co-operation and their attempts at hindrance. This embittered the national feeling of jealousy already existing, and led to that constant hostility between Jews and Samaritans which has continued to this day. The religious separation became final when the Samaritans built a rival temple on Mount Gerizim, and Manasseh, the brother of Juddua, the Jewish High-Priest, having refused to annul his marriage with the daughter of Sanballat, was forced to flee, and became the High-Priest of the new Sanctuary. Henceforth, by impudent falsification of the text of the Pentateuch, Gerizim was declared the rightful centre of worship, and the doctrines and rites of the Samaritans exhibited a curious imitation and adaptation of those prevalent in Judæa. As might be expected, their tendency was Sadducean rather than Pharisaic.

In general it may be said that, while on certain points Jewish opinion remained always the same, the judgment passed on the Samaritans, and especially as to intercourse with them, varied, according as they showed more or less active hostility towards the Jews.[1]

The expression, 'the Jews have no dealings with the Samaritans,'[c] finds its Rabbinic counterpart in this : 'May I never set eyes on a Samaritan ; ' or else, 'May I never be thrown into company with him ! ' A Rabbi in Cæsarea explains, as the cause of these changes of opinion, that formerly the Samaritans had been

a 2 Kings xvii. 30, 31

b 2 Kings xvii. 28-41

c St. John iv. 9

---

[1] For more precise details see the larger work, vol. i. pp. 400, 401.

observant of the Law, which they no longer were. Matters proceeded so far, that they were entirely excluded from fellowship. But at the time of Christ Jewish toleration declared all their food to be lawful, and there would be no difficulty as regarded the purchase of victuals on the part of the disciples of Jesus.

The Samaritans strongly believed in the Unity of God; they held the doctrine of Angels and devils; they received the Pentateuch as of sole Divine authority; they regarded Mount Gerizim as the place chosen of God, maintaining that it alone had not been covered by the Flood, as the Jews asserted of Mount Moriah; they were most strict and zealous in what of Biblical or traditional Law they received; and they looked for the coming of a Messiah, in Whom the promise would be fulfilled, that the Lord God would raise up a Prophet from the midst of them, like unto Moses, in Whom His words were to be, and unto ^{a Deut. xviii. 15, 18} Whom they should hearken.[a] Thus while in some respects access to them would be more difficult than to His own countrymen, yet in others Jesus would find there a soil better prepared for the Divine Seed, or, at least, less encumbered by traditionalism and Pharisaic bigotry.

CHAPTER XVII.

JESUS AT THE WELL OF SYCHAR.

(St. John iv. 1–42.)

THERE is not a district in ' the Land of Promise ' which presents a scene more fair or rich than the plain of Samaria (the modern *Et Mukhna*). As we stand on the summit of the ridge, on the way from Shiloh, the eye travels over the wide sweep, extending more than seven miles northward, till it rests on the twin heights of Gerizim and Ebal, which enclose the Valley of Shechem. Following the straight olive-shaded road from the south to where a spur of Gerizim jutting south-east forms the Vale of Shechem, we stand by that ' Well of Jacob ' to which so many sacred memories attach. North of the entrance to the Vale of Shechem rises Mount Ebal, which also forms, so to speak, the western wall of the northern extension of the Plain of Samaria. Here it bears the name of *El 'Askar*, from Askar, the ancient Sychar, which nestles at the foot of Ebal, at a distance of about two miles from Shechem.

It was, as we judge, about six o'clock of an evening in early summer, when Jesus, accompanied by the small band which formed His disciples, emerged into the rich Plain of Samaria. Far as the eye could sweep, ' the fields ' were ' already white unto the harvest.' They had reached ' the Well of Jacob.' Here Jesus waited, while the others went to the little town of Sychar on their work of ministry. This latter circumstance marks that it was evening, since noon was not the time either for the sale of provisions or for their purchase by travellers. Probably John remained with the Master. They would scarcely have left Him alone, especially in that place ; and the whole narrative reads like that of one who had been present at what passed.

There was another well on the east side of the town, and much nearer to Sychar than ' Jacob's Well ; ' and to it probably the women of Sychar generally resorted. It should also be borne in mind that in those days such work no longer devolved, as in early times, on the matrons and maidens of fair degree, but on women in much humbler station. This Samaritaness may have chosen ' Jacob's Well,' perhaps, because she had been at work or lived in that direction ; perhaps because, if her character was what seems implied in verse 18, the concourse of the more common women at the village-well of an evening might scarcely make such a pleasant place of resort to her.

But whatever the motives which brought her thither, both to Jesus and to the woman the meeting was unsought : providential in the truest sense. The request : ' Give Me to drink,' was natural on the part of the thirsty traveller. Even if He had not spoken, the Samaritaness would have recognised the Jew by His appearance and dress, if, as seems likely, He wore the fringes on the border of His garment.[1] His speech would by its pronunciation place His nationality beyond doubt. Any kindly address, conveying a request not absolutely necessary, would naturally surprise the woman; for, as the Evangelist explanatively adds: 'Jews have no dealings with Samaritans.' Besides, we must remember that this was an ignorant Samaritaness of the lower order. In the mind of such an one, two points would mainly stand out: that the Jews in their wicked pride would have no intercourse with them; and that Gerizim, not Jerusalem, as the Jews falsely asserted, was the place of rightful worship. It was, therefore, genuine surprise which expressed itself in the question: 'How is it, Thou, being a Jew, of me askest to drink?'

And the 'How is it?' of the Samaritan woman soon and fully found its answer. He Who had spoken to her was not like what she thought and knew of the Jews. He was what Israel was intended to have become to mankind; what it was the final object of Israel to have been. Had she but known it, the present relation between them would have been reversed; the Well of Jacob would have been but a symbol of the living water, which she would have asked and He given.

The 'How can these things be?' of Nicodemus finds a parallel in the bewilderment of the woman. Jesus had nothing wherewith to draw from the deep well. Whence, then, the 'living water'? And yet, as Nicodemus' question not only similarly pointed to a physical impossibility, but also indicated his searching after higher meaning and spiritual reality, so that of the woman: 'No! art Thou greater than our father Jacob?'—who at such labour had dug this well, finding no other means than this of supplying his own wants and those of his descendants. Nor did the answer of Jesus now differ in spirit from that which He had given to the Rabbi of Jerusalem. But to this

---

[1] The 'fringes' on the *Tallith* of the Samaritans are blue, while those worn by the Jews are white. The Samaritans do not seem to have worn *phylacteries*. But neither did many of the Jews of old—nor, I feel persuaded, did our Lord.

woman His answer must be much simpler and plainer than
to the Rabbi. It was not water like that of Jacob's Well
which He would give, but 'living water.' In the Old Testament a perennial spring had, in figurative language, been
^a Gen. xxvi. thus designated,^a in significant contrast to water
19 ; Lev. accumulated in a cistern.^b But there was more
xiv. 5
^b Jer. ii. 13 than this : it was water which, in him who had
drunk of it, became a well, not merely quenching the thirst
on this side time, but 'springing up into everlasting life.'

We would mark here that though in many passages
the teaching of the Rabbis is compared to water, it is
never likened to a 'well of water springing up.' The
difference is great. For it is the boast of Rabbinism that
its disciples drink of the waters of their teachers ; chief
merit lies in receptiveness not spontaneity, and higher
praise cannot be given than that of being 'a well-plastered
cistern, which lets not out a drop of water.' But this is
quite the opposite of what our Lord teaches. For it is
only true of what man can give when we read this (in
Ecclus. xxiv. 21) : 'They that drink me shall yet be
thirsty.' At the Feast of Tabernacles, amidst universal
rejoicing, water from Siloam was poured from a golden
pitcher on the altar, as emblem of the outpouring of the
Holy Ghost.[1] But the saying of our Lord to the Samaritaness referred neither to His teaching, nor to the Holy
Ghost, nor yet to faith, but to the gift of that new spiritual
life in Him, of which faith is but the outcome.

If the humble, ignorant Samaritaness had formerly but
imperfectly guessed that there was a higher meaning in
the words of Him Who spake to her, she now believes in
the incredible ; believes it because of Him and in Him ;
believes also in a satisfaction through Him of outward
wants, reaching up beyond this to the everlasting life.
But all these elements are still in strange confusion. And
thus Jesus reached her heart in that dimly conscious longing
which she expressed, though her intellect was incapable of
distinguishing the new truth.

---

[1] See 'The Temple and its Ministry,' pp. 241-243.

It is difficult to suppose that He asked the woman to call her husband with the primary object of awakening in her a sense of sin. Nor does anything in her bearing indicate any such effect; indeed, her reply [a] and her after-reference to it [b] rather imply the contrary. We do not even know for certain whether the five previous husbands had died or divorced her, and, if the latter, with whom the blame lay, although not only the peculiar mode in which our Lord refers to it but the present condition of the woman seem to point to a sinful life in the past. In Judæa a course like hers would have been almost impossible; but we know too little of the social and moral condition of Samaria to judge of what might there be tolerated. On the other hand, we have abundant evidence that, when the Saviour so unexpectedly laid open to her a past which He could only supernaturally have known, the conviction at once arose in her that He was a Prophet, just as in similar circumstances it had been forced upon Nathanael.[c]

a ver. 19
b ver. 29
c St. John i. 48, 49

This conviction, sudden but firm, was already faith in Him; and so the goal had been attained—not, perhaps, faith in His Messiahship, about which she might have only very vague notions, but in Him. We feel that the woman has no after-thought, no covert purpose in what she now asks. All her life long she had heard that Gerizim was the mount of worship, and that the Jews were in deadly error. But here was an undoubted Prophet, and He a Jew. Were they then in error about the right place of worship, and what was she to think and to do?

Once more the Lord answers her question by leading her far beyond all controversy: even on to the goal of all His teaching. 'There cometh an hour, when neither in this mountain, nor yet in Jerusalem, ye shall worship the Father.' Words, these, that pointed to the higher solution in the worship of a common Father, which would be the worship neither of Jews nor of Samaritans, but of children. And yet there was truth in their present differences. 'Ye worship ye know not what: we worship what we know, since salvation is from out the Jews.' The Samaritan was aimless worship, because it wanted the goal of all the Old Testament institutions, that Messiah ' Who was to be of the seed of David '[a]—for of the Jews, ' as concerning the flesh,' was Christ to come.[b] But only of present interest could such distinctions be ; for an hour would come, nay, already was, when the true worshippers would ' worship the Father in spirit and in truth, for the Father also seeketh such for His worshippers. Spirit is God '—and only worship in spirit and in truth could be acceptable to such a God.

[a] Rom. i. 3
[b] Rom. ix. 5

Higher teaching than this could not be uttered. And she who heard thus far understood it, that in the glorious picture, which was set before her, she saw the coming of the Kingdom of the Messiah. ' I know that Messiah cometh. When He cometh, He will tell us all things.' It was then that, according to the need of that untutored woman, He told her plainly what in Judæa, and even by His disciples, would have been carnally misinterpreted and misapplied : that He was the Messiah.

It was the crowning lesson of that day. The disciples had returned from Sychar. That Jesus should converse with a woman was so contrary to all Judæan notions of a Rabbi, that they wondered. Yet, in their reverence for Him, they dared not ask any questions. Meanwhile the woman, forgetful of her errand, and only conscious of that new well-spring of life which had risen within her, had left the unfilled waterpot, and hurried into ' the City.' ' Come, see a man who told me all that I have done. No— is this the Christ ? ' We infer that these strange tidings soon gathered many around her ; that they questioned, and as they ascertained from her the indisputable fact of His superhuman knowledge believed on Him, so far as the woman could set Him before them as object of faith.[c] Under this impression ' they went out of the City, and came on their way towards Him.' [d]

[c] vv. 39, 40
[d] ver. 30

Meantime the disciples had urged the Master to eat of the food which they had brought. But His Soul was otherwise engaged. His words of rebuke made them wonder whether, unknown to them, some one had brought Him

ª St. Matt.
xvi. 6, 7
food. It was not the only nor the last instance of their dulness to spiritual realities.ª

Yet with Divine patience He bore with them : 'My meat is, that I may do the Will of Him that sent Me, and that I may accomplish (bring to a perfect end) His work.' To the disciples that work appeared still in the far future. To them it seemed as yet little more than seed-time; the green blade was only sprouting; the harvest of such a Messianic Kingdom as they expected was still months distant. To correct their mistake, the Divine Teacher, as so often, and as best adapted to His hearers, chose His illustration from what was visible around. To show their meaning more clearly, we venture to reverse the order of the sentences which Jesus spoke: 'Behold, I say unto you, lift up your eyes and look [observantly] at the fields, that they are white to the harvest. [But] do *ye* not say that there are yet four months, and the harvest cometh?'

Notice how the Lord further unfolded His own lesson of present harvesting, and their inversion of what was sowing and what reaping time. 'Already' he that reaped received wages, and gathered fruit unto eternal life (which is the real reward of the Great Reaper, the seeing of the travail of His Soul), so that in this instance the sower rejoiced equally as the reaper. And, in this respect, the otherwise cynical proverb, that one was the sower, another the reaper of his sowing, found a true application. It was indeed so, that the servants of Christ were sent to reap what others had sown, and to enter into their labour. And yet, as in this instance of the Samaritans, the sower would rejoice as well as the reaper.

It was as Christ had said. The Samaritans, who believed 'because of the word' (speech) 'of the woman [what she said] as she testified' of the Christ, 'when they came' to that well, 'asked Him to abide with them. And He abode there two days. And many more believed because of His own word (speech, discourse), and said unto the woman: No longer because of thy speaking do we believe. For we ourselves have heard, and know, that this is truly the Saviour of the world.'

CHAPTER XVIII.

THE CURE OF THE 'NOBLEMAN'S' SON AT CAPERNAUM.

(St. Matt. iv. 12 ; St. Mark i. 14 ; St. Luke iv. 14, 15 ; St. John iv. 43–54.)

WHEN Jesus returned to Galilee, it was in circumstances entirely different from those under which He had left it. As He Himself said,[a] there had, perhaps natur-ally, been prejudices connected with the humble-ness of His upbringing, and the familiarity engendered by knowledge of His home-surroundings. These were over-come when the Galileans had witnessed at the feast in Jerusalem what He had done. Accordingly, they were now prepared to receive Him with the reverent attention which His Word claimed. We may conjecture that it was partially for reasons such as these that He first bent His steps to Cana. The miracle, which had there been wrought,[b] would still further prepare the people for His preaching. Besides, this was the home of Nathanael, in whose house welcome would now await Him. It was here that the second recorded miracle of His Galilean ministry was wrought, with what effect upon the whole district may be judged from the expectancies which the fame of it excited even in Nazareth, the city of His early upbringing.[c]

a St. John iv. 44
b St. John ii. 1–11
c St. Luke iv. 23

It appears that the son of one of Herod Antipas' officers was sick, and at the point of death. When tidings reached the father that the Prophet, or more than Prophet, Whose fame had preceded Him to Galilee, had come to Cana, he resolved in his despair of other means to apply to Him for the cure of his child. We do not assume that this ' court-officer ' was actuated by spiritual belief in the Son of God when applying to Him for help. Rather would we go to almost the opposite extreme, and regard him as simply actuated by what, in the circumstances, might be the views of a devout Jew. Instances are recorded in the Talmud, which may here serve as our guide. Various cases are related in which those seriously ill, and even at the point of death, were restored by the prayers of celebrated Rabbis.

But the great and vital contrast lies alike in what was thought of Him Who was instrumental in the cure and in the moral effects which followed. The profane representation of the relation between God and His servants, the utterly unspiritual view of prayer, which are displayed by the Rabbis, and their daring self-exaltation mark sufficiently the contrast in spirit between the Jewish view and that which underlies the Evangelic narrative.

When, to the request that Jesus would come down to Capernaum to perform the cure, the Master replied, that unless they saw signs and wonders they would not believe, what He reproved was not the request for a miracle, which was necessary, but the urgent plea that He should come down to Capernaum for that purpose. That request argued ignorance of the real character of the Christ, as if He were either merely a Rabbi endowed with special power, or else a miracle-monger. What He intended to teach this man was, that He, Who had life in Himself, could restore life at a distance as easily as by His Presence; by the word of His Power as readily as by personal application. When the 'court-officer' had learned this lesson, he became 'obedient unto the faith,' and 'went his way,'[a] presently to find his faith both crowned and perfected.[b]

Whether this 'royal officer' was *Chuza*, Herod's steward, whose wife, under the abiding impression of this miracle to her child, afterwards gratefully ministered to Jesus,[c] must remain undetermined. Suffice it to mark the progress in the 'royal officer' from belief in the power of Jesus to faith in His word,[d] and thence to absolute faith in Him,[e] with its expansive effect on that whole household. And so are we ever led from the lower stage of belief by what we see Him *do*, to that higher faith which springs from experimental knowledge of what He *is*.

[a] ver. 50
[b] ver. 53
[c] St. Luke viii. 3
[d] ver. 50
[e] ver. 53

CHAPTER XIX.

THE SYNAGOGUE AT NAZARETH—SYNAGOGUE-WORSHIP AND ARRANGEMENTS.

(St. Luke iv. 16.)

THE stay in Cana, though we have no means of determining its length, was probably of only short duration. Perhaps the Sabbath of the same week already found Jesus in the Synagogue of Nazareth.

As the lengthening shadows of Friday's sun closed around the quiet valley, He would hear the well-remembered double blast of the trumpet from the roof of the Synagogue-minister's house, proclaiming the advent of the holy day. Once more it sounded through the still summer-air, to tell all that work must be laid aside. Yet a third time it was heard, ere the 'minister' put it aside close by where he stood, not to profane the Sabbath by carrying it; for now the Sabbath had really commenced, and the festive Sabbath lamp was lit.

Sabbath morn dawned, and early He repaired to that Synagogue where He had so often worshipped in the humble retirement of His rank, sitting, not up there among the elders and the honoured, but far back. The old well-known faces were around Him, the old well-remembered words and services fell on His ear. And now He was again among them, a stranger among His own countrymen; this time, to be looked at, listened to, tested, tried. It was the first time, so far as we know, that He taught in a Synagogue, and this Synagogue that of His own Nazareth.

That Synagogues originated during, or in consequence of, the Babylonish captivity, is admitted by all. The Old Testament contains no allusion to their existence, and the Rabbinic attempts to trace them even to Patriarchal times deserve, of course, no serious consideration. We can readily understand how, during the long years of exile in

H

Babylon, places and opportunities for common worship on Sabbaths and feast-days must have been felt almost a necessity. This would furnish, at least, the basis for the institution of the Synagogue. After the return to Palestine, and still more by 'the dispersed abroad,' such 'meeting-houses' would become absolutely requisite. Here those who were ignorant even of the language of the Old Testament would have the Scriptures read and 'targumed' to them. It was but natural that prayers, and, lastly, addresses, should in course of time be added. Thus the regular Synagogue services would gradually arise; first on Sabbaths and on feast- or fast-days, then on ordinary days, at the same hours as, and with a sort of internal correspondence to, the worship of the Temple. The services on Mondays and Thursdays were special, these being the ordinary market-days, when the country-people came into the towns, and would avail themselves of the opportunity for bringing any case that might require legal decision before the local Sanhedrin, which met in the Synagogue, and consisted of its authorities. Naturally, these two days would be utilised to afford the country-people, who lived far from the Synagogues, opportunities for worship.

A congregation, according to Jewish Law, must consist of at least ten men. Another and perhaps more important rule was as to the direction in which Synagogues were to be built, and which worshippers should occupy during prayer. Prayer towards the east was condemned, on the ground of the false worship towards the east mentioned in Ezek. viii. 16. The prevailing direction in Palestine was towards the west, as in the Temple. It is a mistake to suppose that the men and women sat in opposite aisles, separated by a low wall.

We can with the help given by recent excavations form a conception of these ancient Synagogues. The Synagogue is built of the stone of the country. The flooring is formed of slabs of white limestone; the walls are solid (from 2 even to 7 feet in thickness), and well built of stones, rough in the exterior, but plastered in the interior. The building is

furnished with sufficient windows to admit light. The roof
is flat, the columns being sometimes connected by blocks of
stone, on which massive rafters rest.

Entering by the door at the southern end, and making
the circuit to the north, we take our position in front of
the women's gallery. Those colonnades form the body of
the Synagogue. At the south end, facing north, is a
movable ' Ark,' containing the sacred rolls of the Law and
the Prophets. It was made movable, so that it might be
carried out, as on public fasts. Steps generally led up to
it. In front hangs the *Vilon* or curtain. But the Holy
Lamp is never wanting, in imitation of the undying light

ᵃ Exod.
xxvii. 20 in the Temple.[a] Right before the Ark, and facing
the people, are the seats of honour, for the rulers
ᵇ St. Matt.
xxiii. 6 of the Synagogue and the honourable.[b] The place
for him who leads the devotion of the people is
also in front of the Ark, either elevated, or else, to mark
humility, lowered. In the middle of the Synagogue (so
generally) is the elevation, on which there is the desk, from
which the Law is read. This is also called the chair, or
throne. Those who are to read the Law will stand, while
he who is to preach or deliver an address will sit. Beside
them will be the *Methurgeman*, either to interpret or to
repeat aloud what is said.

To neglect attendance on the services of the Synagogue
would not only involve personal guilt, but bring punishment upon the whole district. Indeed, to be effectual,
prayer must be offered in the Synagogue. At the same
time, the more strict ordinances in regard to the Temple,
such as that we must not enter it carrying a staff, nor with
shoes, nor even dust on the feet, nor with scrip or purse,
do not apply to the Synagogue, as of comparatively inferior
sanctity. However, the Synagogue must not be made a
thoroughfare. We must not behave lightly in it. We
may not joke, laugh, eat, talk, dress, nor resort there for
shelter from sun or rain. Only Rabbis and their disciples,
to whom so many things are lawful, and who, indeed, must
look upon the Synagogue as if it were their own dwelling,
may eat, drink, perhaps even sleep there. Under certain

circumstances also, the poor and strangers may be fed there. But, in general, the Synagogue must be regarded as consecrated to God.

All this, irrespective of any Rabbinic legends, shows with what reverence these ' houses of congregation' were regarded. And now the weekly Sabbath, the pledge between Israel and God, had once more come. To meet it as a bride or queen, each house was adorned on the Friday evening. The Sabbath lamp was lighted; the festive garments put on; the table provided with the best 'which the family could afford; and the benediction spoken over a cup of wine, which, as always, was mixed with water. And as Sabbath morning broke, they hastened with quick steps to the Synagogue; for such was the Rabbinic rule in going, while it was prescribed to return with slow and lingering steps. Jewish punctiliousness defined every movement and attitude in prayer. If those rules were ever observed in their entirety, devotion must have been crushed under their weight. But we have evidence that, in the time of our Lord, and even later, there was room for personal freedom left; for not only was much in the services determined by the usage of each place, but the leader of the devotions might preface the regular service by free prayer, or insert such between certain parts of the liturgy.

The officials are all assembled. The lowest of these [a] St. Luke was the *Chazzan*, or minister,[a] who often acted also iv. 20 as schoolmaster. For this reason, and because the conduct of the services frequently devolved upon him, great care was taken in his selection. Then there were the elders or rulers, whose chief was the *Archisynagogos*. All the rulers of the Synagogue were duly examined as to their knowledge, and ordained to the office. They formed the local Sanhedrin or tribunal. But their election depended on the choice of the congregation; and absence of pride, as also gentleness and humility, are mentioned as special qualifications.

To these regular officials we have to add those who officiated during the service, the delegate of the congregation—who, as its mouthpiece, conducted the devotions— the Interpreter or *Methurgeman*, and those who were called on to read in the Law and the Prophets, or else to preach.

We are now in some measure prepared to follow the worship on that Sabbath in Nazareth. On His entrance into the Synagogue, or perhaps before that, the chief ruler would request Jesus to act for that Sabbath as the *Sheliach Tsibbur*, or delegate of the congregation. For, according to the Mishnah, the person who read in the Synagogue the portion from the Prophets, was also expected to conduct the devotions, at least in greater part. If this rule were enforced at that time, then Jesus would ascend the elevation, and, standing at the lectern, begin the service by two prayers.

After this followed what may be designated as the Jewish Creed. It consisted of three passages from the ^a Pentateuch,^a so arranged that the worshipper took upon himself first the yoke of the Kingdom of Heaven, and only after it the yoke of the commandments. The recitation of these passages was followed by a prayer.

a Deut. vi. 4-9 ; xi. 13- 21 ; Numb. xv. 37-41

This finished, he who officiated took his place before the Ark, and there repeated certain ' Eulogies ' or Benedictions. These are eighteen, or rather nineteen, in number, and date from different periods. But on Sabbaths only the three first and the three last of them, which are also those undoubtedly of greatest age, were repeated, and between them certain other prayers inserted.

After this the Priests, if any were in the Synagogue, spoke the blessing, elevating their hands up to the shoulders (in the Temple above the head). This was called the lifting up of hands.^b In the Synagogue the priestly blessing was spoken in three sections, the people each time responding by an Amen. Lastly, in the Synagogue, the word ' Adonai ' was substituted for Jehovah. If no descendants of Aaron were present, the leader of the devotions repeated the usual

b Comp. 1 Tim. ii. 8

priestly benediction.ᵃ   After the benediction
followed the last Eulogy.

It was the practice of leading Rabbis, probably dating
from very early times, to add at the close of this Eulogy
certain prayers of their own, either fixed or free, of which
the Talmud gives specimens.   From very early times also,
the custom seems to have obtained that the descendants
of Aaron, before pronouncing the blessing, put off their
shoes.   In the benediction the Priests turned towards the
people, while he who led the ordinary prayers stood with
his back to the people, looking towards the Sanctuary.
The public prayers closed with an Amen, spoken by the
congregation.

The liturgical part being thus completed, one of the
most important, indeed, what had been the primary object
of the Synagogue service, began.   The *Chazzan*, or
minister, approached the Ark, and brought out a roll of
the Law.   It was taken from its case and unwound from
those cloths which held it.   The time had now come for
the reading of portions from the Law and the Prophets.
The reading of the Law was both preceded and followed by
brief Benedictions.

Upon the Law followed a section from the Prophets.
As the Hebrew was not generally understood, the
Methurgeman, or Interpreter, stood by the side of the
reader,ᵇ and translated into the Aramæan verse
by verse, and in the section from the Prophets,
after every three verses.   But the *Methurgeman*
was not allowed to read his translation, lest it might
popularly be regarded as authoritative.   This may help us
in some measure to understand the popular mode of Old
Testament quotations in the New Testament.   So long as
the substance of the text was given correctly, the *Methurgeman* might paraphrase for better popular understanding.
Again, it is but natural to suppose that the *Methurgeman*
would prepare himself for his work by such materials as
he would find to hand, among which, of course, the translation of the LXX. would hold a prominent place.   This
may in part account alike for the employment of the LXX.,

ᵇ Comp.
1 Cor. xiv.
27, 28

and for its Targumic modifications, in the New Testament quotations.

The reading of the section from the Prophets was in olden times immediately followed by an address, discourse, or sermon, that is, where a Rabbi capable of giving such instruction, or a distinguished stranger, was present. Neither the leader of the devotions ('the delegate of the congregation'), nor the *Methurgeman*, nor yet the preacher, required ordination. That was reserved for the *rule* of the congregation, whether in legislation or administration, doctrine or discipline. The only points required in the preacher were the necessary qualifications, both mental and moral.

Jewish tradition uses the most extravagant terms to extol the institution of preaching. So it came, that many cultivated this branch of theology. When a popular preacher was expected, men crowded the area of the Synagogue, while women filled the gallery. On such occasions, there was the additional satisfaction of feeling that they had done something specially meritorious in running with quick steps, and crowding into the Synagogue. For, was it not to carry out the spirit of Hos. vi. 3, xi. 10—at least, as Rabbinically understood? Even grave Rabbis joined in this 'pursuit to know the Lord,' and one of them comes to the somewhat caustic conclusion, that 'the reward of a discourse is the haste.'

It is interesting to know that, at the close of his address, the preacher very generally referred to the great Messianic hope of Israel. The service closed with a short prayer, or what we would term an 'ascription.'

We can now picture to ourselves the Synagogue, its worship and teaching. We can see the leader of the people's devotions as (according to Talmudic direction) he first refuses, with mock modesty, the honour conferred on him by the chief ruler; then, when urged, prepares to go; and when pressed a third time, goes up with slow and measured steps to the lectern, and then before the Ark. We can imagine how one after another, standing and facing the people, unrolls and holds in his hand a copy of the Law or of the Prophets, and reads from the Sacred Word, the *Methurgeman* interpreting. Finally, we can picture it, how the preacher would sit down and begin his discourse, none interrupting him with questions till he had finished, when a succession of objections, answers, or inquiries might await the helper, if the preacher had employed such. And help it certainly was not in many cases, to judge by the depreciatory remarks which not unfrequently occur, as to the manners, tone, vanity, self-conceit, and silliness of the *Methurgeman* or *Amora* as he was sometimes called. As he stood beside the Rabbi, he usually thought far more of attracting attention and applause to himself, than of benefiting his hearers. Hence some Rabbis would only employ special and trusted interpreters of their own, who were above fifty years of age. In short, so far as the sermon was concerned, the impression it produced must have been very similar to what we know the addresses of the monks in the Middle Ages to have wrought. All the better can we understand, even from the human aspect, how the teaching of Jesus, alike in its substance and form, in its manner and matter, differed from that of the scribes ; how multitudes would hang entranced on His word ; and how, everywhere and by all, its impression was felt to be overpowering.

CHAPTER XX.

THE FIRST GALILEAN MINISTRY.

(St. Matt. iv. 13–17 ; St. Mark i. 14, 15 ; St. Luke iv. 15–32.)

As there could be no un-Jewish forwardness on the part of Jesus, so would there be none of that mock humility of reluctance to officiate, in which Rabbinism delighted. It seems likely that Jesus commenced the first part of the service, and then pronounced before the ' Ark ' those Eulogies which were regarded as, in the strictest sense, the prayer. And now, one by one, Priest, Levite, and, in succession, five Israelites, had read from the Law. The whole narrative seems to imply that Jesus Himself read the concluding portion from the Prophets. It is most likely that the lesson for that day was taken from the pro-

a Is. lxi. 1, 2
b St. Luke
iv. 18, 19

phecies of Isaiah, and that it included the passage [a] quoted by the Evangelist as read by the Lord Jesus. [b] We know that the ' rolls ' on which the Law was written were distinct from those of the Prophets. In this instance we are expressly told that the minister ' delivered unto Him the book of the prophet Esaias,' and that, ' when He had unrolled the book,' He ' found ' the place from which the Evangelist makes quotation.

It was, indeed, Divine ' wisdom '—' the Spirit of the Lord ' upon Him, which directed Jesus in the choice of the text for His first Messianic Sermon. It struck the key-note to the whole of His Galilean ministry. The ancient

c The other
two being
Is. xxxii. 14,
15 and
Lament.
iii. 50

Synagogue regarded Is. lxi. 1, 2, as one of the three passages, [c] in which mention of the Holy Ghost was connected with the promised redemption. In this view, the application which the passage received in the discourse of our Lord was peculiarly suitable. For the words in which St. Luke reports what followed the introductory text seem rather a summary than either the introduction or part of the discourse of Christ. ' This day is this Scripture fulfilled in your ears.' As regards its form, it would be : so to present the teaching of Holy Scripture, as that it can be drawn together in the focus of one sentence ; as regards its substance, that this be the one focus: all Scripture fulfilled by a present Christ.

There was not a word of that which common Jewish expectancy would have connected with, nay, chiefly accentuated in an announcement of the Messianic redemption ; not a word to raise carnal hopes, or flatter Jewish pride. Truly, it was the most un-Jewish discourse for a Jewish Messiah of those days, with which to open His Ministry. And yet such was the power of these ' words of grace,' that the hearers hung spell-bound upon them. For the time they forgot all else—Who it was that addressed them, even the strangeness of the message, so in contrast to any preaching of Rabbi or Teacher that had been heard in that Synagogue.

The discourse had been spoken, and the breathless silence with which, even according to Jewish custom, it had been listened to, gave place to the usual after-sermon hum of an Eastern Synagogue. On one point all were agreed : that they were marvellous words of grace, which had proceeded out of His mouth. And still the preacher waited for some question, which would have marked the spiritual application of what He had spoken. They were indeed making application of the Sermon to the Preacher, but in quite different manner from that to which His discourse had pointed. It was not the fulfilment of the Scripture in Him, but the circumstance that such an one as the Son of Joseph, their village carpenter, should have spoken such words, that attracted their attention.

They had *heard*, and now they would fain have *seen*. But already the holy indignation of Him, Whom they only knew as Joseph's Son, was kindled. No doubt they would next expect that here in His own city, and all the more because it was such, He would do what they had heard had taken place in Capernaum. It was the world-old saying, as speciously popular as most such sayings : ' Charity begins at home '—or, according to the Jewish proverb, and in application to the special circumstances : ' Physician, heal thyself.' Whereas, if there was any meaning in the discourse He had just spoken, Charity does not begin at home ; and ' Physician, heal thyself' is not of the Gospel for the poor, nor yet the preaching of God's Jubilee, but that of the Devil, whose works Jesus had come to destroy. How could He say this better than by again repeating, though now with different application, that sad experience, ' No prophet is accepted in his own country ; ' [a] and by pointing to those two Old Testament instances of it, whose names and authority were most frequently on Jewish lips ? Not they who were ' their own,' but they who were most receptive in faith—not Israel, but Gentiles, were those most markedly favoured in the ministry of Elijah and of Elisha.

[a] St. John iv. 44

That Jesus should have turned so fully the light upon the Gentiles, and flung its large shadows upon them ; that 'Joseph's Son' should have taken up this position towards them ; that He would make to them spiritual application unto death of His sermon, since they would not make it unto life, stung them to the quick. Away He must out of His city ; it could not bear His Presence any longer, not even on that holy Sabbath. Out they thrust Him from the Synagogue ; out of the city, along the road by the brow of the hill on which the city is built—perhaps to that western angle, at present pointed out as the site. This, with the unspoken intention of crowding Him over the cliff, which there rises abruptly about forty feet out of the valley beneath. If we are correct in indicating the locality, the road here bifurcates, and we can conceive how Jesus, Who had hitherto allowed Himself to be pressed onwards by the surrounding crowd, now turned, and by His look of commanding majesty, which ever and again wrought on those around miracles of subjection, constrained them to halt and give way before Him, while unharmed He passed through their midst.

Cast out of His own city, Jesus pursued His solitary way towards Capernaum. There, at least, devoted friends and believing disciples would welcome Him. There, also, a large draught of souls would fill the Gospel-net. Capernaum would be His Galilean home.[a] Here He would, on the Sabbath-days, preach in that Synagogue, of which the good centurion was the builder,[b] and Jairus the chief ruler.[c] These names, and the memories connected with them, are a sufficient comment on the effect of His preaching : that 'His word was with power.' In Capernaum, also, was the now believing household of the court-officer, whose only son the Word of Christ, spoken at a distance, had restored to life. Here also, or in the immediate neighbourhood, was the home of His earliest and closest disciples, the brothers Simon and Andrew, and of James and John, the sons of Zebedee.

He came ; and now Capernaum was not the only place

a St. Matt. ix. 1

b St. Luke vii. 5

c St. Mark v. 22

where He taught. Rather was it the centre for itinerancy
through all that district, to preach in its Synagogues.[a] Amidst such ministry of quiet 'power,'
chiefly alone and unattended by His disciples, the summer
passed. To the writer of the first Gospel, as, years afterwards,
he looked back on this happy time when he had first seen
the Light, till it had sprung up even to him 'in the region
and shadow of death,' it must have been a time of peculiarly
bright memories. How often, as he sat at the receipt of
custom, must he have seen Jesus passing by; how often
must he have heard His Words, some, perhaps, spoken to
himself, but all preparing him at once to obey the summons when it came: *Follow Me!*

There was a dim tradition in the Synagogue, that this
prediction,[b] 'The people that walk in darkness
see a great light,' referred to the new light, with
which God would enlighten the eyes of those who had
penetrated into the mysteries of Rabbinic lore, enabling
them to perceive concerning 'loosing and binding, concerning what was clean and what was unclean.' Others
regarded it as a promise to the early exiles, fulfilled when
the great liberty came to them. To Levi-Matthew it
seemed as if both interpretations had come true in those
days of Christ's first Galilean ministry.

Marginal notes:
[a] St. Matt. iv. 13-17
[b] Is. ix. 2

CHAPTER XXI.

AT THE 'UNKNOWN' FEAST IN JERUSALEM, AND BY THE POOL OF BETHESDA.

(St. John v.)

THE shorter days of early autumn had come as Jesus passed
from Galilee to what, in the absence of any certain evidence, we must still be content to call 'the Unknown
Feast' in Jerusalem. Thus much, however, seems clear:
that it was either the 'Feast of Wood-offering' on the
15th of Abh (in August), when, amidst demonstrations of

joy, willing givers brought from all parts of the country the wood required for the service of the Altar ; or else the 'Feast of Trumpets' on the 1st of Tishri (about the middle of September), which marked the beginning of the New (civil) Year. The journey of Christ to that Feast and its results are not mentioned in the Synoptic Gospels, because that Judæan ministry lay, in great measure, beyond their historical standpoint. But this and similar events belonged to that grand Self-Manifestation of Christ, with the corresponding growth of opposition consequent upon it, which it was the object of the fourth Gospel to set forth.

It may be inferred that, during the summer of Christ's first Galilean ministry, when Capernaum was His centre of action, the disciples had returned to their homes and usual avocations, while Jesus moved about chiefly alone and unattended. This explains the circumstance of a second call, even to His most intimate and closest followers. It also accords best with that gradual development in Christ's activity, which, commencing with the more private teaching of the new Preacher of Righteousness in the villages by the lake, or in the Synagogues, expanded into that publicity in which He at last appears, surrounded by His Apostles, attended by the loving ministry of those to whom He had brought healing of body or soul, and followed by a multitude which everywhere pressed around Him for teaching and help.

This more public activity commenced with the return of Jesus from 'the Unknown Feast' in Jerusalem. There He had, in answer to the challenge of the Jewish authorities, for the first time set forth His Messianic claims in all their fulness. And there, also, He had for the first time encountered that active persecution unto death, of which Golgotha was the logical outcome. This Feast, then, was the time of critical decision.

It seems only accordant with all the great decisive steps of Him in Whose footprints the disciples trod, after He had marked them, as it were, with His Blood—that He should have gone up to that Feast alone and unattended.

The narrative transports us to what, at the time, seems
to have been a well-known locality in Jerusalem, though
all attempts to identify it, or even to explain the name
Bethesda, have hitherto failed. All we know is, that it
was a pool enclosed within five porches, by the sheep-
market, presumably close to the ' Sheep-Gate.' [a]
This, as seems most likely, opened from the busy
northern suburb of markets, bazaars, and workshops, eastwards upon the road which led over the Mount of Olives
and Bethany to Jericho.

a Neh. iii.
32 ; xii. 39

In the five porches surrounding this pool lay ' a great
multitude of the impotent,' in anxious hope of a miraculous
cure. The popular superstition, which gave rise to a
peculiarly painful exhibition of human misery of body and
soul, is strictly true to the times and the people. Even
now travellers describe a similar concourse of poor crippled
sufferers, on their miserable pallets or on rugs, around the
mineral springs near Tiberias, filling, in true Oriental
fashion, the air with their lamentations. In the present
instance there would be even more occasion for this than
around any ordinary thermal spring. For the popular
idea was, that an Angel [1] descended into the water, causing
it to bubble up, and that only he who *first* stepped into
the pool would be cured. As thus only one person could
obtain benefit, we may imagine the lamentations of the
' many ' who would, perhaps day by day, be disappointed
in their hopes. This bubbling up of the water was, of
course, due not to supernatural but to physical causes.
Such intermittent springs are not uncommon, and to this
day the so-called ' Fountain of the Virgin ' in Jerusalem
exhibits the same phenomenon. The Gospel-narrative
does not ascribe this ' troubling of the waters ' to Angelic
agency, nor endorse the belief, that only the first who
afterwards entered them could be healed. This was
evidently the belief of the impotent man, as of all the
waiting multitude.[b] But the words in verse 4
of our Authorised Version, and perhaps, also,

b St. John v.
7

[1] For the popular Jewish views on Angels see ' The Life and Times,'
&c., Appendix xiii.

the last clause of verse 3, are admittedly an interpolation.

The waters had not yet been 'troubled,' when Jesus stood among that multitude of sufferers and their attendant friends. It was in those breathless moments of intense expectancy, when every eye was fixed on the pool, that the eye of the Saviour searched for the most wretched object among them all. In him, as a typical case, could He best do and teach that for which He had come. This 'impotent' man, for thirty-eight years a hopeless sufferer, without

^a ver 7.
^b ver. 14
^c Comp. St.
John ix. 3

attendant or friend ^a among those whom misery made so intensely selfish; and whose sickness was really the consequence of his sin,^b and not merely in the sense which the Jews attached to it ^c—this now seemed the fittest object for power and grace. It is idle to speak either of faith or of receptiveness on the man's part. The essence of the whole history lies in the utter absence of both; in Christ's raising, as it were, the dead, and calling the things that are not as though they were. The 'Wilt thou be made whole?' with which Jesus drew the man's attention to Himself, was only to probe and lay bare his misery. And then came the word of power or rather the power spoken forth, which made him whole every whit. Away from this pool, in which there was no healing—for the Son of God had come to him with the outflowing of His power and pitying help, and he *was* made whole. Away with his bed, not although it was the holy Sabbath, but just because it was the Sabbath of holy rest and holy delight!

Before the healed man, scarcely conscious of what had passed, had, with new-born vigour, gathered himself up and rolled together his coverlet to hasten after Him, Jesus

^d ver. 13

had already withdrawn.^d In that multitude, all thinking only of their own sorrows and wants, He had come and gone unobserved. But they all now knew and observed this miracle of healing, as they saw this unbefriended one healed, without the troubling of waters or first immersion in them.

The Jews saw him, as from Bethesda he carried home

his ' burden.' Most characteristically, it was this external infringement which they saw, and nothing else ; it was the Person Who had commanded it Whom they would know, not Him Who had made whole the impotent man.

It could not have been long after this that the healed man and his Healer met in the Temple. What He then said to him completed the inward healing. On the ground of his having been healed, let him be whole. As he trusted and obeyed Jesus in the outward cure, so let him now inwardly and morally trust and obey. Here also this looking through the external to the internal, through the temporal to the spiritual and eternal, which is so characteristic of the after-discourse of Jesus, nay, of all His discourses and of His deeds, is most marked. The healed man now knew to Whom he owed faith, gratitude, and trust of obedience ; and the consequences of this knowledge would make him a disciple in the truest sense. And this was the only additional lesson which he, as each of us, must learn individually and personally : that the man healed by Christ stands in quite another position, as regards the morally right, from what he did before—not only before his healing, but even before his felt sickness, so that, if he were to go back to sin, or rather, as the original implies, ' continue to sin,' a thing infinitely worse would come to him.

And yet something further was required. Jesus must speak out in clear, open words, what was the hidden inward meaning of this miracle. The first forthbursting of His Messianic Mission and Character had come in that Temple when He realised it as His Father's House, and His Life as about His Father's business. Again had these thoughts about His Father kindled within Him in that Temple, when, on the first occasion of His Messianic appearance there, He had sought to purge it, that it might be a House of Prayer. And now, once more in that House, it was the same consciousness about God as His Father, and His Life as the business of His Father, which furnished the answer to the angry invectives about His breach of the Sabbath-Law. The Father's Sabbath was His ; the Father worked hitherto and He worked ; the Father's work and His were

• St. John v. the same ; He was the Son of the Father.ᵃ And
17   in this He also taught, what the Jews had never
understood, the true meaning of the Sabbath-Law, by emphasising that which was the fundamental thought of the
Sabbath—' Wherefore the Lord blessed the Sabbath day,
and *hallowed it* : ' not the rest of inactivity, but of blessing
and hallowing.

Once more it was not His whole meaning, but only
this one point, that He claimed to be equal with God, of which
they took hold. As we understand it, the discourse beginning with verse 19 is not a continuation of that which
had been begun in verse 17, but was delivered on another,
though probably proximate occasion. By what He had
said about the Father working hitherto and His working,
He had silenced the multitude, who must have felt that
God's rest was truly that of beneficence, not of inactivity.
But He had raised another question, that of His equality
with God, and for this He was taken to task by the Masters
in Israel. But for the present the majesty of His bearing
overawed His enemies, even as it did to the end, and Christ
could pass unharmed from among them. With this inward
separation and the gathering of hostile parties, closes the
first, and begins the second stage of Christ's Ministry.

CHAPTER XXII.

THE FINAL CALL OF THE FIRST DISCIPLES, AND THE MIRACULOUS DRAUGHT OF FISHES.

(St. Matt. iv. 18-22 ; St. Mark i. 16-20 ; St. Luke v. 1-11.)

WE are once again out of the great City, and by the Lake
of Galilee. They were other men, these honest, simple, impulsive Galileans, than that self-seeking, sophistical, heartless assemblage of Rabbis, whose first active persecution
Jesus had just encountered, and for the time overawed by
the majesty of His bearing. What wonder that, immediately on His return, ' the people pressed upon Him to hear
His word ' ?

I

It seems as if what we are about to relate occurred while Jesus was returning from Jerusalem. But perhaps it followed on the first morning after His return. It had probably been a night of storm on the Lake. For the toil of the

_a St. Luke fishermen had brought them no draught of fishes,^a
v. 5 and they stood by the shore or in the boats drawn up on the beach, casting in their nets to 'wash' them of sand and pebbles, or to mend what had been torn by the violence of the waves. It was a busy scene; for among the many industries by the Lake of Galilee that of fishing was not only the most generally pursued, but perhaps the most lucrative.

Tradition had it, that since the days of Joshua, and by one of his ten ordinances, fishing in the Lake, though under certain necessary restrictions, was free to all. And as fish was among the favourite articles of diet, in health and sickness, on week-days and especially at the Sabbath-meal, many must have been employed in connection with this trade. Frequent and sometimes strange are the Rabbinic advices, what kinds of fish to eat at different times, and in what state of preparation. They were eaten fresh, dried,

_b St. Matt. or pickled;^b a kind of 'relish' or sauce was made
vii. 10; xiii. of them, and the roe also prepared. In truth,
47; xv. 36 these Rabbis are veritable connoisseurs in this delicacy. It is one of their usual exaggerations when we read of 300 different kinds of fish at a dinner given to a great Rabbi, although the common proverb had it to denote what was abundant, that it was like 'bringing fish to Acco.'

Those engaged in the trade of fishing, like Zebedee and his sons, were not unfrequently men of means and standing. This, irrespective of the fact that the Rabbis enjoined some trade or industrial occupation on every man, whatever his station.

Jewish customs and modes of thinking at that time do not help us further to understand the Lord's call, except so far as they enable us to apprehend what the words of Jesus would convey to them. The expression 'Follow Me' would be readily understood, as implying a call to become the permanent disciple of a teacher. Similarly, it was not only the practice of the Rabbis, but regarded as one of the most sacred duties, for a Master to gather around him a circle of disciples. Thus, neither Peter and Andrew, nor the sons of Zebedee, could have misunderstood the call of Christ, or even regarded it as strange. On that memorable return from His temptation in the wilderness they had learned to know Him as the Messiah,[a] and they followed Him. And, now that the time had come for gathering around Him a separate discipleship, when, with the visit to the Unknown Feast, the Messianic activity of Jesus had passed into another stage, that call would not come as a surprise to their minds or hearts.

So far as the Master was concerned, we mark three points. First, the call came after the open breach with, and initial persecution of, the Jewish authorities. It was, therefore, a call to fellowship in His peculiar relationship to the Synagogue. Secondly, it necessitated the abandonment of all their former occupations, and, indeed, of all earthly ties.[b] Thirdly, it was from the first, and clearly, marked as totally different from a call to such discipleship, as that of any other Master in Israel. It was not to learn more of doctrine, nor more fully to follow out a life-direction already taken, but to begin, and to become, something quite new, of which their former occupation offered an emblem. The disciples of the Rabbis, even those of John the Baptist, ' followed,' in order to learn ; they, in order to do, and to enter into fellowship with His Work. ' Follow Me, and I will make you fishers of men.' The more we think of it, the more do we perceive the magnitude of the call and of the decision which it implied—for, without doubt, they understood what it implied, perhaps more clearly than we do. All the deeper, then, must have been their belief in Him, and their earnest attachment, when, with such absolute simplicity and entireness of self-surrender, that it needed not even a spoken *Yea* on their part, they forsook ship and home to follow Him. And so, successively, Simon and Andrew, and John and James— those who had been the first to hear, were also the first to

a St. John i. 37 &c.

b St. Matt. iv. 20, 22

follow Jesus.   And ever afterwards did they remain closest
to Him, who had been the first fruits of His Ministry.

What had passed between Jesus and, first the sons of
Jona, and then those of Zebedee, can scarcely have occupied
many minutes.   But already the people were pressing
around the Master in eager hunger for the Word.   To
such call the Fisher of Men could not be deaf.   The boat of
Peter shall be His pulpit; He had consecrated it by conse-
crating its owner.   We need scarcely ask what He spake.
It would be of the Father, of the Kingdom, and of those
who entered it—like what He spake from the Mount, or
to those who laboured and were heavy laden.   And Peter
had heard it all as he sat close by.   This then was the
teaching of which he had become a disciple; this the
net and the fishing to which he was just called.   Could
such an one as he ever hope, with whatever toil, to be a
successful fisher?

Jesus had read his thoughts, and much more than read
them.   This is another object in Christ's miracles to His
disciples: to make clear their inmost thoughts and longings,
and to point them to the right goal.   'Launch out into the
deep, and let down your nets for a draught.'   That they
toil in vain all life's night only teaches the need of another
beginning.   The 'nevertheless, at Thy word,' marks the
new trust, and the new work as springing from that trust.
Already 'the net was breaking,' when they beckoned to their
partners in the other ship that they should come and help
them.   And now both ships are burdened to the water's edge.

But what did it all mean to Simon Peter?   Jesus could
see to the very bottom of Peter's heart.   And could he
then be a fisher of men, out of whose heart, after a life's
night of toil, the net would come up empty, or rather only
clogged with sand and torn with pebbles?   This is what
he meant when 'he fell down at Jesus' knees, saying:
Depart from me, for I am a sinful man, O Lord.'   And
this is why Jesus comforted him : 'Fear not; from henceforth thou shalt catch men.'

'And when they had brought their ships to land, they
forsook all and followed Him.'

CHAPTER XXIII.

A SABBATH IN CAPERNAUM.

(St. Matt. viii. 14-17 ; St. Mark i. 21-34 ; St. Luke iv. 33-41.)

It was the Holy Sabbath—the first after He had called around Him His first permanent disciples ; the first, also, after His return from the Feast at Jerusalem.

As yet all seemed calm and undisturbed. Those simple, warm-hearted Galileans yielded themselves to the power of His words and works, not discerning hidden blasphemy in what He said, nor yet Sabbath-desecration in His healing on God's holy day. It is morning, and Jesus goes to the Synagogue at Capernaum. To teach there was now His wont. It was not only what He taught, but the contrast with that to which they had been accustomed on the part of ' the Scribes,' which filled His hearers with ' amazement.' There was no appeal to human authority, other than that of the conscience ; no subtle logical distinctions, legal niceties, nor clever sayings. Clear, limpid, and crystalline, His words flowed from out the spring of the Divine Life that was in Him.

Among the hearers in the Synagogue that Sabbath morning was one of a class, concerning whose condition, whatever difficulties may attach to our proper understanding of it, the reader of the New Testament must form some definite idea. The New Testament speaks of those who had a spirit, or a demon, or demons, or an unclean spirit, or the spirit of an unclean demon, but chiefly of persons who were ' demonised.' We find that Jesus not only tolerated the popular opinion regarding the demonised, but that He even made it part of His disciples' commission to [a] St. Matt. ' cast out demons,' [a] and that, when the disciples x. 8. afterwards reported their success in this, Christ [b] St. Luke x. actually made it a matter of thanksgiving to 17, 18 God.[b] The same view underlies His reproof to the disciples,

• St. Matt.
xvii. 21 ;
comp. also
xii. 43 &c.,
also spoken
to the dis-
ciples

when failing in this part of their work [a] ; while in
St. Luke xi. 19, 24, He adopts and argues on this
view as against the Pharisees.

Our next inquiry must be as to the character
of the phenomenon thus designated. In view
of the fact that in St. Mark ix. 21, the demonised had
been such ' of a child,' it is scarcely possible to ascribe it
simply to moral causes. Similarly, personal faith does not
seem to have been a requisite condition of healing. Again,
it is evident that all physical or even mental distempers of
the same class were not ascribed to the same cause : some
might be natural, while others were demoniacal. On the
other hand, there were more or less violent symptoms of
disease in every demonised person, and these were greatly
aggravated in the last paroxysm, when the demon quitted
his habitation. We have therefore to regard the phenomena described as caused by the influence of such ' spirits,'
primarily, upon that which forms the *nexus* between body
and mind, the nervous system, and as producing different
physical effects, according to the part of the nervous
system affected. To this must be added a certain im-
personality of consciousness, so that for the time the
consciousness was not that of the demonised, but the
demoniser, just as in certain mesmeric states the consciousness of the mesmerised is really that of the mesmeriser.
We might carry the analogy farther, and say that the two
states are exactly parallel—the demon or demons taking
the place of the mesmeriser, only that the effects were
more powerful and extensive, perhaps more enduring.
Neither the New Testament, nor even Rabbinic literature,
conveys the idea of permanent demoniac indwelling, to
which the later term ' possession ' owes its origin. On
the contrary, such accounts as that of the scene in the
Synagogue of Capernaum give the impression of a sudden
influence, which in most cases seems occasioned by the
spiritual effect of the Person or of the Words of the
Christ. In our view, it is of the deepest importance
always to keep in mind that the ' demonised ' was not a
permanent state, or possession by the powers of darkness.

For it establishes a moral element, since during the period of their temporary liberty the demonised might have shaken themselves free from the overshadowing power, or sought release from it. Thus the demonised state involved personal responsibility, although that of a diseased and disturbed consciousness.

Whatever want of clearness there may be about the Jewish ideas of demoniac influences,[1] there is none as to the means proposed for their removal. These may be broadly classified as: magical means for the prevention of such influences (such as the avoidance of certain places, times, numbers, or circumstances; amulets, &c.); magical means for the cure of diseases; and direct exorcism (either by certain outward means, or else by formulas of incantation). Again, while the New Testament furnishes no data by which to learn the views of Jesus or of the Evangelists regarding the exact character of the phenomenon, it supplies the fullest details as to the manner in which the demonised were set free. This was always the same. It consisted neither of magical means nor formulas of exorcism, but always in the Word of Power which Jesus spake, or entrusted to His disciples, and which the demons always obeyed. There is here not only difference, but contrariety in comparison with the current Jewish notions, and it leads to the conclusion that there was the same contrast in His views, as in His treatment of the ' demonised.'

In one respect those who were ' demonised ' exhibited the same phenomenon. They all owned the Power of Jesus. It was not otherwise in the Synagogue at Capernaum on that Sabbath morning. What Jesus had spoken produced an immediate effect on the demonised, though one which could scarcely have been anticipated. For there is authority for inserting the word ' straight-way '[a] immediately after the account of Jesus' preaching. Yet, as we think of it, we cannot imagine that the demon would have continued silent, nor

In St. Mark i. 23

---

[1] See ' Life and Times,' Appendix XVI.: ' Jewish Views about Demons and the Demonised.'

yet that he could have spoken other than the truth in the Presence of the God-Man. Involuntarily, in his con-fessed inability of disguise or resistance, he owns defeat even before the contest. ' What have we to do with Thee, Jesus of Nazareth? Thou art come to destroy us! I know Thee Who Thou art, the Holy One of God.' And yet there seems in these words already an emergence of the consciousness of the demonised, at least in so far that there is no longer confusion between him and his tor-mentor, and the latter speaks in his own name. One stronger than the demon had affected the higher part in the demonised.

But this was not all. Jesus had come not only to de-stroy the works of the Devil, but to set the prisoners free. By a word of command He gagged the confessions of the demon, unwillingly made, and even so with hostile intent. It was not by such voices that He would have His Messiahship proclaimed.

The same power which gagged the confession also bade the demon relinquish his prey. One wild paroxysm—and the sufferer was for ever free. But on them all who saw and heard it fell the stupor of astonishment. Each turned to his neighbour with the inquiry: ' What is this? A new doctrine with authority! And He commandeth the un-clean spirits, and they obey Him.'

From the Synagogue we follow the Saviour, in com-pany with His called disciples, to Peter's wedded home. But no festive meal, as was Jewish wont, awaited them there. A sudden access of violent ' burning fever,' such as is even now common in that district, had laid Peter's mother-in-law prostrate. If we had still any lingering thought of Jewish magical cures as connected with those of Jesus, what is now related must dispel it. The Talmud gives this disease precisely the same name, ' burning fever,' and prescribes for it a magical remedy, of which the principal part is to tie a knife wholly of iron by a braid of hair to a thornbush, and to repeat on successive days Exod. iii. 2, 3, then ver. 4, and finally ver. 5, after which the bush is to be cut down, while a certain magical formula is pronounced. How different from this is the Evangelic narrative of the cure of Peter's mother-in-law. Jesus is 'told' of the sickness; He is besought for her who is stricken down. In His Presence disease and misery cannot continue. Bending over the sufferer He 'rebuked the fever,' just as He had rebuked 'the demon' in the Synagogue. Then lifting her by the hand, she rose up, healed, to 'minister' unto them. It was the first *Diaconate* of woman in the Church—a Diaconate to Christ and to those that were His.

The sun was setting, and the Sabbath past. On this autumn evening at Capernaum no one thought of business, pleasure, or rest. There must have been many homes of sorrow, care, and sickness there, and in the populous neighbourhood around. To all had the door of hope now been opened. No disease too desperate, when even the demons owned the authority of His mere rebuke. From all parts they bring them, and the whole city throngs—a hushed, solemnised multitude—expectant, waiting at the door of Simon's dwelling. There they laid them, along the street, up to the market-place, on their beds. Never, surely, was He more truly the Christ than when, in the stillness of that evening, He went through that suffering throng, laying His hands in the blessing of healing on every one of them, and casting out many devils.

CHAPTER XXIV.

SECOND JOURNEY THROUGH GALILEE—THE HEALING OF THE LEPER.

(St. Matt. iv. 23; viii. 2–4; St. Mark i. 35–45; St. Luke iv. 42–44; v. 12–16.)

IT was, so to speak, an inward necessity that the God-Man, when brought into contact with disease and misery, whether from physical or supernatural causes, should remove it by His Presence, by His touch, by His Word. An outward necessity also, because no other mode of teaching equally convincing would have reached those accustomed to Rabbinic disputations, and who must have looked for such a manifestation from One Who claimed such authority.   And yet, so far from being a mere worker of miracles, as we should have expected if the history of His miracles had been of legendary origin, there is nothing more marked than the pain, we had almost said the humiliation, which their necessity seems to have carried to His heart.   ' Except ye see signs and wonders, ye will not believe ; ' ' an evil and adulterous generation seeketh a sign ; ' ' blessed are they that have not seen, and yet have believed '—such are the utterances of Him Who sighed when He opened

^a St. Mark   the ears of the deaf,[a] and bade His Apostles look
vii. 34
^b St. Luke   for higher and better things than power over all
x. 17-20   diseases or even over evil spirits.[b]

And so, thinking of the scene on the evening before, we can understand how, ' very early, while it was still very

^c St. Mark i.   dark,'[c] Jesus rose up, and went into a solitary
35   place to pray.

As the three Synoptists accordantly state, Jesus now entered on His second Galilean journey.   There can be little doubt that the chronological succession of events is here accurately indicated by the more circumstantial narrative in St. Mark's Gospel.

Significantly, His Work began where that of the Rabbis, we had almost said of the Old Testament saints, ended.   Whatever remedies, medical, magical, or sympathetic, Rabbinic writings may indicate for various kinds of disease, leprosy is not included in the catalogue.   They left aside what even the Old Testament marked as moral death, by enjoining those so stricken to avoid all contact with the living, and even to bear the appearance of mourners.   As the leper passed by, his clothes rent, his hair dishevelled, and the lower part of his face and his

^d Lev. xiii.   upper lip covered,[d] it was as one going to death
45   who reads his own burial-service, while the
mournful words, ' Unclean ! Unclean ! ' which he uttered, proclaimed that his was both living and moral death.

Again, the Old Testament, and even Rabbinism, took, in the measures prescribed in leprosy, primarily a moral, or rather a ritual, and only secondarily a sanitary, view of the case.

In the elaborate Rabbinic code of defilements leprosy stood foremost. Not merely actual contact with the leper, but even his entrance defiled a habitation, and everything in it, to the beams of the roof. But beyond this, Rabbinic harshness or fear carried its provisions to the utmost sequences of an unbending logic. Childlessness and leprosy are described as chastisements, which indeed procure for the sufferer forgiveness of sins, but cannot, like other chastisements, be regarded as the outcome of love, nor be received in love. Tradition had it that, as leprosy attached to the house, the dress, or the person, these were to be regarded as always heavier strokes, following as each successive warning had been neglected, and a reference to this was seen in Prov. xix. 29. Eleven sins are mentioned which bring leprosy, among them pre-eminently those of which the tongue is the organ.

Still, if such had been the real views of Rabbinism, one might have expected that compassion would have been extended to those who bore such heavy burden of their sins. Instead of this, their troubles were needlessly increased. True, as wrapped in mourner's garb the leper passed by, his cry ' Unclean ! ' was to incite others to pray for him—but also to avoid him. No one was even to salute him ; his bed was to be low, inclining towards the ground. If he even put his head into a place, it became unclean. No less a distance than four cubits (six feet) must be kept from a leper ; or, if the wind came from that direction, a hundred was scarcely sufficient. Rabbi Meir would not eat an egg purchased in a street where there was a leper. Another Rabbi boasted that he always threw stones at them to keep them far off, while others hid themselves or ran away. To such extent did Rabbinism carry its inhuman logic in considering the leper as a mourner, that it even forbade him to wash his face.

We can now in some measure appreciate the contrast

between Jesus and His contemporaries in His bearing towards the leper. Or, conversely, we can judge by the healing of this leper of the impression which the Saviour had made upon the people. He would have fled from a Rabbi; he came in lowliest attitude of entreaty to Jesus. There was no Old Testament precedent for this approach: not in the case of Moses, nor even in that of Elisha, and there was no Jewish expectancy of it. But to have heard Him teach, to have seen or known Him as healing all manner of disease, must have carried the conviction of His absolute power. And so one can understand this cry: 'If Thou wilt, Thou canst make me clean.' It is not a prayer, but the ground-tone of all prayer—faith in His Power, and absolute committal to Him of our need. And Jesus, touched with compassion, willed it. It almost seems as if it were in the very exuberance of power that Jesus, acting in so direct contravention of Jewish usage, touched the leper. It was fitting that Elisha should disappoint Naaman's expectancy that the prophet would heal his leprosy by the touch of his hand. It was even more fitting that Jesus should surprise the Jewish leper by touching, ere by His Word He cleansed him.

It is not quite so easy at first sight to understand why Christ should with such intense earnestness, almost vehemence, have sent the healed man away—as the term bears, 'cast him out.' Perhaps we may here once more gather how the God-Man shrank from the fame connected with miracles—specially with such an one—which, as we have seen, were rather of inward and outward necessity than of choice in His Mission. Not thronged by eager multitudes of sight-seers, or aspirants for temporal benefits, was the Kingdom of Heaven to be preached and advanced. It would have been the way of a Jewish Messiah, and have led up to His royal proclamation by the populace. But as we study the character of the Christ, no contrast seems more glaring than that of such a scene. And so we read that when, notwithstanding the Saviour's charge to the healed leper to keep silence, it was nevertheless all the more made known by him, He could no more, as before, enter the cities, but remained without in desert places, whither they came to Him from every quarter. And in that withdrawal He spoke, and healed, ' and prayed.'

Christ's injunction of silence to the leper was combined with that of presenting himself to the priest, and conforming to the ritual requirements of the Mosaic Law in such cases. His conforming to the Mosaic Ritual was to be ' a testimony unto them.' The Lord did not wish to have the Law of Moses broken—and broken, not superseded, it would have been, if its provisions had been infringed before His Death, Ascension, and the Coming of the Holy Ghost had brought their fulfilment.

But there is something else here. The course of this history shows that the open rupture between Jesus and the Jewish authorities, which had commenced at the Unknown Feast at Jerusalem, was to lead to practical sequences. On the part of the Jewish authorities, it led to measures of active hostility. The Synagogues of Galilee are no longer the quiet scenes of His teaching and miracles; His Word and deeds no longer pass unchallenged. It had never occurred to these Galileans, as they implicitly surrendered themselves to the power of His words, to question their orthodoxy. But now, immediately after this occur-[a] rence, we find Him accused of blasphemy.[a] They had not thought it breach of God's Law when, on that Sabbath, He had healed in the Synagogue of Capernaum and in the home of Peter; but after this it became sinful to extend like mercy on the Sabbath to him [b] whose hand was withered.[b] They had never thought of questioning the condescension of His intercourse with the poor and needy ; but now they sought to sap the commencing allegiance of His disciples by charging Him with undue intercourse with publicans [c] and sinners,[c] and by inciting against Him even the [d] prejudices and doubts of the half-enlightened followers of His own Forerunner.[d] All these new incidents are due to the presence and hostile watchfulness of the Scribes and Pharisees, who now for the first time appear on the scene of His ministry. Is it too much

a St. Luke v. 21

b St. Luke vi. 7

c St. Luke v. 30

d St. Luke v. 33

then to infer that, immediately after that Feast at Jerusalem, the Jewish authorities sent their familiars into Galilee
after Jesus, and that it was to the presence and influence
of this informal deputation that the opposition to Christ,
which now increasingly appeared, was due? If so, then
we see not only an additional motive for Christ's injunction of silence on those whom He had healed, and for His
own withdrawal from the cities and their throng, but we
can understand how, as He afterwards answered those
whom John had sent to lay before Christ his doubts, by
pointing to His works, so He replied to the sending forth
of the Scribes of Jerusalem to watch, oppose, and arrest
Him, by sending to Jerusalem as His embassy the healed
leper, to submit to all the requirements of the Law.

CHAPTER XXV.

THE RETURN TO CAPERNAUM—CONCERNING THE FORGIVE-
NESS OF SINS—THE HEALING OF THE PARALYSED.

(St. Matt. ix. 1–8; St. Mark ii. 1–12; St. Luke v. 17–26.)

WE are still mainly following the lead of St. Mark, alike
as regards the succession of events and their details.

The second journey of Jesus through Galilee had commenced in autumn; the return to Capernaum was 'after
days,' which, in common Jewish phraseology, meant a considerable interval. As we reckon, it was winter, which
would equally account for Christ's return to Capernaum,
and for His teaching in the house. For, no sooner 'was
it heard that He was in the house,' than so many flocked
to the dwelling of Peter, which at that period may have
been 'the house' or temporary 'home' of the Saviour, as
to fill its limited space to overflowing. The general impression on our minds is, that this audience was rather in
a state of indecision than of sympathy with Jesus. It included 'Pharisees and doctors of the Law,' who had come
on purpose from the towns of Galilee, from Judæa, and

from Jerusalem. These occupied the ' uppermost rooms,' sitting, no doubt, near to Jesus. Their influence must have been felt by the people.

Although in no wise necessary to the understanding of the event, it is helpful to try and realise the scene. We can picture to ourselves the Saviour ' speaking the Word ' to that eager, interested crowd, which would soon become forgetful even of the presence of the watchful ' Scribes.' Though we know a good deal of the structure of Jewish houses,[1] we feel it difficult to be sure of the exact place which the Saviour occupied on this occasion. Meetings for religious study and discussion were certainly held in the *Aliyah* or upper chamber. But, on many grounds, such a *locale* seems unsuited to the requirements of the narrative.

The house of Peter was, probably, one of the better dwellings of the middle classes. In that case Jesus would speak the Word, standing in the covered gallery that ran round the courtyard of such houses, and opened into the various apartments. Perhaps He stood within the entrance of the guest-chamber, while the Scribes sat within that apartment, or beside Him in the gallery. The court before Him was thronged, out into the street. All were absorbedly listening to the Master, when of a sudden those appeared who were bearing a paralytic on his pallet. It had of late become too common a scene to see the sick thus carried to Jesus to attract special attention. And yet one can scarcely conceive that, if the crowd had merely filled an apartment and gathered around its door, it would not have made way for the sick, or that somehow the bearers could not have come within sight, or been able to attract the attention of Christ. But with a courtyard crowded out into the street, all this would be, of course, out of the question. In such circumstances access to Jesus was simply impossible.

Their resolve was quickly taken. If they cannot approach Christ with their burden, they can let it down from above at His feet. Outside the house, as well as inside, a

[1] See ' Sketches of Jewish Life,' pp. 93–96.

stair led up to the roof. They may have ascended it in this wise, or else reached it by what the Rabbis called 'the road of the roofs,' passing from roof to roof, if the house adjoined others in the same street. It would have been comparatively easy to 'unroof' the covering of 'tiles,' and then, 'having dug out' an opening through the lighter framework which supported the tiles, to let down their burden 'into the midst before Jesus.' All this, as done by four strong men, would be but the work of a few minutes. But we can imagine the arresting of the discourse of Jesus, and the surprise of the crowd as this opening through the tiles appeared, and slowly a pallet was let down before them. Busy hands would help to steady it, and bring it safe to the ground. And on that pallet lay one paralysed —his fevered face and glistening eyes upturned to Jesus.

This energy and determination of faith exceeded aught that had been witnessed before. Jesus saw it, and He spake. As yet the lips of the sufferer had not parted to utter his petition. He believed, indeed, in the power of Jesus to heal, with all the certitude that issued in the determination to be laid at His feet. And this open outburst of faith shone out the more brightly from its contrast with the unbelief within the breast of those Scribes, who had come to watch and ensnare Jesus.

As yet no one had spoken, for the silence of expectancy had fallen on them all. But He, Who perceived man's unspoken thoughts, knew that there was not only faith, but also fear, in the heart of that man. Hence the first words which the Saviour spake to him were: 'Be of good cheer.'[a] He had, indeed, got beyond the coarse Judaic standpoint, from which suffering seemed an expiation of sin. But this other Jewish idea was even more deeply rooted, had more of underlying truth, and would, especially in presence of the felt holiness of Jesus, have a deep influence on the soul, that recovery would not be granted to the sick unless his sins had first been forgiven him. It was this, perhaps as yet only partially conscious, want of the sufferer before Him, which Jesus met when He spoke forgiveness to his soul, and that not

a St. Matt. ix. 2

as something to come, but as an act already past : 'Child, thy sins have been forgiven.'

In another sense, also, there was a higher 'need be' for the word which brought forgiveness, before that which gave healing. Let us recall that Jesus was in the presence of those in whom the Scribes would fain have wrought disbelief, not of His power to cure disease—which was patent to all—but in His Person and authority ; that, perhaps, such doubts had already been excited. And here it deserves special notice, that, by first speaking forgiveness, Christ not only presented the deeper moral aspect of His miracles, as against their ascription to magic or Satanic agency, but also established that very claim, as regarded His Person and authority, which it was sought to invalidate. In this forgiveness of sins He presented His Person and authority as Divine, and He proved it such by the miracle of healing which immediately followed.

Thus the inward reasoning of the Scribes, which was open and known to Him Who readeth all thoughts, issued in quite the opposite of what they could have expected. It seemed easy to say : 'Thy sins have been forgiven.' But to Him, Who had 'authority' to do so on earth, it was neither more easy nor more difficult than to say : 'Rise, take up thy bed, and walk.' Yet this latter, assuredly, proved the former, and gave it in the sight of all men unquestioned reality.

CHAPTER XXVI.

THE CALL OF MATTHEW—RABBINIC THEOLOGY AS REGARDS
THE DOCTRINE OF FORGIVENESS IN CONTRAST TO THE
GOSPEL OF CHRIST—THE CALL OF THE TWELVE APOSTLES.

(St. Matt. ix. 9–13 ; St. Mark ii. 13–17 ; St. Luke v. 27–32 ;
St. Matt. x. 2–4 ; St. Mark iii. 13–19 ; St. Luke vi. 12–19.)

IN two things chiefly does the fundamental difference appear between Christianity and all other religious systems,

K

notably Rabbinism. Rabbinism, and every other system down to modern humanitarianism, can only generally point to God for the forgiveness of sin. What here is merely an abstraction has become a concrete reality in Christ. He speaks forgiveness on earth, because He is its embodiment. As regards the second idea, that of the sinner, all other systems would first make him a penitent, and then bid him welcome to God; Christ first welcomes him to God, and so makes him a penitent. The one demands, the other imparts life. And so Christ is the Physician, Whom they that are in health need not, but they that are sick. And so Christ came not to call the righteous, but sinners—not to repentance, as our common text erroneously puts it in St. Matthew ix. 13, and St. Mark ii. 17, but to Himself, to the Kingdom; and this is the beginning of repentance.

Thus it is that Jesus, when His teaching becomes distinctive from that of Judaism, puts these two points in the foreground: the one at the cure of the paralytic, the other in the call of Levi-Matthew. And this, also, further explains His miracles of healing as for the higher presentation of Himself as the Great Physician, while it gives some insight into the *nexus* of these two events, and explains their chronological succession. It was fitting that at the very outset, when Rabbinism followed and challenged Jesus with hostile intent, these two spiritual facts should be brought out, and that, not in a controversial, but in a positive and practical manner. For all the cumbrous observances of Rabbinism—its whole law—were only an attempted answer to the question: How can a man be just with God?

But, as Rabbinism stood self-confessedly silent and powerless as regarded the forgiveness of sins, so it had emphatically no word of welcome or help for the sinner. The very term 'Pharisee,' or 'separated one,' implied the exclusion of sinners. With this the whole character of Pharisaism accorded; perhaps we should have said, that of Rabbinism, since the Sadducean would here agree with the Pharisaic Rabbi. The contempt and avoidance of the unlearned, which was so characteristic of the system, arose not from mere pride of knowledge but from the thought that, as ' the Law ' was the glory and privilege of Israel— indeed, the object for which the world was created and preserved—ignorance of it was culpable. Thus, the unlearned blasphemed his Creator, and missed or perverted his own destiny. It was a principle that 'the ignorant cannot be pious.' The yoke of ' the Kingdom of God ' was the high destiny of every true Israelite. Only to them it lay in external, not internal conformity to the Law of God : ' in meat and drink,' not ' in righteousness, peace, and joy in the Holy Ghost.'

Although Rabbinism had no welcome to the sinner, it was unceasing in its call to repentance and in extolling its merits. Repentance not only averted punishment and prolonged life, but brought good, even the final redemption to Israel and the world at large. But, when more closely examined, we find that this repentance, as preceding the free welcome of invitation to the sinner, was only another form of work-righteousness.

We have already touched the point where, as regards repentance, as formerly in regard to forgiveness, the teaching of Christ is in absolute and fundamental contrariety to that of the Rabbis. According to Jesus Christ, when we have done all, we are to feel that we are but unprofitable servants.[a] According to the Rabbis, as St. Paul puts it, ' righteousness cometh by the Law ; ' and, when it is lost, the Law alone can restore life ; while, according to Christian teaching, it only bringeth death. Thus there was, at the very foundation of religious life, absolute contrariety between Jesus and His contemporaries.

a St. Luke xvii. 10

The nature of repentance has yet to be more fully explained. Its gate is sorrow and shame. In that sense repentance may be the work of a moment, ' as in the twinkling of an eye,' and a life's sins may obtain mercy by the tears and prayers of a few minutes' repentance. To this also refers the beautiful saying, that all which rendered a sacrifice unfit for the altar, such as that it was broken, fitted the penitent for acceptance, since 'the sacrifices of God were a broken and contrite heart.'

In some respects Rabbinic teaching about the need of repentance runs close to that of the Bible. But the vital difference between Rabbinism and the Gospel lies in this : that whereas Jesus Christ freely invited all sinners, whatever their past, assuring them of welcome and grace, the last word of Rabbinism is only despair and a kind of Pessimism. For it is expressly and repeatedly declared in the case of certain sins, and characteristically of heresy, that, even if a man genuinely and truly repented, he must expect immediately to die—indeed, his death would be the evidence that his repentance was genuine, since, though such a sinner might turn from his evil, it would be impossible for him, if he lived, to lay hold on the good, and to do it.

It is in the light of Rabbinic views of forgiveness and repentance that the call of Levi-Matthew must be read, if we would perceive its full meaning.

Few, if any, could have enjoyed better opportunities for hearing and quietly thinking over the teaching of the Prophet of Nazareth, than Levi-Matthew. We do not wonder that in the sequel his first or purely Jewish name of Levi is dropped, and only that of Matthew, which would have been added after his conversion, retained. The latter, which is the equivalent of Nathanael, or of the Greek Theodore (gift of God), seems to have been frequent.

Sitting before his custom-house, as on that day when Jesus called him, Matthew must have frequently heard Him as He taught by the sea-shore. Thither not only the multitude from Capernaum would easily follow; but here was the landing-place for the many ships which traversed the Lake, or coasted from town to town. And this not only for them who had business in Capernaum or that neighbourhood, but also for those who would then strike the great road of Eastern commerce which led from Damascus to the harbours of the West.

We know much about those ' tolls, dues, and customs,'

which made the Roman administration such sore and vexatious exaction to all ' Provincials,' and which in Judæa loaded the very name of publican with contempt and hatred. They who cherished the gravest religious doubts as to the lawfulness of paying any tribute to Cæsar, as involving in principle recognition of a bondage to which they would fain have closed their eyes, and the substitution of heathen kingship for that of Jehovah, must have looked on the publican as the very embodiment of anti-nationalism. The endless vexatious interferences, the unjust and cruel exactions, the petty tyranny, and the extortionate avarice, from which there was neither defence nor appeal, would make it well-nigh unbearable. It is to this that the Rabbis so often refer. If ' publicans' were disqualified from being judges or witnesses, it was, at least so far as regarded witness-bearing, because ' they exacted more than was due.' Hence also it was said that repentance was specially difficult for tax-gatherers and custom-house officers.

It is of importance to notice that the Talmud distinguishes two classes of ' publicans : ' the tax-gatherer in general, and the *douanier* or custom-house official. Although both classes fall under the Rabbinic ban, the *douanier*—such as Matthew was—is the object of chief execration. And this, because his exactions were more vexatious, and gave more scope to rapacity. The tax-gatherer collected the regular dues, which consisted of ground-, income-, and poll-tax. The ground-tax amounted to one-tenth of all grain and one-fifth of the wine and fruit grown—partly paid in kind, and partly commuted into money. The income-tax amounted to 1 per cent.; while the head-money, or poll-tax, was levied on all persons, bond and free, in the case of men from the age of fourteen, in that of women from the age of twelve up to that of sixty-five.

If this offered many opportunities for vexatious exactions and rapacious injustice, the custom-house official might inflict much greater hardship upon the poor people. There was tax and duty upon all imports and exports ; on all that was bought and sold ; bridge-money, road-money, harbour-dues, town-dues, &c. The classical reader knows the ingenuity which could invent a tax and find a name for every kind of exaction. On goods the *ad valorem* duty amounted to from $2\frac{1}{2}$ to 5, and on articles of luxury to even $12\frac{1}{2}$ per cent. But even this was as nothing, compared with the vexation of being constantly stopped on the journey, having to unload all pack-animals, when every bale and package was opened, and the contents tumbled about, private letters opened, and the *douanier* ruled supreme in his insolence and rapacity. This custom-house official was called ' great' if he employed substitutes, and ' small' if he stood himself at the receipt of custom.

What has been described will cast light on the call of Matthew by the Saviour of sinners. For we remember that Levi-Matthew was not only a ' publican,' but of the worst kind : a ' *Mokhes*' or *douanier* ; a ' *little Mokhes*' who himself stood at his custom-house ; of the class to whom, as we are told, repentance offered special difficulties. And, of all such officials, those who had to take toll from ships were perhaps the worst, if we are to judge by the proverb : ' Woe to the ship which sails without having paid the dues.'

But now quite another day had dawned for Matthew. The Prophet of Nazareth was not like those other great Rabbis, or their self-righteous imitators. There was not between Him and one like Matthew, the great, almost impassable gap of repentance. He had seen and heard Him in the Synagogue—and who that had heard His Words or witnessed His power could ever forget or lose the impression ? The people, the rulers, even the evil spirits, had owned His authority. But in the Synagogue Jesus was still the Great One, far away from him ; and he, Levi-Matthew, the ' *little Mokhes*' of Capernaum, to whom, as the Rabbis told him, repentance was next to impossible. But out there, in the open, by the seashore, it was otherwise. All unobserved by others, he observed all, and could yield himself without reserve to the impression.

Perhaps he may have witnessed the call of the first Apostles ; he certainly must have known the fishermen and shipowners of Capernaum. And now it appeared as if Jesus had been brought still nearer to Matthew. For the great ones of Israel, 'the Scribes of the Pharisees,' and their pietist followers, had combined against Him, and would exclude Him, not on account of sin, but on account of the sinners. And so, we take it, long before that eventful day which for ever decided his life, Matthew had, in heart, become the disciple of Jesus. Only he dared not hope for personal recognition—far less for call to discipleship. But when it came, and Jesus fixed on him that look of love which searched the inmost deep of the soul, it needed not a moment's thought or consideration. When He spake it, 'Follow Me,' the past seemed all swallowed up. He said not a word; but he rose up, left the custom-house, and followed Him. That was a gain that day, not of Matthew alone, but of all the poor and needy in Israel—nay, of all sinners from among men, to whom the door of heaven was opened.

It could not have been long after this that the memorable gathering took place in the house of Matthew, which gave occasion to that cavil of the Pharisaic Scribes, which served further to bring out the meaning of Levi's call. It was natural that all the publicans around should, after the call of Matthew, have come to his house to meet Jesus. And it was characteristic that Jesus should improve such opportunity. When we read of 'sinners' as in company with these publicans, it is not necessary to think of gross or open offenders, though such may have been included. For we know what such a term may have included in the Pharisaic vocabulary. Equally characteristic was it, that the Rabbinists should have addressed their objection as to fellowship with such, not to the Master, but to the disciples. Had they been able to lodge this cavil in their minds, it would have fatally shaken the confidence of the disciples in the Master.

From their own standpoint and contention, in their own form of speech, He answered the Pharisees. And

He not only silenced their gainsaying, but further opened up the meaning of His acting—nay, His very purpose and Mission. 'No need have they who are strong and in health [a] of a physician, but they who are ill.' It was the very principle of Pharisaism which He thus set forth, alike as regarded their self-exclusion from Him and His consorting with the diseased. And, as the more Hebraic St. Matthew adds, applying the very Rabbinic formula, so often used when superficial speciousness of knowledge is directed to further thought and information: ' Go and learn ! ' Learn what ? What their own Scriptures meant ; learn that fundamental principle of the spiritual meaning of the Law as explanatory of its mere letter, ' I will have mercy, and not sacrifice.'

[a] The latter in St. Luke v. 31

There was yet another and higher aspect of it, explaining and applying alike this saying and the whole Old Testament, and thus His Own Mission : ' For I am not come to call righteous men, but sinners.' The introduction of the words ' to repentance ' in some manuscripts of St. Matthew and St. Mark shows how early the full meaning of Christ's words was misinterpreted. For Christ called sinners to better and higher than repentance, even to Himself and His Kingdom.

The call of St. Matthew was no doubt speedily followed by the calling of the other Apostles.[b] It appears that only the calling of those to the Apostolate is related, which in some sense is typical, viz. that of Peter and Andrew, of James and John, of Philip and Bartholomew (or Bar Telamyon, or Temalyon, generally supposed the same as Nathanael), and of Matthew the publican. Yet, secondly, there is something which attaches to each of the others. Thomas, who is called Didymus (which means 'twin'), is closely connected with Matthew, both in St. Luke's Gospel and in that of St. Matthew himself. James is expressly named as the son of Alphæus or Clopas.[c] [1] This we know to have been also the name of

[b] St. Matt. x. 2-4 ; St. Mark iii. 13-19 ; St. Luke vi. 12-19

[c] St. John xix. 25

---

[1] Thus he would be the same as ' James the Less,' or rather ' the Little,' a son of Mary, the sister-in-law of the Virgin-Mother.

Matthew-Levi's father. But, as the name was a common one, no inference can be drawn from it, and it does not seem likely that the father of Matthew was also that of James, Judas, and Simon, for these three seem to have been brothers. Judas is designated by St. Matthew as Lebbæus, from the Hebrew for ' *a heart*,' and is also named, both by him and by St. Mark, Thaddæus—a term which we would derive from the Jewish name for '*praise.*' In that case both Lebbæus and Thaddæus would point to the heartiness and the thanksgiving of the Apostle, and hence to his character. St. Luke simply designates him Judas of James, which means that he was the brother (less probably, the son) of James.[a]   Thus his real name would have been Judas Lebbæus, and his surname Thaddæus. Closely connected with these two we have, in all the Gospels, Simon, surnamed Zelotes or Cananæan (not Canaanite), both terms indicating his original connection with the Galilean Zealot party, the 'Zealots for the Law.' His position in the Apostolic Catalogue, and the testimony of Hegesippus, seem to point him out as the son of Clopas, and brother of James, and of Judas Lebbæus. These three were, in a sense, cousins of Christ, since, according to Hegesippus, Clopas was the brother of Joseph, while the sons of Zebedee were real cousins, their mother Salome being a sister of the Virgin. Lastly, we have Judas Iscariot, or *Ish Kerioth*, ' a man of Kerioth,' a town in Judah.[b] Thus the betrayer alone would be of Judæan origin, the others all of Galilean ; and this may throw light on not a little in his after-history.

[a] St. Luke vi. 15 ; comp. St. John xiv. 22

[b] Josh. xv. 25

CHAPTER XXVII.

THE SERMON ON THE MOUNT.

(St. Matt. v.–vii.)

IT was probably on one of those mountain-ranges which stretch to the north of Capernaum, that Jesus had spent the night of lonely prayer which preceded the designation of the twelve to the Apostolate.   As the morning broke, He called up those who had learned to follow Him, and from among them chose the twelve, who were to be His

^{a St. Luke vi. 13} is represented as: Ambassadors and Representatives.[a] But already the eager multitude from all parts had come to the broad level plateau beneath, to bring to Him their need of soul or body.   To them He now descended with words of comfort and power of healing.   As they pressed around Him for that touch which brought virtue of healing to all, He retired again to the mountain height, and through the clear air of the spring day spake what has ever since been known as the 'Sermon on the Mount,' from the place where He sat, or as that 'in the plain' (St. Luke vi. 17), from the place where He had first met the multitude, and which so many must have continued to occupy while He taught.

The first and most obvious, perhaps also most super-ficial thought, is that which brings this teaching of Christ into comparison with the best of the wisdom and piety of the Jewish sages, as preserved in Rabbinic writings.   Its essential difference, or rather contrariety, in spirit and substance, not only when viewed as a whole, but in almost each of its individual parts, will be briefly shown in the sequel.

Turn from a reading of the 'Sermon on the Mount' to the wisdom of the Jewish Fathers in their Talmud.   It matters little what part be chosen for the purpose.   Here, also, the reader is at disadvantage, since his instructors present to him too frequently broken sentences, torn from their connection, words often mistranslated or misapplied; at best, only isolated sentences. There is here wit and logic, quickness and readiness, earnestness and zeal, but by the side of it profanity, uncleanness, superstition, and folly. Taken as a whole, it is not only utterly unspiritual, but anti-spiritual. Not that the Talmud is worse than might be expected of such writings in such times and circumstances, perhaps in many respects much better— always bearing in mind the particular standpoint of narrow nationalism, without which Talmudism itself could not have existed, and which therefore is not an accretion but an essential part of it. But, taken not in abrupt sentences and quotations, but as a whole, it is so utterly and immeasurably unlike the New Testament, that it is not easy to determine which is greater, the ignorance or the presumption of those who put them side by side. And to the reader of such disjointed Rabbinic quotations there is this further source of misunderstanding, that the form and sound of words is so often the same as that of the sayings of Jesus, however different their spirit. For, necessarily, the wine—be it new or old—made in Judæa comes to us in Palestinian vessels. But the ideas underlying terms equally employed by Jesus and the teachers of Israel are, in everything that concerns the relation of souls to God, so absolutely different as not to bear comparison. Whence otherwise the enmity and opposition to Jesus from the first, and not only after His Divine claim had been pronounced?

We can only here attempt a general outline of the 'Sermon on the Mount.' Its great subject is neither righteousness, nor yet the New Law (if such designation be proper in regard to what in no real sense is a Law), but the Kingdom of God. Notably, the Sermon on the Mount contains not any detailed or systematic doctrinal, nor any ritual teaching, nor yet does it prescribe the form of any outward observances.

As from this point of view the Sermon on the Mount differs from all contemporary Jewish teaching, so also is it impossible to compare it with any other system of morality. The difference here is one not of degree, nor

even of kind, but of standpoint. It is indeed true that
the Words of Jesus, properly understood, mark the utmost
limit of all possible moral conception. But every moral
system is a road by which, through self-denial, discipline,
and effort, men seek to reach the goal. Christ begins
with this goal, and places His disciples at once in the
position to which all other teachers point as the end.
They work up to the goal of becoming the 'children of
the Kingdom;' He makes men such, freely, and of His
grace: and this *is* the Kingdom. Accordingly, in the real
sense, there is neither new law nor moral system here, but
entrance into a new life: 'Be ye therefore perfect, as your
Father Which is in heaven is perfect.'

But if the Sermon on the Mount contains not a new,
nor, indeed, any system of morality, and addresses itself
to a new condition of things, it follows that the promises
attaching, for example, to the so-called 'Beatitudes' must not
be regarded as the reward of the spiritual state with which
they are respectively connected, nor yet as their result.
It is not *because* a man is poor in spirit that his is the
Kingdom of Heaven, in the sense that the one state will
grow into the other, or be its result; still less is the one
the reward of the other. The connecting link between
the 'state' and the promise is in each case Christ Himself:
because He stands between our present and our future,
and 'has opened the Kingdom of Heaven to all believers.'
Thus the promise represents the gift of grace by Christ in
the new Kingdom, as adapted to each case.

It is Christ, then, as the King, Who is here flinging
open the gates of His Kingdom. To study it more closely:
in the three chapters, under which the Sermon on the
Mount is grouped in the First Gospel,[a] the Kingdom of God is presented *successively, progressively*,
and *extensively*. Let us trace this with the help of the text
itself.

In the first part of the Sermon on the Mount,[b] the
Kingdom of God is delineated generally, first
positively, and then negatively, marking especially how its righteousness goes deeper than the mere

[a] chs. v.-vii.

[b] St. Matt. v.

letter of even the Old Testament Law. It opens with ten
Beatitudes, which are the New Testament counterpart to
the Ten Commandments. These present to us, not the
observance of the Law written on stone, but the realisation
of that Law which, by the Spirit, is written on the fleshy
tables of the heart.[a]

[a] St. Matt. v.
3-12.
[b] Ex. xix.
3-6
[c] St. Matt. v.
13-16

These Ten Commandments in the Old Covenant were preceded by a Prologue.[b] The ten
Beatitudes have, characteristically, not a Prologue,
but an Epilogue,[c] which corresponds to the Old
Testament Prologue. This closes the first section, of which
the object was to present the Kingdom of God in its
characteristic features. But here it was necessary, in
order to mark the real continuity of the New Testament
with the Old, to show the relation of the one to the other.
And this is the object of verses 17 to 20, the last-men-
tioned verse forming at the same time a grand climax and
transition to the criticism of the Old Testament-Law in its
merely literal application, such as the Scribes and Phari-

[d] vv. 21 to
end of ch. v.

sees made.[d] In this part of the 'Sermon on the
Mount' the careful reader will mark an analogy
to Exod. xxi. and xxii.

This closes the first part of the 'Sermon on the Mount.'
The second part is contained in St. Matt. vi. In this the
criticism of the Law is carried deeper. The question now
is not as concerns the Law in its literality, but as to what
constituted more than a mere observance of the outward
commandments : *piety, spirituality, sanctity.* Three points
here stand out: *alms, prayer,* and *fasting*—or, to put the
latter more generally, the relation of the physical to the
spiritual. These three are successively presented, nega-

[e] *Alms,* vi.
1-4; *Prayer,*
vv. 5-15 ;
Fasting, 16-
18

tively and positively.[e] But even so, this would
have been but the external aspect of them. The
Kingdom of God carries all back to the grand
underlying ideas. What were this or that mode
of giving alms, unless the right idea be apprehended, of
that which constitutes riches, and where they should be
sought ? This is indicated in verses 19 to 21. Again, as to
prayer : what matters it if we avoid the externalism of the

Pharisees, or even catch the right form as set forth in the
' Lord's Prayer,' unless we realise what underlies prayer ?
It is to lay our inner man wholly open to the light of God
in genuine, earnest simplicity, to be quite shone through
by Him.[a] It is, moreover, absolute and undivided self-dedication to God.[b] And in this lies

[a] vv. 22, 23
[b] vv. 22–24

its connection, alike with the spirit that prompts *almsgiving*,
and with that which prompts real *fasting*. That which
underlies all such fasting is a right view of the relation in
which the body with its wants stands to God—the temporal
to the spiritual.[c] It is the spirit of prayer which
must rule alike alms and fasting, and pervade

[c] vv. 25 to
end of ch. vi.

them ; the self-dedication to God, the seeking first after
the Kingdom of God and His Righteousness, that man,
and self, and life may be baptized in it. Such are the
real alms, the real prayers, the real fasts of the Kingdom
of God.

If we have rightly apprehended the meaning of the
first two parts of the ' Sermon on the Mount,' we cannot
be at a loss to understand its third part, as set forth in the
seventh chapter of St. Matthew's Gospel. Briefly, it is
this, as addressed to His contemporaries, nay, with wider
application to the men of all times : First, the Kingdom
of God cannot be *circumscribed*, as you would do it.[d]
Secondly, it cannot be *extended*, as you would do
it, by external means,[e] but cometh to us from
God,[f] and is entered by personal determination

[d] vii. 1–5
[e] ver. 6
[f] vv. 7–12

and separation.[g] Thirdly, it is not *preached*, as too often
is attempted, when thoughts of it are merely of
the external.[h] Lastly, it is not *manifested* in

[g] vv. 13, 14
[h] vv. 15, 16

life in the manner too common among religionists, but is
very real, and true, and good in its effects.[i] And
this Kingdom, as received by each of us, is like

[i] vv. 17–20

a solid house on a solid foundation, which nothing from
without can shake or destroy.[k]

[k] vv. 24–27

The contrast just set forth between the
Kingdom as presented by the Christ and Jewish contemporary teaching is the more striking, that it was expressed
in a form, and clothed in words with which all His hearers

were familiar. It is this which has misled so many in their quotations of Rabbinic parallels to the 'Sermon on the Mount.' They perceive outward similarity, and they straightway set it down to identity of spirit, not understanding that often those things are most unlike in the spirit of them, which are most like in their form. Many of these Rabbinic quotations are, however, entirely inapt, the similarity lying in an expression or turn of words. Occasionally, the misleading error goes even further, and that is quoted in illustration of Jesus' saying which, either by itself or in the context, implies quite the opposite. A few specimens will sufficiently illustrate our meaning.

To begin with the first Beatitude, to the poor in spirit, since theirs is the Kingdom of Heaven. This early Jewish saying is its very counterpart, marking not the optimism, but the pessimism of life: 'Ever be more and more lowly in spirit, since the expectancy of man is to become the food of worms.' Another contrast to Christ's promise of grace to the 'poor in spirit' is presented by the saying of the great Hillel: 'My humility is my greatness, and my greatness my humility,' which, be it observed, is elicited by a Rabbinic accommodation of Ps. cxiii. 5, 6: 'Who is exalted to sit, who humbleth himself to behold.' It is the omission on the part of modern writers of this explanatory addition, which has given the saying of Hillel even the faintest likeness to the first Beatitude.

But even so, what of the promise of 'the Kingdom of Heaven'? What is the meaning which Rabbinism attaches to that phrase, and would it have entered the mind of a Rabbi to promise what he understood as the Kingdom to all men, Gentiles as well as Jews, who were poor in spirit? We recall here the fate of the Gentiles in Messianic days, and, to prevent misstatements, summarise the opening pages of the Talmudic tractate on Idolatry. At the beginning of the coming era of the Kingdom, God is represented as opening the Law, and inviting all who had busied themselves with it to come for their reward. On this, nation by nation appears, but is in turn repelled.

Then all the Gentile nations urge that the Law had not
been offered to them, which is proved to be a vain contention, since God had actually offered it to them, but only
Israel had accepted it. On this the nations reply by a
peculiar Rabbinic explanation of Exod. xix. 17, according
to which God is actually represented as having lifted
Mount Sinai like a cask, and threatened to put it over
Israel unless they accepted the Law. Israel's obedience,
therefore, was not willing, but enforced. On this the
Almighty proposes to judge the Gentiles by the Noachic
commandments, although it is added that, even had they
observed them, these would have carried no reward. And,
although it is a principle that even a heathen if he studied
the Law was to be esteemed like the High-Priest, yet it
is argued, with the most perverse logic, that the reward
of heathens who observed the Law must be less than that
of those who did so because the Law was given them,
since the former acted from impulse, and not from obedience!

Other portions of the context bring out even more
strongly the difference between the largeness of Christ's
World-Kingdom, and the narrowness of Judaism.

It is the same self-righteousness and carnalness of view
which underlies the other Rabbinic parallels to the Beatitudes, pointing to contrast rather than likeness. Thus
the Rabbinic blessedness of mourning consists in this,
that much misery here makes up for punishment hereafter. We scarcely wonder that no Rabbinic parallel can
be found to the third Beatitude, unless we recall the contrast which assigns in Messianic days the possession of
earth to Israel as a nation. Nor could we expect any
parallel to the fourth Beatitude, to those who hunger and
thirst after righteousness. Rabbinism would have quite
a different idea of 'righteousness,' considered as 'good
works,' and chiefly as almsgiving. To such the most
special reward is promised. Similarly, Rabbinism speaks
of the perfectly righteous and the perfectly unrighteous,
or else of the righteous and unrighteous (according as the
good or the evil might weigh heaviest in the scale); and,

besides these, of a kind of middle state. But such a conception as that of 'hunger' and 'thirst' after righteousness would have no place in the system. And, that no doubt may obtain, this sentence may be quoted: 'He that says, I give this "Sela" as alms, in order that my sons may live, and that I may merit the world to come, behold, this is the perfectly righteous.' Along with such assertions of work-righteousness we have this principle often repeated, that all such merit attaches only to Israel, while the good works and mercy of the Gentiles are actually reckoned to them as sin, though it is only fair to add that one voice is raised in contradiction of such teaching.

It seems almost needless to prosecute this subject; yet it may be well to remark that the same self-righteousness attaches to the quality of mercy, so highly prized among the Jews, and which is supposed not only to bring reward, but to atone for sins. With regard to purity of heart, there is, indeed, a discussion between the school of Shammai and that of Hillel—the former teaching that guilty thoughts constitute sin, while the latter expressly confines it to guilty deeds. The Beatitude attaching to peacemaking has many analogies in Rabbinism; but the latter would never have connected the designation of 'children of God' with any but Israel. A similar remark applies to the use of the expression 'Kingdom of Heaven' in the next Beatitude.

One by one, as we place the sayings of the Rabbis by the side of those of Jesus in this Sermon on the Mount, we mark the same essential contrariety of spirit, whether as regards righteousness, sin, repentance, faith, the Kingdom, alms, prayer, or fasting. Only two points may be specially selected, because they are so frequently brought forward by writers as proof that the sayings of Jesus did not rise above those of the chief Talmudic authorities. The first ^{a St. Matt.} of these refers to the well-known words of our ^{vii. 12} Lord:[a] 'Therefore all things whatsoever ye would that men should do to you, do ye even so to them: for this is the law and the prophets.' This is compared

with the following Rabbinic parallel, in which the gentleness of Hillel is contrasted with the opposite disposition
of Shammai. The latter is said to have harshly repelled
an intending proselyte, who wished to be taught the whole
Law while standing on one foot, while Hillel received
him with this saying: 'What is hateful to thee, do not
to another. This is the whole Law, all else is only its explanation.' It will be noticed that the words in which
the Law is thus summed up are really only a quotation
from Tob. iv. 15, although their presentation as the substance of the Law is, of course, original. But apart from
this, there is a vast difference between this negative injunction and the positive direction to do unto others as we would
have them do unto us. The one does not rise above the
standpoint of the Law, while the Christian saying embodies
the nearest approach to absolute love of which human nature
is capable, making that the test of our conduct to others
which we ourselves desire to possess. And, be it observed,
the Lord does not put self-love as the principle of our conduct, but only as its ready test. Besides, the further
explanation in St. Luke vi. 38 should here be kept in
view, as also the explanatory additions in St. Matt. v.
42–48.

The second instance is the supposed similarity between
ª St. Matt.   petitions in the Lord's Prayer ª and Rabbinic
vi. 9–13   prayers. Here we may remark at the outset,
that both the spirit and the manner of prayer are presented
by the Rabbis so externally, and with such details, as to
make it quite different from prayer as our Lord taught His
disciples. That the warning against prayers at the corner
of streets was taken from life appears from the well-
known anecdote concerning one Rabbi Jannai, who was
observed saying his prayers in the public streets of
Sepphoris, and then advancing four cubits to make the so-
called supplementary prayer. Again, a perusal of some
of the recorded prayers of the Rabbis will show how
vastly different many of them were from the petitions
which our Lord taught.

Further details would lead beyond our present scope.

It must suffice to indicate that such sayings as St. Matt.
v. 6, 15, 17, 25, 29, 31, 46, 47 ; vi. 8, 12, 18, 22, 24, 32 ;
vii. 8, 9, 10, 15, 17–19, 22, 23, have no parallel, in any
real sense, in Jewish writings, whose teaching, indeed,
often embodies opposite ideas.

CHAPTER XXVIII.

THE HEALING OF THE CENTURION'S SERVANT.

(St. Matt. viii. 1, 5–15 ; St. Mark iii. 20, 21 ; St. Luke vii. 1–10.)

From the Mount of Beatitudes, it was again to His temporary home at Capernaum that Jesus retired.[a]
Yet not either to solitude or to rest. For of
that multitude which had hung entranced on His Words
many followed Him, and there was now such constant
pressure around Him, that in the zeal of their attendance
upon the wants and demands of those who hungered after
the Bread of Life alike Master and disciples found not
leisure so much as for the necessary sustenance of the
body.

    a St. Mark iii. 19–21

    The circumstances, the incessant work, and the all-
consuming zeal led to the apprehension on the part of ' His
friends' that the balance of judgment might be over-
weighted, and high reason brought into bondage to the
poverty of the earthly frame. On tidings reaching them,
with perhaps Orientally exaggerating details, they hastened
out of their house in a neighbouring street to take possession of Him, as if He had needed their charge. The idea
that He was ' beside Himself' afforded the only explanation of what otherwise would have been to them well-nigh
inexplicable. To the Eastern mind especially this want of
self-possession, the being ' beside ' oneself, would point to
possession by another—God or Devil. It was on the
ground of such supposition that the charge was so constantly raised by the Scribes, and unthinkingly taken up
by the people, that Jesus was mad, and had a devil : not
demoniacal possession, be it marked, but possession by the

Devil, in the absence of self-possessedness. And hence our Lord characterised this charge as really blasphemy against the Holy Ghost. And this also explains how, while unable to deny the reality of His Works, they could still resist their evidential force.

This incident could have caused but brief interruption to His Work. Presently there came the summons of the heathen Centurion and the healing of his servant, which both St. Matthew and St. Luke record.

The Centurion is a real historical personage. He was captain of the troop quartered in Capernaum, and in the service of Herod Antipas. We know that such troops were chiefly recruited from Samaritans and Gentiles of Cæsarea. Nor is there the slightest evidence that this Centurion was a 'proselyte of righteousness.' The accounts both in St. Matthew and in St. Luke are incompatible with this idea. A 'proselyte of righteousness' could have had no reason for not approaching Christ directly, nor would he have spoken of himself as 'unfit' that Christ should come under his roof. But such language quite accorded with Jewish notions of a Gentile, since the houses of Gentiles were considered as defiled, and as defiling those who entered them. On the other hand, the 'proselytes of righteousness' were in all respects equal to Jews, so that the words of Christ concerning Jews and Gentiles, as reported by St. Matthew, would not have been applicable to them. The Centurion was simply one who had learned to love Israel and to reverence Israel's God; one who had built that Synagogue, of which, strangely enough, now after eighteen centuries the remains in their rich and elaborate carvings of cornices and entablatures, of capitals and niches, show with what liberal hand he had dealt his votive offerings.

As the houses of Gentiles were 'unclean,' entrance into them, and still more familiar fellowship, would 'defile.' The Centurion must have known this; and the higher he placed Jesus on the pinnacle of Judaism, the more natural was it for him to communicate with Christ through the elders of the Jews, and not to expect the personal Presence of the Master, even if the application to Him were attended with success.

Closely considered, whatever verbal differences, there is not any real discrepancy between the Judæan presentation of the event in St. Matthew and the fuller Gentile account of it by St. Luke. From both narratives we are led to infer that the house of the Centurion was not in Capernaum itself, but in its immediate neighbourhood, probably on the road to Tiberias.

And in their leading features the two accounts entirely agree. There is earnest supplication for his sick, seemingly dying servant. Again, the Centurion in the fullest sense believes in the power of Jesus to heal, in the same manner as he knows his own commands as an officer would be implicitly obeyed. But in his self-acknowledged 'unfitness' lay the real 'fitness' of this good soldier for membership with the true Israel; and in his deep-felt 'unworthiness' the real 'worthiness' for 'the Kingdom' and its blessings. Here was one who was in the state described in the first clauses of the 'Beatitudes,' and to whom came the promise of the second clauses; because Christ is the connecting link between the two, and because He consciously was such to the Centurion.

And so we mark that participation in the blessedness of the Kingdom is not connected with any outward relationship towards it, nor belongs to our inward consciousness in regard to it; but is granted by the King to that faith which in deepest simplicity realises, and holds fast by Him.

But for the fuller understanding of the words of Christ, the Jewish modes of thought, which He used in illustration, require to be briefly explained. It was a common belief that in the day of the Messiah redeemed Israel would be gathered to a great feast, together with the patriarchs and heroes of the Jewish faith. One thing, however, was clear: Gentiles could have no part in that feast. On this point, then, the words of Jesus in reference to the believing Centurion formed the most marked contrast to Jewish teaching.

In another respect also we mark similar contrariety.
When our Lord consigned the unbelieving to 'outer darkness, where there is weeping and gnashing of teeth,' He
once more used Jewish language, only with opposite application of it.   Gehinnom was a place of darkness, to which,
Amos v. 20 in the day of the Lord,[a] the Gentiles would be
consigned.   On the other hand, the merit of
circumcision would in the day of the Messiah deliver
Jewish sinners from Gehinnom.   It seems a moot question,
[b] St. Matt. whether the expression 'outer darkness'[b] may
viii. 12   not have been intended to designate—besides
the darkness outside the lighted house of the Father, and
even beyond the darkness of Gehinnom—a place of hopeless, endless night.   Associated with it is 'the weeping
and the gnashing of teeth.'   In Rabbinic thought the
former was connected with sorrow, the latter almost always
with anger—not, as generally supposed, with anguish.

To complete our apprehension of the contrast between
the views of the Jews and the teaching of Jesus, we must
bear in mind that, as the Gentiles could not possibly
share in the feast of the Messiah, so Israel had claim and
title to it.   To use Rabbinic terms, the former were
'children of Gehinnom,' but Israel 'children of the King-
[c] St. Matt. dom,'[c] or, in strictly Rabbinic language, 'royal
viii. 12   children,' 'children of God,' 'of heaven,' 'children of the upper chamber,' and 'of the world to come.'

Never, surely, could the Judaism of His hearers have
received more rude shock than by this inversion of all
their cherished beliefs.   There was a feast of Messianic
fellowship, a recognition on the part of the King of all
His faithful subjects, a festive gathering with the fathers
of the faith.   But this fellowship was not of outward, but
of spiritual kinship.   There were 'children of the Kingdom,' and there was an 'outer darkness' with its anguish
and despair.   But this childship was of the Kingdom,
such as He had opened it to all believers; and that outer
darkness theirs, who had only outward claims to present.
And so this history of the believing Centurion is at the
same time an application of the 'Sermon on the Mount,'

and a further carrying out of its teaching. Negatively, it differentiated the Kingdom from Israel; while, positively, it placed the hope of Israel, and fellowship with its promises, within reach of all faith, whether of Jew or Gentile.

CHAPTER XXIX.

THE RAISING OF THE YOUNG MAN OF NAIN.

(St. Luke vii. 11–17.)

IT matters little whether it was the very 'day after' the healing of the Centurion's servant, or 'shortly afterwards,' that Jesus left Capernaum for Nain. Probably it was the morrow of that miracle, and the fact that 'much people,' or rather 'a great multitude,' followed Him seems confirmatory of it. The way was long—as we reckon, more than twenty-five miles; but even if it was all taken on foot, there could be no difficulty in reaching Nain ere the evening, when so often funerals took place. Various roads lead to and from Nain. About ten minutes' walk to the east of Nain lies the now unfenced burying-ground, whither on that spring afternoon they were carrying the widow's son.

Putting aside later superstitions, so little has changed in the Jewish rites and observances about the dead, that from Talmudic and even earlier sources we can form a vivid conception of what had taken place in Nain. The watchful anxiety, the vain use of such means as were known or within reach of the widow would be common features in any such picture. But here we have besides the Jewish thoughts of death and after death; knowledge just sufficient to make afraid, but not to give firm consolation, which make even the most pious Rabbi uncertain of his future; and then the desolate thoughts connected in the Jewish mind with childlessness. We can realise how Jewish ingenuity and wisdom would resort to remedies real or magical; how the neighbours would come in with reverent step, feeling as if the very

S'.ekhinah were, unseen, at the head of the pallet in that humble home; and how they would resort to the prayers of those who were deemed pious in Nain.

But all was in vain. And now the well-known blast of the horn has carried tidings that once more the Angel of Death has done his behest. In passionate grief the mother has rent her upper garment. The last sad offices have been rendered to the dead. The body has been laid on the ground; hair and nails have been cut, and the body washed, anointed, and wrapped in the best the widow could procure.

The mother is left moaning, lamenting. She would sit on the floor, neither eat meat nor drink wine. What scanty meal she would take must be without prayer, in the house of a neighbour, or in another room, or at least with her back to the dead. Pious friends would render neighbourly offices, or busy themselves about the near funeral. If it was deemed duty for the poorest Jew, on the death of his wife, to provide at least two flutes and one mourning woman, we may feel sure that the widowed mother had not neglected what were regarded as the last tokens of affection. In all likelihood the custom obtained even then, though in modified form, to have funeral orations at the grave. For, if charity even provided for an unknown wayfarer the simplest funeral, mourning-women would be hired to chaunt in weird strains the lament: ' Alas, the lion! alas, the hero!' or similar words, while great Rabbis were wont to bespeak for themselves 'a warm funeral oration.'

We can follow in spirit the mournful procession. As it issued chairs and couches were reversed and laid low. Outside, the funeral orator, if such were employed, preceded the bier, proclaiming the good deeds of the dead. Immediately before the dead came the women, this being peculiar to Galilee, the Midrash giving this reason of it, that woman had introduced death into the world. The body was not, as afterwards in preference, carried in an ordinary coffin of wood, if possible cedarwood, but laid on a bier, or in an open coffin. In former times a distinction had been made in these biers between rich and poor. The former were carried, as it were, in state—while the poor were conveyed in a receptacle made of wickerwork, having sometimes at the foot what was termed 'a horn,' to which the body was made fast. But this distinction between rich and poor was abolished by Rabbinic ordinance, and both alike, if carried on a bier, were laid in that made of wickerwork. Commonly, though not in later practice, the face of the dead body was uncovered. The body lay with its face turned up, and its hands folded on the breast. We may add that, when a person had died unmarried or childless, it was customary to put into the coffin something distinctive of them, such as pen and ink, or a key. Over the coffins of bride or bridegroom a baldachino was carried. Sometimes the coffin was garlanded with myrtle. In exceptional cases we read of the use of incense, and even of a kind of libation.

We cannot then, be mistaken in supposing that the body of the widow's son was laid on the 'bed,' or in the 'willow basket,' already described. Nor can we doubt that the ends or handles were borne by friends and neighbours, different parties of bearers, all of them unshod, at frequent intervals relieving each other, so that as many as possible might share in the good work. During these pauses there was loud lamentation; but this custom was not observed in the burial of women. Behind the bier walked the relatives, friends, and then the sympathising 'multitude.' For it was deemed like mocking one's Creator not to follow the dead to his last resting-place, and to all such want of reverence Prov. xvii. 5 was applied. If one were absolutely prevented from joining the procession, although for its sake all work, even study, should be interrupted, reverence should at least be shown by rising up before the dead. And so they would go on to what the Hebrews beautifully designated as the 'house of assembly,' or 'meeting,' the 'hostelry,' the 'place of rest,' or 'of freedom,' the 'field of weepers,' the 'house of eternity,' or 'of life.'

Up from the city close by came this 'great multitude'

that followed the dead, with lamentations, wild chaunts of mourning women, accompanied by flutes and the melancholy tinkle of cymbals, perhaps by trumpets, amidst expressions of general sympathy. Along the road from Endor streamed the great multitude which followed the 'Prince of Life.' Here they met : Life and Death. The connecting link between them was the deep sorrow of the widowed mother. He recognised her as she went before the bier, leading him to the grave whom she had brought into life. She was still weeping ; even after He had hastened a step or two in advance of His followers, quite close to her, she did not heed Him and was still weeping. But, ' beholding her,' the Lord ' had compassion on her.' We remember, by way of contrast, the common formula used at funerals in Palestine, ' Weep with them, all ye who are bitter of heart ! ' It was not so that Jesus spoke to those around, nor to her, but characteristically : ' Be not weeping.' And what He said, that He wrought. He touched the bier, perhaps the very wicker-basket in which the dead youth lay. He dreaded not the greatest of all defilements—that of contact with the dead, which Rabbinism, in its elaboration of the letter of the Law, had surrounded with endless terrors. His was other separation than of the Pharisees : not that of submission to ordinances, but of conquest of what made them necessary.

And as He touched the bier, they who bore it stood still. The awe of the coming wonder—as it were, the shadow of the opening gates of life—had fallen on them. One word of command, ' and he that was dead sat up, and began to speak.' Not of that world of which he had had brief glimpse. For, as one who suddenly passes from dream-vision to waking, in the abruptness of the transition loses what he has seen, so he, who from that dazzling brightness was hurried back to the dim light to which his vision had been accustomed.

And still was Jesus the link between the mother and the son, who had again found each other. And so, in the truest sense, ' He gave him to his mother.'

But on those who saw this miracle at Nain fell the fear of the Divine Presence, and over their souls swept the hymn of Divine praise : fear, because a great Prophet was risen up among them; praise, because God had visited His people.

CHAPTER XXX.

THE WOMAN WHICH WAS A SINNER.

(St. Luke vii. 36–50.)

THE next recorded event in this Galilean journey of the Christ can scarcely have occurred in the quiet little town of Nain. And yet it must have followed almost immediately upon it.

The impression left upon us by St. Matt. xi. 20–30 (which follows on the account of the Baptist's embassy) is that Jesus was on a journey, and it may well be that those words of encouragement and invitation, spoken to the burdened and wearily labouring,[a] formed part, perhaps the substance, of His preaching on that journey. Truly these were ' good tidings,' and not only to those borne down by weight of conscious sinfulness or deep sorrow. ' Good news,' also, to them who would fain have ' learned ' according to their capacity, but whose teachers had weighted 'the yoke of the Kingdom' to a heavy burden, and made the Will of God to them labour, weary and unaccomplishable.

a St. Matt. xi. 28–30

Another point requires notice. It is how, in the unfolding of His Mission to man, the Christ progressively placed Himself in antagonism to the Jewish religious thought of His time, from out of which He had historically sprung. We find this in the whole spirit and bearing of what He did and said—in the house at Capernaum, in the Synagogues, with the Gentile Centurion, at the gate of Nain, and especially here, in the history of the much-forgiven woman who had much sinned. A Jewish Rabbi could not have so acted and spoken ; he would not even have understood Jesus; nay, a Rabbi, however gentle and pitiful, would in word and deed have taken precisely the opposite direction from that of the Christ.

The history itself seems but a fragment. We must try to learn from its structure, where and how it was broken off. We understand the delicacy that left her unnamed, the record of whose ' much forgiveness' and great love had to be joined to that of her much sin. And we mark in contrast the cravings of morbid curiosity, or, for saint-worship, which have associated her history with the name of Mary Magdalene. Another mistake is the attempt of certain critics to identify this history with the much later anointing of Christ at Bethany.[a] Yet the two narratives have really nothing in com- mon, save that in each case there was a ' Simon' —perhaps the commonest of Jewish names; a woman who anointed; and that Christ, and those who were present, spoke and acted in accordance with other passages in the Gospel-history.

> [a] St. Matt. xxvi. 6 &c., and parallels

The invitation of Simon the Pharisee to his table does not necessarily indicate that he had been impressed by the teaching of Jesus. If Jesus had taught in the ' city,' and, as always, irresistibly drawn to Him the multi- tude, it would be only in accordance with the manners of the time if the leading Pharisee invited the distinguished ' Teacher' to his table. As such he undoubtedly treated Him.[b] The question in Simon's mind was, whether He was more than ' Teacher'—even ' Prophet;' and that such question rose within him indi- cates not only that Christ openly claimed a position different from that of Rabbi, and that His followers re- garded Him at least as a Prophet, but also, within the breast of Simon, a struggle in which Jewish prejudice was bearing down the impression of Christ's Presence.

> [b] St. Luke vii. 40

They were all sitting, or rather ' lying,' around the table, the body resting on the couch, the feet turned away from the table in the direction of the wall, while the left elbow rested on the table. And now, from the open court- yard, up the verandah-step, perhaps through an antechamber, and by the open door, passed the figure of a woman into the festive reception-room and dining-hall. How she obtained access little matters—as little as whether she 'had been,' or 'was' up to that day, 'a sinner,' in the terrible acceptation of the term. But we must bear in mind the greatness of Jewish prejudice against any conversation with woman, however lofty her character, fully to realise the incongruity on the part of such a woman in seeking access to the Rabbi, Whom so many regarded as the God-sent Prophet.

We have said before that this story is a fragment ; and here, also, as in the invitation of Simon to Jesus, we have evidence of it. The woman had, no doubt, heard His words that day. What He had said would be, in sub-stance : 'Come unto Me, all ye that labour and are heavy laden, and I will give you rest. . . . Learn of Me, for I am meek and lowly in heart. . . . Ye shall find rest unto your souls. . . .' This was to her the Prophet sent from God with the good news that opened even to her the Kingdom of Heaven, and laid its yoke upon her, not bear-ing her down to very hell, but easy of wear and light of burden. She knew that it was all as He said, in regard to the heavy load of her past ; and, as she listened to those Words, and looked on that Presence, she learned to believe that it was all as He had promised to the heavy-burdened. And she had watched, and followed Him afar off to the Pharisee's house.

The shadow of her form must have fallen on all who sat at meat. But none spake ; nor did she heed any but One. What mattered it to her who was thére, or what they thought ? There was only One Whose Presence she dared not encounter—not from fear of Him, but from knowledge of herself. It was He to Whom she had come. And so she 'stood behind at His Feet.' She had brought with her an *alabastron* (phial, or flask, commonly of alabaster) of perfume. We know that perfumes were much sought after, and very largely in use. Some, such as true balsam, were worth double their weight in silver ; others, like the spikenard, though not equally costly, were also 'precious.' We have evidence that perfumed oils—notably oil of roses, and of the iris plant, but chiefly the mixture known in antiquity as *foliatum*, were largely manufactured and used in Palestine. A flask with this perfume was worn by women round the neck, and hung down below the breast. So common was its use as to be allowed even on the Sabbath. Hence it seems at least not unlikely that the *alabastron* which she brought, who loved so much, was none other than the 'flask of foliatum.'

As she stood behind Him at His Feet, reverently bending, a shower of tears, like sudden summer-rain, 'bedewed' His Feet. As if afraid to defile Him by her tears, she quickly wiped them away with the long tresses of her hair that had fallen down and touched Him as she bent. And, now that her faith had grown bold in His Presence, she is continuing to kiss those Feet which had brought to her the 'good tidings of peace,' and to anoint them out of the *alabastron* round her neck. And still she spake not, nor yet He. For, as on her part silence seemed most fitting utterance, so on His, that He suffered it in silence was best and most fitting answer to her.

Another there was whose thoughts, far other than hers or the Christ's, were also unuttered. A more painful contrast than that of 'the Pharisee' in this scene can scarcely be imagined. We do not insist that the designation 'this Man,'[a] given to Christ in his unspoken thoughts, or the manner in which afterwards he replied to the Saviour's question by a supercilious 'I suppose,' or 'presume,'[b] necessarily imply contempt. But they certainly indicate the mood of his spirit. One thing, at least, seemed now clear to this Pharisee: If 'this Man,' with His strange, novel ways and words, Whom in politeness he must call 'Teacher,' Rabbi, *were* a Prophet, He would have known who the woman was; and, if He had known who she was, then would He never have allowed such approach.

And yet Prophet He was, and in far fuller sense than Simon could have imagined. For He had read Simon's unspoken thoughts. Presently He would show it to him;

[a] ver. 39

[b] ver. 43

yet not by open reproof that would have put him to shame before his guests. What follows is not, as generally supposed, a parable, but an illustration. Accordingly, it must in no way be pressed. With this explanation vanish all the supposed difficulties about the Pharisees being 'little forgiven,' and hence 'loving little.' To convince Simon of the error of his conclusion that, if the life of that woman had been known, the Prophet must have forbidden her touch of love, Jesus entered into the Pharisee's own modes of reasoning. Of two debtors, one of whom owed ten times as much as the other, who would best love the creditor who had freely forgiven them? Though to both the debt might have been equally impossible of discharge, and both might love equally, yet a Rabbi, would, according to his Jewish notions, say that he would love most to whom most had been forgiven. If this was the undoubted outcome of Jewish theology—the so much for so much— let it be applied to the present case. If there were much benefit, there would be much love; if little benefit, little love. And conversely: in such case much love would argue much benefit; little love, small benefit. Let him then apply the reasoning by marking this woman, and contrasting her conduct with his own. To wash the feet of a guest, to give him the kiss of welcome, and especially to anoint him,[a] were not, indeed, necessary attentions at a feast. All the more did they indicate special care, affection, and respect.[b] None of these tokens of regard had marked the merely polite reception of Him by the Pharisee. But, in a twofold climax,[c] of which the intensity can only be indicated, the Saviour now proceeds to show how different it had been with her, to whom, for the first time, He now turned! On Simon's own reasoning, then, he must have received but little, she much benefit. Or, to apply the former illustration, and now to reality: 'Forgiven have been her sins, the many '—not in ignorance, but with knowledge of their being 'many.' This, by Simon's former admission, would explain and account for her much love,

a Comp. St. John xiii. 4
b Gen. xviii. 4; xix. 2; xxiv. 32; Judg. xix. 21; 1 Sam. xxv. 41; Ex. xviii. 7; 2 Sam. xv. 5; xix. 39; Eccl. xix. 8; Amos vi. 6; Ps. xxiii. 5
c vv. 44–46

as the effect of much forgiveness. On the other hand—though the Lord does not actually express it—this other inference would also hold true, that Simon's little love showed that 'little is being forgiven.'

And as formerly for the first time He had turned, so now for the first time He spoke to her : ' Thy sins have been forgiven '—not now ' the many.' Nor does He now heed the murmuring thoughts of those around, who cannot understand Who this is that forgiveth sins also. But to her He said : ' Thy faith has saved thee : go into peace.' Our logical dogmatics would have had it : ' go *in* peace ; ' He, ' *into* peace.' And so she, the first who had come to Him for spiritual healing, went out into the better light, and into the eternal peace of the Kingdom of Heaven.

CHAPTER XXXI.

THE MINISTERING WOMEN—THE RETURN TO CAPERNAUM—
HEALING OF THE DEMONISED DUMB—PHARISAIC CHARGE
AGAINST CHRIST—THE VISIT OF CHRIST'S MOTHER AND
BRETHREN.

(St. Luke viii. 1–3 ; St. Matt. ix. 32–35 ; St. Mark iii. 22, &c. ; St. Matt. xii. 46–50 and parallels.)

ALTHOUGH there are difficulties connected with details, we conclude that Christ was now returning to Capernaum from that Missionary journey[a] of which Nain had been the southernmost point. On this journey He was attended, not only by the Twelve, but by loving, grateful women. Among them three are specially named. ' Mary, called Magdalene,' had received from Him special benefit of healing to body and soul. Her designation as Magdalene was probably derived from her native city, Magdala, just as several Rabbis are spoken of in the Talmud as ' Magdalene.' Magdala, which was a Sabbath-day's journey from Tiberias, was celebrated for its dyeworks, and its manufactories of fine woollen textures, of which eighty are mentioned. Indeed, all that district

[a] St. Luke viii. 1–3 ; St. Matt. ix. 35

seems to have been engaged in this industry. It was also reputed for its traffic in turtle-doves and pigeons for purifications—tradition, with its usual exaggeration of numbers, mentioning three hundred such shops. Accordingly, its wealth was very great, and it is named among the three cities whose contributions were so large as to be sent in a waggon to Jerusalem. But its moral corruption was also great, and to this the Rabbis attributed its final destruction. Of the many towns and villages that dotted the shores of the Lake of Galilee, all have passed away except Magdala, which is still represented by the collection of mud hovels that bears the name of Mejdel. The ancient watch-tower which gave the place its name is still there, probably standing on the same site as that which looked down on Jesus and the Magdalene. To this day Magdala is celebrated for its springs and rivulets, which render it specially suitable for dyeworks; while the shell-fish, with which these waters and the Lake are said to abound, might supply some of the dye.

Such details may help us more clearly to realise the home, and with it, perhaps, also the upbringing and circumstances of her who not only ministered to Jesus in His life, but, with eager avarice of love, watched 'afar off' His dying moments,[a] and then sat over against the new tomb of Joseph in which His Body was laid.[b] And the terrible time which followed she spent with her like-minded friends, who in Galilee had ministered to Christ,[c] in preparing those 'spices and ointments'[d] which the Risen Saviour would never require. But however difficult the circumstances may have been, in which the Magdalene came to profess her faith in Jesus, those of *Joanna* must have been even more trying. She was the wife of *Chuza*, Herod's Steward—possibly, though not likely, the Court-official whose son Jesus had healed by the word spoken in Cana.[e] Only one other of those who ministered to Jesus is mentioned by name. It is *Susanna*, the 'lily.' And they 'ministered to Him of their substance.'

It was on this return-journey to Capernaum, probably

a St. Matt. xxvii. 56

b ver. 61

c St. Luke xxiii. 55

d ver. 56

e St. John iv. 46-54

M

not far from the latter place, that the two blind men had
their sight restored.[a] It was then also that the
healing of the demonised dumb took place, which
is recorded in St. Matt. ix. 32–35, and alluded to in St.
Mark iii. 22–30. This narrative must, of course, not be
confounded with the somewhat similar event told in St.
Matt. xii. 22–32, and in St. Luke xi. 14–26. The latter
occurred at a much later period in our Lord's life, when,
as the whole context shows, the opposition of the Pharisaic
party had assumed much larger proportions, and the language of Jesus was more fully denunciatory of the character
and guilt of His enemies. That charge of the Pharisees,
therefore, that Jesus cast out the demons through the
Prince of the demons,[b] as well as His reply to it,
will best be considered when it shall appear in
its fullest development.

a St. Matt.
ix. 27-31

b St. Matt.
ix. 34

It was on this return-journey to Capernaum from the
uttermost borders of Galilee that the demonised dumb was
restored by the casting out of the demon. The circumstances show that a new stage in the Messianic course had
begun. It is characterised by fuller unfolding of Christ's
teaching and working, and *pari passu* by more fully developed. opposition of the Pharisaic party. For the two
went together, nor can they be distinguished as cause or
effect. That new stage, as repeatedly noted, had opened
on His return from the 'Unknown Feast' in Jerusalem,
whence He seems to have been followed by the Pharisaic
party. We have marked it so early as the call of the four
disciples by the Lake of Galilee. But it first actively
appeared at the healing of the paralytic in Capernaum,
when, for the first time, we noticed the presence and
murmuring of the Scribes, and, for the first time also, the
distinct declaration about the forgiveness of sins on the
part of Jesus. The same twofold element appeared in the
call of the publican Matthew, and the cavil of the Pharisees
at Christ's subsequent eating and drinking with 'sinners.'
It was in further development of this separation from the
old and now hostile element, that the twelve Apostles
were next appointed, and that distinctive teaching of Jesus

addressed to the people in the 'Sermon on the Mount,' which was alike a vindication and an appeal. On the journey through Galilee, which followed, the hostile party does not seem to have actually attended Jesus; but their growing and now outspoken opposition is heard in the discourse of Christ about John the Baptist after the dismissal of his disciples,[a] while its influence appears in the unspoken thoughts of Simon the Pharisee.

<small>ᵃ St. Matt. xi. 16-19</small>

It has already been suggested that the Pharisaic party, as such, did not attend Jesus on His Galilean journey. But we are emphatically told that tidings of the raising of the dead at Nain had gone forth into Judæa.[b] No doubt they reached the leaders at Jerusalem. There seems just sufficient time between this and the healing of the demonised dumb on the return-journey to Capernaum, to account for the presence there of those Pharisees,[c] who are expressly described by St. Mark[d] as 'the Scribes which came down from Jerusalem.'

<small>ᵇ St. Luke vii. 17</small>

<small>ᶜ St. Matt. ix. 34 ᵈ St. Mark iii. 22</small>

Whatever view the leaders at Jerusalem may have taken of the raising at Nain, it could no longer be denied that miracles were wrought by Jesus. At least, what to us seem miracles, yet not to them, since, as we have seen, 'miraculous' cures and the expelling of demons lay within the sphere of their 'extraordinary ordinary'—were not miracles in our sense, since they were, or professed to be, done by their 'own children.' The mere fact, therefore, of such cures would present no difficulty to them. To us a single well-ascertained miracle would form irrefragable evidence of the claims of Christ; to them it would not. They could believe in the 'miracles,' and yet not in the Christ. And here, again, we perceive that it was enmity to the Person and Teaching of Jesus which led to the denial of His claims. The inquiry: By what Power Jesus did these works? they met by the assertion that it was through that of Satan, or the Chief of the Demons. They regarded Jesus, as not only temporarily, but permanently, possessed by a demon, that is, as the constant vehicle of

Satanic influence. And this demon was, according to them, none other than Beelzebub, the Prince of the devils.[a]

a St. Mark iii. 22   Thus, in their view, it was really Satan who acted in and through Him; and Jesus, instead of being recognised as the Son of God, was regarded as an incarnation of Satan; instead of being owned as the Messiah, was denounced and treated as the representative of the Kingdom of Darkness. All this, because the Kingdom which He came to open and which He preached, was precisely the opposite of what they regarded as the Kingdom of God. Thus it was the essential contrariety of Rabbinism to the Gospel of the Christ that lay at the foundation of their conduct towards the Person of Christ.

To regard every fresh manifestation of Christ's Power as only a fuller development of the power of Satan, and to oppose it with increasing determination and hostility, even to the Cross: such was henceforth the natural progress of this history. On the other hand, such a course once fully settled upon, there would and could be no further reasoning with or against it on the part of Jesus. Henceforth His Discourses and attitude to such Judaism must be chiefly denunciatory, while still seeking—as, from the inward necessity of His Nature and the outward necessity of His Mission, He must—to save the elect remnant from this ' untoward generation,' and to lay broad and wide the foundations of the future Church.

The charge of Satanic agency was, indeed, not quite new. It had been suggested that John the Baptist had been under demoniacal influence, and this cunning pretext for resistance to his message had been eminently successful

b St. Matt. xi. 17, 18 ; St. Luke vii. 31-33   with the people.[b] The same charge, only in much fuller form, was now raised against Jesus. As 'the multitude marvelled, saying, it was never so seen in Israel,' the Pharisees, without denying the facts, had this explanation of them : that, both as regarded the casting out of the demon from the dumb man

c St. Matt. ix. 33, 34   and all similar works, Jesus wrought it ' through the Ruler of the Demons.' [c]

Their besetment of the Christ did not cease here. It is to it that we attribute the visit of 'the mother and brethren' of Jesus, which is recorded in the three Synoptic Gospels.[a] Pharisaic opposition had either filled those relatives of Jesus with fear for His safety, or made them sincerely concerned about His proceedings. Only if it meant some kind of interference with His Mission, whether prompted by fear or affection, would Jesus have so disowned their relationship.

a St. Matt.
xii. 46 &c.;
St. Mark
iii. 31 &c.;
St. Luke
viii. 19 &c.

But it meant more than this. Without going so far as to see pride or ostentation in this, that the Virgin-Mother summoned Jesus to her outside the house, since the opposite might as well have been her motive, we cannot but regard the words of Christ as the sternest prophetic rebuke of all Mariolatry, prayer for the Virgin's intercession, and, still more, of the strange doctrines about her freedom from actual and original sin, up to their prurient sequence in the dogma of the 'Immaculate Conception.'

On the other hand, we also remember the deep reverence among the Jews for parents, which found even exaggerated expression in the Talmud. And we feel that of all in Israel He, who was their King, could not have spoken or done what might even seem disrespectful to a mother. There must have been higher meaning in His words. That meaning would be better understood after His Resurrection.

CHAPTER XXXII.

THE PARABLES TO THE PEOPLE BY THE LAKE OF GALILEE, AND THOSE TO THE DISCIPLES IN CAPERNAUM.

(St. Matt. xiii. 1-52 ; St. Mark iv. 1-34 ; St. Luke viii. 4-18.)

WE are once more with Jesus and His disciples by the Lake of Galilee. It was a spring morning, and of such spring-time as only the East, and chiefly the Galilean Lake, knows. Almost suddenly the blood-red anemone, the gay tulip, the spotless narcissus, and the golden ranunculus clothe the fields, while all trees put forth their fragrant promise of fruit. As the imagery employed in the Sermon on the Mount confirmed the inference, otherwise derived, that it was spoken during the brief period after the winter rains, when the ' lilies ' decked the fresh grass, so the scene depicted in the Parables spoken by the Lake of Galilee indicates a more advanced season, when the fields gave first promise of a harvest to be gathered in due time. And as we know that the barley-harvest commenced with the Passover, we cannot be mistaken in supposing that the scene is laid a few weeks before that Feast.

Other evidence of this is not wanting. From the opening verses [a] we infer that Jesus had gone forth from ' the house ' with His disciples only, and that, as He sat by the seaside, the gathering multitude had obliged Him to enter a ship, whence He spake unto them many things in Parables.

[a] St. Matt. xiii. 1, 2

We mark an ascending scale in the three series of Parables, spoken respectively at three different periods in the History of Christ, and with reference to three different stages of Pharisaic opposition and popular feeling. The first series is that,[b] when Pharisaic opposition had just devised the explanation that His works were of demoniac agency, and when misled affection would have converted the ties of earthly relationship into bonds to hold the Christ.

[b] St.Matt. xiii.

The second series of Parables [c] is connected with the climax of Pharisaic opposition as presented in the charge, in its most fully developed form, that Jesus was, so to speak, the incarnation of Satan, the constant medium and vehicle of his activity.[d] This was the blasphemy against the Holy Ghost.

[c] St. Luke x.-xvi., xviii., passim

[d] St. Luke xi. 14-36 ; St. Matt. xii. 22-45 ; St. Mark iii 22 30

In the third series, consisting of eight Parables,[e] the Kingdom of God is presented in its final stage of ingathering, separation, reward and loss, as, indeed, we might expect in the teaching of the Lord immediately before His final rejec-

[e] St. Matt. xviii., xx., xxi., xxii., xxiv., xxv., St.Luke xix.

tion by Israel and betrayal into the hands of the Gentiles.

One thing, however, is common to all the Parables, and forms a point of connection between them. They are all occasioned by some unreceptiveness on the part of the hearers, and that, even when the hearers are professing disciples. This seems indicated in the reason assigned by Christ to the disciples for His use of parabolic teaching: that unto them it was 'given to know the mystery of the Kingdom of God, but unto them that ^{a St. Mark} are without, all these things are done in ^{iv. 11} parables.' [a]

Little information is to be gained from discussing the etymology of the word *Parable*. The word means the placing of one thing by the side of another. Perhaps no other mode of teaching was so common among the Jews as that by Parables. Only in their case they were almost entirely illustrations of what had been said or taught; while, in the case of Christ, they served as the foundation for His teaching. This distinction will be found to hold true, even in instances where there seems the closest parallelism between a Rabbinic and an Evangelic Parable. On further examination, the difference between them, as has been already remarked in regard to other forms of teaching, will appear not merely one of degree, but of kind, or rather of standpoint. This may be illustrated by the Parable of the woman who made anxious search for her lost ^{b St. Luke} coin,[b] to which there is an almost literal Jewish ^{xv. 8-10} parallel. But, whereas in the Jewish Parable the moral is that a man ought to take much greater pains in the study of the Law than in the search for coin, since the former procures an eternal reward, while the coin would, if found, at most only procure temporary enjoyment, the Parable of Christ is intended to set forth, not the merit of study or of works, but the compassion of the Saviour in seeking the lost, and the joy of Heaven in his recovery. It need scarcely be said that comparison between such Parables, as regards their spirit, is scarcely possible, except by way of contrast.

ᵃ St. Matt.
xiii.
ᵇ St. Matt.
xiii. 3, and
parallels
ᶜ St. Matt.
xiii. 34;
St. Mark iv.
33, 34
In the record of this first series,ᵃ the fact that Jesus spake to the people in Parables,ᵇ and only in Parables,ᶜ is strongly marked. It appears, therefore, to have been the first time that this mode of popular teaching was adopted by Him. Accordingly, the disciples not only expressed their astonishment, but inquired the reason of this novel method.ᵈ The answer. of the Lord specially

ᵈ St. Matt.
xiii. 10, and
parallels
marks this as the difference between the teaching vouchsafed to them and the Parables spoken to the people, that the designed effect of the latter was judicial : to complete that hardening which, in its commencement, had been caused by their voluntary rejection

ᵉ St. Matt.
xi. 13–17
of what they had heard.ᵉ To us, at least, it seems clear that the ground of the different effect of the Parables on the unbelieving multitude and on the believing disciples was not caused by the substance or form of these Parables, but by the different standpoint of the two classes of hearers towards the Kingdom of God.

We are now in some measure able to understand why Christ now for the first time adopted parabolic teaching. Its reason lay in the altered circumstances of the case. All His former teaching had been plain, although initial. In it He had set forth by word, and exhibited by fact (in miracles), that Kingdom of God which He had come to open to all believers. The hearers had now ranged themselves into two parties. Those who, whether temporarily or permanently (as the result would show), had admitted these premisses, so far as they understood them, were His professing disciples. On the other hand, the Pharisaic party had now devised a consistent theory, according to which the acts, and hence also the teaching, of Jesus were of Satanic origin. Christ must still preach the Kingdom; for that purpose had He come into the world. Only, the presentation of that Kingdom must now be for *decision*. It must separate the two classes, leading the one to clearer understanding of the mysteries of the Kingdom, while the other class of hearers would now regard these mysteries as wholly unintelligible, incredible, and to be rejected. And

the ground of this lay in the respective positions of these
two classes towards the Kingdom. 'Whosoever hath, to
him shall be given, and he shall have more abundance;
but whosoever hath not, from him shall be taken away
even that he hath.' And the mysterious manner in which
they were presented in Parables was alike suited to, and
corresponded with, the character of these 'mysteries of
the Kingdom,' now set forth, not for initial instruction,
but for final decision.

Thus much in general explanation. The record of the
first series of Parables [a] contains three separate
accounts: that of the Parables spoken to the
people; that of the reason for the use of parabolic teaching,
and the explanation of the first Parables (both addressed
to the disciples); and, finally, another series of Parables
spoken to the disciples. To each of these we must briefly
address ourselves.

On that bright spring morning, when Jesus spoke
from 'the ship' to the multitude that crowded the shore,
He addressed to them these *four Parables*: concerning
Him Who sowed, concerning the Wheat and the Tares,
concerning the Mustard-Seed, and concerning the Leaven.
The first, or perhaps the two first of these, must be supplemented by what may be designated as a *fifth Parable*, that
of the Seed growing unobservedly. This is the only Parable
of which St. Mark alone has preserved the record.[b]
All these Parables refer, as is expressly stated, to
the Kingdom of God; that is, not to any special phase or
characteristic of it, but to the Kingdom itself, or in other
words, to its history.

The first Parable is that of Him Who sowed. We
can almost picture to ourselves the Saviour seated in the
prow of the boat, as He points His hearers to the rich
plain over against Him, where the young corn, still in the
first green of its growing, is giving promise of harvest.
Like this is the Kingdom of Heaven which He has come
to proclaim. The Sower has gone forth to sow the Good
Seed. If we bear in mind a mode of sowing peculiar to
those times, the Parable gains in vividness. According to

Marginal notes:
[a] St. Matt. xiii.
[b] St. Mark iv. 26-29

Jewish authorities there was twofold sowing, as the seed
was either cast by the hand or by means of cattle. In the
latter case, a sack with holes was filled with corn, and
laid on the back of the animal, so that, as it moved onwards, the seed was thickly scattered. Thus it might well
be that it would fall indiscriminately on beaten roadway,
on stony places but thinly covered with soil, or where the
thorns had not been cleared away, or undergrowth from
the thorn-hedge crept into the field, as well as on good
ground. The result in each case need not here be
repeated. But what meaning would all this convey to
the Jewish hearers of Jesus? How could this sowing and
growing be like the Kingdom of God? Certainly not in
the sense in which they expected it. To them it was only
a rich harvest, when all Israel would bear plenteous fruit.
Again, what was the Seed, and who the Sower? or what
could be meant by the various kinds of soil and their
unproductiveness?

To us, as explained by the Lord, all this seems plain.
The initial condition requisite was to believe that Jesus
was the Divine Sower, and His Word the Seed of the
Kingdom. If this were admitted, they had at least the
right premisses for understanding ' this mystery of the
Kingdom.' According to Jewish view the Messiah was to
appear in outward pomp, and by display of power to establish the Kingdom. But this was the very idea of the
Kingdom, with which Satan had tempted Jesus at the outset of His Ministry. In opposition to it was this ' mystery
of the Kingdom,' according to which it consisted in,recep-
tion of the Seed of the Word. That reception would
depend on the nature of the soil, that is, on the mind and
heart of the hearers. The Kingdom of God was *within* ;
it came neither by a display of power, nor even by this,
that Israel, or else the Gospel-hearers, were the field on
which the Seed of the Kingdom was sown.

If even the disciples failed to comprehend the whole
bearing of this ' mystery of the Kingdom,' we can believe
how utterly strange and un-Jewish such a Parable of the
Messianic Kingdom must have sounded to them who had

been influenced by the Pharisaic representations of the
Person and Teaching of Christ.

This appears the fittest place for inserting the Parable
recorded by St. Mark alone,[a] concerning the Seed
growing unobservedly. If the first Parable, that
of the Sower and the Field of Sowing, would prove to
all who were outside the pale of discipleship a ' mystery,'
while to those within it would unfold knowledge of the
very mysteries of the Kingdom, this would even more fully
be the case in regard to this second or supplementary
Parable. In it we are only viewing that portion of the
field which the former Parable had described as good
soil. ' So is the Kingdom of God, as if a man had cast the
seed on the earth, and slept and rose, night and day, and
the seed sprang up and grew : how, he knows not himself.
Automatous [self-acting] the earth beareth fruit : first
blade, then ear, then full wheat in the ear ! But when
the fruit presents itself, immediately he sendeth forth the
sickle, because the harvest is come.' The meaning of all
this seems plain. We can only go about our daily work,
or lie down to rest, as day and night alternate ; we see,
but know not the *how* of the growth of the seed. Yet
assuredly it will ripen, and when that moment has arrived,
immediately the sickle is thrust in, for the harvest is come.
And so also with the Sower. His outward activity on
earth was in the sowing, and it will be in the harvesting.
What lies between them is of that other Dispensation of the
Spirit, till He again send forth His reapers into His field.
But all this must have been to those ' without ' a great
mystery, in no wise compatible with Jewish notions ; while
to them ' within ' it proved a very needful unfolding of the
mysteries of the Kingdom, with wide application of them.

The ' mystery ' is made still further mysterious, or else
it is still further unfolded, in the next Parable concerning
the Tares sown among the Wheat. According to the common view, these Tares represent what is botanically known
as the ' bearded darnel,' a poisonous rye-grass, very common in the East, ' entirely like wheat until the ear appears ; '
or else the ' creeping wheat ' or ' couch-grass ' (*Triticum*

[a] St. Mark iv. 26-29

repens), of which the roots creep underground and become intertwined with those of the wheat. But the Parable gains in meaning if we bear in mind that, according to ancient Jewish (and, indeed, modern Eastern) ideas, the Tares were not of different seed, but only a degenerate kind of wheat.

Once more we see the field on which the corn is growing—we know not how. The sowing time is past. 'The Kingdom of Heaven is become like to a man who sowed good seed in his field. But in the *time* that men sleep came his enemy and over-sowed tares in (upon) the midst of the wheat, and went away.' Thus far the picture is true to nature, since such deeds of enmity were, and still are, common in the East. And so matters would go on unobserved, since, whatever kind of 'tares' may be meant, it would, from their likeness, be for some time impossible to distinguish them from the wheat. 'But when the herbage grew and made fruit, then appeared (became manifest) also the tares.' What follows is equally true to fact, since most strenuous efforts are always made in the East to weed out the tares. But in the present instance separation would have been impossible, without at the same time uprooting some of the wheat. For the tares had been sown right into the midst, and not merely by the side of the wheat; and their roots and blades must have become intertwined. And so they must grow together to the harvest. Then such danger would no longer exist, for the period of growing was past, and the wheat had to be gathered into the barn. Then would be the right time to bid the reapers first gather the tares into bundles for burning, that afterwards the wheat, pure and unmixed, might be stored in the garner.

True to life as the picture is, yet the Parable was, of all others, perhaps the most un-Jewish, and therefore mysterious and unintelligible. Hence the disciples specially asked explanation of this only, which from its main subject they designated as the Parable 'of the Tares.'[a] [a] St. Matt. xiii. 36 Yet this was also perhaps the most important for them to understand. For already 'the Kingdom of Heaven is become like' this, although the appearance of fruit has not yet made it manifest that tares have been sown right into the midst of the wheat. But they would soon have to learn it, in bitter experience and temptation,[a] and not only as regarded the impressionable, fickle multitude, nor even the narrower circle of professing followers of Jesus, but that in their very midst there was a traitor. Most needful, yet most mysterious also, is this other lesson, as the experience of the Church has shown, since almost every period of her history has witnessed not only the recurrence of the proposal to make the wheat unmixed while growing, by gathering out the tares, but actual attempts towards it. All such have proved failures, because the field is the wide 'world,' not a narrow sect; because the tares have been sown into the midst of the wheat, and by the enemy; and because, if such gathering were to take place, the roots and blades of tares and wheat would be found so intertwined, that harm would come to the wheat. But what have we, who are only the owner's servants, to do with it, since we are not bidden of Him? The ' Æon-completion ' will witness the harvest, when the separation of tares and wheat may not only be accomplished with safety, but shall become necessary. For the wheat must be garnered in the heavenly storehouse, and the tares bound in bundles to be burned.

[a] St. John vi. 66-70

More mysterious still, and if possible even more needful, was the instruction that the Enemy who sowed the tares was the Devil. To the Jews, nay, to us all, it may seem a mystery that in ' the Messianic Kingdom of Heaven ' there should be a mixture of tares with the wheat, the more mysterious, that the Baptist had predicted that the coming Messiah would throughly purge His floor. But to those who were capable of receiving it, it would be explained by the fact that the Devil was 'the Enemy' of Christ and of His Kingdom, and that he had sowed those tares. This would, at the same time, be the most effective answer to the Pharisaic charge that Jesus was the incarnation of Satan, and the vehicle of his influence.

The concluding two Parables set forth another equally

mysterious characteristic of the Kingdom : that of its development and power, as contrasted with its small and weak beginnings. In the Parable of the Mustard-seed this is shown as regards the relation of the Kingdom to the outer world; in that of the Leaven in reference to the world within us. The one exhibits the *extensiveness,* the other the *intensiveness* of its power; in both cases at first hidden, almost imperceptible, and seemingly wholly inadequate to the final result.

A few remarks will set the special meaning of these Parables more clearly before us. Here also the illustrations used may have been at hand. The very idea of Parables implies, not strict scientific accuracy, but popular pictorialness. It is characteristic of them to present vivid sketches that appeal to the popular mind, and exhibit such analogies of higher truths as can be readily perceived by all. Thus, as regards the first of these two Parables, the seed of the mustard-plant passed in popular parlance as the smallest of seeds. In fact, the expression, 'small as a mustard-seed,' had become proverbial, and was used, not only by our Lord,[a] but frequently by the Rabbis, to indicate the smallest amount, such as the least drop of blood, the least defilement, or the smallest remnant of sun-glow in the sky. ' But when it is grown, it is greater than the garden-herbs.' Indeed, it looks no longer like a large garden-herb or shrub, but ' becomes,' or rather appears like ' a tree '—as St. Luke puts it, ' a great tree [b]'— of course, not in comparison with other trees, but with garden-shrubs. Such growth of the mustard-seed was also a fact well known at the time, and indeed still observed in the East.

This is the first and main point in the Parable. The other concerning the birds which are attracted to its branches and ' lodge '—literally, ' make tents '— there, or else under the shadow of it,[c] is subsidiary. Pictorial, of course, this trait would be, and we can the more readily understand that birds would be attracted to the branches or the shadow of the mustard-plant, when we know that mustard was in Palestine mixed with or used as

a St. Matt. xvii. 20

b St. Luke xiii. 18, 19

c St. Mark iv. 32

food for pigeons, and presumably would be sought by other birds. And the general meaning would the more easily be apprehended, that a tree, whose wide-spreading branches afforded lodgment to the birds of heaven, was a familiar Old Testament figure for a mighty kingdom that gave shelter to the nations.[a] Indeed, it is specifically used as an illustration of the Messianic Kingdom.[b] Thus the Parable would point to this, so full of mystery to the Jews, so explanatory of the mystery to the disciples : that the Kingdom of Heaven, planted in the field of the world as the smallest seed, in the most humble and unpromising manner, would grow till it far outstripped all other similar plants, and gave shelter to all nations under heaven.

a Ezek. xxxi. 6, 12; Dan. iv. 12, 14, 21, 22

b Ezek. xvii. 23

To this *extensive* power of the Kingdom corresponded its *intensive* character, whether in the world at large or in the individual. This formed the subject of the last of the Parables addressed at this time to the people—that of the Leaven. We need not here resort to ingenious methods of explaining ' the three measures,' or *Seahs*, of meal in which the leaven was hid. Three Seahs were an Ephah, of which the exact capacity differed in various districts. To mix ' three measures ' of meal was common in Biblical, as well as in later times.[c] Nothing further was therefore conveyed than the common process of ordinary, everyday life. And in this, indeed, lies the very point of the Parable : that the Kingdom of God when received within would seem like leaven hid, but would gradually pervade, assimilate, and transform the whole of our common life.

c Comp. Gen. xviii. 6 ; Judg. vi. 19 ; 1 Sam. i. 24

With this most un-Jewish characterisation of the Kingdom of Heaven, the Saviour dismissed the people. Enough had been said to them and for them, if they had but ears to hear. And now He was again alone with the disciples ' in the house ' at Capernaum, to which they had returned.[d] Many new and deeper thoughts of the Kingdom had come to them. But why had He so spoken to the multitude, in a manner so different, as regarded not only the form, but

d St. Matt. xiii. 36 ; comp. ver. 10, and St. Mark iv. 10

even the substance of His teaching? And did they quite understand its solemn meaning themselves? More especially, who was the enemy whose activity would threaten the safety of the harvest? Of that harvest they had ᵃ St. John already heard on the way through Samaria.ᵃ iv. 35   And what were those 'tares,' which were to continue in their very midst till the judicial separation of the end? To these questions Jesus now made answer. His statement of the reason for adopting in the present instance the parabolic mode of teaching would, at the same time, give them farther insight into those very mysteries of the Kingdom which it had been the object of these Parables to set forth. His unsolicited explanation of the details of the first Parable would call attention to points that might readily have escaped their notice, but which, for warning and instruction, it most behoved them to keep in view.

Kindred, or rather closely connected, as are the two Parables of the Treasure hid in the Field and of the Pearl of Great Price—now spoken to the disciples—their differences are sufficiently marked. In the first, one who must probably be regarded as intending to buy a, if not this, field, discovers a treasure hidden there, and in his joy parts with all else to become owner of the field and of the hidden treasure which he had so unexpectedly found. Some difficulty has been expressed in regard to the morality of such a transaction. In reply it may be observed that it was, at least, in entire accordance with Jewish law. If a man had found a treasure in loose coins among the corn, it would certainly be his, if he bought the corn. If he had found it on the ground, or in the soil, it would equally certainly belong to him, if he could claim ownership of the soil, and even if the field were not his own, unless others could prove their right to it. The law went so far as to adjudge to the purchaser of fruits anything found among these fruits.

In the second Parable we have a wise merchantman who travels in search of pearls, and when he finds one which in value exceeds all else, he returns and sells all that he has, in order to buy this unique gem. The supreme value of the Kingdom, the consequent desire to appropriate it, and the necessity of parting with all else for this purpose, are the points common to this and the previous Parable. But in the one case, it is marked that this treasure is hid from common view in the field, and the finder makes unexpected discovery of it, which fills him with joy. In the other case, the merchantman is, indeed, in search of pearls, but he has the wisdom to discover the transcendent value of this one gem, and the yet greater wisdom to give up all further search and to acquire it at the surrender of everything else. Thus, two different aspects of the Kingdom, and two different conditions on the part of those who, for its sake, equally part with all, are here set before the disciples.

Nor was the closing Parable of the Draw-net less needful. Assuredly it became, and would more and more become, them to know that mere discipleship—mere inclusion in the Gospel-net—was not sufficient. That net let down into the sea of this world would include much which, when the net was at last drawn to shore, would prove worthless or even hurtful. To be a disciple, then, was not enough. Even here there would be separation. Not only the tares, which the Enemy had designedly sown into the midst of the wheat, but even much that the Gospel-net cast into the sea had inclosed, would when brought to land prove fit only to be cast away, into 'the oven of the fire where there is the wailing and the gnashing of teeth.'[1]

CHAPTER XXXIII.

THE STORM ON THE LAKE OF GALILEE.

(St. Matt. viii. 18, 23–27; St. Mark iv. 35–41; St. Luke viii. 22–25.)

IT was the evening, and once more great multitudes were gathering to Him. What more could He have said to those to whom He had all that morning spoken in Parables, which hearing they had not heard or understood? In

---

[1] The well-known oven of the well-known fire—Gehenna.

N

truth, after that day's teaching it was better, alike for these multitudes and for His disciples, that He should withdraw. And so 'they took Him even as He was'—that is, probably without refreshment of food, or even preparation of it for the journey. This indicates how readily, nay, eagerly, the disciples obeyed the behest.

Whether in their haste they heeded not the signs of the coming storm; whether they had the secret feeling that ship and sea which bore such burden were safe from tempest; or whether it was one of those storms which so often rise suddenly, and sweep with such fury over the Lake of Galilee, must remain undetermined. He was in 'the ship,' the well-known boat which was always ready for His service, whether as pulpit, resting-place, or means of journeying. But the departure had not been so rapid as to pass unobserved; and the ship was attended by other boats, which bore those who would fain follow Him. In the stern of the ship, on the low bench where the steersman sometimes takes rest, lay Jesus. Weariness, faintness, hunger, exhaustion, asserted their mastery over His true humanity. He, Whom earliest Apostolic testimony [a] pro-
[a] Phil. ii. 6 claimed to have been in 'the form of God,' slept.

Meanwhile the heavens darken, the wild wind swoops down those mountain-gorges, howling over the trembling sea. The danger is increasing—'so that the ship was
[b] St. Mark now filling.' [b] They who watched it might be
iv. 37 tempted to regard the peaceful rest of Jesus as weakness in not being able, even at such a time, to overcome the demands of our lower nature; real indifference, also, to their fate—not from want of sympathy, but of power. In short, it might lead up to the inference that the Christ was a no-Christ, and the Kingdom of which He had spoken in Parables, not His, in the sense of being identified with His Person.

It has been asked, with which of the words recorded by the Synoptists the disciples had wakened the Lord: with
[c] St. Matt. those of entreaty to save them,[c] or with those of
and impatience, perhaps uttered by Peter himself? [d]
St. Luke
[d] St. Mark Similarly, it has been asked, which came first—

the Lord's rebuke of the disciples, and after it that of
the wind and sea,[a] or the converse?[b] But,
may it not be that each recorded that first which
had most impressed itself on his mind—St.
Matthew, who had been in the ship that night, the needful
rebuke to the disciples; St. Mark and St. Luke,
who had heard it from others,[c] the help first, and
then the rebuke?

a St. Matt.
b St. Mark and St. Luke
c St. Mark, probably from St. Peter

Yet it is not easy to understand what the disciples had
really expected, when they wakened the Christ with their
'Lord, save us—we perish!' Certainly not that which
actually happened, since not only wonder but fear came
over them as they witnessed it. Probably theirs would be
a vague, undefined belief in the unlimited possibility of
all in connection with the Christ.

When 'He was awakened'[d] by the voice of
His disciples, 'He rebuked the wind and the sea,'
as Jehovah had of old[e]—just as He had 'rebuked' the fever,[f] and the paroxysm of the demonised.[g] And the sea He commanded as if it
were a sentient being: 'Be silent! Be silenced!'
And immediately the wind was bound, the waves throbbed
into stillness, and a great calm fell upon the Lake. For,
when Christ sleepeth, there is storm; when He waketh,
peace. But over these men who had wakened Him with
their cry, now crept wonderment, awe, and fear. No
longer, as at His first wonder-working in Capernaum, was
it: '*What* is this?'[h] but, '*Who*, then, is this?'
And so the grand question, which the enmity of
the Pharisees had raised, and which, in part, had been
answered in the Parables of teaching, was still more fully
and practically met in what, not only to the disciples, but
to all time, was a Parable of help. And Jesus also
wondered: how was it that they had no faith?

d St. Mark iv. 38
e Ps. cvi. 9; Nah. i. 4
f St. Luke iv. 39
g St. Mark ix. 25

h St. Mark i. 27

CHAPTER XXXV

AT GERASA—THE HEALING OF THE DEMONISED.

(St. Matt viii. 28–34 ; St. Mark v. 1–20 ; St. Luke viii. 26–39.)

MOST writers have suggested that the healing of the demonised on the other side took place at early dawn of the day following the storm on the Lake. But the distance is so short that, even making allowance for the delay by the tempest, the passage could scarcely have occupied the whole night. All the circumstances lead us to regard the healing at Gerasa as a night-scene, following immediately on Christ's arrival from Capernaum, and after the calming of the storm at sea.

We can with confidence describe the exact place where our Lord and His disciples touched the other shore. The ruins right over against the plain of Gennesaret, which still bear the name of *Kersa* or *Gersa*, must represent the ancient Gerasa. The locality entirely meets the requirements of the narrative. About a quarter of an hour to the south of Gersa is a steep bluff, which descends abruptly on a narrow ledge of shore. A terrified herd running down this cliff could not have recovered its foothold, and must inevitably have been hurled into the Lake beneath. Again, the whole country around is burrowed with limestone caverns and rock-chambers for the dead, such as those which were the dwelling of the demonised.

From these tombs the demonised, who is specially singled out by St. Mark and St. Luke, as well as his less prominent companion,[a] came forth to meet Jesus. According to common Jewish superstition, the evil spirits dwelt especially in lonely desolate places, and also among tombs.[1] We must here remember what has previously been explained as to the confusion in the consciousness of the demonised between their own notions

[a] St. Matt. viii. 28

---

[1] See 'Life and Times,' App. XIII., ' Angelology and Demonology ; ' and App. XVI., ' Jewish Views about Demons and the Demonised.'

and the ideas imposed on them by the demons. It is quite in accordance with the Jewish notions of the demonised that, according to the more circumstantial account of St. Luke, he should feel as it were driven into the deserts, and that he was in the tombs, while, according to St. Mark, he was 'night and day in the tombs and in the mountains,' the very order of the words indicating the notion (as in Jewish belief) that it was chiefly at night that evil spirits were wont to haunt burying-places.

In calling attention to this and similar particulars, we repeat that this must be kept in view as characteristic of the demonised, that they were incapable of separating their own consciousness and ideas from the influence of the demon, their own identity being merged, and to that extent lost, in that of their tormentors. In this respect the demonised state was also kindred to madness.

The language and conduct of the demonised, whether seemingly his own, or that of the demons who influenced him, must always be regarded as a mixture of the Jewish-human and the demoniacal. The demonised speaks and acts as a Jew under the control of a demon. Thus, if he chooses solitary places by day, and tombs by night, it is not that demons really preferred such habitations, but that the Jews imagined it, and that the demons, acting on the existing consciousness, would lead him, in accordance with his preconceived notions, to select such places. Here also mental disease offers points of analogy. The fact that in the demonised state a man's identity was not superseded but controlled, enables us to account for many phenomena without either confounding demonism with mania, or else imputing to our Lord such accommodation to the notions of the times, as is not only untenable in itself, but forbidden even by the language of the present narrative.

The description of the demonised, coming out of the tombs to meet Jesus as He touched the shore at Gerasa, is vivid in the extreme. His violence, the impossibility of control by others,[a] the absence of self-control,[b] his homicidal,[c] and almost suicidal,[d] frenzy, are all depicted. Christ, Who had been charged by the Pharisees with being the embodiment and messenger of Satan, is here face to face with the extreme manifestation of demoniac power and influence. It is once more, then, a Miracle in Parable which is about to take place. The question, which had been raised by the enemies, is about to be brought to the issue of a practical demonstration.

With irresistible power the demonised was drawn to Jesus, as He touched the shore at Gerasa. As always, the first effect of the contact was a fresh paroxysm, but in this peculiar case not physical, but moral. As always, also, the demons knew Jesus, and His Presence seemed to constrain their confession of themselves—and therefore of Him.

The strange mixture of the demoniac with the human, or rather, this expression of underlying demoniac thought in the forms and modes of thinking of the Jewish victim, explains the expressed fear of present actual torment, or, as St. Matthew, who, from the briefness of his account, does not seem to have been an eye-witness, expresses it: 'Thou art come to torment us before the time;' and possibly also for the 'adjuration by God.' For, as immediately on the homage and protestation of the demonised: 'What between me and Thee, Jesus, Thou Son of the Most High God?' Christ had commanded the unclean spirit to come out of the man, it may have been that in so doing He had used the Name of the Most High God; or else the 'adjuration' itself may have been the form in which the Jewish speaker clothed the consciousness of the demons, with which his own was identified.

It may be conjectured that it was partly in order to break this identification, or rather to show the demonised that it was not real, and only the consequence of the control which the demons had over him, that the Lord asked his name. To this the man made answer, still in the dual consciousness, 'My name is Legion: for we are many.'

Such might be the subjective motive for Christ's question. Its objective reason may have been to show the power of the demoniac possession in the present instance, thus marking it as an altogether extreme case. It was a common Jewish idea that, under certain circumstances, 'a legion of hurtful spirits' (of course not in the sense of a Roman legion) 'were on the watch for men, saying: When shall he fall into the hands of one of these things, and be taken?'

This identification of the demons with the demonised, in consequence of which he thought with their consciousness, and they spoke not only through him but in his forms of thinking, may also account for the last and most difficult part of this narrative. Their main object and wish was not to be banished from the country and people, or, as St. Luke puts it—again to 'depart into the abyss.' Let us now try to realise the scene. On the very narrow strip of shore, between the steep cliff that rises in the background and the Lake, stands Jesus with His disciples and the demonised. The wish of the demons is not to be sent out of the country—not back into the abyss. Up on that cliff a great herd of swine is feeding; up that cliff, therefore, is 'into the swine;' and this also agrees with Jewish thoughts concerning uncleanness. The rendering of our Authorised Version,[a] that, in reply to the demoniac entreaty, 'forthwith Jesus gave them leave,' has led to misunderstanding. The verb, which is the same in all the three Gospels, would be better rendered by 'suffered' than by 'gave them leave.' With the latter we associate positive permission. None such was either asked or given. The Lord suffered it—that is, He did not actually hinder it. He only 'said unto them, Go!'

a St. Mark v. 13

What followed belongs to the phenomena of supersensuous influences upon animals, of which many instances are recorded, but the *rationale* of which it is impossible to explain. This, however, we can understand: that under such circumstances a panic would seize the herd, that it would madly rush down the steep, on which it could not arrest itself, and so perish in the sea.

The weird scene was past. And now silence has fallen on them. From above, the keepers of the herd had seen it all—alike what had passed with the demonised, and then the issue in the destruction of the herd. From the first, as they saw the demonised, for fear of whom 'no man might pass that way,' running to Jesus, they must have watched with eager interest. In the clear Eastern air not a word that was spoken could have been lost. And now in wild terror they fled, into Gerasa—into the country round about—to tell what had happened.

It is morning, and a new morning-sacrifice and morning-Psalm are about to be offered. He that had been the possession of foul and evil spirits—a very legion of them—and deprived of his human individuality, is now 'sitting at the feet of Jesus,' learning of Him, ' clothed and in his right mind.' He has been brought to God, restored to self, to reason, and to human society—and all this by Jesus, at Whose Feet he is gratefully, humbly sitting, ' a disciple.'

But now from town and country have they come, who had been startled by the tidings which those who fed the swine had brought. It is not necessary to suppose that their request that Jesus would depart out of their coasts was prompted only by the loss of the herd of swine. There could be no doubt in their minds that One possessing supreme and unlimited power was in their midst. Among men superstitious, and unwilling to submit absolutely to the Kingdom which Christ brought, there could only be one effect of what they had heard, and now witnessed in the person of the healed demonised—awe and fear! And in such place and circumstances Jesus could not have continued. As He entered the ship, the healed demonised humbly, earnestly entreated that he might go with his Saviour. It would have seemed to him as if there were calm, safety, and happiness only in His Presence; not far from Him—not among those wild mountains and yet wilder men. So too often do we reason and speak, as regards ourselves or those we love. Not so He Who appoints alike our discipline and our work. To go back,

now healed, to his own, and to publish there, in the city—
nay, through the whole of the large district of the ten con-
federate cities, the Decapolis—how great things Jesus had
done for him, such was henceforth to be his life-work.   In
this there would be both safety and happiness.

'And all men did marvel.'   And presently Jesus Himself came back into that Decapolis, where the healed
demonised had prepared the way for Him.

CHAPTER XXXV.

THE HEALING OF THE WOMAN—THE RAISING OF JAIRUS' DAUGHTER.

(St. Matt. ix. 18–26; St. Mark v. 21–43; St. Luke viii. 40–56.)

ON the shore at Capernaum many were gathered on the
morning after the storm eagerly looking out for the well-
known boat that bore the Master and His disciples.   And,
as He again stepped on the shore, He was soon 'thronged,'
inconveniently pressed upon, by the crowd, eager, curious,
expectant.   The tidings rapidly spread, and reached two
homes where His help was needed; where, indeed, it alone
could now be of possible avail.   The two most nearly concerned must have gone to seek that help about the same
time, and prompted by the same feelings of expectancy.
Both Jairus, the Ruler of the Synagogue, and the woman
suffering these many years from disease, had faith.   But
the weakness of the one arose from excess, and threatened
to merge into superstition, while the weakness of the other
was due to defect, and threatened to end in despair.   In
both cases faith had to be called out, tried, purified, and
so perfected.

Jairus, one of the Synagogue-rulers of Capernaum,
had an only daughter, who at the time of this narrative
had just passed childhood, and reached the period when
Jewish Law declared a woman of age.   Although St.
Matthew, contracting the whole narrative into briefest
summary, speaks of her as dead at the time of Jairus'

application to Jesus, the other two Evangelists, giving fuller details, describe her as on the point of death, literally, ' at the last breath.'

That, in view of his child's imminent death, and with the knowledge he had of the ' mighty deeds ' commonly reported of Jesus, Jairus should have applied to Him, can the less surprise us when we remember how often Jesus must, with consent and by invitation of this Ruler, have spoken in the Synagogue, and what impression His words must have made. There was nothing in what Jairus said which a Jew in those days might not have spoken to a Rabbi, who was regarded as Jesus must have been by all in Capernaum who believed not the charge, which the Judæan Pharisees had just raised. Though we cannot point to any instance where the laying on of a great Rabbi's hands was sought for healing, such combined with prayer would certainly be in entire accordance with Jewish views at the time. The confidence in the result, expressed by the father in the accounts of St. Mark and St. Matthew, is not mentioned by St. Luke. And, perhaps, as being the language of an Eastern, it should not be taken in its strict literality as indicating actual conviction on the part of Jairus, that the laying on of Christ's Hands would certainly restore the maiden.

Be this as it may, when Jesus followed the Ruler to his house, the multitude ' thronging Him ' in eager curiosity, another approached Him whose inner history was far different from that of Jairus. The disease from which this woman had suffered for twelve years would render her Levitically ' unclean.' It must have been not unfrequent in Palestine, and proved as intractable as modern science has found it, to judge by the number and variety of remedies prescribed, and by their character. But what possesses real interest is that, in all cases where astringents or tonics are prescribed, it is ordered that, while the woman takes the remedy, she is to be addressed in the words : ' Arise from thy flux.' It is not only that psychical means are apparently to accompany the therapeutical in this disease, but the coincidence in the command, 'Arise,' with the words used by Christ in raising Jairus' daughter is striking. But here also we mark only contrast to the magical cures of the Rabbis. For Jesus neither used remedies, nor spoke the word 'Arise' to her who had come 'in the press behind' to touch for her healing 'the fringe of His outer garment.'

We can form an approximate idea of the outward appearance of Jesus amidst the throng at Capernaum. He would, we may safely assume, go about in the ordinary although not in the more ostentatious, dress, worn by the Jewish teachers of Galilee. His head-gear would probably be a kind of turban, or perhaps a covering for the head which descended over the back of the neck and shoulders, somewhat like the Indian pugaree. His feet were probably shod with sandals. His inner garment must have been close-fitting, and descended to His feet, since it was not only so worn by teachers, but was regarded as absolutely necessary for anyone who would publicly read or 'Targum' the Scriptures, or exercise any function in the Synagogue. As we know, it was without seam, ^{a St. John xix. 23} woven from the top throughout,[a] and this closely accords with the texture of these garments. Round the middle it would be fastened with a girdle. Over this inner He would most probably wear the square outer garment, or *Tallith*, with the customary fringes of four long white threads with one of hyacinth knotted together at each of the four corners. There is reason to believe that three square garments were made with these 'fringes,' although by way of ostentation, the Pharisees made them particularly wide so as to attract attention, ^{b St. Matt. xxiii. 5} just as they made their phylacteries broad.[b] Although Christ only denounced the latter practice, not the phylacteries themselves, it is impossible to believe that Himself ever wore them, either on the forehead or the arm. There was certainly no warrant for them in Holy Scripture, and only Pharisaic externalism could represent their use as fulfilling the import of Exod. xiii. 9, 16; Deut. vi. 8; xi. 18. The admission that neither the officiating priests, nor the representatives of the people, wore them in the Temple, seems to imply that this practice was not quite universal.

One further remark may be allowed before dismissing this subject. Our inquiries enable us in this matter also to confirm the accuracy of the Fourth Gospel. We read [a]
that the quaternion of soldiers who crucified
Christ made division of the riches of His poverty, taking each one part of His dress, while for the fifth, which, if divided, would have had to be rent in pieces, they cast lots. This incidental remark carries evidence of the Judæan authorship of the Gospel in the accurate knowledge which it displays. The four pieces of dress to be divided would be the head-gear, the more expensive sandals or shoes, the long girdle, and the coarse *Tallith*— all about equal in value. And the fifth undivided and comparatively most expensive garment, 'without seam, woven from the top throughout,' probably of wool, as befitted the season of the year, was the inner garment.

[a] St. John
xix. 23

We do not wonder that this Jewish woman, 'having heard the things concerning Jesus,' with her imperfect knowledge, in the weakness of her strong faith, thought that, if she might but touch His garment, she would be made whole.

We can picture her to our minds as, mingling with those who thronged and pressed upon the Lord, she put forth her hand and 'touched the border of His garment,' most probably the long fringes of one of the corners of the outer garment. We can understand how, with a disease which not only rendered her Levitically defiling, but where womanly shamefacedness would make public speech so difficult, she, thinking of Him Whose Word spoken at a distance had brought healing, might thus seek to have her heart's desire. Yet in the very strength of her faith lay also its weakness. She believed so much in Him, that she felt as if it needed not personal appeal to Him ; she felt so deeply the hindrances to her making request of Himself, that, believing so strongly in Him, she deemed it sufficient to touch, not even Himself, but that which in itself had no power nor value, except as it was in contact with His Divine Person.

Very significantly, the Lord disappointed not her faith, but corrected the error of its direction and manifestation. No sooner had she so touched the border of His garment than 'she knew in the body that she was healed of the scourge.' No sooner, also, had she so touched the border of His garment than He knew, 'perceived in Himself,' what had taken place: the forthgoing of the Power that is from out of Him.

And this was neither unconscious nor unwilled on His part. It was caused by her faith, not by her touch. 'Thy faith hath made thee whole.' And the question of Jesus could not have been misleading, when 'straightway' He 'turned Him about in the crowd and said, 'Who touched My garments?' That He knew who had done it, and only wished, through self-confession, to bring her to clearness in the exercise of her faith, appears from what is immediately added: 'And He looked round about,' not to see who had done it, but 'to see her that had done this thing.' And as His look was at last fixed on her alone in all that crowd, which, as Peter rightly said, was thronging and pressing Him, 'the woman saw that she was not hid,'[a] and came forward to make full confession. Thus, while in His mercy He had borne with her weakness, and in His faithfulness not disappointed her faith, its twofold error was also corrected. She learned that it was not from the garment, but from the Saviour, that the power proceeded; she learned also that it was not the touch of it, but the faith in Him, that made whole— and such faith must ever be of personal dealing with Him. And so He spoke to her the Word of twofold help and assurance: 'Thy faith hath made thee whole—go forth into peace, and be healed of thy scourge.'

a St. Luke viii. 47

Brief as is the record of this occurrence, it must have caused considerable delay in the progress of our Lord to the house of Jairus. For in the interval the maiden, who had been at the last gasp when her father went to entreat the help of Jesus, had not only died, but the house of mourning was already filled with relatives, hired mourners, wailing women, and musicians, in preparation for the funeral. The intentional delay of Jesus when summoned ᵃ St. John to Lazarus ᵃ leads us to ask whether similar xi. 6 purpose may not have influenced His conduct in the present instance. But even were it otherwise, no outcome of God's Providence is of chance, but each is designed. The circumstances, which in their concurrence make up an event, may all be of natural occurrence, but their conjunction is of Divine ordering and to a higher purpose, and this constitutes Divine Providence. It was in the interval of this delay that the messengers came, who informed Jairus of the actual death of his child. Jesus overhead it, as they whispered to the Ruler not to trouble the Rabbi any further, but He heeded it not, save so far as it affected the father. The emphatic admonition, not to fear, only to believe, gives us an insight into the threatening failure of the Ruler's faith ; perhaps, also, into the motive which prompted the delay of Christ. The utmost need, which would henceforth require the utmost faith on the part of Jairus, had now come. But into that which was to pass within the house no stranger must intrude. Even of the Apostles only those, who now for the first time became, and henceforth continued, the innermost circle, might witness what was about to take place.

Within, ' the tumult ' and weeping, the wail of the mourners, real or hired, and the melancholy sound of the mourning flutes—sad preparation for, and pageantry of, an Eastern funeral —broke discordantly on the calm of assured victory over death, with which Jesus had entered the house of mourning. But even so He would tell them that the damsel was not dead, but only sleeping. The Rabbis also frequently have the expression ' to sleep ' (when the sleep is overpowering and oppressive), instead of ' to die.' It may well have been that Jesus made use of this word of double meaning in some such manner as this : ' the maiden sleepeth.' And they understood Him well in their own way, yet understood Him not at all.

For did they not verily know that she had actually

died, even before the messengers had been despatched to prevent the needless trouble of His coming? Yet even this their scorn served a higher purpose. For it showed these two things : that to the certain belief of those in the house the maiden was really dead, and that the Gospel-writers regarded the raising of the dead as not only beyond the ordinary range of Messianic activity, but as something miraculous even among the miracles of Christ.

The first thing to be done by Christ was to ' put out ' the mourners, whose proper place this house no longer was, and who by their conduct had proved themselves unfit to be witnesses of Christ's great manifestation. The impression which the narrative leaves on the mind is that all this while the father of the maiden was stupefied, passive rather than active in the matter. The great fear, which had come upon him when the messengers apprised him of his only child's death, seemed still to numb his faith.

Christ now led the father and the mother into the chamber where the dead maiden lay, followed by the three Apostles, witnesses of His chiefest working and of His utmost earthly glory, but also of His inmost sufferings. Without doubt or hesitation He took her by the hand, and spoke only these two words : *Talyetha Qum [Kum]* Maiden, arise! ' And straightway the damsel arose.' But the great astonishment which came upon them, as well as the ' strait charge ' that no man should know it, are further evidence, if such were required, how little their faith had been prepared for that which in its weakness was granted to it. And thus Jesus, as He had formerly corrected in the woman that weakness of faith which came through very excess, so now in the Ruler of the Synagogue the weakness which was by failure.

CHAPTER XXXVI.

SECOND VISIT TO NAZARETH—THE MISSION OF THE TWELVE.

(St. Matt. xiii. 54–58; x. 1, 5–42; xi. 1; St. Mark vi. 1–13;
St. Luke ix.1–6.)

How Jesus conveyed Himself away from Capernaum, whether through another entrance into the house, or by 'the road of the roofs,' we are not told.   But assuredly He must have avoided the multitude.   Presently we find Him far from Capernaum.   Probably He had left it immediately on quitting the house of Jairus.

It almost seems as if the departure of Jesus from the town marked a crisis in its history.   From henceforth it ceases to be the centre of His activity, and is only occasionally, and in passing, visited.   Indeed, the concentration and growing power of Pharisaic opposition, and the proximity of Herod's residence at Tiberias, would have rendered a permanent stay there impossible at this stage in our Lord's history.   Henceforth, He has no certain dwelling-place: in His own language, ' He hath not where to lay His Head.'

a St. Mark vi. 1   The notice in St. Mark's Gospel,[a] that His disciples followed Him, seems to connect the arrival of Jesus in ' His own country ' (at Nazareth) with the departure from the house of Jairus, into which He had allowed only three of His Apostles to accompany Him. The circumstances of the present visit, as well as the tone of His countrymen at this time, are entirely different from what is recorded of His former sojourn at Nazareth.[b]

b St. Luke iv. 16–31   Nazareth would have ceased to be Nazareth, had its people felt or spoken otherwise than they had before.   That His fame had so grown in the interval would only stimulate the conceit of the village-town.

And now He had come back to them, after nine or ten months, in totally different circumstances.   No one could any longer question His claims, whether for good or for evil. As on the Sabbath He stood up once more in that Synagogue to teach, they were astonished. But their astonishment was that of unbelief. Whence had 'this One' 'these things,' 'and what the wisdom which' was ᵃ St. Mark 'given to this One—and these mighty works vi. 2 done by His Hands?'ᵃ

'And He marvelled because of their unbelief.' In view of their own reasoning it was most unreasonable.

But it would have been impossible for Christ to have finally given up His own town of Nazareth without one further appeal and one further opportunity for repentance. As He had begun, so He closed this part of His Galilean Ministry, by preaching in His own Synagogue of Nazareth. Save in the case of a few who were receptive, on whom He laid His Hands for healing, His visit passed away without such 'mighty works' as the Nazarenes had heard of. He will not return again to Nazareth. Henceforth He will make commencement of sending forth His disciples. For His Heart compassionated the many who were ignorant and out of the way.

Viewing the discourse with which Christ now sent out ᵇ St. Matt. x. the Twelve in its fullest form,ᵇ it is to be noted 5 to the end that it consists of *five* parts: vv. 5 to 15; vv. 16 to 23; vv. 24 to 33; vv. 34 to 39; vv. 40 to the end.

ᶜ St. Matt. Its first partᶜ applies entirely to this first x. 5-15 Mission of the Twelve, although the closing words point forward to 'the judgment.'ᵈ Accordingly it has its ᵈ ver. 15 parallels, although in briefer form, in the other ᵉ St. Mark two Gospels.ᵉ vi. 7-11 ; St. Luke 1. The Twelve were to go forth two and two,ᶠ ix. 1-5 ᶠ St. Mark furnished with authority—or, as St. Luke more vi. 7 fully expresses it, with 'power and authority'— alike over all demons and to heal all manner of diseases. The special commission, for which they received such power, was to proclaim the near advent of the Kingdom, and, in manifestation as well as in evidence of it, to heal the sick, cleanse the lepers, and cast out demons. They were to speak good and to do good in the highest sense, and that in a manner which all would feel to be good: freely,

o

even as they had received it. Again, they were not to make any special provision for their journey, beyond the absolute immediate present. They were but labourers, yet as such they had claim to support. Their Employer would provide, and the field in which they worked might well be expected to supply it.[a]

a Comp. for this latter aspect 1 Tim. v. 18

Before entering into a city, they were to make inquiry, literally to ' search out,' who in it was ' worthy,' and of them to ask hospitality ; not seeking during their stay a change for the gratification of vanity or for self-indulgence. If the report on which they had made choice of a host proved true, then the ' Peace with thee ! with which they had entered their temporary home, would become a reality. Christ would make it such.

But even if the house should prove unworthy, the Lord would none the less own the words of His messengers and make them real ; only, in such case the ' Peace with thee !' would return to them who had spoken it. Yet another case was possible. The house to which their inquiries had led them, or the city into which they had entered, might refuse to receive them, because they came as Christ's ambassadors. Greater, indeed, would be their guilt than that of the Cities of the Plain, since these had not known the character of the heavenly guests to whom they refused reception ; and more terrible would be their future punishment. So Christ would vindicate their authority as well as His own, and show the reality of their commission : on the one hand, by making their word of peace a reality to those who had proved ' worthy ; ' and, on the other, by punishment if their message were refused. Lastly, in their present Mission they were not to touch either Gentile or Samaritan territory. This direction—so different in spirit from what Jesus Himself had previously said and done, and from their own later commission—was, of course, only ' for the present necessity.' It would have been a fatal anticipation of their inner and outer history to have attempted more, and it would have defeated the object of our Lord of disarming prejudices when making a final appeal to the Jews of Galilee.

Even these considerations lead us to expect a strictly Jewish cast in this Discourse to the Disciples. The command to abstain from any religious fellowship with Gentiles and Samaritans was in temporary accommodation to the prejudices of His disciples and of the Jews. And the distinction between 'the way of the Gentiles' and 'any city of the Samaritans' is the more significant, when we bear in mind that even the dust of a heathen road was regarded as defiling, while the houses, springs, roads, and certain food of the Samaritans were declared clean. At the same time, religiously and as regarded fellowship, the Samaritans were placed on the same footing with Gentiles. Nor would the injunction, to impart their message freely, sound strange in Jewish ears. It was, in fact, what the Rabbis themselves most earnestly enjoined in regard to the teaching of the Law and traditions, however different their practice may have been. Indeed, the very argument that they were to impart freely, because they had received freely, is employed by the Rabbis, and derived from the language and example of Moses in Deut. iv. 5. Again, the directions about not taking staff, shoes, nor money-purse, exactly correspond to the Rabbinic injunction not to enter the Temple-precincts with staff, shoes (mark, not sandals), and a money-girdle. The symbolic reasons underlying this command would, in both cases, be probably the same: to avoid even the appearance of being engaged on other business, when the whole being should be absorbed in the service of the Lord. Nor could they be in doubt what severity of final punishment a doom heavier than that of Sodom and Gomorrah would imply, since, according to early tradition, their inhabitants were to have no part in the world to come. And most impressive to a Jewish mind would be the symbolic injunction, to shake off the dust of their feet for a testimony against such a house or city. The expression, no doubt, indicated that the ban of the Lord was resting on it, and the symbolic act would, as it were, be the solemn pronouncing that 'nought of the cursed
^{a Deut. xiii. 17} thing' clave to them.[a] In this sense, anything that clave to a person was metaphorically called

o 2

'the dust,' as, for example, ' the dust of an evil tongue,'
' the dust of usury,' as, on the other hand, to ' dust to
idolatry' meant to cleave to it.   Even the injunction not
to change the dwelling, where a reception had been given,
was in accordance with Jewish views, the example of Abra-

^a According
to Gen. xiii.
3

ham being quoted, who ^a ' returned to the place
where his tent had been at the beginning.'

^b St. Matt. x.
1-15
^c St. Matt. x.
16-23

These remarks show how closely the Lord
followed, in this first part of His charge to the
disciples,^b Jewish forms of thinking and modes of
expression.   It is not otherwise in the second,^c although the
difference is here very marked.   We have no longer merely
the original commission, as it is given in almost the same
terms by St. Mark and St. Luke.   But the horizon is now
enlarged, and St. Matthew reports that which the other
Evangelists record at a later stage of the Lord's Ministry.

Without here anticipating the full inquiry into the
promise of His immediate Coming, it is important to
avoid, even at this stage, any possible misunderstanding on
the point.   The expectation of the Coming of ' the Son of

^d Dan. vii.
13

Man' was grounded on a prophecy of Daniel,^d in
which that Advent, or rather manifestation, was
associated with judgment.   The same is the case in this
charge of our Lord.   The disciples in their work are described ' as sheep in the midst of wolves,' a phrase which
the Midrash applies to the position of Israel amidst a
hostile world, adding : How great is that Shepherd, Who
delivers them, and vanquishes the wolves!   Similarly,
the admonition to ' be wise as serpents and harmless as
doves' is reproduced in the Midrash, where Israel is described as harmless as the dove towards God, and wise as
serpents towards the hostile Gentile nations.   Such and
even greater would be the enmity which the disciples, as
the true Israel, would have to encounter from Israel after
the flesh.   They would be handed over to the various
Sanhedrin, and visited with such punishments as these

^e St. Matt. x.
17

tribunals had power to inflict.^e   More than this,
they would be brought before governors and
kings—primarily, the Roman governors and the Hero-

dian princes.[a] And so determined would be this persecution, as to break the ties of the closest kinship, and to bring
on them the hatred of all men.[b] The only support
in those terrible circumstances was the assurance
of such help from above, that, although unlearned
and humble, they need have no care, nor make preparation
in their defence. And with this they had the promise
that he who endured to the end would be saved, and the
prudential direction, so far as possible, to avoid persecution
by timely withdrawal, which could be the more readily
achieved, since they would not have completed their circuit
of the cities of Israel before the ' Son of Man be come.'

It is of the greatest importance to keep in view that,
at whatever period of Christ's Ministry this prediction and
promise were spoken, and whether only once or oftener,
they refer exclusively to a *Jewish* state of things. The
persecutions are exclusively Jewish. This appears from
verse 18, where the answer of the disciples is promised to
be ' for a testimony against them,' who had delivered them
up, that is, here, evidently the Jews, as also against ' the
Gentiles.' And the Evangelistic circuit of the disciples
in their preaching was to be *primarily Jewish* ; and not
only so, but in the time when there were still ' cities of
Israel,' that is, previous to the final destruction of the Jewish commonwealth. The reference, then, is to that period of
Jewish persecution and of Apostolic preaching in the cities
of Israel, which is bounded by the destruction of Jerusalem.
Accordingly, the ' Coming of the Son of Man,' and ' the
end '‹here spoken of, must also have the same application.
It was, as we have seen, according to Dan. vii. 13, a coming
in judgment. To the Jewish persecuting authorities, who
had rejected the Christ, in order, as they imagined, to save
their City and Temple from the Romans,[c] and to
whom Christ had testified that He would come
again, this judgment on their city and state, this destruction of their polity, was ' the Coming of the Son of Man '
in judgment, and the only coming which the Jews, as a
state, could expect.

The disciples must have the more readily applied this

a St. Matt. x.
18
b vv. 21, 22

c St. John
xi. 48

prediction of His Coming to Palestine, since 'the woes' connected with it so closely corresponded to those expected by the Jews before the Advent of Messiah. Even the direction to flee from persecution is repeated by the Rabbis in similar circumstances, and established by the example of Jacob, of Moses, and of David.

In the next section of this Discourse of our Lord, as reported by St. Matthew,[a] the horizon is enlarged. The statements are still primarily applicable to the early disciples, and their preaching among the Jews and in Palestine. But their ultimate bearing is already wider, and includes predictions and principles true to all time. In view of the treatment which their Master received, the disciples must expect misrepresentation and evil-speaking. Nor could it seem strange to them, since even the common Rabbinic proverb had it : ' It is enough for a servant to be as his lord.' As we hear it from the lips of Christ, we remember that this saying afterwards comforted those who mourned the downfall of wealthy and liberal homes in Israel, by thoughts of the greater calamity which had overthrown Jerusalem and the Temple. And very significant is its application by Christ : ' If they have called the Master of the house Beelzebul, how much more them of His household.'

But they were not to fear such misrepresentations. In due time the Lord would make manifest both His and their true character.[b] Nor were they to be deterred from announcing in the clearest and most public manner, in broad daylight, and from the flat roofs of houses, that which had been first told them in the darkness, as Jewish teachers communicated the deepest and highest doctrines in secret to their disciples, or as the preacher would whisper his discourse into the ear of the interpreter. But, from a much higher point of view, how different was the teaching of Christ from that of the Rabbis! The latter laid it down as a principle, which they tried to prove from Scripture,[c] that, in order to save one's life, it was not only lawful, but even duty, if necessary, to commit any kind of sin,

* St. Matt. x. 24–34

b St. Matt. x. 26

c Lev. xviii. 5.

except idolatry, incest, or murder. Nay, even idolatry was allowed, if only it were done in secret, so as not to profane the Name of the Lord—than which death was infinitely preferable. Christ, on the other hand, not only ignored this vicious Jewish distinction of public and private as regarded morality, but bade His followers set aside all regard for personal safety, even in reference to the duty of preaching the Gospel. There was a higher fear than of men : that of God—and it should drive out the fear of those who could only kill the body. Besides, why fear? God's Providence extended even over the meanest of His creatures. Two sparrows cost only about the third of a penny. Yet even one of them would not perish without the knowledge of God. No illustration was more familiar to the Jewish mind than that of His watchful care even over the sparrows.

Nor could even the additional promise of Christ: ' But of you even the hairs of the head are all numbered,' surprise His disciples. But it would convey to them the assurance that, in doing His Work, they were performing the Will of God, and were specially in His keeping. And it would carry home to them what Rabbinism expressed in a realistic manner by the common sayings, that whither a man was to go, thither his feet would carry him ; and, that a man could not injure his finger on earth, unless it had been so decreed of him in heaven. And in later Rabbinic writings we read, in almost the words of Christ: ' Do I not number all the hairs of every creature ? ' And yet an even higher outlook was opened to the disciples. All preaching was confessing, and all confessing a preaching of Christ; and our confession or denial would, almost by a law of nature, meet with similar confession or denial on the part of Christ before His Father in heaven. This, also, was an application of that fundamental principle, that ' nothing is covered that shall not be revealed.'

ᵃ St. Matt. x. 34   What follows in our Lord's Discourse [d] still further widens the horizon. It describes the condition and laws of His Kingdom, until the final revelation of that which is now covered and hidden. So long as His claims were set before a hostile world, they could only provoke war. On the other hand, so long as such decision was necessary, in the choice of either those nearest and dearest, of ease, nay, of life itself, or else of Christ, there could be no compromise. Not that, as is sometimes erroneously supposed, a very great degree of love to the dearest on earth amounts to loving them more than Christ. The love which Christ condemneth differs not in degree, but in kind, from rightful affection. It is one which takes the place of love to Christ—not which is placed by the side of that of Christ. For, rightly viewed, the two occupy different provinces. Wherever and whenever the two affections come into comparison, they also come into collision. And so the questions of not being worthy of Him, and of the true finding or losing of our life, have their bearing on our daily life and profession.

But even in this respect the disciples must, to some extent, have been prepared to receive the teaching of Christ. It was generally expected that a time of great tribulation would precede the Advent of the Messiah. Again, it was a Rabbinic axiom that the cause of the teacher, to whom a man owed eternal life, was to be taken in hand before that of his father, to whom he owed only the life of this world. Even the statement about taking up the Cross in following Christ, although prophetic, could not sound quite strange. Crucifixion was, indeed, not a Jewish punishment, but the Jews must have become sadly familiar with it. Indeed, the expression ' bearing the cross,' as indicative of sorrow and suffering, is so common, that we read, Abraham carried the wood for the sacrifice of Isaac, ' like one who bears his cross on his shoulder.'

Nor could the disciples be in doubt as to the meaning of the last part of Christ's address.[a] They were old Jewish forms of thought, only filled with the new wine of the Gospel. The Rabbis taught, but in extravagant terms, the merit attaching to the reception and entertainment of sages. The very expression ' in the name of ' a prophet, or a righteous man, is strictly Jewish,

a St. Matt. x. 40–42

and means for the sake of, or with intention in regard to.
It appears to us that Christ introduced His own distinctive teaching by the admitted Jewish principle, that
hospitable reception for the sake of, or with the intention
of doing it to, a prophet or a righteous man, would procure a share in the prophet's or righteous man's reward.
Thus, tradition had it that the Obadiah of King Ahab's
court [a] had become the prophet of that name,
because he had provided for the hundred prophets. And we are repeatedly assured that to receive
a sage, or even an elder, was like receiving the Shekhinah
itself. But the concluding promise of Christ, concerning
the reward of even ' a cup of cold water ' to ' one of these
little ones ' ' in the name of a disciple,' goes far beyond
the farthest conceptions of His contemporaries. Yet, even
so, the expression would, so far as its form is concerned,
perhaps bear a fuller meaning to them than to us. These
' little ones' were 'the children,' who were still learning
the elements of knowledge, and who would by-and-by
grow into ' disciples.' For, as the Midrash has it : ' Where
there are no little ones, there are no disciples ; and where
no disciples, no sages ; where no sages, there no elders ;
where no elders, there no prophets ; and where no prophets, there does God not cause His Shekhinah to rest.'

We have been particular in marking the Jewish parallelisms in this Discourse, first, because it seemed important
to show that the words of the Lord were not beyond the
comprehension of the disciples. Starting from forms of
thought and expressions with which they were familiar,
He carried them far beyond Jewish ideas and hopes. But,
secondly, it is just in this similarity of form, which proves
that it was of the time and to the time, as well as to us
and to all times, that we best see how far the teaching of
Christ transcended all contemporary conception.

[a] 1 Kings
xviii. 4

CHAPTER XXXVII.

WHILE the Apostles went forth by two and two on their
first Mission, Jesus Himself taught and preached in the
towns around Capernaum.[a] This period of undisturbed activity seems, however, to have been
of brief duration. That it was eminently successful, we infer not only from direct notices,[b]
but also from the circumstance that, for the first time, the
attention of Herod Antipas was now called to the Person
of Jesus. We suppose that, during the nine or ten
months of Christ's Galilean Ministry, the Tetrarch had
resided in his Peræan dominions (east of the Jordan),
either at Julias or at Machærus, in which latter fortress
the Baptist was beheaded. We infer that the labours of
the Apostles had also extended thus far, since they attracted the notice of Herod. In the popular excitement
caused by the execution of the Baptist, the miraculous
activity of the messengers of the Christ Whom John had
announced, would naturally attract wider interest, while
Antipas would, under the influence of fear and superstition, give greater heed to them. We can scarcely be
mistaken in supposing that this accounts for the abrupt
termination of the labours of the Apostles, and their return to Jesus. At any rate, the arrival of the disciples
of John, with tidings of their master's death, and the
return of the Apostles, seem to have been contempora-
neous.[c] Finally, we conjecture that it was
among the motives which influenced the removal of Christ and His Apostles from Capernaum. Temporarily to withdraw Himself and His dis-

[a] St. Matt.
xi. 1

[b] St. Mark
vi. 12, 13;
St. Luke ix.
6

[c] St. Matt.
xiv. 12, 13;
St. Mark vi.
30

ciples from Herod, to give them a season of rest and further preparation after the excitement of the last few weeks, and to avoid being involved in the popular movements consequent on the murder of the Baptist—such we may venture to indicate as among the reasons of the departure of Jesus and His disciples, first into the dominions of the Tetrarch Philip, on the eastern side of the Lake,[a] and after that 'into the borders of Tyre and Sidon.'[b] Thus the fate of the Baptist was, as might have been expected, decisive in its influence on the History of the Christ and of His Kingdom. But we have yet to trace the incidents in the life of John, so far as recorded in the Gospels, from the time of his last contact with Jesus to his execution.

[a] St. John vi. 1
[b] St. Mark vii. 24

1. It was[c] in the early summer of the year 27 of our era, that John was baptizing in Ænon, near to Salim. In the neighbourhood Jesus and His disciples were similarly engaged. The Presence and activity of Jesus in Jerusalem at the Passover[d] had determined the Pharisaic party to take active measures against Him and His Forerunner, John. As the first outcome of this plan we notice the discussions on the question of 'purification,' and the attempt to separate between Christ and the Baptist by exciting the jealousy of the latter.[e] But the result was far different. His disciples might have been influenced, but John himself was too true a man, and too deeply convinced of the reality of Christ's Mission, to yield even for a moment to such temptation.

[c] St. John iii. 22 to iv. 3

[d] St. John ii. 13 to iii. 21

[e] St. John iii. 25 &c.

It was not the greatness of the Christ, to his own seeming loss, which could cloud the Baptist's convictions. In simple Judæan illustration, he was only 'the friend of the Bridegroom,' with all that popular association or higher Jewish allegory connected with that relationship. He claimed not the bride. His was another joy—that of hearing the Voice of her rightful Bridegroom, Whose 'groomsman' he was. In the sound of that Voice lay the fulfilment of his office.

2. The scene has changed, and the Baptist has become

the prisoner of Herod Antipas. The dominions of the latter embraced, in the north : Galilee, west of the Jordan and of the Lake of Galilee; and in the south : Peræa, east of the Jordan. To realise events we must bear in mind that, crossing the Lake eastwards, we should pass from the possessions of Herod to those of the Tetrarch Philip, or else come upon the territory of the 'Ten Cities' or Decapolis, a kind of confederation of townships, with constitution and liberties, such as those of the Grecian cities. By a narrow strip northwards, Peræa just slipped in between the Decapolis and Samaria. It is impossible with certainty to localise the Ænon, near Salim, where John baptized. We believe that the place was close to, perhaps actually in, the north-eastern angle of the province of Judæa, where it borders on Samaria. We are now on the western bank of Jordan. The other, or eastern, bank of the river would be that narrow northern strip of Peræa which formed part of the territory of Antipas. Thus a few miles, or the mere crossing of the river, would have brought the Baptist into Peræa. There can be no doubt but that the Baptist must either have crossed into, or else that Ænon, near Salim, was actually within the dominions of Herod. It was on that occasion that Herod seized on his person,[a] and that Jesus, Who was still within Judæan territory, withdrew from the intrigues of the Pharisees and the proximity of Herod, through Samaria, into Galilee.[b]

[a] St. John iii. 24
[b] St. John vi. 1

Supposing Antipas to have been at his palace in the Peræan Julias, he would have been in close proximity to the scene of the Baptist's last recorded labours at Ænon. We can now understand, not only how John was imprisoned by Antipas, but also the threefold motives which influenced it. According to Josephus, the Tetrarch was afraid that his absolute influence over the people, who seemed disposed to carry out whatever he advised, might lead to a rebellion. This circumstance is also indicated in the remark of St. Matthew[c] that Herod was afraid to put the Baptist to death on account of the people's opinion of him. On the other hand, the

[c] St. Matt. xiv. 5

ᵃ St. Matt. xiv. 3, 4; St. Mark vi. 17, 18 Evangelic statement ᵃ that Herod had imprisoned John on account of his declaring his marriage with Herodias unlawful, is in no way inconsistent with the reason assigned by Josephus. Not only might both motives have influenced Herod, but there is an obvious connection between them. For John's open declaration of the unlawfulness of Herod's marriage, as alike incestuous and adulterous, might, in view of the influence which the Baptist exercised, have easily led to a rebellion. The reference to the Pharisaic spying and to their comparisons between the influence of Jesus and of ᵇ St. John iv. 1, 2 John,ᵇ which led to the withdrawal of Christ into Galilee, seems to imply that the Pharisees had something to do with the imprisonment of John. Their connection with Herod appears even more clearly in the attempt to induce Christ's departure from Galilee, on pretext of Herod's machinations. It will be remembered that the Lord unmasked their hypocrisy by bidding them go back to Herod, showing that He fully knew that real danger threatened Him, not from the Tetrarch, but from ᶜ St. Luke xiii. 31-33 the leaders of the party in Jerusalem.ᶜ Our inference, therefore, is that Pharisaic intrigue had a very large share in giving effect to Herod's fear of the Baptist and of his reproofs.

3. Machærus (the modern *M'khaur*) marked the extreme point south, as Pella that north, in Peræa. As the boundary fortress in the south-east (towards Arabia), its safety was of the greatest importance, and everything was done to make a place, exceedingly strong by nature, impregnable.

'A rugged line of upturned squared stones' shows the old Roman paved road leading to the fortress, in which, according to Josephus, the Baptist was confined. Ruins covering quite a square mile, on a group of undulating hills, mark the site of the ancient town of Machærus. Although surrounded by a wall and towers, its position is supposed not to have been strategically defensible. Only a mass of ruins here, with traces of a temple to the Syrian Sun-God, broken cisterns, and desolateness all around.

Crossing a narrow deep valley, about a mile wide, we climb up to the ancient fortress on a conical hill. Altogether it covered a ridge of more than a mile. The key of the position was a citadel to the extreme east of the fortress. It occupied the summit of the cone, was isolated, and almost impregnable, but very small. Descending a steep slope about 150 yards towards the west, we reach the oblong flat plateau that formed the fortress, containing Herod's magnificent palace.

No traces of the royal palace are left, save foundations and enormous stones upturned. Within the area of the keep are a well of great depth, and a deep cemented cistern with the vaulting of the roof still complete, and two dungeons, one of them deep down, its sides scarcely broken in, 'with small holes still visible in the masonry where staples of wood and iron had once been fixed.' As we look down into its hot darkness, we shudder in realising that this terrible keep had for nigh ten months been the prison of that son of the free 'wilderness,' the bold herald of the coming Kingdom, the humble, earnest, self-denying John the Baptist.

4. In these circumstances we scarcely wonder at the feelings of John's disciples, as months of his weary captivity passed. Uncertain what to expect, they seem to have oscillated between Machærus and Capernaum. Any hope of their Master's vindication and deliverance lay in the possibilities involved in the announcement he had made of Jesus as the Christ. And it was to Him that their Master's finger had pointed them. Indeed, some of Jesus' earliest and most intimate disciples had come from their ranks; and, as themselves had remarked, the multitude had turned to Jesus even before the Baptist's im-

ª St. John iii. 26

prisonment.ª And yet, in their view, there must have been a terrible contrast between him who lay in the dungeon of Machærus, and Him Who sat down to eat and drink at a feast of the publicans.

His reception of publicans and sinners they could understand; their own Master had not rejected them. But why eat and drink with them? Was not fasting always,

but more especially now, appropriate? The Pharisees, in
their anxiety to separate between Jesus and His Forerunner, must have told them all this again and again, and
pointed to the contrast.

At any rate, it was at the instigation of the Pharisees,
and in company with them, that the disciples of John propounded to Jesus this question about fasting and prayer,
immediately after the feast in the house of the converted
Levi-Matthew.[a] We must bear in mind that
fasting and prayer, or else fasting and alms, or
all the three, were always combined. Fasting
represented the negative, prayer and alms the positive
element, in the forgiveness of sins. Fasting, as self-
punishment and mortification, would avert the anger of
God and calamities. Most extraordinary instances of the
purposes in view in fasting, and of the results obtained,
are told in Jewish legend, which (as will be remembered)
went so far as to relate how a Jewish saint was thereby
rendered proof against the fire of Gehenna, of which a
realistic demonstration was given when his body was
rendered proof against ordinary fire.

[a] St. Matt.
ix. 14-17
and parallels

To the Jews, fasting was the readiest means of turning
aside any threatening calamity, such as drought, pesti-
lence, or national danger. The second and fifth days of
the week (Monday and Thursday) were those appointed
for public fasts, because Moses was supposed to have gone
up the Mount for the second Tables of the Law on a
Thursday, and to have returned on a Monday.

It may well have been that it was on one of these
weekly fasts that the feast of Levi-Matthew had taken
place, and that this explains the expression: 'And John's
disciples and the Pharisees were fasting.'[b] This
would give point to their complaint, 'Thy
disciples fast not.' Looking back upon the standpoint
from which they viewed fasting, it is easy to perceive
why Jesus could not have sanctioned, nor even tolerated, the practice, among His disciples, as little as St.
Paul could tolerate among Judaising Christians the, in
itself indifferent, practice of circumcision. But it was

[b] St. Mark
ii. 18

not so easy to explain this at the time to the disciples of John.

The last recorded testimony of the Baptist had pointed to Christ as 'the Bridegroom.'[a] As explained in a previous chapter, John applied this in a manner which appealed to popular custom. As he had pointed out, the Presence of Jesus marked the marriage-week. By universal consent and according to Rabbinic law, this was to be a time of unmixed festivity. During the marriage-week all mourning was to be suspended— even the obligation of the prescribed daily prayers ceased. It was regarded as a religious duty to gladden the bride and bridegroom. Was it not, then, inconsistent on the part of John's disciples to expect 'the sons of the bride-chamber' to fast, so long as the Bridegroom was with them?

a St. John iii. 29

But let it not be thought that it was to be a time of unbroken joy to the disciples of Jesus. The Bridegroom would be violently taken from them, and then would be the time for mourning and fasting. Not that this necessarily implies literal fasting, any more than it excludes it, provided the great principles, more fully indicated immediately afterwards, are kept in view. Painfully minute, Judaistic self-introspection is contrary to the spirit of the joyous liberty of the children of God. It is only a sense of sin, and the felt absence of the Christ, which should lead to mourning and fasting, though not in order thereby to avert either the anger of God or outward calamity.

In general, the two illustrations employed—that of the piece of undressed cloth (or, according to St. Luke, a piece torn from a new garment) sewed upon the rent of an old garment, and that of the new wine put into the old wine-skins—must not be too closely pressed in regard to their language. They seem chiefly to imply this: You ask, why do we fast often, but Thy disciples fast not? You are mistaken in supposing that the old garment can be retained, and merely its rents made good by patching it with a piece of new cloth. The old garment will not bear mending with the 'undressed cloth.' Christ's was not merely a reformation : all things must become new. Or, again, take the other view of it—the new wine of the Kingdom cannot be confined in the old forms. It would burst those wine-skins. The spirit must, indeed, have its corresponding form of expression ; but that form must be adapted, and correspond to it. Such are the two final principles—the one primarily addressed to the Pharisees, the other to the disciples of John, by which the illustrative teaching concerning the marriage-feast, with its bridal garment and wine of banquet, is carried beyond the original question of the disciples of John, and receives an application to all time.

5. Weeks had passed, and the disciples of John had come back and showed their Master of all these things. He still lay in the dungeon of Machærus ; his circumstances unchanged—perhaps, more hopeless than before. For Herod was in that spiritually most desperate state : he had heard the Baptist, and was much perplexed. This we can understand, since he ' feared him, knowing that he was a righteous man and holy,' and thus fearing ' heard him.' But that, being ' much perplexed,' he still ' heard him gladly,'[a] constituted the hopelessness of his case. But was the Baptist right ? Did it constitute part of his Divine calling to have not only denounced, but apparently directly confronted Herod on his adulterous marriage ? Had he not attempted to lift himself the axe which seemed to have slipt from the grasp of Him, of Whom the Baptist had hoped and said that He would lay it to the root of the tree ?

Such thoughts may have been with him, as he passed from his dungeon to the audience of Herod, and from such bootless interviews back to his deep keep. Strange as it may seem, it was, perhaps, better for the Baptist when he was alone. The state of mind and experience of his disciples has already appeared, even in the slight notices concerning them. Indeed, had they fully understood him, and not ended where he began—which, truly, is the characteristic of all sects—they would not have remained his disciples. Their very affection for him, and their zeal

a St. Mark
vi. 20

P

for his credit (as shown in the almost coarse language of their inquiry : ' John the Baptist hath sent us unto Thee, saying, Art Thou He that cometh, or look we for another ? '), as well as their tenacity of unprogressiveness—were all, so to speak, marks of his failure. And if he had failed with them, had he succeeded in anything ?

And yet further and more searching questions rose in that dark dungeon. What if after all there had been some horrible mistake on his part ? At any rate the logic of events was against him. He was now the fast prisoner of that Herod, to whom he had spoken with authority; in the power of that bold adulteress, Herodias. If he were Elijah, the great Tishbite had never been in the hands of Ahab and Jezebel. And the Messiah, Whose Elijah he was, moved not ; could not, or would not, but feasted with publicans and sinners ! Was it all a reality ? It must have been a terrible hour, and the power of darkness. At the end of a life, and that of such self-denial and suffering, and with a conscience so alive to God, which had —when a youth—driven him burning with holy zeal into the wilderness, to have the question meeting him : Art Thou He, or do we wait for another ?

In that conflict John overcame, as we all must overcome. His very despair opened the door of hope. The helpless doubt, which none could solve but One, he brought to Him around Whom it had gathered. When John asked the question : Do we wait for another ? light was already struggling through darkness. It was incipient victory even in defeat. When he sent his disciples with this question straight to Christ, he had already conquered; for such a question addressed to a possibly false Messiah had no meaning.

The designation ' The Coming One,' though a most truthful expression of Jewish expectancy, was not one ordinarily used of the Messiah. But it was invariably used in reference to the Messianic age as the coming world or Æon. In the mouth of John it might therefore mean chiefly this : Art Thou He that is to establish the Messianic Kingdom in its outward power, or have we to

wait for another ? In that case, the manner in which the
Lord answered it would be all the more significant. The
messengers came just as He was engaged in healing body
^a St. Luke and soul.ᵃ Without interrupting His work, or
vii. 21 otherwise noticing their inquiry, He bade them
tell John for answer what they had seen and heard, and
ᵇ St. Matt. that 'the poor ᵇ are evangelised.' To this, as the
xi. 5 inmost characteristic of the Messianic Kingdom,
He only added, not by way of reproof nor even of warning,
but as a fresh 'Beatitude': 'Blessed is he, whosoever
shall not be scandalised in Me.' And such knowledge
of Christ's distinctive Work and Word is the only true
answer to our questions, whether of head or heart.

But a harder saying than this did the Lord speak
amidst the forthpouring of His testimony to John, when
his messengers had left. He to Whom John had formerly
borne testimony now bore testimony to him ; and that,
not in the hour when John had testified for Him, but when
his testimony had wavered and almost failed. Again we
mark that the testimony of Christ is as from a higher
standpoint. And it is a full vindication as well as unstinted
praise, spoken, not as in his hearing, but after his
messengers—who had met a seemingly cold reception—
had left.

6. The scene once more changes, and we are again at
Machærus. Weeks have passed since the return of John's
messengers. We cannot doubt that the sunlight of faith
has again fallen into the dark dungeon, nor yet that the
peace of conviction has filled the martyr of Christ.
He must have known that his end was at hand, and been
ready to be offered up. Nor would he any longer expect
from the Messiah assertions of power on his behalf. He
now understood that for which 'He had come ;' he knew
the better liberty, triumph, and victory which He brought.
His life-work had been done, and there was nothing further
that fell to him or that he could do, and the weary servant
of the Lord must have longed for his rest.

It was early spring, shortly before the Passover, the
anniversary of the death of Herod the Great and of the

accession of (his son) Herod Antipas to the Tetrarchy. A
fit time this for a Belshazzar-feast, when such an one as
Herod would gather to a grand banquet 'his lords,' and
the military authorities, and the chief men of Galilee.   It is
evening, and the castle-palace is brilliantly lighted up.   The
noise of music and the shouts of revelry come across the
slope into the citadel, and fall into the deep dungeon where
waits the prisoner of Christ.   And now the merriment in
the great banqueting-hall has reached its utmost height.
The king has nothing further to offer his satiated guests,
no fresh excitement.   So let it be the sensuous stimulus
of dubious dances, and, to complete it, let the dancer be
the fair young daughter of the king's wife, the very
descendant of the Asmonæan priest-princes !   To viler
depth of coarse familiarity even a Herod could not have
descended.

She has come, and she has danced, this princely
maiden.   And she has done her best in that wretched
exhibition, and pleased Herod and them that sat at meat
with him.   And now, amidst the general plaudits, she
shall have her reward—and the king swears it to her with
loud voice, that all around hear it—even to the half of his
kingdom.   The maiden steals out of the banquet-hall to
ask her mother what it shall be.   Can there be doubt or
hesitation in the mind of Herodias ?   If there was one object
she had at heart, which these ten months she had in vain
sought to attain, it was the death of John the Baptist.
She remembered it all only too well—her stormy, reckless
past.   The daughter of Aristobulus, the ill-fated son of the
ill-fated Asmonæan princess Mariamme (I.), she had been
married to her half-uncle, Herod Philip, the son of Herod
the Great and of Mariamme (II.), the daughter of the
High-Priest (Boëthos).   At one time it seemed as if Herod
Philip would have been sole inheritor of his father's dominions.
But the old tyrant had changed his testament, and Philip
was left with great wealth, but as a private person living
in Jerusalem.   This little suited the woman's ambition.
It was when his half-brother, Herod Antipas, came on a
visit to him at Jerusalem, that an intrigue began between

the Tetrarch and his brother's wife. It was agreed that,
after the return of Antipas from his impending journey to
Rome, he should repudiate his wife, the daughter of Aretas,
king of Arabia, and wed Herodias. But Aretas' daughter
heard of the plot, and having obtained her husband's consent to go to Machærus, she fled thence to her father.
This, of course, led to enmity between Antipas and Aretas.
Nevertheless, the adulterous marriage with Herodias
followed. In a few sentences the story may be carried to
its termination. The woman proved the curse and ruin of
Antipas. First came the murder of the Baptist, which
sent a thrill of horror through the people, and to which all
the later misfortunes of Herod were attributed. Then
followed a war with Aretas, in which the Tetrarch was
worsted. And, last of all, his wife's ambition led him to
Rome to solicit the title of king, lately given to Agrippa,
the brother of Herodias. Antipas not only failed, but was
deprived of his dominions, and banished to Lyons in Gaul.
The pride of the woman in refusing favours from the
Emperor, and her faithfulness to her husband in his fallen
fortunes, are the only redeeming points in her history.
As for Salome, she was first married to her uncle, Philip
the Tetrarch. Legend has it that her death was retribu-
tive, being in consequence of a fall on the ice.

Such was the woman who had these many months
sought to rid herself of the hated person who alone had
dared publicly denounce her sin, and whose words held her
weak husband in awe. The opportunity had now come for
obtaining from the vacillating monarch what her entreaties
could never have secured. As the Gospel puts it,[a]
'instigated' by her mother, the damsel hesitated
not. 'With haste,' as if no time were to be lost, she went
up to the king: 'I will that thou forthwith give me in a
charger the head of John the Baptist.' Silence must
have fallen on the assembly. Even into their hearts such
a demand from the lips of little more than a child must
have struck horror. They all knew John to be a righteous
and a holy man. Wicked as they were, in their superstition, if not religiousness, few, if any of them, would have

[a] St. Matt. xiv. 8

willingly lent himself to such work. And they all knew
also why Salome, or rather Herodias, had made this
demand. What would Herod do? 'The king was exceeding sorry.' For months he had striven against this.
His conscience, fear of the people, inward horror of the
deed, all would have kept him from it. But he had sworn
to the maiden, who now stood before him, claiming that
the pledge be redeemed, and every eye in the assembly
was fixed upon him. Unfaithful to his God, to his conscience, to truth and righteousness; not ashamed of any
crime or sin, he would yet be faithful to his half-drunken
oath, and appear honourable and true before such companions!

It has been but the contest of a moment. 'Straightway' the king gives the order to one of the body-guard.
No time for preparation is given, or needed. A few
minutes more, and the gory head of the Baptist is brought
to the maiden in a charger, and she gives the ghastly dish
to her mother.

It is all over! As the pale morning light streams into
the keep, the faithful disciples, who had been told of it,
come reverently to bear the headless body to the burying.
They go forth for ever from that accursed place, which is
so soon to become a mass of shapeless ruins. They go to
tell it to Jesus, and henceforth to remain with Him. We
can imagine what welcome awaited them. But the people
ever afterwards cursed the tyrant, and looked for those
judgments of God to follow, which were so soon to descend
on him. And he himself was ever afterwards restless,
wretched, and full of apprehensions. He could scarcely
believe that the Baptist was really dead, and when the
fame of Jesus reached him, and those around suggested
that this was Elijah, a prophet, or as one of them, Herod's
mind, amidst its strange perplexities, still reverted to the
man whom he had murdered. It was a new anxiety,
perhaps even so a new hope; and as formerly he had
often and gladly heard the Baptist, so now he would fain
ª St. Luke ix. have seen Jesus.[a] He would see Him: but not
9   now. In that dark night of betrayal, he, who at

the bidding of the child of an adulteress, had murdered the Forerunner, might, with the approbation of a Pilate, have rescued Him Whose faithful witness John had been. But night was to merge into yet darker night. For it was the time and the power of the Evil One. And yet: Jehovah reigneth!

CHAPTER XXXVIII.

THE MIRACULOUS FEEDING OF THE FIVE THOUSAND.

(St. Matt. xiv. 13–21; St. Mark vi. 30–44; St. Luke ix. 10–17; St. John vi. 1–14.)

IN the circumstances described in the previous chapter, Jesus resolved at once to leave Capernaum; and this probably, as we have seen, alike for the sake of His disciples, who needed rest; for that of the people, who might have attempted a rising after the murder of the Baptist; and temporarily to withdraw Himself and His followers from the power of Herod. For this purpose He chose the place, outside the dominions of Antipas, nearest to Capernaum. This was Beth-Saida ('the house of fishing') on the eastern border of Galilee, just within the territory of the Tetrarch Philip. Originally a small village, Philip had converted it into a town, and named it Julias, after Cæsar's daughter. It lay on the eastern bank of Jordan, just before that stream enters the Lake of Galilee.[1]

Only a few hours' sail from Capernaum, and even a shorter distance by land, lay the district of Bethsaida Julias. It was natural that Christ, wishing to avoid public attention, should have gone ' by ship,' and equally so that the many ' seeing them departing, and knowing' —viz. what direction the boat was taking—should have followed on foot, and been joined by others from the neighbouring villages. The circumstance that the Passover was

---

[1] This Bethsaida must not be confounded with the other 'Fishertown' or Bethsaida, on the western shore of the Lake, which the Fourth Gospel distinguishes from the Eastern as 'Bethsaida of Galilee' (St. John xii. 21; comp. i. 44; St. Mark vi. 45).

nigh at hand, so that many must have been starting on their journey to Jerusalem, round the Lake and through Peræa, partly accounts for the immense number of 'about 5,000 men, beside women and children,' which is mentioned. And this, perhaps in conjunction with the effect on the people of John's murder, may also explain their ready and eager gathering to Christ.

As we picture it to ourselves, our Lord with His disciples, and perhaps followed by those who had outrun the rest, first retired to the top of a height, and there rested in teaching converse with them.[a] Presently, as He saw the great multitudes gathering, He was ' moved with compassion towards them.' [b] There could be no question of retirement or rest in view of this. He must work while it was called to-day, ere the night of judgment came. It was this depth of pity which now ended the Saviour's rest, and brought Him down from the hill to meet the gathering multitude in the 'desert' plain beneath.

a St. John vi. 3
b St. Matt. xiv. 14

And what a sight—these thousands of men, besides women and children; and what thoughts of the past, the present, and the future, would be called up by the scene. These Passover-pilgrims and God's guests, now streaming out into this desert after Him; with a murdered John just buried, and no earthly teacher, guide, or help left ! Truly they were 'as sheep having no shepherd.'[c] The very surroundings seemed to give to the thought the vividness of a picture : this wandering, straying multitude, the desert sweep of country, the very want of provisions. A Passover, indeed, but of which He would be the Paschal Lamb, the Bread which He gave the Supper, and around which He would gather those scattered, shepherdless sheep into one flock of many ' companies,' to which His Apostles would bring the bread He had blessed and broken, to their sufficient and more than sufficient nourishment ; and from which they would carry the remnant-baskets full, after the flock had been fed, to the poor in the outlying places of far-off heathendom.

c St. Mark vi. 34

Meantime the Saviour was moving among them—
'beginning to teach them many things,'[a] and
'healing them that had need of healing.'[b] Yet,
as He so moved and thought of it all, from the
first 'He Himself knew what He was about to do.'[c]

a St. Mark
vi. 34
b St. Luke
ix. 11
c St. John
vi. 6

And now the sun had passed its meridian, and
the shadows fell on the surging crowd. Full of the
thoughts of the great Supper, which was symbolically to
link the Passover of the past with that of the future, and
its Sacramental continuation to all time, He turned to
Philip with this question : 'Whence are we to buy bread,
that these may eat?' Perhaps there was something in
Philip which made it specially desirable that the question
should be put to him.[d] At any rate, the answer
of Philip showed that there had been a 'need be'
for it. This—'two hundred denarii (between

d Comp. St.
John xiv.
8, 9

six and seven pounds) worth of bread is not sufficient for
them, that every one may take a little,' is the realism, not
of unbelief, but of an absence of faith which, entirely
ignoring any higher possibility, has not even its hope left
in a 'Thou knowest, Lord.'

But there is evidence, also, that the question of Christ
worked deeper thinking and higher good. As we understand it, Philip told it to Andrew, and they to the others.
While Jesus taught and healed, they must have spoken
together of this strange question of the Master. They
knew Him sufficiently to judge that it implied some
purpose on His part. Did He intend to provide for all
that multitude? They counted them roughly. They
thought of all the means for feeding such a multitude.
How much had they of their own? As we judge by combining the various statements, there was a lad there who
carried the humble provisions of the party—perhaps a
fisher-lad brought for the purpose from the boat.[e]
It would take quite what Philip had reckoned—
about two hundred denarii—if the Master meant
them to go and buy victuals for all that multitude.
Probably the common stock—at any rate as computed by Judas, who carried the bag—did not contain that

e Comp. St.
John vi. 9
with St.
Matt. xiv.
17 ; St. Mark
vi. 38 ; St.
Luke ix. 13

amount. In any case, the right and the wise thing was to
dismiss the multitude, that they might go into the towns
and villages and buy for themselves victuals, and find
lodgment.

Already what was called ' the first evening ' had set in,
when the disciples, whose anxiety must have been growing
with the progress of time, asked the Lord to dismiss the
people. But it was as they had thought. He would have
them give the people to eat! How many loaves had they?
Let them go and see.[a] And when Andrew went
to see what store the fisher-lad carried for them,
he brought back the tidings, ' He hath five barley loaves
and two small fishes,' to which he added, half in disbelief,
half in faith's rising expectancy of impossible possibility :
' But what are they among so many?'[b] It is
to the fourth Evangelist alone that we owe the
record of this remark, which we instinctively feel gives to
the whole the touch of truth and life. It is to him also
that we owe two other minute traits of deep interest, and
of greater importance than at first sight appears.

When we read that these five were *barley*-loaves, we
learn that, no doubt from voluntary choice, the fare of the
Lord and of His followers was the poorest. Indeed, barley-
bread was, almost proverbially, the meanest. The other
minute trait in St. John's Gospel consists in the use of a
peculiar word for ' fish '—' opsarion,' which properly means
what was eaten along with the bread, and specially refers
to the small and generally dried or pickled fish eaten with
bread, like our ' sardines,' or the ' caviar ' of Russia, the
pickled herrings of Holland and Germany, or a peculiar
kind of small dried fish, eaten with the bones, in the North
of Scotland. Now the Lake of Galilee was particularly
rich in these fishes, and we know that both the salting
and pickling of them was a special industry among its
fishermen. For this purpose a small kind was specially
selected. The diminutive used by St. John, of which our
Authorised Version no doubt gives the meaning fairly by
rendering it 'small fishes,' refers, most likely, to those small
fishes (probably a kind of sardine), of which millions were

a St. Mark
vi. 38

b St. John
vi. 9

caught in the Lake, and which, dried and salted, would form the most common ' savoury ' with bread for the fisher-population along the shores.

Only once again does the same expression occur, and that once more in the fourth Gospel. On that morning, when the Risen One manifested Himself by the Lake of Galilee to them who had all the night toiled in vain, He had provided for them miraculously the meal, when on the ' fire of charcoal ' they saw the well-remembered ' little fish,' and, as He bade them bring of the ' little fish ' which they had miraculously caught, Peter drew to shore the net full, not of ' little ' but ' of great fishes.' And yet it was not of those ' great fishes ' that He gave them, but ' He took ^a St. John the bread and gave them, and the *opsarion* like-xxi. 9, 10, 13 wise.' [a]

There is one proof at least of the implicit faith, or rather trust, of the disciples in their Master. They had given Him account of their own scanty provision, and yet, as He bade them make the people sit down to the meal, they hesitated not to obey. We can picture to ourselves the expanse of ' grass,' [b] ' green,' and fresh,[c] ' much grass ; ' [d] then the people in their ' companies ' [e] of fifties and hundreds, reclining,[f] and looking in their regular divisions, and with their bright many-coloured dresses, like ' garden-beds ' [g] on the turf. But on One Figure must every eye have been bent. Around Him stood His Apostles. They had laid before Him the scant provision made for their own wants, and which was now to feed this great multitude. As was wont at meals on the part of the head of the household, Jesus took the bread, ' blessed ' or, as St. John puts it, ' gave thanks,' and ' brake ' it. The expression recalls that connected with the Holy Eucharist, and leaves little doubt on the mind that, in the Discourse delivered in the Synagogue of Capernaum,[h] there is also reference to the Lord's Supper. As of comparatively secondary import-ance, yet helping us better to realise the scene, we recall the Jewish ordinance, that the head of the house was only to

^b St. Matt. xiv. 19
^c St. Mark vi. 39
^d St. John vi. 10
^e St. Mark vi. 39.
^f St. Luke ix. 14
^g St. Mark vi. 40

^h St. John vi. 48–58

speak the blessing if he himself shared in the meal. Yet if they who sat down to it were not merely guests, but his children, or his household, then might he speak it, even if he himself did not partake of the bread which he had broken.

There can be little doubt that the words which Jesus spake, whether in Aramæan, Greek, or Hebrew, were those so well known : ' Blessed art Thou, Jehovah our God, King of the world, Who causest to come forth bread from the earth.' Assuredly it was this threefold thought : the up-ward thought, the recognition of the creative act as regards every piece of bread we eat, and the thanks-giving—which was realised anew in all its fulness when, as He distributed to the disciples, the provision miracu-lously multiplied in His Hands. And still they bore it from His Hands from company to company, laying before each a store. When they were all filled, He that had pro-vided the meal bade them gather up the fragments before each company. So doing, each of the twelve had his basket filled. Here also we have another life-touch. Those ' baskets ' known in Jewish writings by a similar name, made of wicker or willows, were in common use, but considered of the poorest kind. There is a sublimeness of contrast that passes description between this feast to the five thousand, besides women and children, and the poor's provision of barley-bread and the two small fishes ; and, again, between the quantity left and the coarse wicker baskets in which it was stored. Nor do we forget to draw mentally the parallel between this Messianic feast and that banquet of ' the latter days ' which Rabbinism pictured so realistically. But as the wondering multitude watched, as the disciples gathered from company to com-pany the fragments into their baskets, the murmur ran through the ranks : ' This is truly the Prophet, " the Coming One." '

CHAPTER XXXIX.

THE NIGHT OF MIRACLES ON THE LAKE OF GENNESARET.

(St. Matt. xiv. 22–36; St. Mark vi. 45–56; St. John vi. 15–21.)

THE last question of the Baptist spoken in public had been : ' Art Thou the Coming One, or look we for another ? ' It had in part been answered, as the murmur had passed through the ranks : ' This One is truly the Prophet, the Coming One ! ' So, then, they had no longer to wait, nor to look for another! An irresistible impulse seized the people. They would proclaim Him King, then and there ; and as they knew, probably from previous utterances, perhaps when similar movements had to be checked, that He would resist, they would constrain Him to declare Himself, or at least to be proclaimed by them.

'Jesus, therefore, perceiving that they were about to come, and to take Him by force, that they might make Him King, withdrew again into the mountain, Himself alone,' or, as it might be rendered, though not quite in the modern usage of the expression, ' became an anchorite again . . . Himself alone.'[a] He withdrew to pray ; and He stilled the people, and sent them, no doubt solemnised, to their homes, by telling them that He withdrew to pray. And He did pray till far on, when the (second) evening had come,[b] and the first stars shone out over the Lake of Galilee.

[a] St. John vi. 15

[b] St. Matt. xiv. 23

For whom and for what He prayed alone on that mountain, we dare not inquire. And as He prayed, out on the Lake, where the bark which bore His disciples made for the other shore, ' a great wind ' ' contrary to them ' was rising. And still He was ' alone on the land,' but looking out after them, as the ship was ' in the midst of the sea,' and they toiling and ' distressed in rowing.'

Thus far, to the utmost verge of their need, but not farther. The Lake is altogether about six miles wide, and they had as yet made little more than half the distance. Already it was ' the fourth watch of the night,' what might be termed the morning watch,[1] when the well-known Form seemed to be passing them, 'walking upon the sea.' There can, at least, be no question that such was the impression, not only of one or another, but that all saw Him. They tell us that they regarded His Form moving on the water as ' a spirit,' and cried out for fear ; and again, that the impression produced by the whole scene, even on them that had witnessed the miracle of the previous evening, was one of overwhelming astonishment. This walking on the water, then, was even to them within the domain of the truly miraculous, and it affected their minds equally, perhaps even more than ours, from the fact that in their view so much which to us seems miraculous lay within the sphere of what might be expected in the course of such a history.

As regards what may be termed the credibility of this miracle this may again be stated, that this and similar instances of ' dominion over the creature,' are not beyond the range of what God had originally assigned to man, when He made him a little lower than the angels, and crowned him with glory and honour, made him to have dominion over the works of His Hands, and all things were put under his feet.[a] Indeed, this ' dominion over the sea ' seems to exhibit the Divinely human rather than the humanly Divine aspect of Christ's Person, if such distinction may be lawfully made.

[a] Ps. viii. 5, 6 ; comp. Heb. ii. 6-9

This, however, deserves special notice : that there is one marked point of difference between the account of this miracle and what will be found a general characteristic in legendary narratives. In the latter the miraculous, however extraordinary, is the expected ; it creates no surprise and it is never mistaken for something that might have occurred in the ordinary course of events. For it is characteristic of the mythical that the miraculous is not only introduced in the most realistic manner, but forms the essential element in the conception of things. Now the opposite is the case in the present narrative. Had it been mythical or legendary, we should have expected that

[1] Probably from 3 to about 6 A.M.

the disciples would have been described as immediately recognising the Master as He walked on the sea, and worshipping Him. Instead of this, they 'are troubled' and 'afraid.' 'They supposed it was an apparition' (this in accordance with popular Jewish notions), and 'cried out for fear.' Even afterwards, when they had received Him into the ship, 'they were sore amazed in themselves,' and 'understood not,' while those in the ship (in contradistinction to the disciples) burst forth into an act of worship. This much then is evident, that the disciples expected not the miraculous; that they were unprepared for it; that they explained it on what to them seemed natural grounds; and that, even when convinced of its reality, the impression of wonder which it made was of the deepest.

But their fear, which made them almost hesitate to receive Him into the boat, even though the outcome of error and superstition, brought His ready sympathy and comfort, in language which has so often converted misapprehension into thankful assurance: 'It is I, be not afraid!'

And they were no longer afraid, though truly His walking upon the waters might seem more awesome than any 'apparition.' The storm in their hearts, like that on the Lake, was commanded by His Presence. We must still bear in mind their former excitement, now greatly intensified by what they had just witnessed, in order to understand the request of Peter: 'Lord, if it be Thou, bid me come to Thee on the water.' They are the words of a man whom the excitement of the moment has carried beyond all reflection. And yet, with reverence be it said, Christ could not have left the request ungranted, even though it was the outcome of yet unreconciled and untransformed doubt and presumption. And so He bade him come upon the water to transform his doubt, but left him to his own feelings unassured from without as he saw the wind, in order to transform his presumption; while by stretching out His Hand to save him from sinking, and by the words of correction which He spake, He did actually so point to their transformation in that hope, of which St. Peter is the special representative, and the preacher in the Church.

And presently, as they two came into the boat, the wind ceased, and immediately the ship was at the land. But ' they that were in the boat '—apparently in contradistinction to the disciples, though the latter must have stood around in sympathetic reverence—' worshipped Him, saying, Of a truth Thou art the Son of God.' The first full public confession this of the fact, and made not by the disciples, but by others. But in the disciples also the thought was striking deep root; and presently, by the Mount of Transfiguration, would it be spoken in the name of all by Peter, not as demon nor as man taught, but as taught of Christ's Father Who is in Heaven.

CHAPTER XL.

CONCERNING ' PURIFICATION,' ' HAND-WASHING,' AND ' VOWS.'

(St. Matt. xv. 1–20 ; St. Mark vii. 1–23.)

IT is quite in accordance with the abrupt departure of Jesus from Capernaum, and its motives, that when, far from finding rest and privacy at Bethsaida (east of the Jordan), a greater multitude than ever had there gathered around Him, which would fain have proclaimed Him King, He resolved on immediate return to the western shore, with the view of seeking a quieter retreat, even though it were in ' the coasts of Tyre and Sidon.' [a] From the fact that St. Mark [b] names Bethsaida, and St. John [c] Capernaum, as the original destination of the boat, we would infer that Bethsaida was the fishing quarter of, or rather close to, Capernaum, even as we so often find in our own country a ' Fisherton ' adjacent to larger towns.

[a] St. Matt. xv. 21
[b] St. Mark vi. 45
[c] St. John vi. 17

Christ had directed the disciples to steer thither. But we gather from the expressions used [d] that the boat which bore them had drifted out of its course—probably owing to the wind—and touched land, not where they had intended, but at Gennesaret, where they moored it early on the Friday morning. There can be no question

[d] St. Mark vi. 53

that by this term is meant 'the Plain of Gennesaret,' the richness and beauty of which Josephus and the Rabbis describe in such glowing language. To this day it bears marks of having been the most favoured spot in this favoured region.

As the tidings spread of His arrival and of the miracles which had so lately been witnessed, the people from the neighbouring villages and towns flocked around Him, and brought their sick for the healing touch. So passed the greater part of the forenoon. Meantime the report of all this must have reached the neighbouring Capernaum. This brought immediately on the scene those Pharisees and Scribes 'who had come from Jerusalem' on purpose to watch, and, if possible, to compass the destruction of Jesus. As we conceive it, they met the Lord and His disciples on their way to Capernaum.

Although the cavil of the Jerusalem Scribes may have been occasioned by seeing some of the disciples eating without first having washed their hands, we cannot banish the impression that it reflected on the miraculously provided meal of the previous evening, when thousands had sat down to food without the previous observance of the Rabbinic ordinance. Neither in that case, nor in the present, had the Master interposed. He was, therefore, guilty of participation in their offence. But, in another aspect, the objection of the Scribes was not a mere cavil.

It has already been shown that the Pharisees accounted for the miracles of Christ as wrought by the power of Satan, whose special representative—almost incarnation— they declared Jesus to be. This would not only turn the evidential force of these signs into an argument against Christt, but vindicate the resistance of the Pharisees to His claims. The second charge against Jesus was, that He was 'not of God;' that He was 'a sinner.'[a] If this could be established it would, of course, prove that He was not the Messiah, but a deceiver who misled the people, and whom it was the duty of the Sanhedrin to unmask and arrest. The way in which they attempted to establish this, perhaps persuaded themselves

a St. John ix. 16, 24

Q

that it was so, was by proving that He sanctioned in others, and Himself committed, breaches of the traditional law. The third and last charge against Jesus, which finally decided the action of the Council, could only be fully made at the close of His career. It might be formulated so as to meet the views of either the Pharisees or Sadducees. To the former it might be presented as a blasphemous claim to equality with God—the Very Son of the Living God. To the Sadducees it would appear as a movement on the part of a most dangerous enthusiast—if honest and self-deceived, all the more dangerous; one of those pseudo-Messiahs who led away the ignorant, superstitious, and excitable people; and which, if unchecked, would result in persecutions and terrible vengeance by the Romans, and in loss of the last remnants of their national independence. To each of these three charges, of which we are now watching the opening or development, there was (from the then standpoint) only one answer: faith in His Person. To this faith Jesus was now leading His disciples, till, fully realised in the great confession of Peter, it became, and has ever since proved, the Rock on which that Church is built, against which the very gates of Hades cannot prevail.

It was in support of the second of these charges that the Scribes now blamed the Master for allowing His disciples to eat without having previously washed, or, as St. Mark—indicating in the word the origin of the custom—expresses it: ' with common hands.' This practice is expressly admitted to have been, not a Law of Moses, but ' a tradition of the elders.' Still, it was so strictly enjoined that to neglect it was like being guilty of gross carnal defilement. Its omission would lead to temporal destruction, or, at least, to poverty. Bread eaten with unwashen hands was as if it had been filth. In fact, although at one time it had only been one of the marks of a Pharisee, yet at a later period to wash before eating was regarded as affording the ready means of recognising a Jew.

Let us try to realise the attitude of Christ in regard to the ordinances about purification, and seek to understand the reason of His bearing. That, in replying to the charge of the Scribes against His disciples, He neither vindicated their conduct, nor apologised for their breach of Rabbinic ordinances, implied at least an attitude of indifference towards traditionalism. This is the more noticeable, since, as we know, the ordinances of the Scribes were declared more precious and of more binding importance than those of Holy Scripture itself. But, even so, the question might arise, why Christ should have provoked such hostility by placing Himself in marked antagonism to what, after all, was in itself indifferent. The answer to this inquiry will require a disclosure of that aspect of Rabbinism which has hitherto been avoided.

It has elsewhere been told how Rabbinism, in the madness of its self-exaltation, represented God as busying Himself by day with the study of the Scriptures, and by night with that of the Mishnah ; and how, in the heavenly Sanhedrin, over which the Almighty presided, the Rabbis sat in the order of their greatness, and the Halakhah was discussed, and decisions taken in accordance with it. It is even more terrible to read of God wearing the *Tallith*, or that He puts on the Phylacteries, which is deduced from Is. lxii. ˙8. In like manner the Almighty is supposed to submit to purifications. Similarly He immersed in a bath of fire, after the defilement of the burial of Moses.

Such details will explain how Jesus could not have assumed merely an attitude of indifference towards traditionalism. His antagonism was never more pronounced that in what He said in reply to the charge of neglect of the ordinance about ' the washing of hands.' It was an admitted Rabbinic principle that, while the ordinances of Scripture required no confirmation, those of the Scribes needed such, and that no Halakhah (traditional law) might contradict Scripture. When Christ, therefore, next proceeded to show that in a very important point—nay, in ' many such like things '—the Halakhah was utterly incompatible with Scripture, that, indeed, they made ' void the Word of God ' by their traditions which they had

received,ᵃ He dealt the heaviest blow to traditionalism. Rabbinism stood self-condemned;
on its own showing it was to be rejected as incompatible with the Word of God.

It is not so easy to understand why the Lord should, out of 'many such things,' have selected in illustration the Rabbinic ordinance concerning vows, as in certain circumstances contravening the fifth commandment. Of course, the 'Ten Words' were the Holy of Holies of the Law; nor was there any obligation more rigidly observed than that of honour to parents. In both respects, then, this was a specially vulnerable point, and it might well be argued that if in this Law Rabbinic ordinances came into conflict with the demands of God's Word, the essential contrariety between them must, indeed, be great.

At the outset it must be admitted that Rabbinism did *not* encourage the practice of promiscuous vowing. The Jewish proverb had it: 'In the hour of need a vow; in time of ease excess.' Towards such work-righteousness and religious gambling the Eastern, and especially the Rabbinic Jew, would be particularly inclined. But even the Rabbis saw that its encouragement would lead to the profanation of what was holy. Of many sayings con-demnatory of the practice one will suffice to mark the general feeling: 'He who makes a vow, even if he keep it, deserves the name of wicked.' Nevertheless, the practice must have attained serious proportions, whether as regards the number of vows, the lightness with which they were made, or the kind of things which became their object. It was not necessary to use the express words of vowing. Not only the word ' *Qorban* ' [*Korban*]—' given to God '— but any similar expression would suffice; the mention of anything laid upon the altar (though not of the altar it-self), such as the wood or the fire, would constitute a vow, nay, the repetition of the form which generally followed on the votive *Qonam* or *Qorban* had binding force, even though not preceded by these terms.

It is in explaining this strange provision, intended both to uphold the solemnity of vows, and to discourage the rash use of words, that the Talmud makes use of the word ' *hand* ' in a connection which might, by association of ideas, have suggested to Christ the contrast between what the Bible and what the Rabbis regarded as ' sanctified hands,' and hence between the commands of God and the traditions of the Elders. For the Talmud explains that when a man simply says : ' That (or if) I eat or taste such a thing,' it is imputed as a vow, and he may not eat or taste of it, ' because the hand is on the Qorban '—the mere touch of Qorban had sanctified it and put it beyond his reach, just as if it had been laid on the altar itself. Here then was a contrast. According to the Rabbis, the touch of ' a common ' hand defiled God's good gift of meat, while the touch of ' a sanctified ' hand in rash or wicked words might render it impossible to give anything to a parent, and so involve the grossest breach of the Fifth Commandment! Such, according to Rabbinic Law, was the ' common ' and such the ' sanctifying ' touch of the hands. And did such traditionalism not truly ' make void the Word of God ' ?

A few further particulars may serve to set this in clearer light. It must not be thought that the pronunciation of the votive word ' *Qorban*,' although meaning ' a gift,' or ' given to God,' necessarily dedicated a thing to the Temple. The meaning might simply be, and generally was, that it was to be regarded like *Qorban*—that is, the thing termed was to be considered as if it were *Qorban*, laid on the altar, and put entirely out of their reach. For although included under the one name, there were really two kinds of vows : those of consecration to God, and those of personal obligation—and the latter were the most frequent.

The legal distinctions between a vow, an oath, and ' the ban,' are clearly marked both in reason and in Jewish Law. The oath was an absolute, the vow a conditional undertaking. The ' ban ' might refer to one of three things : those dedicated for the use of the priesthood, those dedicated to God, or else to a sentence pronounced by the Sanhedrin. Absolutions from a vow might be obtained before a ' sage,' or, in his absence, before three laymen, when all

obligations became null and void. At the same time the
Mishnah admits that this power of absolving from vows
received little (or, as *Maimonides* puts it, no) support from
Scripture.

There can be no doubt that the words of Christ referred
to such vows of personal obligation. By these a person
might bind himself in regard to men or things, or else put
that which was another's out of his own reach, or that which
was his own out of the reach of another, and this as completely
as if the thing or things had been *Qorban*, a gift given
to God. And so stringent was the ordinance that (almost
in the words of Christ) it is expressly stated that such a vow
was binding, even if what was vowed involved a breach of
the Law. Such vows in regard to parents were certainly
binding, and were actually made. Thus the charge brought
by Christ is in fullest accordance with the facts of the case.
More than this, the seemingly inappropriate addition to our
Lord's mention of the Fifth Commandment of the words:
' He that revileth father or mother, he shall (let him)
surely die,'[a] is not only explained but vindicated
by the common usage of the Rabbis, to mention
along with a command the penalty belonging to its breach,
so as to indicate the importance which Scripture attached
to it. On the other hand, the words of St. Mark: ' Qorban (that is to say, gift [viz. to God]) that by which
thou mightest be profited by me,' are a most exact tran-
scription into Greek of the common formula of vowing,
as given in the Mishnah and Talmud.

But Christ did not merely show the hypocrisy of the
system of traditionalism in conjoining in the name of religion the greatest outward punctiliousness with the grossest
breach of real duty. Never was prophecy more clearly vindicated than the words of Isaiah to Israel: ' This people
honoureth Me with their lips, but their heart is far from
Me. Howbeit, in vain do they worship Me, teaching
for doctrines the commandments of men.' In thus setting
forth for the first time the real character of traditionalism,
and placing Himself in open opposition to its fundamental
principles, the Christ enunciated also for the first time the

[a] Ex. xxi. 17

fundamental principle of His own interpretation of the Law. That Law was not a system of externalism, in which outward things affected the inner man. It was moral, and addressed itself to man as a moral being. Not from without inwards, but from within outwards : such was the principle of the new Kingdom, as setting forth the Law in its fulness and fulfilling it. 'There is nothing from without the man, that, entering into him, can defile him ; but the things which proceed out of the man, those are they that defile the man.' It is in this essential contrariety of principle, rather than in any details, that the unspeakable difference between Christ and all contemporary teachers appears.

As we read it, the discussion had taken place between the Scribes and the Lord, while the multitude perhaps stood aside. But when enunciating the grand principle of what constituted real defilement, ' He called to Him the multitude.' [a] It was probably while pursuing their way to Capernaum, when this conversation had taken place, that His disciples afterwards reported that the Pharisees had been offended by that saying of His to the multitude. Even this implies the weakness of the disciples : that they were not only influenced by the good or evil opinion of these religious leaders of the people, but in some measure sympathised with their views. The answer which the Lord gave bore a twofold aspect : that of warning concerning the inevitable fate of every plant which God had not planted, and that of warning concerning the character and issue of Pharisaic teaching, as being the leadership of the blind by the blind, which must end in ruin to both.

But even so the words of Christ are represented in the Gospel as sounding strange and difficult to the disciples. They were earnest, genuine men ; and when they reached the home in Capernaum, Peter, as the most courageous of them, broke the reserve—half of fear and half of reverence—which, despite their necessary familiarity, seems to have subsisted between the Master and His disciples. He would seek for himself and his fellow-disciples explanation of

[a] St. Matt. xv. 10 ; St. Mark vii. 14

what seemed to him parabolic in the Master's teaching.
He received it in the fullest manner. There was, indeed,
one part even in the teaching of the Lord, which accorded
with the higher views of the Rabbis. Those sins which
Christ set before them as sins of the outward and inward
man, and of what connects the two : our relation to others,
were the outcome of 'evil thoughts.' And this the Rabbis
taught, explaining with much detail how the heart was
alike the source of strength and of weakness, of good
and 'of evil thoughts, loved and hated, envied, lusted and
deceived, proving each statement from Scripture. But
never before could they have realised that anything entering from without could not defile a man. Least of all
could they perceive the final inference which St. Mark

ª St. Mark
vii. 19,
last clause long afterwards derived from this teaching of the
Lord : ' *This He said*, making all meats clean.' ª

CHAPTER XLI.

THE GREAT CRISIS IN POPULAR FEELING—CHRIST THE BREAD OF LIFE—'WILL YE ALSO GO AWAY?'

(St. John vi. 22-71.)

THE narrative now returns to those who, on the previous
evening, had after the miraculous meal been 'sent away'
to their homes. We remember that this had been after
an abortive attempt on their part to take Jesus by force
and make Him their Messiah-King. We can understand
how the resistance of Jesus to their purpose not only
weakened, but in great measure neutralised, the effect of
the miracle which they had witnessed. In fact, we look
upon this check as the first turning of the tide of popular
enthusiasm. Let us bear in mind what ideas and expectations of an altogether external character those men connected with the Messiah of their dreams. At last, by
some miracle more notable even than the giving of the
Manna in the wilderness, enthusiasm had been raised to
the highest pitch, and thousands were determined to give

up their pilgrimage to the Passover, and then and there proclaim the Galilean Teacher Israel's King. If He were the Messiah, such was His rightful title. Why then did He so strenuously and effectually resist it? In ignorance of His real views concerning the Kingship, they would naturally conclude that it must have been from fear, from misgiving, from want of belief in Himself. At any rate, He could not be the Messiah, Who would not be Israel's King. Enthusiasm of this kind, once repressed, could never again be kindled. Henceforth there were continuous misunderstanding, doubt, and defection among former adherents, growing into opposition and hatred unto death. Even to those who took not this position, Jesus, His Words and Works, were henceforth a constant mystery. And so it came that the morning after the miraculous meal found the vast majority of those who had been fed either in their homes or on their pilgrim-way to the Passover at Jerusalem. Only comparatively few came back to seek Him, where they had eaten bread at His Hand. And even they sought both 'a sign' to guide, and an explanation to give them its understanding.

It is this view of the mental and moral state of those who, on the morning after the meal, came to seek Jesus which alone explains the questions and answers of the interview at Capernaum. As we read it: 'the day following, the multitude which stood on the other [the eastern] side of the sea' 'saw that Jesus was not there, neither ᵃ St. John   His disciples.'ᵃ But of two facts they were vi. 22, 24   cognisant. They knew that on the evening before only one boat had come over, bringing Jesus and His disciples; and that Jesus had not returned in it with His disciples, for they had seen them depart, while Jesus remained to dismiss the people. In these circumstances they probably imagined that Christ had returned on foot by land, being, of course, ignorant of the miracle of that night. But the wind which had been contrary to the disciples had also driven over to the eastern shore a number of fishing-boats from Tiberias. These they now hired, and came to Capernaum, making inquiry for Jesus. It

is difficult to determine whether the conversation and outlined address of Christ took place on the Friday afternoon
and Sabbath morning, or only on the Sabbath.   All that
we know for certain is that the last part (at any
rate [a]) was spoken 'in Synagogue, as He taught
in Capernaum.' [b]

 a St. John
vi. 53–58
b ver. 59

We have to bear in mind that the Discourse in question was delivered in the city which had been the scene
of so many of Christ's great miracles, and the centre of
His teaching, and in the Synagogue built by the good
Centurion, and of which Jairus was the chief ruler. Again,
it was delivered after that miraculous feeding which had
raised the popular enthusiasm to the highest pitch, and
also after that chilling disappointment of their Judaistic
hopes in Christ's utmost resistance to His Messianic proclamation.   They now came ' seeking for Jesus,' in every
sense of the word.   They were outwardly prepared for the
very highest teaching, to which the preceding events had
led up, and therefore they must receive such, if any. But
they were not inwardly prepared for it, and therefore they
could not understand it. Secondly, and in connection
with it, we must remember that two high-points had been
reached—by the people, that Jesus was the Messiah-
King; by the ship's company, that He was the Son of
God. However imperfectly these truths may have been
apprehended, yet the teaching of Christ must start from
them, and then point onwards.

c vv. 25–29   1. The question: [c] 'Rabbi, when camest
Thou hither?' with which they from the eastern
shore greeted Jesus, seems to imply that they were perplexed about, and that some perhaps had heard a vague
rumour of the miracle of His return to the western shore.
It was the beginning of that unhealthy craving for the
miraculous which the Lord had so sharply to reprove. In
His own words: they sought Him not because they ' saw
signs,' but because they ' ate of the loaves,' and, in their
love for the miraculous, ' were filled.' What brought them
was not that they had discerned either the higher meaning of that miracle, or the Son of God, but those carnal

Judaistic expectancies which had led them to proclaim Him
King. What they waited for was a Kingdom of God—
not in righteousness, joy, and peace in the Holy Ghost,
but in meat and drink—a kingdom with miraculous wil-
derness-banquets to Israel, and coarse miraculous triumphs
over the Gentiles. Not to speak of the fabulous Messianic banquet which a sensuous realism expected, or of the
achievements for which it looked, every figure in which
prophets had clothed the brightness of those days was first
literalised, and then exaggerated, till the most glorious
poetic descriptions became incongruous caricatures of
spiritual Messianic expectancy. The fruit-trees were every
day, or at least every week or two, to yield their riches,
the fields their harvests; the grain was to stand like palm
trees, and to be reaped and winnowed without labour.
Similar blessings were to visit the vine; ordinary trees
would bear like fruit-trees, and every produce of every
clime would be found in Palestine in such abundance and
luxuriance as only the wildest imagination could conceive.

Such were the carnal thoughts about the Messiah and
His Kingdom of those who sought Jesus because they ' ate
of the loaves, and were filled.' What a contrast between
them and the Christ, as He pointed them from the search
for such meat to ' work for the meat which He would give
them,' not as a merely Jewish Messiah, but as ' the Son
of Man.' And yet in uttering this strange truth, Jesus
could appeal to something they would understand when He
added, ' for Him the Father hath sealed, even God.' The
words, which seem almost inexplicable in this connection,
become clear when we remember that this was a well-
known Jewish expression. According to the Rabbis, ' the
seal of God was *Truth*,' the three letters of which this
word is composed in Hebrew being, as was significantly
pointed out, respectively the first, the middle, and the last
letters of the alphabet. Thus the words of Christ would
convey to His hearers that for the real meat, which would
endure to eternal life—for the better Messianic banquet—
they must come to Him, because God had impressed upon

Him His own seal of truth, and so authenticated His Teaching and Mission.

ᵃ St. John vi. 30-36 2. Probably what now follows ᵃ took place at a somewhat different time—perhaps on the way to the Synagogue. Among the ruins of the Synagogue of Capernaum the lintel has been discovered : it bears the device of a pot of manna, ornamented with a flowing pattern of vine leaves and clusters of grapes. Here then were the outward emblems, which would connect themselves with the Lord's teaching on that day. The miraculous feeding of the multitude in the ' desert place ' the evening before, and the Messianic thoughts which gathered around it, would naturally suggest to their minds remembrance of the manna. That manna, which was angels' food, distilled (as they imagined) from the upper light, ' the dew from above '—miraculous food, of all manner of taste, and suited to every age, according to the wish or condition of him who ate it, but bitterness to Gentile palates—they expected the Messiah to bring again from heaven. For all that the first deliverer, Moses, had done, the second—Messiah—would also do. And here, over their Synagogue, was the pot of manna—symbol of what God had done, earnest of what the Messiah would do : that pot of manna, which was now among the things hidden, but which Elijah, when he came, would restore again.

In their view the events of yesterday must lead up to some such sign, if they had any real meaning. They had been told to believe on Him as the One authenticated by God with the seal of truth, and Who would give them meat to eternal life. By what sign would Christ corroborate His assertion that they might see and believe? What work would He do to vindicate His claim ? Their fathers had eaten manna in the wilderness. To understand the reasoning of the Jews, implied but not fully expressed, as also the answer of Jesus, it is necessary to bear in mind that it was the oft and most anciently expressed opinion that, although God had given them this bread out of heaven, yet it was given through the merits of Moses, and ceased with his death. This the Jews had probably

in view, when they asked : ' What workest Thou ? ' and
this was the meaning of Christ's emphatic assertion that
it was not Moses who gave Israel that bread. And then,
by what may be designated a peculiarly Jewish turn of
reasoning, such as only those familiar with Jewish literature can fully appreciate, the Saviour makes quite different,
yet to them familiar, application of the manna. Moses
had not given it—his merits had not procured it—but His
Father gave them the true bread out of heaven. ' For,'
as He explained, ' the bread of God is that which cometh
down from heaven, and giveth life unto the world.' Again,
this very Rabbinic tradition which described in such glowing language the wonders of that manna, also further explained its other and real meaning to be that if Wisdom
said ' Eat of my bread and drink of my wine,' [a]
it indicated that the manna and the miraculous
water-supply were the sequence of Israel's receiving the
Law and the Commandments—for the real bread from
heaven was the Law.

[a] Prov. ix. 5

It was a reference which the Jews understood, and to
which they could not but respond. Yet the mood was
brief. As Jesus, in answer to the appeal that He would
evermore give them this bread, once more directed them
to Himself—from works of men to the Works of God and
to faith—the passing gleam of spiritual hope had already
died out, for they had seen Him and ' yet did not believe.'

With these words Jesus turned away from His questioners. The solemn sayings which now followed [b]
could not have been spoken to, and they would
not have been understood by, the multitude. And accordingly we find that, when the conversation of the Jews is
once more introduced, [c] it takes up the thread
where it had been broken off, when Jesus spake
of Himself as the Bread Which had come down from
heaven.

[b] St. John vi. 37-40

[c] ver. 41

3. Regarding these words of Christ as addressed to the
disciples, there is nothing in them beyond their standpoint.
Believing that Jesus was the Messiah, it might not be
quite strange nor new to them as Jews—although not

commonly received—that He would at the end of the world raise the pious dead. Indeed, one of the names given to the Messiah has by some been derived from this very expectancy. Again, He had said that it was not any Law, but His Person that was the bread which came down from heaven and gave life, not to Jews only, but unto the world—and they had seen Him and believed not. But none the less would the purpose of God be accomplished in the totality of His true people, and its reality be experienced by every individual among them : ' All that [the total number] which the Father giveth Me shall come unto Me [shall reach Me], and him that cometh unto Me [the coming one to Me] I will not cast out outside.' The totality of the God-given must reach Him, despite all hindrances, for the object of His Coming was to do the Will of His Father ; and those who came would not be cast outside, for the Will of Him that had sent Him, and which He had come to do, was that of ' *the* all which He has given' Him, He ' should not lose *anything* out of this, but raise it up in the last day.' Again, it was the Will of Him that sent Him ' that everyone who intently looketh at the Son, and believeth on Him, should have eternal life ; ' and the coming ones would not be cast outside, since this was His undertaking and promise as the Christ in regard to each : ' And raise him up will I at the last day.' [a]

ᵃ St. John vi. 39, 40

4. What now follows [b] is again spoken to ' the Jews,' and may have occurred just as they were entering the Synagogue. To those spiritually unenlightened, the point of difficulty seemed how Christ could claim to be the Bread come down from heaven. His known parentage and early history forbade anything like a literal interpretation of His Words.

ᵇ vv. 41-51

Yet we mark that what Jesus now spake to ' the Jews ' was the same in substance as, though different in application from, what He had just uttered to the disciples. This, not merely in regard to the Messianic prediction of the Resurrection, but even in what He pronounced as the judgment on their murmuring. The words : ' No man can come to Me, except the Father Which hath sent Me draw him,' present only the converse aspect of those to the disciples: ' All that which the Father giveth Me shall come unto Me, and him that cometh unto Me I will in no wise cast out.' No man can come to the Christ—such is the condition of the human mind and heart that coming to Christ as a disciple is not an outward, but an inward, impossibility— except the Father ' draw him.' And this, again, not in the sense of any constraint, but in that of the personal moral influence and revelation, to which Christ afterwards refers when He saith : ' And I, if I be lifted up from the earth, will draw all men unto myself.' [a]

a St. John xii. 32

Nor did Jesus, while uttering these entirely un-Jewish truths, forget that He was speaking to Jews. The appeal to their own Prophets was the more telling, that Jewish tradition also applied these two prophecies (Is. liv. 13; Jer. xxxi. 34) to the teaching by God in the Messianic Age. But the explanation of the manner and issue of God's teaching was new : ' Everyone that hath heard from the Father, and learned, cometh unto Me.' And this, not by some external or realistic contact with God, such as they regarded that of Moses in the past, or expected for themselves in the latter days; only ' He Which is from God, He hath seen the Father.' But even this might sound general and without exclusive reference to Christ. So, also, might this statement seem : ' He that believeth hath eternal life.' Not so the final application, in which the subject was carried to its ultimate bearing, and all that might have seemed general or mysterious plainly set forth. The Personality of Christ *was* the Bread of Life : ' I am the Bread of Life.' [b] The Manna had not been bread of life, for those who ate it had died, their carcases had fallen in the wilderness. Not so in regard to this, the true Bread from heaven. To share in that Food was to have everlasting life, a life which the sin and death of unbelief and judgment would not cut short, as it had that of them who had eaten the Manna and died in the wilderness : ' the Bread that I will give is My Flesh, for the life of the world.'

b St. John vi. 48

5. These words, so significant to us, as pointing out the true meaning of all His teaching, must have sounded most mysterious. Yet the fact that they strove about their meaning shows that they must have had some glimmer of apprehension that they bore on His self-surrender, or, as they might view it, His martyrdom. This last point is set forth in the concluding Discourse,[a] which we know to have been delivered in the Synagogue, whether before, during, or after, His regular Sabbath address. It was not a mere martyrdom for the life of the world, in which all who benefited by it would share—but personal fellowship with Him. Eating the Flesh and drinking the Blood of the Son of Man, such was the necessary condition of securing eternal life. It is impossible to mistake the primary reference of these words to our personal application of His Death and Passion to the deepest need and hunger of our souls; most difficult, also, to resist the feeling that, secondarily, they referred to that Holy Feast which shows forth that Death and Passion, and is to all time its remembrance, symbol, seal, and fellowship.

> [a] St. John vi. 53–58

6. But to them that heard it, nay even to many of His disciples, this was an hard saying. It was a thorough disenchantment of all their Judaic illusions, an entire upturning of all their Messianic thoughts. The 'meat' and 'drink' from heaven which had the Divine seal of 'truth' were, according to Christ's teaching, not 'the Law,' nor yet Israel's privileges, but fellowship with the Person of Jesus in that state of humbleness ('the son of Joseph'[b]), nay, of martyrdom, which His words seemed to indicate, 'My Flesh is the true meat, and My Blood is the true drink;'[c] and what even this fellowship secured consisted only in abiding in Him and He in them;[d] or, as they would understand it, in inner communion with Him, and in sharing His condition and views.

> [b] ver. 42
> [c] ver. 55
> [d] ver. 56

Though they spake it not, this was the rock of offence over which they stumbled and fell. And Jesus read their thoughts. If they stumbled at this, what when they came to contemplate the far more mysterious and un-Jewish

ᵃ St. John vi. facts of the Messiah's Crucifixion and Ascension!ᵃ
62   Truly, not outward following, but only inward
and spiritual life-quickening could be of profit—even in
the case of those who heard the very Words of Christ,
which were spirit and life. Thus it again appeared, and
most fully, that, morally speaking, it was absolutely im-
ᵇ ver. 65 ;   possible to come to Him, even if His Words
comp. vv.   were heard, except under the gracious influence
37, 44   from above.ᵇ

And so this was the great crisis in the History of the
Christ. We have traced the gradual growth and development of the popular movement, till the murder of the
Baptist stirred popular feeling to its inmost depth. With
his death it seemed as if the Messianic hope, awakened by
his preaching and testimony to Christ, were fading from
view. It was a terrible disappointment, not easily borne.
Now must it be decided whether Jesus were really the
Messiah. His Works, notwithstanding what the Pharisees
said, seemed to prove it. That miraculous feeding, that
wilderness-cry of Hosanna to the Galilean King-Messiah
from thousands of Galilean voices—what were they but its
beginning? All the greater was the disappointment : first,
in the repression of the movement—so to speak, the retreat
of the Messiah, His voluntary abdication, rather, His
defeat ; then, next day, the incongruousness of a King,
Whose few unlearned followers, in their ignorance and un-
Jewish neglect of most sacred ordinances, outraged every
Jewish feeling, and whose conduct was even vindicated by
their Master in a general attack on all traditionalism, that
basis of Judaism—as it might be represented, to the contempt of religion and even of common truthfulness in the
denunciation of solemn vows ! This was not the Messiah
ᶜ St. Matt.   Whom the many—nay, Whom almost any—
xv. 12   would own.ᶜ

Here, then, we are at the parting of the two ways ;
and, just because it was the hour of decision, did Christ so
clearly set forth the highest truths concerning Himself, in
opposition to the views which the multitude entertained
about the Messiah. The result was yet another and a sorer

R

defection. 'Upon this many of His disciples went back,
ᵃ St. John
vi. 66 and walked no more with Him.'ᵃ Nay, the
searching trial reached even unto the hearts of
the Twelve. But one thing kept them true. It was the
experience of the past. This was the basis of their present
faith and allegiance. They could not go back to their old
past; they must cleave to Him. So Peter spake it in
name of them all: ' Lord, to whom shall we go? Words
of Eternal Life hast Thou!' Nay, and more than this,
as the result of what they had learned: 'And we have
ᵇ vv. 68, 69 believed and know that Thou art the Holy One
of God.'ᵇ

But of these Twelve Christ knew one to be ' a devil'—
like that Angel, fallen from highest height to lowest depth.
The apostasy of Judas had already commenced in his heart.
And the greater the popular expectancy and disappointment had been, the greater the reaction and the enmity
that followed.

CHAPTER XLII.

JESUS AND THE SYRO-PHŒNICIAN WOMAN.

(St. Matt. xv. 21–28; St. Mark vii. 24–30.)

THE purpose of Christ to withdraw His disciples from the
excitement of Galilee, and from what might follow the
execution of the Baptist, had been interrupted by the
events at Bethsaida-Julias, but it was not changed.

A comparatively short journey would bring Jesus and
His companions from Capernaum 'into the parts,' or, as
St. Mark more specifically calls them, ' the borders of Tyre
and Sidon.' At that time this district extended, north of
Galilee, from the Mediterranean to the Jordan. But the
event about to be related occurred, as all circumstances
show, not within the territory of Tyre and Sidon, but on
its borders, and within the limits of the Land of Israel.

The whole circumstances seem to point to more than a
night's rest in that distant home. Possibly, the two first

Passover-days may have been spent here. According to
St. Mark, Jesus 'would have no man know' His Presence
in that place, 'but He could not be hid,' and the fame of
His Presence spreading into the neighbouring district of
Tyre and Sidon reached the mother of the demonised child.
All this implies a stay of two or three days. And with
this also agrees the after-complaint of the disciples: 'Send
her away, for she crieth after us.' [a] As the
Saviour apparently received the woman in the
house,[b] it seems that she must have followed
some of the disciples into Galilee, entreating their help or
intercession in a manner that attracted the attention which,
according to the will of Jesus, they would fain have avoided,
before, in her despair, she ventured into the presence of
Christ within the house.

 She who now sought His help was, as St. Matthew
calls her, from the Jewish standpoint, 'a Ca-
naanitish [c] woman,' by which term a Jew would
designate a native of Phœnicia, or, as St. Mark calls her,
a Syro-Phœnician (to distinguish her country from Lybo-
Phœnicia), and 'a Greek'—that is, a heathen. But we
can understand how she would, on hearing of the Christ
and His mighty deeds, seek His help for her child with the
most intense earnestness, and that, in so doing, she would
approach Him with lowliest reverence, falling
at His Feet. [d] But what, in our view, furnishes
the explanation of the Lord's bearing towards this woman
is her mode of addressing Him : 'O Lord, Thou Son of
David!' This was the most distinctively Jewish appellation
of the Messiah ; and yet it is emphatically stated of her
that she was a heathen.

 Spoken by a heathen, these words were, if used without knowledge, an address to a Jewish Messiah, Whose
works were only miracles, and not also and primarily signs.
Now this was exactly the error of the Jews which Jesus
had encountered and combated, alike when He resisted the
attempt to make Him King, in His reply to the Jerusalem Scribes, and in His Discourses at Capernaum. To
have granted her the help she so entreated would have been,

Marginal notes:
[a] St. Matt. xv. 23
[b] St. Mark vii. 24, 25
[c] Ezra ix. 1
[d] St. Mark vii. 25

R 2

as it were, to reverse the whole of His Teaching, and to make His works of healing merely works of power. In her mouth, the designation meant something to which Christ could not have yielded. And yet He could not refuse her petition. And so He first taught her, in such manner as she could understand, that which she needed to know— the relation of the heathen to the Jewish world, and of both to the Messiah, and then He gave her what she asked.

She had spoken, but Jesus had answered her not a word. When the disciples—in some measure, probably, still sharing the views of this heathen, that He was the Jewish Messiah—without, indeed, interceding for her, asked that she might be sent away, because she was troublesome to them, He replied that His Mission was only to the lost sheep of the house of Israel. This was true, as regarded His Work while upon earth ; and true, in every sense, as we keep in view the world-wide bearing of the Davidic reign and promises, and the real relation between Israel and the world. Thus baffled, as it might seem, she cried no longer 'Son of David,' but 'Lord, help me.' It was then that the special teaching came in the manner she could understand. If it were as 'the Son of David' that He was entreated—if the heathen woman as such applied to the Jewish Messiah as such, what, in the Jewish view, were the heathens but 'dogs,' and what would be fellowship with them but to cast to the dogs—house-dogs, it may be—what should have been the children's bread? And, certainly, no expression more common in the mouth of the Jews than that which designated the heathens as dogs. Most harsh as it was, as the outcome of national pride and Jewish self-assertion, yet in a sense it was true, that those *within* were the children, and those 'without' 'dogs.'[a]

* Rev. xxii. 15

Two lessons did she learn with that instinct-like rapidity which Christ's personal Presence seemed ever and again to call forth. 'Yea, Lord,' it is as Thou sayest: heathenism stands related to Judaism as the house-dogs to the children, and it were not meet to rob the children of their bread in order to give it to dogs. But Thine own words show that such would not now be the case. If they are house-dogs, then they are the Master's and under His table, and when He breaks the bread to the children, in the breaking of it the crumbs must fall around.

But in so saying she was no longer 'under the table,' but had sat down at the table with Abraham, Isaac, and Jacob, and was partaker of the children's bread. He was no longer to her the Jewish Messiah, but truly 'the Son of David.' She now understood what she prayed, and she *was* a daughter of Abraham. And that which had taught her all this was faith in His Person and Work, as not only just enough for the Jews, but enough and to spare for all—children at the table and dogs under it; that in and with Abraham, Isaac, Jacob, and David, all nations were blessed in Israel's King and Messiah. And so it was that the Lord said it: 'O woman, great is thy faith: be it done unto thee even as thou wilt.' Or, as St. Mark puts it, not quoting the very sound of the Lord's words, but their impression upon Peter: 'For this saying go thy way; the devil is gone out of thy daughter.' 'And her daughter was healed from that hour.'[a] 'And she went away unto her house, and found her daughter prostrate [indeed] upon the bed, and [but] the demon gone out.'

[a] St. Matt. xv. 28

CHAPTER XLIII.

A GROUP OF MIRACLES AMONG A SEMI-HEATHEN POPULATION.

(St. Matt. xv. 29-31; St. Mark vii. 31-37; viii. 22-26;
St. Matt. xi. 27-31.)

IF even the brief stay of Jesus in that friendly Jewish home by the borders of Tyre could not remain unknown, the fame of the healing of the Syro-Phœnician maiden would soon have rendered impossible that privacy and retirement, which had been the chief object of His leaving Capernaum. Accordingly, when the two Paschal days were ended, He resumed His journey, extending it far beyond any previously undertaken. The borders of

Palestine proper, though not of what the Rabbis reckoned as belonging to it, [1] were passed. Making a long circuit through the territory of Sidon, He descended—probably through one of the passes of the Hermon range—into the country of the Tetrarch Philip. Thence He continued 'through the midst of the borders of Decapolis,' till He once more reached the eastern, or south-eastern, shore of the Lake of Galilee. It will be remembered that the Decapolis, or confederacy of 'the Ten Cities,' was wedged in between the Tetrarchies of Philip and Antipas. Their political constitution was that of the free Greek cities. They were subject only to the Governor of Syria, and formed part of Cœle-Syria, in contradistinction to Syro-Phœnicia.

It is important to keep in view that, although Jesus was now within the territory of ancient Israel, the district and all the surroundings were essentially heathen, although in closest proximity to that which was purely Jewish. St.
[a] St. Matt. xv. 29-31 Matthew [a] gives a general description of Christ's activity there.

They have heard of Him as the wonder-worker, these heathens in the land so near to, and yet so far from, Israel; and they have brought to Him 'the lame, blind, dumb, maimed, and many others,' and laid them at His Feet. All disease vanishes in presence of Heaven's Own Life Incarnate. It is a new era—Israel conquers the heathen world, not by force, but by love; not by outward means, but by the manifestation of life-power from above. Truly, this is the Messianic conquest and reign: 'and they glorified the God of Israel.'

One special instance of miraculous healing is recorded by St. Mark, not only from its intrinsic interest, but, perhaps, also, as in some respects typical.

1. Among those brought to Him was one deaf, whose speech had, probably in consequence of this, been so affected as practically to deprive him of its power. This circumstance, and that he is not spoken of as so afflicted from his

---

[1] For the Rabbinic views of the boundaries of Palestine see 'Sketches of Jewish Social Life,' ch. ii.

birth, leads us to infer that the affection was the result of disease, and not congenital. Remembering that alike the subject of the miracle and they who brought him were heathens, but in constant and close contact with Jews, what follows is vividly true to life. The entreaty to 'lay His Hand upon him' was heathen, and yet semi-Jewish also. Quite peculiar it is, when the Lord took him aside from the multitude; and again that, using a means of healing accepted in popular opinion of Jew and Gentile, 'He spat,' applying it directly to the diseased organ. We read of the direct application of saliva only here and in the healing of the blind man at Bethsaida.[a] We are disposed to regard this as peculiar to the healing of Gentiles. Peculiar, also, is the term expressive of burden on the mind, when, 'looking up to heaven, He sighed.' Peculiar, also, is the 'thrusting' of His Fingers into the man's ears, and the touch of his tongue. Only the upward look to heaven, and the command 'Ephphatha' —'be opened'—seem the same as in His everyday wonders of healing. But we mark that all here seems more elaborate than in Israel. The reason of this must, of course, be sought in the moral condition of the person healed. There is an accumulation of means, yet each and all inadequate to effect the purpose, but all connected with His Person. This elaborate use of such means would banish the idea of magic; it would arouse the attention, and fix it upon Christ as using these means, which were all connected with His own Person.

a St. Mark viii. 23

It was in vain to enjoin silence. Wider and wider spread the unbidden fame, till it was caught up in this hymn of praise: 'He hath done all things well—He maketh even the deaf to hear, and the dumb to speak.'

b St. Mark viii. 22-26

2. Another miracle is recorded by St. Mark,[b] as wrought by Jesus in these parts, and, as we infer, on a heathen. All the circumstances are kindred to those just related. It was in Bethsaida-Julias that one blind was brought unto Him, with the entreaty that He would touch him,—just as in the case of the deaf and dumb. Here, also, the Saviour took him aside—'led him

out of the village '—and 'spat on his eyes, and put His Hands upon him.' We mark not only the similarity of the means employed, but the same, and even greater elaborateness in the use of them, since a twofold touch is recorded before the man saw clearly. So far as we can judge, the object was, by a gradual process of healing, to disabuse the man of any idea of magical cure, while at the same time the process of healing again markedly centred in the Person of Jesus. With this also agrees (as in the case of the deaf and dumb) the use of spittle in the healing. We may here recall that the use of saliva was a well-known Jewish remedy for affections of the eyes.

3. Yet a third miracle of healing requires to be here considered, although related by St. Matthew in another connection.[a] But we have learned enough of the structure of the first Gospel to know that its arrangement is determined by the plan of the writer rather than by the chronological succession of events. The manner in which the Lord healed the two blind men, the injunction of silence, and the notice that none the less they spread His fame in *all that land*, seem to imply that He was not on the ordinary scene of His labours in Galilee. Nor can we fail to mark an internal analogy between this and the other two miracles enacted amidst a chiefly Grecian population. And, strange though it may sound, the cry with which the two blind men who sought His help followed Him, 'Son of David, have mercy on us,' comes more frequently from Gentile than from Jewish lips. It was, of course, pre-eminently the Jewish designation of the Messiah, the basis of all Jewish thought of Him. But we can understand how to Gentiles who resided in Palestine the Messiah of Israel would chiefly stand out as 'the Son of David.' It was the most ready, and, at the same time, the most universal, form in which the great Jewish hope could be viewed by them.

Peculiar to this history is the testing question of Christ, whether they really believed what their petition implied, that He was able to restore their sight; and, again, His stern, almost passionate, insistence on their

a St. Matt. ix. 27-31

silence as to the mode of their cure. Only on one other occasion do we read of the same insistence. It is, when the leper had expressed the same absolute faith in Christ's ability to heal if He willed it, and Jesus had, as in the case of these two blind men, conferred the benefit by the ^a St. Mark i. touch of His Hand.^a In both these cases, it is 40, 41 remarkable that, along with strongest faith of those who came to Him, there was rather an implied than an expressed petition on their part. The leper who knelt before Him only said: 'Lord, if Thou wilt, Thou canst make me clean ;' and the two blind men : ' Have mercy on us, Thou Son of David.' Thus it is the highest and most realising faith which is most absolute in its trust, and most reticent as regards the details of its request.

CHAPTER XLIV.

THE TWO SABBATH-CONTROVERSIES—THE PLUCKING OF THE
EARS OF CORN BY THE DISCIPLES, AND THE HEALING
OF THE MAN WITH THE WITHERED HAND.

(St. Matt. xii. 1–21 ; St. Mark ii. 23–iii. 6 ; St. Luke vi. 1–11.)

IN grouping together the three miracles of healing described in the last chapter, we do not wish to convey that it is certain they had taken place in precisely that order. From their position in the Evangelic narratives we inferred that they happened at that particular period and east of the Jordan. They differ from the events about to be related by the absence of the Jerusalem Scribes, who hung on the footsteps of Jesus. While the Saviour tarried on the borders of Tyre, and thence passed through the territory of Sidon into the Decapolis and to the southern and eastern shores of the Lake of Galilee, they were in Jerusalem at the Passover. But after the two festive days, which would require their attendance in the Temple, they seem to have returned. And the events about to be related are chronologically distinguished from those that had preceded by this presence and opposition of the Pharisaic party. The contest now becomes more decided and sharp, and we are rapidly nearing the period when He, Who had hitherto been chiefly preaching the Kingdom, and healing body and soul, will, through the hostility of the leaders of Israel, enter on the second, or prevailingly negative stage of His Work.

Where fundamental principles were so directly contrary, the occasion for conflict could not be long wanting. Indeed, all that Jesus taught must have seemed to these Pharisees strangely un-Jewish in cast and direction, even if not in form and words. But chiefly would this be the case in regard to that on which, of all else, the Pharisees laid most stress: the observance of the Sabbath. On no other subject is Rabbinic teaching more minute and more manifestly incongruous to its professed object. For, if we rightly apprehend what underlay the complicated and intolerably burdensome laws and rules of the Pharisaic Sabbath-observance, it was to secure, negatively, absolute rest from all labour, and, positively, to make the Sabbath a delight. The Mishnah includes Sabbath-desecration among those most heinous crimes for which a man was to be stoned. This, then, was their first care: by a series of complicated ordinances to make a breach of the Sabbath-rest impossible. The next object was, in a similarly external manner, to make the Sabbath a delight. A special Sabbath dress, the best that could be procured; the choicest food, even though a man had to work for it all the week, or public charity were to supply it—such were some of the means by which the day was to be honoured and men were to find pleasure therein. The strangest stories are told, how, by the purchase of the most expensive dishes, the pious poor had gained unspeakable merit, and obtained, even on earth, Heaven's manifest reward. And yet, by the side of these and similar misdirections of piety, we come also upon that which is touching, beautiful, and even spiritual. On the Sabbath there must be no mourning, for to the Sabbath

^a In Prov. x. 22 applies this saying: ^a 'The blessing of the Lord, it maketh rich, and He addeth no sorrow with it.'

Quite alone was the Sabbath among the measures of time. Every other day had been paired with its fellow : not so the Sabbath. And so any festival, even the Day of Atonement, might be transferred to another day : not so the observance of the Sabbath. Nay, when the Sabbath complained before God that of all days it alone stood solitary, God had wedded it to Israel ; and this holy union God had bidden His people ' remember,' [a] when they stood before the Mount. Even the tortures of Gehenna were intermitted on that holy, happy day.

a Ex. xx. 8

Jewish Law sufficiently explains the controversies in which the Pharisaic party now engaged with Jesus. Of these the first was when, going through the cornfields on the Sabbath, His disciples began to pluck and eat the ears of corn.

This first Sabbath-controversy is immediately followed by that connected with the healing of the man with the withered hand. From St. Matthew and St. Mark it might appear as if this had occurred on the same day as the plucking of the ears of corn, but St. Luke corrects any possible misunderstanding by telling us that it happened ' on another Sabbath '—perhaps that following the walk through the cornfields.

It was probably on the Sabbath after the Second Paschal Day that, as Christ and His disciples passed through cornfields, His disciples, being hungry,[b] as they went,[c] plucked ears of corn and ate them, having rubbed off the husks in their hands.[d] On any ordinary day this would have been lawful,[e] but on the Sabbath it involved, according to Rabbinic statutes, at least two sins. For, according to the Talmud, what was really one labour, would, if made up of several acts, each of them forbidden, amount to several acts of labour, each involving sin, punishment, and a sin-offering. Now in this case there were at least two such acts involved : that of plucking the ears of corn, ranged under the sin of reaping, and that of rubbing them, which might be ranged under sifting in a sieve, threshing, sifting out fruit, grinding, or fanning.

b St. Matthew
c St. Mark
d St. Luke
e Deut. xxiii.

Holding views like these, the Pharisees, who witnessed the conduct of the disciples would naturally condemn what they must have regarded as gross desecration of the Sabbath. Yet it was clearly not a breach of the Biblical, but of the Rabbinic Law. Not only to show them their error, but to lay down principles which would for ever apply to this difficult question, was the object of Christ's reply. Unlike the others of the Ten Commandments, the Sabbath Law has in it two elements : the moral and the ceremonial; the eternal, and that which is subject to time and place; the inward and spiritual, and the outward (the one as the mode of realising the other). In their distinction and separation lies the difficulty of the subject. In its spiritual and eternal element, the Sabbath Law embodied the two thoughts of rest for worship, and worship which pointed to rest. The keeping of the seventh day, and the Jewish mode of its observance, were the temporal and outward form in which these eternal principles were presented. Even Rabbinism, in some measure, perceived this. It was a principle that danger to the life of an Israelite, but not of a heathen or Samaritan, superseded the Sabbath Law, and, indeed, all other obligations. It was argued that a man was to keep the commandments that he might live—certainly not, that by so doing he might die. Yet this other and kindred principle did Rabbinism lay down, that every positive commandment superseded the Sabbath-rest. This was the ultimate vindication of work in the Temple, although certainly not its explanation. Lastly, we should, in this connection, include this important canon, laid down by the Rabbis: 'a single Rabbinic prohibition is not to be heeded, where a graver matter is in question.'

These points must be kept in view for the proper understanding of the words of Christ to the Scribes. For, while going far beyond the times and notions of His questioners, His reasoning must have been within their comprehension. Hence the first argument of our Lord, as recorded by all the Synoptists, was taken from Biblical history. When, on his flight from Saul, David had, 'when an hungered,' eaten of the shewbread, and given it to his followers, although, by the letter of the Levitical Law,[a] it was only to be eaten by the priests, Jewish tradition vindicated his conduct on the plea that 'danger to life superseded the Sabbath-Law,' and hence all laws connected with it ; while, to show David's zeal for the Sabbath-Law, the legend was added that he had reproved the priests of Nob, who had been baking the shewbread on the Sabbath. To the first argument of Christ St. Matthew adds this as His second, that the priests, in their services in the Temple, necessarily broke the Sabbath-Law without thereby incurring guilt.

a Lev. xxiv. 5-9.

In truth, the Sabbath-Law was not one merely of rest, but of rest for worship. The Service of the Lord was the object in view. The priests worked on the Sabbath, because this service was the object of the Sabbath ; and David was allowed to eat of the shewbread, not because there was danger to life from starvation, but because he pleaded that he was on the service of the Lord, and needed this provision.

To this St. Mark adds as a corollary : ' The Sabbath was made for man, and not man for the Sabbath.' It is remarkable that a similar argument is used by the Rabbis. When insisting that the Sabbath-Law should be set aside to avoid danger to life, it is urged : ' the Sabbath is handed over to you; not, ye are handed over to the Sabbath.' Lastly, the three Evangelists record this as the final outcome of His teaching on this subject, that ' The Son of Man is Lord of the Sabbath also.' The Service of God, and the Service of the Temple, by universal consent, superseded the Sabbath-Law. But Christ was greater than the Temple, and His Service more truly that of God, and higher than that of the outward Temple—and the Sabbath was intended for man, to serve God : therefore Christ and His Service were superior to the Sabbath-Law. Thus much would be intelligible to these Pharisees, although they would not receive it, because they believed not on Him as the Sent of God.

But to us the words mean more than this. We are

free while we are doing anything for Christ; God loves
mercy, and demands not sacrifice; His sacrifice is the
service of Christ, in heart, and life, and work. We are
not free to do anything we please; but we are free to do
anything needful or helpful, while we are doing any service to Christ. He is the Lord of the Sabbath, Whom we
serve in and through the Sabbath.

The question as between Christ and the Pharisees was
not, however, to end here. 'On another Sabbath'—probably that following — He was in their Synagogue.
Whether or not the Pharisees had brought 'the man with
the withered hand' on purpose, or otherwise raised the
question, certain it is that their secret object was to commit Christ to some word or deed, which would lay Him
open to the capital charge of breaking the Sabbath-Law.
It does not appear whether the man with the withered
hand was consciously or unconsciously their tool. But in
this they judged rightly: that Christ would not witness
disease without removing it—or, as we might express it,
that disease could not continue in the Presence of Him
Who was the Life. He read their inward thoughts of evil,
and yet He proceeded to do the good which He purposed.

So much unclearness prevails as to the Jewish views
about healing on the Sabbath that some connected information on the subject seems needful. We have already
seen that in their view only actual danger to life warranted
a breach of the Sabbath-Law. But this opened a large
field for discussion. Thus, according to some, disease of
the ear, according to some throat-disease, while, according
to others, such a disease as angina, involved danger, and
superseded the Sabbath-Law. All applications to the outside of the body were forbidden on the Sabbath. As
regarded internal remedies, such substances as were used
in health, but had also a remedial effect, might be taken,
although here also there was a way of evading the Law.
A person suffering from toothache might not gargle his
mouth with vinegar, but he might use an ordinary tooth-
brush and dip it in vinegar. Medical aid might be called
in if a person had swallowed a piece of glass; a splinter

might be removed from the eye, and even a thorn from the body.

But although the man with the withered hand could not be classed with those dangerously ill, it could not have been difficult to silence the Rabbis on their own admissions. Clearly, their principle implied that it was lawful on the Sabbath to do that which would save life or prevent death. But if so, did it not also, in strictly logical sequence, imply this far wider principle, that it must be lawful to do good on the Sabbath? There was no answer to such an argument; St. Mark expressly records that they dared not attempt a reply.[a] On the other hand, St. Matthew, while alluding to this challenge,[b] records yet another and a personal argument. It seems that Christ publicly appealed to them: If any poor man among them, who had one sheep, were in danger of losing it through it having fallen into a pit, would he not lift it out? To be sure, the Rabbinic Law ordered that food and drink should be lowered to it, or else that some means should be furnished by which it might either be kept up in the pit, or enabled to come out of it. And was not the life of a human being to be more accounted of?

a St. Mark iii. 4
b St. Matt. xii. 12

We can now imagine the scene in that Synagogue. The place is crowded. Christ probably occupies a prominent position as leading the prayers or teaching: a position whence He can see, and be seen by all. Here, eagerly bending forward, are the dark faces of the Pharisees, expressive of curiosity, malice, cunning. They are looking round at a man whose right hand is withered,[c] perhaps putting him forward, drawing attention to him, loudly whispering, 'Is it lawful to heal on the Sabbath-day?' The Lord takes up the challenge. He bids the man stand forth—right in the midst of them, where they might all see and hear. By one of those telling appeals, which go straight to the conscience, He puts the analogous case of a poor man who was in danger of losing his only sheep on the Sabbath: would he not rescue it; and was not a man better than a sheep? Nay, did they not themselves enjoin a breach of the Sabbath-Law to save

c St. Luke vi. 6

human life ? Then must He not do so; might He not do good rather than evil ?

They were speechless. But a strange mixture of feeling was in the Saviour's heart: 'And when He had looked round about on them with anger, being grieved at the hardening of their heart.' It was but for a moment, and then He bade the man stretch forth his hand. Withered it was no longer, when the Word had been spoken. A fresh life had streamed into it, as, following the Saviour's Eye and Word, he slowly stretched it forth. And as he stretched it forth, his hand was restored. The Saviour had broken their Sabbath-Law, and yet He had not broken it, for neither by remedy, nor touch, nor outward application had He healed him. He had broken the Sabbath-rest, as God breaks it, when He sends, or sustains, or restores life, or does good.

They had all seen it, this miracle of almost new creation. As they saw it, ' they were filled with madness.' [a] They could not gainsay, but they went forth and took counsel with the Herodians against Him, how they might destroy Him. Presumably, then, He was within, or quite close by, the dominions of Herod, east of the Jordan. And the Lord withdrew once more, as it seems to us, into Gentile territory, probably that of the Decapolis. For, as He went about healing all that needed it in that great multitude that followed His steps, yet enjoining silence on them, this prophecy of Isaiah blazed into fulfilment: ' Behold My Servant, Whom I have chosen, My Beloved, in Whom My soul is well-pleased; I will put My Spirit upon Him, and He shall declare judgment to the Gentiles. He shall not strive nor cry aloud, neither shall any hear His Voice in the streets. A bruised reed shall He not break, and smoking flax shall He not quench, till He send forth judgment unto victory. And in His Name shall the Gentiles trust.'

[a] St. Luke vi. 11

CHAPTER XLV.

THE FEEDING OF THE FOUR THOUSAND—'THE SIGN FROM HEAVEN'

(St. Matt. xv. 32–xvi. 12; St. Mark viii. 1–21.)

IT is remarkable that each time Christ's prolonged stay and Ministry in a district were brought to a close with some supper, so to speak, some festive entertainment on His part. The Galilean Ministry had closed with the feeding of the five thousand, the guests being mostly from Capernaum and the towns around, as far as Bethsaida (Julias), many in the number probably on their way to the Paschal Feast at Jerusalem. But now at the second provision for the four thousand, with which His Decapolis Ministry closed, the guests were not strictly Jews, but semi-Gentile inhabitants of that district and its neighbourhood. Lastly, His Judæan Ministry closed with the Last Supper. At the first 'Supper,' the Jewish guests would fain have proclaimed Him Messiah-King; at the second, as 'the Son of Man,' He gave food to those Gentile multitudes which, having been with Him those days, and consumed all their victuals during their stay with Him, He could not send away fasting, lest they should faint by the way. And on the last occasion, as the true Priest and Sacrifice, He fed His own with the true Paschal Feast ere He sent them forth alone into the wilderness. Thus these three 'Suppers' seem connected, each leading up, as it were, to the other.

There can be little doubt that this second feeding of the multitude took place in the Gentile Decapolis, and that those who sat down to the meal were chiefly the inhabitants of that district. If it be lawful, departing from strict history, to study the symbolism of this event, as compared with the previous feeding of the five thousand who were Jews, somewhat singular differences will present themselves

S

to the mind. On the former occasion there were five thousand fed with five loaves, when twelve baskets of fragments were left. On the second occasion, four thousand were fed from seven loaves, and seven baskets of fragments collected. It is at least curious that the number *five* in the provision for the Jews is that of the Pentateuch, just as the number *twelve* corresponds to that of the tribes and of the Apostles. On the other hand, in the feeding of the Gentiles we mark the number *four*, which is the signature of the world, and *seven*, which is that of the Sanctuary.

On all general points the narratives of the twofold miraculous feeding run so parallel that it is not necessary again to consider this event in detail. But the attendant circumstances are quite unlike. There are broad lines of difference as to the number of persons, the provision, and the quantity of fragments left. On the former occasion the repast was provided in the evening for those who had gone after Christ, and listened to Him all day; who had been so busy for the Bread of Life that they had forgotten that of earth. But on this second occasion, of the feeding of the Gentiles, the multitude had been three days with Him, and what sustenance they had brought must have failed, when, in His compassion, the Saviour would not send them to their homes fasting, lest they should faint by the way. And it must be kept in view that Christ dismissed them, not, as before, because they would have made Him their King. Yet another marked difference lies even in the designation of ʻ the baskets ʼ in which the fragments left were gathered. At the first feeding they were, as the Greek word shows, the small wicker-baskets which each of the Twelve would carry in his hand. At the second feeding they were the large baskets, in which provisions, chiefly bread, were stored or carried for longer voyages. For on the first occasion, when they passed into Israelitish territory—and, as they might think, left their home for a very brief time—there was not the same need to make provision for storing necessaries as on the second, when they were on a lengthened journey, and passing through or tarrying in Gentile territory.

But the most noteworthy difference seems to us this: that on the first occasion they who were fed were Jews; on the second, Gentiles. There is a little trait in the narrative which affords striking, though undesigned, evidence of this. In referring to the blessing which Jesus spake over the first meal, it was noted that, in strict accordance with Jewish custom, He only rendered thanks once over the bread. But no such custom would rule His conduct when dispensing the food to the Gentiles; and, indeed, His speaking the blessing only over the bread, while He was silent when distributing the fishes, would probably have given rise to misunderstanding. Accordingly, we find it expressly stated that He not only gave *a St. Mark* thanks over the bread, but also spake the bless- *viii. 6, 7* ing over the fishes.[a] Nor should we, when marking such undesigned evidence, omit to notice that on the first occasion, which was immediately before the Passover, the guests were, as three of the Evangelists expressly *b St. Matt.* state, ranged on 'the grass,'[b] while, on the *xiv. 19 ;* present occasion, which must have been several *St. Mark vi.* *39; St.John* weeks later, when in the East the grass would *vi. 10* be burnt up, we are told by the two Evangelists that they sat on 'the ground.'

On the occasion referred to in the preceding narrative, those who had lately taken counsel together against Jesus— the Pharisees and the Herodians, or, to put it otherwise, the Pharisees and Sadducees—were not present. For those who, politically speaking, were 'Herodians' might also, though perhaps not religiously speaking, yet from the Jewish standpoint of St. Matthew, be designated as, or else include, Sadducees. But they were soon to reappear on the scene, as Jesus came close to the Jewish territory of Herod. As Jesus sent away the multitude whom He had fed, He took ship with His disciples, and 'came into *c St. Matt.* the borders of Magadan,'[c] or, as St. Mark puts it, *xv. 39* 'the parts of Dalmanutha.' Neither 'Magadan' nor 'Dalmanutha' has been identified. This only we infer, that the place was close to, yet not within the boundary of strictly Jewish territory; since on His arrival there the

s 2

Pharisees are said to 'come forth' [a]—a word which
a St. Mark viii. 11 implies that they resided elsewhere, though, of
course, in the neighbourhood. We can quite
understand the challenge on the part of Sadducees of 'a
sign from heaven.' They would disbelieve the heavenly
Mission of Christ, or, indeed, to use a modern term, any
supra-naturalistic connection between heaven and earth.
But in the mouth of the Pharisees also it had a special
meaning. Certain supposed miracles had been either witnessed by, or testified to them, as done by Christ. As
they now represented it—since Christ laid claims which
in their view were inconsistent with the doctrine received
in Israel, preached a Kingdom quite other than that of
Jewish expectancy, was at issue with all Jewish customs,
more than this, was a breaker of the Law, in its most
important commandments, as they understood them—it
followed that, according to Deut. xiii., He was a false
prophet, who was not to be listened to. Then, also, must
the miracles which He did have been wrought by the power
of Beelzebul, 'the lord of idolatrous worship,' the very
prince of devils. But had there been real signs, and
might it not all have been an illusion? Let Him show
them 'a sign,' and let that sign come direct from heaven!

It is said that Rabbi Eliezer, when his teaching was
challenged, successfully appealed to certain 'signs.' First, a
locust tree moved at his bidding one hundred, or according
to some, four hundred cubits. Next the channels of water
were made to flow backwards. Then the walls of the
Academy leaned forward, and were only arrested at the
bidding of another Rabbi. Lastly, Eliezer exclaimed: 'If
the Law is as I teach, let it be proved from heaven!' when
a voice fell from the sky: 'What have ye to do with Rabbi
Eliezer, for the Halakhah is as he teaches?'

It was, therefore, no strange thing, when the Pharisees
asked of Jesus 'a sign from heaven,' to attest His claims
and teaching. The answer which He gave was among
the most solemn which the leaders of Israel could have
heard. They had asked Him virtually for some sign of
His Messiahship; some striking vindication from heaven

of His claims. It would be given them only too soon.
By the light of the flames of Jerusalem and the Sanctuary
were the words on the Cross to be read again. The burning of Jerusalem was God's answer to the Jews' cry,
' Away with Him—we have no king but Cæsar;' the
thousands of crosses on which the Romans hanged their
captives, the terrible counterpart of the Cross on Golgotha.

It was to this that Jesus referred in His reply to the
Pharisees and ' Sadducean' Herodians. Men could discern by the appearance of the sky whether the day would
be fair or stormy. And yet, when all the signs of the
gathering storm that would destroy their city and people,
were clearly visible, they, the leaders of the people, failed
to perceive them! Israel asked for ' a sign '—but none
should be given the doomed land and city other than that
which had been given to Nineveh: ' the sign of Jonah.'
The only sign to Nineveh was Jonah's solemn warning
and call to repentance; and the only sign now, or rather,
' unto this generation no sign,' [a] was the warn- [a St. Mark viii. 12]
ing cry of judgment and the loving call to [b St. Luke xix. 41-44]
repentance.[b]

It was but a natural sequence that ' He left them
and departed.' Once more the ship bore Him and His
disciples towards the coast of Bethsaida-Julias. He was
on his way to the utmost limit of the land, to Cæsarea
Philippi, in pursuit of His purpose to delay the final conflict. For the great crisis must begin, as it would end,
in Jerusalem, and at the Feast; it would begin at the
Feast of Tabernacles,[c] and it would end at the [c St. John vii.]
following Passover. But by the way the disciples
themselves showed how little even they, who had so long
and closely followed Christ, understood His teaching, and
how prone to misapprehension their spiritual dulness
rendered them.

When the Lord touched the other shore, His mind and
heart were still full of the scene from which He had lately
passed. For truly on this demand for a sign did the
future of Israel seem to hang. And now, when they
landed, they carried ashore the empty provision baskets;

for, as, with his usual attention to details, St. Mark notes,
they had only brought one loaf of bread with them. In
fact, in the excitement and hurry 'they forgot to take
bread.' Whether or not something connected with this
arrested the attention of Christ, He broke the silence,
speaking that which was so much on His mind. He
warned them, as greatly they needed it, of the leaven
with which Pharisees and Sadducees had, each in their
own manner, leavened, and so corrupted, the holy bread
of Scripture-truth. The disciples, aware that in their
hurry and excitement they had forgotten bread, misunderstood these words of Christ. They thought the words
implied that in His view they had not forgotten to bring
bread, but purposely omitted to do so, in order, like the
Pharisees and Sadducees, to 'seek of Him a sign' of His
Divine Messiahship—nay, to oblige Him to show such:
that of miraculous provision in their want. The mere
suspicion showed what was in their minds, and pointed to
their danger. This explains how, in His reply, Jesus reproved them, not for utter want of discernment, but only
for 'little faith.' It was their lack of faith—the very
leaven of the Pharisees and Sadducees—which had suggested such a thought. Again, if the experience of the
past had taught them anything, it should have been to
believe that the needful provision of their wants by Christ
was not 'a sign,' such as the Pharisees had asked, but
what faith might ever expect from Christ, when following
after or waiting upon Him. Then understood they
truly that it was not of the leaven of bread that He had
bidden them beware, but pointed to the far more real
danger of 'the teaching of the Pharisees and Sadducees,'
which had underlain the demand for a sign from heaven.

CHAPTER XLVI.

THE GREAT CONFESSION—THE GREAT COMMISSION

(St. Matt. xvi. 13-28; St. Mark viii. 27-ix. 1; St. Luke ix. 18-27.)

IF we are right in identifying the little bay—Dalmanutha —with the neighbourhood of Tarichæa, yet another link of strange coincidence connects the prophetic warning spoken there with its fulfilment. From Dalmanutha our Lord passed across the Lake to Cæsarea Philippi. From Cæsarea Philippi did Vespasian pass through Tiberias to Tarichæa, when the town and people were destroyed, and the blood of the fugitives reddened the Lake, and their bodies choked its waters. Even amidst the horrors of the last Jewish war, few spectacles could have been so sickening as that of the wild stand at Tarichæa, ending with the butchery of 6,500 on land and sea; and lastly, the vile treachery by which they to whom mercy had been promised were lured into the circus at Tiberias, when the weak and old, to the number of about 1,200, were slaughtered, and the rest—upwards of 30,400—sold into slavery. Well might He, who foresaw and foretold that terrible end, standing on that spot, deeply sigh in spirit as He spake to them who asked ʻ a sign,ʼ and yet saw not what even ordinary discernment might have perceived of the red and lowering sky overhead.

From Dalmanutha, across the Lake, then by the plain where so lately the five thousand had been fed, and near to Bethsaida, would the road of Christ and His disciples lead to the capital of the Tetrarch Philip, the ancient Paneas, or, as it was then called, Cæsarea Philippi, the modern Banias.

The situation of the ancient Cæsarea Philippi (1,147 feet above the sea) is, indeed, magnificent. Nestling amid three valleys on a terrace in the angle of Hermon, it is almost shut out from view by cliffs and woods. The

western side of a steep mountain, crowned by the ruins of
an ancient castle, forms an abrupt rock-wall. Here from
out an immense cavern bursts a river. These are 'the
upper sources' of the Jordan. This cave, an ancient
sanctuary of Pan, gave its earliest name of Paneas to the
town. Here Herod, when receiving the tetrarchy from
Augustus, built a temple in his honour. On the rocky
wall close by, votive niches may still be traced, one of them
bearing the Greek inscription, 'Priest of Pan.' When
Herod's son, Philip, received the tetrarchy, he enlarged
and greatly beautified the ancient Paneas, and called it in
honour of the Emperor, Cæsarea Philippi.

It was into this chiefly Gentile district that the Lord
now withdrew with His disciples after that last and decisive question of the Pharisees. It was here that as His
question, like Moses' rod, struck their hearts, there leaped
from the lips of Peter the living, life-spreading waters of
his confession. It may have been that this rock-wall
below the castle, from under which sprang Jordan, or the
rock on which the castle stood, supplied the material suggestion for Christ's words : 'Thou art Peter, and on this
rock will I build My Church.' In Cæsarea, or its immediate neighbourhood, did the Lord spend with His disciples six days after this confession ; and here, close by,
on one of the heights of snowy Hermon, was the scene of
the Transfiguration, the light of which shone
for ever into the hearts of the disciples on their
dark and tangled path.[a]

[a] 2 Pet. i. 19

The trial to which Jesus had put His disciples' faith at
Capernaum was only renewed and deepened by all that
followed. It should be remembered that His refusal to
meet the challenge of 'a sign' of the Sadducees must have
left the impression of a virtual defeat, while His subsequent
'hard sayings' led to the defection of many. Undoubtedly the faith of the disciples had been greatly tried,
as appears also from the question of Christ: 'Will ye also
go away ?' But here it was their whole past experience in
following Him which enabled them to overcome. Almost
like a cry of despair goes up that shout of victory : 'Lord,

to whom shall we go? Thou hast the words of eternal life.'

We shall, perhaps, best understand the progress of this trial when following it in him who, at last, made shipwreck of his faith: Judas Iscariot. Without attempting to penetrate the Satanic element in his apostasy, we may trace his course in its psychological development. We must not regard Judas as a monster, but as one with like passions as ourselves. True, there was one terrible master-passion in his soul—covetousness; but that was only the downward, lower aspect of what seems, and to many really is, that which leads to the higher and better—ambition. It had been thoughts of Israel's King which had first set his imagination on fire, and brought him to follow the Messiah. Gradually, increasingly, came the disenchantment. It was quite another Kingdom, that of Christ; quite another Kingship than what had set Judas aglow. This feeling was deepened as events proceeded. His confidence must have been rudely shaken when the Baptist was beheaded. Then came the next disappointment, when Jesus would not be made King. Why not—if He were King? And so on, step by step, till the final depth was reached, when Jesus would not, or could not—which was it?—meet the public challenge of the Pharisees. We take it that it was then that the leaven pervaded and leavened Judas in heart and soul.

We repeat that what so permanently penetrated Judas could not (as Christ's warning shows) have left the others wholly unaffected. The very presence of Judas with them must have had its influence. The littleness of their faith required correction; it must grow and become strong. And so we can understand what follows. It was after solitary prayer—no doubt for them [a]—that, with reference to the challenge of the Pharisees, ' the leaven ' that threatened them, He now gathered up all their experience of the past by putting to them the question, what men, the people who had watched His Works and heard His Words, regarded Him as being. Even on them some conviction had been wrought by their observance of

[a] St. Luke ix. 18

Him.   It marked Him out (as the disciples said) as different from all around, nay, from all ordinary men : like
the Baptist, or Elijah, or as if He were one of the old
prophets alive again.   But, if even the multitude had
gathered such knowledge of Him, what was their experience
who had always been with Him ?   Answered he, who most
truly represented the Church, because he combined with
the most advanced experience of the three most intimate
disciples the utmost boldness of confession : ' Thou art the
Christ ! '

And so in part was this ' leaven ' of the Pharisees
purged !   Yet not wholly.   For then it was that Christ
spake to them of His sufferings and death, and that the
resistance of Peter showed how deeply that leaven had
penetrated.   And then followed the grand contrast presented by Christ, between minding the things of men
and those of God, with the warning which it implied, and
the monition as to the necessity of bearing the cross of
contempt, and the absolute call to do so, as addressed
to those who would be His disciples.   Here, then, the
contest about ' the sign,' or rather the challenge about the
Messiahship, was carried from the mental into the moral
sphere, and so decided.   Six days more of quiet waiting
and growth of faith, and it was met, rewarded, crowned, and
perfected by the sight on the Mount of Transfiguration ;
yet, even so, perceived only as through the heaviness of sleep.

We are probably correct in supposing that popular
opinion did not point to Christ as literally the Baptist,
Elijah, Jeremiah, or one of the other prophets who had
long been dead.   Rather would it mean that some saw in
Him the continuation of the work of John, as heralding
and preparing the way of the Messiah, or, if they did not
believe in John, of that of Elijah ; while to others He
seemed a second Jeremiah, denouncing woe on Israel, and
calling to tardy repentance : or else one of those old prophets, who had spoken either of the near judgment or of
the coming glory.   But however men differed on these
points, in this all agreed, that they regarded Him not as
an ordinary man or teacher, but His Mission as straight

from heaven ; and in this also, that they did not view Him as the Messiah.

There is a significant emphasis in the words with which Jesus turned from the opinion of ' the multitudes ' to elicit the faith of the disciples : ' But you, whom do *you* say that I am ? ' In that moment it leaped, by the power of God, to the lips of Peter : ' Thou art the Christ (the Messiah), the Son of the Living God.' [a] St. Chrysostom has beautifully designated Peter as ' the mouth of the Apostles '—and we recall, in this connection, the words of St. Paul as casting light on the representative character of Peter's confession as that of the Church, and hence on the meaning of Christ's reply, and its equally representative application : ' With the mouth confession is made unto salvation.' [b] The words of the confession are given somewhat differently by the three Evangelists. From our standpoint, the briefest form (that of St. Mark) : ' Thou art the Christ,' means quite as much as the fullest (that of St. Matthew) : ' Thou art the Christ, the Son of the Living God.' We can thus understand how the latter might be truthfully adopted, and, indeed, would be the most truthful, accurate, and suitable in a Gospel primarily written for the Jews. And here we notice that the most exact form of the words seems that in the Gospel of St. Luke : ' The Christ of God.'

Previously to the confession of Peter, the ship's company, that had witnessed His walking on the water, had owned : ' Of a truth Thou art the Son of God,' [c] but not in the sense in which a well-informed, believing Jew would hail Him as the Messiah, and ' the Son of the Living God,' designating both His Office and His Nature—and these two in their combination. Again, Peter himself had made a confession of Christ, when, after His Discourse at Capernaum, so many of His disciples had forsaken Him. It had been : ' We have believed, and know that Thou art the Holy One of God.' [d]

But now he has consciously reached the firm ground of Messianic acknowledgment. All else is implied in this,

[a] St. Matt. xvi. 16

[b] Rom. x. 10

[c] St. Matt. xiv. 33

[d] St. John vi. 69

and would follow from it.   It is the first real confession
of the Church.   We can understand how it followed after solitary prayer by Christ [a]—we can
scarcely doubt, for that very revelation by the Father, which
He afterwards joyously recognised in the words of Peter.

The reply of the Saviour is only recorded by St.
Matthew.   The whole form is Hebraistic.   The 'blessed
art thou' is Jewish; the address, 'Simon bar Jona,' proves
that the Lord spake in Aramaic.   The expression 'flesh
and blood,' as contrasted with God, occurs not only in that
Apocryphon of strictly Jewish authorship, the Wisdom of
the Son of Sirach,[b] and in the letters of St. Paul,[c]
but in almost innumerable passages in Jewish
writings, as denoting man in opposition to God;
while the revelation of such a truth by 'the
Father Which is in Heaven,' represents not only
both Old and New Testament teaching, but is clothed in
language familiar to Jewish ears.

Not less Jewish in form are the succeeding words of
Christ: 'Thou art Peter (*Petros*), and upon this Rock
(*Petra*) will I build My Church.'   We notice in the original the change from the masculine gender, 'Peter'
(Petros), to the feminine, 'Petra' ('Rock'), which seems
the more significant, that *Petros* is used in Greek for
'stone,' and also sometimes for 'rock,' while *Petra* always
means a 'rock.'   The change of gender must therefore
have a definite object.   The Greek word Rock ('on this
Petra [Rock] will I build my Church') was used in the
same sense in Rabbinic language.   According to Jewish
ideas, the world would not have been created, unless it
had rested, as it were, on some solid foundation of piety
and acceptance of God's Law—in other words, it required
a moral, before it could receive a physical foundation.   It
is, so runs the comment, as if a king were going to build
a city.   One and another site is tried for a foundation,
but in digging they always come upon water.   At last
they come upon *a Rock.*   So, when God was about to build
His world, He could not rear it on the generation of Enos,
nor on that of the flood, who brought destruction on the

[a] St. Luke
ix. 18

[b] Ecclus. xiv.
18; xvii. 31
[c] 1 Cor. xv.
50; Gal. i.
16; Eph. vi.
12

world; but 'when He beheld that Abraham would arise in the future, He said: Behold I have found a Rock to build on it, and to found the world,' whence also Abraham is called a Rock, as it is said : [a] 'Look unto the Rock whence ye are hewn.' The parallel between Abraham and Peter might be carried even further. If, from a misunderstanding of the Lord's promise to Peter, later Christian legend represented the Apostle as sitting at the gate of heaven, Jewish legend represents Abraham as sitting at the gate of Gehenna, so as to prevent all who had the seal of circumcision from falling into its abyss.

[a] Is. li. 1

But to return. Believing that Jesus spoke to Peter in the Aramaic, we can now understand how the words *Petros* and *Petra* would be purposely used by Christ to mark the difference which their choice would suggest. Perhaps it might be expressed in this somewhat clumsy paraphrase : 'Thou art Peter (Petros)—a Stone or Rock—and upon this Petra—the Rock, the Petrine—will I found My Church.' If, therefore, we would not entirely limit the reference to the words of Peter's confession, we would certainly apply them to that which was the Petrine in Peter : the heaven-given faith which manifested itself in his confession. And we can further understand how, just as Christ's contemporaries may have regarded the world as reared on the rock of faithful Abraham, so Christ promised that He would build His Church on the Petrine in Peter— on his faith and confession. Nor would the term 'Church' sound strange in Jewish ears. The same Greek word (ἐκκλησία), as the equivalent of the Hebrew which is rendered in our version 'convocation,' 'the called,' was apparently in familiar use at the time. In Hebrew use it referred to Israel, not in their national but in their religious unity. As here employed, it would convey the prophecy that His disciples would in the future be joined together in a religious unity; that this religious unity or 'Church' would be a building of which Christ was the Builder ; that it would be founded on 'the Petrine' of heaven-taught faith and confession ; and that this religious unity, this Church, was not only intended for a time, like a school of

thought, but would last beyond death and the disembodied
state: that, alike as regarded Christ and His Church—
'the gates of Hades shall not prevail against it.'

Viewing 'the Church' as a building founded upon 'the
Petrine,' it was not to vary. To carry on the same meta-
phor, Christ promised to give to him who had spoken as representative of the Apostles—'the stewards of the mysteries
of God'—'the keys of the Kingdom of Heaven.' For, as
the religious unity of His disciples, or the Church, represented 'the royal rule of heaven,' so, figuratively, entrance
into the gates of this building, submission to the rule of
God—to that Kingdom of which Christ was the King.
And we remember how, in a special sense, this promise was
fulfilled to Peter. Even as he had been the first to utter
the confession of the Church, so was he also privileged to
be the first to open its hitherto closed gates to the Gentiles, when God made choice of him, that, through his
mouth, the Gentiles should first hear the words of
the Gospel,[a] and at his bidding first be baptized.[b]

[a] Acts xv. 7
[b] Acts x. 48

Our primary inquiry must here be, what the further
words of Christ would convey to the person to whom the
promise was addressed. And here we recall that no other
terms were in more constant use in Rabbinic Canon-Law
than those of 'binding' and 'loosing.' The words are the
literal translation of the Hebrew 'to bind,' in the sense of
prohibiting, and 'to loose,' in the sense of permitting. The
power of 'binding and loosing' was one claimed by the
Rabbis. It represented the *legislative*, while another pretension, that of declaring 'free' or else 'liable,' i.e. guilty,
expressed their claim to the *judicial* power. By the first
of these they 'bound' or 'loosed' acts or things; by the
second they 'remitted' or 'retained,' declared a person
free from, or liable to punishment, to compensation, or to
sacrifice. These two powers—the legislative and judicial—
which belonged to the Rabbinic office, Christ now transferred, and that not in their pretension, but in their reality,
to His Apostles: the first here to Peter as their
Representative, the second after His Resurrection
to the Church.[c]

[c] St. John xx. 23

On the second of these powers we need not at present dwell. That of ' binding ' and ' loosing ' included all the legislative functions for the new Church. In the view of the Rabbis heaven was like earth, and questions were discussed and settled by a heavenly Sanhedrin. Now, in regard to some of their earthly decrees, they were wont to say that ' the Sanhedrin above' confirmed what ' the Sanhedrin beneath ' had done. But the words of Christ, as they avoided the foolish conceit of His contemporaries, left it not doubtful, but conveyed the assurance that, under the guidance of the Holy Ghost, whatsoever they bound or loosed on earth would be bound or loosed in heaven.

But all this that had passed between them could not be matter of common talk—least of all, at that crisis in His History, and in that locality. Accordingly, all the three Evangelists record—each with distinctive emphasis— that the open confession of His Messiahship, which was virtually its proclamation, was not to be made public. Among the people it could only have led to results the opposite of those to be desired. How unprepared even that Apostle was, who had made proclamation of the Messiah, for what his confession implied, and how ignorant of the real meaning of Israel's Messiah, appeared only too soon. The Evangelists, indeed, write it down in plain language, as fully taught them by later experience, that He was to be rejected by the rulers of Israel, slain, and to rise again the third day. And there can be as little doubt that Christ's language (as afterwards they looked back upon it) must have clearly implied all this, as that at the time they did not fully understand it. They could well understand His rejection by the Scribes—a sort of figurative death, or violent suppression of His claims and doctrines, and then, after briefest period, their resurrection, as it were—but not these terrible details in their full literality.

But, even so, there was enough of realism in the words of Jesus to alarm Peter. His very affection, intensely human, to the Human Personality of his Master would lead him astray. He put it in the very strongest language, although the Evangelist gives only a literal translation of the Rabbinic expression—God forbid it, ' *God* be merciful to Thee : ' no, such never could, nor should be to the Christ! It was an appeal to the Human in Christ, just as Satan had, in the great Temptation after the forty days' fast, appealed to the purely Human in Jesus.

Yet Peter's words were to be made useful, by affording to the Master the opportunity of correcting what was amiss in the hearts of all His disciples, and teaching them such general principles about His Kingdom, and about that implied in true discipleship, as would, if received in the heart, enable them in due time victoriously to bear those trials connected with that rejection and Death of the Christ, which at the time they could not understand. Not a Messianic Kingdom, with glory to its heralds and chieftains —but self-denial, and the voluntary bearing of that cross on which the powers of this world would nail the followers of Christ. They knew the torture which their masters —the power of the world—the Romans, were wont to inflict: such must they, and similar must we all, be prepared to bear, and in so doing begin by denying self. In such a contest to lose life would be to gain it, to gain would be to lose life. And if the issue lay between these two, who could hesitate what to choose, even if it were ours to gain or lose a whole world? For behind it all there was a reality—a Messianic triumph and Kingdom—not, indeed, such as they imagined, but far higher, holier : the Coming ᵃ St. Matt. of the Son of Man in the glory of His Father, xvi. 24–27 and with His Angels, and then eternal gain or loss, according to our deeds.ᵃ

But why speak of the future and distant? ' A sign ' —a terrible sign of it ' from heaven,' a vindication of the Christ Whom they had slain, invoking His Blood on their City and Nation, a vindication such as alone these men could understand, of the reality of His Resurrection and Ascension, was in the near future. The flames of the City and Temple would be the light in that nation's darkness, by which to read the inscription on the Cross. All this

not afar off. Some of those who stood there would not
'taste death,' till in those judgments they would see
that the Son of Man had come in His Kingdom.[a]

ᵃ St. Matt.
xvi. 28

CHAPTER XLVII.

THE TRANSFIGURATION.

(St. Matt. xvii. 1-8; St. Mark ix. 2-8; St. Luke ix. 28-36.)

THE great confession of Peter, as the representative
Apostle, had laid the foundations of the Church as such.
In contradistinction to the varying opinions of even those
best disposed towards Christ, it openly declared that Jesus
was the Very Christ of God, the fulfilment of all Old
Testament prophecy, the heir of Old Testament promise,
the realisation of the Old Testament hope for Israel, and,
in Israel, for all mankind. Without this confession,
Christians might have been a Jewish sect, a religious
party, or a school of thought, and Jesus a Teacher, Rabbi,
Reformer, or Leader of men. But the confession which
marked Jesus as the Christ also constituted His followers
the Church. It separated them, as it separated Him, from
all around; it gathered them into One, even Christ; and
it marked out the foundation on which the building made
without hands was to rise. Never was illustrative answer
so exact as this: 'On this Rock'—bold, outstanding, well-
defined, immovable—'will I build My Church.'

Without doubt this confession also marked the high-
point of the Apostles' faith. Never afterwards, till His
Resurrection, did it reach so high. Nay, what followed
seems rather a retrogression from it: beginning with their
unwillingness to receive the announcement of His Decease,
and ending with their unreadiness to share His sufferings
or to believe in His Resurrection.

Perhaps it was the Sabbath when Peter's great confession was made; and the 'six days' of St. Matthew and
St. Mark become the 'about eight days' of St. Luke, when
we reckon from that Sabbath to the close of another, and
suppose that at even the Saviour ascended the Mount of

T

Transfiguration with the three Apostles: Peter, James, and John. There can scarcely be a reasonable doubt that Christ and His disciples had not left the neighbourhood of Cæsarea, and hence that 'the mountain' must have been one of the slopes of gigantic, snowy Hermon.

It was then, as we have suggested, the evening after the Sabbath, when the Master and those three of His disciples, who were most closely linked to Him in heart and thought, climbed the path that led up to one of these heights.

As St. Luke alone informs us, it was 'to pray' that Jesus took them apart up into that mountain. 'To pray,' no doubt in connection with 'those sayings;' since their reception required quite as much the direct teaching of the Heavenly Father, as had the previous confession of Peter, of which it was, indeed, the complement. And the Transfiguration, with its attendant glorified Ministry and Voice from heaven, was God's answer to that prayer.

On that mountain-top 'He prayed.' And, with deep reverence be it said, for Himself also did Jesus pray. He needed prayer, that in it His Soul might lie calm and still in the unruffled quiet of His Self-surrender, and the victory of His Sacrificial Obedience. And He needed prayer also, as the introduction to, and preparation for, His Transfiguration. Truly, He stood on Hermon. It was the highest ascent, the widest prospect into the past, present, and future, in His Earthly Life.

As we understand it, the prayer with them had ceased, or merged into silent prayer of each, or Jesus now prayed alone and apart, when what gives this scene such a truly human and truthful aspect ensued. It was but natural for these men of simple habits, at night, and after the long ascent, and in the strong mountain-air, to be heavy with sleep. 'They were heavy—weighted—with sleep,' as afterwards in Gethsemane their eyes were weighted.[a]

[a] St. Matt. xxvi. 43; St. Mark xiv. 40   Yet they struggled with it, and it is quite consistent with experience that they should continue in that state of semi-stupor during what passed between Moses and Elijah and Christ, and also be 'fully awake' 'to see His Glory, and the two men who stood with Him.'

What they saw was their Master, while praying,

'transformed.' The 'form of God' shone through the 'form of a servant;' 'the appearance of His Face became

^a St. Luke
^b St. Matthew

other,'[a] it 'did shine as the sun.'[b] Nay, the whole Figure seemed bathed in light, the very garments whiter far than the snow on which the moon shone—'so as no fuller on earth can white them,'[c]

^c St. Mark
^d St. Luke
^e St. Luke

'glittering,'[d] 'white as the light.' And more than this they saw and heard. They saw 'with Him two men,'[e] whom, in their heightened sensitiveness to spiritual phenomena, they could have no difficulty in recognising, by such of their conversation as they heard, as Moses and Elijah. The column was now complete: the base in the Law; the shaft in that Prophetism of which Elijah was the great Representative; and the apex in Christ Himself—a unity completely fitting together in all its parts. And they heard also that they spake of 'His Exodus—outgoing—which He was about to fulfil at Jerusalem.'[f] Although the term

^f St. Luke

'Exodus,' 'outgoing,' occurs otherwise for 'death,' we must bear in mind its meaning as contrasted with that in which the same Evangelic writer designates

^g Acts xiii. 24

the Birth of Christ, as His 'incoming.'[g] In truth, it implies not only His Decease, but its manner, and even His Resurrection and Ascension. In that sense we can understand the better, as on the lips of Moses and Elijah, this about His fulfilling that Exodus: accomplishing it in all its fulness, and so completing Law and Prophecy, type and prediction.

And still that night of glory had not ended. A strange peculiarity has been noticed about Hermon: in 'a few minutes a thick cap forms over the top of the mountain, and as quickly disperses and entirely disappears.' Suddenly a cloud passed over the clear brow of the mountain—not an ordinary, but 'a luminous cloud,' a cloud uplit, filled with light. As it laid itself between Jesus and the two Old Testament Representatives, it parted, and presently enwrapped them. Most significant is it, suggestive of the Presence of God, revealing, yet concealing—a cloud, yet luminous. And this cloud overshadowed the disciples: the shadow of its light fell upon them. A nameless terror seized them. Fain would they have held what seemed to escape their grasp. Such vision had never before been vouchsafed to mortal man as had fallen on their sight; they had heard Heaven's converse; they had tasted Angels' Food, the Bread of His Presence. Could the vision not be perpetuated—at least prolonged? In the confusion of their terror they knew not how otherwise to word it, than by an expression of ecstatic longing for the continuance of what they had, of their earnest readiness to do their little best, if they could but secure it—make booths for the heavenly Visitants—and themselves wait in humble service and reverent attention on what their dull heaviness had prevented them from enjoying and profiting by to the full. They knew and felt it: 'Lord'—'Rabbi'—'Master'—'it is good for us to be here.' 'They wist not what they said.' In presence of the luminous cloud that enwrapped those glorified Saints, they spake from out that darkness which compassed them about.

And now the light-cloud was spreading; presently its fringe fell upon them. Heaven's awe was upon them: for the touch of the heavenly strains, almost to breaking, the bond betwixt body and soul. 'And a Voice came out of the cloud, saying, This is My Beloved Son: hear Him.' It had needed only One other Testimony to seal it all; One other Voice, to give both meaning and music to what had been the subject of Moses' and Elijah's speaking. That Voice had now come—not in testimony to any fact, but to a Person—that of Jesus as His 'Beloved Son,' and in gracious direction to them. They heard it, falling on their faces in awestruck worship.

How long the silence had lasted, and the last rays of the cloud had passed, we know not. Presently, it was a gentle touch that roused them. It was the Hand of Jesus, as with words of comfort He reassured them: 'Arise, and be not afraid.' And as, startled, they looked round about them, they saw no man save Jesus only. The heavenly Visitants had gone, the last glow of the light-cloud had faded away, the echoes of Heaven's Voice had died out. It was night, and they were on the Mount with Jesus, and with Jesus only.

CHAPTER XLVIII.

THE MORROW OF THE TRANSFIGURATION.

(St. Matt. xvii. 9–21; St. Mark ix. 9–29; St. Luke ix. 37–43.)

IT was the early dawn of another summer's day when the Master and His disciples turned their steps once more towards the plain. They had seen His Glory; they had had the most solemn witness which, as Jews, they could have; and they had gained a new knowledge of the Old Testament. It all bore reference to the Christ, and it spake of His Decease. Perhaps on that morning better than in the previous night did they realise the vision, and feel its calm happiness.

It would be only natural that their thoughts should also wander to the companions and fellow-disciples whom on the previous evening they had left in the valley beneath. A light had been shed upon that hard saying concerning His Rejection and violent Death. They—at least these three— had formerly simply submitted to the saying of Christ because it was His, without understanding it; but now they had learned to see it in quite another light. How they must have longed to impart it to those whose difficulties were at least as great, perhaps greater; who perhaps had not yet recovered from the rude shock which their Messianic thoughts and hopes had so lately received.

But it was not to be so. Evidently it was not an event to be made generally known, either to the people or even to the great body of the disciples. They could not have understood its real meaning; in their ignorance they would have misapplied to carnal Jewish purposes its heavenly lessons. But even the rest of the Apostles must not know of it: that they were not qualified to witness it, proved that they were not prepared to hear of it.

And so it was that, when the silence of that morning-descent was broken, the Master laid on them the command to tell no man of this vision, till after the Son of Man were risen from the dead. The silence thus enjoined was the first step into the Valley of Humiliation. It was also a test whether they had understood the spiritual teaching of the vision. And their strict obedience, not questioning even the grounds of the injunction, proved that they had learned it. So entire, indeed, was their submission that they dared not even ask the Master about a new and seemingly greater mystery than they had yet heard: the ª St. Mark ix. 10 meaning of the Son of Man rising from the dead.ª Did it refer to the general Resurrection; was the Messiah to be the first to rise from the dead, and to waken the other sleepers—or was it only a figurative expression for His triumph and vindication? Evidently they knew as yet nothing of Christ's Personal Resurrection as separate from that of others, and on the third day after His Death. Among themselves, then and many times ᵇ St. Mark ix. 10 afterwards, in secret converse, they questioned what the rising again from the dead should mean.ᵇ

There was another question, and it they might ask of Jesus, since it concerned not the mysteries of the future but the lessons of the past. Thinking of that vision, of the appearance of Elijah and of his speaking of the Death of the Messiah, why did the Scribes say that Elijah should first come—and, as was the universal teaching, for the purpose of restoring all things? If, as they had seen, Elijah had come—but only for a brief season, not to abide together with Moses as they had wished when they proposed to rear them booths; if he had come not to the people but to Christ, in view of only them three—and they were not even to tell of it; and if it had been not to prepare for a spiritual restoration, but to speak of what implied the opposite: the Rejection and violent Death of the Messiah —then, were the Scribes right in their teaching, and what was its real meaning? The question afforded the opportunity of presenting to the disciples not only a solution of their difficulties, but another insight into the necessity of His Rejection and Death. They had failed to distinguish between the coming of Elijah and its alternative sequence. Truly ' Elias cometh first ' and Elijah had ' come already' in the person of John the Baptist. The Divinely intended object of Elijah's coming was to 'restore all things.' This, of course, implied a moral element in the submission of the people to God, and their willingness to receive his message. Otherwise there was this Divine alternative in the prophecy of Malachi: 'Lest I come to smite the land with the ban.' Elijah had come; if the people had received his message there would have been the promised restoration of all things. As the Lord had said on a previous occasion:ª 'If ye are willing to receive *him*, this is Elijah, which is to come.' Similarly, if Israel had received the Christ, He would have gathered them as a hen her chickens for protection; He would not only have been, but have visibly appeared as their King. But Israel did not know their Elijah, and did unto him whatsoever they listed; and so, in logical sequence, would the Son of Man also suffer of them. And thus has the other part of Malachi's prophecy been fulfilled, and the land of Israel been smitten with the ban.

ª St. Matt. xi. 14

Amidst such conversation the descent from the mountain was accomplished. Presently they found themselves in view of a scene, which only too clearly showed that unfitness of the disciples for the heavenly vision of the preceding night, to which reference has been made.

It was, indeed, a terrible contrast between the scene below and that vision of Moses and Elijah, when they had spoken of the Exodus of the Christ, and the Divine Voice had attested the Christ from out the luminous cloud. A concourse of excited people—among them once more ' Scribes,' who had tracked the Lord and come upon His weakest disciples in the hour of their greatest weakness—is gathered about a man who had in vain brought his lunatick son for healing. He is eagerly questioned by the multitude, and moodily answers; or, as it might almost seem from St. Matthew,ᵇ he is leaving the crowd and those from whom he had vainly sought help. This was the hour of triumph for these Scribes. The Master had refused the challenge in Dalmanutha, and the disciples, accepting it, had signally failed. There they were, ' ques-

ᵇ St. Matt. xvii. 14

tioning with them' noisily, discussing this and all similar phenomena, but chiefly the power, authority, and reality of the Master. It reminds us of Israel's temptation in the wilderness, and we should scarcely wonder if they had even questioned the return of Jesus, as they of old did that of Moses.

At that very moment Jesus appeared with the three. We cannot wonder that, ' when they saw Him, they were ^{a St. Mark} greatly amazed and running to Him saluted Him.'ᵃ Before the Master's inquiry about the cause of this violent discussion could be answered, the man who had been its occasion came forward and, ' kneel-^{b St. Matthew} ing to Him,'ᵇ addressed Jesus. Describing the symptoms of his son's distemper, which were those of epilepsy and mania—although both the father and Jesus rightly attributed the disease to demoniac influence—he told how he had come in search of the Master, but only found the nine disciples, and how they had attempted and failed in the desired cure.

Why had they failed? For the same reason that they had not been taken into the Mount of Transfiguration—because they were ' faithless,' because of their ' unbelief.' They had that outward faith of the ' probatum est ' (' it is proved '); they believed because of what they had seen ; but that deeper faith, which consisted in the spiritual view of that which was the unseen in Christ, and that higher power, which flows from such apprehension, they had not. In such faith as they had, they repeated forms of exorcism, tried to imitate their Master. But they signally failed, as did those seven Jewish Priest-sons at Ephesus. In that hour of crisis, in the presence of questioning Scribes and a wondering populace, and in the absence of the Christ, only one power could prevail, that of spiritual faith ; and ' that kind ' could ' not come out but by prayer.'

For one moment we have a glimpse into the Saviour's soul : the poignant sorrow of His disappointment at the unbelief of the ' faithless and perverse generation,' with which He had so long borne ; the patience and condescension, the Divine ' need be ' of His having thus to bear even with His own, together with the humiliation which it involved; and the almost home-longing, as it has been called, of His soul. These things are mysteries. The next moment Jesus turns Him to the father. At His command the lunatick is brought to Him. In the Presence of Jesus, and in view of the coming contest between Light and Darkness, one of those paroxysms of demoniac operation ensues, such as we have witnessed on all similar occasions. This was allowed to pass in view of all. But both this, and the question as to the length of time the lunatick had been afflicted, together with the answer and the description of the dangers involved which it elicited, were evidently intended to point the lesson of the need of a higher faith. To the father, however, who knew not the mode of treatment by the Heavenly Physician, they seemed like the questions of an earthly healer who must consider the symptoms before he could attempt to cure. ' If Thou canst do anything, have compassion on us, and help us.'

There is all the calm majesty of Divine self-consciousness, yet without trace of self-assertion, when Jesus, utterly ignoring the ' if Thou canst,' turns to the man and tells him that, while with the Divine Helper there is the possibility of all help, it is conditioned by a possibility in ourselves, by man's receptiveness, by his faith. ' If thou canst believe, all things are possible to him that believeth.'

It was a lesson, of which the reality was attested by the hold which it took on the man's whole nature. While by one great out-going of his soul he overleapt all, to lay hold on the fact set before him, he felt all the more the dark chasm of unbelief behind him. Thus through the felt unbelief of faith he attained true faith by laying hold on the Divine Saviour, when he cried out and said : ' Lord, I believe ; help Thou mine unbelief.'

Such cry could not be, and never is, unheard. It was a reality, and not accommodation to Jewish views, when, as He saw ' the multitude running together, He rebuked the unclean spirit, saying to him : Dumb and deaf spirit, I command thee, come out of him, and no more come into him.'

Another and a more violent paroxysm, so that the by-standers almost thought him dead. But the unclean spirit had come out of him. And with strong gentle Hand the Saviour lifted him, and delivered him to his father.

CHAPTER XLIX.

THE LAST EVENTS IN GALILEE:—THE TRIBUTE-MONEY, THE DISPUTE BY THE WAY AND THE FORBIDDING OF HIM WHO COULD NOT FOLLOW WITH THE DISCIPLES.

(St. Matt. xvii. 22—xviii. 22; St. Mark ix. 30-50; St. Luke ix. 43-50.)

Now that the Lord's retreat at Cæsarea Philippi was known to the Scribes, and that He was again surrounded and followed by the multitude, there could be no further object in His retirement. Indeed, the time was coming that He should meet that for which He had been, and was still, preparing the minds of His disciples—His Decease at Jerusalem. Accordingly, we find Him once more with His disciples in Galilee—not to abide there, but prepara-tory to His journey to the Feast of Tabernacles. The few events of this brief stay, and the teaching connected with it, may be summed up as follows.

1. Prominently, perhaps, as the summary of all, we have now the clear and emphatic repetition of the predic-tion of His Death and Resurrection. The announcement filled their hearts with exceeding sorrow; they compre-hended it not; nay, they were—perhaps not unnaturally—afraid to ask Him about it.

2. It is to the depression caused by His insistence on this terrible future, to the constant apprehension of near danger, and the consequent desire not to 'offend,' and so provoke those at whose hands Christ had told them He was to suffer, that we trace the incident of the tribute-money. We can scarcely believe that Peter would have

answered as he did, without previous permission of his
Master, had it not been for such thoughts and fears. It
was another mode of saying, ' That be far from Thee '—or,
rather, trying to keep it as far as he could from Christ.

It is well known that, on the ground of the injunction
in Exod. xxx. 13 &c., every male in Israel, from twenty
years upwards, was expected annually to contribute to the Temple-Treasury the sum of one
half-shekel of the Sanctuary,[a] equivalent to about
1*s*. 2*d*. or 1*s*. 3*d*. of our money. Whether or not
the original Biblical ordinance had been intended to institute a regular annual contribution, the Jews of the Dis-
persion would probably regard it in the light of a patriotic
as well as religious act.

It will be remembered that, shortly before the previous
Passover, Jesus with His disciples had left Capernaum,
that they returned to the latter city only for the Sabbath,
and that, as we have suggested, they passed the first
Paschal days on the borders of Tyre. It must have been
known that He had not gone up to Jerusalem for the
Passover. Accordingly, when it was told in Capernaum
that the Rabbi of Nazareth had once more come to what
seems to have been His Galilean home, it was only natural
that they who collected the Temple-tribute should have
applied for its payment. It is quite possible that their
application may have been, if not prompted, yet quickened,
by the wish to involve Him in a breach of so well-known
an obligation, or else by a hostile curiosity.

We picture it to ourselves on this wise. Those who
received the Tribute-money had come to Peter, and perhaps met him in the court or corridor, and asked him :
' Your Teacher (Rabbi), does He not pay the didrachma ? '
While Peter hastily responded in the affirmative, and then
entered into the house to procure the coin, or else to report
what had passed, Jesus, Who had been in another part of
the house, but was cognisant of all, ' anticipated him.'
Addressing him in kindly language as ' Simon,' He pointed
out the real state of matters by an illustration which must,
of course, not be too literally pressed, and of which the

a Comp.
2 Kings xii.
4 ; 2 Chron.
xxiv. 6 ;
Neh. x. 32

meaning was : Whom does a King intend to tax for the maintenance of his palace and officers? Surely not his own family, but others. The inference from this, as regarded the Temple-tribute, was obvious. As in all similar Jewish parabolic teaching, it was only indicated in general principle : 'Then are the children free.' But even so, be it as Peter had wished, although not from the same motive. Let no needless offence be given; for, assuredly, they would not have understood the principle on which Christ would have refused the Tribute-money, and all misunderstanding on the part of Peter was now impossible. Yet Christ would still further vindicate His royal title. He will pay for Peter also, and pay, as heaven's King, with a *stater*, or four-drachm piece, miraculously provided.

If we wish to mark the difference between the sobriety of this record and the extravagances of legend, we may remind ourselves of a somewhat kindred Jewish Haggadah intended to glorify the Jewish mode of Sabbath observance. One Joseph, known as 'the honourer' of the Sabbath, had a wealthy heathen neighbour, to whom the Chaldæans had prophesied that all his riches would come to Joseph. To render this impossible, the wealthy man converted all his property into one magnificent gem, which he carefully concealed within his head-gear. Then he took ship, so as for ever to avoid the dangerous vicinity of the Jew. But the wind blew his head-gear into the sea, and the gem was swallowed by a fish. And, lo! it was the holy season, and they brought to the market a splendid fish. Who should purchase it but Joseph? for none as he would prepare to honour the day by the best which he could provide. But when they opened the fish, the gem was found in it—the moral being : 'He that borroweth for the Sabbath, the Sabbath will repay him.'

3. The event next recorded in the Gospels took place partly on the way from the Mount of Transfiguration to Capernaum, and partly in Capernaum itself, immediately after the scene connected with the Tribute-money. It is recorded by the three Evangelists, and it led to explana-

tions and admonitions, which are told by St. Mark and
St. Luke, but chiefly by St. Matthew. This circumstance
seems to indicate that the latter was the chief actor in
that which occasioned this special teaching and warning of
Christ, and that it must have sunk very deeply into his
heart.

^a St. Mark ix. 34 — As St. Mark puts it,[a] by the way they had
disputed among themselves which of them should
^b St. Matt. xviii. 1 — be the greatest—as St. Matthew explains,[b] in
the Messianic Kingdom of Heaven. Of a dispute
serious and even violent, among the disciples, we have
evidence in the exhortation of the Master, as reported by
^c St. Mark ix. 42-50 — St. Mark,[c] in the direction of the Lord how to
deal with an offending brother, and in the
^d St. Matt. xviii. 15, 21 — answering inquiry of Peter.[d] Nor can we be at
a loss to perceive its occasion. The distinction just
bestowed on the three in being taken up the Mount, may
have roused feelings of jealousy in the others, perhaps
of self-exaltation in the three. Alike the spirit which
John displayed in his harsh prohibition of the man that
^e St. Mark ix. 38 — did not follow with the disciples,[e] and the self-
righteous bargaining of Peter about forgiving the
^f St. Matt. xviii. 21 — supposed or real offences of a brother,[f] give evi-
dence of this.

In truth, the Apostles were still greatly under the influence of the old spirit. It was the common Jewish view
that there would be distinctions of rank in the Kingdom
of Heaven. It can scarcely be necessary to prove this by
Rabbinic quotations, since the whole system of Rabbinism
and Pharisaism, with its separation from the vulgar and
ignorant, rests upon it. But even within the circle of
Rabbinism there would be distinctions, due to learning,
merit, and even to favouritism. In this world there were
God's special favourites, who could command anything at
His hand—to use the Rabbinic illustration, like a spoilt
child from its father. And in the Messianic age God would
assign booths to each according to his rank.

How deep-rooted were such thoughts and feelings
appears not only from the dispute of the disciples by the

way, but from the request proffered by the mother of Zebedee's children and her sons at a later period.ª

We have already seen that there was quite sufficient occasion and material for such a dispute on the way from the Mount of Transfiguration to Capernaum. We suppose Peter to have been only at the first with the others. To judge by the latter question, how often he was to forgive the brother who had sinned against him, he may have been so deeply hurt that he left the other disciples, and hastened on with the Master, Who would, at any rate, sojourn in his house. For neither he nor Christ seems to have been present when John and the others forbade the man, who would not follow with them, to cast out demons in Christ's Name. Again, the other disciples only came into Capernaum, and entered the house, just as Peter had gone for the stater, with which to pay the Temple-tribute for the Master and himself. And, if speculation be permissible, we would suggest that the brother, whose offences Peter found it so difficult to forgive, may have been none other than Judas. In such a dispute by the way, Judas, with his Judaistic views, would be particularly interested; perhaps he may have been its chief instigator; certainly, he, whose natural character amidst its sharp contrasts to that of Peter presented so many points of resemblance to it, would on many grounds be specially jealous of and antagonistic to him.

Quite natural in view of this dispute by the way is another incident of the journey, which is afterwards
related.ᵇ As we judge, John seems to have been the principal actor in it; perhaps in the absence of Peter he claimed the leadership. They had met one who was casting out demons in the Name of Christ —whether successfully or not, we need scarcely inquire. So widely had faith in the power of Jesus extended; so real was the belief in the subjection of the demons to Him; so reverent was the acknowledgment of Him. A man who, thus forsaking the methods of Jewish exorcists, owned Jesus in the face of the Jewish world, could not be

far from the Kingdom of Heaven. John had, in name of the disciples, forbidden him, because he had not cast in his lot wholly with them. To forbid a man in such circumstances would be either prompted by the spirit of the dispute by the way, or else must be grounded on evidence that the motive was, or the effect would ultimately be (as in the case of the sons of Sceva), to lead men 'to speak evil' of Christ, or to hinder the work of His disciples. Assuredly, such could not have been the case with a man who invoked His Name, and perhaps experienced Its efficacy. More than this—and here is an eternal principle: 'He that is not against us is for us;' a saying still more clear, when we adopt the better reading in St. Luke,[a] 'He that is not against you is for you.'

ᵃ St. Luke ix. 50

The lesson is of the most deep-reaching character. Not that it is unimportant to follow with the disciples, but that it is not ours to forbid any work done, however imperfectly, in His Name, and that only one question is really vital—whether or not a man is decidedly with Christ.

Such were the incidents by the way. And now, while withholding from Christ their dispute, and, indeed, anything that might seem personal in the question, the disciples, on entering the house where He was in Capernaum, addressed to Him this inquiry: 'Who then is greatest in the Kingdom of Heaven?' It was a general question— but Jesus perceived the thought of their heart;[b] He knew about what they had disputed by the way,[c] and now asked them concerning it. The account of St. Mark is most graphic. Conscience-stricken 'they held their peace.' It seems as if the Master had at first gone to welcome the disciples on their arrival, and they, 'full of their dispute,' had without delay addressed their inquiry to Him in the court or antechamber, where they met Him. Leading the way into the house, 'He sat down,' not only to answer their inquiry, but to teach them what they needed to learn. He called a little child—perhaps Peter's little son—and put him in the midst of them. Not to strive who was to be greatest, but to be utterly without

ᵇ St. Luke

ᶜ St. Mark ix. 33

self-consciousness, like a child — thus to become turned and entirely changed in mind, 'converted,' was the condition for entering into the Kingdom of Heaven. Then, as to the question of greatness there, it was really one of greatness of service, and that was greatest service which implied most self-denial. Suiting the action to the teaching, the Blessed Saviour took the happy child in His Arms. Not to teach, to preach, to work miracles, nor to do great things, but to do the humblest service for Christ's sake, was to receive Christ—nay, to receive the Father. And the smallest service, as it might seem—even the giving a cup of cold water in such spirit—would not lose its reward.

These words about receiving Christ, and 'receiving in the Name of Christ,' had stirred the memory and conscience of John, and made him half wonder, half fear, whether what they had done by the way, in forbidding the man to do what he could in the Name of Christ, had been right. And so he told it, and received the further and higher teaching on the subject. St. Mark and St. Matthew record further instruction in connection with this, to which St. Luke refers at a somewhat later period.[a] The love of Christ goes deeper than the condescension of receiving a child, utterly un-Pharisaic and un-Rabbinic as this is.[b] A man may enter into the Kingdom and do service—yet, if in so doing he disregard the law of love to the little ones, far better his work should be abruptly cut short; better one of those large millstones turned by an ass were hung about his neck and he cast into the sea! We pause to note, once more, the Judaic, and therefore evidential setting of the Evangelic narrative. The Talmud also speaks of two kinds of millstones—the one turned by hand, referred to in St. Luke xvii. 35 : the other turned by an ass. Similarly, the figure about a millstone hung round the neck occurs also in the Talmud —although there as figurative of almost insuperable difficulties. Again, the expression, 'it were better for him,' is a well-known Rabbinic expression. Lastly, according

a St. Luke xvii. 1–7

b St. Matt. xviii. 2–6, and parallels

to St. Jerome, the punishment which seems alluded to in the words of Christ, and which we know to have been inflicted by Augustus, was actually practised by the Romans in Galilee on some of the leaders of the insurrection under Judas of Galilee.

And yet greater guilt would only too surely be incurred! Woe unto the world![a] Occasions of stumbling and offence would surely come, but woe to the man through whom such havoc was wrought. What then is the alternative? If it be a question as between offence and some part of ourselves, a limb or member, however useful—the hand, the foot, the eye— then let it rather be severed from the body, however painful, or however seemingly great the loss. It cannot be so great as that of the whole being in the eternal fire of Gehenna, where their worm dieth not, and the fire is not quenched. Be it hand, foot, or eye—practice, pursuit, or research—which consciously leads us to occasions of stumbling, it must be resolutely put aside in view of the incomparably greater loss of eternal remorse and anguish.

Here St. Mark abruptly breaks off with a saying in which the Saviour makes general application, although the narrative is further continued by St. Matthew.[b] It seems to us that, turning from this thought that even members which are intended for useful service may, in certain circumstances, have to be cut off to avoid the greatest loss, the Lord gave to His disciples this as the final summary and explanation of all: 'For every one shall be salted for the fire'—or, as a very early gloss which has strangely crept into the text paraphrased and explained it, 'Every sacrifice shall be salted with salt.' No one is fit for the sacrificial fire nor can offer anything as a sacrifice, unless it have been first, according to the Levitical Law, covered with salt, symbolic of the incorruptible. 'Salt is good; but if the salt,' with which the spiritual sacrifice is to be salted for the fire, 'have lost its savour, wherewith will ye season it?' Hence, 'have salt in yourselves,' but do not let that salt be corrupted by making it an occasion of offence to others, or among your·

*St. Matt. xviii. 7-9; St. Mark ix. 43-48

b St. Mark ix. 49, 50

U

selves, as in the dispute by the way, or in the disposition of mind that led to it, or in forbidding others to work who follow not with you, but ' be at peace among yourselves.'

To this explanation of the words of Christ it may, perhaps, be added that, from their form, they must have conveyed a special meaning to the disciples. It was a well-known law that every sacrifice burned on the Altar must be salted with salt.[a] Indeed, according to the Talmud, not only every such offering, but even the wood with which the sacrificial fire was kindled, was sprinkled with salt. Salt symbolised to the Jews of that time the incorruptible and the higher. The Bible was compared to salt, so was acuteness of intellect, so was the soul. Lastly, the question : ' If the salt have lost its savour, wherewith will ye season it ? ' seems to have been proverbial, and occurs in exactly the same words in the Talmud, apparently to denote a thing that is impossible.

a Lev. ii. 13

Most thoroughly anti-Pharisaic and anti-Rabbinic as all this was, what St. Matthew further reports leads still farther in the same direction. We seem to see Jesus still holding this child, and, with evident reference to the Jewish contempt for that which is small, point to him and apply, in quite other manner than they had ever heard, the Rabbinic teaching about the Angels. In the Jewish view, only the chiefest of the Angels were before the Face of God within the curtained Veil, while the others, ranged in different classes, stood outside and awaited His behest. The distinction which the former enjoyed was always to behold His Face, and to hear and know directly the Divine counsels and commands. This distinction was, therefore, one of knowledge ; Christ taught that it was one of love. Look up from earth to heaven ; those representative, it may be guardian Angels nearest to God, are not those of deepest knowledge of God's counsel and commands, but those of simple, humble grace and faith—and so learn not only not to despise one of these little ones, but who is truly greatest in the Kingdom of Heaven !

Yet a further depth of Christian love remained to be

shown, that which sought not its own, but the things of others. Hitherto it had been a question of not seeking self, nor minding great things, but, Christ-like and God-like, to condescend to the little ones.   What if actual wrong had been done, and just offence given, by a 'brother'?[a] In such case, also, the principle of the Kingdom —which, negatively, is that of self-forgetfulness, positively, that of service of love—would first seek the good of the offending brother.   We mark here the contrast to Rabbinism, which directs that the first overtures must be made by the offender, not the offended; and even prescribes this to be done in presence of numerous witnesses, and, if needful, repeated three times.   As regards the duty of showing to a brother his fault, and the delicate tenderness of doing this in private so as not to put him to shame, Rabbinism speaks the same as the Master of Nazareth. Yet, in practice, matters were very different; and neither could those be found who would take reproof, nor yet such as were worthy to administer it.

Quite other was it in the Kingdom of Christ, where the theory was left undefined, but the practice clearly marked.   Here, by loving dealing, to convince of his wrong him who had done it, was not humiliation nor loss of dignity or of right, but real gain: the gain of our brother to us, and eventually to Christ Himself.   But even if this should fail, the offended must not desist from his service of love, but conjoin in it others with himself so as to give weight and authority to his remonstrances, as not being the outcome of personal feeling or prejudice—perhaps, also, to be witnesses before the Divine tribunal.   If this failed, a final appeal should be made on the part of the Church as a whole, which, of course, could only be done through her representatives and rulers, to whom Divine authority had been committed.   And if that were rejected, the offer of love would, as always in the Gospel, pass into danger of judgment.   Not, indeed, that such was to be executed by man; but that such an offender, after the first and second admonition, was to be rejected.[b] He was to be treated as was the custom in regard

[a] St. Matt. xviii. 15

[b] Titus iii. 10

to a heathen or a publican—not persecuted, despised, or avoided, but not received in Church-fellowship (a heathen), nor admitted to close familiar intercourse (a publican). And this, as we understand it, marks out the mode of what is called Church discipline in general, and specifically as regards wrong done to a brother. Discipline so exercised (which may God restore to us) has the highest Divine sanction, and the most earnest reality attaches to it. For in virtue of the authority which Christ had committed to the Church in the persons of her rulers and representatives, what they bound or loosed—declared obligatory or non-obligatory—was ratified in heaven. Nor was this to be wondered at. The Incarnation of Christ was the link which bound earth to heaven; through it whatever was agreed upon in the fellowship of Christ as that which was to be asked, would be done for them of His Father Which was in heaven.[a] Thus the power of the Church reached up to heaven through the power of prayer in His Name Who made God our Father. And so, beyond the exercise of discipline and authority, there was the omnipotence of prayer—'if two of you shall agree . . . as touching anything . . . it shall be done for them'—and with it also the possibility of a higher service of love. For in the smallest gathering in the Name of Christ His Presence would be, and with it the certainty of nearness to, and acceptance with, God.[b]

It is bitterly disappointing that, after such teaching, even a Peter could come to the Master—either immediately, or perhaps after he had had time to think it over, and apply it—with the question how often he was to forgive an offending brother, imagining that he had more than satisfied the new requirements, if he extended it to seven times.[c] Such traits show better than elaborate discussions the need of the mission and the renewing of the Holy Ghost. And yet there is something touching in the simplicity and honesty with which Peter goes to the Master, as if he had fully entered into His teaching, yet with such a misapprehension of its spirit.

[a] St. Matt. xviii. 19

[b] vv. 19, 20

[c] ver. 21

Surely, the new wine was bursting the old bottles. It was a principle of Rabbinism that, even if the wrongdoer had made full restoration, he would not obtain forgiveness till he had asked it of him whom he had wronged, but that it was cruelty in such circumstances to refuse pardon. The Jerusalem Talmud adds the beautiful remark: 'Let this be a token in thine hand—each time that thou showest mercy, God will show mercy on thee; and if thou showest not mercy, neither will God show mercy on thee.' But it was a settled rule, that forgiveness should not be extended more than three times. Even so, the practice was very different.

It must have seemed to Peter, in his ignorance, quite a stretch of charity to extend forgiveness to seven, instead of three offences. It did not occur to him that the very act of numbering offences marked an externalism which had never entered into, nor comprehended the spirit of Christ. Until seven times? Nay, until seventy times seven! The evident purport of these words was to efface all such landmarks. Peter had yet to learn what we too often forget: that Christ's forgiveness, as that of the Christian, must not be computed by numbers. It is *qualitative*, not *quantitative*: Christ forgives sin, not sins —and he who has experienced it follows in His footsteps.

CHAPTER L.

THE JOURNEY TO JERUSALEM—FIRST INCIDENTS BY THE WAY.

(St. John vii. 1–16; St. Luke ix. 1–56, 57–62; St. Matt. viii. 19–22.)

THE part in the Evangelic History which we have now reached has this peculiarity and difficulty, that the events are recorded by only one of the Evangelists. The section in St. Luke's Gospel from chapter ix. 51 to chapter xviii. 14 stands absolutely alone. St. John mentions three appearances of Christ in Jerusalem at that period : at the Feast of Tabernacles,[a] at that of the Dedication,[b] and His final entry, which is referred to by all the other Evangelists.[c] But, while the narrative of St. John confines itself exclusively to what happened in Jerusalem or its immediate neighbourhood, it also either mentions or gives sufficient indication that on two out of these three occasions Jesus left Jerusalem for the country east of the Jordan (St. John x. 19–21 ; St. John x. 39–43, where the words in ver. 39, 'they sought again to take Him,' point to a previous similar attempt and flight). Besides these, St. John also records a journey to Bethany—though not to Jerusalem—for the raising of Lazarus,[d] and after that a council against Christ in Jerusalem, in consequence of which He withdrew out of Judæan territory into a district near ' the wilderness '[e]— as we infer, that in the north, where John had been baptising and Christ been tempted, and whither He had afterwards withdrawn.[f] We regard this ' wilderness ' as on the eastern bank of the Jordan, and extending northward towards the eastern shore of the Lake of Galilee.[g]

a St. John
vii. to x.

b x. 22-42

c St. Matt.
xx. 17 &c.;
St. Mark x.
32 &c.; St.
Luke xvii.
11 &c.

d St. John xi.

e xi. 54

f St. Luke
iv. 1; v. 16;
vii. 24

g St. Luke
viii. 29

If St. John relates three appearances of Jesus at this time in Jerusalem, St. Luke records three journeys to Jerusalem,[h] the last of which agrees, in regard to its starting point, with the notices of the other Evangelists.[i]

h St. Luke
ix. 51 ; xiii.
22 ; xviii. 31

i St. Matt.
xix. 1;
St. Mark x. 1

St. Luke's account of the three journeys to Jerusalem fits into the narrative of Christ's three appearances in Jerusalem as described by St. John. The unique section in St. Luke[j] supplies the record of what took place before, during, and after those journeys, of which the upshot is told by St. John. We have now some insight into the plan of St. Luke's Gospel, as compared with that of the others. We see that St. Luke forms a kind of transition between the other two Synoptists and St. John. The Gospel by St. Matthew has for its main object the Discourses or teaching

j St. Luke
ix. 51-xviii.
14

of the Lord, around which the History groups itself. It is intended as a demonstration, primarily addressed to the Jews, and in a form peculiarly suited to them, that Jesus was the Messiah, the Son of the Living God. The Gospel by St. Mark is a rapid survey of the History of the Christ as such. It deals mainly with the Galilean Ministry. The Gospel by St. John, which gives the highest, the reflective, view of the Eternal Son as the Word, deals almost exclusively with the Jerusalem Ministry. And the Gospel by St. Luke complements the narratives in the other two Gospels (St. Matthew and St. Mark), and it supplements them by tracing, what is not done otherwise: the Ministry in Peræa.

The subject primarily before us is the journeying of Jesus to Jerusalem. In that wider view which St. Luke takes of this whole history, he presents what really were three separate journeys as one—that towards the great end.

St. John goes farther back, and speaks of the circumstances which preceded Christ's journey to Jerusalem. The events chronicled in the sixth chapter of St. John's Gospel took place immediately before the Passover,[a] which was on the fifteenth day of the first ecclesiastical month (*Nisan*), while the Feast of Tabernacles [b] began on the same day of the seventh ecclesiastical month (*Tishri*). The six or seven months between the Feast of Passover [c] and that of Tabernacles,[d] and all that passed within them, are covered by this brief remark: 'After these things Jesus walked in Galilee: for He would not walk in Judæa, because the Jews [the leaders of the people] sought to kill Him.'

But now the Feast of Tabernacles was at hand. The pilgrims would probably arrive in Jerusalem before the opening day of the Festival. For besides the needful preparations—which would require time, especially on this Feast, when booths had to be constructed in which to live during the festive week—it was the common practice to offer such sacrifices as might have previously become due at any of the great Feasts to which the people might go

[a] St. John vi. 4

[b] vii. 2

[c] ch. vi.

[d] ch. vii.

up. Remembering that five months had elapsed since the
last great Feast (that of Weeks), many such sacrifices
must have been due. Accordingly, the ordinary festive
companies of pilgrims, which would travel slowly, must
have started from Galilee some time before the beginning
of the Feast. These circumstances fully explain the details
of the narrative. They also afford another illustration of
the loneliness of Christ in His Work. His disciples had
failed to understand His teaching. In the near prospect
of His Death they either displayed gross ignorance, or else
disputed about their future rank. And His own 'brethren'
did not believe in Him. The whole course of late events,
especially the unmet challenge of the Scribes for ' a sign
from heaven,' had deeply shaken them. If He really did
these ' Works,' let Him manifest Himself before the world
—in Jerusalem, the capital of their world, and before those
who could test the reality of them. Let Him come forward, at one of Israel's great Feasts, in the Temple, and
especially at this Feast which pointed to the Messianic ingathering of all nations. Let Him now go up with them
in the festive company into Judæa, that so His disciples—
not the Galileans only, but all—might have the opportunity
of ' gazing ' on His Works.

As the challenge was not new, so from the worldly
point of view it can scarcely be called unreasonable. To
manifest Himself! This truly would He do, though not
in their way. For this ' the season ' had not yet come,
though it would soon arrive. Their ' season '—that for
such Messianic manifestations as they contemplated—was
' always ready.' And this naturally, for ' the world ' could
not ' hate ' them ; they and their demonstrations were quite
in accordance with the world and its views. But towards
Him the world cherished personal hatred, because of their
contrariety of principle, because Christ was manifested,
not to restore an earthly kingdom to Israel, but to bring
the Heavenly Kingdom upon earth—' to destroy the works
of the Devil.' Hence, He must provoke the enmity of
that world which lay in the Wicked One. Another manifestation than that which they sought would He make,

when His 'season was fulfilled;' soon, beginning at this very Feast, continued at the next, and completed at the last Passover; such manifestation of Himself as the Christ, as could alone be made in view of the essential enmity of the world.

And so He let them go up in the festive company, while Himself tarried. When the noise and publicity (which He wished to avoid) were no longer to be apprehended, He also went up, but privately, not publicly, as they had suggested. Here St. Luke's account begins. It almost reads like a commentary on what the Lord had just said to His brethren about the enmity of the world, and His mode of manifestation. ' He came unto His own, and His own received Him not. But as many as received Him, to them gave He power to become children of God . . . which were born . . . of God.'

The first purpose of Christ seems to have been to take the more direct road to Jerusalem, through Samaria, and not to follow that of the festive pilgrim-bands, which travelled to Jerusalem through Peræa, in order to avoid the land of their hated rivals. But His intention was soon frustrated. In the very first Samaritan village to which the Christ had sent beforehand to prepare for Himself and His company, His messengers were told that the Rabbi could not be received; that neither hospitality nor friendly treatment could be extended to One Who was going up to the Feast at Jerusalem. The messengers who brought back this strangely un-Oriental answer met the Master and His followers on the road. It was not only an outrage on common manners, but an act of open hostility to Israel, as well as to Christ, and the 'Sons of Thunder,' whose feelings for their Master were, perhaps, the more deeply stirred as opposition to Him grew more fierce, proposed to vindicate the cause, alike of Israel and its Messiah-King, by the open and Divine judgment of fire called down from heaven to destroy that village. Did they in this connection think of the vision of Elijah, ministering to Christ on the Mount of Transfiguration—and was this their application of it? But He Who had come, not to destroy, but to save, turned and rebuked them, and passed from Samaritan into Jewish territory.

This journey was decisive not only as regarded the Master, but those who followed Him. Henceforth it must not be as in former times, but wholly and exclusively as into suffering and death. It is thus that we view the next three incidents of the way.

It seems that as, after the rebuff of these Samaritans, they ' were going' towards another, and a Jewish village, ' one' of the company, and as we learn from St. Matthew, ' a Scribe,' in the generous enthusiasm of the moment— perhaps stimulated by the wrong of the Samaritans, per- haps touched by the love which would rebuke the zeal of the disciples, but had no word of blame for the unkindness of others—broke into a spontaneous declaration of readiness to follow Him absolutely and everywhere. But there was one eventuality which that Scribe, and all of like enthusiasm, reckoned not with—the utter homelessness of the Christ in this world; and this, not from accidental circumstances, but because He was ' the Son of Man.'

The intenseness of the self-denial involved in following Christ, and its contrariety to all that was commonly re- ceived among men, was immediately brought out. This Scribe had proffered to follow Jesus. Another of His dis- ciples He asked to follow Him, and that in circumstances
ᵃ St. Luke   of peculiar trial and difficulty.ᵃ   The expression
ix. 59   ' to follow' a Teacher would, in those days, be universally understood as implying discipleship. Again, no other duty would be regarded as more sacred than that they, on whom the obligation naturally devolved, should bury the dead. To this everything must give way—even prayer, and the study of the Law. Lastly, we feel certain that when Christ called this disciple to follow Him, He was fully aware that at that very moment his father lay dead. Thus, He called him not only to homelessness—for this he might have been prepared—but to set aside what alike natural feeling and the Jewish Law seemed to impose on him as the most sacred duty. In the apparently strange reply which Christ made to the request to be allowed first

to bury his father, we pass over the consideration that, according to Jewish Law, the burial and mourning for a dead father and the subsequent purifications would have occupied many days, so that it might have been difficult, perhaps impossible, to overtake Christ. We would rather abide by the simple words of Christ. They teach us this searching lesson, that there are higher duties than either those of the Jewish Law, or even of natural reverence, and a higher call than that of man.

Yet another hindrance to following Christ was to be faced. Another in the company would go with Him, but he asked permission first to go and bid farewell to those whom he had left in his home. It almost seems as if this request had been one of those ' tempting ' questions addressed to Christ. It shows that to follow Christ was regarded as a duty, and to leave those in the earthly home as a trial; and it betokens not merely a divided heart, but one not fit for the Kingdom of God. For how can he draw a straight furrow in which to cast the seed, who, as he puts his hand to the plough, looks around or behind him ?

Thus, these are the three vital conditions of following Christ : absolute self-denial and homelessness in the world ; immediate and entire self-surrender to Christ and His Work ; and a heart and affections simple, undivided, and set on Christ and His Work—while there is no other trial of parting like that which would involve parting from Him, no other or higher joy than that of following Him.

CHAPTER LI.

THE MISSION AND RETURN OF THE SEVENTY—THE HOME AT BETHANY.

(St. Luke x. 1–16 ; St. Matt. ix. 36–38 ; xi. 20–24 ; St. Luke x. 17–24 ;
St. Matt. xi. 25–30 ; xiii. 16 ; St. Luke x. 25, 38–42.)

IT seems most likely that it was on His progress south-wards at this time that Jesus ' designated ' those ' seventy '

' others,' who were to herald His arrival in every town and village.

With all their similarity, there are notable differences between the Mission of the Twelve and this of ' the other Seventy.' Let it be noted that the former is recorded by the three Evangelists, so that there could have been no confusion on the part of St. Luke.[a] But the Mission of the Twelve was on their appointment to the Apostolate ; it was evangelistic and mission- ary ; and it was in confirmation and manifesta- tion of the ' power and authority' given to them. We regard it, therefore, as symbolical of the Apostolate just instituted, with its work and authority. On the other hand, no power or authority was formally conferred on the Seventy, their mission being only temporary; its primary object was to prepare for the coming of the Master in the places to which they were sent; and their selection was from the wider circle of disciples, the number being now Seventy instead of Twelve. Even these two numbers, as well as the difference in the functions of the two classes of messengers, seem to indicate that the Twelve symbolised the princes of the tribes of Israel, while the Seventy were the symbolical representatives of these tribes, like the seventy elders appointed to assist Moses.[b] This symbolical meaning of the number Seventy con- tinued among the Jews. We can trace it in the LXX (supposed) translators of the Bible into Greek, and in the seventy members of the Sanhedrin, or supreme court.

We mark that, what may be termed ' the Preface' to the Mission of the Seventy, is given by St. Matthew (in a somewhat fuller form) as that to the appointment and mission of the Twelve Apostles;[c] and it may have been, that kindred words had preceded both. Partially, indeed, the expressions reported in St. Luke x. 2 had been employed long before.[d] Those ' multi- tudes ' throughout Israel—nay, those also which ' are not of that flock'—appeared to His view like sheep without a true shepherd's care, ' distressed and prostrate,' and their mute misery appealed to His Divine com-

[a] St. Matt. x. 5 &c.; St. Mark vi. 7 &c.; St. Luke ix. 1 &c.

[b] Num. xi. 16

[c] St. Matt. ix. 36-38

[d] St. John iv. 35

passion. This constituted the ultimate ground of the Mission of the Apostles, and now of that of the Seventy, into a harvest that was truly great. Compared with the extent of the field, and the urgency of the work, how few were the labourers! Yet, as the field was God's, so also could He alone 'thrust forth labourers' willing and able to do His work, while it must be ours to pray that He would be pleased to do so.

On these introductory words,[a] which ever since have formed 'the bidding prayer' of the Church in her work for Christ, followed the commission and special directions to the thirty-five pairs of disciples who went on this embassy. In almost every particular they are the same as those formerly given to the Twelve. We mark, however, that both the introductory and the concluding words addressed to the Apostles are wanting in what was said to the Seventy. It was not necessary to warn them against going to the Samaritans, since the direction of the Seventy was to those cities of Peræa and Judæa, on the road to Jerusalem, through which Christ was about to pass. Nor were they armed with precisely the same supernatural powers as the Twelve.[b] Naturally, the personal directions as to their conduct were in both cases substantially the same. We mark only three peculiarities in those addressed to the Seventy. The direction to 'salute no man by the way' was suitable to a temporary and rapid mission, which might have been interrupted by making or renewing acquaintances. Both the Mishnah and the Talmud lay it down, that prayer was not to be interrupted to salute even a king, nay, to uncoil a serpent that had wound round the foot. All agreed that immediately before prayer no one should be saluted, to prevent distraction, and it was advised rather to summarise or to cut short than to interrupt prayer, though the latter might be admissible in case of absolute necessity. None of these provisions, however, seems to have been in the mind of Christ. If any parallel is to be sought, it would be found in the similar direction of Elisha to Gehazi, when sent to lay the prophet's staff on the dead child of the Shunammite.

[a] St. Luke x. 2

[b] St. Matt. x. 7, 8; comp. St. Luke x. 9

The other two peculiarities in the address to the Seventy seem verbal rather than real. The expression,[a] 'if the Son of Peace be there,' is a Hebraism, equivalent to 'if the house be worthy,'[b] and refers to the character of the head of the house and the tone of the household. Lastly, the direction to eat and drink such things as were set before them[c] is only a further explanation of the command to abide in the house which had received them, without seeking for better entertainment. On the other hand, the whole most important close of the address to the Twelve— which, indeed, forms by far the largest part of it[d] —is wanting in the commission to the Seventy, thus clearly marking its merely temporary character.

In St. Luke's Gospel, the address to the Seventy is followed by a denunciation of Chorazin and Bethsaida.[e] This is evidently in its right place there, after the Ministry of Christ in Galilee had been completed and finally rejected. In St. Matthew's Gospel, it stands immediately after the Lord's rebuke of the popular rejection of the Baptist's message.[f] The ' woe ' pronounced on those cities, in which ' most of His mighty works were done,' is in proportion to the greatness of their privileges. The denunciation of Chorazin and Bethsaida is the more remarkable, that Chorazin is not otherwise mentioned in the Gospels, nor yet any miracles recorded as having taken place in (the western) Bethsaida. From this two inferences seem inevitable. First, if this history were legendary, Jesus would not be represented as selecting the names of places, which the writer had not connected with the legend. Again, apparently no record has been preserved in the Gospels of most of Christ's miracles—only those being narrated, which were necessary in order to present Jesus as the Christ, in accordance with the respective plans on which each of the Gospels was constructed.[g]

Chorazin and Bethsaida are compared with Tyre and Sidon, which under similar admonitions would have repented, while Capernaum, which, as for so long the home

[a] St. Luke
x. 6
[b] St. Matt.
x. 13

[c] St. Luke
x. 7, 8

[d] St. Matt.
xi. 16-42

[e] St. Luke
x. 13-16

[f] St. Matt.
xi. 20-24

[g] St. John
xxi. 25

of Jesus, had truly 'been exalted to heaven,' is compared
with Sodom.   And such guilt involved a still greater
punishment.   The very site of Bethsaida and Chorazin
cannot be fixed with certainty.   The former probably represents the 'Fisherton' of Capernaum; the latter St.
Jerome places two miles from Capernaum.   If so, it may
be represented by the modern Kerâzeh, somewhat to the
north-west of Capernaum.   As for Capernaum itself—
standing on that vast field of ruins and upturned stones
which marks the site of the modern *Tell Hûm*, we feel
that no description of it could be more pictorially true
than that in which Christ prophetically likened the city
in its downfall to the desolateness of death and 'Hades.'

Whether or not the Seventy actually returned to Jesus
before the Feast of Tabernacles, it is convenient to consider
in this connection the result of their Mission.   It had
filled them with 'joy;' nay, the result had exceeded their
expectations, just as their faith had gone beyond the mere
letter unto the spirit of His Words.   As they reported it
to Him, even the demons had been subject to them through
His Name.   In this they had exceeded the letter of Christ's
commission; but as they made experiment of it, their faith
had grown, and they had applied His command to 'heal
the sick' to the worst of all sufferers, those grievously
vexed by demons.   The Prince of Light and Life had
vanquished the Prince of Darkness and Death.   The
Prince of this world must be cast out.[a]   In
spirit, Christ gazed on 'Satan falling as lightning
from heaven.'   He sees of the travail of His soul, and is
satisfied!

a St. John xii. 31

What the faith of the Seventy had attained was now
to be made permanent to the Church, whose representatives
they were.   For the words in which Christ now gave
authority and power to tread on serpents and scorpions,
and over all the power of the Enemy, and the promise
that nothing should hurt them, could not have been addressed to the Seventy for a Mission which had now come
to an end, except in so far as they represented the Church
Universal.   Yet it is not this power or authority which is

to be the main joy either of the Church or the individual, but the fact that our names are written in heaven. And so Christ brings us back to His great teaching about the need of becoming children, and wherein lies the secret of true greatness in the Kingdom.

The joy of the disciples was met by that of the Master, and His teaching presently merged into a prayer of thanksgiving. Throughout the occurrences since the Transfiguration, we have noticed an increasing antithesis to the teaching of the Rabbis. But it almost reached its climax in the thanksgiving, that the Father in heaven had hid these things from the wise and the understanding, and revealed them unto babes. As we view it in the light of those times, we know that 'the wise and understanding' —the Rabbi and the Scribe—could not, from their standpoint, have perceived them. And so it must ever be the law of the Kingdom and the fundamental principle of Divine Revelation that, not as 'wise and understanding,' but only as 'babes'—as 'converted,' 'like children'—we can share in that knowledge which maketh wise unto salvation. This truly is the Gospel, and the Father's good pleasure.

The words [a] with which Christ turned from this address

ᵃ St. Luke x. to the Seventy and thanksgiving to God, seem almost like the Father's answer to the prayer of the Son. They refer to and explain the authority which Jesus had bestowed on His Church: 'All things were delivered to Me of My Father;' and they afford the highest *rationale* for the fact that these things had been hid from the wise and revealed unto babes. For as no man, only the Father, could have full knowledge of the Son, and conversely no man, only the Son, had true knowledge of the Father, it followed that this knowledge came to us, not of wisdom or learning, but only through the Revelation of Christ: 'No one knoweth Who the Son is, save the Father; and Who the Father is, save the Son, and he to whomsoever the Son willeth to reveal Him.'

St. Matthew, who also records this—although in a different connection—concludes this section by words which have ever since been the grand text of those who, following in the wake of the Seventy, have been ambassadors for Christ.[a] On the other hand, St. Luke concludes this part of his narrative by adducing words equally congruous to the occasion,[b] which, indeed, are not new in the mouth of the Lord.[c] From their suitableness to what had preceded, we can have little doubt that both that which St. Matthew, and that which St. Luke report were spoken on this occasion. Because knowledge of the Father came only through the Son, and because these things were hidden from the wise and revealed to 'babes,' did the gracious Lord open His Arms and bid all that laboured and were heavy laden come to Him. These were the sheep, distressed and prostrate, whom to gather, that He might give them rest, He had sent forth the Seventy on a work for which He had prayed the Father to thrust forth labourers, and which He has since entrusted to the faith and service of love of the Church. And the true wisdom, which qualified for the Kingdom, was to take up His yoke, which would be found easy, not like that unbearable yoke of Rabbinic conditions;[d] and the true understanding to be sought was by learning of Him. In that wisdom of entering the Kingdom by taking up its yoke, and in that knowledge which came by learning of Him, Christ was Himself alike the true lesson and the best teacher for those 'babes.' For He is meek and lowly in heart, and so, by coming unto Him, would true rest be found for the soul.

These words, as recorded by St. Matthew—the Evangelist of the Jews—must have sunk the deeper into the hearts of Christ's Jewish hearers, that they came in their own old familiar form of speech, yet with such contrast of spirit. One of the most common figurative expressions of the time was that of 'the yoke,' to indicate submission to an occupation or obligation. Thus we read not only of the 'yoke of the Law,' but of that of 'earthly governments,' and ordinary 'civil obligations.' This yoke might be 'cast off,' as the ten tribes had cast off that 'of God,' and thus brought on themselves their exile. On the other hand, to

a St. Matt. xi. 28–30

b St. Luke x. 23, 24

c Comp. St. Matt. xiii. 16

d Acts xv. 10

X

'take upon oneself the yoke' meant to submit to it of free choice and deliberate resolution. Of Isaiah it was said that he had been privileged to prophesy of so many blessings, 'because he had taken upon himself the yoke of the Kingdom of Heaven with joy.' And, as previously stated, it was set forth that in the ' *Shema*,' or Creed—which was repeated every day—the words, Deut. vi. 4–9, were recited before those in xi. 13–21, so as first generally to ' take upon ourselves the yoke of the Kingdom of Heaven, and only afterwards that of the commandments.' And this yoke all Israel had taken upon itself, thereby gaining the merit ever afterwards imputed to them.

Yet, practically, ' the yoke of the Kingdom' was none other than that ' of the Law ' and ' of the commandments ; ' one of laborious performances and of impossible self-righteousness. It was ' unbearable,' not ' the easy ' yoke of Christ, in which the Kingdom of God was of faith, not of works. This voluntary making of the yoke as heavy as possible, the taking on themselves as many obligations as possible, was the ideal of Rabbinic piety. There was, therefore, peculiar teaching and comfort in the words of Christ; and well might He add, as St. Luke reports,[a] that blessed were they who saw and heard these things.

[a] St. Luke x. 23, 24

It seems not unlikely, that the scene next recorded by St. Luke [b] stands in its right place. Such an inquiry on the part of a ' certain lawyer,' as to what he should do to inherit eternal life, together with Christ's Parabolic teaching about the Good Samaritan, is evidently congruous to the previous teaching of Christ about entering into the Kingdom of Heaven. Possibly, this Scribe may have understood the words of the Master about these things being hid from the wise, and the need of taking up the yoke of the Kingdom, as enforcing the views of those Rabbinic teachers who laid more stress upon good works than upon study.

[b] x. 25 &c.

From this interruption, which, but for the teaching of Christ connected with it, would have formed a discord in the heavenly harmony of this journey, we turn to a far

other scene. It must mark the close of Christ's journey to
the Feast of Tabernacles, since the home of Martha and
Mary, to which it introduces us, was in Bethany, close to
Jerusalem, almost one of its suburbs. From the narrative
of Christ's reception in the house of Martha, we gather
that Jesus had arrived in Bethany with His disciples, but
^{a St. Luke x.} that He alone was the guest of the two sisters.^a
³⁸ We infer that Christ had dismissed His disciples
to go into the neighbouring City for the Feast, while Himself tarried in Bethany. With this agrees the notice in
St. John vii. 14, that it was not at the beginning, but
'about the midst of the feast,' that 'Jesus went up into
the Temple.' Although travelling on the two first festive
days was not actually unlawful, yet we can scarcely conceive
that Jesus would have done so—especially on the Feast of
Tabernacles; and the inference is obvious, that Jesus had
tarried in the immediate neighbourhood, as we know He
did at Bethany in the house of Martha and Mary.

Other things, also, do so explain themselves—notably,
the absence of the brother of Martha and Mary, who probably spent the festive days in the City itself. It was the
beginning of the Feast of Tabernacles, and the scene recorded by St. Luke ^b would take place in the
^{b x. 38-42} open leafy booth which served as the sitting
apartment during the festive week. For, according to
law, it was duty during the festive week to eat, sleep, pray,
study—in short, to live—in these booths, which were to
be constructed of the boughs of living trees. And, although
this was not absolutely obligatory on women, yet the rule
which bade all make 'the booth the principal, and the
house only the secondary dwelling,' would induce them to
make this leafy tent at least the sitting apartment alike
for men and women. They were high enough, and yet
not too high; chiefly open in front; close enough to be
shady, and yet not so close as to exclude sunlight and air.
Such would be the apartment in which what is recorded
passed; and, if we add that this booth stood probably in
the court, we can picture to ourselves Martha moving
forwards and backwards on her busy errands, and seeing,

as she went, Mary still sitting a rapt listener, not heeding
what passed around; and, lastly, how the elder sister could,
as the language of verse 40 implies, enter so suddenly the
Master's Presence, bringing her complaint.

To understand this history, we must dismiss from our
minds preconceived, though, perhaps, attractive thoughts.
There is no evidence that the household of Bethany had
previously belonged to the circle of Christ's professed disciples. It was, as the whole history shows, a wealthy home.
Although we know not how it came so to be, the house
was evidently Martha's, and into it she received Jesus on
His arrival in Bethany. It would have been no uncommon
occurrence in Israel for a pious, wealthy lady to receive a
great Rabbi into her house. But the present was not an
ordinary case. Martha must have heard of Him, even if
she had not seen Him. But, indeed, the whole narrative
^a Comp. St. implies ^a that Jesus had come to Bethany with
Luke x. 38 the view of accepting the hospitality of Martha,
which probably had been proffered when some of those
' Seventy,' sojourning in the worthiest house at Bethany,
had announced the near arrival of the Master. Still, her
bearing affords only indication of being drawn towards
Christ—at most, of a sincere desire to learn the good news,
not of actual discipleship.

And so Jesus came. He was to lodge in one of the
booths, the sisters in the house, and the great booth in the
middle of the courtyard would be the common living apartment of all. This festive season was a busy time for the
mistress of a wealthy household, especially in the near
neighbourhood of Jerusalem, whence her brother might,
after the first two festive days, bring with him any time
that week honoured guests from the City. To these cares
was now added that of doing sufficient honour to such a
Guest—for she must already have deeply felt His greatness.
And so she hurried to and fro through the courtyard,
literally, ' distracted about much serving.'

Her younger sister, also, would do Him all highest
honour; but not as Martha. Her homage consisted in
forgetting all else but Him, Who spake as none had ever

done. ' She sat at the Lord's Feet, and heard His Word.'
And so, time after time, as Martha passed on her busy
way, she still sat listening and living. At last the sister,
who in her impatience could not think that a woman
could in such manner fulfil her duty or show forth her
religious profiting, broke in with what sounds like a
querulous complaint: ' Lord, dost Thou not care that my
sister did leave me to serve alone?' Mary had served with
her, but she had now left her to do the work alone. With
tone of gentle reproof and admonition, the affectionateness
of which appeared even in the repetition of her name,
' Martha, Martha '—as similarly, on a later occasion, ' Simon,
Simon '—did He teach her in words which, however simple
in their primary meaning, are so full that they have ever
since borne the most many-sided application: ' Thou art
careful and anxious about many things : but one thing is
needful; and Mary hath chosen that good part, which
shall not be taken away from her.'

CHAPTER LII.

AT THE FEAST OF TABERNACLES—FIRST DISCOURSE IN THE TEMPLE.

(St. John vii. 11–36.)

IT was the non-sacred part of the festive week, the half-
holy days. Jerusalem wore quite another than its usual
aspect; other, even, than when its streets were thronged
by festive pilgrims during the Passover-week, or at Pentecost. For this was pre-eminently the Feast for foreign
pilgrims, coming from the farthest distance, whose Temple-
contributions were then received and counted. As the
Jerusalemite would look with proud self-consciousness, not
unmingled with kindly patronage, on the swarthy strangers,
yet fellow-countrymen, or the eager-eyed Galilean curiously
stare after them, the pilgrims would in turn gaze with
mingled awe and wonderment on the novel scene.
All day long the smoke of the burning, smouldering

sacrifices rose in slowly-widening column, and hung between the Mount of Olives and Zion; the chant of Levites and the solemn responses of the *Hallel* were borne on the breeze, or the clear blast of the Priests' silver trumpets seemed to waken the echoes far away. And then, at night, how all these vast Temple-buildings stood out, illuminated by the great Candelabras that burned in the Court of the Women, and by the glare of torches, when strange sound of mystic hymns and dances came floating over the intervening darkness! Truly, well might Israel designate the Feast of Tabernacles as ' *the* Feast,' and the Jewish historian describe it as ' the holiest and greatest.'

Early on the 14th Tishri (corresponding to our September or early October), all the festive pilgrims had arrived. Then it was indeed a scene of bustle and activity. Hospitality had to be sought and found; guests to be welcomed and entertained; all things required for the Feast to be got ready. Booths must be erected everywhere—in court and on housetop, in street and square, for the lodgment and entertainment of that vast multitude; leafy dwellings everywhere, to remind of the wilderness-journey, and now of the goodly land. Only that fierce castle, Antonia, which frowned above the Temple, was undecked by the festive spring into which the land had burst. To the Jew it must have been a hateful sight, that castle, which guarded and dominated his own City and Temple. Yet, for all this, Israel could not read on the lowering sky the signs of the times, nor yet knew the day of their merciful visitation. And this, although of all festivals that of Tabernacles should have most clearly pointed them to the future.

Indeed, the whole symbolism of the Feast, beginning with the completed harvest, for which it was a thanksgiving, pointed to the future. The Rabbis themselves admitted this. The strange number of sacrificial bullocks —seventy in all—they regarded as referring to ' the seventy nations ' of heathendom. The ceremony of the outpouring of water, which was considered of such vital importance as to give to the whole festival the name of ' House of Outpouring,' was symbolical of the outpouring of the Holy

Spirit. As the brief night of the great Temple-illumination closed, there was solemn testimony made before Jehovah against heathenism. It must have been a stirring scene, when from out the mass of Levites, with their musical instruments, who crowded the fifteen steps that led from the Court of Israel to that of the Women, stepped two Priests with their silver trumpets. As the first cockcrowing intimated the dawn of morn, they blew a threefold blast, another on the tenth step, and yet another threefold blast as they entered the Court of the Women. And, still sounding their trumpets, they marched through the Court of the Women to the Beautiful Gate. Here, turning round and facing westwards to the Holy Place, they repeated: 'Our fathers, who were in this place, they turned their backs on the Sanctuary of Jehovah, and their faces eastward, for they worshipped eastward, the sun; but we, our eyes are towards Jehovah.' 'We are Jehovah's—our eyes are towards Jehovah.' Nay, the whole of this night- and morning-scene was symbolical: the Temple-illumination, of the light which was to shine from out the Temple into the dark night of heathendom; then, at the first dawn of morn the blast of the Priests' silver trumpets, of the army of God, as it advanced with festive trumpet-sound and call to awaken the sleepers, marching on to quite the utmost bounds of the Sanctuary, to the Beautiful Gate, which opened upon the Court of the Gentiles—and then again facing round to utter solemn protest against heathenism, and make solemn confession of Jehovah!

But Jesus did not appear in the Temple during the first two festive days. The pilgrims from all parts of the country had expected Him there, for everyone would now speak of Him—'not openly,' in Jerusalem, for they were afraid of their rulers. But they sought Him, and inquired after Him—a low, confused discussion of the *pro* and *con*. in this great controversy among the 'multitudes,' or festive bands from various parts. Some said: 'He is a good man,' while others declared that He only led astray the common, ignorant populace. And now, all at once, in the half-holy-days, Jesus Himself appeared in the Temple, and taught.

We know that on a later occasion [a] He walked and taught

[a] St. John x. 23
[b] Acts v. 12

in 'Solomon's Porch,' and, from the circumstance
that the early disciples made this their common meeting-place,[b] we may draw the inference
that it was here the people now found Him.   Although
neither Josephus nor the Mishnah mentions this 'Porch' by
name, we have every reason for believing that it was the
eastern colonnade, which abutted against the Mount of
Olives and faced 'the Beautiful Gate,' that formed the
principal entrance into the 'Court of the Women,' and so
into the Sanctuary.   For all along the inside of the great
wall which formed the Temple-enclosure ran a double
colonnade—each column a monolith of white marble, 25
cubits high, covered with cedar-beams.   These colonnades,
which, from their ample space, formed alike places for quiet
walk and for larger gatherings, had benches in them—and,
from the liberty of speaking and teaching in Israel, Jesus
might here address the people in the very face of His
enemies.

We know not what was the subject of Christ's teaching on this occasion.   But the effect on the people was
one of general astonishment.   They knew what common

[c] St. John vii. 15
[d] Comp. Acts xxvi. 24

unlettered Galilean tradesmen were—but this,
whence came it?[c] 'How does this one know literature (letters, learning),[d] never having learned?'
To the Jews there was only one kind of learning—that of
Theology; and only one road to it—the Schools of the Rabbis.
Their *major* was true, but their *minor* false, and Jesus
hastened to correct it.   He had, indeed, 'learned,' but in
a School quite other than those which alone they recognised.
Yet, on their own showing, it claimed submission.
Among the Jews a Rabbi's teaching derived authority
from the fact of its accordance with tradition—that it
accurately represented what had been received from a
previous great teacher, and so on upwards to Moses, and to
God Himself.   On this ground Christ claimed the highest
authority.   His doctrine was not His own invention: it
was the teaching of Him that sent Him.   The doctrine
was God-received, and Christ was sent direct from God to

bring it. He was God's messenger of it to them.[a]
Everyone who in his soul felt drawn towards God,
each one who really 'willeth to do His Will,'
would know 'concerning this teaching, whether it is of
God,' or whether it was of man. It was this felt, though
unrealised influence, which had drawn all men after Him,
so that they hung on His lips.

St. John vii. 16, 17

Jesus had said: 'He shall know of the teaching,
whether it be of God, or whether I speak from Myself.'
From Myself? Why, there is this other test of it: 'Who
speaketh from himself, seeketh his own glory'—there can
be no doubt or question of this, but do I seek My own
glory?—'But He Who seeketh the glory of Him Who
sent Him, He is true [a faithful messenger], and unrighteousness is not in Him.'[b] Thus did Christ
appeal and prove it: My doctrine is of God, and
I am sent of God!

[b] ver. 18

Sent of God, no unrighteousness in Him! And yet at
that very moment there hung over Him the charge of defiance of the Law of Moses, nay, of that of God, in an open
breach of the Sabbath-commandment—there, in that very
City, the last time He had been in Jerusalem; for which,
as well as for His Divine Claims, the Jews were even then
seeking 'to kill Him.'[c] And this forms the transition to what may be called the second part of
Christ's address. Here He argues as a Jew would argue
with Jews, only the substance of the reasoning is to all
times and people. In His reply the two threads of the
former argument are taken up. Doing is the condition of
knowledge—and a messenger had been sent from God!
Admittedly, Moses was such, and yet every one of them
was breaking the Law which he had given them; for were
they not seeking to kill Him without right or justice?
This, put in the form of a double question,[d] represents a peculiarly Jewish mode of argumentation, behind which lay the truth, that those whose hearts
were so little longing to do the Will of God, not only must
remain ignorant of His Teaching as that of God, but had
also rejected that of Moses.

[c] St. John v. 18

[d] ch. vii. 19, 20

A general disclaimer, a cry 'Thou hast a demon' (art possessed), 'who seeks to kill Thee?' here broke in upon the Speaker. But He would not be interrupted, and continued : 'One work I did, and all you wonder on account of it'—referring to His healing on the Sabbath, and their utter inability to understand His conduct. Well, then, Moses was a messenger of God, and I am sent of God. Moses gave the law of circumcision—not, indeed, that it was of his authority, but had long before been God-given —and, to observe this law, no one hesitated to break the Sabbath, since, according to Rabbinic principle, a positive ordinance superseded a negative. And yet when Christ, as sent from God, made a man every whit whole on the Sabbath ('made a whole man sound'), they were angry with Him !ᵃ Every argument which might have been urged in favour of the postponement of Christ's healing to a week-day, would equally apply to that of circumcision ; while every reason that could be urged in favour of Sabbath-circumcision, would tell an hundredfold in favour of the act of Christ. Let them not judge, then, after the mere outward appearance, but 'judge the right judgment.'

ᵃ St. John vii. 21-24

From the reported remarks of some Jerusalemites in the crowd we learn that the fact that He, Whom they sought to kill, was suffered to speak openly, seemed incomprehensible.ᵇ Could it be that the authorities were shaken in their former ideas about Him, and now regarded Him as the Messiah ? But it could not be. It was a settled popular belief, and in a sense not quite unfounded, that the appearance of the Messiah would be sudden and unexpected. He might be there, and not be known ; or He might come, and be again hidden for a time. As they put it, when Messiah came no one would know whence He was ; but they all knew ' whence this One ' was. And with this rough and ready argument they, like so many among us, settled off-hand and once for all the great question. But Jesus could not, even for the sake of His disciples, let it rest there. ' Therefore' He lifted up His voice, that it reached the dispersing, receding multitude. Yes, they thought they knew both Him and whence He came.

ᵇ vv. 25-27

It would have been so had He come from Himself. But He had been sent, and He that sent Him 'was real; 'though they knew Him not. And so, with a reaffirmation of His two-

^a St. John vii. 29

fold claim, His Discourse closed.^a But they had understood His allusions, and in their anger would fain have laid hands on Him, but His hour had not come. Yet others were deeply stirred to faith. As they parted they spoke of it among themselves, and the sum of it all was : 'The Christ, when He cometh, will He do more miracles (signs) than this One did ? '

So ended the first teaching of that day in the Temple. And as the people dispersed, the leaders of the Pharisees —-who, no doubt aware of the presence of Christ in the Temple, yet unwilling to be in the number of His hearers, had watched the effect of His Teaching—overheard the furtive, half-spoken remarks ('the murmuring') of the people about Him. Presently they conferred with the heads of the priesthood and the chief Temple-officials. Although there was neither meeting, nor decree of the Sanhedrin about it, nor, indeed, could be, orders were given to the Temple-guard on the first possible occasion to seize Him. Jesus was aware of it, and as, either on this or another day, He was moving in the Temple, watched by the spies of the rulers and followed by a mingled crowd of disciples and enemies, deep sadness in view of the end filled His heart. ' Jesus therefore said '—no doubt to His disciples, though in the hearing of all—' Yet a little while am I with you, then I go away to Him that sent Me. Ye shall seek Me, and not find Me; and where I am,

^b vv. 33, 34

thither ye cannot come.'^b Mournful words, these, which were only too soon to become true. But those who heard them naturally failed to comprehend their meaning. Was He about to leave Palestine, and go among the dispersed who lived in heathen lands, to teach the Greeks ? Or what could be His meaning ?

CHAPTER LIII.

'IN THE LAST, THE GREAT DAY OF THE FEAST.'

(St. John vii. 37–viii. 11.)

IT was ' the last, the Great Day of the Feast,' and Jesus was once more in the Temple. We have in this Feast the only Old Testament type yet unfulfilled; the only Jewish festival which has no counterpart in the cycle of the Christian year, just because it points forward to that great, yet unfulfilled hope of the Church: the ingathering of Earth's nations to the Christ.

The celebration of the Feast corresponded to its meaning. Not only did all the priestly families minister during that week, but it has been calculated that not fewer than 446 Priests, with, of course, a corresponding number of Levites, were required for its sacrificial worship. In general, the services were the same every day, except that the number of bullocks offered decreased daily from thirteen on the first to seven on the seventh day. Only during the first two, and on the last festive day (as also on the Octave of the Feast), was strict Sabbatic rest enjoined. On the intervening half-holy days, although no new labour was to be undertaken, unless in the public service, the ordinary and necessary avocations of the home and of life were carried on, and especially all done that was required for the festive season. But ' the last, the Great Day of the Feast,' was marked by special observances.

Let us suppose ourselves in the number of worshippers who are leaving their ' booths ' at daybreak to take part in the service. The pilgrims are all in festive array. In his right hand each carries a myrtle and willow-branch tied together with a palm-branch between them. This was supposed to be in fulfilment of the command, Lev. xxiii. 40. 'The fruit (A.V. ' boughs ') of the goodly trees,' mentioned in the same verse of Scripture, was supposed to be the so-called Paradise-apple, a species of citron. This each worshipper carries in his left hand.

Thus provided, the festive multitude would divide into three bands. Some would remain in the Temple to attend the preparation of the Morning Sacrifice. Another band would go in procession ' below Jerusalem ' to a place which some have sought to identify with the Emmaus of the Resurrection-Evening. Here they cut down willow-branches, with which, amidst the blasts of the Priests' trumpets, they adorned the altar, forming a leafy canopy about it. Yet a third company was taking part in a still more interesting service. To the sound of music a procession started from the Temple. It followed a Priest who bore a golden pitcher, capable of holding about two pints. Onwards it passed, probably through Ophel, which recent investigations have shown to have been covered with buildings to the very verge of Siloam, down the edge of the Tyropœon Valley, where it merges into that of the Kedron. To this day terraces mark where the gardens, watered by the living spring, extended from the King's Gardens down to the entrance into the Tyropœon.

When the Temple-procession had reached the Pool of Siloam, the Priest filled his golden pitcher from its waters. Then they went back to the Temple, so timing it that they should arrive just as the pieces of the sacrifice were being laid on the great Altar of Burnt-offering towards the close of the ordinary Morning-Sacrifice service. A threefold blast of the Priests' trumpets welcomed the arrival of the Priest, as he entered through the ' Water-gate,' which obtained its name from this ceremony, and passed straight into the Court of the Priests. Here he was joined by another Priest, who carried the wine for the drink-offering. The two Priests ascended ' the rise ' of the altar, and turned to the left. There were two silver funnels here, with narrow openings, leading down to the base of the altar. Into that at the east, which was some-what wider, the wine was poured, and, at the same time, the water into the western and narrower opening.

Immediately after ' the pouring of water,' the great ' Hallel,' consisting of Psalms cxiii. to cxviii. (inclusive), was chanted antiphonally, or rather with responses, to the

accompaniment of the flute. As the Levites intoned the
first line of each Psalm, the people repeated it; while to
each of the other lines they responded by *Hallelu Yah*
('Praise ye the Lord'). But in Psalm cxviii. the people
not only repeated the first line, 'O give thanks to the
Lord,' but also these, 'O then, work now salvation, Jehovah,'[a] 'O Lord, send now prosperity;'[b] and
again, at the close of the Psalm, 'O give thanks
to the Lord.' As they repeated these lines,
they shook towards the altar the branches which they held
in their hands—as if with this token of the past to express
the reality and cause of their praise, and to remind God of
His promises. It is this moment which should be chiefly
kept in view.

[a] Ps. cxviii.
25
[b] ver. 25

The festive morning-service was followed by the offering of the special sacrifices for the day, with their drink-
offerings, and by the Psalm for the day, which, on 'the
last, the Great Day of the Feast,' was Psalm lxxxii. from
verse 5. The Psalm was, of course, chanted as always
to instrumental accompaniment, and at the end of each of
its three sections the Priests blew a threefold blast, while
the people bowed down in worship. In further symbolism
of this Feast, as pointing to the ingathering of the heathen
nations, the public services closed with a procession round
the altar by the Priests, who chanted, 'O then, work now
salvation, Jehovah! O Jehovah, send now prosperity.'[c]
But on 'the last, the Great Day of the Feast,'
this procession of Priests made the circuit of the
altar, not only once but seven times, as if they were again
compassing, but now with prayer, the Gentile Jericho
which barred their possession of the promised land. Hence
the seventh or last day of the Feast was also called that
of 'the Great Hosannah.' As the people left the Temple,
they saluted the altar with words of thanks, and on the
last day of the Feast they shook off the leaves on the
willow-branches round the altar, and beat their palm-
branches to pieces. On the same afternoon the 'booths'
were dismantled, and the Feast ended.

[c] Ps. cxviii.
25

We can have little difficulty in determining at what

part of the services of 'the last, the Great Day of the Feast,' Jesus stood and cried, 'If any one thirst, let him come unto Me and drink!' It must have been with special reference to the ceremony of the outpouring of the water, which was considered the central part of the service. Moreover, all would understand that His words must refer to the Holy Spirit, since the rite was universally regarded as symbolical of His outpouring. The forthpouring of the water was immediately followed by the chanting of the *Hallel*. But after that there must have been a short pause to prepare for the festive sacrifices. It was then, immediately after the symbolic rite of water-pouring, immediately after the people had responded by repeating those lines from Psalm cxviii.—given thanks, and prayed that Jehovah would send salvation and prosperity, and had shaken their branches towards the altar, thus praising 'with heart and mouth and hands,' and then silence had fallen upon them—that there rose, so loud as to be heard throughout the Temple, the Voice of Jesus. He interrupted not the services, for they had for the moment ceased : He interpreted, and He fulfilled them.

Of those who had heard Him, none but must have understood that, if the invitation were indeed real, and Christ the fulfilment of all, then the promise also had its deepest meaning, that he who believed on Him would not only receive the promised fulness of the Spirit, but give it forth to the fertilising of the barren waste around. It was, truly, the fulfilment of the Scripture-promise, not of one but of all: that in Messianic times the 'prophet,' literally the 'weller forth,' viz., of the Divine, should not be one or another select individual, but that He would pour out on all His handmaidens and servants of His Holy Spirit, and thus the moral wilderness of this world be changed into a fruitful garden. What was new to them was that all this was treasured up in the Christ, that out of His fulness men might receive. And yet even this was not quite new. For was it not the fulfilment of that old prophetic cry : 'The Spirit of the Lord Jehovah is upon Me : therefore has He Messiahed (anointed) Me to preach good tidings unto the poor'? So, then, it was nothing new, only the happy fulfilment of the old, when He thus 'spake of the Holy Spirit, Which they who believed on Him should receive,' not then, but upon His Messianic exaltation.

And so we scarcely wonder that many on hearing Him said, though not with that heart-conviction which would have led to self-surrender, that He was the Prophet promised of old, even the Christ; while others, by their side, regarding Him as a Galilean, the Son of Joseph, raised the ignorant objection that He could not be the Messiah, since the latter must be of the seed of David and come from Bethlehem. Nay, such was the anger of some against what they regarded a dangerous seducer of the poor people, that they would fain have laid violent hands on Him. But amidst all this, the strongest testimony to His Person and Mission remains to be told. It came, as so often, from a quarter whence it could least have been expected. Those Temple-officers, whom the authorities had commissioned to watch an opportunity for seizing Jesus, now returned without having done their behest, and that when, manifestly, the scene in the Temple might have offered the desired ground for His imprisonment. To the question of the Pharisees, they could only give this reply, which has ever since remained unquestionable fact of history, admitted alike by friend and foe : ' Never man so spake as this Man.'

The scene which followed is so thoroughly Jewish, that it alone would suffice to prove the Jewish, and hence Johannine, authorship of the Fourth Gospel. The harsh sneer : ' Are ye also led astray ? ' is succeeded by pointing to the authority of the learned and great, who with one accord were rejecting Jesus. ' But this people '—the country-people, the ignorant, unlettered rabble—' are cursed.'

But there was one standing among the Temple-authorities, whom an uneasy conscience would not allow to remain quite silent. It was the Sanhedrist Nicodemus. He could not hold his peace, and yet he dared not speak for Christ. So he made compromise of both by taking the part of, and speaking as a righteous, rigid Sanhedrist. ' Does our Law judge (pronounce sentence upon) a man, except it first hear from himself and know what he doeth ? ' From the Rabbinic point of view, no sounder judicial saying could have been uttered. Yet such common-place helped not the cause of Jesus, and it disguised not the advocacy of Nicodemus. We know what was thought of Galilee in the Rabbinic world. ' Art thou also of Galilee ? Search and see, for out of Galilee ariseth no prophet.' [1]

CHAPTER LIV.

TEACHING IN THE TEMPLE ON THE OCTAVE OF THE FEAST OF TABERNACLES.

(St. John viii. 12–59.)

THE addresses of Jesus which followed must have been delivered either later on that day, or, as seems more likely, chiefly, or all, on the next day, which was the Octave of the Feast, when the Temple would be once more thronged by worshippers.

On this occasion we find Christ first in ' the Treasury,' [a] and then [b] in some unnamed part of the sacred building, in all probability one of the ' Porches.' Greater freedom could be here enjoyed, since these ' Porches,' which enclosed the Court of the Gentiles, did not form part of the Sanctuary in the stricter sense. Discussions might take place, in which not, as in ' the Treasury,' only ' the Pharisees,' [c] but the people generally, might propound questions, answer, or assent. Again, as regards the requirements of the present narrative, since the Porches opened upon the Court, the

[a] St. John viii. 20
[b] ver. 21
[c] ver. 13

---

[1] The reader will observe that the narrative of the woman taken in adultery, as also the previous verse (St. John vii. 53–viii. 11) have been left out in this History—although with great reluctance. By this it is not intended to characterise that section as Apocryphal. All that we feel bound to maintain is that the narrative in its present form did *not* exist in the Gospel of St. John.

Y

Jews might there pick up stones to cast at Him (which would have been impossible in any part of the Sanctuary itself), while, lastly, Jesus might easily pass out of the Temple in the crowd that moved through the Porches to the outer gates.

But the narrative first transports us into 'the Treasury,' where 'the Pharisees'—or leaders—would alone venture to speak. This would be within 'the Court of the Women,' the common meeting-place of the worshippers, and, as we may say, the most generally attended part of the Sanctuary. Here, in the hearing of the leaders of the people, took place the first Dialogue between Christ and the Pharisees.

It opened with what probably was an allusion alike to one of the great ceremonies of the Feast of Tabernacles, to its symbolic meaning, and to an express Messianic expectation of the Rabbis. As the Mishnah states: On the first, or, as the Talmud would have it, on every night of the festive week, 'the Court of the Women' was brilliantly illuminated, and the night spent in the demonstrations already described. This was called 'the joy of the Feast.' This 'festive joy,' of which the origin is obscure, was no doubt connected with the hope of earth's great harvest-joy in the conversion of the heathen world, and so pointed to 'the days of the Messiah.' In connection with this we mark that the term 'light' was specially applied to the Messiah. In a very interesting passage of the Midrash we are told that, while commonly windows were made wide within and narrow without, it was the opposite in the Temple of Solomon, because the light issuing from the Sanctuary was to lighten that which was without. This

^a St. Luke ii. 32 reminds us of the language of devout old Simeon in regard to the Messiah,^a as 'a light to lighten the Gentiles, and the glory of His people Israel.' We ought to refer to a passage in another Midrash, where, after a remarkable discussion on such names of the Messiah as 'the Lord our Righteousness,' 'the Branch,' 'the Comforter,' 'Shiloh,' 'Compassion,' His Birth is connected with the destruction, and His return with the restoration of the Temple. But in that very passage the Messiah is also

specially designated as the ' Enlightener,' the words : ' the
light dwelleth with Him,' [a] being applied to
Him.

ᵃ Dan. ii. 22

What has just been stated shows that the Pharisees could
not have mistaken the Messianic meaning in the words of
Jesus, in their reference to the past festivity : ' I am the
Light of the world.' Substantially, the Discourses which
follow are a continuation of those previously delivered at
this Feast. What Jesus had gradually communicated to
the disciples, who were so unwilling to receive it, had now
become an acknowledged fact. It was no longer a secret
that the leaders of Israel and Jerusalem were compassing
the Death of Jesus. This underlies all His Words. And
He sought to turn them from their purpose, not by appealing to their pity or to any lower motive, but by claiming
as His right that for which they would condemn Him. He
was the Sent of God, the Messiah ; although, to know Him
and His mission, it needed moral kinship with Him that
had sent Him. But this they did not possess; nay, no
man possessed it, till given him of God. This was not
exactly new in these Discourses of Christ, but it was now
far more clearly stated and developed.

As a corollary He would teach that Satan was not a
merely malicious being, working outward destruction, but
that there was a moral power of evil which held us all—not
the Gentile world only, but even the most favoured, learned,
and exalted among the Jews. Of this power Satan was
the concentration and impersonation; the prince of the
power of ' darkness.' This opens up the reasoning of
Christ, alike as expressed and implied. He presented
Himself to them as the Messiah, and hence as the Light of
the World. It resulted that only in following Him would
a man ' not walk in the darkness,' but have the light—and
that, be it marked, not the light of knowledge,
but of life.[b] On the other hand, it also followed
that all who were not within this light were in darkness
and in death.

ᵇ St. John
viii. 12

It was an appeal to the moral in His hearers. The
Pharisees sought to turn it aside by an appeal to the

external and visible. They asked for some witness, or pal-
a St. John
viii. 13
pable evidence, of what they called His testimony
about Himself,[a] well knowing that such could
only be through some external, visible, miraculous manifestation, just as they had formerly asked for a sign from
heaven. The Bible, and especially the Evangelic history,
is full of what men ordinarily, and often thoughtlessly, call
the miraculous. But in this case the miraculous would
have become the magical, which it never is. If Christ had
yielded to their appeal, and transferred the question from
the moral to the coarsely external sphere, He would have
ceased to be the Messiah of the Incarnation, Temptation,
and Cross, the Messiah-Saviour. A miracle or sign would
at that moment have been a moral anachronism—as much
as any miracle would be in our days, when the Christ
makes His appeal to the moral, and is met by a demand
for the external and material evidence of His witness.

The interruption of the Pharisees [b] was thoroughly
b ver. 13
Jewish, and so was their objection. It had to be
met, and that in the Jewish form in which it had
been raised, while the Christ must at the same time continue His former teaching to them concerning God and
their own distance from Him. Their objection had proceeded on this fundamental judicial principle—'A person
is not accredited about himself.' Harsh and unjust as this
principle sometimes was, it evidently applied only in judicial cases, and hence implied that these Pharisees sat in
judgment on Him as one suspected, and charged with guilt.
The reply of Jesus was plain. Even if His testimony about
Himself were unsupported, it would still be true, and He
was competent to bear it, for He knew as a matter of fact
whence He came and whither He went—His own part in
this Mission, and its goal, as well as God's—whereas they
knew not either.[c] But more than this: their
c ver. 14
demand for a witness had proceeded on the assumption of their being the judges, and He the panel—a
relation which only arose from their judging after the
flesh. Spiritual judgment upon that which was within
belonged only to Him Who searcheth all secrets. Christ,

while on earth, judged no man; and, even if He did so, it must be remembered that He did it not alone, but with, and as the Representative of, the Father. Hence such ^a St. John judgment would be true.[a] But as for their viii. 15, 16 main charge, was it either true or good in law? In accordance with the Law of God, there were two witnesses to the fact of His Mission: His own, and the frequently-shown attestation of His Father. And, if it were objected that a man could not bear witness in his own cause, the same Rabbinic canon laid it down, that this only applied if his testimony stood alone. But if it were corroborated, although by only one male or female slave—who ordinarily were unfit for testimony—it would be credited.

The reasoning of Christ, without for a moment quitting the higher ground of His teaching, was quite unanswerable from the Jewish standpoint. The Pharisees felt it, and, though well knowing to Whom He referred, tried to evade it by the sneer—where (not Who) His Father was? This gave occasion for Christ to return to the main subject of His address, that the reason of their ignorance of Him ^b ver. 19 was that they knew not the Father, and, in turn, that only acknowledgment of Him would bring true knowledge of the Father.[b]

Such words would only ripen in the hearts of such men the murderous resolve against Jesus. Yet, not till His hour had come! Presently we find Him again, now in one of the Porches—probably that of Solomon—teaching, this time, 'the Jews.' We imagine they were chiefly, if not all, Judæans—perhaps Jerusalemites, aware of the murderous intent of their leaders—not His own Galileans, whom He addressed. It was in continuation of what had gone before—alike of what He had said to them, and of what they felt towards Him. The words are Christ's farewell to His rebellious people, His tear-words over lost Israel; abrupt also, as if they were torn sentences, or else headings for special discourses: 'I go My way'—'Ye shall seek Me, and in your sin shall ye die'—'Whither I go, ye cannot come!' They thought that He spoke of His dying, and not, as He did, of that which came after it. But how

could His dying establish such separation between them?
ª St. John
viii. 22 This was the next question which rose in their
minds.ª Would there be anything so peculiar
about His dying, or did His expression about going
indicate a purpose of taking away His Own life?

It was this misunderstanding which Jesus briefly but
emphatically corrected by telling them, that the ground of
their separation was the difference of their nature: they
were from beneath, He from above; they of this world,
He not of this world. Hence they could not come where
ᵇ vv. 23, 24 He would be, since they must die in their sin,
as He had told them—'if ye believe not that
I am.' ᵇ

The words were intentionally mysteriously spoken, as
to a Jewish audience. Believe not that Thou art! But
'Who art Thou?' Their question condemned themselves.
In His broken sentence, Jesus had tried them—to see how
they would complete it. All this time they had not yet
learned Who He was; had not even a conviction on that
point either for or against Him, but were ready to be
swayed by their leaders! 'Who I am?' Has My testimony by word or deed ever swerved on this point? I am
what all along, from the beginning, I tell you. Then,
ᶜ vv. 25, 26 putting aside this interruption, He resumed His
argument.ᶜ Many other things had He to say
and to judge concerning them, besides the bitter truth of
their perishing if they believed not that it was He—but He
that had sent Him was true, and He must ever speak into the
world the message which He had received. When Christ
ᵈ ver. 26 referred to it as that which 'He heard from
Him,' ᵈ He evidently wished thereby to emphasise
the fact of His Mission from God, as constituting His
claim on their obedience of faith. But it was this very
ᵉ ver. 27 point which, even at that moment, they were not
understanding.ᵉ And they would only learn it,
not by His Words, but by the event, when they had
ᶠ ver. 28 'lifted Him up,' as they thought to the Cross, but
really on the way to His Glory.ᶠ Then would
they perceive the meaning of the designation He had

given of Himself, and the claim founded on it: [a] 'Then

a St. John viii. 28 (comp. ver. 24) shall ye perceive that I am.' Meantime: 'And of Myself do I nothing, but as the Father taught Me, these things do I speak. And He that sent Me is with Me. He hath not left Me alone, because what pleases Him I do always.'

If the Jews failed to understand the expression 'lifting up,' which might mean His Exaltation, though it did mean in the first place His Cross, there was that in His appeal to His Words and Deeds as bearing witness to His Mission and to the Divine Help and Presence in it, which by its sincerity and reality found its way to the hearts of many. Instinctively they felt and believed that His Mission must be Divine. Whether or not this found articulate expression, Jesus now addressed Himself to those who thus far—at least for the moment—believed on Him. They were at the crisis of their spiritual history, and He must press home on them what He had sought to teach at the first. By nature far from Him, they were bondsmen. Only if they abode in His Word would they know the truth, and the truth would make them free. The result of this knowledge would be moral, and hence that knowledge consisted not in merely believing on Him, but in making His Word and teaching their dwelling—abiding in it.[b] But it was this very

b vv. 30-32 moral application which they resisted. In this also Jesus had used their own forms of thinking and teaching, only in a much higher sense. For their own tradition had it, that he only was free who laboured in the study of the Law. Yet the liberty of which He spoke came not through study of the Law, but from abiding in the Word of Jesus. But they ignored the spiritual, and fell back upon the national application of the words of Christ. As this is once more evidential of the Jewish authorship of this Gospel, so also the characteristically Jewish boast, that as the children of Abraham they had never been and never could be in real servitude. It would take too long to enumerate all the benefits supposed to be derived from descent from Abraham. Suffice here the almost fundamental principle: 'All Israel are the children of Kings,' and its application even to common life, that as 'the children of Abraham, Isaac, and Jacob, not even Solomon's feast could be too good for them.'

Not so, however, would the Lord allow them to pass it by. He pointed them to another servitude which they ^{a St. John viii. 34} knew not, that of sin,^a and, entering at the same time also on their own ideas, He told them that continuance in this servitude would also lead to national bondage and rejection: 'For the servant abideth not in the house for ever.' On the other hand, the Son abode there for ever; whom He made free by adoption into His Family, they would be free in reality and essentially.^b ^{b ver. 35} Then, for their very dulness, He would turn to their favourite conceit of being Abraham's seed. There was, indeed, an obvious sense in which, by their natural descent, they were such. But there was a moral descent—and that alone was of real value. Abraham's seed? But they entertained purposes of murder, and that because the Word of Christ had not free course, made not way in them. His Word was what he had *seen* with (before) the Father, not heard—for His Presence there was eternal. Their deeds were what they had *heard* from their father—the word 'seen' in our common text depending on a wrong reading. And thus He showed them—in answer to their interpellation—that their father could not have been Abraham, so far as spiritual descent ^{c vv. 37–40} was concerned.^c They had now a glimpse of His meaning, but only to misapply it, according to their Jewish prejudice. Their spiritual descent, they urged, must be of God, since their descent from ^{d ver. 41} Abraham was legitimate.^d But the Lord dispelled even this conceit by showing that if theirs were spiritual descent from God, then would they not reject His Message, nor seek to kill Him, but recognise ^{e ver. 42} and love Him.^e ^{f vv. 43–47} But whence all this misunderstanding of His speech?^f Because they were morally incapable of hearing it—and this because of the sinfulness of their nature: an element which Judaism had never taken into account.

And so, with infinite wisdom, Christ once more brought back His Discourse to what He would teach them concerning man's need, whether he be Jew or Gentile, of a Saviour and of renewing by the Holy Ghost. If the Jews were morally unable to hear His Word and cherished murderous designs, it was because, morally speaking, their descent was of the Devil. Very differently from Jewish ideas did He speak concerning the moral evil of Satan, as both a murderer and a liar—a murderer from the beginning of the history of our race, and one who ' stood not in the truth, because truth is not in him.' Hence ' whenever he speaketh a lie'—whether to our first parents, or now concerning the Christ—' he speaketh from out his own (things), for he (Satan) is a liar, and the father of such an one (who telleth or believeth lies).' Which of them could convict Him of sin? If therefore He spake truth and they believed Him not, it was because they were not of God, but, as He had shown them, of their father, the Devil.

The argument was unanswerable, and there seemed only one way to turn it aside—a Jewish *Tu quoque*, an adaptation of the ' Physician, heal thyself': ' Do we not say rightly, that Thou art a Samaritan, and hast a demon?' By no strain of ingenuity is it possible to account for the designation ' Samaritan,' as given by the Jews to Jesus, if it is regarded as referring to nationality. But in the language which they spoke, what is rendered into Greek by ' Samaritan,' while literally meaning such, is almost as often used in the sense of ' *heretic*.' But it is also sometimes used as the equivalent of *Ashmedai*, the prince of the demons. If this, therefore, were the term applied by the Jews to Jesus, it would literally mean, ' Child of the Devil.'

This would also explain why Christ only replied to the charge of having a demon, since the two charges meant substantially the same: 'Thou art a child of the devil and hast a demon.' In wondrous patience and mercy He almost passed it by, dwelling rather, for their teaching, on the fact that, while they dishonoured Him, He honoured His Father. He heeded not their charges. His concern was the glory of His Father; the vindication of His own honour would be brought about by the Father—though, alas! in judgment on those who were casting such dis-

ᵃ St. John viii. 50

honour on the Sent of God.ᵃ Then He once more pressed home the great subject of His Discourse, that only 'if a man keep'—both have regard to, and observe—His 'Word,' 'he shall not gaze at death [intently behold it] unto eternity'—for ever shall he not come within close and terrible gaze of what is really death, of what became such to Adam in the hour of his Fall.

It was, as repeatedly observed, this death as the consequence of the Fall, of which the Jews knew nothing. And so they once more misunderstood it as of physical death, and, since Abraham and the prophets had died, regarded Christ as setting up a claim higher than theirs.ᵇ

ᵇ vv. 52, 53

The Discourse had contained all that He had wished to bring before them, and their objections were degenerating into wrangling. It was time to break it off by a general application. The question, He added, was not of what *He* said, but of what God said of Him— that God, Whom they claimed as theirs, and yet knew not, but Whom He knew, and Whose Word He 'kept.' But, as for Abraham—he had 'exulted' in the thought of the coming day of the Christ, and, seeing its glory, he was glad. Even Jewish tradition could scarcely gainsay this, since there were two parties in the Synagogue of which one believed that, when that horror of great dark-

ᶜ Gen. xv. 17

ness fell on him,ᶜ Abraham had in vision been shown not only this, but the coming world— and not only all events in the present 'age,' but also those in Messianic times. And now theirs was not misunderstanding, but wilful misinterpretation. He had spoken of Abraham seeing His day; they took it of His seeing Abraham's day, and challenged its possibility. Whether or not they intended thus to elicit an avowal of His claim to eternal duration, and hence to Divinity, it was not time any longer to forbear the full statement, and, with Divine emphasis, He spake the words which could not be mistaken : ' Verily, verily, I say unto you, before Abraham was, I AM.'

It was as if they had only waited for this. Furiously they rushed from the Porch into the Court of the Gentiles —with symbolic significance even in this—to pick up stones, and to cast them at Him. But, once more, His hour had not yet come, and their rage proved impotent. Hiding Himself for the moment, as might so easily be done, in one of the many chambers, passages, or gateways of the Temple, He presently passed out.

It had been the first plain disclosure and avowal of His Divinity, and it was ' in the midst of His enemies,' and when most contempt was cast upon Him. Presently would that avowal be renewed both in Word and by Deed ; for ' the end ' of mercy and judgment had not yet come, but was drawing terribly nigh.

CHAPTER LV.

THE HEALING OF THE MAN BORN BLIND.

(St. John ix.)

AFTER the scene in the Temple described in the last chapter, and Christ's consequent withdrawal from His enemies, we are led to infer that no long interval of time elapsed before the healing of the man born blind. Probably it happened the day after the events just recorded.

It was the Sabbath, the day after the Octave of the Feast, and Christ with His disciples was passing—presumably when going into the Temple—where this blind beggar was wont to sit, probably soliciting alms, perhaps in some such terms as these, which were common at the time : ' Gain merit by me ; ' or ' O tenderhearted, by me gain merit, to thine own benefit.' But on the Sabbath he would of course neither ask nor receive alms, though his presence in the wonted place would secure wider notice, and perhaps lead to many private gifts. Indeed, the blind were regarded as specially entitled to charity; and the Jerusalem Talmud relates instances of the delicacy displayed towards them. As the Master, and His disciples passed the blind beggar, Jesus 'saw' him with that look which they who followed Him knew to be full of meaning. Yet, so thoroughly Judaised were they by their late contact with the Pharisees, that no thought of possible mercy came to them, only a question addressed to Him expressly and as 'Rabbi:' through whose guilt this blindness had befallen him—through his own, or that of his parents.

Thoroughly Jewish the question was. Many instances could be adduced in which one or another sin is said to have been punished by some immediate stroke, disease, or even by death; and we constantly find Rabbis, when meeting such unfortunate persons, asking them how, or by what sin this had come to them. But, as this man was 'blind from his birth,' the possibility of some actual sin before birth would suggest itself, at least as a speculative question, since the 'evil impulse' might even then be called into activity. At the same time, both the Talmud and the later charge of the Pharisees, 'In sins wast thou born altogether,' imply that in such cases the alternative explanation would be considered, that the blindness might be caused by the sin of his parents. It was a common Jewish view that the merits or demerits of the parents would appear in the children. Certain special sins in the parents would result in specific diseases in their offspring, and one is mentioned as causing blindness in the children. But the impression left on our minds is that the disciples felt not sure as to either of these solutions of the difficulty. It seemed a mystery, inexplicable on the supposition of God's infinite goodness, and to which they sought to apply the common Jewish solution.

Putting aside the clumsy alternative suggested by the disciples, Jesus told them that it was so in order 'that the works of God might be made manifest in him.' They wanted to know the 'why,' He told them the 'in order to,' of the man's calamity; they wished to understand its reason as regarded its origin, He told them its reasonableness in regard to the purpose which it and all similar suffering should serve, since Christ has come, the Healer of evil—because the Saviour from sin. Thus He transferred the question from intellectual ground to that of the moral purpose which suffering might serve.

To make this the reality to us, was 'the work of Him' Who sent, and for which He sent the Christ. And rapidly now must He work it, for perpetual example, during the few hours still left of His brief working-day.[a] This figure was not unfamiliar to the Jews, though it may well be that, by thus emphasising the briefness of the time, He may also have anticipated any objection to His healing on the Sabbath.

a St. John ix. 4, 5

Once more we notice how in His Deeds, as in His Words, the Lord adopted the forms known and used by His contemporaries, while He filled them with quite other substance. It has already been stated that saliva was commonly regarded as a remedy for diseases of the eye, although, of course, not for the removal of blindness. With this He made clay, which He now used, adding to it the direction to go and wash in the Pool of Siloam, a term which literally meant 'sent.' A symbolism this, of Him Who was the Sent of the Father.

And so, what the Pharisees had sought in vain, was freely vouchsafed when there was need for it. With perfect simplicity the man's obedience and healing are recorded. We judge that his first impulse when healed must have been to seek for Jesus, naturally, where he had first met Him. On his way, probably past his own house to tell his parents, and again on the spot where he had so long sat begging, all who had known him must have noticed the great change that had passed over him. So marvellous indeed did it appear, that while part of the crowd that gathered would, of course, acknowledge his identity, others would say: 'No, but he is like him;' in their suspiciousness looking for some imposture. For there can be little doubt that on his way he must have learned more about Jesus than merely His Name,[b] and in turn have communicated to his informants the story of his healing. Similarly,

b ver. 11

the formal question now put to him by the Jews was as
much, if not more, a preparatory inquisition than the outcome of a wish to learn the circumstances of his healing.
And so we notice in his answer the cautious desire not to
say anything that could incriminate his Benefactor. He
tells the facts truthfully, plainly ; he accentuates by what
means he had ' recovered,' not received, sight ; but otherwise gives no clue by which either to discover
or to incriminate Jesus.[a]

* St. John
ix. 12

Presently they bring him to the Pharisees, not to take
notice of his healing, but to found on it a charge against
Christ. The ground on which the charge would rest was
plain : the healing involved a manifold breach of the
Sabbath-Law. The first of these was that Jesus had made
clay. Next, it would be a question whether any remedy
might be applied on the holy day. Such could only be
done in diseases of the internal organs (from the throat
downwards), except when danger to life or the loss of an
organ was involved. It was, indeed, declared lawful to
apply, for example, wine to the outside of the eyelid, on the
ground that this might be treated as washing; but it was
sinful to apply it to the inside of the eye. And as regards
saliva, its application to the eye is expressly forbidden, on
the ground that it was evidently intended as a remedy.

There was, therefore, abundant legal ground for a
criminal charge. And, although on the Sabbath the
Sanhedrin would not hold any formal meeting, and even
had there been such, the testimony of one man would not
have sufficed, yet ' the Pharisees ' set the inquiry regularly
on foot. First, as if not satisfied with the report of those
who had brought the man, they made him repeat it.[b] The
wondrous fact could neither be denied nor explained. The alternative, therefore, was : whether
their traditional law of Sabbath-observance, or else He
Who had done such miracles, was Divine ? Was Christ not
of God, because He did not keep the Sabbath in their way ?
But then, could an open transgressor of God's Law do
such miracles ? In this dilemma they turned to the simple
man before them. ' Seeing that He opened ' his eyes, what

b ver. 15

did he say of Him? what was the impression left on his
ᵃ St. John ix.
17 and
following
verses mind, who had the best opportunity for judging? ᵃ

There is something very peculiar, and, in one
sense, most instructive, as to the general opinion entertained
even by the best disposed who had not yet been taught the
higher truth, in his reply, so simple, so comprehensive in
its sequences, and yet so utterly inadequate by itself: ' He
is a Prophet.' One possibility still remained. After all,
the man might not have been really blind; and they
might, by cross-examining the parents, elicit that about
his original condition which would explain the pretended
cure. But on this most important point, the parents,
with all their fear of the anger of the Pharisees, remained
unshaken. He had been born blind; but as to the manner
of his cure, they declined to offer any opinion.

For to persons so wretchedly poor as to allow their son
to live by begging, the consequences of being ' un-Syna-
gogued,' or put outside the congregation—which was to be
the punishment of any one who confessed Jesus as the
Messiah—would have been dreadful. Talmudic writings
speak of two, or rather, we should say, of three, kinds of
' excommunication,' of which the first two were chiefly disciplinary, while the third was the real ' casting out,' ' un-
Synagoguing,' ' cutting off from the congregation.' The
first and lightest degree was, properly, ' a rebuke,' an in-
veighing. Ordinarily, its duration extended over seven
days; but, if pronounced by the Head of the Sanhedrin,
it lasted for thirty days. In later times, however, it only
rested for one day on the guilty person. Perhaps St. Paul
referred to this ' rebuke ' in the expression which he used
ᵇ 1 Tim. v. 1 about an offending Elder.ᵇ He certainly adopted
the practice in Palestine, when he would not
have an Elder ' rebuked,' although he went far beyond it
when he would have such ' entreated.' Yet another
direction of St. Paul's is evidently derived from these
arrangements of the Synagogue, although applied in a far
different spirit. When the Apostle wrote : ' An heretic
after the first and second admonition reject,' there must

have been in his mind the second degree of Jewish excommunication, called from the verb to thrust, thrust out, cast out. This lasted for thirty days at the least, although among the Babylonians only for seven days. At the end of that term there was 'a second admonition,' which lasted other thirty days. If still unrepentant, the third, or real excommunication, was pronounced, which was called the ban, and of which the duration was indefinite. Henceforth he was like one dead. He was not allowed to study with others, no intercourse was to be held with him, he was not even to be shown the road. He might, indeed,

ᵃ Comp. 1 Cor. v. 11 buy the necessaries of life, but it was forbidden to eat or drink with such an one.ᵃ

When we remember what such an anathema would involve to persons in the rank of life, and so poor as the parents of· that blind man, we no longer wonder at their evasion of the question put by the Sanhedrin. And if we ask ourselves, on what ground so terrible a punishment could be inflicted to all time and in every place—for the ban once pronounced applied everywhere—simply for the confession of Jesus as the Christ, the answer is not difficult. The Rabbinists enumerate twenty-four grounds for excommunication, of which more than one might serve the purpose of the Pharisees. But in general, to resist the authority of the Scribes, or any of their decrees, or to lead others either away from ' the commandments,' or to what was regarded as profanation of the Divine Name, was sufficient to incur the ban, while it must be borne in mind that excommunication by the President of the Sanhedrin extended to all places and persons.

As nothing could be elicited from his parents, the man who had been blind was once more summoned before the Pharisees. It was no longer to inquire into the reality of his alleged blindness, nor to ask about the cure, but simply to demand of him recantation, though this was put in the most specious manner. Thou hast been healed: own that it was only by God's Hand miraculously stretched forth, and that 'this man' had nothing to do with it, save that the coincidence may have been allowed to try the faith of

Israel. It could not have been Jesus Who had done it, for they knew Him to be ' a sinner.' Of the two alternatives they had chosen that of the absolute rightness of their own Sabbath-traditions as against the evidence of His Miracles. Virtually, then, this was the condemnation of Christ and the apotheosis of traditionalism.

The renewed inquiry as to the manner in which Jesus had healed him [a] might have had for its object to betray the man into a positive confession, or to elicit something demoniacal in the mode of the cure. The blind man had now fully the advantage. He had already told them. As he put it half ironically : Was it because they felt the wrongness of their own position, and that they should become His disciples ? It stung them to the quick ; they lost all self-possession, and with this their moral defeat became complete. ' Thou art the disciple of that Man, but we (according to the favourite phrase) are the disciples of Moses.' Of the Divine Mission of Moses they knew, but of the Mission of Jesus they knew nothing.[b] The unlettered man had now the full advantage in the controversy. ' In this, indeed,' there was ' the marvellous,' that the leaders of Israel should confess themselves ignorant of the authority of One, Who had power to open the eyes of the blind—a marvel which had never before been witnessed. If He had that power, whence had He obtained it, and why ? It could only have been from God. They said, He was ' a sinner '—and yet there was no principle more frequently repeated by the Rabbis, than that answers to prayer depended on a man being ' devout ' and doing the Will of God. There could therefore be only one inference : If Jesus had not Divine Authority, He could not have had Divine Power.

The truthful reasoning of that untutored man, which confounded the acuteness of the sages, shows the effect of these manifestations on all whose hearts were open to the truth. The Pharisees had nothing to answer, and, as not unfrequently in analogous cases, could only in their fury cast him out with bitter reproaches. Would he teach them—he, whose very disease showed him to have been a

a St. John
ix. 26

b ver. 29

z

child conceived and born in sin, and who, ever since his birth, had been among ignorant, Law-neglecting 'sinners'?

But there was Another Who watched and knew him: He Whom, so far as he knew, he had dared to confess, and for Whom he was content to suffer. Let him now have the reward of his faith, even its completion. Ten-
ᵃ St. John
ix. 35 derly did Jesus seek him out,ᵃ and, as He found him, this one question did He ask, whether the conviction of his experience was not growing into the higher faith of the yet unseen: 'Dost thou believe on the Son of God?'

To such a soul it needed only the directing Word of Christ. 'And Who is He, Lord, that I may believe on
ᵇ ver. 36 Him?'ᵇ It seems as if the question of Jesus had kindled in him the conviction of what was the right answer. To such readiness there could be only one answer. In language more plain than He had ever before used, Jesus answered, and with immediate confession of implicit faith the man worshipped. And so it was that the first time he saw his Deliverer, it was to worship Him.

There were those who still followed Him—not convinced by, nor as yet decided against Him—Pharisees, who well understood the application of His Words. Formally, it had been a contest between traditionalism and the Work of Christ. They also were traditionalists—were they also blind? But nay, they had misunderstood Him by leaving out the moral element, thus showing themselves blind indeed. It was not the calamity of blindness; but it was a blindness in which they were guilty, and for which they
ᶜ ver. 41 were responsible,ᶜ which indeed was the result of their deliberate choice: therefore their sin—not their blindness only—remained.

CHAPTER LVI.

THE 'GOOD SHEPHERD.'

(St. John x. 1–21.)

IT was in accordance with the character of the Discourse presently under consideration, that Jesus spake it, not indeed in Parables in the strict sense (for none such are recorded in the fourth Gospel), but in an allegory in the Parabolic form,[a] hiding the higher truths from those who having eyes had not seen, but revealing them to such whose eyes had been opened. If the scenes of the last few days had made anything plain, it was the utter unfitness of the teachers of Israel for their professed work of feeding the flock of God. The Rabbinists also called their spiritual leaders 'feeders.' The term comprised the two ideas of 'leading' and 'feeding,' which are separately insisted on in the Lord's allegory. It only required to recall the Old Testament language about the shepherding of God, and that of evil shepherds, to make the application to what had so lately happened. They were, surely, not shepherds, who had cast out the healed blind man, or who so judged of the Christ, and would cast out all His disciples. They had entered into God's Sheepfold, but not by the door by which the Owner, God, had brought His flock into the fold. To it the entrance had been His love, His thoughts of pardoning, His purpose of saving mercy. Not by that door, as had so lately fully appeared, had Israel's rulers come in. They had climbed up to their place in the fold some other way—with the same right, or by the same wrong, as a thief or a robber. They had wrongfully taken what did not belong to them—cunningly and undetected, like a thief; they had allotted it to themselves, and usurped it by violence, like a robber. What more accurate description could be given of the means by which the Pharisees and Sadducees had attained the rule over God's flock, and claimed it for themselves?

How different He, Who comes in and leads us through

a St. John x. 6

God's door of covenant-mercy and Gospel-promise—the door by which God had brought, and ever brings, His flock into His fold! This was the true Shepherd. The allegory must, of course, not be too closely pressed; but, as we remember how in the East the flocks are at night driven into a large fold, and charge of them is given to an under-shepherd, we can understand how, when the shepherd comes in the morning, 'the doorkeeper' or 'guardian' opens to him. And when a true spiritual shepherd comes to the true spiritual door, it is opened to him by the guardian from within—that is, he finds ready and imme-diate access. Equally pictorial is the progress of the allegory. Having thus gained access to his flock, it has not been to steal or rob, but the shepherd knows and calls them, each by his name, and leads them out. We mark that in the expression: 'when he has *put forth* all his own,'—the word is a strong one. For they have to go each singly, and perhaps they are not willing to go out each by himself, or even to leave that fold, and so he 'puts' or thrusts them forth, and he does so to 'all his own.' Then the Eastern shepherd places himself at the head of his flock, and goes before them, guiding them, making sure of their following simply by his voice, which they know. So would His flock follow Christ, for they know His Voice, and in vain would strangers seek to lead them away, as the Pharisees had tried. It was not the known Voice of their own Shepherd, and they would only flee from it.[a]

[a] St. John x. 4, 5

We can scarcely wonder that they who heard it did not understand the allegory, for they were not of His flock and knew not His Voice. But His own knew it then, and would know it for ever. 'Therefore,'[b] both for the sake of the one and the other, He continued, now dividing for greater clearness the two leading ideas of His allegory, and applying each separately for better com-fort. These two ideas were: *entrance* by the *door*, and the characteristics of the *good Shepherd*—thus affording a twofold test by which to recognise the true, and distin-guish it from the false.

[b] ver. 7

I. *The Door.*—Christ was the Door.[a] All the Old

[a] St. John x. Testament institutions, prophecies, and promises,

[7-9] so far as they referred to access into God's fold,

meant Christ. And all those who went before Him, pretending to be the door—whether Pharisees, Sadducees, or
Nationalists—were only thieves and robbers : that was
not the door into the Kingdom of God. And the sheep,
God's flock, did not hear them ; for although they might
pretend to lead the flock, the voice was that of strangers.
The transition now to another application of the allegorical
idea of the ' door ' was natural and almost necessary,
though it appears somewhat abrupt. Even in this it is
peculiarly Jewish. We must understand this transition
as follows : I am the Door ; those who professed otherwise
to gain access to the fold have climbed in some other way.
But if I am the only, I am also truly the Door. And,
dropping the figure, if any man enters by Me, he shall be
saved, securely go out and in (where the language is not
to be closely pressed), in the sense of having liberty and
finding pasture.

II. This forms also the transition to the second
leading idea of the allegory : *the True and Good Shepherd.*
Here we mark a fourfold progression of thought, which
reminds us of the poetry of the Book of Psalms. There
the thought expressed in one line or one couplet is carried
forward and developed in the next, forming what are
called the Psalms of Ascent (' of Degrees '). And in the
Discourse of Christ also the final thought of each couplet
of verses is carried forward, or rather leads upward in the
next. Thus we have here a Psalm of Degrees concerning
the Good Shepherd and His Flock, and, at the same time,
a New Testament version of Psalm xxiii. Accordingly its
analysis might be formulated as follows :

1. *Christ the Good Shepherd, in contrast to*

[b] ver. 10 *others who falsely claimed to be the shepherds.*[b]

2. *The Good Shepherd Who layeth down His life for
His sheep !*

3. *For the sheep that are Mine, whom I know, and for
whom I lay down My Life !*

4. In the final Step of 'Ascent' [a] the leading thoughts
[a] St. John x. of the whole Discourse are taken up and carried
17, 18 to the last and highest thought. *The Good Shepherd that brings together the One Flock!* Yes—by laying down His Life, but also by taking it up again. Both are necessary for the work of the Good Shepherd : nay, the life is laid down in the surrender of sacrifice, in order that it may be taken up again, and much more fully, in the Resurrection-Power. And therefore His Father loveth Him as the Messiah-Shepherd, Who so fully does the work committed to Him, and so entirely surrenders Himself to it.

And all this, in order to be the Shepherd-Saviour—to die, and rise for His Sheep, and thus to gather them all, Jews and Gentiles, into one flock, and to be their Shepherd. This, neither more nor less, was the Mission which God had given Him ; this, ' the *commandment*' which He had received of His Father—*that which God had*
[b] ver. 18 *given Him to do.*[b]

It was a noble close of the series of those Discourses in the Temple, which had it for their object to show that He was truly sent of God.

And, in a measure, they attained that object. To some, indeed, it all seemed unintelligible, incoherent, madness ; and they fell back on the favourite explanation of all this strange drama—He hath a demon ! But others there were, not yet His disciples, to whose hearts these words went straight. ' These utterances are not of a demonised' — and then it came back to them : ' Can a demon open the eyes of the blind ? '

And so, once again, the Light of His Words and of His Person fell upon His Works, and, as ever, revealed their character, and made them clear.

CHAPTER LVII.

DISCOURSE CONCERNING THE TWO KINGDOMS.

(St. Matt. xii. 22-45; St. Luke xi. 14-36.)

IT was well that Jesus should, for the present, have parted from Jerusalem with words like these. Even ' the schism ' that had come among them[a] concerning His Person made it possible not only to continue His Teaching, but to return to the City once more ere His final entrance. For His Peræan Ministry, which extended from after the Feast of Tabernacles to the week preceding the last Passover, was, so to speak, cut in half by the brief visit of Jesus to Jerusalem at the Feast of the Dedication.[b] Of these six months we have (with the solitary exception of St. Matthew xii. 22-45), no other account than that furnished by St. Luke,[c] although, as usually, the Jerusalem and Judæan incidents of it are described by St. John.[d]

a St. John x. 19

b St. John x. 22-39

c St. Luke xi. 14 to xvii. 11

d St. John x. 22-42; xi. 1-45; xi. 46-54

It will be noticed that this section is peculiarly lacking in incident. It consists almost exclusively of Discourses and Parables, with but few narrative portions interspersed. And this chiefly from the character of His Ministry in Peræa. We remember that, similarly, the beginning of Christ's Galilean Ministry had been chiefly marked by Discourses and Parables. In fact, His Peræan was substantially a resumption of His early Galilean Ministry, only modified and influenced by the much fuller knowledge of the people concerning Christ, and the greatly developed enmity of their leaders. Thus, to begin with, we can understand how He would, at this initial stage of His Peræan, as in that of His Galilean Ministry, repeat, when asked for instruction concerning prayer, those sacred words ever since known as the Lord's Prayer. The variations are so slight as to be easily accounted for by the individuality of the reporter. They afford, however, the occasion for remarking on the two principal differences. In St. Luke the prayer is for the forgiveness of 'sins,' while St. Matthew uses the Hebraic term 'debts,' which has passed even into the Jewish Liturgy, denoting our guilt as indebtedness. Again the ' day by day ' of St. Luke, which further explains the petition for 'daily bread,' common both to St. Matthew and St. Luke, may be illustrated by the beautiful Rabbinic teaching, that the Manna fell only for each day, in order that thought of their daily dependence might call forth constant faith in our ' Father Which is in heaven.'

From the introductory expression : ' When (or whenever) ye pray, say '—we venture to infer, that this prayer was intended, not only as the model, but as furnishing the words for the future use of the Church. Yet another suggestion may be made. The request, ' Lord, teach us to ^{a St. Luke} pray, as John also taught his disciples,' [a] seems ^{xi. 1} to indicate what was 'the certain place,' which, now consecrated by our Lord's prayer, became the school for ours. It seems at least likely, that the allusion of the disciples to the Baptist may have been prompted by the circumstance that the locality was that which had been the scene of John's labours—of course, in Peræa. This chapter will be devoted to the briefest summary of the Lord's Discourses in Peræa, previous to His return to Jerusalem for the Feast of the Dedication of the Temple.

The first of these was on the occasion of His casting ^{b St. Luke} out a demon,[b] and restoring speech to the de- ^{xi. 14} monised; or if, as seems likely, the cure is the same as that recorded in St. Matt. xii. 22, both sight and speech, which had probably been paralysed. This is one of the cases in which it is difficult to determine whether narratives in different Gospels, with slightly varying details, represent different events or only differing modes of narration. When recording similar events the Evangelists would naturally tell them in much the same manner. Hence it does not follow that two similar narratives in different Gospels always represent the same event. But in this instance it seems likely.

It is the Pharisees' charge that He was an instrument of Satan which forms the main subject of Christ's address,

^a St. Mark iii. 22 His language being now much more explicit than formerly,^a even as the opposition of the Pharisees had more fully ripened. The following are the leading features of Christ's reply: 1st, It was utterly unreason-

^b St. Matt. xii. 25 able,^b and inconsistent with their own premisses,^c showing that their ascription of Satanic agency

^c vv. 27-30 to what Christ did was only prompted by hostility to His Person. This mode of turning the argument against the arguer was peculiarly Hebraic, and it does not imply any assertion on the part of Christ as to whether or not the disciples of the Pharisees really cast out demons. Mentally we must supply—according to your own pro-fessions, your disciples cast out demons. If so, by whom are they doing it?

But 2ndly, beneath this logical argumentation lies spiritual instruction, closely connected with the late teaching during the festive days in Jerusalem. It is directed against the superstitious and unspiritual views entertained by Israel alike of the Kingdom of evil and of that of God. For if we ignore the moral aspect of Satan and his kingdom, all degenerates into the absurdities and superstitions of the Jewish view concerning demons and Satan. On the other hand, introduce the ideas of moral evil, of the concentration of its power in a kingdom of which Satan is the representative and ruler, and of our own inherent sinfulness, which makes us his subjects—and all becomes clear. Then, truly, can Satan not cast out Satan—else how could his kingdom stand? Then, also, is the casting out of Satan only by 'God's Spirit,' or 'Finger:'

^d vv. 25-28 and this *is* the Kingdom of God.^d Nay, by their own admission, the casting out of Satan was part of the work of Messiah. Then had the Kingdom of God indeed come to them—for in this was the Kingdom of God; and He was the God-sent Messiah, come not for the glory of Israel, nor for anything outward or intellectual,

but to engage in mortal conflict with moral evil, and with Satan as its representative. In that contest Christ, as the Stronger, bindeth ' the strong one,' spoils his house (divideth his spoil), and takes from him the armour in which his strength lay ('he trusted') by taking away the power of sin.[a] This is the work of the Messiah—and, therefore, also, no one can be indifferent towards Him, because all, being by nature in a certain relation towards Satan, must, since the Messiah had commenced His Work, occupy a definite relationship towards the Christ Who combats Satan.[b]

_{a St. Matt. xii. 29}

_{b ver. 30}

But it is conceivable that a man may not only try to be passively, but even be actively on the enemy's side, and this not by merely speaking against the Christ, which might be the outcome of ignorance or unbelief, but by representing that as Satanic which was the object of His Coming.[c] Such perversion represents sin in its absolute completeness, and for which there can be no pardon, since the state of mind of which it is the outcome admits not the possibility of repentance, because its essence lies in this, to call that Satanic which is the very object of repentance.

_{c vv. 31, 32}

3rdly. Recognition of the spiritual, which was the opposite of the sin against the Holy Ghost, was, as Christ had so lately explained in Jerusalem, only to be attained by spiritual kinship with it.[d] The tree must be made good, if the fruit were to be good ; tree and fruit would correspond to each other. How then could these Pharisees ' speak good things,' since the state of the heart determined speech and action ? Hence, a man would have to give an account even of every idle word, since however trifling it might appear to others or to oneself, it was really the outcome of ' the heart,' and showed the inner state. And thus, in reality, would a man's future in judgment be determined by his words ; a conclusion the more solemn, when we remember its bearing on what His disciples on the one side, and the Pharisees on the other said concerning Christ and the Spirit of God.

_{d vv. 33–37}

4thly. Both logically and morally the Words of Christ

were unanswerable ; and the Pharisees fell back on the old
device of challenging proof of His Divine Mission by some
^{a St. Matt.} visible sign.^a But this was an attempt to shift
^{xii. 38} the argument from the moral to the physical.
It was the moral that was at fault, or rather, wanting in
them ; and no amount of physical evidence or demonstration
could have supplied that. Hence, as under previous similar
^{b St. Matt.} circumstances,^b He would offer them only one
^{xvi. 1-4} sign, that of Jonas the prophet. But whereas on
the former occasion Christ chiefly referred to Jonas' preaching (of repentance), on this He rather pointed to the
allegorical history of Jonas as the Divine attestation of his
Mission. As he appeared in Nineveh, he was himself ' a
^{c St. Luke} sign unto the Ninevites ; ' ^c the fact that he had
^{xi. 30} been three days and nights in the whale's belly,
and that thence he had, so to speak, been sent forth alive
to preach in Nineveh, was evidence to them that he had
been sent of God. And so would it be again. After three
days and three nights ' in the heart of the earth '—which
is a Hebraism for ' in the earth '—would His Resurrection
Divinely attest to this generation His Mission. The
Ninevites did not question, but received this attestation of
Jonas ; nay, an authentic report of the wisdom of Solomon
had been sufficient to bring the Queen of Sheba from so
far ; in the one case it was because they felt their sin ; in
the other, because she felt need and longing for better
wisdom than she possessed. But these were the very
elements wanting in the men of this generation ; and so
both Nineveh and the Queen of Sheba would stand up,
not only as mute witnesses against, but to condemn, them.
For, the great Reality of which the preaching of Jonas had
been only the type, and for which the wisdom of Solomon
^{d St. Matt.} had been only the preparation, had been presented
^{xii. 39-42} to them in Christ.^d

5thly. And so, having put aside this cavil, Jesus returned
to His former teaching ^e concerning the Kingdom
^{e vv. 43-45} of Satan and the power of evil. Here, also, it
must be remembered that, as the words used by our Lord
were allegorical and illustrative, they must not be too

closely pressed. As compared with the other nations of the world, Israel was like a house from which the demon of idolatry had gone out with all his attendants—really the 'Beel-Zibbul' whom they dreaded. And then the house had been swept of all the foulness and uncleanness of idolatry, and garnished with all manner of Pharisaic adornments. Yet all this while it was left really empty; God was not there; the Stronger One, Who alone could have resisted the Strong One, held not rule in it. And so the demon returned to it again, to find the house whence he had come out, swept and garnished indeed—but also empty and defenceless. The folly of Israel lay in this, that they thought of only one demon—him of idolatry—Beel-Zibbul, with all his foulness. So, to continue the illustrative language of Christ, Satan came back 'with seven other spirits more wicked than himself'—pride, self-righteousness, unbelief, and the like, the number seven being general—and thus the last state—Israel without the foulness of gross idolatry, and garnished with all the adornments of Pharisaic devotion to the study and practice of the Law—was really worse than had been the first with all its open repulsiveness.

6thly. Once more was the Discourse interrupted, this time by a truly Jewish incident. A woman in the crowd burst into exclamations about the blessedness of the Mother who had borne and nurtured such a Son.[a] The phraseology seems to have been not uncommon, since it is equally applied by the Rabbis to Moses, and even to a great Rabbi.

[a] St. Luke xi. 27

And yet such praise must have been peculiarly unwelcome to Christ, as being the exaltation of only His Human Personal excellence, intellectual or moral. It quite looked away from that which He would present: His Work and Mission as the Saviour. This praise of the Christ through His Virgin-Mother was as unacceptable and unsuitable as the depreciation of the Christ, which really, though unconsciously, underlay the loving care of the Virgin-Mother when she would have arrested Him in His Work, and which (perhaps for this very reason) St. Matthew relates in

the same connection.[a] Accordingly, the answer in both
[a] St. Matt. xii. 46, 47
cases is substantially the same : to point away
from His merely Human Personality to His Work
and Mission—in the one case: ' Whosoever shall do the
Will of My Father Which is in heaven, the same is My
brother, and sister, and mother ; ' in the other : ' Yea
rather, blessed are they that hear the Word of God and
keep it.'

7thly. And now the Discourse draws to a close [b] by a fresh
[b] St. Luke xi. 33–36
application of what, in some other form or connection, Christ had taught at the outset of His
[c] St. Matt. v. 15 ; vi. 22, 23
public Ministry in the ' Sermon on the Mount.' [c]
Rightly to understand its present connection,
we must pass over the various interruptions of Christ's
Discourse, and join this as the conclusion to the previous
part, which contained the main subject. This was, that
spiritual knowledge presupposed spiritual kinship. As
here put, it is that spiritual receptiveness is ever the condition of spiritual reception. What was the object of
lighting a lamp ? Surely, that it may give light. But if
so, no one would put it into a vault, or under the bushel,
but on the stand. Should we then expect that God would
light the spiritual lamp, if it be put in a dark vault ? Or, to
take an illustration of it from the eye, which, as regards
the body, serves the same purpose as the lamp in a house.
Does it not depend on the state of the eye whether or not
we have the sensation, enjoyment, and benefit of the light ?
Let us therefore take care, lest by placing, as it were, the
lamp in a vault, the light in us be really only darkness.
On the other hand, if by means of a good eye the light is
transmitted through the whole system, then shall we be
wholly full of light. And this, finally, explains the reception or rejection of Christ : how, in the words of an Apostle,
the same Gospel would be both a savour of life unto life,
and of death unto death.

CHAPTER LVIII.

THE MORNING-MEAL IN THE PHARISEE'S HOUSE.

(St. Luke xi. 37–54.)

BITTER as was the enmity of the Pharisaic party against Jesus, it had not yet so far spread, nor become so avowed, as in every place to supersede the ordinary rules of courtesy. It is thus that we explain that invitation of a Pharisee to the morning-meal, which furnished the occasion for the second recorded Peræan Discourse of Christ. It is the last address to the Pharisees recorded in the Gospel of St. Luke. A similar last appeal is recorded in a much ^{a St. Matt.} later portion of St. Matthew's Gospel,[a] only ^{xxiii.} that St. Luke reports that spoken in Peræa, St. Matthew that made in Jerusalem. This may also partly account for the similarity of language in the two Discourses.

What makes it almost certain that some time must have elapsed between this and the previous Discourse (or rather that, as we believe, the two events happened in different places), is, that the invitation of the Pharisee was to the ' morning-meal.' We know that this took place early, immediately after the return from morning-prayers in the Synagogue. It is, therefore, scarcely conceivable that all that is recorded in connection with the first Discourse should have occurred before this first meal. On the other hand, it may well have been, that what passed at the Pharisee's table may have some connection with something that had occurred just before in the Synagogue, for we conjecture that it was the Sabbath-day. We infer this from the circumstance that the invitation was not to the principal meal, which on a Sabbath ' the Lawyers ' (and, indeed, all householders) would, at least ordinarily, have in their own homes. We can picture to ourselves the scene. The week-day family-meal was simple enough, whether breakfast or dinner—the latter towards evening, although

sometimes also in the middle of the day, but always before
actual darkness, in order, as it was expressed, that the
sight of the dishes by daylight might excite the appetite.
The Babylonian Jews were content to make a meal without meat; not so the Palestinians. With the latter the
favourite food was young meat: goats, lambs, calves. Beef
was not só often used, and still more rarely fowls. Bread
was regarded as the mainstay of life, without which no
entertainment was considered as a meal. Indeed, in a sense
it constituted the meal. For the blessing was spoken over
the bread, and this was supposed to cover all the rest of the
food that followed, such as the meat, fish, or vegetables—in
short, all that made up the dinner, but not the dessert.
Similarly, the blessing spoken over the wine included all
other kinds of drink. Otherwise it would have been necessary to pronounce a separate benediction over each different
article eaten or drunk. He who neglected the prescribed
benedictions was regarded as if he had eaten of
[a] Ps. xxiv. 1 things dedicated to God, since it was written:
'The earth is the Lord's and the fulness thereof.'[a]

Let us suppose the guests assembled. To such a morning-meal they would not be summoned by slaves, nor be
received in such solemn state as at feasts. First, each
would observe, as a religious rite, 'the washing of hands.'
Next, the head of the house would cut a piece from the
whole loaf—on the Sabbath there were two loaves—and
speak the blessing. But this only if the company reclined
at table, as at dinner. If they sat, as probably always at the
early meal, each would speak the benediction for himself.
The same rule applied in regard to the wine.

At the entertainment of this Pharisee, as indeed generally, our Lord omitted the prescribed 'washing of hands'
before the meal. But as this rite was in itself indifferent,
He must have had some definite object, which will be explained in the sequel.

In regard to the position of the guests, we know that
the uppermost seats were occupied by the Rabbis. The
Talmud formulates it in this manner: That the worthiest
lies down first, on his left side, with his feet stretching

back.   If there are two 'cushions' (divans), the next
worthiest reclines above him, at his left hand; if there are
three cushions, the third worthiest lies below him who had
lain down first (at his right), so that the chief person is in
the middle (between the worthiest guest at his left and the
less worthy one at his right hand).   The water before
eating is first handed to the worthiest, and so in regard to
the washing after meat.   But if a large number are present,
you begin after dinner with the least worthy, till you come
to the last five, when the worthiest in the company washes
his hands, and the other four after him.   The guests being
thus arranged, the head of the house, or the chief person at
table, speaks the blessing, and then cuts the bread.   Then,
generally, the bread was dipped into salt, or something
salted, etiquette demanding that where there were two
they should wait one for the other, but not where there
were three or more.

The wine was mixed with water, and, indeed, some
thought that the benediction should not be pronounced till
the water had been added to the wine.   Various vintages
are mentioned : among them a red wine of Saron, and a
black wine.   Spiced wine was made with honey and pepper.
Another mixture, chiefly used for invalids, consisted of old wine, water, and balsam ; yet another
was 'wine of myrrh.'[a]   Palm wine was also in
use, and foreign drinks.

a Mentioned
in St. Mark
xv. 23

As regards the various kinds of grain, meat, fish, and
fruits used by the Jews, either in their natural state or
preserved, almost everything known to the ancient world
was embraced.   At feasts there was an introductory course,
followed by the dinner itself, which finished with dessert,
consisting of pickled olives, radishes and lettuce, and fruits,
among which even preserved ginger from India is mentioned.   Fish was a favourite dish, and never wanting at a
Sabbath-meal.   It was a saying, that both salt and water
should be used at every meal, if health was to be preserved.
Very different were the meals of the poor—locusts, eggs,
or a soup made of vegetables : the poorer still would satisfy
their hunger with bread and cheese or bread and fruit.

At meals the rules of etiquette were strictly observed, especially as regarded the sages. According to some, it was not good breeding to speak while eating. The learned and most honoured occupied not only the chief places, but were sometimes distinguished by a double portion. According to Jewish etiquette, a guest should conform in everything to his host, even though it were unpleasant. Although hospitality was the greatest and most prized social virtue, which, to use a Rabbinic expression, might make every home a sanctuary and every table an altar, an unbidden guest, or a guest who brought another guest, was proverbially an unwelcome apparition. Sometimes, by way of self-righteousness, the poor were brought in, and the best part of the meal ostentatiously given to them.[1] After dinner, the formalities concerning handwashing and prayer already described were gone through, and then frequently aromatic spices burnt, over which a special benediction was pronounced. We have only to add, that on Sabbaths it was deemed a religious duty to have three meals, and to procure the best that money could obtain, even though one were to save and fast for it all the week. Lastly, it was regarded as a special obligation and honour to entertain sages.

We have no difficulty now in understanding what passed at the table of the Pharisee. When the water for purification was presented to Him, Jesus would either refuse it; or if, as seems more likely at a morning-meal, each guest repaired by himself for the prescribed purification, He would omit to do so, and sit down to meat without this formality. No one who knows the stress which Pharisaism laid on this rite would argue that Jesus might have conformed to the practice. Indeed, the controversy was long and bitter between the Schools of Shammai and Hillel on such a point as whether the hands were to be washed before the cup was filled with wine, or after that, and where the towel was to be deposited. A religion which spent its energy on such trivialities must have lowered the moral tone. All the more that Jesus insisted

For fuller details see ' Life and Times, &c.,' vol. ii. p. 209.

so earnestly, as the substance of His teaching, on that corruption of our nature which Judaism ignored, and on that spiritual purification which was needful for the reception of His doctrine, would He publicly and openly set aside ordinances of man which diverted thoughts of purity into questions of the most childish character. On the other hand, we can also understand what bitter thoughts must have filled the mind of the Pharisee, whose guest Jesus was, when he observed His neglect of the cherished rite. It was an insult to himself, a defiance of Jewish Law, a revolt against the most cherished traditions of the Synagogue. Remembering that a Pharisee ought not to sit down to a meal with such, he might even feel that he should not have asked Jesus to his table.

What our Lord said on that occasion will be considered in detail in another place. Suffice it here to mark that He first exposed the mere externalism of the Pharisaic law of purification, to the utter ignoring of the higher need of
^a St. Luke xi. 39 — inward purity, which lay at the foundation of all.^a
If the primary origin of the ordinance was to prevent the eating of sacred offerings in defilement, were these outward offerings not a symbol of the inward sacrifice, and was there not an inward defilement as well as the
^b ver. 40 — outward?^b To consecrate what we had to God
in His poor, instead of selfishly enjoying it, would not, indeed, be a purification of them (for such was not needed), but it would, in the truest sense, be to eat God's
^c ver. 41 — offerings in cleanness.^c We mark here a progress and a development as compared with the former occasion when Jesus had publicly spoken on the
^d St. Matt. xv. 1–9 — same subject.^d Formerly He had treated the
ordinance of the Elders as a matter not binding; now He showed how this externalism militated against thoughts of the internal and spiritual. Formerly He had shown how traditionalism came into conflict with the written Law of God; now, how it superseded the first principles which underlay that Law. Formerly He had
^e St. Matt. xv. 10, 11 — laid down the principle that defilement came not
from without inwards but from within outwards; ^e

now He unfolded this highest principle that higher consecration imparted purity.

The same principle, indeed, would apply to other things,
such as to the Rabbinic law of tithing. At the same time
it may have been, as already suggested, that something
which had previously taken place, or was the subject of
conversation at table, had given occasion for the further
remarks of Christ.[a] Thus, the Pharisee may
have wished to convey his rebuke of Christ by
referring to the subject of tithing. And such covert mode
of rebuking was very common among the Jews. It was
regarded as utterly defiling to eat of that which had not
been tithed. Indeed, the three distinctions of a Pharisee
were : not to make use nor to partake of anything that
had not been tithed ; to observe the laws of purification ;
and, as a consequence of these two, to abstain from familiar
intercourse with all non-Pharisees. This separation formed
the ground of their claim to distinction.[b] It will
be noticed that it is exactly to these three things
our Lord adverts : so that these sayings of His are not,
as might seem, unconnected, but in the strictest internal
relationship. Our Lord shows how Pharisaism, as regarded
the outer, was connected with the opposite tendency as regarded the inner man : outward purification with ignorance
of the need of that inward purity, which consisted in
God-consecration, and with the neglect of it ; strictness of
outward tithing with ignorance and neglect of the principle
which underlay it, viz. the acknowledgment of God's right
over mind and heart (judgment and the love of God) ;
while, lastly, the Pharisaic pretence of separation, and
consequent claim to distinction, issued only in pride and
self-assertion. Thus, tried by its own tests, Pharisaism
failed. It was hypocrisy, although that word was not
mentioned till afterwards ;[c] and that both negatively and positively : the concealment of what
it was, and the pretension to what it was not. And the
Pharisaism which pretended to the highest purity was
really the greatest impurity—the defilement of graves,
only covered up not to be seen of men !

It was at this point that one of 'the Scribes' at table broke in. Remembering in what contempt some of the learned held the ignorant bigotry of the Pharisees, we can understand that he might have listened with secret enjoyment to denunciations of their 'folly.' As the common saying had it, 'the silly pietist,' 'a woman Pharisee,' and the (self-inflicted) 'blows of Pharisaism,' were among the plagues of life. But, as the Scribe rightly remarked, by attacking, not merely their practice but their principles, the whole system of traditionalism, which they represented,

a St. Luke xi. 45 was condemned.[a] And so the Lord assuredly meant it. The 'Scribes' were the exponents of the traditional law: those who bound and loosed in Israel. They did bind on heavy burdens, but they never loosed one; all these grievous burdens of traditionalism they laid on the poor people, but not the slightest effort

b ver. 46 did they make to remove any of them.[b] Tradition, the ordinances that had come down—they would not reform nor put aside anything, but claim and proclaim all that had come down from the fathers as a sacred inheritance to which they clung. So be it! let them be judged by their own words. The fathers had murdered the prophets, and they built their sepulchres; that also was a tradition—that of guilt which would be avenged. Tradition, learning, exclusiveness—alas! it was only taking away from the poor the key of knowledge; and while they themselves entered not by 'the door' into the Kingdom, they hindered those who would have gone in. And truly so did they prove that theirs was the in-

c vv. 47–52 heritance, the 'tradition,' of guilt in hindering and banishing the Divine teaching of old, and murdering its Divine messengers.[c]

There was terrible truth and solemnity in what Jesus spake, and in the Woe which He denounced on them. But after such denunciations, the entertainment in the Pharisee's house must have been broken up. With what feelings they parted from Him appears from the sequel.

'And when He was come out from thence, the Scribes

and the Pharisees began to press upon Him vehemently, and to provoke Him to speak of many things; laying wait for Him, to catch something out of His Mouth.'

CHAPTER LIX.

TO THE DISCIPLES—TWO EVENTS AND THEIR MORAL.

(St. Luke xii. 1–xiii. 17.)

THE record of Christ's last warning to the Pharisees, and of the feelings of murderous hate which it called forth, is followed by a summary of Christ's teaching to His disciples. The tone is still that of warning, but entirely different from that to the Pharisees. It is a warning of sin that threatened, not of judgment that awaited; it was for prevention, not in denunciation. The same teaching, because prompted by the same causes, had been mostly delivered also on other occasions. Yet there are notable, though seemingly slight, divergences, accounted for by the difference of the writers or of the circumstances, and which mark the independence of the narratives.

1. The first of these Discourses [a] naturally connects itself with what had passed at the Pharisee's table, an account of which must soon have spread. Although the Lord is reported as having addressed the same language chiefly to the Twelve when sending them on their first Mission,[b] we mark characteristic variations. The address—or probably only its summary—is introduced by the following notice of the circumstances: 'In the mean time, when the many thousands of the people were gathered together, so that they trode upon each other, He began to say to His disciples: "First [above all], beware of the leaven of the Pharisees, which is hypocrisy."' There is no need to point out the connection between this warning and the denunciation of Pharisaism and traditionalism at the Pharisee's table. Although the word 'hypocrisy' had not been spoken there, it was the sum and substance of His contention

[a] St. Luke xii. 1–12

[b] St. Matt. x.

that Pharisaism, while pretending to what it was not, concealed what it was. And it was this which, like ' leaven,' pervaded the whole system of Pharisaism. Not that as individuals they were all hypocrites, but that the system was hypocrisy. And here it is characteristic of Pharisaism, that Rabbinic Hebrew has not even a word equivalent to the term ' hypocrisy.' The only expression used refers either to flattery of, or pretence before men, not to that unconscious hypocrisy towards God which our Lord so truly describes as ' the leaven ' that pervaded all the Pharisees said and did.

After all, hypocrisy was only self-deception.[a] ' But there is nothing covered that shall not be revealed.' Hence, what they had said in the darkness would be revealed, and what they had spoken about in the store-rooms would be proclaimed on the housetops. Nor should fear influence them.[b] Man could only kill the body, but God held body and soul. And as fear was foolish, so was it needless in view of that Providence which watched over even the meanest of God's creatures.[c] Rather let them, in the impending struggle with the powers of this world, rise to consciousness of its full import. And this contest was not only opposition to Christ, but, in its inmost essence, blasphemy against the Holy Ghost. Therefore, to succumb implied the deepest spiritual danger.[d] Nay, but let them not be apprehensive; their acknowledgment would be not only in the future. Even now, in the hour of their danger, would the Holy Ghost help them, and give them an answer before their accusers and judges, whoever they might be—Jews or Gentiles. Thus, if they fell victims, it would be with the knowledge—not by neglect —of their Father ; in their own hearts, before the Angels, before men, would He give testimony for those who were His witnesses.[e]

2. The second Discourse recorded in this connection was occasioned by a request for judicial interposition on the part of Christ. This He answered by a Parable,[f] which will be explained in conjunction

[a] St. Luke xii. 2.

[b] ver. 4

[c] vv. 6, 7

[d] vv. 8-10

[e] vv. 11, 12

[f] vv. 16-21

with the other Parables of that period. The outcome of
this Parable, as to the uncertainty of this life, and the
consequent folly of being so careful for this world while
neglectful of God, led Him to make warning application
to His Peræan disciples.[a] Only here the negative injunction that preceded the Parable, ' beware of covetousness,' is, when addressed to ' the disciples,'
carried back to its positive underlying principle : to dismiss
all anxiety, even for the necessaries of life, learning from
the birds and the flowers to have absolute faith and trust
in God, and to labour for only one thing—the Kingdom
of God.   But even in this they were not to be careful,
but to have absolute faith and trust in their
Father, ' Who was well pleased to give ' them
' the Kingdom.'[b]

a St. Luke xii. 22-34

b ver. 32

With but slight variations the Lord had used the same
language, even as the same admonition had been needed,
at the beginning of His Galilean Ministry, in the Sermon
on the Mount.[c] Perhaps we may here also
regard the allusion to the springing flowers as a
mark of time.   Only, whereas in Galilee this would mark
the beginning of spring, it would, in the more favoured
climate of certain parts of Peræa, indicate the beginning
of December, about the time of the Feast of the Dedication
of the Temple.   More important, perhaps, is it to note,
that the expression [d] rendered in the Authorised
and Revised Versions, ' neither be ye of doubtful
mind,' really means, ' neither be ye uplifted,' in the sense
of not aiming, or seeking after great things.[e]
The context here shows that the term must refer
to the disciples coveting great things, since only to this
the remark could apply, that the Gentile world sought
such things, but that our Father knew what was really
needful for us.   Of deep importance is the final consolation, to dismiss all care and anxiety, since the Father was
pleased to give to this ' little flock ' the Kingdom.   The expression ' flock ' carries us back to the language which Jesus
had held ere parting from Jerusalem.[f]   Henceforth this designation would mark His people.

c St. Matt. vi. 25-33

d St. Luke xii. 29

e Comp. Jer. xlv. 5

f St. John x.

These admonitions, alike as against covetousness, and as to absolute trust and a self-surrender to God, which would count all loss for the Kingdom, are finally set forth, alike in their present application and their ultimate and permanent principle, in what we regard as the concluding part of this Discourse.[a] Its first sentence, 'Sell that ye have, and give alms,' which is only recorded by St. Luke, indicates not a general principle, but its application to that particular period, when the faithful disciple required to follow the Lord unencumbered by worldly cares or possessions.[b] The general principle underlying it is that expressed by St. Paul,[c] and finally resolves itself into this: that the Christian should have as not holding, and use what he has not for self nor sin, but for necessity.

a St. Luke xii. 33, 34

b Comp. St. Matt. xix. 21

c 1 Cor. vii. 30

3. Closely connected with, and yet quite distinct from the previous Discourse, is that about the waiting attitude of the disciples in regard to their Master. The Discourse itself consists of three parts and a practical application.

(1) *The Disciples as Servants in the absence of their Master:*[d] *their duty and their reward.*[e] This part, containing what would be so needful to these Peræan disciples, is peculiar to St. Luke. The Master is supposed to be absent, at a wedding, so that the exact time of his return could not be known to the servants who waited at home. In these circumstances, they should hold themselves in readiness, that, whatever hour it might be, they should be able to open the door at the first knocking. Such eagerness and devotion of service would naturally meet its reward, and the Master would, in turn, consult the comfort of those who had not allowed themselves their evening-meal, nor lain down, but watched for him. Hungry and weary as they were from their zeal for him, he would now, in turn, minister to their personal comfort. And this applied to servants who so watched—it mattered not how long, whether into the second or the third of the watches into which the night was divided.

d St. Luke xii.

e vv. 35-38

The ' Parable ' now passes into another aspect of the

case, which is again referred to in the last Discourses of
Christ.[a] Conversely—suppose the other case,
of people sleeping : the house might be broken
into. If one had known the hour when the thief would
come, sleep would not have been indulged in ; but it is
just this uncertainty and suddenness which should keep
the people in the house ever on their watch till Christ
came.[b]

a St. Matt.
xxiv. 43, 44

b St. Luke
xii. 39, 40

It was at this particular point that a question
of Peter interrupted the Discourse of Christ. To whom
did this ' Parable ' apply about ' the good man ' and ' the
servants ' who were to watch : to the Apostles, or also to
all ? We can understand how Peter might entertain the
Jewish notion, that the Apostles would come with the
Master from the marriage-supper, rather than wait for His
return and work while waiting. It is to this that the
reply of Christ refers. If the Apostles or others are rulers,
it is as stewards, and their reward of faithful and wise
stewardship will be advance to higher administration.
But as stewards they are servants—servants of Christ, and
ministering servants in regard to the other and general
servants. What becomes them in this twofold capacity
is faithfulness to the absent yet ever near Lord, and to
their work, avoiding on the one hand the masterfulness
of pride and of harshness, and on the other the self-
degradation of conformity to evil manners, either of which
would entail sudden and condign punishment in the sudden
and righteous reckoning at His appearing. The ' Parable,'
therefore, alike as to the waiting and the reckoning,
applied to work for Christ, as well as to personal relationship towards Him.

In this Peræan Discourse, as reported by St. Luke,[c]
there now follows what must be regarded, not
indeed as a further answer to Peter's inquiry,
but as referring to the question of the relation
between special work and general discipleship

c St. Luke
xii. 42–46 ;
comp.
St. Matt.
xxiv. 45–51

which had been raised. For, in one sense, all disciples
are servants, not only to wait, but to work. As regarded
those who, like the professed stewards or labourers, knew

their work, but neither 'made ready,' nor did according to His Will, their punishment and loss (where the illustrative figure of ' many ' and ' few stripes ' must not be too closely pressed) would naturally be greater than that of them who knew not—though this also involves guilt— that their Lord had any will towards them, that is, any

^a St. Luke xii. 47, 48 work for them.^a

(2) In the absence of their Master! *A period this of work*, as well as of waiting; *a period of trial also.*^b Here also the two opening verses, in

^b vv. 49–53 their connection with the subject-matter under the first head of this Discourse, but especially with the closing sentences about work for the Master, are peculiar to St. Luke's narrative. The Church had a work to do in His absence—the work for which He had come. He ' came to cast fire on earth '—that fire which was kindled when the Risen Saviour sent the Holy Ghost, and of which the tongues of fire were the symbol. That fire must they spread : this was the work in which, as disciples, each one

^c vv. 49, 50 must take part.^c Again, in that Baptismal Agony of His they also must be prepared to share. It was *fire* : burning up, as well as purifying and giving light. And here it was in place to repeat to His Peræan disciples the prediction already addressed to the

^d St. Matt. x. 34–36 Twelve when going on their Mission,^d as to the certain and necessary trials connected with carrying ' the fire ' which Christ had cast on earth, even to the burning up of the closest bonds of association and

^e St. Luke xii. 51–53 kinship.^e

^f ver. 54 (3) Thus far the disciples. And now for its application to ' the multitudes.'^f Let them not think that all this only concerned the disciples. Were they so blinded as not ' to know how to interpret the

^g ver. 56 time '^g—they who had no difficulty in interpret-

^h ver. 57 ing it when a cloud rose from the sea, or the sirocco blew from the south ?^h Why then did they not of themselves judge what was fitting and necessary, in view of the gathering tempest ?

What was it ? Even what He had told them before in

Galilee,[a] for the circumstances were the same. What
a St. Matt. v. 25, 26 common sense and common prudence would
dictate to every one whom his accuser or creditor
haled before the magistrate : to come to an agreement
with him before it was too late, before sentence had been
b St. Luke xii. 58, 59 pronounced and executed.[b] Although the illustration must not be pressed, its general meaning
would be the more readily understood that there was a
similar Rabbinic proverb, although with very different
practical application.

4. Besides these Discourses, two events are recorded
before Christ's departure to the 'Feast of the Dedication.'
Each of these led to a brief Discourse, ending in a
Parable.

The first records two circumstances not mentioned by
the Jewish historian *Josephus*, nor in any other historical
notice of the time, either by Rabbinic or other writers.

It appears that then, or soon afterwards, some persons
told Christ about a number of His own Galileans, whom
Pilate had ordered to be cut down, as we infer, in the Tem-
c St. Luke xiii. 1-5 ple, while engaged in offering their sacrifices ; [c]-
so that, in the pictorial language of the East,
their blood had mingled with that of their sacrifices.
Clearly, their narration of this event must be connected
with the preceding Discourse of Jesus. He had asked
them whether they could not discern the signs of the
terrible national storm that was nearing. And it was in
reference to this, as we judge, that they repeated this story.
To understand their object, we must attend to the answer
of Christ. It is intended to refute the idea, that these
Galileans had in this been visited by a special punishment
of some special sin against God.

Very probably these Galileans were thus murdered
because of their real or suspected connection with the
Nationalist movement, of which Galilee was the focus.
It is as if these Jews had said to Jesus : Yes, signs of the
times and of the coming storm ! These Galileans of yours,
your own countrymen, involved in a kind of Pseudo-
Messianic movement, a kind of 'signs of the times' rising,

something like that towards which you want us to look—
was not their death a condign punishment? This latter
inference they did not express in words, but implied in
their narration of the fact. But the Lord read their
thoughts and refuted their reasoning. For this purpose
^a St. Luke   He adduced another instance,^a when a tower at
xiii. 4   the Siloam-Pool had fallen on eighteen persons
and killed them, perhaps in connection with that construction of an aqueduct into Jerusalem by Pilate, which
called forth on the part of the Jews the violent opposition
which the Roman so terribly avenged. As good Jews
they would probably think that the fall of the tower,.
which had buried in its ruins these eighteen persons
who were perhaps engaged in the building of that cursed
structure, was a just judgment of God! For Pilate had
used for it the sacred money which had been devoted to
Temple-purposes, and many there were who perished in
the tumult caused by the Jewish resistance to this act of
profanation. But Christ argued that it was as wrong to
infer that Divine judgment had overtaken His Galilean
countrymen, as it would be to judge that the Tower of
Siloam had fallen to punish these Jerusalemites. Not
one party only, nor another; not the supposed Messianic
tendency (in the shape of a national rising), nor, on the
other hand, the opposite direction of absolute submission
to Roman domination, was in fault. The whole nation
was guilty; and the coming storm, to the signs of which
He had pointed, would destroy all, unless there were
spiritual repentance on the part of the nation.

Having thus answered the implied objection, the Lord
^b vv. 6–9   next showed, in the Parable of the Fig-tree,^b the
need and urgency of national repentance.

The second event recorded by St. Luke in this connec-
^c vv. 10–17   tion^c recalls the incidents of the early Judæan^d
^d St. John   and of the Galilean Ministry.^e In Jerusalem there
v. 16   is neither reasoning nor rebuke on the part of
^e St. Matt.   the Jews, but absolute persecution. There also
xii. 9–13   the Lord enters on the higher exposition of His
^f St. John   actions, motives, and Mission.^f In Galilee there
v. 16, 17 &c.

is questioning, and cunning intrigue against Him on the part of the Judæans who dogged His steps. But while no violence can be attempted against Him, the people do not venture openly to take His part.[a] But in Peræa we are confronted by the clumsy zeal of a country-Archisynagogos (Chief Ruler of a Synagogue), who is very angry, but not very wise ; who admits Christ's healing power, and does not dare to attack Him directly, but instead rebukes, not Christ, not even the woman who had been healed, but the people who witnessed it, at the same time telling them to come for healing on other days, not perceiving, in his narrow-minded bigotry, what this admission implied.

a St. Matt. xii. 1-21

Little more requires to be added about this incident in 'one of the Synagogues' of Peræa. Let us only briefly recall the scene. Among those present in this Synagogue had been a poor woman, who for eighteen years had been a sufferer, as we learn, through demoniac agency. In fact, she was, both physically and morally, not sick, but sickly, and most truly was hers ' a spirit of infirmity,' so that ' she was bowed together, and could in no wise lift herself up.' For we mark that hers was not demoniac possession at all —and yet, though she had not yielded, she had not effectually resisted, and so she was ' bound' by ' a spirit of infirmity,' both in body and soul.

We recognise the same ' spirit of infirmity ' in the circumstances of her healing. When Christ, seeing her, called her, she came ; when He said unto her, ' Woman, thou hast been loosed from thy sickliness,' she *was* unbound, and yet in her weakliness she answered not, nor straightened herself, till Jesus ' laid His Hands on her,' and so strengthened her in body and soul, and then she was immediately ' made straight, and glorified God.'

As for the Archisynagogos, we have, as already hinted, such characteristic portraiture of him that we can almost see him ; confused, irresolute, perplexed, and very angry, bustling forward and scolding the people who had done nothing, yet not venturing to silence the woman, now no longer infirm—far less to reprove the great Rabbi, Who had just done such a 'glorious thing,' but speaking at Him through those who had been the astounded eye-witnesses. He was easily and effectually silenced, and all who sympathised with him put to shame. 'Hypocrites!' spake the Lord—on your own admissions your practice and your Law condemn your speech. Every one on the Sabbath looseth his ox or ass, and leads him to the watering. The Rabbinic law expressly allowed this, and even to draw the water, provided the vessel were not carried to the animal. If, as you admit, I have the power of 'loosing' from the bonds of Satan, and she has been so bound these eighteen years, should she—a daughter of Abraham—not have that done for her which you do for your beasts of burden?

The retort was unanswerable; it covered the adversaries with shame. And the Peræans in that Synagogue felt also, at least for the time, the freedom which had come to that woman. They took up the echoes of her hymn of praise, and 'rejoiced for all the glorious things that were done by Him.' And He answered their joy by setting before them 'the Kingdom,' which He had come both to preach and to bring, in its reality and all-pervading energy, as exhibited in the two Parables of 'the Mustard-seed' and 'the Leaven,' spoken before in Galilee. These were now repeated, as specially suited to the circumstances. And the practical application of these Parables must have been obvious to all.

CHAPTER LX.

AT THE FEAST OF THE DEDICATION OF THE TEMPLE.

(St. Luke xiii. 22; St. John x. 22–42.)

ABOUT two months had passed since Jesus had left Jerusalem after the Feast of Tabernacles. At the Feast of the Dedication of the Temple we find Christ once more in the Temple.

There seems special fitness in Christ's spending what,

by a computation of dates, we may regard as the last anniversary season of His Birth, in the Temple at that Feast. It was not of Biblical origin, but had been instituted by Judas Maccabæus in 164 B.C., when the Temple, which had been desecrated by Antiochus Epiphanes, was once more purified, and re-dedicated to the service of Jehovah. Accordingly, it was designated as 'the Dedication of the Altar.'

During the eight days of the Feast the series of Psalms known as the *Hallel* [a] was chanted in the Temple, the people responding as at the Feast of Tabernacles. Other rites resembled those of the latter Feast. Thus, originally, the people appeared with palm-branches.[b] This however does not seem to have been afterwards observed, while another rite, not mentioned in the Book of Maccabees—that of illuminating the Temple and private houses—became characteristic of the Feast. Tradition had it, that when the Temple-Services were restored by Judas Maccabæus, the oil was found to have been desecrated. Only one flagon was discovered of that which was pure, sealed with the very signet of the High-Priest. The supply proved just sufficient to feed for one day the Sacred Candlestick, but by a miracle the flagon was continually replenished during eight days, till a fresh supply could be brought from Thekoah. In memory of this, it was ordered the following year, that the Temple be illuminated for eight days on the anniversary of its 'Dedication.' But the 'Lights' in honour of the Feast were lit not only in the Temple, but in every home. One would have sufficed for the whole household on the first evening, but pious householders lit a light for every inmate of the home, so that, if ten burned on the first, there would be eighty on the last night of the Festival. According to the Talmud, the light might be placed at the entrance to the house or room, or, according to circumstances, in the window, or even on the table. According to modern practice the light is placed at the left on entering a room (the Mezuzah, or folded scroll of the Law, is on the right). Certain benedictions are spoken on lighting these lights, all work is stayed, and the festive time spent in merriment. The first

a Ps. cxiii.-cxviii.

b 2 Macc. x. 7

night is specially kept in memory of Judith, who is supposed to have slain Holofernes, and cheese is freely partaken of as the food of which, according to legend, she gave him so largely, to incite him to thirst and drunkenness. Lastly, during this Festival all fasting and public mourning were prohibited, though some minor acts of private mourning were allowed.

This Festival, like the Feast of Tabernacles, commemorated a Divine victory, which again gave to Israel their good land, after they had once more undergone sorrows like those of the wilderness: it was another harvest-feast, and pointed forward to yet another ingathering. As the once extinguished light was relit in the Temple, it grew day by day in brightness, till it shone out into the heathen darkness, that once had threatened to quench it. That He Who purified the Temple, was its True Light, and brought the Great Deliverance, should (as hinted) have spent the last anniversary season of His Birth at that Feast in the Sanctuary, shining into their darkness, seems most fitting.

Thoughts of the meaning of this Feast and of what was associated with it, will be helpful as we listen to the words which Jesus spake to the people in ' Solomon's Porch.' It is winter, and Christ is walking in the covered Porch in front of the ' Beautiful Gate,' which formed the principal entrance into the ' Court of the Women ' As He walks up and down, the people are literally barring His way—' came round about' Him. From the whole circumstances we cannot doubt that the question which they put, ' How long holdest Thou us in suspense ?.' had not in it an element of genuine inquiry. Their desire that He should tell them ' plainly ' if He were the Christ, had no other motive than that of grounding on it an accusation. The more clearly we perceive this, the more wonderful appear the forbearance of Christ and the wisdom of His answer Briefly He puts aside their hypocrisy. What need is there of fresh speech ? He told them before, and they ' believe not.' From words He appeals to the indisputable witness of deeds : the works which He wrought in His Father's Name. Their non-belief in presence of these facts was due to their not being of His Sheep. As He had said unto them before it was characteristic of His Sheep (as generally of every flock in regard to its own shepherd) to hear—recognise, listen to—His Voice and follow Him. We mark in the words of Christ a triplet of double parallelisms concerning the Sheep and the Shepherd, in ascending climax,[a] as follows :

ᵃ St. John x. 27, 28

My sheep hear My Voice,	And I know them,
And they follow Me :	And I give unto them eternal life ;
And they shall never perish.	And no one shall snatch them out of My Hand.

Richer assurance could not have been given. But something special has here to be marked. The two first parallelisms always link the promise of Christ to the attitude of the sheep ; not, perhaps, conditionally, but as a matter of sequence and of fact. But in the third parallelism there is no reference to anything on the part of the sheep ; it is all promise, and the second clause only explains and intensifies what is expressed in the first. If it indicates attack of the fiercest kind, and by the strongest and most cunning of enemies, be they men or devils, it also marks the watchfulness and absolute superiority of Him Who hath them, as it were, in His Hand—perhaps a Hebraism for ' power '—and hence their absolute safety. And, as if to carry twofold assurance of it, He reminds His hearers that His Work, being ' the Father's Commandment,' is really the Father's Work, given to Christ to do, and no one could snatch them out of the Father's Hand.

One logical sequence is unavoidable. Rightly understood, it is not only the last and highest announcement, but it contains and implies everything else. If the Work of Christ is really that of the Father, and His Working also that of the Father, then it follows that He ' and the Father are One ' (' one ' is in the neuter). This identity of work (and purpose) implies the identity of Nature (Essence) ; that of working, the identity of Power. And so, evidently, the Jews understood it when they again took up stones with the intention of stoning Him—no

B B

doubt because He expressed, in yet more plain terms, what they regarded as His blasphemy. Once more the Lord appealed from His Words, which were doubted, to His Works, which He hath 'showed from the Father,' any one of which might have served as evidence of His Mission. And when the Jews ignored this line of evidence, and insisted that He had been guilty of blasphemy, since, being a Man, he had made Himself God, the Lord replied in a manner that calls for our special attention. From the peculiarly Hebraistic mode of designating a quotation from the Psalms [a] as 'written in the Law,' we gather that we have here a literal transcript of the very words of our Lord. He had claimed to be One with the Father in work and working; from which, of course, the necessary inference was, that He was also One with Him in Nature and Power. Let us see whether the claim was strange. In Ps. lxxxii. 6 the titles 'God' and 'Sons of the Highest' had been given to Judges as the Representatives and Vicegerents of God, wielding His delegated authority, since to them had come His Word of authorisation. But here was authority not transmitted by 'the word,' but personal and direct consecration and Mission on the part of God. The comparison made was not with Prophets, because they only told the word and message from God, but with Judges, who, as such, did the very act of God. If those who, in so acting, had received an indirect commission, were 'gods,' the very representatives of God, could it be blasphemy when He claimed to be the Son of God, Who had received, not authority through a word transmitted through long centuries, but direct personal command, to do the Father's Work; had been directly and personally consecrated to it by the Father, and directly and personally sent by Him, not to say, but to do, the work of the Father?

All would, of course, depend on this, whether Christ really did the works of the Father.[b] If He did the works of His Father, then let them believe, if not the words, yet the works, and thus would they arrive at the knowledge, 'and understand'—distin-

[a] Ps. lxxxii. 6

[b] St. John x. 37

guishing here the act from the state—that ' in Me is the Father, and I in the Father.' In other words, recognising the Work as that of the Father, they would come to understand that the Father worked in Him, and that the root of His Work was in the Father.

The stones that had been taken up were not thrown, for the words of Christ rendered impossible the charge of explicit blasphemy which alone would, according to Rabbinic law, have warranted such summary vengeance. But ' they sought again to seize Him,' so as to drag Him before their tribunal. His time, however, had not yet come, ' and He went forth out of their hand.'

CHAPTER LXI.

THE SECOND SERIES OF PARABLES—THE TWO PARABLES OF HIM WHO IS NEIGHBOUR TO US.

(St. Luke x. 25–37 ; xi. 5–13.)

THE period between Christ's return from the ' Feast of the Dedication' and His last entry into Jerusalem, may be arranged into two parts, divided by the brief visit to Bethany for the purpose of raising Lazarus from the dead.

The Parables of this period look back upon the past, and forward into the future. Those spoken by the Lake of Galilee were purely symbolical. This second series of Parables could be understood by all. They were typical, using the word ' type ' as an example, or perhaps more correctly, an exemplification.[a] Accordingly, they are also intensely practical. Their prevailing character is not descriptive, but hortatory ; and they bring the Gospel, in the sense of glad tidings to the lost, to the hearts of all who hear them.

a As in 1 Cor. x. 6, 11 ; Phil. iii. 17 ; 1 Thess. i. 7 ; 2 Thess. iii. 9 ; 1 Tim. iv. 12 ; Tit. ii. 7 ; 1 Pet. v. 3

Of the Parables of the third series it will for the present suffice to say that they are neither symbolical nor typical, but their prevailing characteristic is prophetic.

The Parables of the second (or Peræan) series, which are typical and hortatory, and ' Evangelical ' in character, are thirteen in number, and, with the exception of the last, are either peculiar to, or else most fully recorded in, the Gospel by St. Luke.

ª St. Luke x. 25-37   1. *The Parable of the Good Samaritan.*ª— This Parable is connected with a question addressed to Jesus by a 'lawyer'—not one of the Jerusalem Scribes or Teachers, but probably an expert in Jewish Canon Law, who possibly made it more or less a profession in that district, though perhaps not for gain. We have suggested that the words of this lawyer referred, or else that himself belonged, to that small party among the Rabbinists who, at least in theory, attached greater value to good works than to study. Knowing the habits of his class, we do not wonder that he put his question to 'tempt'—test, try—the great Rabbi of Nazareth.

We seem to witness the opening of a regular Rabbinic contest as we listen to this speculative problem: 'Teacher, what having done shall I inherit eternal life?' At the foundation lay the notion that eternal life was the reward of merit, of works: the only question was, what these works were to be. The idea of guilt had not entered his mind; he had no conception of sin within. There was a way in which a man might inherit eternal life, not indeed as having absolute claim to it, but in consequence of God's Covenant on Sinai. And so our Lord, using the common Rabbinic expression, 'What readest thou?' pointed him to the Scriptures of the Old Testament.

The reply of the 'lawyer' is remarkable, not only on its own account, but as substantially that given on two ᵇ St. Matt. xix. 16-22; xxii. 34-40 other occasions by the Lord Himself.ᵇ The question therefore naturally arises, whence did this lawyer, who certainly had not spiritual insight, derive his reply? As regarded the duty of absolute love to God, indicated by the quotation of Deut. vi. 5, there could, of course, be no hesitation in the mind of a Jew. The primary obligation of this is frequently referred to, and, indeed, taken for granted, in Rabbinic teaching. The repetition of this command formed part of the daily paayers. When Jesus referred the lawyer to the Scriptures, he could scarcely fail to quote this first paramount obligation.

Hillel had summed up the Law, in briefest compass, in these words: ' What is hateful to thee, that do not to another. This is the whole Law ; the rest is only its explanation.' Still, the two principles just mentioned are not enunciated in conjunction by Rabbinism, nor seriously propounded as either containing the whole Law or as securing heaven. They are also subjected to grave modifications.

On the ground of works—if that had been tenable—the lawyer's answer really pointed to the right solution of the question : this was the way to heaven. To understand any other answer would have required a sense of sin ; and it is the preaching of the Law which awakens in the mind a sense of sin.[a] But the difficulty of this ' way ' would soon suggest itself to a Jew.

[a] Rom. vii. 7

Whatever complexity of motives there may have been, there can be no doubt as to the main object of the lawyer's question : ' But who is my neighbour ? ' He wished ' to justify himself,' in the sense of vindicating his original question, and showing that it was not quite so easily settled as the answer of Jesus seemed to imply. And here it was that Christ could in a ' Parable ' show how far orthodox Judaism was from even a true understanding, much more from such perfect observance of this Law as would gain heaven.

Some one coming from the Holy City, the Metropolis of Judaism, is pursuing the solitary desert-road, those twenty-one miles to Jericho, a district notoriously insecure, when he ' fell among robbers, who, having both stripped and inflicted on him strokes, went away leaving him just as he was, half dead.' This is the first scene. The second opens with an expression which, theologically, as well as exegetically, is of the greatest interest. The word rendered ' by chance ' occurs only in this place, for Scripture commonly views matters in relation to agents rather than to results. The real meaning of the word is ' concurrence,' much like the corresponding Hebrew term. And better definition could not be given, not, indeed, of ' Providence,'

which is a heathen abstraction for which the Bible has no
equivalent, but for the concrete reality of God's providing.
He provides through a concurrence of circumstances, all in
themselves natural and in the succession of ordinary
causation (and this distinguishes it from the miracle),
but the concurring of which is directed and overruled by
Him.   And this helps us to put aside those coarse tests
of the reality of prayer and of the direct rule of God which
men sometimes propose.

It was by such a ' concurrence ' that first a priest, then
a Levite, came down that road, when each successively
' when he saw him, passed by over against (him).'   It
was the principle of questioning, ' Who is my neighbour ? '
which led both priest and Levite to such conduct.   Who
knew what this wounded man was, and how he came
to lie there; and were they called upon, in ignorance of this, to take all the trouble, perhaps incur the
risk of life, which care of him would involve ?   Thus
Judaism (in the persons of its chief representatives) had,
by its exclusive attention to the letter, come to destroy
the spirit of the Law.   Happily, there came yet another
that way, not only a stranger, but one despised, a semi-
heathen Samaritan.   He asked not who the man was,
but what was his need.   Whatever the wounded Jew
might have felt towards him, the Samaritan proved a
true ' neighbour.'   ' He came towards him, and beholding
him, he was moved with compassion.'   He first bound up
his wounds, and then, taking from his travelling provision
wine and oil, made of them what was regarded as the
common dressing for wounds.   Next, having ' set ' (lifted)
him on his own beast, he walked by his side, and brought
him to one of those khans, or hostelries, by the side of
unfrequented roads, which afforded free lodgment to the
traveller.   Generally they also offered entertainment,
in which case, of course, the host, commonly a non-
Israelite, charged for the victuals supplied to man or
beast, or for the care taken.   In the present instance the
Samaritan seems himself to have tended the wounded
man all that evening.   But even thus his care did not

end. The next morning, before continuing his journey, he gave to the host two dinars—about one shilling and threepence of our money, the amount of a labourer's wages for two days [a]—as it were, two days' wages for his care of him, with this provision, that if any further expense were incurred, he would pay it when he next came that way.

a St. Matt.
xx. 2

So far the Parable: its lesson ' the lawyer ' is made himself to enunciate. ' Which of these three seems to thee to have become neighbour of him that fell among the robbers ? ' Though unwilling to take the hated name of Samaritan on his lips, especially as the meaning of the Parable and its anti-Rabbinic bearing were so evident, the 'lawyer' was obliged to reply: 'He that showed mercy on him,' when the Saviour answered, ' Go, and do thou likewise.'

The Parable implies not a mere enlargement of the Jewish ideas, but a complete change of them. The whole old relationship of mere duty is changed into one of love. Thus matters are placed on an entirely different basis from that of Judaism. The question now is not ' Who is my neighbour ? ' but ' Whose neighbour am I ? ' The Gospel answers the question of duty by pointing us to love. Wouldst thou know who is thy neighbour ? Become a neighbour to all by the utmost service thou canst do them in their need. And so the Gospel would not only abolish man's enmity, but bridge over man's separation.

2. The Parable which follows in St. Luke's narrative [b] seems closely connected with that just commented upon. It is also a story of a good neighbour who gives in our need, but presents another aspect of the truth to which the Parable of the Good Samaritan had pointed. Love bends to our need: this is the objective manifestation of the Gospel. Need looks up to love, and by its cry elicits the boon which it seeks. And this is the subjective experience of the Gospel. The one underlies the story of the first Parable, the other that of the second.

b St. Luke
xi. 5-13

This second Parable is strung to the request of some

disciples to be taught what to pray.[a]   A man has a
a St. Luke
xi. 1 friend who, long after nightfall, unexpectedly
comes to him from a journey. He has nothing
in the house, yet he must provide for his need, for hospitality
demands it. Accordingly, though it be so late, he goes to
his friend and neighbour to ask him for three loaves, stating
the case. On the other hand, the friend so asked refuses,
since at that late hour he has retired to bed with his
children, and to grant his request would imply not only
inconvenience to himself, but the disturbing of the whole
household. It is not ordinary but, so to speak, extraordinary prayer, which is here alluded to.

To return to the Parable: the question (abruptly
broken off from the beginning of the Parable in ver. 5)
is, what each of us would do in the circumstances just
b ver. 8 detailed. The answer is implied in what follows.[b]
It points to continued importunity, which would
at last obtain what it needs. 'I tell you, even if he will
not give him, rising up, because he is his friend, yet at
least on account of his importunity, he will rise up and
give him as many as he needeth.'   It is a gross misunderstanding to describe this as presenting a mechanical view
of prayer; as if it implied either that God was unwilling
to answer, or else that prayer, otherwise unheard, would
be answered merely for its importunity. The lesson is
that where, for some reasons, there are or seem special
difficulties to an answer to our prayers, the importunity
arising from the sense of our absolute need, and the
knowledge that He is our Friend and that He has bread,
will ultimately prevail. The difficulty is not as to the
giving, but as to the giving *then*—'rising up;' and this
is overcome by perseverance, so that (to return to the
Parable) if he will not rise up because he is his friend,
yet at least he will rise because of his importunity, and
not only give him 'three' loaves, but, in general, 'as
many as he needeth.'

So important is the teaching of this Parable that
Christ makes detailed application of it. He bids us 'ask,'
and that earnestly and believingly; 'seek,' and that

energetically and instantly; 'knock,' and that intently and loudly. Ask—He is a Friend, and we shall 'receive;' 'seek'—it is there, and we shall 'find;' 'knock'—our need is absolute, and it shall be opened to us. And such importunity applies to 'every one,' whoever he be, and whatever the circumstances which would seem to render his prayer specially difficult of answer.

More than this, God will not deceive by the appearance of what is not reality. He will even give the greatest gift. The Parabolic relation is now not that of friends, but of father and son. If the son ask for bread, will the father give what seems such, but is only a stone? If he ask for a fish, will he tender him what looks such, but is a serpent? If he seeks an egg, will he hand to him what breeds a scorpion? The need, the hunger, of the child will not, in answer to its prayer, receive at the Father's Hands that which seems, but gives not the reality of satisfaction —rather is poison. Let us draw the inference. Such is our conduct—how much more shall our heavenly Father give His Holy Spirit to them that ask Him?

CHAPTER LXII.

THE THREE PARABLES OF WARNING: THE FOOLISH RICH MAN—THE BARREN FIG-TREE—THE GREAT SUPPER.

(St. Luke xii. 13-21 ; xiii. 6-9 ; xiv. 16-24.)

THE three Parables which successively follow in St. Luke's Gospel may generally be designated as those 'of warning.' This holds especially true of the last two of them, which refer to the civil and the ecclesiastical polity of Israel. Each of the three Parables was spoken under circumstances which gave occasion for such illustration.

ª St. Luke xii. 13-21   1. *The Parable of the Foolish Rich Man.*[a] It appears that some one among them that listened to Jesus, conceived the idea that the authority of the Great Rabbi of Nazareth might be used for his own selfish purposes. Evidently Christ must have attracted and deeply moved multitudes, or His interposition would not have been sought; and, equally evidently, what He preached had made upon this man the impression that he might possibly enlist Him as his champion. On the other hand, Christ had not only no legal authority for interfering, but the Jewish law of inheritance was so clearly defined, and we may add so just, that if this person had had any just or good cause, there could have been no need for appealing to Jesus. Hence it must have been ' covetousness,' in the strictest sense, which prompted it—perhaps a wish to have, besides his own share as a younger brother, half of that additional portion which, by law, came to the eldest son of the family.

This accounts for the immediate reference of our Lord to covetousness, the folly of which He showed by this almost self-evident principle—that ' not in the superabounding to any one [not in that wherein he has more than enough] consisteth his life, from the things which he possesseth.' In other words, that part of the things which a man possesseth by which his life is sustained, consists not in what is superabundant : his life is sustained by that which he needs and uses ; the rest, the superabundance, forms no part of his life, and may, perhaps, never be of use to him. And herein lies the danger : the love of these things will engross mind and heart, and care about them will drive out higher thoughts and aims. The moral as regarded the Kingdom of God, and the warning not to lose it for thought of what ' perisheth with the using,' are obvious.

The Parable itself consists of two parts, of which the first shows the folly, the second the sin and danger of that care for what is beyond our present need, which is the characteristic of covetousness. The rich man is surveying his land, which is bearing plentifully—evidently beyond its former yield, since the old provision for storing the corn appears no longer sufficient. In the calculations which he now makes, he looks into the future, and sees there progressive increase and riches. As yet, the harvest was not reaped ; but he was already considering what to do, reckon-

ing upon the riches that would come to him. And so he
resolved to pull down the old, and build larger barns, where
he would store his future possessions. In these plans for
the future—and it was his folly to make such absolutely—
he thought not of God. His whole heart was set on the
acquisition of earthly riches, not on the service of God.
He remembered not his responsibility; all that he had was
for himself, and absolutely his own, to batten upon : ' Soul,
thou hast much goods laid up for many years ; take thine
ease, eat, drink, be merry.' He did not even remember
that there was a God Who might cut short his years.

And now comes the quick, sharp contrast. ' But God
said unto him '—not by revelation, nor through inward
presentiment, but with awful suddenness, in those unspoken words of fact which cannot be gainsaid or answered :
' Thou fool ! this very night '—which follows on thy plans
and purposings—' thy soul is required of thee. But the
things which thou hast prepared, whose shall they be ? '
Here, with the obvious evidence of the folly of such state
of mind, the Parable breaks off. Its sinfulness—nay, and
beyond this negative aspect of it, the wisdom of righteousness in laying up the good treasure which cannot be taken
from us, appears in this concluding remark of Christ—' So
is he who layeth up treasure (treasureth) for himself, and
is not rich towards God.'

It was a barbed arrow, we might say, out of the Jewish
quiver, but directed by the Hand of the Lord. For we
read in the Talmud that a Rabbi told his disciples,
' Repent the day before thy death ; ' and when his disciples asked him : ' Does a man know the day of his
death ? ' he replied, that on that very ground he should
repent to-day, lest he should die to-morrow. And so
would all his days be days of repentance. The Son of
Sirach, the Talmud, and the Midrash furnish similar warnings and parallels. But we miss in them the spiritual
application made by Christ.

2. The special warning intended to be conveyed by
the Parable of *the Barren Fig-tree*[a] sufficiently appears from the context. As previously

[a] St. Luke
xiii. 6-9

explained, the Lord had not only corrected the erroneous interpretations which the Jews were giving to certain recent national occurrences, but pointed them to this higher moral of all such events, that, unless speedy national repentance followed, the whole people would perish. This Parable offers not merely an exemplification of this general prediction of Christ, but sets before us that which underlies it : Israel in its relation to God; the need of repentance; Israel's danger; the nature of repentance, and its urgency; the relation of Christ to Israel; the Gospel; and the final judgment on impenitence.

As regards the details of this Parable, we mark that the fig-tree had been specially planted by the owner in his vineyard, which was the choicest situation. This, we know, was not unusual. Fig-trees, as well as palm- and olive-trees, were regarded as so valuable, that to cut them down, if they yielded even a small measure of fruit, was popularly deemed to deserve death at the Hand of God. Ancient Jewish writings supply interesting particulars of this tree and its culture. On account of its repeated crops, it was declared not subject to the ordinance which enjoined that fruit should be left in the corners for the poor. Its artificial inoculation was known. The practice mentioned in the Parable of digging about the tree and dunging it, is frequently mentioned in Rabbinic writings, and by the same designations. Curiously, *Maimonides* mentions three years as the utmost limit within which a tree should bear fruit in the land of Israel. Lastly, as trees were regarded as by their roots undermining and deteriorating the ground, a barren tree would be of threefold disadvantage : it would yield no fruit; it would fill valuable space, which a fruit-bearer might occupy; and it would needlessly deteriorate the land. Accordingly, while it was forbidden to destroy fruit-bearing trees, it would, on the grounds above stated, be duty to cut down a 'barren' or 'empty' tree.

These particulars will enable us more fully to understand the details of the Parable. Allegorically, the fig-tree served in the Old Testament as emblem of the Jewish nation [a]; in the Talmud, rather as that of Israel's lore, and

a Joel i. 7

hence of the leaders and the pious of the people.
The vineyard is in the New Testament the
symbol of the Kingdom of God, as distinct from the nation
of Israel.[b] Thus far then, the Parable may be

b St. Matt.
xx. 1 &c. ;
xxi. 33 &c.
In Jewish
thought the
two were
scarcely
separated.

thus translated : God called Israel as a nation,
and planted it in the most favoured spot—as a
fig-tree in the vineyard of His own Kingdom.
'And He came seeking,' as He had every right to
do, 'fruit thereon, and found none.' It was the
third year (not after three years, but evidently in the third
year, when the third year's crop should have appeared),
that He had vainly looked for fruit, when He turned to His
Vinedresser—the Messiah, to Whom the vineyard is committed as its King—with this direction : 'Cut it down—
why doth it also deteriorate the soil ?' It is barren,
though in the best position ; as a fig-tree it ought to bear
figs, and here the best; it fills the place which a good tree
might occupy ; and besides, it deteriorates the soil. And
its three years' barrenness has established (as before explained) its utterly hopeless character. Then it is that
the Divine Vinedresser, in His infinite compassion, pleads,
and with far deeper reality than either Abraham or Moses
could have entreated, for the fig-tree which Himself had
planted and tended, that it should be spared 'this year
also,' 'until then that I shall dig about it, and dung it'—
till He labour otherwise than before, even by His Own
Presence and Words, nay, by laying to its roots His most
precious Blood. 'And if then it bear fruit'—here the
text abruptly breaks off, as implying that in such case it
would, of course, be allowed to remain ; 'but if not, *then*
against the future (coming) year shalt thou cut it down.'
The Parable needs no further commentation.

3. The third Parable of warning—that of *the Great*

c St. Luke
xiv. 16-24

Supper [c]—refers not to the political state of Israel,
but to their ecclesiastical *status*, and their continuance as the possessors and representatives of the
Kingdom of God. It was spoken after the return of Jesus
from the Feast of the Dedication, and therefore carries us

beyond the point in this history which we have reached. Accordingly, the attendant circumstances will be explained in the sequel.

What led up to the Parable of 'the Great Supper' happened after these things : after His healing of the man with the dropsy in sight of them all on the Sabbath, after His twofold rebuke of their perversion of the Sabbath-Law, and of those marked characteristics of Pharisaism, which showed how far they were from bringing forth fruit worthy of the Kingdom, and how they misrepresented ^{a St. Luke} the Kingdom, and were utterly unfit ever to do ^{xiv. 1-11} otherwise.[a] The Lord had spoken of making a feast, not for one's kindred, nor for the rich—whether such outwardly, or mentally and spiritually from the standpoint of the Pharisees—but for the poor and afflicted. This would imply true spirituality, because that fellowship of giving, which descends to others in order to raise them as brethren, not condescends, in order to be raised by them as their ^{b vv. 12, 13} Master and Superior.[b] And He had concluded with these words : 'And thou shalt be blessed— because they have not to render back again to thee, for ^{c ver. 14} it shall be rendered back to thee again in the Resurrection of the Just.'[c]

It was this last clause—but separated, in true Pharisaic spirit, from that which had preceded and indicated the motive—on which one of those present now commented, probably with a covert, perhaps a provocative, reference to what formed the subject of Christ's constant teaching : 'Blessed whoso shall eat bread in the Kingdom of Heaven.' An expression this, which to the Pharisee meant the common Jewish expectancy of a great feast at the beginning of the Messianic Kingdom. Whether or not it was the object of his exclamation, as sometimes religious commonplaces or platitudes are in our days, to interrupt the course of Christ's rebukes, or as before hinted, to provoke Him to unguarded speech, must be left undetermined. What is chiefly apparent is, that this Pharisee separated what Christ said about the blessings of the first Resurrection from that with which He had connected them as logically their moral antecedent: viz. love, in opposition to self-assertion and self-seeking. The Pharisee's words imply that like his class he, at any rate, fully expected to share in these blessings as a matter of course, and because he was a Pharisee. Thus to leave out Christ's anteceding words was not only to set them aside, but to pervert His saying, and to place the blessedness of the future on the very opposite basis from that on which Christ had rested ^{a St. Luke} it. Accordingly, it was to this man personally ^a ^{xiv. 16} that the Parable was addressed.

ª St. Luke
xiv. 16

There can be no difficulty in understanding the main ideas underlying the Parable. The man who made the ' Great Supper' was He Who had, in the Old Testament, prepared ' a feast of fat things.' ^b The ' bidding many ' preceded the actual announcement of the day and hour of the feast. This general announcement was made in the Old Testament institutions and prophecies, and the guests bidden were those in the city, the chief men—not the ignorant and those out of the way, but the men who knew, and read, and expounded these prophecies. At last the preparations were ended, and the Master sent out His Servant—referring to whomsoever He would employ for that purpose. It was to intimate to the persons formerly bidden, that everything was now ready. Then it was that, however differing in their special grounds for it, or expressing it with more or less courtesy, they were all at one in declining to come. The feast to which they had been bidden some time before, and to which they had apparently agreed to come, was, when actually announced as ready, not what they had expected, at any rate not what they regarded as more .desirable than what they had, and must give up in order to come to it. For—and this seems one of the principal points in the Parable—to come to that feast, to enter into the Kingdom, implies the giving up of something that seems, if not necessary, yet most desirable, and the enjoyment of which appears only reasonable.

b Is. xxv. 6, 7

Then let the feast be for those who were in need of it, and to whom it would be a feast: the poor and those afflicted—the maimed, and blind and lame, on whom those great citizens who had been first bidden would look down. This, with reference to, and in higher spiritual explanation of what Christ had previously said about bidding such to *St. Luke* our feasts of fellowship and love.[a] Accordingly, xiv. 13 the Servant is now directed to ' go out quickly into the (larger) streets and the (narrow) lanes of the City ' —a trait which shows that the scene is laid in ' the City,' the professed habitation of God. The importance of this circumstance is evident. It not only explains who the first bidden chief citizens were, but also that these poor were the despised ignorant, and the maimed, lame, and blind—such as the publicans and sinners. These are they in ' the streets ' and ' lanes ; ' and the Servant is directed, not only to invite, but to ' bring them in,' as otherwise they might naturally shrink from coming to such a feast. But even so, ' there is yet room ; ' for the Lord of the house has, in His liberality, prepared a very great feast for very many. And so the Servant is once more sent, so that the Master's ' house may be filled.' But now he is bidden to ' go out,' outside the City, outside the Theocracy, ' into the highways and hedges,' to those who travel along the world's great highway, or who have fallen down weary, and rest by its hedges; into the busy, or else weary, heathen world. This reference to the heathen world is the more apparent that, according to the Talmud, there were commonly no hedges round the fields of the Jews. And this time the direction to the Servant is not, as in regard to those naturally bashful outcasts of the City—who would scarcely venture to the great house—to ' bring them in,' but ' constrain ' [without a pronoun] ' to come in.' Their being invited by a Lord Whom they had not known, per- haps never heard of before, to a City in which they were strangers, and to a feast for which—as wayfarers, or as resting by the hedges, or else as working within their en- closure—they were wholly unprepared, required special urgency, ' a constraining,' to make them either believe in it, or come to it from where the messengers found them, and that without preparing for it by dress or otherwise. And so the house would be filled.

Here the Parable abruptly breaks off. What follows are the words of our Lord in explanation and application of it to the company then present: 'For I say unto you, that none of those men which were bidden shall taste of My Supper.' And this was the final answer to this Pharisee and to those with him at that table, and to all such perversion of Christ's Words and misapplication of God's Promises as he and they were guilty of.

CHAPTER LXIII.

THE THREE PARABLES OF THE GOSPEL: THE LOST SHEEP, THE LOST DRACHM, THE LOST SON.

(St. Luke xv.)

A SIMPLE perusal of the three Parables grouped together in the fifteenth chapter of St. Luke's Gospel, will convince us of their connection. They are peculiarly Gospel Parables 'of the recovery of the lost:' in the first instance, through the unwearied labour; in the second, through the anxious care, of the owner; and in the third Parable, through the never-ceasing love of the Father.

Properly to understand these Parables, the circumstances which elicited them must be kept in view. As Jesus preached the Gospel of God's call, not to those who had, as they imagined, prepared themselves for the Kingdom by study and good works, but as that of a door open, and a welcome free to all, 'all the publicans and sinners were [constantly] drawing near to Him.' It has been shown, that the Jewish teaching concerning repentance was quite other than, nay, contrary to, that of Christ. Theirs was not a Gospel to the lost: they had nothing to say to sinners. They called upon them to 'do penitence,' and then Divine Mercy, or rather Justice, would have its reward for the penitent. Christ's Gospel was to the lost as such. It told them of forgiveness, of what the Saviour was doing, and the Father purposed and felt for them; and that, not in the future and as reward of their penitence, but now in the immediate present. From what we know of the Pharisees, we can scarcely wonder that ' they were murmuring at Him, saying, This man receiveth " sinners," and eateth with them.' Whether or not Christ had on this, as on other occasions,[a] joined at a meal with such persons, their charge was so far true, that ' this One,' in contrariety to the principles and practice of Rabbinism, ' received sinners ' as such, and consorted with them.

* St. Matt. ix. 10, 11

These three Parables proceed on the view that the work of the Father and of Christ, as regards ' the Kingdom,' is the same; that Christ was doing the work of the Father, and that they who know Christ know the Father also. That work was the restoration of the lost; Christ had come to do it, and it was the longing of the Father to welcome the lost home again. Further, and this is only second in importance, the lost was still God's property; and he who had wandered farthest was a child of the Father, and considered as such.

In other particulars there are, however, differences, all the more marked that they are so finely shaded. These concern the *lost*, their *restoration*, and its *results*.

1. *The Parable of the Lost Sheep.*—The Lost Sheep is only one among a hundred : not a very great loss. Yet which among us would not, even from the common motives of ownership, leave the ninety-and-nine, and go after it, all the more that it has strayed into the wilderness ? At the outset we remark that this Parable and the next, that of the Lost Drachm, are intended as an answer to the Pharisees. Hence they are addressed to them. Should not the Christ do even as they would have done to the straying and almost lost sheep of His own flock ? We think not only of those sheep which Jewish pride and superciliousness had left to go astray, but of our own natural tendency to wander. And we recall the saying of St. Peter, which, no doubt, looked back upon this Parable : ' Ye were as sheep going astray; but are now returned unto the Shepherd and Bishop of your souls.'[b] It is not difficult in imagination to follow the Parabolic picture : how in its folly and ignorance the sheep strayed further and

b 1 Pet. ii. 25

further, and at last was lost in solitude and among stony places; how the shepherd followed and found it, weary and footsore; and then with tender care lifted it on his shoulder, and carried it home, glad that he had found the lost. And not only this, but when, after long absence, he returned home with his found sheep, that now nestled close to its Saviour, he called together his friends, and bade them rejoice with him over the erst lost and now found treasure.

To mark here the contrast between the teaching of Christ and that of the Pharisees, we put down in all its nakedness the message which Pharisaism brought to the lost. Christ said to them : ' There is joy in heaven over one sinner that repenteth.' Pharisaism said—and we quote literally—' There is joy before God when those who provoke Him perish from the world.'

2. In proceeding to the second Parable, that of *the Lost Drachm*, we must keep in mind that in the first the danger of being lost arose from the natural tendency of the sheep to wander. In the second Parable it is no longer our natural tendency to which our loss is attributable. The drachm (about 7½d. of our money) has been lost, as the woman, its owner, was using or counting her money. The loss is the more sensible as it is one out of only ten, which constitute the owner's property. But it is still in the house—not like the sheep that had gone astray—only covered by the dust that is continually accumulating from the work and accidents around. And so it is more and more likely to be buried under it, or swept into chinks and corners, and less and less likely to be found as time passes. But the woman lights a lamp, sweeps the house, and seeks diligently till she has found it. And then she calleth together those around, and bids them rejoice with her over the finding of the lost part of her possessions. And so there is joy in the presence of the Angels over one sinner that repenteth. The interest of this Parable centres in the *search*.

3. If it has already appeared that the two first Parables are not merely a repetition, in different form, of the

same thought, but represent two different aspects and causes of the ' being lost'—the essential difference between them appears even more clearly in the third Parable, that of *the Lost Son*. Before indicating it in detail, we may mark the similarity in form, and the contrast in spirit, of analogous Rabbinic Parables. The Midrash [a] relates how when Moses fed the sheep of Jethro in the wilderness, and a kid had gone astray, he went after it, and found it drinking at a spring. As he thought it might be weary, he laid it on his shoulder and brought it back ; when God said that, because he had shown pity on the sheep of a man, He would give him His own sheep, Israel, to feed. As a parallel to the second Parable, this may be quoted as similar in form, though very different in spirit, when a Rabbi notes that, if a man had lost a *sela* (drachm) or anything else of value in his house, he would light ever so many lights till he had found what provides for only one hour in this world. How much more, then, should he search, as for hidden treasures, for the words of the Law, on which depends the life of this and of the world to come! And in regard to the high place which Christ assigned to the repenting sinner, we may note that, according to the leading Rabbis, the penitents would stand nearer to God than the ' perfectly righteous, since, in Is. lvii. 19, peace was first bidden to those who had been afar off, and then only to those near.

on Ex. iii. 1

It may be added that besides illustrations, to which reference will be made in the sequel, Rabbinic tradition supplies a parallel to at least part of the third Parable, that of the Lost Son. It tells us that while prayer may sometimes find the gate of access closed, it is never shut against repentance, and it introduces a Parable in which a king sends a tutor after his son, who, in his wickedness, had left the palace, with this message : ' Return, my son! ' to which the latter replied : ' With what face can I return ? I am ashamed ! ' On which the father sends this message : ' My son, is there a son who is ashamed to return to his father— and shalt thou not return to thy father ? Thou shalt return.' So, continues the Midrash, had God sent Jeremiah after Israel in the hour of their sin with the call to return,[a] and the comforting reminder that it was to their Father.

a Jer. iii. 12

In the Parable of ' *the Lost Son,*' the main interest centres in his restoration. It is not now to the innate tendency of his nature, nor yet to the work and dust in the house that the loss is attributable, but to the personal, free choice of the individual. He does not stray; he does not fall aside—he wilfully departs, and under aggravated circumstances. It is the younger of two sons of a father who is equally loving to both, and kind even to his hired servants, whose home, moreover, is one not only of sufficiency but of wealth. The demand which he makes for the ' portion of property falling' to him is founded on the Jewish Law of Inheritance. Presumably, the father had only these two sons. The elder would receive two portions, the younger the third of all movable property. The father could not have disinherited the younger son, although, if there had been several younger sons, he might have divided the property falling to them as he wished, provided he expressed only his disposition, and did not add that such or such of the children were to have a less share or none at all. On the other hand, a man might, during his lifetime, dispose of all his property by gift, as he chose, to the disadvantage or even the total loss of the firstborn, or of any other children; nay, he might give all to strangers.

It thus appears that the younger son was, by law, fully entitled to his share of the possessions, although, of course, he had no right to claim it during his father's lifetime. His conduct, whatever his motives, was most heartless as regarded his father, and sinful as before God. Such a disposition could not prosper. The father had yielded to his demand, and, to be as free as possible from control and restraint, the younger son had gone into a far country. There the natural sequences soon appeared, and his property was wasted in riotous living.

The next scene in the history is misunderstood when the objection is raised, that the young man's misery is there represented as the result of Providential circumstances rather than of his own misdoing.   For our awakening, indeed, we are frequently indebted to what is called the Providence, but what is really the manifold working together of the grace of God.   And so we find special meaning in the occurrence of this famine.   That in his want ' he clave to one of the citizens of that country,' seems to indicate that the man had been unwilling to engage the dissipated young stranger, and only yielded to his desperate importunity.   This also explains how he employed him in the lowest menial service, that of feeding swine.   To a Jew there was more than degradation in this, since the keeping of swine (although perhaps the ownership rather than the feeding) was prohibited to Israelites under a curse.   And even in this demeaning service he was so evil entreated, that for very hunger he would fain have ' filled his belly with the carob-pods that the swine did eat.'   But here the same harshness which had sent him to such employment met him on the part of all the people of that country : 'and no man gave unto him,' even sufficient of such food.   What perhaps gives additional meaning to this description is the Jewish saying, ' When Israel is reduced to the carob-tree, they become repentant.'

It was this pressure of extreme want which first showed to the younger son the contrast between the country and the circumstances to which his sin had brought him, and the plentiful provision of the home he had left, and the kindness which provided bread enough and to spare for even the hired servants.   There was only a step between what he said, ' having come into himself,' and his resolve to return, though its felt difficulty seems implied in the expression, ' I will arise.'   Nor would he go back with the hope of being reinstated in his position as son, seeing he had already received and wasted in sin his portion of the patrimony.   All he sought was to be made as one of the hired servants.   And alike from true feeling, and to show that this was all his pretence, he would preface his request by the confession, that he had sinned ' against heaven '—a frequent Hebraism for ' against

God'—and in the sight of his father, and hence could no longer lay claim to the name of son.

But the result was far other than he could have expected. When we read that, 'while he was yet afar off, his father saw him,' we must evidently understand it in the sense, that his father had been always on the outlook for him, an impression which is strengthened by the later command to the servants to 'bring the calf, the fatted one,'[a] as if it had been specially fattened against his return. As he now saw him, 'he was moved with compassion, and he ran, and he fell on his neck, and covered him with kisses.' Such a reception rendered the purposed request, to be made as one of the hired servants, impossible. The father's love had anticipated his confession, and rendered its self-spoken sentence of condemnation impossible. And so he only made confession of his sin and wrong—not only as preface to the request to be taken in as a servant, but as the outgoing of a humbled, grateful, truly penitent heart. Here it deserves special notice, as marking the absolute contrast between the teaching of Christ and Rabbinism, that we have in one of the oldest Rabbinic works a Parable exactly the reverse of this, when the son of a friend is redeemed from bondage, not as a son, but to be a slave, that so obedience might be demanded of him. The inference drawn is, that the obedience of the redeemed is not that of filial love of the pardoned, but the enforcement of the claim of the master.

They have reached the house. And now the father would not only restore the son, but convey to him the evidence of it, and he would do so before, and by the servants. The three tokens of wealth and position are to be furnished him. 'Quickly' the servants are to bring forth the '*stola*,' the upper garment of the higher classes, and that 'the first'—the best, and this instead of the tattered, coarse raiment of the foreign swineherd. Similarly, the finger-ring for his hand, and the sandals for his unshod feet, would indicate the son of the house. And to mark this still further, the servants are not only to bring these articles, but themselves to 'put them on' the son,

[a] St. Luke xv. 23

so as thereby to own his mastership. And yet further, the calf, 'the fatted one' for this very occasion, was to be killed, and there was to be a joyous feast, for 'this' his son 'was dead, and is come to life again; was lost and is found.'

While this was going on, so continues the Parable, the elder brother was still in the field. On his return home, he inquired of a servant the reason of the festivities which he heard within the house. The harsh words of reproach with which he next set forth his own apparent wrongs could have only one meaning: his father had never rewarded him for his services.

But in this very thing lay the error of the elder son, and to apply it—the fatal mistake of Pharisaism. The elder son regarded all as of merit and reward, as work and return. But it is not so. We mark, first, that the same tenderness which had welcomed the returning son now met the elder brother. The father spoke to the angry man, not in the language of merited reproof, but addressed him lovingly as ' son,' and reasoned with him. And then, when he had shown him his wrong, he would fain recall him to better feeling by telling him of the other as his ' brother.' [a]

[a] St. Luke xv. 32   But the main point is this. There can be here no question of desert. So long as the son is in His Father's house, He gives in His great goodness to His child all that is the Father's. But this poor lost one—still a son and a brother—he has not got any reward, only been taken back again by a Father's love, when he had come back to Him in the misery of his need. This son, or rather, as the other should view him, this ' brother,' had been dead, and was come to life again; lost, and was found. And over this ' it was meet to make merry and be glad,' not to murmur. Such murmuring came from thoughts of work and pay—wrong in themselves, and foreign to the proper idea of Father and son; such joy, from a Father's heart. The elder brother's were the thoughts of a servant: of service and return; the younger brother's was the welcome of a son in the mercy and everlasting love of a Father.

CHAPTER LXIV.

THE UNJUST STEWARD—DIVES AND LAZARUS.

(St. Luke xvi.)

ALTHOUGH widely differing in their object and teaching, the last group of Parables spoken during this part of Christ's Ministry is, at least outwardly, connected by a leading thought. The word by which we would string them together is *Righteousness.* There are three Parables of the *Un*righteous: the Unrighteous Steward, the Unrighteous Owner, and the Unrighteous Dispenser, or Judge. And these are followed by two other Parables of the *Self*-righteous: Self-righteousness in its Ignorance, and its dangers as regards oneself; and Self-Righteousness in its Harshness, and its dangers as regards others. But when this outward connection has been marked, we have gone the utmost length. Much more close is the internal connection between some of them.

I. *The Parable of the Unjust Steward.*—Here we dis-

^{a St. Luke xvi. 1-8} tinguish—1. The illustrative Parable.^a 2. Its ^{b ver. 9} moral.^b 3. Its application in the combination ^{c vv. 10-13} of the moral with some of the features of the Parable.^c

1. The illustrative Parable.^d This may be said to ^{d vv. 1-8} converge to the point brought out in the conclud-^{e ver. 8} ing verse:^e the prudence which characterises the dealings of the children of this world in regard to their own generation—or, to translate the Jewish forms of expression into our own phraseology, the wisdom with which those who care not for the world to come choose the means most effectual for attaining their worldly objects. It is this prudence by which their aims are so effectually secured, and it alone, which is set before 'the children of light,' as that from which to learn. And the lesson is the more practical, that those primarily addressed had hitherto been among these men of the world. Let them learn from the serpent its wisdom, and from the dove its harm-

lessness; from the children of this world, their prudence as regarded their generation, while, as children of the new light, they must remember the higher aim for which that prudence was to be employed. Thus would that Mamon which is ' of unrighteousness ' and which certainly ' faileth,' become to us treasure in the world to come—welcome us there, and, so far from ' failing,' prove permanent— welcome us in everlasting tabernacles. Thus also shall we have made friends of the ' Mamon of unrighteousness,' and that, which from its nature must fail, become eternal gain.

The connection between this Parable and what the Lord had previously said concerning returning sinners, is evidenced by the use of the term ' wasting ' in the charge against the steward, just as the prodigal son had ' wasted ' his substance.[a] Only, in the present instance, the property had been entrusted to his adminis- tration. As regards the owner, his designation as ' rich ' seems intended to mark how large was the property com- mitted to the steward. The ' steward ' was not, as in St. Luke xii. 42–46, a slave, but one employed for the adminis- tration of the rich man's affairs, subject to notice of dismissal.[b] He was accused—the term implying malevolence, but not necessarily a false charge— not of fraud, but of wasting his master's goods. And his master seems to have convinced himself that the charge was true, since he at once gives him notice of dismissal. The latter is absolute, and not made dependent on the ' account of his stewardship,' which is only asked when he gives up his office. Nor does the steward either deny the charge or plead any extenuation. His great concern rather is, during the time still left of his stewardship, before he gives up his accounts, to provide for his future support. The only alternative before him in the future is that of manual labour or mendicancy. But for the former he has not strength ; from the latter he is restrained by shame.

Then it is that his ' prudence ' suggests a device by which, after his dismissal, he may without begging be

[a] St. Luke xv. 13

[b] St. Luke xvi. 2, 3

received into the houses of those whom he has made friends. It must be borne in mind that he is still steward, and, as such, has full power of disposing of his master's affairs. When, therefore, he sends for one after another of his master's debtors, and tells each to alter the sum in the bond, he does not suggest to them forgery or fraud, but, in remitting part of the debt, he acts, although unrighteously, yet strictly within his rights. Thus neither the steward nor the debtors could be charged with criminality, and the master must have been struck with the cleverness of a man who had thus secured a future provision by making friends, so long as he had the means of so doing (ere his Mamon of unrighteousness failed).

A few archæological notices may help the interpretation of details. It seems likely, that the ' bonds,' or rather 'writings,' of these debtors were written acknowledgments of debt. In the first case they are stated as ' a hundred *bath* of oil,' in the second as ' a hundred *cor* of wheat.' In regard to these quantities we have the preliminary difficulty, that three kinds of measurement were in use in Palestine—that of the ' Wilderness,' or the original Mosaic ; that of ' Jerusalem,' which was more than a fifth larger ; and that of Sepphoris, probably the common Galilean measurement, which, in turn, was more than a fifth larger than the Jerusalem measure. Assuming the measurement to have been the Galilean, one *bath* would have been equal to about 39 *litres*. In the Parable, the first debtor was owing 100 of these *bath*, or, according to the Galilean measurement, about 3,900 *litres* of oil. The value of the oil would probably amount to about 10*l.* of our money, and the remission of the steward, of course, to 5*l.*

The second debtor owed ' a hundred *cor* of wheat '— that is, in dry measure, ten times the amount of the oil of the first debtor, since the *cor* was ten *ephah* or *bath*, the *ephah* three *seah*, the *seah* six *qabh*, and the *qabh* four *log*. This must be borne in mind, since the dry and the fluid measures were precisely the same ; and here, also, their threefold computation (the ' Wilderness,' the ' Jerusalem,' and the ' Galilean ') obtained. Striking an average between the various prices mentioned we infer that the hundred _cor_ would represent a debt of from 100*l.* to 125*l.*, and the remission of the steward (of 20 _cor_), a sum of 20*l.* to 25*l.* Comparatively small as these sums may seem, they are in reality large, remembering the value of money in Palestine, which, on a low computation, would be five times as great as in our own country. These two debtors are only mentioned as instances, and so the unjust steward would easily secure for himself friends by the ' Mamon of unrighteousness '—the term _Mamon_, we may note, being derived from the Syriac and Rabbinic word of the same kind (signifying to apportion).

Another point on which acquaintance with the history and habits of those times throws light is, how the debtors could so easily alter the sum mentioned in their respective bonds. For the text implies that this, and not the writing of a new bond, is intended; since in that case the old one would have been destroyed, and not given back for alteration.

The materials on which the Jews wrote were of the most diverse kind : leaves, as of olives, palms, the carob, &c. ; the rind of the pomegranate, the shell of walnuts, &c. ; the prepared skins of animals (leather and parchment) ; and the product of the papyrus, used long before the time of Alexander the Great for the manufacture of paper, and known in Talmudic writings by the same name. But what interests us more, as we remember the ' tablet ' on which Zacharias wrote the name of the future Baptist,[a]

[a] St. Luke i. 63

is the circumstance that it bears not only the same name, but that it seems to have been of such common use in Palestine. It consisted of thin pieces of wood fastened or strung together. The Mishnah enumerates three kinds of them : those where the wood was covered with papyrus, those where it was covered with wax, and those where the wood was left plain to be written on with ink. The latter was of different kinds. Black ink was prepared of soot, or of vegetable or mineral substances. Gum Arabic and Egyptian and vitriol seem also to have been used in writing. A pen made of reed was employed, and the reference in an Apostolic Epistle[a] to writing 'with ink and pen' finds even its verbal counterpart in the Midrash. Indeed, the public 'writer'—a trade very common in the East—went about with a reed-pen behind his ear, as badge of his employment. With the reed-pen we ought to mention its necessary accompaniments: the pen-knife, the inkstand (which, when double, for black and red ink, was sometimes made of earthenware), and the ruler—it being regarded by the stricter set as unlawful to write any words of Holy Writ on any unlined material, no doubt to ensure correct writing and reading.

In all this we have not referred to the practice of writing on leather specially prepared with salt and flour, nor to the parchment in the stricter sense. For we are here chiefly interested in the common mode of writing, that on the 'tablet,' and especially on that covered with wax. Indeed, a little vessel holding wax was generally attached to it. On such a tablet they wrote, of course, not with a reed-pen, but with a *stylus*, generally of iron. This instrument consisted of two parts, which might be detached from each other: the hard pointed 'writer,' and the 'blotter,' which was flat and thick for smoothing out letters and words which had been written or rather graven in the wax. There can be no question that acknowledgments of debt, and other transactions, were ordinarily written down on such wax-covered tablets; for not only is direct reference made to it, but there are special provisions in regard to documents where there are such erasures, or rather effacements—such as, that they require to be noted in the document, under what conditions and how the witnesses are in such cases to affix their signatures, &c.—just as there are particular injunctions how witnesses who could not write are to affix their mark.

2. We return to notice the moral of the Parable.[b] It is put in these words: 'Make to yourselves friends out of [by means of] the Mamon of unrighteousness, that, when it shall fail, they may receive you into ever-

lasting tabernacles.' From what has been previously stated the meaning of these words offers little serious difficulty. We recall the circumstance that they were primarily addressed to converted publicans and sinners, to whom the expression ' Mamon of unrighteousness '—of which there are close analogies, and even an exact transcript in the Targum—would have an obvious meaning. Again, the addition of the definite article leaves no doubt, that ' the everlasting tabernacles' mean the well-known heavenly home; in which sense the term ' tabernacle' is, indeed, already used in the Old Testament. But as a whole we regard it as an adaptation to the Parable of the well-known Rabbinic saying, that there were certain graces of which a man enjoyed the benefit here, while the capital, so to speak, remained for the next world. And if a more literal interpretation were demanded, we cannot but feel the duty incumbent on those converted publicans, nay, in a sense, on us all, to seek to make for ourselves of the Mamon—be it of money, of knowledge, of strength, or opportunities—which to many has, and to all may so easily become that ' of unrighteousness '—such lasting and spiritual application : gain such friends by means of it, that, ' when it fails,' as fail it must when we die, all may not be lost, but rather meet us in heaven. Thus would each deed done for God with this Mamon become a friend to greet us as we enter the eternal world.

3. The suitableness both of the Parable and of its application to the audience of Christ appears from its similarity to what occurs in Jewish writings. We almost seem to hear the very words of Christ: ' He that is faithful in that which is least, is faithful also in much,' in this of the Midrash : ' The Holy One, blessed be His Name, does not give great things to a man until he has been tried in a small matter ; ' which is illustrated by the history of Moses and of David, who were both called to rule from the faithful guiding of sheep.

Considering that the Jewish mind would be familiar with such modes of illustration, there could have been no misunderstanding of the words of Christ. These converted publicans might think that theirs was a very narrow sphere of service, one of little importance ; or else, like the Pharisees, that faithful administration of the things of this world ('the Mamon of unrighteousness') had no bearing on the possession of the true riches in the next world. In answer to the first difficulty, Christ points out that the principle of service is the same, whether applied to much or to little ; that the one was, indeed, meet preparation for, and, in truth, the test of the other.[a] Therefore, if a man failed in faithful service of God in his worldly matters, could he look for the true Mamon, or riches of the world to come ? Would not his unfaithfulness in the lower stewardship imply unfitness for the higher ? And—still in the language of the Parable—if they had not proved faithful in mere stewardship, ' in that which was another's,' could it be expected that they would be exalted from stewardship to proprietorship ? And the ultimate application of all was this, that dividedness was impossible in the service of God.[b] There is absolutely no distinction to the disciple between spiritual matters and worldly, and our common usage of the words secular and spiritual is derived from a serious misunderstanding and mistake. To the secular, nothing is spiritual ; and to the spiritual, nothing is secular : No servant *can* serve two Masters ; ye cannot serve God and Mamon.

[a] St. Luke xvi. 10

[b] ver. 13

II. The Parable of *Dives and Lazarus.*[c]—Although primarily spoken to the Pharisees, and not to the disciples, yet, as will presently appear, it was spoken for the disciples.

[c] vv. 14–31

The words of Christ had touched more than one sore spot in the hearts of the Pharisees. It is said that they derided Him—literally, ' turned up their noses at Him.' [d] The mocking gestures, with which they pointed to His publican-disciples, would be accompanied by mocking words in which they would extol and favourably compare their own claims and standing with that of those new disciples of Christ. But one by one their pleas were taken up and shown to be untenable. They were persons who by outward righteousness and

[d] ver. 14

pretences sought to appear just before men, but God
knew their hearts; and that which was exalted among
men, their Pharisaic standing and standing aloof, was
abomination before Him.[a] These two points form
the main subject of the Parable. Its first object
was to show the great difference between the ' before men '
and the ' before God;' between Dives as he appears to
men in this world, and as he is before God and will be in
the next world. Again, the second main object of the
Parable was to illustrate that their Pharisaic standing and
standing aloof—the bearing of Dives in reference to a
Lazarus—which was the glory of Pharisaism before men,
was an abomination before God. Yet a third object of the
Parable was in reference to their covetousness, the selfish
use which they made of their possessions—their Mamon.
But a selfish was an unrighteous use; and, as such, would
meet with sorer retribution than in the case of an unfaithful steward.

[a] St. Luke xvi. 15

Christ then proceeds to combat these grounds of their
bearing, that they were the custodians and observers of
the Law and of the Prophets, while those poor sinners had
no claims upon the Kingdom of God. Yes—but the Law
and the Prophets had their *terminus ad quem* in John the
Baptist, who ' brought the good tidings of the Kingdom of
God.' Since then ' every one ' had to enter it by personal
resolution and ' force.'[b] It was true that the
Law could not fail in one tittle of it.[c] But,
notoriously and in everyday life, the Pharisees,
who thus spoke of the Law and appealed to it,
were the constant and open breakers of it. Witness here their teaching and practice concerning
divorce, which really involved a breach of the seventh
commandment.[d]

[b] Comp. St. Matt. xi. 12, and our remarks on the passage
[c] St. Luke xvi. 16, 17
[d] ver. 18

Bearing in mind that we have here only the ' headings,'
or rather the ' stepping stones,' of Christ's argument—from
notes by a hearer at the time, which were afterwards given
to St. Luke—we perceive how closely connected are the
seemingly disjointed sentences which preface the Parable,
and how aptly they introduce it. The Parable itself is

strictly of the Pharisees and their relation to the 'publicans and sinners' whom they despised, and to whose steward-ship they opposed thoughts of their own proprietorship. It tells in two directions: in regard to their selfish use of the literal riches—their covetousness; and in regard to their selfish use of the figurative riches—their Pharisaic righteousness, which left poor Lazarus at their door to the dogs and to famine, not bestowing on him aught from their supposed rich festive banquets.

It will be necessary in the interpretation of this Parable to keep in mind that its Parabolic details must not be ex-ploited, nor doctrines of any kind derived from them, either as to the character of the other world, the question of the duration of future punishments, or the possible moral improvement of those in *Gehinnom.* All such things are foreign to the Parable, which is only a type and illus-tration of what is intended to be taught.

1. *Dives and Lazarus before and after death.*[a]—The Parable opens by presenting to us 'a rich man' 'clothed in purple and byssus, joyously faring every day in splendour.' Byssus and purple were the most expensive materials, only inferior to silk, which if genuine and unmixed—for at least three kinds of silk are mentioned in ancient Jewish writings—was worth its weight in gold.

[a] St. Luke xvi. 16-22

Quite in accordance with this luxuriousness was the feasting every day, the description of which conveys the impression of company, merriment, and splendour. This is intended to set forth the selfish use which this man made of his wealth, and to point the contrast of his bearing to-wards Lazarus. Here also every detail is meant to mark the pitiableness of the case, as it stood out before Dives. The very name—not often mentioned in any other real, and never in any other Parabolic story—tells it: *Lazarus, Laazar,* a common abbreviation of *Elazar,* as it were, 'God help *him!*' Then we read that he 'was cast' at his gate-way, as if to mark that the bearers were glad to throw down their unwelcome burden. Laid there, he was in full view of the Pharisee as he went out or came in, or sat in his courtyard. And as he looked at him, he was covered with a loathsome disease; as he heard him, he uttered a piteous request to be filled with what fell from the rich man's table. Yet nothing was done to help his bodily misery, and, as the word 'desiring' implies, his longing for the 'crumbs' remained unsatisfied. So selfish in the use of his wealth was Dives, so wretched Lazarus in his view; so self-satisfied and unpitying was the Pharisee, so miserable in his sight and so needy the publican and sinner. 'Yea, even the dogs came and licked his sores'— for it is not to be understood as an alleviation, but as an aggravation of his ills, that he was left to the dogs, which in Scripture are always represented as unclean animals.

So it was before men. But how was it before God? There the relation was reversed. The beggar died—no more of him here. But the Angels 'carried him away into Abraham's bosom.' Leaving aside for the present the Jewish teaching concerning the 'after death,' we are struck with the sublime simplicity of the figurative language used by Christ, as compared with the wild and sensuous fancies of later Rabbinic teaching on the subject. It is, indeed, true that we must not look in this Parabolic language for Christ's teaching about the 'after death.' On the other hand, while He would say nothing that was essentially divergent from the purest views entertained on the subject at that time, yet whatever He did say must, when stripped of its Parabolic details, be consonant with fact. Thus, the carrying up of the soul of the righteous by Angels is certainly in accordance with Jewish teaching, though stripped of all legendary details, such as about the number and the greetings of the Angels. But it is also fully in accordance with Christian thought of the ministry of Angels. Again, as regards the expression 'Abraham's bosom,' it occurs, although not frequently, in Jewish writings. On the other hand, the appeal to Abraham as our father is so frequent, his presence and merits are so constantly invoked; notably, he is so expressly designated as he who receives the penitent into Paradise, that we can see how congruous, especially to the higher Jewish teaching which dealt not in coarsely sensuous descriptions of Paradise, the phrase 'Abraham's bosom' must have been.

2. *Dives and Lazarus after death* :[a] The 'great contrast' fully realised, and how to enter into the
Kingdom.—Here also the main interest centres
in Dives. He also has died and been buried. Thus ends
all his exaltedness before men. The next scene is in *Hades*
or *Sheol*, the place of the disembodied spirits before the
final Judgment. It consists of two divisions: the one of
consolation, with all the faithful gathered unto Abraham as
their father; the other of fiery torment. Thus far in accordance with the general teaching of the New Testament.
As regards the details, they evidently represent the views
current at the time among the Jews. According to them,
the Garden of Eden and the Tree of Life were the abode of
the blessed. Nay, in common belief, the words of Gen.
ii. 10 : ' a river went out of Eden to water the garden,' indicated that this Eden was distinct from, and superior to, the
garden in which Adam had been originally placed. With
reference to it, we read that the righteous in Paradise see
the wicked in *Gehinnom*, and rejoice ; and, similarly, that
the wicked in *Gehinnom* see the righteous sitting beatified
in Paradise, and their souls are troubled. Again, it is
consonant with what were the views of the Jews, that conversations could be held between dead persons, of which
several legendary instances are given in the Talmud. The
torment, especially of thirst, of the wicked, is repeatedly
mentioned in Jewish writings. The righteous is seen beside delicious springs, and the wicked with his tongue
parched at the brink of a river, the waves of which are
constantly receding from him. But there is this very
marked and characteristic contrast, that in the Jewish
legend the beatified is a Pharisee, while the sinner tormented with thirst is a Publican! Above all, we notice
that there is no analogy in Rabbinic writings to the statement in the Parable, that there is a wide and impassable
gulf between Paradise and Gehenna.

To return to the Parable. When we read that Dives
in torments 'lifted up his eyes,' it was, no doubt, for help,
or, at least, alleviation. Then he first perceived and recognised the reversed relationship. The text emphatically

[a] St. Luke xvi. 23-26

D D 2

repeats here : ' And he,'—literally, this one, as if now for the first time he realised, but only to misunderstand and misapply it, how easily superabundance might minister relief to extreme need—'calling (viz. upon = invoking) said : " Father Abraham, have mercy upon me, and send Lazarus." ' The invocation of Abraham, as having the power, and of Abraham as ' Father,' was natural on the part of a Jew. All the more telling is it, that the rich Pharisee should behold in the bosom of Abraham, whose child he specially claimed to be, what, in his sight, had been poor Lazarus, covered with moral sores, and, religiously speaking, thrown down outside his gate. And it was the climax of the contrast that he should now have to invoke, and that in vain, his ministry, seeking it at the hands of Abraham. And here we also recall the previous Parable about making, ere it fail, friends by means of the Mamon of unrighteousness, that they may welcome us in the everlasting tabernacles.

It should be remembered that Dives now limits his request to the humblest dimensions, asking only that Lazarus might be sent to dip the tip of his finger in the cooling liquid, and thus give him even the smallest relief. To this Abraham replies, though in a tone of pity : ' Child,' yet decidedly—showing him, first, the rightness of the present position of things ; and, secondly, the impossibility of any alteration, such as he had asked. Dives had in his lifetime received his good things ; those had been his, he had chosen them as his part, and used them for self, without communicating of them. And Lazarus had received evil things. Now Lazarus was comforted and Dives in torment. It was the right order—not that Lazarus was comforted because in this world he had suffered, nor yet that Dives was in torment because in this world he had had riches. But Lazarus received there the comfort which had been refused to him on earth, and the man who had made this world his good, and obtained there his portion, of which he had refused even the crumbs to the most needy, now received the meet reward of his unpitying, unloving, selfish life. But, besides all this, Dives had asked what

was impossible: no intercourse could be held between
Paradise and Gehenna, and on this account a great and
impassable chasm existed between the two, so that even if
they would, they could not pass from heaven to hell, nor
yet from hell to those in bliss.

ᵃ St. Luke   3. *Application of the Parable*,ᵃ showing how
xvi. 27–31   the Law and the Prophets cannot fail, and how
we must now press into the Kingdom.

We now find Dives pleading that Lazarus might be
sent to his five brothers, who, as we infer, were of the same
disposition and life as himself had been, to 'testify unto
them'—the word implying earnest testimony.   Presumably, what he so asked to be attested was, that he, Dives,
was in torment ; and the expected effect, not of the testi-
              mony but of the mission of Lazarus,ᵇ whom they
ᵇ ver. 30   are supposed to have known, was that these his
brothers might not come to the same place.   At the same
time, the request seems to imply an attempt at self-justification, as if during his life he had not had sufficient
warning.   Accordingly, the reply of Abraham is no longer
couched in a tone of pity, but implies stern rebuke of Dives.
They need no witness-bearer : they have Moses and the
Prophets, let them hear them.   If testimony be needed,
theirs has been given and it is sufficient—a reply this,
which would specially appeal to the Pharisees.   And when
Dives, now, perhaps, as much bent on self-justification as
on the message to his brothers, remonstrates that although
they had not received such testimony, yet 'if one come to
them from the dead,' they would repent, the final, and as
history has shown since the Resurrection of Christ, the true
answer is, that 'if they hear not [give not hearing to]
Moses and the Prophets, neither will they be influenced
[moved : their intellects to believe, their wills to repent]
if one rose from the dead.'

And here the Parable, and the warning to the Pharisees,
abruptly break off.   When next we hear the Master's
              voice,ᶜ it is in loving application to the disciples
ᶜ ch. xvii.   of some of the lessons which were implied in what
He had spoken to the Pharisees.

CHAPTER LXV.

THE THREE LAST PARABLES OF THE PERÆAN SERIES: THE
UNRIGHTEOUS JUDGE—THE PHARISEE AND THE PUBLICAN
—THE UNMERCIFUL SERVANT.

(St. Luke xviii. 1–14 ; St. Matt. xviii. 23–35.)

We must bear in mind that between the Parable of
Dives and Lazarus and that of the *Unjust Judge*, most
momentous events had intervened.   These were : the visit
of Jesus to Bethany, the raising of Lazarus, the Jerusalem

ᵃ St. John
xi.
council against Christ, the flight to Ephraim,ᵃ a
brief stay and preaching there, and the commence-

ᵇ St. Luke
xvii. 11
ment of His last journey to Jerusalem.ᵇ   During
this last slow progress from the borders of Galilee

ᶜ St. Luke
xvii.
to Jerusalem, we suppose the Discoursesᶜ and
the Parable about the Coming of the Son of Man
to have been spoken.   And although such utterances will
be best considered in connection with Christ's later and
full Discourses about 'The Last Things,' we readily perceive, even at this stage, how, when He set His Face
towards Jerusalem, there to be offered up, thoughts and
words concerning the ' End ' may have entered into all
His teaching.

The most common but also the most serious mistake
in reference to the Parable of ' the Unjust Judge,' is to
regard it as implying that, just as the poor widow
insisted in her petition and was righted because of her
insistence, so the disciples should persist in prayer, and
would be heard because of their insistence.   The inference
from the Parable is not that the Church will be ultimately
vindicated because she perseveres in prayer, but that she
so perseveres, because God will surely right her cause : it
is not that insistence in prayer is the cause of its answer,
but that the certainty of that which is asked for should
lead to continuance in prayer, even when all around seems
to forbid the hope of answer.   This is the lesson to be
learned from a comparison of the Unjust Judge with the

Just and Holy God in His dealings with His own.   If the
widow persevered, knowing that although no other consideration, human or Divine, would influence the Unjust
Judge, yet her insistence would secure its object, how much
more should we 'not faint,' but continue in prayer, who
are appealing to God, Who has His people and His cause
at heart, even though He delay—remembering also that
even this is for their sakes who pray !   And this is fully
expressed in the introductory words : ' He spake also a
Parable to them with reference to the need be of their
always praying, and not fainting.'

If it be asked, how the conduct of the Unjust Judge
could serve as illustration of what might be expected from
God, we answer, that the lesson in the Parable is not from
the similarity, but from the contrast between the Unrighteous human and the Righteous Divine Judge.   'Hear
what the Unrighteous Judge saith.   But God [mark the
emphatic position of the word], shall He not indeed vindicate [the injuries of, do judgment for] His elect . . . ? '
In truth, this mode of argument is perhaps the most
common in Jewish Parables, and occurs on almost every
page of ancient Rabbinic commentaries.   It is called the
' light and heavy,' and answers to our reasoning *a fortiori*
or *de minore ad majus* (from the less to the greater).   According to the Rabbis, ten instances of such reasoning occur
in the Old Testament itself.[1]   In the present Parable the
reasoning would be : ' If the Judge of Unrighteousness '
said that he would vindicate, shall not the Judge of all
Righteousness do judgment on behalf of His Elect ?   In
fact, we have an exact Rabbinic parallel to the thought
underlying, and the lesson derived from, this Parable.
When describing how at the preaching of Jonah Nineveh
repented and cried to God, His answer to the loud persistent cry of the people is thus explained : ' The bold (he who
is unabashed) conquers even a wicked person [to grant him
his request], how much more the All-Good of the world ! '

---

[1] These ten passages are: Gen. xliv. 8; Exod. vi. 9, 12; Numb. xii.
14; Deut. xxxi. 27; two instances in Jerem. xii. 5; 1 Sam. xxiii. 3;
Prov. xi. 31; Esth. ix. 12; and Ezek. xv. 5.

The Parable opens by laying down as a general principle
the necessity and duty of the disciples always to pray—
the precise meaning being defined by the opposite, or
limiting clause: 'not to faint,' that is, not 'to become
weary.' The word 'always' must be understood in the sense
of under all circumstances, however apparently adverse,
when it might seem as if an answer could not come, and
we should therefore be in danger of 'fainting' or becoming
weary. Thus it is argued even in Jewish writings, that a
man should never be deterred from, nor cease praying—the
illustration being from the case of Moses, who knew that it
was decreed he should not enter the land, and yet continued
praying about it.

The Parable introduces to us a Judge in a city, and a
widow. Except where a case was voluntarily submitted
for arbitration rather than judgment, or judicial advice was
sought of a sage, one man could not have formed a Jewish
tribunal. Besides, his mode of speaking and acting is
inconsistent with such a hypothesis. He must therefore
have been one of the Judges, or municipal authorities,
appointed by Herod or the Romans—perhaps a Jew, but
not a *Jewish* Judge. Possibly, he may have been a police-
magistrate, or one who had some function of that kind
delegated to him. We know that, at least in Jerusalem,
there were two stipendiary magistrates, whose duty it was
to see to the observance of all police-regulations and the
prevention of crime. At any rate there were in every
locality police-officials, who watched over order and law.
Frequent instances are mentioned of gross injustice and
bribery in regard to the non-Jewish Judges in Palestine.

It is to such a Judge that the Parable refers—one who
was avowedly [a] inaccessible to the highest motive,
the fear of God, and not even restrained by the
lower consideration of regard for public opinion. It is an
extreme case, intended to illustrate the exceeding unlikeli-
hood of justice being done. For the same purpose, the
party seeking justice at his hands is described as a poor,
unprotected widow. This widow came to the Unjust
Judge (the imperfect tense in the original indicating

[a] St. Luke
xviii. 4

repeated coming), with the urgent demand to be vindicated
of her adversary : that is, that the Judge should make
legal inquiry, and by a decision set her right as against
him at whose hands she was suffering wrong. For reasons
of his own he would not; and this continued for a while.
At last, not from any higher principle, nor even from regard
for public opinion—both of which, indeed, as he avowed to
himself, had no weight with him—he complied with her
request, as the text (literally translated) has it : ' Yet at any
rate ^a because this widow troubleth me, I will do

^a Comp. St.
Luke xi. 8

justice for her, lest, in the end, coming she bruise
me '—do personal violence to me, attack me bodily. Then
follows the grand inference from it : If the ' Judge of
Unrighteousness' speak thus, shall not the Judge of all
Righteousness—God—do judgment, vindicate [by His
Coming to judgment and so setting right the wrong done
to His Church] 'His Elect, which cry to Him day and
night, although He suffer long on account of them '—delay
His final interposition of judgment and mercy, and that,
not as the Unjust Judge, but for their own sakes, in order
that the number of the Elect may all be gathered in, and
they fully prepared ?

2. *The Parable of the Pharisee and the Publican*, which
follows,^b is only internally connected with that of

^b St. Luke
xviii. 9-14

' the Unjust Judge.' It is not of unrighteousness, but of self-righteousness—and this, both in its positive and negative aspects : as trust in one's own state, and
as contempt of others. Again, it has also this connection
with the previous Parable, that, whereas that of the Unrighteous Judge pointed to continuance, this to humility
in prayer.

Probably something had taken place which is not
recorded, to occasion this Parable, which, if not directly
addressed to the Pharisees, is to such as are of Pharisaic
spirit. It brings before us two men going up to the
Temple—whether ' at the hour of prayer,' or otherwise is
not stated. Remembering that, with the exception of the
Psalms for the day and the interval for a certain prescribed
prayer, the service in the Temple was entirely sacrificial,

we are thankful for such glimpses which show that, both in
the time of public service, and still more at other times,
the Temple was made the place of private prayer.[a]   On
the present occasion the two men, who went together to the entrance of the Temple, represented
the two religious extremes in Jewish society.
To the entrance of the Temple, but no farther, did the
Pharisee and the Publican go together.   Within the sacred
enclosure—before God, where man should least have made
it, began their separation.   ' The Pharisee put himself by
himself, and prayed thus : O God, I thank Thee that I am
not as the rest of men—extortioners, unjust, adulterers—
nor also as this Publican [there].'   Never, perhaps, were
words of thanksgiving spoken in less thankfulness than
these.   They referred not to what he had received, but to
the sins of others by which they were separated from him,
and to his own meritorious deeds by which he was separated
from them.   Thus his words expressed what his attitude
indicated ; and both were the expression, not of thankfulness, but of boastfulness.   It was the same as their
bearing at feasts and in public places ; the same as their
contempt and condemnation of ' the rest of men,' and especially ' the publicans ; ' the same that even their designation
—'Pharisees,' 'Separated ones'—implied.   The 'rest of men'
might be either the Gentiles, or more probably, the common
unlearned people, whom they accused or suspected of every
possible sin, according to their fundamental principle :
' The unlearned cannot be pious.'   And it must be added
that, as we read the Liturgy of the Synagogue, we come
ever and again upon such and similar thanksgiving—that
they are ' not as the rest of men.'

But this was not all.   From looking down upon others
the Pharisee proceeded to look up to himself.   Here
Talmudic writings offer parallelisms.   They are full of
references to the merits of the just, to ' the merits and
righteousness of the fathers,' or else of Israel in taking upon
itself the Law.   And for the sake of these merits and of that
righteousness, Israel, as a nation, expects general acceptance, pardon, and temporal benefits.   All spiritual benefits

Israel as a nation, and the pious in Israel individually, possess already, nor do they need to get them from heaven, since they can and do work them out for themselves. And here the Pharisee in the Parable significantly dropped even the form of thanksgiving. The religious performances which he enumerated are those which mark the Pharisee among the Pharisees : 'I fast twice a week, and I give tithes of all that I acquire.' The first of these was in pursuance of the custom of some ' more righteous than the rest,' who, as previously explained, fasted on the second and fifth days of the week. But, perhaps, we should not forget that these were also the regular market days, when the country-people came to the towns, and there were special Services in the Synagogues, and the local Sanhedrin met—so that these saints in Israel would, at the same time, attract and receive special notice for their fasts. As for the boast about giving tithes of all that he acquired—and not merely of his land, fruits, &c.—it has already been explained that this was one of the distinctive characteristics of ' the sect of the Pharisees.' Their practice in this respect may be summed up in these words of the Mishnah : ' He tithes all that he eats, all that he sells, and all that he buys, and he is not a guest with an unlearned person [so as not possibly to partake of what may have been left untithed].'

Although it may not be necessary, yet a quotation will help to show how truly this picture of the Pharisee was taken from life. Thus, the following prayer of a Rabbi is recorded : ' I thank Thee, O Lord my God, that Thou hast put my part with those who sit in the Academy, and not with those who sit at the corners [money-changers and traders]. For I rise early, and they rise early : I rise early to the words of the Law, and they to vain things. I labour and they labour : I labour and receive a reward, they labour and receive no reward. I run and they run : I run to the life of the world to come, and they to the pit of destruction.' We also recall such painful sayings as those of Rabbi Simeon ben Jochai, to which reference has already been made—notably this, that if there were only two righteous men in the world, he and his son were these; and if only one, it was he!

The second picture, or scene, in the Parable sets before us the reverse state of feeling from that of the Pharisee. Only we must bear in mind, that as the Pharisee is not blamed for his giving of thanks, nor yet for his good-doing, real or imaginary, so the prayer of the Publican is not answered because he was a sinner. In both cases what decides the rejection or acceptance of the prayer is, whether or not it was *prayer*. The Pharisee retains the righteousness which he had claimed for himself, whatever its value; and the Publican receives the righteousness which he asks: both have what they desire before God. If the Pharisee ' stood by himself,' apart from others, so did the Publican: ' standing afar off,' viz. from the Pharisee —quite far back, as became one who felt himself unworthy to mingle with God's people. In accordance with this: ' He would not so much as lift his eyes to heaven,' as men generally do in prayer, ' but smote his breast '—as the Jews still do in the most solemn part of their confession on the Day of Atonement—' saying, God be merciful to me the sinner.' The one appealed to himself for justice, the other appealed to God for mercy.

Once more, as between the Pharisee and the Publican, the seeming and the real, that before men and before God, there is sharp contrast; and the lesson which Christ had so often pointed is again set forth, not only in regard to the feelings which the Pharisees entertained, but also to the glad tidings of pardon to the lost: ' I say unto you, This man went down to his house justified above the other.' In other words, the sentence of righteousness as from God with which the Publican went home was above, far better than, the sentence of righteousness as pronounced by himself, with which the Pharisee returned. This saying casts also light on such comparisons as between ' the righteous ' elder brother and the pardoned prodigal, or the ninety-nine that ' need no repentance ' and the lost that was found, or on such an utterance as this : ' Except your righteousness shall exceed the righteousness of the Scribes and Pharisees, ye shall in no case enter into the Kingdom of Heaven.'^a

a St. Matt. v. 20 And so the Parable ends with the general principle, so often enunciated : ' For every one that exalteth himself shall be abased; and he that humbleth himself shall be exalted.' And with this fully accords the instruction of Christ to His disciples concerning the reception of little children, which im-

b St. Luke xviii. 15-17 mediately follows.^b

c St. Matt. xviii. 23-35 3. The parable with which this series closes— that of the *Unmerciful Servant* ^c—can be treated more briefly, since the circumstances leading up to it have already been explained. We are now reaching the point where the solitary narrative of St. Luke again merges with those of the other Evangelists. The Parable of the Unmerciful Servant belongs to the Peræan series, and closes it.

Its connection with the Parable of the Pharisee and the Publican lies in this, that Pharisaic self-righteousness and contempt of others may easily lead to unforgiveness and unmercifulness, which are utterly incompatible with a sense of our own need of Divine mercy and forgiveness. And so in the Gospel of St. Matthew this Parable follows on the exhibition of a self-righteous, unmerciful spirit, which would reckon up how often we should forgive, forgetful of our own need of absolute and unlimited pardon

d St. Matt. xviii. 15-22 at the hands of God^d—a spirit, moreover, of harshness, that could look down upon Christ's ' little ones,' in forgetfulness of our own need perhaps of cutting off even a right hand or foot to enter the Kingdom of Heaven.^e

e St. Matt. xviii. 1-14, passim In studying this Parable, we must once more remind ourselves of the general canon of the need of distinguishing between what is essential in a Parable, as directly bearing on its lessons, and what is merely introduced for the sake of the Parable itself, to give point to its main teaching.

Keeping apart the essentials of the Parable from the accidents of its narration, we have three distinct scenes, or parts, in this story. In the first, our new feelings towards our brethren are traced to our new relation towards God, as the proper spring of all our thinking, speaking, and acting. Notably, as regards forgiveness, we are to remember the Kingdom of God : ' Therefore has the Kingdom of God become like '—' therefore ' : in order that thereby we may learn the duty of absolute, not limited, forgiveness—not that of ' seven,' but of ' seventy times seven.' And now this likeness of the Kingdom of Heaven is set forth in the Parable of ' a man, a King ' (as the Rabbis would have expressed it. ' a king of flesh and blood '), who would ' make his reckoning ' ' with his servants '—not his bond-servants, but probably the governors of his provinces, or those who had charge of the revenue and finances. ' But after he had begun to reckon '—not necessarily at the very beginning of it—' one was brought to him, a debtor of ten thousand talents.' Reckoning them only as Attic talents this would amount to the enormous sum of about two and a quarter millions sterling. No wonder that one who during his administration had been guilty of such peculation, or else culpable negligence, should, as the words ' brought to him ' imply, have been reluctant to face the king. The Parable further implies that the debt was admitted ; and hence, in the course of ordinary judicial procedure—according to the Law of Moses,[a] and the universal code of antiquity—that 'servant,' with his family and all his property, was ordered to be sold, and the returns paid into the treasury.

[a] Ex. xxii. 3 ; Lev. xxv. 39, 47

It is not suggested that the ' payment ' thus made would have met his debt. This trait belongs not to the essentials of the Parable. Nor does the promise : ' I will pay thee all.' In truth, the narrative takes no notice of this, but on the other hand, states : ' But, being moved with compassion, the lord of that servant released him [from the bondage decreed, and which had virtually begun with his sentence], and the debt forgave he him.' A more accurate representation of our relation to God could not be made. We are the debtors to our heavenly King, Who has entrusted to us the administration of what is His, and which we have purloined or misused, incurring an unspeakable debt, which we can never discharge, and of which, in the course of justice, unending bondage, misery, and ruin would be the proper sequence. But if in humble repentance we cast ourselves at His Feet, He is ready in infinite compassion, not only to release us from meet punishment, but—O blessed revelation of the Gospel !—to forgive us the debt.

It is this new relationship to God which must be the foundation and the rule for our new relationship towards our fellow-servants. And this brings us to the second part, or scene, in this Parable. Here the lately pardoned servant finds one of his fellow-servants, who owes him the small sum of 100 dinars, about 4*l*. 10*s*. In the first case, it was the servant brought to account, and that before the king; here it is a servant finding, and that his fellow-servant; in the first case he owed talents, in the second dinars (a six-thousandth part of them); in the first, ten thousand talents; in the second, one hundred dinars. Again, in the first case payment is only demanded, while in the second the man takes his fellow-servant by the throat—a not uncommon mode of harshness on the part of Roman creditors—and says : ' Pay what,' or, according to the better reading, ' if thou owest anything.' And lastly, although the words of the second debtor are almost the same as those in which the first debtor besought the king's patience, yet no mercy is shown, but he is ' cast ' [with violence] into prison, till he have paid what was due.

It can scarcely be necessary to show the incongruousness or the guilt of such conduct. But this is the object of the third part, or scene, in the Parable. Here the other servants are introduced as exceedingly sorry, no doubt about the fate of their fellow-servant. Then they come to their lord, and ' clearly set forth,' or ' explain ' what had happened, upon which the Unmerciful Servant is summoned, and addressed as ' wicked servant,' not only because he had not followed the example of his lord, but because, after having received such immense favour as the entire remission of his debt on entreating his master, to have refused to the entreaty of his fellow-servant even a brief delay in the payment of a small sum argued want of all mercy and

positive wickedness. And the words are followed by the
manifestation of righteous anger. As he has done, so is it
done to him—and this is the final application of the Para-
ᵃ St. Matt. ble.ᵃ He is delivered 'to the tormentors:' in other
xviii. 35 words, he is sent to the hardest and severest prison,
there to remain till he should pay all that was due by him
—that is, in the circumstances, for ever. And here we may
remark that as sin has incurred a debt which can never
be discharged, so the banishment, or rather the loss and
misery of the sinner, will be endless.

We pause to notice how near Rabbinism has come to
this Parable, and yet how far it is from its sublime teaching. At the outset we recall that unlimited forgiveness—
or, indeed, for more than the farthest limit of three times
—was not the doctrine of Rabbinism. It did, indeed,
teach how freely God would forgive Israel, and it introduces
a similar Parable of a debtor appealing to his creditor, and
receiving the fullest and freest release of mercy, and it also
draws from it the moral, that man should similarly show
mercy; but it is not the mercy of forgiveness from the
heart, but of forgiveness of money debts to the poor, or of
various injuries, and the mercy of benevolence and beneficence to the wretched. But, however beautifully Rabbinism at times speaks on the subject, the Gospel conception
of forgiveness, even as that of mercy, could only come by
experience of the infinitely higher forgiveness, and the incomparably greater mercy, which the pardoned sinner has
received in Christ from our Father in Heaven.

CHAPTER LXVI.

CHRIST'S DISCOURSES IN PERÆA—CLOSE OF THE PERÆAN MINISTRY.

(St. Luke xiii. 23-30, 31-35; xiv. 1 11, 25-35; xvii. 1-10.)

FROM the Parables we now turn to such Discourses of the
Lord as belong to this period of His Ministry. Their consideration may be the more brief, that throughout we find
points of correspondence with previous or later portions of
His teaching.

1. The words of our Lord, as recorded by St. Luke,[a] are not spoken, as in 'The Sermon on the Mount,'[b] in connection with His teaching to His disciples, but are in reply to a question addressed to Him by some one—probably, a representative of the Pharisees : [c] 'Lord, are they few, the saved ones [that are being saved] ?' We can scarcely doubt that the word 'saved' bore reference, not to the eternal state of the soul, but to admission to the benefits of the Kingdom of God—the Messianic Kingdom, with its privileges and its judgments, such as the Pharisees understood it. The question, whether 'few' were to be saved, could not have been put from the Pharisaic point of view, if understood of personal salvation ; while, on the other hand, if taken as applying to part in the near-expected Messianic Kingdom, it has its distinct parallel in the Rabbinic statement, that, as regarded the days of the Messiah (His Kingdom), it would be similar to what it had been at the entrance into the land of promise, when only two (Joshua and Caleb) out of all that generation were allowed to have part in it.

[a] St. Luke
xiii. 23-30
[b] ver. 24,
comp. St.
Matt. vii. 13,
14 ; vv. 25-
27, comp.
St. Matt. vii.
21-23
[c] See also
St. Luke xiii.
31.

As regards entrance into the Messianic Kingdom, this Pharisee, and those whom he represented, are told that the Kingdom was not theirs, as a matter of course— their question as to the rest of the world being only whether few or many would share in it—but that all must 'struggle [agonise] to enter in through the narrow door.' 'When once the Master of the house is risen up,' to welcome His guests to the banquet, and has shut to the door, while they standing without vainly call upon Him to open it, and He replies : 'I know you not whence ye are,' would they begin to remind Him of those covenant-privileges on which, as Israel after the flesh, they had relied ('we have eaten and drunk in Thy Presence, and Thou hast taught in our streets'). To this He would reply by a repetition of His former words, grounding alike His disavowal and His refusal to open on their inward contrariety to the King and His Kingdom: 'Depart from Me, all ye workers of iniquity.' It was a banquet to the

E E

friends of the King: the inauguration of His Kingdom. When they found the door shut, they would indeed knock, in the confident expectation that their claims would at once be recognised, and they admitted. And when the Master of the house did not recognise them as they had expected, and they reminded Him of their outward connection, He only repeated the same words as before, since it was not outward but inward relationship that qualified the guests, and theirs was not friendship, but antagonism to Him. Terrible would then be their sorrow and anguish, when they would see their own patriarchs ('we have eaten and drunk in Thy Presence') and their own prophets ('Thou hast taught in our streets') within, and yet themselves were excluded from what was peculiarly theirs— while from all parts of the heathen world the welcome guests would flock to the joyous feast. And here pre-eminently would the saying hold good, in opposition to Pharisaic claims and self-righteousness: 'There are last which shall be first, and there are first which shall be last.'[a]

[a] Comp. also St. Matt. xix. 30; xx. 16

2. The next Discourse, noted by St. Luke,[b] had been spoken 'in that very day,' as the last. It was occasioned by a pretended warning of 'certain of the Pharisees' to depart from Peræa, which, with Galilee, was the territory of Herod Antipas, as else the Tetrarch would kill Him. Probably the danger of which these Pharisees spoke might have been real enough, and from their secret intrigues with Herod they might have special reasons for knowing of such. But their suggestion that Jesus should depart could only have proceeded from a wish to get Him out of Peræa, where, evidently, His works of healing were largely attracting and influencing the people.

[b] St. Luke xiii. 31-35

But if our Lord would not be deterred by the fears of His disciples from going into Judæa,[c] feeling that each one had his appointed working day, in the light of which he was safe, and during the brief duration of which he was bound to 'walk,' far less would He recede before His enemies. Pointing to their secret

[c] St. John xi. 8

intrigues, He bade them, if they chose, go back to 'that fox,' and give to his low cunning, and to all similar attempts to hinder or arrest His Ministry, what would be a decisive answer, since it unfolded what He clearly foresaw in the near future. 'Depart?'—yes, 'depart' ye to tell 'that fox,' I have still a brief and an appointed time to work, and then 'I am perfected,' in the sense in which we all readily understand the expression, as applying to His Work and Mission. 'I know that at the goal is death : yet not at the hands of Herod, but in Jerusalem, the slaughter-house of them that "teach in her streets."'

But the thought of Jerusalem—of what it was, what it might have been, and what would come to it—may well have forced from the lips of Him Who wept over it a cry of mingled anguish, love, and warning.[a] It may be that these very words, which are reported by St. Matthew in another connection,[b] are here quoted by St. Luke, because they fully express the thought to which Christ here first gave distinct utterance. But some such words, we can scarcely doubt, He did speak even now, when pointing to His near Decease in Jerusalem.

a St. Luke xiii. 34, 35
b St. Matt. xxiii. 37-39

3. The next in order of the Discourses recorded by St. Luke[c] is that which prefaced the Parable of 'the Great Supper,' expounded in a previous chapter.[d] A very brief commentation will here suffice. It appears that the Lord accepted the invitation to a Sabbath-meal in the house 'of one of the Rulers of the Pharisees' —perhaps one of the Rulers of the Synagogue in which they had just worshipped, and where Christ may have taught. His acceptance was made use of to 'watch Him.' The man with the dropsy had, no doubt, been introduced for a treacherous purpose, although it is not necessary to suppose that he himself had been privy to it. On the other hand, it is characteristic of the gracious Lord, that, with full knowledge of their purpose, He sat down with such companions, and that He did His Work of power and love unrestrained by their evil thoughts. But, even so, He must turn their wickedness also to good account. Yet

c St. Luke xiv. 1-11
d Chapter lxii.

we mark that He first dismissed the man healed of the
ª St. Luke xiv. 4 dropsy before He reproved the Pharisees.ª It
was better so—for the sake of the guests, and
for the healed man himself.

And after his departure the Lord first spake to them,
as was His wont, concerning their misapplication of the
Sabbath-Law, to which, indeed, their own practice gave
the lie. They deemed it unlawful ' to heal ' on the Sabbath-
day, though, when He read their thoughts and purposes as
against Him, they would not answer His question on the
point. And yet, if ' a son,[1] or even an ox,' of any of them
had ' fallen into a pit,' they would have found some valid
legal reason for pulling him out ! Their Sabbath-feast,
and their invitation to Him, when thereby they wished to
lure Him to evil—and, indeed, their much-boasted hospitality—was all characteristic, only external show, with
utter absence of all real love ; only self-assumption, pride,
and self-righteousness, together with contempt of all who
were regarded as religiously or intellectually beneath them.
Even among themselves there was strife about ' the first
places '—such as, perhaps, Christ had on that occasion
witnessed, amidst mock professions of humility, when,
perhaps, the master of the house had afterwards, in true
Pharisaic fashion, proceeded to re-arrange the guests according to their supposed dignity. And even the Rabbis
ᵇ ver. 10 had given advice to the same effect as Christ's ᵇ—
and of this His words may have reminded them.

But further—addressing him who had so treacherously
bidden Him to this feast, Christ showed how the principle
of Pharisaism consisted in self-seeking, to the necessary
exclusion of all true love. This self-righteousness appeared
even in what, perhaps, they most boasted of—their hospitality. For if in an earlier Jewish record we read the
beautiful words : ' Let thy house be open towards the
street, and let the poor be the sons of thy house,' we have
also this later comment on them, that Job had thus had
his house opened to the four quarters of the globe for the
poor, and that when his calamities befell him, he remon-

---

[1] So—and not ' ass '—according to the best reading.

strated with God on the ground of his merits in this respect,
to which answer was made that he had in this matter
come very far short of the merits of Abraham. So entirely
self-introspective and self-seeking did Rabbinism become,
and so contrary was its outcome to the spirit of Christ, the
inmost meaning of Whose Work, as well as Words, was
entire self-forgetfulness and self-surrender in love.

4. In the fourth Discourse recorded by St. Luke,[a] we
pass from the parenthetic account of that Sabbath-
meal in the house of the ' Ruler of the Pharisees,'
back to where the narrative of the Pharisees'
threat about Herod and the reply of Jesus had left us.[b]

<small>ᵃ St. Luke xiv. 25-35
ᵇ xiii. 31-35</small>

At the outset we mark that we are not told what constituted the true disciple, but what would prevent a man
from becoming such. Again, it was now no longer (as in
the earlier address to the Twelve), that he who loved the
nearest and dearest of earthly kin more than Christ—and
hence clave to such rather than to Him—was not worthy
of Him; nor that he who did not take his cross and follow
after Him was not worthy of the Christ. Since then the
enmity had ripened, and discipleship became impossible
without actual renunciation of the nearest relationship,
and, more than that, of life itself.[c] The term
' hate ' points to this, that, as outward separation
consequent upon men's antagonism to Christ was before
them in the near future, so in the present inward separation, a renunciation in mind and heart, preparatory to that
outwardly, was absolutely necessary. And this immediate
call was illustrated in twofold manner. A man who was
about to begin building a tower, must count the cost of his
undertaking.[d] It was not enough that he was
prepared to defray the expense of the foundations; he must look to the cost of the whole. So must
they in becoming disciples look not on what was involved
in the present following of Christ, but remember the cost
of the final acknowledgment of Jesus. Again, if a king
went to war, common prudence would lead him to consider
whether his forces were equal to the great contest before
him ; else it were far better to withdraw in time, even

<small>ᶜ St. Luke xiv. 26</small>

<small>ᵈ vv. 28-30</small>

though it involved humiliation, from what, in view of his weakness, would end in miserable defeat.[a] So, and much more, must the intending disciple make complete inward surrender of all, deliberately counting the cost, and in view of the coming trial ask himself whether he had indeed sufficient inward strength—the force of love to Christ—to conquer.

Or else, and here Christ breaks once more into that pithy Jewish proverb—' Salt is good;' ' salt, if it have lost its savour, wherewith shall it be salted?'[b] We have preferred quoting the proverb in its Jewish form to show its popular origin. Salt in such condition was neither fit to improve the land, nor on the other hand to be mixed with the manure. The disciple who had lost his distinctiveness would neither benefit the land, nor was he even fit, as it were, for the dunghill, and could only be cast out. And so, let him that hath ears to hear, hear the warning!

5. We have still to consider the last Discourses of Christ before the raising of Lazarus.[c] As being addressed to the disciples,[d] we have to connect them with the Discourse just commented upon. In point of fact, part of these admonitions had already been spoken on a previous occasion, and that more fully, to the disciples in Galilee.[e] Only we must again bear in mind the difference of circumstances. Here they immediately precede the raising of Lazarus,[f] and they form the close of Christ's public Ministry in Peræa. Hence they come to us as Christ's parting admonitions to His Peræan followers.

They are intended to impress on the new disciples these four things: to be careful to give no offence [g]; to be careful to take no offence [h]; to be simple and earnest in their faith, and absolutely to trust its all-pervading power [i]; and yet, when they had made experience of it, not to be elated, but to remember their relation to their Master, that all was in His service, and that, after all, when everything had been

marginal notes:

[a] St. Luke xiv. 31, 32

[b] vv. 34, 35

[c] St. Luke xvii. 1–10
[d] ver. 1

[e] vv. 1–4, comp. St. Matt. xviii. 6–35 ; ver. 6, comp. St. Matt. xvii. 20
[f] St. John xi.

[g] St. Luke xvii. 1, 2
[h] vv. 3, 4
[i] ver. 6

done, they were but unprofitable servants.[a] In other words, they urged upon the disciples holiness, love, faith, and service of self-surrender and humility.

a St. Luke xvii. 7-10

The four parts of this Discourse are broken by the prayer of the Apostles, who had formerly expressed their difficulty in regard to these very requirements : [b] 'Add unto us faith.' It was upon this that the Lord spake to them, for their comfort, of the absolute power of even the smallest faith,[c] and of the service and humility of faith.[d] The latter was couched in a Parabolic form, well calculated to impress on them those feelings which would keep them lowly. They were but servants; and, even though they had done their work, the Master expected them to serve Him, before they sat down to their own meal and rest. Yet meal and rest there would be in the end. Only, let there not be self-elation, nor weariness, nor impatience; but let the Master and His service be all in all. Surely, if ever there was emphatic protest against the fundamental idea of Pharisaism, as claiming merit and reward, it was in the closing admonition of Christ's public Ministry in Peræa : ' When ye shall have done all those things which are commanded you, say, We are unprofitable servants; we have done that which was our duty to do.'

b St. Matt. xviii. 1-6, &c., 21, 22
c St. Luke xvii. 6
d vv. 7-10

And with these parting words did He most effectually and for ever separate, in heart and spirit, the Church from the Synagogue.

CHAPTER LXVII.

THE DEATH AND THE RAISING OF LAZARUS.

(St. John xi. 1-54.)

FROM listening to the teaching of Christ, we turn once more to follow His working. It will be remembered that the visit to Bethany divides the period from the Feast of the Dedication to the last Paschal week into two parts. It also forms the prelude and preparation for the awful events of the End. For it was on that occasion that the members of the Sanhedrin formally resolved on His Death. It now only remained to settle and carry out the plans for giving effect to their purpose.

At the outset, we must here once more meet, however briefly, the preliminary difficulty in regard to Miracles, of which the raising of Lazarus is the most notable. Undoubtedly, a Miracle runs counter not only to our experience, but to the facts on which our experience is grounded; and can only be accounted for by a direct Divine interposition, which also runs counter to our experience, although it cannot logically be said to run counter to the facts on which that experience is grounded. Beyond this it is impossible to go, since the argument on other grounds than of experience—be it phenomenal [observation and historical information] or real [knowledge of laws and principles]—would necessitate knowledge alike of all the laws of Nature and of all the secrets of Heaven.

On the other hand, to argue this point only on the ground of experience (phenomenal or real), were not only reasoning *à priori*, but in a vicious circle. It would really amount to this: A thing has not been, because it cannot be ; and it cannot be, because, so far as I know, it is not and has not been. But to deny on such *à priori* prejudgment the possibility of Miracles ultimately involves a denial of a Living, Reigning God. For the existence of a God implies at least the possibility, it may be the rational necessity, of Miracles. And the same grounds of experience, which tell against the occurrence of a Miracle, would equally apply against belief in a God. We have as little ground in experience (of a physical kind) for the one as for the other. This is not said to deter inquiry, but for the sake of our argument. For we confidently assert, and challenge experiment of it, that disbelief in a God, or Materialism, involves infinitely more difficulties, and that at every step and in regard to all things, than the faith of the Christian.

We may now follow this solemn narrative itself. Perhaps the more briefly we comment on it the better.

It was while in Peræa, that this message suddenly reached the Master from the well-remembered home at Bethany, ' the village of Mary and her sister Martha,' concerning their (younger) brother Lazarus : ' Lord, behold he whom Thou lovest is sick ! ' We note as an important fact that the Lazarus, who had not even been mentioned in the only account preserved to us of a previous visit of Christ a St. Luke x. to Bethany,[a] is described as ' he whom Christ 38 &c. loved.' What a gap of untold events between the two visits of Christ to Bethany—and what modesty should it teach us as regards inferences from the circumstance that certain events are not recorded in the Gospels ! The messenger was apparently dismissed by Christ with this reply : ' This sickness is not unto death, but for the glory of God, in order that the Son of God may be glorified thereby.' This answer was heard by such of the Apostles as were present at the time. They would naturally infer from it that Lazarus would not die, and that his restoration would glorify Christ, either as having foretold it, or prayed for it, or effected it by His Will.

And yet, probably at the very time when the messenger received his answer, and ere he could have brought it to the sisters, Lazarus was already dead. Nor did this awaken doubt in the minds of the sisters. We seem to hear the very words, which at the time they said to each other, when each of them afterwards repeated to the Lord : ' Lord, if Thou hadst been here, my brother would not have died.' They probably thought the message had reached Him too late. Even in their keenest anguish, there was no failure of trust. Yet all this while Christ knew that Lazarus had died, and still He continued two whole days where He was, finishing His work. And yet—and this is noted before anything else, alike in regard to His delay and to His after-conduct—He ' loved Martha, and her sister, and Lazarus.' Christ is never in haste, because He is always sure.

It was only after these two days that Jesus broke silence as to His purposes and as to Lazarus. Though thoughts of him must have been present with the disciples, none dared ask aught, although not from misgiving, nor yet from fear. This also of faith and of confidence. At last, when His work in that part had been completed, He spoke of leaving, but even so not of going to Bethany, but into Judæa. For, in truth, His work in Bethany was not only geographically, but really, part of His work in Judæa; and He told the disciples of His purpose, just because He knew their fears and would teach them, not only for this but for every future occasion, what principle applied to them. For when in their care and affection they reminded the ' Rabbi ' that the Jews ' were even now seeking to stone ' Him, He replied by telling them in figurative language that we have each our working day from God, and that while it lasts no foe can shorten it or break up our work. The day had twelve hours, and while these lasted no mishap would befall him that walked in the way [he stumbleth not, because he seeth the light of this world]. It was otherwise when the day was past and the night had come. When our God-given day has set, and with it the light been withdrawn which hitherto prevented our stumbling—then, if a man went in his own way and at his own time, might such mishap befall him, ' because,' figuratively as to light in the night-time, and really as to guidance and direction in the way, ' the light is not in him.'

But this was only part of what Jesus said to His disciples in preparation for a journey that would issue in such tremendous consequences. He next spoke of Lazarus, their ' friend,' as ' fallen asleep '—in the frequent Jewish figurative sense of it, and of His going there to wake him out of sleep. The disciples would naturally connect this mention of His going to Lazarus with His proposed visit to Judæa, and, in their eagerness to keep Him from the latter, interposed that there could be no need for going to Lazarus, since sleep was according to Jewish notions one of the six, or, according to others, five symptoms or crises in recovery from dangerous illness. And when the Lord then plainly stated it, ' Lazarus died,' adding, what should have aroused their attention, that for their sakes He was glad He had not been in Bethany before the event, because now that would come which would work faith in them, and proposed to go to the dead Lazarus—even then, their whole attention was so absorbed by the certainty of danger to their loved Teacher, that Thomas had only one thought: since it was to be so, let them go and die with Jesus.

We already know the quiet happy home of Bethany. When Jesus reached it, 'He found'—probably from those who met Him by the way [a]—that Lazarus had been already four days in the grave. According to custom, he would be buried the same day that he had died.

a Comp. St. John xi. 20

This may be a convenient place for adding to the account already given, in connection with the burying of the widow's son at Nain, such further particulars of the Jewish observances and rites, as may illustrate the present history. Referring to the previous description, we resume, in imagination, our attendance at the point where Christ met the bier at Nain and again gave life to the dead. But we remember that, as we are now in Judæa, the hired mourners—both mourning-men and mourning-women—would follow, and not, as in Galilee, precede the body. From the narrative we infer that the burial of Lazarus did not take place in a common burying-ground, which was never nearer a town than 50 cubits, dry and rocky places being chosen in preference. Here the graves must be at least a foot and a half apart. It was deemed a dishonour to the dead to stand on, or walk over, the turf of a grave. Roses and other flowers seem to have been planted on graves. But cemeteries, or common burying-places, appear in earliest times to have been used only for the poor,[b] or for strangers.[c] In Jerusalem there were also two places where executed criminals were buried. All these, it is needless to say, were outside the City. But there is abundant evidence that every place had not its own burying-ground; and that, not unfrequently, provision had to be made for the transport of bodies. Indeed, a burying-place is not mentioned among the ten requisites for every fully-organised Jewish commu-

b 2 Kings xxiii. 6 ; Jer. xxvi. 23
c St. Matt. xxvii. 7 ;
Acts i. 19

nity.[1] The names given, both to the graves and to the burying-place itself, are of interest. As regards the former, we mention such as ' the house of silence ; ' ' the house of stone ; ' ' the hostelry,' or literally, ' place where you spend the night ; ' ' the couch ; ' ' the resting-place ; ' ' the valley of the multitude,' or ' of the dead.' The cemetery was called ' the house of graves ; ' or ' the court of burying ; ' and ' the house of eternity.' By a euphemism, ' to die ' was designated as ' going to rest ; ' ' being completed ; ' ' being gathered to the world,' or ' to the home of light ; ' ' being withdrawn,' or ' hidden.' Burial without coffin seems to have continued the practice for a considerable time, and rules are given how a pit, the size of the body, was to be dug, and surrounded by a wall of loose stones to prevent the falling in of earth. It is interesting to learn that, for the sake of peace, just as the poor and sick of the Gentiles might be fed and nursed as well as those of the Jews, so their dead might be buried with those of the Jews, though not in their graves. On the other hand, a wicked person should not be buried close to a sage. Suicides were not accorded all the honours of those who had died a natural death, and the bodies of executed criminals were laid in a special place, whence the relatives might after a time remove their bones. The burial terminated by casting earth on the grave.

But, as already stated, Lazarus was, as became his station, not laid in a cemetery, but in his own private tomb in a cave—probably in a garden, the favourite place of interment. Though on terms of close friendship with Jesus, he was evidently not regarded as an apostate from the Synagogue. For every indignity was shown at the burial of an apostate ; people were even to array themselves in white festive garments to make demonstration of joy. Here, on the contrary, every mark of sympathy, respect, and sorrow had been shown by the people in the district and by friends in the neighbouring Jerusalem. In such

[1] These were: a law court, provision for the poor, a synagogue, a public bath, a *secessus*, a doctor, a surgeon, a scribe, a butcher, and a schoolmaster.

case it would be regarded as a privilege to obey the Rabbinic direction of accompanying the dead, so as to shew honour to the departed and kindness to the survivors. As the sisters of Bethany were ' disciples,' we may well believe that some of the more extravagant demonstrations of grief were, if not dispensed with, yet modified. We can scarcely believe that the hired ' mourners ' would alternate between extravagant praises of the dead and calls upon the attendants to lament; or that, as was their wont, they would strike on their breasts, beat their hands, and dash about their feet, or break into wails and mourning songs, alone or in chorus. In all probability, however, the funeral oration would be delivered—as in the case of all distinguished persons—either in the house, or at one of the stations where the bearers changed, or at the burying-place ; perhaps, if they passed it, in the Synagogue. It has previously been noted what extravagant value was in later times attached to these orations, as indicating both a man's life on earth and his place in heaven. The dead was supposed to be present, listening to the words of the speaker and watching the expression on the faces of the hearers.

When thinking of these tombs in gardens, we naturally revert to that which for three days held the Lord of Life. It is, perhaps, better to give details here rather than afterwards to interrupt, by such inquiries, our solemn thoughts in presence of the Crucified Christ. Not only the rich, but even those moderately well-to-do, had tombs of their own, which probably were acquired and prepared long before they were needed, and treated and inherited as private and personal property. In such caves, or rock-hewn tombs, the bodies were laid, having been anointed with many spices, with myrtle, aloes, and, at a later period, also with hyssop, rose-oil, and rose-water. The body was dressed and, at a later period, wrapped, if possible, in the worn cloths in which originally a Roll of the Law had been held. The ' tombs ' were either ' rock-hewn,' or natural ' caves,' or else large walled vaults, with niches along the sides. Such a ' cave ' or ' vault ' 6 feet in width, 9 feet in length, and 6 feet in height, contained 'niches' for eight bodies. The larger caves or vaults held thirteen bodies. These figures apply, of course, only to what the Law required, when a vault had been contracted for. At the entrance to the vault was 'a court' 9 feet square, to hold the bier and its bearers. After a time the bones were collected and put into a box or coffin, having first been anointed with wine and oil, and being held together by wrappings of cloth. This circumstance explains the existence of the mortuary chests, or *osteophagi*, so frequently found in the tombs of Palestine by late explorers, who have been unable to explain their meaning. Inscriptions appear to have been graven either on the lid of the mortuary chest, or on the great stone 'rolled' at the entrance to the vault, or to the 'court' leading into it, or else on the inside walls of yet another erection, made over the vaults of the wealthy, and which was supposed to complete the burying-place.

These small buildings surmounting the graves may have served as shelter to those who visited the tombs. They also served as 'monuments,' of which we read in the Bible, in the Apocrypha and in *Josephus*. But of gravestones with inscriptions we cannot find any record in Talmudic works. At the same time, the place where there was a vault or a grave was marked by a stone, which was kept whitened, to warn the passer-by against defilement.

We are now able fully to realise all the circumstances and surroundings in the burial and raising of Lazarus.

Jesus had come to Bethany. But in the house of mourning they knew it not. As Bethany was only about two miles from Jerusalem, many from the City, who were on terms of friendship with what was evidently a distinguished family, had come in obedience to one of the most binding Rabbinic directions—that of comforting the mourners. In the funeral procession the sexes had been separated, and the practice probably prevailed even at that time for the women to return alone from the grave. This may explain why afterwards the women went and returned alone to the Tomb of our Lord. The mourning, which began before the burial, had been shared by the friends who sat silent on the ground, or were busy preparing the mourning meal. As the company left the dead, each had taken leave of the deceased with a 'Depart in peace!' Then they had formed into lines, through which the mourners passed amidst expressions of sympathy, repeated (at least seven times) as the procession halted on the return to the house of mourning. Then began the mourning in the house, which really lasted thirty days, of which the first three were those of greatest, the others, during the seven days, or the special week of sorrow, of less intense mourning. But on the Sabbath, as God's holy day, all mourning was intermitted—and so 'they rested on the Sabbath, according to the commandment.'

In that household of disciples this mourning would not have assumed such violent forms, as when we read that the women were in the habit of tearing out their hair, or of a Rabbi who publicly scourged himself. But we know how the dead would be spoken of. In death the two worlds were said to meet and kiss. And now they who had passed away beheld God. They were at rest. Such beautiful passages as Ps. cxii. 6, Prov. x. 7, Is. xi. 10, last clause, and Is. lvii. 2, were applied to them. Nay, the holy dead should be called 'living.' In truth, they knew about us, and unseen still surrounded us. Nor should they ever be mentioned without adding a blessing on their memory.

In this spirit, we cannot doubt, the Jews were now 'comforting' the sisters. They may have repeated words like those quoted as the conclusion of such a consolatory speech: 'May the Lord of consolations comfort you! Blessed be He Who comforteth the mourners!' But they could scarcely have imagined how literally a wish like this was about to be fulfilled. For already the message had reached Martha, who was probably in one of the outer apartments of the house: Jesus is coming! She hastened to meet the Master. Not a word of complaint, not a murmur, nor doubt, escaped her lips—only what during those four bitter days these two sisters must have been so often saying to each other, when the luxury of solitude was allowed them, that if He had been there, their brother would not have died. And still she held fast by it, that even now God would give Him whatsoever He asked. Her words could scarcely have been the expression of any real hope of the miracle about to take place, or Martha would not have afterwards sought to arrest Him, when He bade them roll away the stone. And yet is it not even so, that when that comes to us which our faith had once dared to suggest, if not to hope, we feel as if it were all too great and impossible—that a very physical ' cannot be ' separates us from it ?

It was in very truth and literality that the Lord meant it, when He told Martha her brother would rise again, although she understood His Words of the Re- surrection at the Last Day. In answer, Christ pointed out to her the connection between Himself and the Resurrection; and, what He spoke, that He did when He raised Lazarus from the dead. The Resurrection and the Life are not special gifts either to the Church or to humanity, but are connected with the Christ—the out- come of Himself. Most literally He *is* the Resurrection and the Life—and this, the new teaching about the Resurrection, was the object and the meaning of the raising of Lazarus.

It is only when we think of the meaning of Christ's previous words that we can understand the answer of Martha to His question: ' Believest thou this ? Yea, Lord, I have believed that Thou art the Christ, the Son of God [with special reference to the original message of ^a St. John Christ ^a], He that cometh into the world ' [' the xi. 4 Coming One into the world ' = the world's promised, expected, come Saviour].

What else passed between them we can only gather from the context. It seems that the Master ' called ' for Mary. This message Martha now hasted to deliver, although ' secretly.' Mary was probably sitting in the chamber of mourning, with its upset chairs and couches, and other melancholy tokens of mourning, as was the custom; surrounded by many who had come to comfort them. As she heard of His coming and call, she rose 'quickly,' and the Jews followed her, under the impression that she was again going to visit and to weep at the tomb of her brother. For it was the practice to visit the grave, especially during the first three days. When she came to Jesus, where He still stood, outside Bethany, she was forgetful of all around. She could only fall at His Feet, and repeat the poor words with which she and her sister had these four weary days tried to cover the nakedness of their sorrow: poor words of faith, which she did not, like her sister, make still poorer by adding the poverty of her hope to that of her faith. To Martha that had been the *maximum*, to Mary it was the *minimum* of her faith; for the rest, it was far better to add nothing more, but simply to worship at His Feet.

It must have been a deeply touching scene: the outpouring of her sorrow, the absoluteness of her faith, the mute appeal of her tears. And the Jews who witnessed it were moved as she, and wept with her. What follows is difficult to understand. But if with a realisation of Christ's Condescension to, and union with humanity as its Healer, by taking upon Himself its diseases, we combine the statement formerly made about the Resurrection, as not a gift or boon but the outcome of Himself—we may, in some way, not understand, but be able to gaze into the unfathomed depth of that Theanthropic fellow-suffering which was both vicarious and redemptive, and which, before He became the Resurrection to Lazarus, shook His whole inner Being, when, in the words of St. John, ' He vehemently moved His Spirit and troubled Himself.'

And now every trait is in accord. ' Where have ye laid him ?' As they bade Him come and see, the tears that fell from Him were not like the violent lamentation that burst from Him at sight and prophetic view of doomed Jerusalem.[a] Yet we can scarcely think that the Jews rightly interpreted it, when they ascribed it only to His love for Lazarus. But surely there was not a touch either of malevolence or of irony, only what we feel to be quite natural in the circumstances, when some of

ᵃ St. Luke
xix. 41

F F

them asked aloud : ' Could not this One, Which opened the eyes of the blind, have wrought so that [in order] this one also should not die ? ' Scarcely was it even unbelief. They had so lately witnessed in Jerusalem that Miracle, such as had ' not been heard' ' since the world began,' [a] that it seemed difficult to understand how, seeing there was the will (in His affection for Lazarus), there was not the power—not to raise him from the dead, for that did not occur to them, but to prevent his dying. Was there, then, a barrier in death ? And it was this, and not indignation, which once more caused that Theanthropic recurrence upon Himself, when again ' He vehemently moved His Spirit.'

[a] St. John ix. 32

And now they were at the cave which was Lazarus' tomb. He bade them roll aside the great stone which covered its entrance. Amidst the awful pause which preceded obedience, one voice only was raised. It was that of Martha. Jesus had not spoken of raising Lazarus. But what was about to be done ? She could scarcely have thought that He merely wished to gaze once more upon the face of the dead. Something nameless had seized her. She dared not believe ; she dared not disbelieve. Did she, perhaps, not dread a failure, but feel misgivings, when thinking of Christ as in presence of commencing corruption before these Jews—and yet, as we so often, still love Him even in unbelief ? It was the common Jewish idea that corruption commenced on the fourth day, that the drop of gall, which had fallen from the sword of the Angel and caused death, was then working its effect, and that, as the face changed, the soul took its final leave from the resting-place of the body. Only one sentence Jesus spake of gentle reproof, of reminder of what He had said to her just before, and of the message He had sent when first He heard of Lazarus' illness.[b] And now the stone was rolled away. We all feel that the fitting thing here was prayer—yet not petition, but thanksgiving that the Father ' heard ' Him, not as regarded the raising of Lazarus, which was His Own Work, but in the ordering and

[b] St. John xi. 4

arranging of all the circumstances—alike the petition and
the thanksgiving having for their object them that stood
by, for He knew that the Father always heard Him : that
so they might believe that the Father had sent Him.
Sent of the Father—not come of Himself, not sent of
Satan—and sent to do His Will !

One loud command spoken into that silence ; one loud
call to that sleeper, and the wheels of life again moved at
the outgoing of The Life.   And, still bound hand and foot
with graveclothes, and his face with the napkin, Lazarus
stood forth, shuddering and silent, in the cold light of
earth's day.   In that multitude, now more pale and shuddering than the man bound in the graveclothes, the only
one majestically calm was He, Who before had been so
deeply moved and troubled Himself, as He now bade them
' Loose him, and let him go.'

We know no more.   What happened afterwards—how
they loosed him, what they said, and what were Lazarus' first
words, we know not.   Did Lazarus remember aught of the
late past, or was not rather the rending of the grave a real
rending from the past : the awakening so sudden, the
transition so great, that nothing of the bright vision remained, but its impress—just as a marvellously beautiful
Jewish legend has it, that before entering this world, the
soul of a child has seen all of heaven and hell, of past,
present, and future ; but that, as the Angel strikes it on
the mouth to waken it into this world, all of the other has
passed from the mind ?   Again we say : We know not—
and it is better so.

And here abruptly breaks off this narrative.   Some of
those who had seen it believed on Him ; others hurried
back to Jerusalem to tell it to the Pharisees.   Then was
hastily gathered a meeting of the Sanhedrists, not to judge
Him, but to deliberate what was to be done.   They had
not the courage of, though the wish for judicial murder,
till he who was the High-Priest, Caiaphas, reminded them
of the well-known Jewish adage, that it ' is better one man
should die, than the community perish.'

This was the last prophecy in Israel ; with the sentence

F F 2

of death on Israel's true High-Priest died prophecy in Israel, died Israel's High Priesthood. It had spoken sentence upon itself.

This was the first Friday of dark resolve. Henceforth it only needed to concert plans for carrying it out. Some one, perhaps Nicodemus, sent word of the secret meeting and resolution of the Sanhedrists. That Friday and the next Sabbath Jesus rested in Bethany, with the same majestic calm which He had shown at the grave of Lazarus. Then He withdrew far away to the obscure bounds of Peræa and Galilee, to a city of which the very location is now unknown. And there He continued with His disciples, withdrawn from the Jews—till He would make His final entrance into Jerusalem.

CHAPTER LXVIII.

ON THE JOURNEY TO JERUSALEM—HEALING OF TEN LEPERS —ON DIVORCE—THE BLESSING TO LITTLE CHILDREN.

(St. Matt. xix. 1, 2; St. Mark x. 1; St. Luke xvii. 11; 12–19; St. Matt. xix. 3–12; St. Mark x. 2–12; St. Matt. xix. 13–15; St. Mark x. 13–16; St. Luke xviii. 15–17.)

THE brief time of rest and quiet converse with His disciples in the retirement of Ephraim was past, and the Saviour of men prepared for His last journey to Jerusalem. All the three Synoptic Gospels mark this, although with varying details.[a] From the mention of Galilee by St. Matthew, and by St. Luke of Samaria and Galilee—or more correctly, 'between (along the frontiers of) Samaria and Galilee,' we may conjecture that, on leaving Ephraim, Christ made a very brief detour along the northern frontier to some place at the southern border of Galilee—perhaps to meet at a certain point those who were to accompany Him on His final journey to Jerusalem. The whole company would then form one of those festive bands which travelled to the Paschal Feast, nor would

a St. Matt. xix. 1, 2; St. Mark x. 1; St. Luke xvii. 11

there be anything strange or unusual in the appearance
of such a band, in this instance under the leadership of
Jesus.

Another notice, furnished by SS. Matthew and Mark,
is that during this journey through Peræa, ' great multitudes' resorted to, and followed Him, and that
' He healed'[a] and 'taught them.'[b] This will
account for the incidents and Discourses by the
way, and also how, from among many deeds, the Evangelists may have selected for record what to them seemed the
most important or novel, or else best accorded with the
plans of their respective narratives.

1. St. Luke alone relates the very first incident
by the way,[c] and the first Discourse.[d]

It is a further confirmation of our suggestion as to the
road taken by Jesus, that of the ten lepers whom, at the
outset of His journey, He met when entering into a village,
one was a Samaritan. It may have been that the district
was infested with leprosy ; or these lepers may, on tidings
of Christ's approach, have hastily gathered there. It was
in strict accordance with Jewish Law, that these lepers
remained both outside the village and far from Him to
Whom they now cried for mercy. And, without either
touch or even command of healing, Christ bade them go
and show themselves as healed to the priests. For this it
was not necessary to repair to Jerusalem. Any priest
might declare ' unclean' or ' clean,' provided the applicants
presented themselves singly, and not in company, for
his inspection. And they went at Christ's bidding, even
before they had actually experienced the healing ! So
great was their faith, and, may we not almost infer, the
general belief throughout the district, in the Power of ' the
Master.' And as they went, the new life coursed in their
veins.

But now the characteristic difference between these
men appeared. Of the ten, equally recipients of the
benefit, the nine Jews continued their way—presumably
to the priests—while the one Samaritan in the number at
once turned back, with a loud voice glorifying God. No

a St. Mat-
thew
b St. Mark

c St. Luke
xvii. 12–19
d vv. 20–37

longer now did he remain afar off, but fell on his face at the Feet of Him to Whom he gave thanks. This Samaritan had received more than new bodily life and health : he had found spiritual life and healing.

But why did the nine Jews not return ? Assuredly, they must have had some faith when first seeking help from Christ, and still more when setting out for the priests before they had experienced the healing. But perhaps we may over-estimate the faith of these men. Bearing in mind the views of the Jews at the time, and what constant succession of miraculous cures had been witnessed these years, it cannot seem strange that lepers should apply to Jesus. Nor yet perhaps did it, in the circumstances, involve very much greater faith to go to the priests at His bidding— implying, of course, that they were or would be healed. But it was far different to turn back and to fall down at His Feet in worship and thanksgiving. That made a man a disciple.

And the Lord emphasised the contrast in this between the children of the household and 'this stranger.' According to the Gospels, a man might either seek benefit from Christ, or else receive Christ through such benefit. In the one case the benefit sought was the object, in the other the means : in the one it ultimately led away from, in the other it led to Christ and to discipleship. And so Christ now spake to this Samaritan : 'Arise, go thy way ; thy faith has made thee whole.'

2. The Discourse concerning the Coming of the Kingdom, which is reported by St. Luke immediately after the healing of the ten lepers,[a] will be more conveniently considered in connection with the fuller statement of the same truths at the close of our Lord's Ministry.[b]

a St. Luke xvii. 20-37

b St. Matt. xxiv.

3. This brings us to what we regard as, in point of time, the next Discourse of Christ on this journey, recorded both by St. Matthew and, in briefer form, by St. Mark.[c]

c St. Matt. xix. 3-12; St. Mark x. 2-12

Christ had advanced farther on His journey, and now once more encountered the hostile Pharisees. It will be remembered that He had met them before in the same

part of the country,ᵃ and answered their taunts
and objections, among other things, by charging
them with breaking in spirit that Law of which they professed to be the exponents and representatives. And this
He had proved by reference to their views and teaching
on the subject of divorce.ᵇ This seems to have
ᵇ vv. 17, 18 rankled in their minds. Probably they also
imagined, it would be easy to show on this point a marked
difference between the teaching of Jesus and that of Moses
and the Rabbis, and to enlist popular feeling against Him.
Accordingly, when these Pharisees again encountered Jesus,
now on His journey to Judæa, they resumed the subject precisely where it had been broken off when they had last met
Him, only now with the object of 'tempting Him.' Perhaps
it may also have been in the hope that, by getting Christ
to commit Himself against divorce in Peræa—the territory
of Herod—they might enlist against Him, as formerly
against the Baptist, the implacable hatred of Herodias.

But their main object evidently was to involve Christ
in controversy with some of the Rabbinic Schools. This
appears from the form in which they put the question,
ᶜ St. Matt. whether it was lawful to put away a wife 'for
xix. 3 every cause'?ᶜ St. Mark, who gives only a very
condensed account, omits this clause; but in Jewish circles
the whole controversy between different teachers turned
upon this point. All held that divorce was lawful, the only
question being as to its grounds. There can however be
no question that the practice was discouraged by many of
the better Rabbis, alike in word and by their example:
nor yet, that the Jewish Law took the most watchful care
of the interests of the woman. In fact, if any doubt were
raised as to the legal validity of a letter of divorce, the
Law always pronounced against the divorce. At the same
time, in popular practice, divorce must have been very
frequent; while the principles underlying Jewish legislation on the subject are most objectionable.

No real comparison is possible between Christ and
even the strictest of the Rabbis, since none of them actually

prohibited divorce, except in case of adultery, nor yet laid down those high eternal principles which Jesus enunciated. But we can understand how from the Jewish point of view 'tempting Him,' they would put the question, whether it was lawful to divorce a wife ' for every cause.' Avoiding their cavils, the Lord appealed straight to the highest authority—God's institution of marriage. He Who at the beginning had made them male and female had in the marriage-relation ' joined them together;' to the breaking of every other, even the nearest, relationship, to be ' one flesh '—that is, to a union which was unity. Such was the fact of God's ordering. It followed that they were one —and what God had willed to be one, man might not put asunder. Then followed the natural Rabbinic objection, why, in such case, Moses had commanded a bill of divorce-ment. Our Lord replied by pointing out that Moses had not commanded divorce, only tolerated it on account of their hardness of heart, and in such case commanded to give a bill of divorce for the protection of the wife. And this argument would appeal the more forcibly to them, that the Rabbis themselves taught that a somewhat similar con-

[margin note: ᵃ Deut. xxi. 11] cession had been made ᵃ by Moses in regard to female captives of war—as the Talmud has it, ' on account of the evil impulse.' But such a separation, our Lord continued, had not been provided for in the original institution, which was a union to unity. Only one thing could put an end to that unity—its absolute breach. Hence, to divorce one's wife (or husband) while this unity lasted, and to marry another, was adultery, because, as the divorce was null before God, the original marriage still subsisted—and in that case the Rabbinic Law would also have forbidden it. The next part of the Lord's inference, that ' whoso marrieth her which is put away doth commit adultery,' is more difficult of interpretation. Generally, it is understood as implying that a woman divorced for adultery might not be married. Be this as it may, the Jewish Law, which regarded marriage with a woman divorced under any circumstances as unadvisable, absolutely forbade that of the adulterer with the adulteress.

That the Pharisees had rightly judged, when 'tempting Him,' what the popular feeling on the subject would be, appears even from what 'His disciples' [not necessarily the Apostles] afterwards said to Him. They waited to ex-

ᵃ St. Mark press their dissent till they were alone with Him
x. 10 'in the house,' ᵃ and then urged that, if it were
as Christ had taught, it would be better not to marry at
ᵇ St. Matt. all. To which the Lord replied,ᵇ that 'this say-
xix. 10-12 ing' of the disciples, 'it is not good to marry,'
could not be received by all men, but only by those to whom it was 'given.' For there were three cases in which abstinence from marriage might lawfully be contemplated. In two of these it was, of course, natural; and, where it was not so, a man might, 'for the Kingdom of Heaven's sake'—that is, in the service of God and of Christ—have all his thoughts, feelings, and impulses so engaged that others were no longer existent. It is this which requires to be 'given' of God; and which 'he that is able to receive it'—who has the moral capacity for it—is called upon to receive.

4. The next incident is recorded by the three Evange-
ᶜ St. Matt. lists.ᶜ It probably occurred in the same house
xix. 13-15; where the disciples had questioned Christ about
St. Mark x. His teaching on the Divinely sacred relationship
Luke xviii. of marriage. And the account of His blessing of
15-17 'infants' and 'little children' most aptly follows on the former teaching. We can understand how, when One Who so spake and wrought rested in the house, Jewish mothers should have brought their 'little children,' and some their 'infants,' to Him, that He might 'touch,' 'put His Hands on them, and pray.' What power and holiness must these mothers have believed to be in His touch and prayer; what life to be in, and to come from Him; and what gentleness and tenderness must His have been, when they dared so to bring these little ones! For how utterly contrary it was to all Jewish notions, and how incompatible with the supposed dignity of a Rabbi, appears from the rebuke of the disciples. It was an occasion and an act when, as the fuller and more pictorial account of St. Mark

informs us, Jesus 'was much displeased'—the only time this strong word is used of our Lord—and said unto them : ' Suffer the little children to come to Me, hinder them not, for of such is the Kingdom of God.' Then He gently reminded His own disciples of their grave error, by repeating what they had apparently forgotten,[a] that, in order to enter the Kingdom of God, it must be received as by a little child—that here there could be no question of intellectual qualification, nor of distinction due to a great Rabbi, but only of humility, receptiveness, meekness, and a simple application to, and trust in the Christ. And so He folded these little ones in His Arms, put His Hands upon them, and blessed them.

* St. Matt. xviii. 3

CHAPTER LXIX.

THE LAST INCIDENTS IN PERÆA—THE YOUNG RULER WHO WENT AWAY SORROWFUL—PROPHECY OF CHRIST'S PASSION —THE REQUEST OF SALOME, AND OF JAMES AND JOHN.

(St. Matt. xix. 16–22 ; St. Mark x. 17–22 ; St. Luke xviii. 18–23 ; St. Matt. xix. 23–30 ; St. Mark x. 23–31 ; St. Luke xviii. 24–30 ; St. Matt. xx. 17–19 ; St. Mark x. 32–34 ; St. Luke xviii. 31–34 ; St. Matt. xx. 20–28 ; St. Mark x. 35–45.)

As we near the goal, the story seems to grow in tenderness and pathos. It is as if all the loving condescension of the Master were to be crowded into these days ; all the pressing need also and the human weaknesses of His disciples.

As ' He was going forth into the way '—probably at early morn, as He left the house where He had blessed the children brought to Him by believing parents—His progress was arrested. It was ' a young man,' ' a ruler,'[b] probably of the local Synagogue, who came with all haste, ' running,' and kneeling,[c] to ask what to him, to us all, is the most important question.

b St. Luke

* St. Mark

The actual question of the young Ruler is one which repeatedly occurs in Jewish writings, as put to a Rabbi by his disciples. Amidst the different answers given, we scarcely wonder that they also pointed to observance of the Law. And the saying of Christ seems the more adapted to the young Ruler when we recall this sentence from the Talmud : 'There is nothing else that is good but the Law.' But here again the similarity is only of form, not of substance. For it will be noticed that, in the fuller account by St. Matthew, Christ leads the young Ruler upwards through the table of the prohibitions of deeds to the first positive command of deed, and then, by a rapid transition, to the substitution for the tenth commandment in its negative form of this wider positive and all-embracing command : [a] 'Thou shalt love thy neighbour as thyself.' Any Jewish 'Ruler,' but especially one so earnest, would have at once answered a challenge on the first four commandments by 'Yes'—and that not self-righteously but sincerely, though of course in ignorance of their real depth. And this was not the time for lengthened discussion and instruction : only for rapid awakening, to lead up, if possible, from a heart-drawing towards the Master to real discipleship. Best here to start from what was admitted as binding—the ten commandments—and to lead from that in them which was least likely to be broken, step by step, upwards to that which was most likely to awaken consciousness of sin.

[a] Lev. xix. 18

And the young Ruler did not, as that other Pharisee, reply by trying to raise a Rabbinic disputation over the 'Who is neighbour to me ?'[b] but in the sincerity of an honest heart answered that he had kept— that is, so far as he knew them—'all these things from his youth.' On this St. Matthew puts into his mouth the question—'What lack I yet ?' What he had seen and heard of the Christ had quickened to greatest intensity all in him that longed after God and heaven, and had brought him in this supreme moral earnestness to the Feet of Him in Whom, as he felt, all perfectness was, and from Whom all perfectness came. He had not been first drawn to Christ, and thence to the pure, as were the publicans and sinners ; but, like so many—even as Peter, when in that hour of soul-agony he said : 'To whom shall we go ? Thou

[b] St. Luke x. 29

hast the words of eternal life,'—he had been drawn to the pure and the higher, and therefore to Christ.

And Jesus saw what he lacked; and what He saw, He showed him. For, 'looking at him' in his sincerity and earnestness, 'He loved him.' One thing was needful for this young man: that he should not only become His disciple, but that, in so doing, he should 'come and follow' Christ. It seems as if to some it needed, not only the word of God, but a stroke of some Moses'-rod to make the water gush forth from the rock. And thus would this young Ruler have been 'perfect;' and what he had given to the poor have become, not through merit nor by way of reward, but really, 'treasure in heaven.'

What he lacked—was earth's poverty and heaven's riches: a heart fully set on following Christ; and this could only come to him through willing surrender of all.

There is something deeply pathetic in the mode in which St. Mark describes what follows: 'he was sad'— the word painting a dark gloom that overshadowed the face of the young man. We need scarcely here recall the almost extravagant language in which Rabbinism describes the miseries of poverty; we can understand his feelings without that. Such a possibility had never entered his mind: the thought of it was terribly startling. Rabbinism had never asked this; if it demanded alms-giving, it was in odious boastfulness; while it was declared even unlawful to give away all one's possessions—at most, only a fifth of them might be dedicated.

And so, with clouded face he gazed down into what he lacked—within; but also gazed up in Christ on what he needed. And, although we hear no more of him who that day went back to his rich home very poor, because 'very sorrowful,' we cannot but believe that he whom Jesus loved yet found in the poverty of earth the treasure of heaven.

Nor was this all. The deep pity of Christ for him who had gone that day, speaks also in His warning to His disciples.[a] But surely those are not only riches in the literal sense which make it so

a St. Mark x. 23

difficult for a man to enter into the Kingdom of Heaven
—so difficult, as to amount almost to that impossibility
which was expressed in the common Jewish proverb,
that a man did not even in his dreams see an elephant
pass through the eye of a needle? But when in their
perplexity the disciples put to each other the question:
Who then can be saved? He taught them that what was
impossible of achievement by man in his own strength,
God would work by His Almighty Grace.

It almost jars on our ears when Peter, perhaps as
spokesman of the rest, seems to remind the Lord that they
had forsaken all to follow Him. St. Matthew records also
the special question which Simon added to it: 'What
shall we have therefore?' The Lord's reply bore on two
points: on the reward which all who left everything to
follow Christ would obtain; [a] and on the special
acknowledgment awaiting the Apostles of Christ.[b]
In regard to the former we mark, that it is twofold. They who had forsaken all 'for His sake'[c]
'and the Gospel's,'[d] 'for the Kingdom of God's
sake'—and these three expressions explain and
supplement each other—would receive 'in this
time' 'manifold more' of new, and better, and
closer relationships of a spiritual kind for those which they
had surrendered, although, as St. Mark significantly adds,
to prevent all possible mistakes, 'with persecutions.' But
by the side of this stands out unclouded and bright the
promise for 'the world to come' of 'everlasting life.' As
regarded the Apostles personally, some mystery lies on
the special promise to them (that 'in the regeneration'
they should 'sit on thrones judging the twelve tribes of
Israel'). We could quite understand that the distinction
of rule to be bestowed on them might have been worded
in language taken from the expectations of the time,
in order to make the promise intelligible to them. But,
unfortunately, we have here no explanatory information
to offer. The Rabbis, indeed, speak of a renovation or
regeneration of the world which was to take place after
the 7,000 or else 5,000 years of the Messianic reign.

[a] St. Matt. xix. 29; St. Mark x. 29, 30; St. Luke xviii. 29, 30
[b] St. Matt. xix. 28
[c] St. Matthew and St. Mark
[d] St. Mark

Such a renewal of all things is not only foretold by the prophets,[a] and dwelt upon in later Jewish writings,[b] but frequently referred to in Rabbinic literature. But as regards the special rule or 'judgment' of the Apostles, or ambassadors of the Messiah, we have not, and, of course, cannot expect any parallel in Jewish writings. Yet that the delegation of such rule and judgment to the Apostles is in accordance with Old Testament promise will be seen from Dan. vii. 9, 10, 14, 27; and there are few references in the New Testament to the blessed consummation of all things in which such renewal of the world,[c] and even the rule and judgment of the representatives of the Church,[d] are not referred to.

The reference to the blessed future with its rewards was followed by a Parable, recorded as with one exception all of that series, only by St. Matthew. It will best be considered in connection with the last series of Christ's Parables. But it was accompanied by a most needful warning.[e] Thoughts of the future Messianic reign, its glory, and their own part in it might have so engrossed the minds of the disciples as to make them forgetful of the terrible present, immediately before them. In such case they might not only have lapsed into that most fatal Jewish error of a Messiah-King Who was not Saviour—the Crown without the Cross—but have even suffered shipwreck of their faith, when the storm broke on the Day of His Condemnation and Crucifixion. How truly such preparation was required by the disciples appears from the narrative itself.

There was something sad and mysterious in the words with which Christ had closed His Parable, that the last should be first and the first last[f]—and it had carried misgiving to those who heard it. Yet the disciples could not have indulged in illusions. His own sayings on at least two previous occasions,[g] however ill or partially understood, must have led them to expect at any rate grievous

[a] As for example Is. xxxiv. 4; li. 6; lxv. 17
[b] Book of Enoch xci. 16, 17; 4 Esd. vii. 28
[c] Acts iii. 21; Rom. viii. 19-21; 2 Pet. iii. 13; Rev. xxi. 1
[d] 1 Cor. vi. 2, 3; Rev. xx. 4; xxi. 14
[e] St. Matt. xx. 17-19
[f] St. Matt. xx. 16; St. Mark x. 31
[g] St. Matt. xvi. 21; xvii. 22, 23

opposition and tribulations in Jerusalem, and their endeavour to deter Christ from going to Bethany, to raise Lazarus, proves that they were well aware of the
St. John danger which threatened the Master in Judæa.[a]
xi. 8, 16 Yet not only ' was He now going up to Jerusalem,' but there was that in His bearing which was quite unusual. As St. Mark writes, ' And going before them was Jesus; and they were amazed [utterly bewildered, viz. the Apostles]; and those who were following, were afraid.' It was then that Jesus took the Apostles apart, and, in language more precise than ever before, told them how all things that were ' written by the prophets shall be accomplished on the Son of Man ' [b]—not
[b] St. Luke merely, that all that had been written concerning
xviii. 31 the Son of Man should be accomplished, but a far deeper truth, all-comprehensive as regards the Old Testament: that all its prophecy ran up into the Sufferings of the Christ. As the three Evangelists report it, the Lord gave them full details of His Betrayal, Crucifixion, and Resurrection. And yet we may, without irreverence, doubt whether on that occasion He had really entered into all those particulars. In such case it would seem difficult to explain how, as St. Luke reports, ' they understood none of these things, and the saying was hid from them, neither knew they the things which were spoken ; ' and again, how afterwards the actual events and the Resurrection could have taken them so by surprise. Rather do we think that the Evangelists report what Jesus had said, in the light of after-events. At the time they may have thought that it pointed only to His rejection by Jews and Gentiles, to Sufferings and Death—and then to a Resurrection, either of His Mission or to such a reappearance of the Messiah, after His temporary disappearance, as Judaism expected.

One other incident, and the Peræan stay is for ever ended. It almost seems as if the fierce blast of temptation, the very breath of the destroyer, were already sweeping over the little flock, as if the twilight of the night of betrayal and desertion were already falling

around. And now it has fallen on the two chosen disciples, James and John—'the sons of thunder,' and one
of them, 'the beloved disciple!' Peter, the third in that
band most closely bound to Christ, had already had his
^{a St. Matt.} temptation,^a and would have it more fiercely—to
^{xvi. 23} the uprooting of life, if the Great High-Priest
had not specially interceded for him. And, as regards
^{b St. Matt.} these two sons of Zebedee and of Salome,^b we
^{xxvii. 56;} know what temptation had already beset them,—
^{comp. St.}
^{Mark xv. 40} how John had forbidden one to cast out devils,
^{c St. Mark}
^{ix. 38} because he followed not with them,^c and how
both he and his brother, James, would have called down
fire from heaven to consume the Samaritans who would
^{d St. Luke} not receive Christ.^d It was essentially the same
^{ix. 54} spirit that now prompted the request which
their mother Salome preferred, not only with their full
^{e By St.} concurrence, but, as we are expressly told,^e with
^{Mark (x. 35)} their active participation. There is the same
faith in the Christ, the same allegiance to Him, but also
the same unhallowed earnestness, the same misunderstanding—and, let us add, the same latent self-exaltation,
as in the two former instances, in the present request that,
as the most honoured of His guests, and also as the nearest
to Him, they might have their places at His Right Hand
^{St. Matt.} and at His Left in His Kingdom.^f Terribly in-
^{xx. 20-28;}
^{St. Mark x.} congruous as is any appearance of self-seeking
³⁵⁻⁴⁵ at that moment and with that prospect before
them, we cannot but feel that there is also an intenseness
of faith almost sublime, when the mother steps forth from
among those who follow Christ to His Suffering and
Death, to proffer such a request with her sons, and for
them.

And so the Saviour seems to have viewed it. He,
Whose Soul is filled with the contest before Him, bears
with the weakness and selfishness which could cherish such
ambitions at such a time. To correct them, He points to
that near prospect, when the Highest is to be made low.
'Ye know not what ye ask!' The King is to be King
through suffering—are they aware of the road which leads

to that goal ? Those nearest to the King of Sorrows must reach the place nearest to Him by the same road as He. Are they prepared for it; prepared to drink that cup of soul-agony, which the Father will hand to Him—to submit to, to descend into that Baptism of consecration, when the floods will sweep over Him ? In their ignorance, and listening only to the promptings of their hearts, they imagine that they are. Nay, in some measure it would be so; yet, finally to correct their mistake : to sit at His Right and at His Left Hand, these were not marks of mere favour for Him to bestow—in His own words : it 'is not Mine to give except to them for whom it is prepared of My Father.'

But as for the other ten, when they heard of it, it was only the pre-eminence which, in their view, James and John had sought, that stood out before them, to their envy and indignation.[a] And so in that solemn hour would the fire of controversy have broken out among them who should have been most closely united—had not Jesus hushed it into silence when He spoke to them of the grand contrast between the princes of the Gentiles as they 'lord it over them,' or the 'great among them' as they 'domineer' over men, and their own aims—how, whosoever would be great among them, must seek his greatness in service— not greatness through service, but the greatness of service ; and whosoever would be chief or rather 'first' among them, let it be in service. The Son of Man Himself—let them look back, let them look forward—He came not to be ministered unto, but to minister. And then, breaking through the reserve that had held Him, and revealing to them the inmost thoughts which had occupied Him when He had been alone, going before them on the way, He spoke for the first time fully what was the deepest meaning of His Life, Mission, and Death : 'to give His Life a ransom for many,'[b] to pay with His Life-Blood the price of their redemption, to lay down His Life for them : in their room and stead, and for their salvation.

These words must have sunk deep into the heart of

[a] St. Matt. xx. 24, &c. ; St. Mark x. 41, &c.

[b] St. Matt. xx. 28 ; St. Mark x. 45

one at least in that company. A few days later, and the beloved disciple tells us of this Ministry of His Love at the Last Supper,[a] and ever afterwards, in his writings and in his life, does he seem to bear them about with him, and to re-echo them. Ever since also have they remained the foundation-truth on which the Church has been built: the subject of her preaching, and the object of her experience.[b]

a St. John
xiii.
b Rom. iii.
24; 1 Cor.
vi. 20;
1 Tim. ii. 6;
1 Pet. i. 19;
1 John iv. 10

CHAPTER LXX.

IN JERICHO—A GUEST WITH ZACCHÆUS—THE HEALING OF
BLIND BARTIMÆUS—AT BETHANY, AND IN THE HOUSE OF
SIMON THE LEPER.

(St. Luke xix. 1–10; St. Matt. xx. 29–34; St. Mark x. 46–52; St. Luke
xviii. 35–43; St. John xi. 55–xii. 1; St. Matt. xxvi. 6–13; St. Mark
xiv. 3–9; St. John xii. 2–11.)

ONCE more, and now for the last time, were the fords of Jordan passed, and Christ was on the soil of Judæa proper. Behind Him were Peræa and Galilee; behind Him the Ministry of the Gospel by Word and Deed; before Him the final Act of His Life, towards which all had consciously tended. And He was coming openly, at the head of His Apostles, and followed by many disciples—a festive band going up to the Paschal Feast, of which Himself was to be 'the Lamb' of sacrifice.

The first station reached was Jericho, the 'City of Palms,' a distance of only about six hours from Jerusalem. The ancient City occupied not the site of the present wretched hamlet, but lay about half an hour to the north-west of it, by the so-called Elisha-Spring. A second spring rose an hour further to the north-north-west. The water of these springs distributed by aqueducts gave, under a tropical sky, unsurpassed fertility to the rich soil along the 'plain' of Jericho, which is about twelve or fourteen miles wide. Herod the Great had first plundered, and then partially rebuilt, fortified, and adorned Jericho. It was here that he died. Long before, it had recovered its ancient fame for fertility and its prosperity. If to its special advantages of climate, soil, and productions we add that it lay on the caravan-road from Damascus and Arabia, that it was a great commercial and military centre, and lastly, its nearness to Jerusalem, to which it formed the last ' station ' on the road of the festive pilgrims from Galilee and Peræa —it will not be difficult to understand either its importance or its prosperity.

We can picture to ourselves the scene, as our Lord on that afternoon in early spring beheld it. There it was, indeed, already summer, for, as *Josephus* tells us, even in winter the inhabitants could only bear the lightest clothing of linen. It is protected by walls, flanked by four forts. These walls, the theatre, and the amphitheatre, have been built by Herod; the new palace and its splendid gardens are the work of Archelaus. All around wave groves of palms, rising in stately beauty; stretch gardens of roses, and especially sweet-scented balsam - plantations — the largest behind the royal gardens, of which the perfume is carried by the wind almost out to sea, and which may have given to the city its name (Jericho, ' the perfumed '). And in the streets of Jericho a motley throng meets : pilgrims from Galilee and Peræa, priests who have a ' station ' here, traders from all lands, who have come to purchase or to sell, or are on the great caravan-road from Arabia and Damascus—robbers and anchorites, wild fanatics, soldiers, courtiers, and busy publicans—for Jericho was the central station for the collection of tax and custom, both on native produce and on that brought from across Jordan.

It was through Jericho that Jesus, ' having entered,' was passing.[a] Tidings of the approach of the band, consisting of His disciples and Apostles, and headed by the Master Himself, must have preceded Him these six miles from the fords of Jordan. His Name, His Works, His Teaching—perhaps Himself, must have been known to the people of Jericho, just as they must have been aware of the feelings of the leaders of the people,

[a] St. Luke xix. 1-10

perhaps of the approaching great contest between them and the Prophet of Nazareth. Was He a good man; had He wrought those great miracles in the power of God or by Satanic influence—was He the Messiah or the Antichrist; would He bring salvation to the world, or entail ruin on His own nation: conquer or be destroyed? Close by was Bethany, whence tidings had come, most incredible yet unquestioned and unquestionable, of the raising of Lazarus. And yet the Sanhedrin—it was well known—had resolved on His death! At any rate there was no concealment about Him; and here, in face of all, and accompanied by His followers—humble and unlettered, but thoroughly convinced of His superhuman claims, and deeply attached—Jesus was going up to Jerusalem to meet His enemies!

It was the custom when a festive band passed through a place, that the inhabitants gathered in the streets to bid their brethren welcome. And on that afternoon surely scarce any one in Jericho but would go forth to see this pilgrim-band. A solid wall of onlookers before their gardens was this ' crowd ' along the road by which Jesus ' was to pass.' Would He only pass through the place, or be the guest of some of the leading priests in Jericho; would He teach or work any miracle, or silently go on His way to Bethany? Only one in all that crowd seemed unwelcome; alone, and out of place. It was the ' chief of the Publicans '—the head of the tax and customs department. As his name shows, he was a Jew: but yet that very name Zacchæus, ' Zakkai ' ' the just ' or 'pure,' sounded like mockery. We know in what repute Publicans were held, and what opportunities of wrong-doing and oppression they possessed. And from his after-confession it is only too evident that Zacchæus had to the full used them for evil. And he had got that for which he had given up alike his nation and his soul: ' he was rich.' If, as Christ had taught, it was harder for any rich man to enter the Kingdom of Heaven than for a camel to pass through the eye of a needle, what of him who had gotten his riches by such means?

The narrative is singularly detailed and pictorial.

Zacchæus, trying to push his way through ' the press,' and repulsed ; Zacchæus, ' little of stature,' and unable to look over the shoulders of others.

Needless questions have been asked as to the import of Zacchæus' wish ' to see who Jesus was.' It is just this vagueness of desire, which Zacchæus himself does not understand, that is characteristic. And since he cannot otherwise succeed, he climbs up one of those wide-spreading sycamores in a garden, perhaps close to his own house, along the only road by which Jesus can pass—' to see Him.' Now the band is approaching, through that double living wall : first, the Saviour, viewing the crowd, but with different thoughts from theirs—surrounded by His Apostles, the face of each expressive of such feelings as were uppermost ; conspicuous among them, he who ' carried the bag,' with furtive, uncertain glance here and there, as one who seeks to gather himself up to a terrible deed. Behind them are the disciples, men and women, who are going up with Him to the Feast. Of all persons in that crowd the least noted, the most hindered in coming—and yet the one most concerned, was the Chief Publican. Never more self-unconscious was Zacchæus than at the moment when Jesus was entering that garden-road and passing under the overhanging branches of that sycamore, the crowd closing up behind, and following as He went along. Only one thought—without ulterior conscious object, temporal or spiritual—filled his whole being. The present absolutely held him—when those Eyes out of which heaven itself seemed to look upon earth, were upturned, and that Face of infinite grace, never to be forgotten, beamed upon him the welcome of recognition, and He uttered the self-spoken invitation in which the invited was the real Inviter, the guest the true Host.

As bidden by Christ, Zacchæus ' made haste and came down.' Under the influence of the Holy Ghost he ' received Him rejoicing.' Nothing was as yet clear to him, and yet all was joy within his soul. But a few steps farther, and they were at the house of the Chief Publican. But now the murmur of disappointment and anger ran through the accompanying crowd—which perhaps had not before heard what had passed between Jesus and the Publican—because He was gone to be guest with a man that was a sinner. And it was this sudden shock of opposition which awoke Zacchæus to full consciousness. In that moment Zacchæus saw it all: what his past had been, what his present was, what his future must be. Standing forth, not so much before the crowd as before the Lord, and scarcely conscious of the confession it implied—Zacchæus vowed fourfold restoration, as by a thief,[a] of what had become his through false accusation, as well as the half of all his goods to the poor. And so the whole current of his life had been turned in those few moments; and Zacchæus the public robber, the rich Chief of the Publicans, had become an almsgiver.

[a] Ex. xxii. 1

It was then that Jesus spake in the hearing of all for their and our teaching : ' This day became—arose—there salvation to this house,' ' forasmuch as,' truly and spiritually, ' this one also is a son of Abraham.' And as regards this man and all men, so long as time endureth : ' For the Son of Man came to seek and to save that which was lost.'

The Evangelic record passes with significant silence over that night in the house of Zacchæus. It was in the morning, when the journey in company with His disciples was resumed, that the next public incident occurred in the healing of the blind by the wayside.[b] It may have been that, as St. Matthew relates, there were *two* blind men sitting by the wayside, and that St. Luke and St. Mark mention only one—the latter by name as ' Bar Timæus '—because he was the spokesman.

[b] St. Matt. xx. 29-34; St. Mark x. 46-52; St. Luke xviii. 35-43

Once more the crowd was following Jesus, as He resumed the journey with His disciples. And there by the wayside, begging, sat the blind men. As they heard the tramp of many feet and the sound of many voices, they learned that Jesus of Nazareth was passing by. But what must their faith have been, when there, in Jericho, they not only owned Him as the true Messiah, but cried—in a

mode of address significant, as coming from Jewish lips:
'Jesus, Thou Son of David, have mercy on me!' It was
in accordance with what one might almost have expected—
certainly with the temper of Jericho, as we learnt it on
the previous evening, when 'many,' the 'multitude,' 'they
which went before,' would have bidden that cry for help
be silent as an unwarrantable intrusion and interruption.
But only all the louder and more earnest rose the petition,
as the blind felt that they might for ever be robbed of the
opportunity that was slipping past. And He, Who listens
to every cry of distress, heard this. He stood still, and
commanded the blind to be called. Then it was that the
sympathy of sudden hope seized the 'multitude'—the
wonder about to be wrought fell upon them, as they comforted the blind in the agony of rising despair with the
words, 'He calleth thee.'[a] As so often, we are
indebted to St. Mark for the vivid sketch of
what passed. We can almost see Bartimæus as, on receiving Christ's summons, he casts aside his upper garment
and hastily comes. That question: what he would that
Jesus should do unto him, must have been meant for those
around more than for the blind. The cry to the Son of
David had been only for mercy. It might have been for
alms—though, as the address, so the gift bestowed in
answer, would be right royal—'after the order of David.'
But the faith of the blind rose to the full height of the
Divine possibilities opened before them. Their inward
eyes had received capacity for The Light, before that of
earth lit up their long darkness. In the language of St.
Matthew, 'Jesus had compassion on them, and touched their
eyes.' This is one aspect of it. The other is that given by
St. Mark and St. Luke, in recording the words with which
He accompanied the healing: 'Thy faith hath saved thee.'

And these two results came of it: 'all the people,
when they saw it, gave praise unto God;' and as for
Bartimæus, though Jesus had bidden him 'go thy way,'
yet 'immediately he received his sight,' he 'followed Jesus in the way,' glorifying God.[b]

The arrival of the Paschal band from Galilee and Peræa

[a] St. Mark x. 49

[b] St. Luke

was not in advance of many others. In truth, most pilgrims from a distance would probably come to the Holy City some days before the Feast, for the sake of purification in the Temple, since those who for any reason needed such—and there would be few families that did not—generally deferred it till the festive season brought them to Jerusalem. We owe this notice, and that which follows,

^a St. John xi. 55-57 to St. John,[a] and in this again recognise the Jewish writer of the Fourth Gospel. It was only natural that these pilgrims should have sought for Jesus, and, when they did not find Him, discuss among themselves the probability of His coming to the Feast. His absence would, after the work which He had done these three years, the claim which He made, and the defiant denial of it by the priesthood and the Sanhedrin, have been regarded as a virtual surrender to the enemy. There was a time when He need not have appeared at the Feast —when, as we see, it was better He should not come. But that time was past. The chief priests and the Pharisees also knew it, and they 'had given commandment that, if any one knew where He was, he should show it, that they might take Him.' It would be better to ascertain where He lodged, and to seize Him before He appeared in public, in the Temple.

But it was not as they had imagined. Without concealment Christ came to Bethany, where Lazarus lived, whom He had raised from the dead. He came there six days before the Passover—and yet His coming was such

^b St. John xii. 1 that they could not 'take Him.'[b] They might as well take Him in the Temple; nay, more easily. For the moment His stay in Bethany became known, 'much people of the Jews' came out, not only for His sake, but to see that Lazarus whom He had raised from the dead. And of those who so came many went away believing. Thus one of their plans was frustrated. The Sanhedrin could perhaps not be moved to such flagrant

^c St. John xii. 10, 11 outrage of all Jewish Law, but 'the chief priests,' who had no such scruples, consulted how they might put Lazarus also to death.[c]

Yet, not until His hour had come could man do aught against Christ or His disciples. And in contrast to such scheming, haste, and search, we mark the calm and quiet of Him Who knew what was before Him. Jesus had arrived at Bethany six days before the Passover—that is, on a Friday. The day after was the Sabbath, and 'they made Him a supper.'ª It was the special festive meal of the Sabbath. The words of St. John seem to indicate that the meal was a public one, as if the people of Bethany had combined to do Him this honour, and so share the privilege of attending the feast. In point of fact, we know from St. Matthew and St. Mark that it took place 'in the house of Simon the Leper'—not, of course, an actual leper—but one who had been such. Among the guests is Lazarus; and, prominent in service, Martha; and Mary (the unnamed woman of the other two Gospels, which do not mention that household by name) is also true to her character. She had 'an alabaster' of 'spikenard genuine,' which was very precious. It held 'a litra,' which was 'a Roman pound,' and its value could not have been less than nearly 9*l*.

Remembering the fondness of Jewish women for such perfumes, it is, at least, not unreasonable to suppose that Mary may have had that 'alabaster' of very costly ointment from olden days, before she had learned to serve Christ. Then, when she came to know Him, and must have learned how constantly that Decease, of which He ever spoke, was before His Mind, she may have put it aside, 'kept it, against the day of His burying.' And now the decisive hour had come. Jesus may have told her, as He had told the disciples, what was before Him in Jerusalem at the Feast, and she would be far more quick to understand, even as she must have known far better than they, how great was the danger from the Sanhedrin. And it is this believing apprehension of the mystery of His Death on her part, and this preparation of deepest love for it—this mixture of sorrow, faith, and devotion—which made her deed so precious, that, wherever in the future the Gospel should be preached, this also that she had done should be

ª St. John
xii. 1

recorded for a memorial of her.[a]   And the more we think

a St. Matt. xxvi. 13

of it, the better can we understand how, at that last feast of fellowship, when all the other guests realised not—not even His disciples—how near the end was, she would 'come aforehand to anoint His Body for

b St. Mark xiv. 8

the burying.'[b]   Her faith made it a twofold anointing: that of the best Guest at the last feast, and that of preparation for that Burial which, of all others, she apprehended as so terribly near.   And so she poured the precious ointment over His Head, over His Feet—then, stooping over them, wiped them with her hair, as if not only in evidence of service and love, but in fellowship of His Death.[c]   'And the house was

c St. John

filled'—as to all time His House, the Church, is filled—'with the odour of the ointment.'

It is ever the light which throws the shadows of objects —and this deed of faith and love now cast the features of Judas in dark outlines against the scene.   He knew the nearness of Christ's Betrayal, and hated the more; she knew of the nearness of His precious Death, and loved the more.   It was not that he cared for the poor, when, taking the mask of charity, he simulated anger that such costly ointment had not been sold and the price given to the poor.   For he was essentially dishonest, ' a thief,' and covetousness was the underlying master-passion of his soul.   The money, claimed for the poor, would only have been used by himself.   Yet such was his pretence of righteousness, such his influence as 'a man of prudence' among the disciples, and such their weakness, that they,

d St. Mark xiv. 41

or at least ' some,'[d] expressed indignation among themselves and against her who had done the deed of love.   There is something inexpressibly sad, yet patient and tender, in Christ's 'Let her alone.'   That He Who was ever of the poor and with them, Who for our sakes became poor that through His poverty we might be made rich, should have to plead for a last service of love to Himself, and for Mary, and as against a Judas, seems indeed the depth of self-abasement.   Yet, even so, has this falsely-spoken plea for the poor become a real plea, since He has left us this, as it were, as His last charge, and that by His own Death, that we have the poor always with us. And so do even the words of covetous dishonesty become transformed into the command of charity, and the Church does constant service to Christ in the ministry to His poor.

CHAPTER LXXI.

THE FIRST DAY IN PASSION-WEEK—THE ROYAL ENTRY INTO JERUSALEM.

(St. Matt. xxi. 1–11; St. Mark xi. 1–11; St. Luke xix. 29–44; St. John xii. 12–19.)

AT length the time of the end had come. Jesus was about to make Entry into Jerusalem as King: King of the Jews, as Heir of David's royal line, with all of symbolic, typic, and prophetic import attaching to it. Yet not as Israel after the flesh expected its Messiah was the Son of David to make triumphal entrance, but as deeply and significantly expressive of His Mission and Work, and as of old the rapt seer had beheld afar off the outlined picture of the Messiah-King; not in the proud triumph of war-conquests, but in the ' meek ' rule of peace.

It was a day in the early spring of the year 29, when the festive procession set out from the home at Bethany. There can be no reasonable doubt as to the locality of that hamlet (the modern *El-'Azarîye*, ' of Lazarus '), perched on a broken rocky plateau on the other side of Olivet. More difficulty attaches to the identification of *Bethphage*, which is associated with it, the place not being mentioned in the Old Testament, though repeatedly, but with contradictory statements of locality, in Jewish writings. Perhaps the name Bethphage—' house of figs '—was given alike to that district generally, and to a little village close to Jerusalem where the district began.

Although all the four Evangelists relate Christ's Entry into Jerusalem, they seem to do so from different standpoints. The Synoptists accompany Him from Bethany, while St. John, in accordance with the general scheme of his narrative, seems to follow from Jerusalem that multitude which, on tidings of His approach, hastened to meet Him. It was probably soon after His outset that He sent the 'two disciples'—possibly Peter and John [a] —into 'the village over against' them—presumably Bethphage. There they would find by the side of the road an ass's colt tied, whereon never man had sat. We mark the significant symbolism of the latter, in connection with the general conditions of consecration to Jehovah [b] — and note in it, as also in the Mission of the Apostles, that this was intended by Christ to be His Royal and Messianic Entry. This colt they were to loose and to bring to Him.

[a] Comp. St. Luke xxii. 8

[b] Num. xix. 2; Deut. xxi. 3

The disciples found all as He had said. When they reached Bethphage, they saw by a doorway where two roads met the colt tied by its mother. As they loosed it, 'the owners' and 'certain of them that stood by' [c] asked their purpose, to which, as directed by the Master, they answered: 'The Lord [the Master, Christ] hath need of him,' when, as predicted, no further hindrance was offered.

[c] St. Mark; comp. also St. Matthew

We can understand how, so soon as from the bearing and the peculiar words of the disciples they understood their purpose, the owners of the ass and colt would grant the use of the colt for the solemn Entry into the City of the Teacher of Nazareth, Whom the multitude was so eagerly expecting; and again how, as from the gates of Jerusalem tidings spread of what had passed in Bethphage, the multitude would stream forth to meet Jesus.

Meantime Christ and those who followed Him from Bethany had entered on the well-known caravan-road from Jericho to Jerusalem. It is the most southern of three which converge close to the City, perhaps at the very place where the colt had stood tied. 'The road soon loses sight of Bethany. It is now a rough, but still broad and well-defined mountain-track, winding over rock and loose stones; a steep declivity on the left; the sloping shoulder of Olivet above on the right; fig-trees below and above, here and

there growing out of the rocky soil.' Somewhere here
the disciples who brought 'the colt' must have met Him.
They were accompanied by many, and immediately followed
by more. For, as already stated, Bethphage—we presume
the village—formed almost part of Jerusalem, and during
Easter-week must have been crowded by pilgrims, who
could not find accommodation within the City walls. And
the announcement that disciples of Jesus had just fetched
the beast of burden on which Jesus was about to enter
Jerusalem, must have quickly spread among the crowds
which thronged the Temple and the City. With these
went also a number of 'Pharisees,' their hearts full of
jealousy and hatred. As we shall presently see, it is of
importance to keep in mind this composition of the
'multitude.'

As the two disciples, accompanied or immediately followed by the multitude, brought 'the colt' to Christ, 'two
streams of people met'—the one coming from the City,
the other from Bethany. The disciples, who understood

a St. John
xii. 16 not,[a] till the light of the Resurrection-glory had
been poured on their minds, the significance of
'these things,' even after they had occurred, seem not even
to have guessed that it was of set purpose Jesus was about
to make His Royal Entry into Jerusalem. Their enthusiasm
seems only to have been kindled when they saw the procession from the town come to meet Jesus with palm-
branches cut down by the way, and greeting Him with
Hosanna-shouts of welcome. Then they spread their garments on the colt, and set Jesus thereon. Then also in
their turn they cut down branches from the trees and gardens
through which they passed, or plaited and twisted palm-

b St. Luke
xix. 37, 38 branches, and strewed them as a rude matting in
His way, while they joined in, and soon raised
to a much higher pitch [b] the Hosanna of welcoming praise.

They had now ranged themselves : the multitude which
had come from the City preceding, that which had come
with Him from Bethany following the triumphant progress
of Israel's King, 'meek, and sitting upon an ass, and a colt
the foal of an ass.' 'Gradually the long procession swept

up and over the ridge where first begins "the descent of the Mount of Olives" towards Jerusalem. At this point the first view is caught of the south-eastern corner of the City. The Temple and the more northern portions are hid by the slope of Olivet on the right; what is seen is only Mount Zion, now for the most part a rough field.' But at that time it rose, terrace upon terrace, from the Palace of the Maccabees and that of the High-Priest, a very city of palaces, till the eye rested in the summit on that castle, city, and palace, with its frowning towers and magnificent gardens, the royal abode of Herod, supposed to occupy the very site of the Palace of David. They had been greeting Him with Hosannas! But enthusiasm, especially in such a cause, is infectious. They were mostly stranger-pilgrims that had come from the City, chiefly because they had heard of the raising of Lazarus.[a] And now they must have questioned them which came from Bethany, who in turn related that of which themselves had been eyewitnesses.[b] It may have been just as the precise point of the road was reached where 'the City of David' first suddenly emerges into view, 'at the descent of the Mount of Olives,' 'that the whole multitude of the disciples began to rejoice and praise God with a loud voice for all the mighty works that they had seen.'[c] As the burning words of joy and praise, the record of what they had seen, passed from mouth to mouth, and they caught their first sight of 'the City of David,' adorned as a bride to welcome her King— Davidic praise to David's Greater Son wakened the echoes of old Davidic Psalms. 'Hosanna to the Son of David! Blessed be He that cometh in the Name of the Lord. . . . Blessed the Kingdom that cometh, the Kingdom of our father David. . . . Blessed be He that cometh in the Name of the Lord. . . . Hosanna . . . Hosanna in the highest. . . . Peace in heaven, and glory in the highest.'

They were but broken utterances, partly based upon Ps. cxviii., partly taken from it—the 'Hosanna,' or 'Save now,' and the 'Blessed be He that cometh in the Name of the Lord,'[d] forming part of the re-

a St. John xii. 18

b ver. 17

c St. Luke

d Ps. cxviii. 25, 26

sponses by the people with which this Psalm was chanted on certain of the most solemn festivals. At the same time it must be remembered that, according to Jewish tradition, Ps. cxviii. vv. 25–28 was also chanted antiphonally by the people of Jerusalem, as they went to welcome the festive pilgrims on their arrival, the latter always responding in the second clause of each verse, till the last verse of the Psalm [a] was reached, which was sung by both parties in unison, Psalm ciii. 17 being added by way of conclusion. But as 'the shout rang through the long defile,' carrying evidence far and wide, that, so far from condemning and forsaking, more than the ordinary pilgrim-welcome had been given to Jesus—the Pharisees, who had mingled with the crowd, turned to one another with angry frowns : ' Behold [see intently], how ye prevail nothing ! See—the world is gone after Him !' Then they made a desperate appeal to the Master Himself, Whom they so bitterly hated, to check and rebuke the honest zeal of His disciples. He had been silent hitherto, but now, with a touch of quick and righteous indignation, He pointed to the rocks and stones, telling those leaders of Israel that, if the people held their peace, the very stones would cry out.[b] Silence has fallen these many centuries upon Israel ; but the very stones of Jerusalem's ruin and desolateness have cried out that He, Whom in their silence they rejected, has come as King in the Name of the Lord.

[a] ver. 29

[b] St. Luke

' Again the procession advanced. The road descends a slight declivity, and the glimpse of the City is again withdrawn behind the intervening ridge of Olivet. A few moments and the path mounts again, it climbs a rugged ascent, it reaches a ledge of smooth rock, and in an instant the whole City bursts into view. . . . It is hardly possible to doubt that this rise and turn of the road—this rocky ledge—was the exact point where the multitude paused again, and " He, when He beheld the City, wept over it." ' Not with still weeping, as at the grave of Lazarus, but with loud and deep lamentation. The contrast was indeed terrible between the Jerusalem that rose before Him in all its beauty, glory, and security, and the Jerusalem which He saw in vision dimly rising on the sky, with the camp of the enemy round about it on every side, and the very 'stockade' which the Roman Legions raised; then, another scene in the shifting panorama, and the City laid with the ground, the bodies of her children among her ruins; and yet another scene: the silence and desolateness of death by the Hand of God—not one stone left upon another!

But for the present, on that bright spring-day, the weak, fickle populace streamed before Him through the City-gates, through the narrow streets, up the Temple-mount. Everywhere the tramp of their feet and the shout of their exclamations brought men, women, and children into the streets and on the housetops. The City was moved, and from mouth to mouth the question passed among the eager crowd of curious onlookers: 'Who is He?' And the multitude answered—not, this is Israel's Messiah-King, but: 'This is Jesus the Prophet of Nazareth of Galilee.' And so up into the Temple!

He alone spake not, but only looked round about upon all things, as if to view the field on which He was to suffer and die. And now the shadows of evening were creeping up; and, weary and sad, He once more returned with the twelve disciples to the shelter and rest of Bethany.

CHAPTER LXXII.

THE SECOND DAY IN PASSION-WEEK—THE BARREN FIG-TREE
—THE CLEANSING OF THE TEMPLE—THE HOSANNA OF
THE CHILDREN.

(St. Matt. xxi. 12–22; St. Mark xi. 15–26; St. Luke xix. 45–48.)

How the King of Israel spent the night after the triumphal

a St. Mark i. 35; St. Luke v. 16; St. Matt. xiv. 23; St. Luke vi. 12; ix. 28

Entry into His City and Temple, we may venture reverently to infer. We know how often His nights had been spent in lonely prayer,[a] and surely it is not too bold to associate such thoughts with the first night in Passion-week Thus also we can most readily account for that exhaustion and faintness of hunger, which next morning made Him seek fruit on the fig-tree on His way to the City.

It was very early on the morning of the second day in Passion-week (Monday), when Jesus with His disciples left Bethany. In the fresh, crisp, spring air, after the exhaustion of that night, 'He hungered.' By the roadside, as so often in the East, a solitary tree grew in the rocky soil. It must have stood on an eminence, where it caught the sunshine and warmth, for He saw it 'afar off,'[a] green, against the sky. 'It was not the season of figs,' but the tree, covered with leaves, attracted His attention. It might have been that they hid some of the fruit which hung through the winter, or else the springing fruits of the new crop. For it is a well-known fact that in Palestine 'the fruit appears before the leaves;' and that this fig-tree, whether from its exposure or soil, was precocious, is evident from the fact that it was in leaf, which is quite unusual at that season on the Mount of Olives. The old fruit would, of course, have been edible, and in regard to the unripe fruit we have the evidence of the Mishnah, confirmed by the Talmud, that the unripe fruit was eaten so soon as it began to assume a red colour—as it is expressed, 'in the field, with bread,' or, as we understand it, by those whom hunger overtook in the fields, whether working or travelling. But in the present case there was neither old nor new fruit, 'but leaves only.' It was evidently a barren fig-tree, cumbering the ground, and to be hewn down. Our mind almost instinctively reverts to the Parable of the Barren Fig-tree, which Jesus had so lately spoken.[b] To Him, Who but yesterday had wept over the Jerusalem that knew not the day of its visitation, and over which the sharp axe of judgment was already lifted this fig-tree with its luxuriant leaves must have recalled, with pictorial vividness, the scene of the previous day. Israel was that barren fig-tree; and the leaves only covered their nakedness, as erst they had that of our first parents after their Fall. And the judgment symbolically

[a] St. Mark

[b] St. Luke xiii. 6-9

H H

spoken in the Parable must be symbolically executed in this leafy fig-tree, barren when searched for fruit by the Master. According to the more detailed account of St. Mark, it was only next morning, when they again passed by, that they noticed the fig-tree had withered from its very roots. The spectacle attracted their attention, and vividly recalled the Words of Christ, to which on the previous day they had, perhaps, scarcely attached sufficient importance. And it was the suddenness and completeness of the judgment that had been denounced which now struck Peter, rather than its symbolic meaning. Peter's words are at least capable of this interpretation, that the fig-tree had withered in consequence of, rather than by the Word of Christ. His answer combined all that they needed to learn. It pointed to the typical lesson of what had taken place: the need of realising, simple faith, the absence of which was the cause of Israel's leafy barrenness, and which, if present and active, could accomplish all, however impossible it might seem by outward means. To one who 'shall not doubt in his heart, but shall believe that what he saith cometh to pass, it shall be to him.' And this general principle of the Kingdom, which to the reverent believer needs neither explanation nor limitation, received its further application, specially to the Apostles in their coming need: 'Therefore I say unto you, whatsoever things, praying, ye ask for, believe that ye have received them [not, in the counsel of God, but actually, in answer to the prayer of faith], and it shall be to you.'

On the previous afternoon, when Christ had come to the Temple, the services were probably over, and the Sanctuary comparatively empty of worshippers and of those who there carried on their traffic. When treating of the first cleansing of the Temple, at the beginning of Christ's Ministry, sufficient has been said to explain the character and mode of that nefarious traffic, the profits of which went to the leaders of the priesthood, as also how popular indignation was roused alike against this trade and the traders. We need not here recall the words of Christ; Jewish authorities sufficiently describe, in even stronger terms, this transformation of ' the House of Prayer' into ' a den of robbers.' If, when beginning to do the ' business' of His Father, and for the first time publicly presenting Himself with Messianic claim, it was fitting He should take such authority, and first ' cleanse the Temple,' much more was this appropriate now, at the close of His Work, when as King He had entered His City and publicly claimed authority. At the first it had been for teaching and warning, now it was in symbolic judgment; what and as He then began, that and so He now finished. Accordingly, as we compare the words, and even some of the acts, of the first ' cleansing' with those accompanying and explaining the second, we find the latter bearing a different character —that of final judicial sentence.

Nor did the Temple-authorities now, as on the former occasion, seek to raise the populace against Him, or challenge His authority by demanding the warrant of ' a sign.' The contest had reached quite another stage. They heard what He said in their condemnation, and with bitter hatred in their hearts sought for some means to destroy Him. But fear of the people restrained their violence. For marvellous indeed was the power which He wielded. With rapt attention the people hung on His lips,[a] 'astonished' at those new and blessed truths which dropped from them. By His authority the Temple was cleansed of the unholy, thievish traffic which a corrupt priesthood carried on, and so for the time restored to the solemn Service of God; and that purified House now became the scene of Christ's teaching, when He spake those words of truth and of comfort concerning the Father— thus realising the prophetic promise of ' a House of Prayer for all the nations.'[b] And as those traffickers were driven from the Temple, and He spake, there flocked in from porches and Temple-Mount sufferers —the blind and the lame—to get healing to body and soul. It was truly spring-time in that Temple, and the boys that gathered about their fathers, and looked in turn from their faces of wonderment and enthusiasm to the Godlike Face

[a] St. Luke

[b] St. Mark

of the Christ, and then on those healed sufferers, took up the echoes of the welcome at His entrance into Jerusalem —in their simplicity understanding and applying them better—as they burst into 'Hosanna to the Son of David!'

It rang through the courts and porches of the Temple, this Children's Hosanna. They heard it, whom the wonders He had spoken and done, so far from leading to repentance and faith, had only filled with indignation. Once more in their impotent anger they sought, as the Pharisees had done on the day of His Entry, by a hypocritical appeal to His reverence for God, not only to mislead, and so to use His very love of the truth against the truth, but to betray Him into silencing those Children's voices. But not from the great, the wise, nor the learned, but ' out of the mouth of babes and sucklings ' has He ' perfected praise.'

CHAPTER LXXIII.

THE THIRD DAY IN PASSION-WEEK—THE QUESTION OF CHRIST'S AUTHORITY—THE QUESTION OF TRIBUTE TO CÆSAR—THE WIDOW'S FARTHING—THE GREEKS WHO SOUGHT TO SEE JESUS.

(St. Matt. xxi. 23–27 ; St. Mark xi. 27–33 ; St. Luke xx. 1–8 ; St. Matt. xxii. 15–22 ; St. Mark xii. 13–17 ; St. Luke xx. 20–26 ; St. Matt. xxii. 41–46 ; St. Luke xxi. 1–4 ; St. John xii. 20–50.)

THIS chapter will be devoted to the *events* of the third day in Passion-Week.

1. As usually, the day commenced[a] with teaching in the Temple.[b] We gather this from the expression : ' as He was walking,'[c] viz., in one of the Porches, where, as we know, considerable freedom of meeting, conversing, or even teaching, was allowed. It will be remembered that on the previous day the authorities had been afraid to interfere with Him. But with the night and morning other counsels had come. From the

[a] St. Matthew
[b] St. Luke
[c] St. Mark

formal manner in which ' the chief priests, the scribes, and the elders' are introduced,[a] and from the circumstance that they so met Christ immediately on His entry into the Temple, we can scarcely doubt that a meeting, although informal, of the authorities had been held to concert measures against the growing danger. Yet, even so, they dared not directly oppose Him, but endeavoured, by attacking Him on the one point where He seemed to lay Himself open to it, to arrogate to themselves the appearance of strict legality, and so to turn popular feeling against Him.

[a] St. Mark

For there was no principle more firmly established by universal consent than that authoritative teaching required previous authorisation. Indeed, this logically followed from the principle of Rabbinism. All teaching must be authoritative, since it was traditional—approved by authority, and handed down from teacher to disciple. The highest honour of a scholar was that he was like a well-plastered cistern, from which not a drop had leaked of what had been poured into it. The ultimate appeal in cases of discussion was always to some great authority, whether an individual Teacher or a Decree by the Sanhedrin. And to decide differently from authority was either the mark of ignorant assumption or the outcome of daring rebellion, in either case to be visited with ' the ban.' And this was at least one aspect of the controversy as between the chief authorities and Jesus. No one would have thought of interfering with a mere Haggadist —a popular expositor, preacher, or teller of legends. But authoritatively to teach required other warrant. In fact, there was regular ordination to the office of Rabbi, Elder, and Judge, for the three functions were combined in one.

At whatever periods this practice may have been introduced, it is at least certain that, at the time of our Lord, no one would have ventured authoritatively to teach without proper Rabbinic authorisation. The question therefore with which the Jewish authorities met Christ, while teaching, was one which had a very real meaning, and appealed to the habits and feelings of the people who listened to Jesus. Otherwise also it was cunningly framed. For it did not merely challenge Him for teaching, but also asked for His authority in what He did; referring not only to His Work generally, but perhaps especially to what had happened on the previous day. They were not there to oppose Him; but when a man did as He had done in the Temple, it was their duty to verify his credentials. Finally, the alternative question reported by St. Mark: ' or '—if Thou hast not proper Rabbinic commission—' who gave Thee this authority to do these things?' seems clearly to point to their contention, that the power which Jesus wielded was delegated to Him by none other than Beelzebul.

But the Lord answered their question, though He also exposed the cunning and cowardice which prompted it. To the challenge for His authority, and the dark hint about Satanic agency, He replied by an appeal to the Baptist. He had borne full witness to the Mission of Christ from the Father, and ' all men counted John, that he was a prophet indeed.' Were they satisfied? What was their view of the Baptism in preparation for the Coming of Christ? They would not, or could not, answer. If they said the Baptist was a prophet, this implied not only the authorisation of the Mission of Jesus, but the call to believe on Him. On the other hand, they were afraid publicly to disown John. And so they were self-condemned, when they pleaded ignorance—a plea so grossly and manifestly dishonest, that Christ could refuse further discussion with them on this point.

2. Foiled in their endeavour to involve Him with the ecclesiastical, they next attempted the more dangerous device of bringing Him into collision with the civil authorities. Remembering the ever watchful jealousy of Rome, the tyranny of Pilate, and the low artifices of Herod, ● St. Luke who was at that time in Jerusalem,[a] we instinc- xxiii. 7 tively feel how even the slightest compromise on the part of Jesus in regard to the authority of Cæsar would have been absolutely fatal. If it could have been proved on undeniable testimony that Jesus had declared

Himself on the side of, or even encouraged, the so-called
' Nationalist' party, He would have quickly perished,
like Judas of Galilee.[a] The Jewish leaders
would thus have readily accomplished their object, and its unpopularity have recoiled only on the
hated Roman power. How great the danger was which
threatened Jesus may be gathered from this, that, despite
His clear answer, the charge that He perverted the
nation, forbidding to give tribute to Cæsar, was actually among those brought against Him before
Pilate.[b]

a Acts v. 37

b St. Luke
xxiii. 2

The object of the plot was to ' spy ' out His inmost
thoughts,[c] and, if possible, ' entangle ' Him in
His talk.[d] For this purpose it was not the old
Pharisees whom He knew and would have dis-
trusted, who came, but some of their disciples—apparently
earnest conscientious men. With them had combined
certain of ' the Herodians '—not a sect nor religious school,
but a political party at the time. We know comparatively
little of the deeper political movements in Judæa; but we
cannot be greatly mistaken in regarding the Herodians
as a party which honestly accepted the House of Herod as
occupants of the Jewish throne.

c St. Luke
d St. Mat-
thew

Feigning themselves just men, these now came to
Jesus with honeyed words, intended not, only to disarm
His suspicions, but, by an appeal to His fearlessness and
singleness of moral purpose, to induce Him to commit
Himself without reserve. Was it lawful for them to give
tribute unto Cæsar, or not ? were they to pay the capita-
tion tax of one drachm, or to refuse it ? We know how
later Judaism would have answered such a question. It
lays down the principle that the right of coinage implies
the authority of levying taxes, and indeed constitutes such
evidence of *de facto* government as to make it duty absolutely to submit to it. On the other hand, there was
a strong party in the land, with which, not only politically
but religiously, many of the noblest spirits would sym-
pathise, which maintained that to pay the tribute-money
to Cæsar was virtually to own his royal authority, and

so to disown that of Jehovah, Who alone was Israel's King. The scruple expressed by these men would therefore, if genuine, have called forth sympathy. But what was the alternative here presented to Christ? To have said *No*, would have been to command rebellion; to have said simply *Yes*, would have been to give a painful shock to deep feeling, and, in a sense, in the eyes of the people, the lie to His own claim of being Israel's Messiah-King.

But the Lord escaped from this 'temptation'—because, being true, it was no real temptation to Him. Their hypocrisy He immediately perceived and exposed, in this also responding to their appeal of being 'true.' It was a very real answer, when, pointing to the image and inscription on the coin for which He had called, He said, 'What is Cæsar's render to Cæsar, and what is God's to God.'[a] It did far more than rebuke their hypocrisy and presumption; it answered not only that question of theirs to all earnest men of that time, as it would present itself to their minds, but it settles to all time and for all circumstances the principle underlying it. Christ's Kingdom is not of this world; a true Theocracy is not inconsistent with submission to the secular power in things that are really its own; politics and religion neither include, nor yet exclude, each other: they are side by side, in different domains. The State is Divinely sanctioned, and religion is Divinely sanctioned—and both are equally the ordinance of God.

a St. Mark xii. 17

It was an answer which elevated the controversy into quite another sphere, where there was no conflict between what was due to God and to man. Nor did it speak harshly of the Nationalist aspirations, nor yet plead the cause of Rome. It said not whether the rule of Rome was right or should be permanent—but only what all must have felt to be Divine. And so they who had come to 'entangle' Him 'went away,' not convinced nor converted, but marvelling exceedingly.

3. Weary with the contention, the Master had left those to whom He had spoken in the Porches, and while the crowd wrangled about His Words or His Person, had

ascended the flight of steps which led from 'the Terrace' into the Temple-building. From these steps He could gain full view into ' the Court of the Women,' into which they opened. On these steps, or within the gate (for in no other place was it lawful), He sat Him down, watching the multitude. The time of Sacrifice was past, and those who still lingered had remained for private devotion, for private sacrifices, or to pay their vows and offerings. Although the topography of the Temple, especially of this part of it, is not without its difficulties, we know that under the colonnades which surrounded ' the Court oᶜ the Women,' but still left in the middle room for more than 15,000 worshippers, provision was made for receiving religious and charitable contributions. All along these colonnades were the thirteen trumpet-shaped boxes; somewhere here also we must locate two chambers: that of ' the silent,' for gifts to be distributed in secret to the children of the pious poor, and that where votive vessels were deposited. Perhaps there was here also a special chamber for offerings. These ' trumpets' bore each inscriptions, marking the objects of contribution—whether to make up for past neglect, to pay for certain sacrifices, to provide incense, wood, or for other gifts.

As they passed to this or that treasury-box, some wore an appearance of self-righteousness, some of ostentation, some as cheerfully performing a happy duty. ' Many that were rich cast in much '—for such was the tendency that (as already stated) a law had to be enacted, forbidding the gift to the Temple of more than a certain proportion of one's possessions.

And as Jesus sat watching on these steps, His gaze was riveted by a solitary figure. The words of St. Mark sketch a story of singular pathos ' It was one pauper widow.' We can see her coming alone, as if ashamed to mingle with the crowd of rich givers; ashamed to have her offering seen; ashamed perhaps to bring it; a ' widow,' in the garb of a desolate mourner; her condition, appearance, and bearing that of a ' pauper.' He observed her closely and read her truly. She held in her hand only the smallest coins : 'two Perutahs '—and it should be known that it was not lawful to contribute a less amount. Together these two Perutahs made what was the ninety-sixth part of a *denar*, itself of the value of about sevenpence. But it was 'all her living.' And of this she now made humble offering unto God. He spake not to her words of encouragement, for she walked by faith ; He offered not promise of return, for her reward was in heaven. Yet though He spake not to her, the sunshine of His words must have fallen into the desolateness of her heart ; and, though perhaps she knew not why, that must have been a happy day when she gave up 'her whole living ' unto God. And so perhaps is every sacrifice for God all the more blessed, when we know not of its blessedness.

4. One other event remains to be recorded on that day.[a] But so closely is it connected with what the Lord afterwards spoke, that the two cannot be separated. It is narrated only by St. John, who tells it as one of a series of progressive manifestations of the Christ : first, in His Entry into the City, and then in the Temple—successively, to the Greeks, by the Voice from Heaven, and before the people.

a St. John xii. 20-50

It was, as we suppose, the evening of a long day of teaching. As the sun had been hastening towards its setting in red, He had spoken of that other sun-setting, with the sky all aglow in judgment, and of the darkness that was to follow—but also of the better Light that would rise in it. And in those Temple-porches they had been hearing Him—seeing Him in His wonder-working yesterday, hearing Him in His wonder-speaking that day—those ' men of other tongues.' They were ' Proselytes,' Greeks by birth, who had groped their way to the porch of Judaism, just as the first streaks of the light were falling within upon its altar.

And so, as the shadows gathered around the Temple-court and porches, they would fain have ' seen ' Him, not afar off, but near : spoken to Him. They had become ' Proselytes of Righteousness,' they would become disciples of 'the Lord our Righteousness ; ' as Proselytes they had

come to Jerusalem 'to worship,' and they would learn to
praise. Yet, in the modesty of their religious childhood,
they dared not go to Jesus directly, but came with their
request to Philip of Bethsaida. We know not why to him:
whether from family connections, or that his education
or previous circumstances connected Philip with these
'Greeks,' or whether anything in his position in the Apostolic circle, or something that had just occurred, influenced
their choice. And he also—such was the ignorance of the
Apostles of the inmost meaning of their Master—dared
not go directly to Jesus, but went to his own townsman,
who had been his early friend and fellow-disciple, and now
stood so close to the Person of the Master—Andrew, the
brother of Simon Peter. Together the two came to Jesus,
Andrew apparently foremost. The answer of Jesus implies
what, at any rate, we should have expected, that the
request of these Gentile converts was granted, though this
is not expressly stated, and it is extremely difficult to
determine whether, and what portion of what He spake
was addressed to the Greeks, and what to the disciples.

But it is sufficiently clear to us that our Lord spake
primarily to these Greeks, and secondarily to His disciples,
of the meaning of His impending Death, of the necessity
of faithfulness to Him in it, and of the blessing attaching
thereto. He was not unconscious of the awful realities
which this involved.[a] He was true Man, and
His Human Soul was troubled in view of it:
True Man, therefore He felt it; True Man, therefore He
spake it, and so also sympathised with them in their coming
struggle. Truly Man, but also truly more than Man—and
hence both the expressed desire, and at the same time the
victory over that desire: 'What shall I say? "Father,
save Me from this hour? But for this cause came I unto
this hour!"' And the seeming discord is resolved, as
both the Human and the Divine in the Son—faith and
sight—join in glorious accord: 'Father, glorify Thy
Name!'

Such appeal and prayer, made in such circumstances,
could not have remained unacknowledged, if He was the

a St. John xii. 27, 28 a

Messiah, Son of God. As at His Baptism, so at this Baptism of self-humiliation and absolute submission to suffering, came the Voice from Heaven, audible to all, but its words intelligible only to Him : ' I both glorified it, and will again glorify it ! ' ᵃ Words these, which carried the Divine seal of confirmation to all Christ's past work, and assured it for that which was to come. The words of confirmation could only be for Himself; ' the Voice' was for all. What mattered it, that some spoke of it as thunder on a spring-evening, while others, with more reason, thought of Angel-Voices ? To Him it bore the assurance, which had all along been the ground of His claims, as it was the comfort in His Sufferings, that, as God had in the past glorified Himself in the Son, so would it be in the future in the perfecting of the work given Him to do. And this He now spake, as, looking on those Greeks as the emblem and first-fruits of the work finished in His Passion, He saw of the travail of His Soul and was satisfied. Of both He spake in the prophetic present. To His view judgment had already come to this world, as it lay in the power of the Evil One, since the Prince of it was cast out from his present rule. And in place of it the Crucified Christ, ' lifted up out of the earth ' —in the twofold sense—was, as the result of His Work, drawing, with sovereign, conquering power, ' all' unto Him, and up with Him.

ᵃ St. John xii. 28 b-33

The Jews who heard it so far understood Him, that His words referred to His removal from earth, or His Death, since this was a common Jewish mode of expression.ᵇ But even in what they understood, they had a difficulty. They understood Him to imply that He would be taken from earth ; and yet they had always been taught from the Scriptures that the Messiah was, when fully manifested, to abide for ever, or, as the Rabbis put it, that His Reign was to be followed by the Resurrection. Or did He refer to any other One by the expression ' Son of Man ' ? Into the controversial part of their question the Lord did not enter ; nor would it have been fitting to have done so in that ' hour.' But to their inquiry He fully

ᵇ vv. 34-36 a

replied, and that with such earnest, loving admonition as became His last address in the Temple. Yes; it was so! But a little while would the Light be among them. Let them hasten to avail themselves of it, lest darkness overtake them—and he that walked in darkness knew not whither he went. While they still had 'the Light,' would that they might learn to believe in the Light, that so they might become the children of Light!

They were His last words of appeal to them, ere He *a* St. John withdrew to spend His Sabbath of soul before the xii. 36 *b* Great Contest.[a] And the writer of the fourth Gospel gathers up, by way of epilogue, the great contrast between Israel and Christ.[b] Although He had *b* vv. 37-43 shown so many miracles, they believed not on Him—and this their wilful unbelief was the fulfilment of Esaias' prophecy of old concerning the *c* Is. liii. 1 Messiah.[c]

Such was Israel. On the other hand, what was the summary of the Christ's activity? His testimony now rose so *d* St. John loud as to be within hearing of all ('Jesus cried').[d] xii. 44 From first to last that testimony had pointed from Himself up to the Father. Its substance was the reality and the realisation of that which the Old Testament had infolded and gradually unfolded to Israel, and through Israel to the world: the Fatherhood of God. To believe on Him *e* vv. 45-48 was really not faith in Him, but faith in Him that sent Him. A step higher: To behold Christ was to behold Him that had sent Him.[e]

Once more, and more emphatic than ever, was the final *f* vv. 49, 50 appeal to His Mission by the Father.[f] From first to last it had not been His own work: what He should say, and what He should speak, the Father 'Himself' had given Him commandment. Nay, this commandment, and what He spoke in it, was not mere teaching, nor Law: it was Life everlasting. The things which He spake, He spake as the Father said unto Him.

These two things: concerning the history of Israel and their necessary unbelief, and concerning the Christ as God-sent, God-witnessed, God-revealing, bringing light and life as the Father's gift and command—the Christ as absolutely surrendering Himself to this Mission and embodying it—are the sum of the Gospel-narratives. They explain their meaning, and set forth their object and lessons.

CHAPTER LXXIV.

THE THIRD DAY IN PASSION-WEEK—THE SADDUCEES AND THE RESURRECTION—THE SCRIBE AND THE GREAT COMMANDMENT—QUESTION TO THE PHARISEES, AND FINAL WARNING AGAINST THEM.

(St. Matt. xxii. 23–33; St. Mark xii. 18–27; St. Luke xx. 27–39; St. Matt. xxii. 34–40; St. Mark xii. 28–34; St. Matt. xxii. 41–46; St. Mark xii. 35–40; St. Luke xx. 40–47; St. Matt. xxiii.)

WE remember that during the whole previous history Christ had only on one occasion come into public conflict with the Sadducees, when, characteristically, they had ᵃ St. Matt. asked of Him 'a sign from heaven.'[a] Their xvi. 1 Rationalism would lead them to treat the whole movement as the outcome of ignorant fanaticism. Nevertheless, when Jesus assumed such a position in the Temple, and was evidently to such extent swaying the people, it behoved them, if only to guard their position, no longer to stand by. Possibly, the discomfiture and powerlessness of the Pharisees may also have had their influence. At any rate, the impression left is that those of them who now went to Christ were delegates, and that the question which they put had been well planned.

Their object was certainly not serious argument, but to use the much more dangerous weapon of ridicule. Persecution the populace might have resented; for open opposition all would have been prepared; but to come with icy politeness and philosophic calm, and by a well-turned question to reduce the renowned Galilean Teacher to silence, and show the absurdity of His teaching, would have been to inflict on His cause the most damaging blow.

Had the Sadducees succeeded, they would at the same time have gained a signal triumph for their tenets, and defeated, together with the Galilean Teacher, their own Pharisaic opponents. The subject of attack was to be the Resurrection—the same which is still the favourite topic for the appeals of the coarser forms of infidelity to 'the common sense' of the masses.

The Sadducees here would allow no appeal to the highly poetic language of the Prophets, to whom, at any rate, they attached less authority; but demanded proof from that clear and precise letter of the Law, every tittle and iota of which the Pharisees exploited for their doctrinal inferences, and from which alone they derived them. Here, also, it was the Nemesis of Pharisaism, that the postulates of their system laid it open to attack. In vain would the Pharisees appeal to Isaiah, Ezekiel, Daniel, or the Psalms. To such an argument as from the words, 'this people will rise up,'[a] the Sadducees would rightly reply that the context forbade the application to the Resurrection; to the quotation of Isaiah xxvi. 19, they would answer that that promise must be understood spiritually, like the vision of the dry bones in Ezekiel; while such a reference as to this, 'causing the lips of those that are asleep to speak,'[b] would scarcely require serious refutation.

a Deut. xxxi. 16
b Cant. vii. 9

And the additions with which the Pharisees had encumbered the doctrine of the Resurrection would not only surround it with fresh difficulties, but deprive the simple fact of its majesty. Thus, it was a point in discussion whether a person would rise in his clothes, which one Rabbi tried to establish by a reference to the grain of wheat, which was buried 'naked,' but rose clothed. Indeed, some Rabbis held that a man would rise in exactly the same clothes in which he had been buried, while others denied this. On the other hand, it was beautifully argued that body and soul must be finally judged together, so that, in their contention to which of them the sins of man had been due, justice might be meted out to each—or rather to the two in their combination, as in their combination they had sinned. Again, it was inferred from the apparition of Samuel[a] that the risen would look exactly as in life—have even the same bodily defects, such as lameness, blindness, or deafness. It was argued that they were only afterwards to be healed, lest enemies might say that God had not healed them when they were alive, but that He did so when they were dead, and that they were perhaps not the same persons. In some respects even more strange was the contention that, in order to secure that all the pious of Israel should rise on the sacred soil of Palestine,[b] there were cavities underground in which the body would roll till it reached the Holy Land, there to rise to newness of life.

[a] 1 Sam. xxviii. 14

[b] Is. xlii. 5

But all the more that it was so keenly controverted by heathens, Sadducees, and heretics, as appears from many reports in the Talmud, and that it was so encumbered with realistic legends, should we admire the tenacity with which the Pharisees clung to this doctrine. The hope of the Resurrection-world appears in almost every religious utterance of Israel. It is one of the few dogmas denial of which involves, according to the Mishnah, the loss of eternal life, the Talmud explaining—almost in the words of Christ—that in the retribution of God this is only ' measure according to measure.' It is venerable even in its exaggeration that only our ignorance fails to perceive it in every section of the Bible, and to hear it in every commandment of the Law.

But in the view of Christ the Resurrection would necessarily occupy a different place. It was the innermost shrine in the Sanctuary of His Mission, towards which He steadily tended ; it was also, at the same time, the living corner-stone of that Church which He had builded, and its spire, which, as with uplifted finger, ever pointed all men heavenwards. But of such thoughts connected with His Resurrection Jesus could not have spoken to the Sadducees; they would have been unintelligible at that time even to His own disciples. He met the cavil of the Sadducees with words most lofty and spiritual, yet such as they could understand, and which, if they had received them, would have led them far beyond the standpoint of the Pharisees.

The story under which the Sadducees conveyed their sneer was also intended covertly to strike at their Pharisaic opponents. The ancient ordinance of marrying a brother's
^{a Deut. xxv. 5 &c.} childless widow [a] had more and more fallen into discredit, as its original motive ceased to have influence. But what here most interests us is, that what are called in the Talmud the ' Samaritans,' but, as we judge, the Sadducees, held the opinion that the command to marry a brother's widow only applied to a betrothed wife, not to one that had actually been wedded. This gives point to their controversial question, as addressed to Jesus.

A case such as they told, of a woman who had successively been married to seven brothers, might, according to Jewish Law, have really happened. Their question now was, whose wife she was to be in the Resurrection. This, of course, on the assumption of the grossly materialistic views of the Pharisees. In this the Sadducean cavil was, in a sense, anticipating certain objections of modern materialism. It proceeded on the assumption that the relations of time would apply to eternity, and the conditions of the things seen hold true in regard to those that are unseen. But perchance it is otherwise; and the future may reveal what in the present we do not see.

In His argument against the Sadducees Christ first
^{b St. Matt. xxii. 29, 30, and parallel} appealed to the power of God.[b] What God would work was quite other than they imagined · not a mere re-awakening, but a transformation. The world to come was not to be a reproduction of that which had passed away—else why should it have passed away?—but a regeneration and renovation ; and the body with which we were to be clothed would be like that which Angels bear. What, therefore, in our present relations is of the earth, and of our present body of sin and corruption, will cease; what is eternal in them will continue. But the power of God will transform all—the present terrestrial into the future heavenly, the body of humiliation into one of exaltation. Nor ought questions here to rise, like dark

clouds, such as of the perpetuity of those relations which
on earth are not only so precious to us, but so holy.
Assuredly they will endure, as all that is of God and good ;
only what in them is earthly will cease, or rather be transformed with the body. Nay, and we shall also recognise each
other, not only by the fellowship of the soul ; but as even
now the mind impresses its stamp on the features, so
then, when all shall be quite true, shall the soul body
itself forth, fully impress itself on the outward appearance,
and for the first time shall we then fully recognise those
whom we shall now fully know—with all of earth that was
in them left behind, and all of God and good fully developed
and ripened into perfectness of beauty.

But our Lord would not merely reply, He would
answer the Sadducees. Of course, as speaking to the
Sadducees, He remained on the ground of the Pentateuch ;
and yet it was not only to the Law but to the whole Bible
that He appealed, nay, to that which underlay Revelation
itself : the relation between God and man. He Who, not
only historically but in the fullest sense, calls Himself the
God of Abraham, of Isaac, and of Jacob, cannot leave them
dead. Revelation implies, not merely a fact of the past—
as is the notion which traditionalism attaches to it—a dead
letter ; it means a living relationship. ' He is not the
God of the dead, but of the living, for all live unto Him.'

The Sadducees were silenced, the multitude was
astonished, and even from some of the Scribes the admission was involuntarily wrung : ' Teacher, Thou hast
beautifully said.' One point, however, still claims our
attention. It is curious that, as regards both these argu-
ments of Christ, Rabbinism offers statements closely
similar. Thus, it is recorded as one of the frequent sayings of a later Rabbi, that in the world to come there
would be neither eating nor drinking, fruitfulness nor
increase, business nor envy, hatred nor strife, but that the
just would sit with crowns on their heads, and feast on the
splendour of the Shekhinah. This reads like a Rabbinic
adaptation of the saying of Christ. As regards the other
point, the Talmud reports a discussion on the Resurrection

between 'Sadducees,' or perhaps Jewish heretics (Jewish-Christian heretics), in which Rabbi Gamaliel II. at last silences his opponents by an appeal to the pro-mise [a] 'that ye may prolong your days in the land which the Lord sware unto your fathers to give unto them'—'unto *them*,' emphasises the Rabbi, not 'unto you.' Although this almost entirely misses the spiritual meaning conveyed in the reasoning of Christ, it is impossible to mistake its Christian origin. The point opens such further questions as these: In the constant intercourse between Jewish Christians and Jews, what did the latter learn? and may there not be much in the Talmud which is only an appropriation and adaptation of what had been derived from the New Testament?

2. The answer of our Lord was not without its further results. As we conceive it, among those who listened to the brief but decisive passage between Jesus and the Sadducees were some 'Scribes'—or, as they are also designated, 'lawyers,' 'teachers of the Law,' experts, ex-pounders, practitioners of the Jewish Law. One of them, perhaps he who exclaimed: Beautifully said, Teacher! hastened to the knot of Pharisees, whom it requires no stretch of the imagination to picture gathered in the Temple on that day, watching the Saviour's every move-ment. As 'the Scribe' came up to them, he would relate how Jesus had literally 'gagged' and 'muzzled' the Sadducees—just as, according to the will of God, we are 'by well-doing to gag the want of knowledge of senseless men.' There can be little doubt that the report would give rise to mingled feelings, in which that pre-vailing would be, that, although Jesus might thus have discomfited the Sadducees, He would be unable to cope with other questions, if only properly propounded by Pharisaic learning. And so we can understand how once of the number, perhaps the same Scribe, would volunteer to undertake the office; [a] and how his question was, as St. Matthew reports, in a sense really intended to 'tempt' Jesus.

We dismiss here the well-known Rabbinic

[Margin notes:]
[a] Deut. xi. 9

[a] Comp. the two ac-counts in St. Matt. xxii. 34-40 and in St. Mark xii. 28-34

distinctions of 'heavy' and 'light' commandments, because Rabbinism declared the 'light' to be as binding as the 'heavy,' those of the Scribes more 'heavy' (or binding) than those of Scripture, and that one commandment was not to be considered to carry greater reward, and to be therefore more carefully observed, than another. That such thoughts were not in the mind of the questioner, but rather the general problem—however himself might have answered it—appears even from the form of his inquiry: 'Which is the great—the first [a] commandment in the Law?' So challenged, the Lord could have no hesitation in replying. Not to silence him, but to speak the absolute truth, He quoted the words which every Jew was bound to repeat in his devotions, and which were ever to be on his lips, living or dying, as the inmost expressions of his faith: 'Hear, O Israel, the Lord our God is one Lord.' And then continuing, He repeated the command concerning love to God which is the outcome of that profession. But to have stopped here would have been to propound a theoretic abstraction without concrete reality, a mere Pharisaic worship of the letter. As God is love—His Nature so manifesting itself—so is love to God also love to man. And so this second is 'like' 'the first and great commandment.' It was a full answer to the Scribe when He said: 'There is none other commandment greater than these.'

a St. Mark xii. 28

But it was more than an answer when, as St. Matthew reports, He added: 'on these two commandments hang all the Law and the Prophets.' [b] It little matters for our present purpose how the Jews at the time understood and interpreted these two commandments. They would know what it meant that the Law and the prophets 'hung' on them, for it was a Jewish expression. For the moment, at least, traditionalism lost its sway; and, as Christ pointed to it, the Scribe saw the exceeding moral beauty of the Law. He was not far from the Kingdom of God. [c]

b St. Matt. xxii. 4

c St. Mark xii. 33, 34

3. Without addressing any one in particular, Christ now set before them all, what perhaps was the most

familiar subject in their theology, that of the descent of Messiah. Whose Son was He? And when they replied: 'The Son of David,' He referred them to the opening words of Psalm cx., in which David called the Messiah 'Lord.' The argument proceeded, of course, on the twofold supposition that the Psalm was Davidic and that it was Messianic. Neither of these statements would have been questioned by the ancient Synagogue.

But we should greatly err if we thought that, in calling the attention of His hearers to this apparent contradiction about the Christ, the Lord only intended to show the utter incompetence of the Pharisees to teach the higher truths of the Old Testament. Far beyond this, as in the proof which He gave for the Resurrection, and in the view which He presented of the great commandment, He would point to the grand harmonious unity of Revelation. Viewed separately, the two statements, that Messiah was David's Son, and that David owned Him Lord, would seem incompatible. But in their combination in the Person of the Christ, how harmonious and how full of teaching—to Israel of old, and to all men—concerning the nature of Christ's Kingdom and of His Work!

It was but one step from this demonstration of the incompetence of Israel's teachers for the position they claimed to a solemn warning on this subject.

To begin with—Christ would have them understand that He neither wished for Himself nor His disciples the place of authority which they claimed, nor yet sought to incite the people to resistance thereto. On the contrary, so long as they held the place of authority, they were to be regarded—in the language of the Mishnah—as if instituted by Moses himself, as sitting in Moses' seat, and were to be obeyed, so far as merely outward observances were concerned. We also recall that the ordinances to which Christ made reference were those of the Jewish canon-law, and did not involve anything which could really affect the conscience—except that of the ancient, or of our modern Pharisees. But while they thus obeyed their outward directions, they were equally to eschew the spirit

which characterised their observances.   In this respect a
twofold charge is laid against them : of want of spiritual
earnestness and love,[a] and of mere externalism,
vanity, and self-seeking.[b]   And here Christ interrupted His Discourse to warn His disciples
against the first beginnings of what had led to such fear-
ful consequences, and to point them to the
better way.[c]

a St. Matt.
xxiii. 3, 4
b vv. 5-7

c vv. 8-12

This constitutes the first part of Christ's charge.
Before proceeding to those which follow, we may give a
few illustrative explanations.   Of the opening accusation
about the binding of heavy burdens and grievous to be
borne, and laying them on men's shoulders, proof can
scarcely be required.   As frequently shown, Rabbinism
placed the ordinances of tradition above those of the Law,
and this by a necessity of the system, since they were pro-
fessedly the authoritative exposition and the supplement
of the written Law.   And although it was a general rule
that no ordinance should be enjoined heavier than the
congregation could bear, yet it was admitted that, whereas
the words of the Law contained what 'lightened' and what
'made heavy,' the words of the Scribes contained only
what 'made heavy.'   Again, it was another principle
that, where an 'aggravation' or increase of the burden
had once been introduced, it must continue to be observed.
Thus the burdens became intolerable.   And the blame
rested equally on both the great Rabbinic Schools.

It is not so easy to understand the second part of
Christ's accusation.   There were, indeed, many hypocrites
among them, who might, in the language of the Talmud,
alleviate for themselves and make heavy for others.   Yet
the charge of not moving them with the finger could
scarcely apply to the Pharisees as a party—not even in
this sense, that Rabbinic ingenuity mostly found some
means of evading what was unpleasant.   We would understand the word then in the sense that they did not 'alleviate'
where they might have done so, or else with reference to
their admitted principle, that their ordinances always
made heavier, never lighter.

With this charge of unreality and want of love, those of externalism, vanity, and self-seeking are closely connected. Here we can only make selection from the abundant evidence in support of it. By a merely external interpretation of Exod. xiii. 9, 16, and Deut. vi. 8, xi. 18, the practice of wearing Phylacteries, or, as they were called, *Tephillin*, 'prayer-fillets,' was introduced. These, as will be remembered, were square capsules, covered with leather, containing on small scrolls of parchment these four sections of the law: Exod. xiii. 1–10, 11–16; Deut. vi. 4–9; xi. 13-21. The Phylacteries were fastened by long leather straps to the forehead, and round the left arm, near the heart. Most superstitious reverence was attached to them, and in later times they were even used as amulets. Nevertheless, the Talmud itself gives confirmation that the practice of constantly wearing Phylacteries—or, it might be, making them broad, and enlarging the borders of the garments—was intended '*for to be seen of men.*' Nay, the Rabbis had in so many words to lay it down as a principle, that the Phylacteries were not to be worn for show.

Detailed proof is scarcely required of the charge of vanity and self-seeking in claiming marked outward honours, such as the uppermost places at feasts and in the Synagogue, respectful salutations in the market, the ostentatious repetition of the title 'Rabbi,' or 'Abba,' 'Father,' or 'Master,' or the distinction of being acknowledged as 'greatest.' The very earnestness with which the Talmud sometimes warns against such motives for study or for piety sufficiently establishes it.

The Law of the Kingdom, as repeatedly taught,[a] was the opposite. As regarded aims, they were to seek the greatness of service; and as regarded that acknowledgment which would come from God, it would be the exaltation of humiliation.

[a] St. Mark ix. 35; St. Luke xiv. 11; xviii. 14

It was not a break in the Discourse, rather an intensification of it, when Christ now turned to make final denunciation of Pharisaism in its sin and hypocrisy.[b] Corresponding to the eight Beatitudes

[b] St. Matt. xxiii. 13-33

in the Sermon on the Mount with which His public
Ministry began, He now closed it with eight denunciations
of woe. These are the forthpouring of His holy wrath,
the last and fullest testimony against those whose guilt
would involve Jerusalem in common sin and common
judgment.

The first Woe against Pharisaism was on their shutting
the Kingdom of God against men by their opposition to
the Christ. All knew how exclusive were their pretensions
in confining piety to the possession of knowledge, and that
they declared it impossible for an ignorant person to be
pious.

The second Woe was on their covetousness and hypocrisy. They made long prayers, but how often did it only
cover the vilest selfishness, even to the 'devouring' of
widows' houses!

The third Woe was on their proselytism, which issued
only in making their converts twofold more the children of
hell than themselves. Against this charge, rightly understood, Judaism has in vain sought to defend itself.

But the Lord may have referred here, not to conversion
to Judaism in general, but to proselytism to the sect of the
Pharisees, which was undoubtedly sought to the compassing
of sea and land.

The fourth Woe is denounced on the moral blindness
of these guides rather than on their hypocrisy. It seems
likely that our Lord refers to oaths or adjurations in connection with vows, where the casuistry was of the most
complicated kind.

The fifth Woe referred to one of the best-known and
strangest Jewish ordinances, which extended the Mosaic
law of tithing, in most burdensome minuteness, even to
the smallest products of the soil that were esculent and
could be preserved, such as anise. Of these, according
to some, not only the seeds, but in certain cases even
the leaves and stalks, had to be tithed. We remember
that this conscientiousness in tithing constituted one of
the characteristics of the Pharisees; but we could scarcely
be prepared for such an instance of it, as when the Talmud

gravely assures us that the ass of a certain Rabbi had been so well trained as to refuse corn of which the tithes had not been taken!

From tithing to purification the transition was natural. It constituted the second characteristic of Pharisaic piety. We have seen with what punctiliousness questions of outward purity of vessels were discussed. But woe to the hypocrisy which, caring for the outside, heeded not whether that which filled the cup and platter had been procured by extortion or was used for excess. And, alas for the blindness which perceived not that internal purity was the real condition of that which was outward!

Woe similarly to another species of hypocrisy, of which, indeed, the preceding were but the outcome: that of outward appearance of righteousness, while heart and mind were full of iniquity—just as those annually-whited sepulchres of theirs seemed so fair outwardly, but within were full of dead men's bones and all uncleanness. Woe, lastly, to that hypocrisy which built and decorated sepulchres of prophets and righteous men, and by so doing sought to shelter itself from share in the guilt of those who had killed them. It was not spiritual repentance, but national pride, which actuated them in this, the same spirit of self-sufficiency, pride, and impenitence which had led their fathers to commit the murders. And were they not about to imbrue their hands in the blood of Him to Whom all the prophets had pointed? Fast were they in the Divine judgment filling up the measure of their fathers.

And thicker and heavier than ever before fell the hailstorm of His denunciations, as· He foretold the certain doom which awaited their national impenitence.[a] ^a ^(a St. Matt. xxiii. 34-36) Prophets, wise men, and scribes would be sent them of Him; and only murders, sufferings, and persecutions would await them—not reception of their message and warnings. And so would they become heirs of all the blood of martyred saints, from that of him whom Scripture records as the first one murdered, down to that last martyr of Jewish unbelief of whom tradition spoke in such

terms—Zechariah,[1] stoned by the king's command in the
^{a 2 Chron. xxiv. 20-22} Court of the Temple,[a] whose blood, as legend had
it, did not dry up those two centuries and a half,
but still bubbled on the pavement, when Nebuzar-adan
entered the Temple and at last avenged it.

And yet it would not have been Jesus, if, while denouncing certain judgment on them who, by continuance
and completion of the crimes of their fathers, through the
same unbelief, had proved themselves heirs to all their
guilt, He had not also added to it the passionate lament of
a love which, even when spurned, lingered with longing
^{b St. Matt. xxiii. 37-39} over the lost.[b] They all knew the common illus-
tration of the hen gathering her young brood for
shelter, and they knew also what of Divine protection,
blessing, and rest it implied, when they spoke of being
gathered under the wings of the Shekhinah. Fain and
often would Jesus have given to Israel, His people, that
shelter, rest, protection, and blessing—but they would not.
Looking around on those Temple-buildings—that House,
it shall be left to them desolate! And He quitted its
courts with these words, that they of Israel should not see
Him again till, the night of their unbelief past, they would
welcome His return with a better Hosanna than that which
had greeted His Royal Entry three days before.

---

[1] We need scarcely remind the reader that this Zechariah was the
son of Jehoiada. The difference in the text of St. Matthew may either
be due to family circumstances, unknown to us, which might admit of
his designation as 'the son of Barachias' (the reading is undoubtedly
correct), or an error may have crept into the text—how, we know not,
and it is of little moment. There can be no question that the reference
is to this Zacharias.

CHAPTER LXXV.

THE THIRD DAY IN PASSION-WEEK—THE LAST SERIES OF
PARABLES: OF THE LABOURERS IN THE VINEYARD—OF
THE TWO SONS—OF THE EVIL HUSBANDMEN—OF THE
MARRIAGE OF THE KING'S SON AND OF THE WEDDING
GARMENT.

(St. Matt. xix. 30-xx. 16; xxi. 28-32, 33-46; St. Mark xii. 1-12;
St. Luke xx. 9-19; St. Matt. xxii. 1-14.)

ALTHOUGH it may not be possible to mark their exact
succession, it will be convenient here to group together
the last series of Parables. Most, if not all of them, were
spoken on that third day in Passion-week : the first four
to a more general audience; the last three (to be treated
in another chapter) to the disciples, when, on the evening
of that third day, on the Mount of Olives,[a] He
told them of the 'Last Things.' They are the
Parables of Judgment, and in one form or another
treat of 'the End.'

St. Matt. xxiv. 1; St. Luke xxi. 37

1. *The Parable of the Labourers in the Vine-yard.*[b]—As treating of 'the End,' this Parable
evidently belongs to the last series, although it
may have been spoken previously to Passion-week.

b St. Matt. xix. 30-xx. 16

We remember that on the occasion of the rich young
ruler's failure to enter the Kingdom, to which he was so
near, Christ had uttered an earnest warning on the
danger of 'riches.'[c] In the low spiritual stage
which the Apostles had as yet attained, it was,
perhaps, only natural that Peter should, as spokesman of
the rest, have in a kind of spiritual covetousness clutched
at the promised reward, and that in a tone of self-righteousness he should have reminded Christ of the sacrifices which
they had made. It was most incongruous, yet part of
what the Lord had always to bear from their ignorance
and failure to understand Him and His work. Only

c St. Matt. xix. 23, 24

there was here danger to the disciples: danger of
lapsing into feelings kindred to those with which the
Pharisees viewed the pardoned Publicans, or the elder son
in the Parable his younger brother; danger of misunderstanding the right relations, and with it the very character
of the Kingdom, and of work in and for it. It is to this
that the Parable of the Labourers in the Vineyard refers.

The principle which Christ lays down is that, while
nothing done for Him shall lose its reward, yet, from one
reason or another, no forecast can be made, no inferences
of self-righteousness may be drawn. It does not by any
means follow that most work done—at least, to our seeing
and judging—shall entail a greater reward.

Of this the Parable of the Labourers is an illustration.
It teaches nothing beyond this. But while illustrating
how it may come that some who were first are 'last,' and
how utterly mistaken or wrong is the thought that they
must necessarily receive more than others, who seemingly
have done more—how, in short, work for Christ is not a
ponderable quantity, so much for so much, nor yet we the
judges of when and why a worker has come—it also conveys much besides.

We mark, first, the bearing of 'the householder, who
went out to hire labourers into his vineyard.' That he
did not send his steward, but went himself,[a] and
with the dawn of morning, shows both that there
was much work to do, and the householder's anxiety to
have it done. That householder is God, and the vineyard
His Kingdom; the labourers, whom with earliest morning
He seeks in the market-place of busy life, are His Servants.
With these he agreed for a *denarius* a day, which was the
ordinary wages for a day's labour, and so sent them into
the vineyard: in other words, he told them he would pay
the reward promised to labourers. About the third hour
(the Jewish working day being reckoned from sunrise to
sunset) he went out again, and as he saw 'others' standing
idle in the market-place, he said to them, 'Go ye also into
the vineyard.' There was more than enough to do in that
vineyard; enough and more to employ them. And when

a St. Matt.
xx. 1

he came, they had stood in the market-place ready and waiting to go to work, yet 'idle'—unemployed as yet. It might not have been precisely their blame that they had not gone before; they were 'others' than those in the market-place when the Master had first come, and they had not been there at that time. Only as he now sent them, he made no definite promise. They felt that in their special circumstances they had no claim ; he told them that whatsoever was right he would give them ; and they implicitly trusted to his word, to his justice and goodness. And so happened it yet again, both at the sixth and at the ninth hour of the day. Neither did the Master in any case make, nor they ask for, other promise than that implied in his word and character.

And now the time for working is past, and the Lord of the vineyard bids His Steward [here the Christ] pay His labourers. But here the first surprise awaits them. The order of payment is the inverse of that of labour : 'beginning from the last unto the first.' This is almost a necessary part of the Parable. For, if the first labourers had been paid first, they would either have gone away without knowing what was done to the last, or, if they had remained, their objection could not have been urged, except on the ground of manifest malevolence towards their neighbours. Again we notice, as indicating the disposition of the later labourers, that those of the third hour did not murmur, because they had not got more than they of the eleventh hour. This is in accordance with their not having made any bargain at the first, but trusted entirely to the householder. But they of the first hour had their cupidity excited. Seeing what the others had received, they expected to have more than their due. When they likewise received every man a *denarius*, they murmured, as if injustice had been done them. And, as mostly in like circumstances, truth and fairness seemed on their side. For selecting the extreme case of the eleventh hour labourers, had not the householder made those who had wrought only one hour equal to them who had 'borne the burden of the day and the heat'? Yet, however fair their reasoning might seem, they had no claim in truth or equity. They had gone to work with a stipulated sum as their hire distinctly in view. They now appealed to justice; but from first to last they had had justice. This as regards the ' so much for so much ' principle of claim, law, work, and pay.

But there was yet another aspect than that of mere justice. Those other labourers, who had felt that, owing to the lateness of their appearance, they had no claim, had made no bargain, but trusted to the Master. And as they had believed, so was it unto them. Not because they made or had any claim—'I will, however, to give unto this last, even as unto thee'—the word 'I will,' being emphatically put first to mark ' the good pleasure ' of His grace as the ground of action. Such a Master could not have given less to those who had come when called, trusting to His goodness, and not in their deserts. The reward was now reckoned, not of work nor of debt, but of grace.[a]

[a] Rom. iv. 4-6; xi. 6

And so, in this illustrative case of the Parable, ' the first shall be last, and the last first.'

Another point still remains to be noticed. If anywhere, we expect in these Parables, addressed to the people, forms of teaching and speaking with which they were familiar—in other words, Jewish parallels. But we equally expect that the teaching of Christ, while conveyed under illustrations with which the Jews were familiar, would be entirely different in spirit. And such we find it notably in the present instance. To begin with, according to Jewish Law, if a man engaged a labourer without any definite bargain, but on the statement that he would be paid as one or another of the labourers in the place, he was, according to some, only bound to pay the lowest wages in the place; but, according to the majority, the average between the lowest and the highest.

The same spirit of work and pay appears in the following illustrative Parable. A king had a garden, for which he hired labourers without telling them what their wages would be. In the evening he called them, and having ascertained from each under what tree he had been working, he paid them according to the value of the trees on which they had been engaged. And when they said that he ought to have told them which trees would bring the labourers most pay, the king replied that thereby a great part of his garden would have been neglected. So had God in like manner only revealed the reward of the greatest of the commandments, ᵃ Ex. xx. 12 that to honour father and mother,ᵃ and that of the ᵇ Deut. xxii.7 least, about letting the mother-bird fly away ᵇ— attaching to both precisely the same reward.

To these, if need were, might be added other illustrations of that painful reckoning about work, or else sufferings, and reward, which characterises Jewish theology, as it did those labourers in the Parable.

2. The second Parable in this series—or perhaps rather illustration—was spoken within the Temple. The Saviour had been answering the question of the Pharisees as to His authority by an appeal to the testimony of the Baptist. This led Him to refer to the twofold reception of that testimony—on the one hand, by the Publicans and harlots, and on the other, by the Pharisees.

ᶜ St. Matt. xxi. 28-32   The Parable ᶜ which now follows introduces a man who has two sons. He goes to the first, and in language of affection bids him go and work in his vineyard. The son curtly and rudely refuses; but afterwards he changes his mind and goes. Meantime the father, when refused by the one, has gone to his other son on the same errand. The contrast here is marked. The tone is most polite, and the answer of the son contains not only a promise, but we almost see him going: ' I, sir!—and he did not go.' The application was easy. The first son represented the Publicans and harlots, whose curt and rude refusal of the Father's call was implied in their life of reckless sin. But afterwards they changed their mind—and went into the Father's vineyard. The other son, with his politeness of tone and ready promise, but utter neglect of obligations undertaken, represented the Pharisees with their hypocritical and empty professions. And Christ obliged them to make application of the Parable. When challenged by the Lord, which of the two had done the will of his father, they could not avoid the answer. Then it was that in language equally stern and true He pointed the moral. The Baptist had come preaching righteousness, and, while the self-righteous Pharisees had not believed him, those sinners had. And yet, even when the Pharisees saw the effect on these former sinners, they changed not their minds that they might believe. Therefore the Publicans and harlots would and did go into the Kingdom before them.

3. Closely connected with the two preceding Parables, ᵃ St. Matt. and, indeed, with the whole tenor of Christ's xxi. 33 &c. sayings at that time, is that about the Evil Hus- and parallels bandmen in the Vineyard.ᵃ

The Parable opens, like that in Is. v., with a description of the complete arrangements made by the Owner of the Vineyard, to show how everything had been done to ensure a good yield of fruit, and what right the Owner had to expect at least a share in it. In the Parable, as in the prophecy, the Vineyard represents the Theocracy, although in the Old Testament, necessarily, as identified with the ᵇ Is. v. 7 nation of Israel,ᵇ while in the Parable the two are distinguished, and the nation is represented by the labourers to whom the Vineyard was 'let out.' In- deed, the whole structure of the Parable shows that the husbandmen are Israel as a nation, although they are addressed and dealt with in the persons of their represen- ᶜ St. Luke tatives and leaders. And so it was spoken 'to xx. 9 ᵈ St. Matt. the people,'ᶜ and yet 'the chief priests and Phari- xxi. 45 sees' rightly 'perceived that He spake of them.' ᵈ

This vineyard the owner had let out to husbandmen, while he himself 'travelled away' [abroad], as St. Luke adds, 'for a long time.' From the language it is evident that the husbandmen had the full management of the vine- yard. We remember that there were three modes of dealing with land. According to one of these ' the labourers' employed received a certain portion of the fruits, say, a third or a fourth of the produce. In such cases it seems, at least sometimes, to have been the practice, besides giving them a proportion of the produce, to provide also the seed (for a field) and to pay wages to the labourers. The other two modes of letting land were, either that the tenant paid a money rent to the proprietor, or else that he agreed to give the owner a definite amount of produce, whether the harvest had been good or bad. Such leases were given by the year or for life; sometimes the lease was even hereditary, passing from father to son. There can scarcely be a doubt that it is the latter kind of lease which is referred to in the Parable, the lessees being bound to give the owner a certain amount of fruits in their season.

Accordingly, 'when the time of the fruits drew near, he sent his servants to the husbandmen to receive his fruits'— the part of them belonging to him, or, as St. Mark and St. Luke express it, ' of the fruits of the vineyard.' We gather that it was a succession of servants, who received increasingly ill treatment from these evil husbandmen. We might have expected that the owner would now have taken severe measures; but instead of this he sent, in his patience and goodness, 'other servants'—not 'more,' but 'greater than the first,' no doubt with the idea that their greater authority would command respect. And when these also received the same treatment, we must regard it as involving increased guilt on the part of the husbandmen. Once more a fresh and still greater display of the owner's patience and unwillingness to believe that these husbandmen were so evil. As St. Mark pathetically puts it, indicating not only the owner's goodness, but the spirit of determined rebellion and the wickedness of the husbandmen : ' He had yet one, a beloved son—he sent him last unto them,' on the supposition that they would reverence him. The result was different. The appearance of the legal heir made them apprehensive of their tenure. Practically, the vineyard was already theirs; by killing the heir, the only claimant to it would be put out of the way, and so the vineyard become in every respect their own. For the husbandmen proceeded on the idea that, as the owner was ' abroad' ' for a long time,' he would not personally inter-

K K

fere—an impression strengthened by the circumstance that he had not avenged the former ill-usage of his servants, but only sent others in the hope of influencing them by gentleness. So the labourers, 'taking him [the son], cast him forth out of the vineyard, and killed him'—the first action indicating that by violence they thrust him out of his possession, before they wickedly slew him.

The meaning of the Parable is sufficiently plain. The Owner of the vineyard, God, had let out His Vineyard— the Theocracy—to His people of old. The covenant having been instituted, He withdrew, as it were—the former direct communication between Him and Israel ceased. Then in due season He sent 'His Servants,' the prophets, to gather His fruits—they had had theirs in all the temporal and spiritual advantages of the covenant. But instead of returning the fruits meet unto repentance, they only ill-treated His messengers, and that increasingly even unto death. In His longsuffering He next sent on the same errand 'greater' than them—John the Baptist.[a] And when he also received the same treatment, He sent last His own Son, Jesus Christ. His appearance made them feel that it was now a decisive struggle for the Vineyard—and so in order to gain its possession for themselves, they cast the rightful Heir out of His own possession, and then killed Him.

a St. Luke vii. 26

And they must have understood the meaning of the Parable, who had proved themselves heirs to their fathers in the murder of all the prophets,[b] who had just been convicted of the rejection of the Baptist's message, and whose hearts were even then full of murderous thoughts against the rightful Heir of the Vineyard. But, even so, they must speak their own judgment. In answer to His challenge, what in their view the owner of the vineyard would do to these husbandmen, the chief priests and Pharisees could only reply: 'As evil men evilly will He destroy them. And the vineyard will He let out to other husbandmen, which shall render Him the fruits in their seasons.'[c]

b St. Matt. xxiii. 34-36

c St. Matt. xxi. 41

The application was obvious, and it was made by

Christ, first, as always, by a reference to the prophetic testimony. And then followed, in plain and unmistakable language, the terrible prediction, first nationally, that the Kingdom of God would be taken from them, and ' given to a nation bringing forth the fruits thereof: ' and then individually, that whosoever stumbled at that stone and fell over it, in personal offence or hostility, should be broken in pieces, but whosoever stood in the way of, or resisted its progress, and on whom therefore it fell, it would ' scatter him as dust.'

Once more was their wrath roused, but also their fears. They knew that He spake of them, and would fain have laid hands on Him; but they feared the people, who in those days regarded Him as a prophet. And so for the present they left Him, and went their way.

4. If Rabbinic writings offer scarcely any parallel to the preceding Parable, that of the Marriage-Feast of the King's Son and the Wedding Garment [a] seems almost reproduced in Jewish tradition. A King is represented as inviting to a feast, without, however, fixing the exact time for it. The wise adorn themselves in time, and are seated at the door of the palace, so as to be in readiness, since, as they argue, no elaborate preparation for a feast can be needed in a palace; while the foolish go away to their work, arguing there must be time enough, since there can be no feast without preparation. But suddenly comes the King's summons to the feast, when the wise appear festively adorned, and the King rejoices over them, and they are made to sit down, eat and drink; while he is wroth with the foolish, who appear squalid, and are ordered to stand by and look on in anguish, hunger and thirst.

[a] St. Matt. xxii. 1-14

When we turn to the Parable of our Lord, its meaning is not difficult to understand. The King made a marriage for his Son, and sent his Servants to call them that were bidden to the wedding. Evidently, as in the Jewish Parable, and as before in that of the guests invited to the great Supper,[b] a preliminary general invitation had preceded the announcement that all was

[b] St. Luke xiv. 16, 17

ready. But those invited would not come. It reminds us both of the Parable of the Labourers for the Vineyard, sought at different times, and of the repeated sending of messengers to those Evil Husbandmen for the fruits that were due, when we are next told that the King sent forth other servants to tell them to come, for he had made ready his 'early meal,' and that, no doubt with a view to the later meal, the oxen and fatlings were killed. These repeated endeavours to call, to admonish, and to invite, form a characteristic feature of these Parables, showing that it was one of the central objects of our Lord's teaching to exhibit the longsuffering and goodness of God. Instead of giving heed to these repeated and pressing calls, in the words of the Parable : ' But they [the one class] made light of it, and went away, the one to his own land, the other unto his own merchandise.'

So the one class; the other made not light of it, but acted even worse than the first. ' But the rest laid hands on his servants, entreated them shamefully, and killed them.' The sin was the more aggravated that he was their king, and the messengers had invited them to a feast, and that one in which every loyal subject should have rejoiced to take part. Theirs was therefore not only murder, but also rebellion against their sovereign. On this the king in his wrath sent forth his armies, which— and here the narrative in point of time anticipates the event—destroyed the murderers, and burnt their city.

[a] St. Matt. xxii. 8   ' Then '[a]— after the king had given commandment for his armies to go forth, he said to his servants, ' The wedding indeed is ready, but they that were bidden were not worthy. Go ye therefore into the partings of the highways [where a number of roads meet and cross], and, as many as ye shall find, bid to the marriage.' We remember that the Parable here runs parallel to that other, when first the outcasts from the city-lanes, and then the wanderers on the world's high-[b] St. Luke xiv. 21-24   way, were brought in to fill the place of the invited guests.[b]

We have already in part anticipated the interpretation

of this Parable. 'The Kingdom' is here, as so often in the Old and in the New Testament, likened to a feast, and more specifically to a marriage-feast. But we mark as distinctive, that the King makes it for His Son. Thus Christ, as Son and Heir of the Kingdom, forms the central Figure in the Parable. The next point is that the chosen, invited guests were the ancient Covenant-people—Israel. To them God had sent first under the Old Testament. And, although they had not given heed to His call, yet a second class of messengers was sent to them under the New Testament. And the message of the latter was that 'the early meal was ready [Christ's first coming], and that all preparations had been made for the great evening-meal [Christ's Reign]. Another prominent truth is set forth in the repeated message of the King, which points to the goodness and longsuffering of God. Next, our attention is drawn to the refusal of Israel, which appears in the contemptuous neglect and preoccupation with their own things of one party, and the hatred, resistance, and murder by the other. Then follow in quick succession the command of judgment on the nation, and the burning of their city—God's army being, in this instance, the Romans—and finally, the direction to go into the crossways to invite all men, alike Jews and Gentiles.

With verse 10 begins the second part of the Parable. The 'Servants'—that is, the New Testament messengers —had fulfilled their commission ; they had brought in as many as they found, both bad and good : that is, without respect to their previous history, or their moral and religious state up to the time of their call: and 'the wedding was filled with guests'—that is, the table at the marriage-feast was filled with those who as guests 'lay around it.' But if ever we are to learn that we must not expect on earth—not even at the King's marriage-table—a pure Church, it is surely from what now follows. The King entered to see his guests, and among them he descried one who had not on a wedding-garment. Manifestly, the quickness of the invitation, and the previous unpreparedness of the guests did not prevent the procuring of such a garment. As the guests had been travellers, and as the feast was in the King's palace, we cannot be mistaken in supposing that such garments were supplied in the palace itself to all those who sought them. And with this agrees the circumstance that the man so addressed ' was speechless' [literally, ' gagged,' or ' muzzled ']. His conduct argued utter insensibility as regarded that to which he had been called—ignorance of what was due to the King, and what became such a feast. And whereas it is said in the Parable that only one was descried without this garment, this is intended to teach that the King will not only generally view His guests, but that each will be separately examined, and that no one will be able to escape discovery amidst the mass of guests, if he has not the ' wedding-garment.' In short, in that day of trial it is not a scrutiny of Churches, but of individuals in the Church. And so the King bade the servants, not the same who had previously carried the invitation, but evidently here the Angels, His ' ministers,' to bind him hand and foot, and to ' cast him out into the darkness, the outer '—that is, unable to offer resistance and as a punished captive, he was to be cast out into that darkness which is outside the brilliantly lighted guest-chamber of the King. And still further to mark that darkness outside, it is added that this is the well-known place of suffering and anguish : ' there shall be the weeping and the gnashing of teeth.'

And here the Parable closes with the general statement, applicable alike to the first part of the Parable—to the first invited guests, Israel—and to the second, the guests from all the world : ' For' (this is the meaning of the whole Parable) 'many are called, but few chosen.' [a]

ᵃ St. Matt. xxii. 14

CHAPTER LXXVI.

THE EVENING OF THE THIRD DAY IN PASSION-WEEK—
DISCOURSE TO THE DISCIPLES CONCERNING THE LAST
THINGS.

(St. Matt. xxiv.; St. Mark xiii.; St. Luke xxi. 5-38; xii. 35-48.)

THE last and most solemn denunciation of Jerusalem had
been uttered, the last and most terrible prediction of judgment upon the Temple spoken. It was as if Jesus had
cast the dust off His shoes against ' the House ' that was to
be ' left desolate.' And so He quitted for ever the Temple
and them that held office in it.

They had left the Sanctuary and the City, had crossed
black Kidron, and were slowly climbing the Mount of
Olives. A sudden turn in the road, and the Sacred Building was once more in full view. In the setting, even more
than in the rising sun, the vast proportions, the sym-
metry, and the sparkling sheen of this mass of snowy marble
and gold must have stood out gloriously. And across
the valley, and up the slopes of Olivet, lay the shadows
of those gigantic walls built of massive stones, some of
them nearly twenty-four feet long. Even the Rabbis,
despite their hatred of Herod, grow enthusiastic, and
dream that the very Temple-walls would have been covered
with gold, had not the variegated marble, resembling the
waves of the sea, seemed more beauteous. It was probably
as they now gazed on all this grandeur and strength, that
they broke the silence imposed on them by gloomy thoughts
of the near desolateness of that House, which the Lord had
predicted.[a] One and another pointed out to Him
those massive stones and splendid buildings, or
spake of the rich offerings with which the Temple was
adorned.[b] It was but natural that the contrast
between this and the predicted desolation should
have impressed them; natural also, that they should refer

[a] St. Matt. xxiii. 37-39

[b] St. Matt. xxiv. 1

to it—not as matter of doubt, but rather as of question.[a]

a St. Matt.
xxiv. 3
Then Jesus, turning to His questioners,[b] spoke fully of that terrible contrast between the present

b St. Mark
xiii. 1
and the near future, when, as fulfilled with almost incredible literality, not one stone would be left upon another that was not upturned.

In silence they pursued their way. Upon the Mount of Olives they sat down, right over against the Temple. Whether or not the others had gone farther, or Christ had sat apart with these four, Peter and James and John and

c St. Mark
xiii. 3
Andrew are named[c] as those who now asked Him further of what must have weighed so heavily on their hearts. It was not idle curiosity, although inquiry on such a subject, even merely for the sake of information, could scarcely have been blamed in a Jew. But it did concern them personally, for had not the Lord conjoined the desolateness of that 'House' with His own absence? He had explained the former as meaning the ruin of the City and the utter destruction of the Temple. But to His prediction of it had been added these words: 'Ye shall not see Me henceforth, till ye shall say, ·Blessed is He that cometh in the Name of the Lord.' In their view, this could only refer to His Second Coming, and to the end of the world as connected with it. This explains the twofold question which the four now addressed to Christ: 'Tell us, when shall these things be? and what shall be the sign of Thy Coming, and of the consummation of the age?'

Irrespective of other sayings in which a distinction between these two events is made, the disciples could scarcely have conjoined the desolation of the Temple with the immediate Advent of Christ and the end of the world. For in the very saying which gave rise to their question, Christ had placed an indefinite period between the two. Between the desolation of the House and their new welcome to Him, would intervene a period of indefinite length, during which they would not see Him again.

Keeping this in mind, the question of the disciples would appear to have been twofold: *When* would these things be? and, What would be the *signs* of His Royal Advent and the consummation of the 'Age'? On the former the Lord gave no information; to the latter His Discourse on the Mount of Olives was directed. On one point the statement of the Lord had been so novel as almost to account for their question. Jewish writings speak very frequently of the so-called 'sorrows of the Messiah.' These were partly those of the Messiah, and partly—perhaps chiefly—those coming on Israel and the world previous to, and connected with the Coming of the Messiah. They may generally be characterised as marking a period of internal corruption and of outward distress, especially of famine and war, of which the land of Palestine was to be the scene, and in which Israel were to be the chief sufferers. But as a matter of fact, none of them refers to desolation of the City and Temple as one of the 'signs' or 'sorrows' of the Messiah. When Christ therefore proclaimed the desolation of 'the House,' and even placed it in indirect connection with His Advent, He taught that which must have been alike new and unexpected.

This may be the most suitable place for explaining the Jewish expectation connected with the Advent of the Messiah.[1] Into many points connected with it we cannot enter here. Suffice it to say that, according to general opinion, the Birth of the Messiah would be unknown to His contemporaries; that He would appear, carry on His work, then disappear—probably for forty-five days; then reappear, and destroy the hostile powers of the world, notably 'Edom,' 'Armilos,' the Roman power—the fourth and last world-empire (sometimes it is said: through Ishmael). Ransomed Israel would now be miraculously gathered from the ends of the earth, and brought back to their own land, the ten tribes sharing in their restoration, but this only on condition of their having repented of their former sins. According to the Midrash, all circumcised Israel would then be released from Gehenna, and the dead be raised—according to some authorities, by

---

[1] On the expectation of a double Messiah see 'Life and Times, &c.,' vol. ii. pp. 434-436.

the Messiah, to Whom God would give 'the Key of the Resurrection of the Dead.' This Resurrection would take place in the land of Israel, and those of Israel who had been buried elsewhere would have to roll under ground— not without suffering pain—till they reached the sacred soil. Probably the reason of this strange idea, which was supported by an appeal to the direction of Jacob and Joseph as to their last resting-place, was to induce the Jews, after the final desolation of their land, not to quit Palestine. This resurrection, which is variously supposed to take place at the beginning or during the course of the Messianic manifestation, would be announced by the blowing of the great trumpet. It would be difficult to say how many of these strange and confused views pre-vailed at the time of Christ; which of them were uni-versally entertained as real dogmas; or from what sources they had been originally derived. Probably many of them were popularly entertained, and afterwards further de-veloped—as we believe, with elements distorted from Christian teaching.

We have now reached the period of the ' coming age.' All the resistance to God would be concentrated in the great war of Gog and Magog, and with it the prevalence of all wickedness be conjoined. And terrible would be the straits of Israel. Three times would the enemy seek to storm the Holy City. But each time would the assault be repelled—at the last with complete destruction of the enemy. The sacred City would now be wholly rebuilt and inhabited. But oh, how different from of old! Its Sabbath-boundaries would be strewed with pearls and precious gems. The City itself would be lifted to a height of some nine miles—nay, with realistic applica-tion of Is. xlix. 20, it would reach up to the throne of God, while it would extend from Joppa as far as the gates of Damascus. For Jerusalem was to be the dwelling-place of Israel, and the resort of all nations. But most glorious in Jerusalem would be the new Temple which the Messiah was to rear, and to which those five things were to be restored which had been wanting in the former

Sanctuary: the golden candlestick, the Ark, the Heaven-lit fire on the Altar, the Holy Ghost, and the Cherubim. And the land of Israel would then be as wide as it had been sketched in the promise which God had given to Abraham, and which had never before been fulfilled— since the largest extent of Israel's rule had only been over seven nations, whereas the Divine promise extended it over ten, if not over the whole earth.

Strangely realistic and exaggerated by Eastern imagination as these hopes sound, there is connected with them a point of interest on which remarkable divergenco of opinion prevailed. It concerns the Services of the re-built Temple, and the observance of the Law in Messianic days. One party here insisted on the restoration of all the ancient Services, and the strict observance of the Mosaic and Rabbinic Law—nay, on its full imposition on the Gentile nations. But the most liberal view, and, as we may suppose, that most acceptable to the enlightened, was that in the future only these two festive seasons would be observed: The Day of Atonement, and the Feast of Esther (or else that of Tabernacles); and that of all the sacrifices only thankofferings would be continued. Nay, opinion went even further, and many held that in Messianic days the distinctions of pure and impure, law-ful and unlawful, as regarded food, would be abolished. There can be little doubt that these different views were entertained even in the days of our Lord and in Apostolic times, and they account for the exceeding bitterness with which the extreme Pharisaic party in the Church at Jerusalem contended that the Gentile converts must be circumcised, and the full weight of the yoke of the Law laid on their necks.

It only remains briefly to describe the beatitude of Israel, both physical and moral, in those days. Morally, this would be a period of holiness, of forgiveness, and of peace. Without, there would be no longer enemies or oppressors. And within the City and Land a more than Paradisiacal state would prevail, which is depicted in even more than the usual realistic Eastern language. And it is one of the strangest mixtures of self-righteousness and realism with deeper and more spiritual thoughts, when the Rabbis prove by references to the prophetic Scriptures that every event and miracle in the history of Israel would find its counterpart, or rather larger fulfilment, in Messianic days.

But by the side of this we find much coarse realism. The land would spontaneously produce the best dresses and the finest cakes; the wheat would grow as high as palm-trees, nay, as the mountains, while the wind would miraculously convert the grain into flour, and cast it into the valleys. Every tree would become fruit-bearing; nay, they were to break forth and to bear fruit every day; daily was every woman to bear child, so that ultimately every Israelitish family would number as many as all Israel at the time of the Exodus. All sickness and disease, and all that could hurt, would pass away. Lastly, such physical and outward loss as Rabbinism regarded as the consequence of the Fall, would be again restored to man.

The same literalism prevails in regard to the reign of King Messiah over the nations of the world. Jerusalem would, as the residence of the Messiah, become the capital of the world, and Israel take the place of the (fourth) world-monarchy, the Roman Empire.

A great war, which seems a continuation of that of Gog and Magog, would close the Messianic era. The nations, who had hitherto given tribute to Messiah, would rebel against Him, when he would destroy them by the breath of His mouth, so that Israel alone would be left on the face of the earth. The duration of that period of rebellion is stated to be seven years. It seems at least a doubtful point, whether a second or general Resurrection was expected, the more probable view being that there was only one Resurrection, and that of Israel alone, or, at any rate, only of the studious and the pious, and that this was to take place at the beginning of the Messianic reign. If the Gentiles rose at all, it would only be immediately again to die.

Then the final Judgment would commence. We must here once more make distinction between Israel and the Gentiles, with whom, nay, as more punishable than they, certain notorious sinners, heretics, and all apostates, were to be ranked. Whereas to Israel the Gehenna, to which all but the perfectly righteous had been consigned at death, had proved a kind of purgatory, from which they were all ultimately delivered by Abraham, or, according to some, by the Messiah, no such deliverance was in prospect for the heathen nor for sinners of Israel. At the time of Christ the punishment of the wicked was regarded as of eternal duration, while annihilation would await the less guilty.

The contrast between the Jewish picture of the last Judgment and that outlined in the Gospels is so striking, as alone to vindicate (were such necessary) the eschatological parts of the New Testament, and to prove what infinite distance there is between the Teaching of Christ and the Theology of the Synagogue.

After the final Judgment we must look for the renewal of heaven and earth. In the latter neither physical nor moral darkness would any longer prevail, since the 'Evil impulse' would be destroyed. And renewed earth would bring forth all without blemish and in Paradisiacal perfection, while alike physical and moral evil had ceased. Then began the 'world to come.' The question whether any functions or enjoyments of the body would continue, is variously answered. The reply of the Lord to the question of the Sadducees about marriage in the other world seems to imply that materialistic views on the subject were entertained at the time. On the other hand, passages may be quoted in which the utterly unmaterial character of the 'world to come' is insisted upon in most emphatic language.

The many and persistent attempts, despite the gross inconsistencies involved to represent the teaching of Christ concerning 'the Last Things' as only the reflection of contemporary Jewish opinion, have rendered some

evidence necessary.[1]   When, with the information just
summarised, we again turn to the questions addressed to
Him by the disciples, we recall that they could not have
conjoined the 'when' of 'these things'—that is, of the
destruction of Jerusalem and the Temple—with the
'when' of His Second Coming and the end of the 'Age.'
We would also suggest that Christ referred to His Advent, as
to His disappearance, from the Jewish standpoint of Jewish, rather than from the general cosmic view-point of
universal history.

As regards the answer of the Lord to the two questions of His disciples, it may be said that the first part of
^a St. Matt.   His Discourse ^a is intended to supply information
xxiv. 4-35,   on the two facts of the future : the destruction
and parallels
of the Temple, and His Second Advent and the
end of the 'Age,' by setting before them the signs indicating the approach or beginning of these events.   But
even here the exact period of each is not defined, and the
teaching given is intended for purely practical purposes.
^b St. Matt.   In the second part of His Discourse ^b the Lord dis-
xxiv. 36 to   tinctly tells them what they are not to know,
end, and
parallels   and why ; and how all that was communicated to
them was only to prepare them for that constant watchfulness, which has been to the Church at all times the
proper outcome of Christ's teaching on the subject.   This
then we may take as a guide in our study ; that the words
of Christ contain nothing beyond what was necessary for
the warning and teaching of the disciples and of the
Church.

^c vv. 4-35   The first part of Christ's Discourse ^c consists
^d vv. 4-8 ; 9-   of four Sections,^d of which the first describes
14 ; 15-28 ;
29-35   'the beginning of the birth-woes' ^e of the new
^e ver. 8 ;   'Age' about to appear.
St. Mark
xiii. 8
^f St. Matt.   1. The purely practical character of the Dis-
xxiv. 4   course appears from its opening words.^f   They
contain a warning, addressed to the disciples in their
individual, not in their corporate capacity, against being

---

[1] For details as to the opinions on this subject expressed in the
Pseudepigraphic Writings, see 'Life and Times, &c.,' vol. ii. pp. 442–445.

'led astray.' This, more particularly in regard to Judaic seductions leading them after false Christs. Though in the multitude of impostors, who in the troubled times between the rule of Pilate and the destruction of Jerusalem promised Messianic deliverance to Israel, few names and claims of this kind have been specially recorded, yet the hints in the New Testament,[a] and the refer- ences, however guarded, by the Jewish historian, imply the appearance of many such seducers. But taking a wider view, they might also be misled by either rumours of war at a distance, or by actual warfare, so as to believe that the dissolution of the Roman Empire, and with it the Advent of Christ, was at hand.[b] This also would be a misapprehension, grievously. misleading, and to be carefully guarded against.

> [a] Acts v. 36; viii. 9; xxi. 38
> [b] St. Matt. xxiv. 6-8

2. From the warning to Christians as individuals, the Lord next turns to give admonition to the Church in her corporate capacity. Here we mark that the events now described[c] must not be regarded as following, with strict chronological precision, those referred to in the previous verses. Rather is it intended to indicate a general *nexus* with them, so that these events begin partly before, partly during, and partly after, those formerly predicted. They form, in fact, the continuation of the 'birth-woes.' As regards the admonition itself, ex- pressed in this part of the Lord's Discourse,[d] we notice that, as formerly to individuals, so now to the Church, two sources of danger are pointed out: internal, from heresies ('false prophets') and the decay of faith;[e] and external, from persecutions, whether Judaic and from their own kindred, or from the secular powers throughout the world. But along with these two dangers, two consoling facts are also pointed out. As regards the persecutions in prospect, full Divine aid is promised to Christians—alike to individuals and to the· Church. And as for the other and equally consoling fact: despite the persecution of Jews and Gentiles, before the End cometh 'this the Gospel of the Kingdom shall be preached in all the inhabited earth for a testimony to all

> [c] St. Matt. xxiv. 9-14, and parallels
> [d] St. Matt. xxiv. 9-14, and parallels
> [e] St. Matt. xxiv. 10-13

the nations.[a] This, then, is really the only sign of 'the
End' of the present 'Age.'

3. From these general predictions, the Lord proceeds, in the third part of this Discourse,[b] to adver-
tise the Disciples of the great historic fact immediately before them, and of the dangers which
might spring from it. In truth, we have here
His answer to their question, 'When shall these
things be?'[c] not, indeed, as regards the *when*,
but the *what* of them. And with this He conjoins
the present application of His general warning regarding
false Christs, given in the first part of this Discourse.[d] The fact is the destruction of Jerusalem.
Its twofold dangers would be—outwardly, the difficulties
and perils which at that time would necessarily beset men,
and especially the members of the infant-Church; and
religiously, the pretensions and claims of false Christs or
prophets at a period when all Jewish thinking and expectancy would lead men to anticipate the near Advent of the
Messiah. There can be no question that from both these
dangers the warning of the Lord delivered the Church.
As for Jerusalem, the prophetic vision initially fulfilled in
the days of Antiochus[e] would once more, and now
fully, become reality, and 'the abomination of
desolation' stand in the Holy Place. Nay, so dreadful would
be the persecution, that, if Divine mercy had not interposed
for the sake of the followers of Christ, the whole Jewish
race that inhabited the land would have been
swept away.[f] But on the morrow of that day
no new Maccabee would arise, no Christ come, as Israel
fondly hoped; but over that carcase would the
vultures gather;[g] and so through all the Age of
the Gentiles, till converted Israel should raise the welcoming
shout: 'Blessed be He that cometh in the Name of the
Lord!'

4. The Age of the Gentiles,[h] 'the end of the
Age,' and with it the new allegiance of His now
penitent people Israel; 'the sign of the Son of Man in
heaven,' perceived by them; the conversion of all the

[a] St. Matt. xxiv. 14
[b] St. Matt. xxiv. 15-28, and parallels; note especially the language of St. Luke
[c] St. Matt. xxiv. 3
[d] vv. 4, 5
[e] 2 Macc. vi. 1-9
[f] St. Matt. xxiv. 22
[g] ver. 28
[h] vv. 29-31

world, the Coming of Christ, the last Trumpet, the Resurrection of the dead—such, in most rapid sketch, is the outline which the Lord draws of His Coming and the End of the world.

It will be remembered that this had been the second question of the disciples.^a We again recall that the disciples could not have connected, as immediately subsequent events, the destruction of Jerusalem and His Second Coming, since He had expressly placed between them the period—apparently protracted—of His Absence,^b with the many events that were to happen in it—notably, the preaching of the Gospel over the whole inhabited earth.^c Hitherto the Lord had, in His Discourse, dwelt in detail only on those events which would be fulfilled before this generation should pass.^d

<small>a St. Matt. xxiv. 3</small>

<small>b xxiii. 38, 39</small>

<small>c xxiv. 14</small>

<small>d ver. 34</small>

More than this concerning the future of the Church could not have been told, without defeating the very object of the admonition and warning which Christ had exclusively in view, when answering the question of the disciples. Accordingly, what follows in ver. 29, describes the history, not of the Church—far less any visible physical signs in the literal heavens—but in prophetic imagery, the history of the hostile powers of the world, with its lessons. A constant succession of empires and dynasties would characterise politically the whole period after the extinction of the Jewish State.^e Immediately after that would follow the appearance to Israel of the ' Sign' of the Son of Man in heaven, and with it the conversion of all nations (as previously predicted),^f the Coming of Christ,^g and finally, the blast of the last Trumpet and the Resurrection.^h

<small>e ver. 30</small>

<small>f ver. 14</small>

<small>g ver. 30</small>

<small>h ver. 31</small>

5. From this rapid outline of the future the Lord once more turned to make present application to the disciples; application, also, to all times. From the fig-tree, under which on that spring-afternoon they may have rested on the Mount of Olives, they were to learn a ' parable.'ⁱ We can picture Christ taking one of its twigs, just as its softening tips were bursting into young leaf.

<small>i vv. 32, 33</small>

Surely, this meant that summer was nigh—not that it had actually come. The distinction is important. For it seems to prove that ' all these things,' which were to indicate to them that it was near, even at the doors, and which were to be fulfilled ere this generation had passed away, could not have referred to the last signs connected with the immediate Advent of Christ,[a] but must apply to the previous prediction of the destruction of Jerusalem and of the Jewish Commonwealth. At the same time we again admit, that the language of the Synoptists indicates that they had not clearly understood the words of the Lord which they reported, and that in their own minds they had associated the ' last signs ' and the Advent of Christ with the fall of the City. Thus may they have come to expect that blessed Advent even in their own days.

II. It is at least a question whether the Lord, while distinctly indicating these facts, had intended to remove the doubt and uncertainty of their succession from the minds of His disciples. To have done so would have necessitated that which, in the opening sentence of the second division of this Discourse,[b] He had expressly declared to lie beyond their ken. The ' *when* '—the day and the hour of His coming— was to remain hidden from men and Angels.[c] Nay, even the Son Himself—as they viewed Him and as He spake to them—knew it not. It formed no part of His present Messianic Mission, nor subject for His Messianic Teaching. The Church would not have been that of the New Testament, had she known the mystery of that day and hour, and not ever waited as for the immediate Coming of her Lord and Bridegroom.

To the world this uncertainty would indeed become the occasion for utter carelessness and practical disbelief of the coming Judgment.[d] As in the days of Noah the long delay of threatened judgment had led to absorption in the ordinary engagements of life, to the entire disbelief of what Noah had preached, so would it be in the future. But that day would come certainly and unexpectedly, to the sudden separation of those who

a St. Matt. xxiv. 29-31

b St. Matt. xxiv. 36 to end

c St. Matt. xxiv. 36

d vv. 37-40

were engaged in the same daily business of life, of whom
one might be taken up, the other left to the destruction of the coming Judgment.[a]

• St. Matt.
xxiv. 40, 41

But this very mixture of the Church with the world in
the ordinary avocations of life indicated a great danger.
As in all such, the remedy which the Lord would set before
us is not negative in the avoidance of certain things, but
positive.[b] We shall best succeed, not by going
out of the world, but by being watchful in it,
and keeping fresh on our hearts, as well as on our minds,
the fact that He is our Lord, and that we are always
to look and long for His return.

b vv. 42–51

CHAPTER LXXVII.

EVENING OF THE THIRD DAY IN PASSION-WEEK — LAST
PARABLES: OF THE TEN VIRGINS — OF THE TALENTS —
OF THE MINAS.

(St. Matt. xxv. 1-13; 14–30; St. Luke xix. 11–28.)

1. As might have been expected, the Parables concerning
the Last Things are closely connected with the Discourse
of the Last Things, which Christ had just spoken to His
Disciples. In fact, that of the Ten Virgins is, in its
main object, only an illustration of the last part of Christ's
Discourse.[c] Its outlines may be thus summa-
rised: Be ye personally prepared; be ye prepared for any length of time; be ye prepared to go to
Him directly.

c St. Matt.
xxiv. 36–51

It is late at even—the world's long day seems past,
and the Coming of the Bridegroom must be near. The
day and the hour we know not, for the Bridegroom has
been far away. Only this we know, that it is the evening
of the Marriage which the Bridegroom had fixed, and
that His word of promise may be relied upon. Therefore
all has been made ready within the bridal house, and is in
waiting there; and therefore the Virgins prepare to go
forth to meet Him on His arrival. The Parable proceeds

on the assumption that the Bridegroom is not in the town, but somewhere far away; so that it cannot be known at what precise hour He may arrive. But it is known that He will come that night; and the Virgins who are to meet Him have gathered—presumably in the house where the Marriage is to take place—waiting for the summons to go forth and welcome the Bridegroom. The common mistake, that the Virgins are represented in verse 1 as having gone forth *on the road* to meet the Bridegroom, is not only irrational—since it is scarcely credible that they would all have fallen asleep by the wayside, and with lamps in their hands—but incompatible with the circumstance [a] that at midnight the cry is suddenly raised to go forth and meet Him. In these circumstances, no precise parallel can be derived from the ordinary Jewish marriage-processions, where the bridegroom, accompanied by his groomsmen and friends, went to the bride's house, and thence conducted the bride, with her attendant maidens and friends, into his own or his parents' home. But in the Parable, the Bridegroom comes from a distance and goes to the bridal house. Accordingly, the bridal procession is to meet Him on His arrival, and escort Him to the bridal place.

[a] St. Matt. xxv. 6

Another archæological inquiry will, perhaps, be helpful to our understanding of this Parable. The ' lamps '—not ' torches '—which the Ten Virgins carried, were of well-known construction. They consisted of a round receptacle for pitch or oil for the wick. This was placed in a hollow cup or deep saucer—which was fastened by a pointed end into a long wooden pole, on which it was borne aloft. According to Jewish authorities, it was the custom in the East to carry in a bridal procession about ten such lamps. We have the less reason to doubt that such was also the case in Palestine, since, according to rubric, ten was the number required to be present at any office or ceremony, such as at the benedictions accompanying the marriage-ceremonies. And, in the peculiar circumstances supposed in the Parable, Ten Virgins are represented as going forth to meet the Bridegroom, each bearing her lamp.

The first point which we mark is that the Ten Virgins brought ' their own lamps.' Emphasis must be laid on this. Thus much was there of personal preparation on the part of all. But while the five that were wise brought also ' oil in the vessels' [presumably the hollow receptacles in which the lamp proper stood], the five foolish Virgins neglected to do so, no doubt expecting that their lamps would be filled out of some common stock in the house. In the text the foolish Virgins are mentioned before the wise, because the Parable turns on this. We cannot be at a loss to interpret the meaning of it. The Bridegroom far away is Christ, Who is come for the Marriage-Feast from 'the far country'—the Home above—certainly on that night, but we know not at what hour of it. The ten appointed bridal companions who are to go forth to meet Him are His professed disciples, and they gather in readiness to welcome His arrival. It is night, and a marriage-procession: therefore they must go forth with their lamps. All of them have brought their own lamps, they all have the Christian, or the Church-profession: the lamp in the hollow cup on the top of the pole. But only the wise Virgins have more than this—the oil in the vessels, without which the lamps cannot give their light. The Christian or Church-profession is but an empty vessel without the oil. We here remember the words of Christ: ' Let your light so shine before men, that they may see your good ᵃ St. Matt. works, and glorify your Father Which is in v. 16 heaven.' ᵃ The foolishness of the Virgins, which consisted in this, that they had omitted to bring their oil, is thus indicated in the text: ' All they which *were* foolish, when they brought their own lamps, brought not with them oil:' they brought their own lamps, but not their own oil. They had no conception either of any personal obligation in this matter, nor that the call would come so suddenly, nor yet that there would be so little interval between the arrival of the Bridegroom and 'the closing of the door.'

For—and here begins the second scene in the Parable —the interval between the gathering of the Virgins in readiness to meet Him and the arrival of the Bridegroom is much longer than had been anticipated. And so it came, that both the wise and the foolish Virgins 'slumbered and slept.' What follows is intended to bring into prominence the startling suddenness of the Bridegroom's Coming. It is midnight—when sleep is deepest—when suddenly 'there was a cry, Behold, the Bridegroom cometh! Come ye out to the meeting of Him. Then all those Virgins awoke, and prepared (trimmed) their lamps.' This, not in the sense of heightening the low flame in their lamps, but in that of hastily drawing up the wick and lighting it, when, as there was no oil in the vessels, the flame, of course, immediately died out. 'Then the foolish said unto the wise, Give us of your oil; for our lamps are going out. But the wise answered, saying: Not at all—it will never suffice for us and you! Go ye rather to the sellers, and buy for your own selves.'

This advice must not be regarded as given in irony. The trait is introduced to point out the proper source of supply —to emphasise that the oil must be their own, and also to prepare for what follows. 'But while they were going to buy, the Bridegroom came ; and the ready ones [they that were ready] went in with Him to the Marriage-Feast, and the door was shut.' It is of no importance here, whether or not the foolish Virgins finally succeeded in obtaining oil, since it could no longer be of any possible use, as its object was to serve in the festive procession, which was now past. Nevertheless, and when the door was shut, those foolish Virgins came, calling on the Bridegroom to open to them. But they had failed in that which could alone give them a claim to admission. Professing to be bridesmaids, they had not been in the bridal procession, and so, in truth and righteousness, He could only answer from within: 'Verily I say unto you, I know you not.' This, not only in punishment, but in the right order of things.

The personal application of this Parable to the disciples, which the Lord makes, follows almost of necessity. 'Watch therefore, for ye know not the day, nor the hour.'

Not enough to be in waiting with the Church; His Coming will be far on in the night; it will be sudden; it will be rapid : be prepared therefore, be ever and personally prepared! To present the necessity of this in the most striking manner, the Parable takes the form of a dialogue, first between the foolish and the wise Virgins, in which the latter only state the bare truth when saying that each has only sufficient oil for what is needed when joining the marriage-procession, and no one what is superfluous. Lastly, we are to learn from the dialogue between the foolish Virgins and the Bridegroom, that it is impossible in the day of Christ's Coming to make up for neglect of previous preparation, and that those who have failed to meet Him, even though of the bridal Virgins, shall be finally excluded as being strangers to the Bridegroom.

2. *The Parable of the Talents*—their use and mis-use [a] — follows closely on the admonition to watch, in view of the sudden and certain Return of Christ, and the reward or punishment which will then be meted out. Only that, whereas in the Parable of the Ten Virgins the reference was to the personal state, in that of 'the Talents' it is to the personal work of the Disciples. In the former instance, they are portrayed as the bridal maidens who are to welcome His Return ; in the latter, as the servants who are to give an account of their stewardship.

[a] St. Matt. xxv. 14–30

From its close connection with what precedes, the Parable opens almost abruptly with the words : 'For [it is] like a Man going abroad, [who] called his own servants, and delivered to them his goods.' The emphasis rests on this, that they were his own *servants*, and to act for his interest. His property was handed over to them, not for safe custody, but that they might do with it as best they could in the interest of their Master. This appears from what immediately follows : ' and so to one he gave five talents (about 1,170*l.*), but to one two (about 468*l.*), and to one one (=6,000 denarii, about 234*l.*), to each according to his own capability '—that is, he gave to each according to his capacity, in proportion as he deemed

them severally qualified for larger or smaller administration. 'And he journeyed abroad straightway.'

Thus far we can have no difficulty in understanding
the meaning of the Parable. Our Lord, Who has left us
for the Father's Home, is He Who has gone on the journey
abroad, and to His own servants has He entrusted, not
for custody, but to use for Him in the time between His
departure and His return, what He claims as His own
'goods.' We must not limit this to the administration of
His Word, nor to the Holy Ministry, although these may
have been pre-eminently in view. It refers generally to
all that a man has, wherewith to serve Christ : his time,
money, opportunities, talents, or learning. And to each
of us He gives according to our capacity for working—
mental, moral, and even physical—to one five, to another
two, and to another one 'talent.'

And here the characteristic difference appears. 'He
that received the five talents went and traded with them,
and made other five talents. In like manner he *that had
received* the two gained other two.' As each had received
according to his ability, so each worked according to his
power, as good and faithful servants of their Lord. If the
outward result was different, their labour, devotion, and
faithfulness were equal. It was otherwise with him who
had least to do for his Master, since only one talent had
been entrusted to him. He 'went away, digged up earth,
and hid the money of his Lord.' The prominent fact
here is, that he did not employ it for the Master, as a
good servant, but shunned alike the labour and the responsibility. In so doing he was not only unfaithful to
his trust, but practically disowned that he was a servant
of his Lord.

And now the second scene opens. 'But after a long
time cometh the Lord of those servants, and maketh
reckoning.' The first of the servants, without speaking
of his labour in trading, or his merit in 'making' money,
answers with simple joyousness : 'Lord, five talents
deliveredst thou unto me. See, other five talents have I
gained besides.' His Master's approval was all that the

faithful servant had looked for, for which he had toiled during that long absence. And we can understand how the Master welcomed and owned that servant, and assigned to him meet reward. The latter was twofold. Having proved his faithfulness and capacity in a comparatively limited sphere, one much greater would be assigned to him. Hence also the second part of his reward—that of entering into the joy of his Lord—must not be confined to sharing in the festive meal at his return, still less to advancement from the position of a servant to that of a friend who shares his Master's lordship. It implies far more than this : even satisfied heart-sympathy with the aims and gains of his Master, and participation in them, with all that this conveys.

A similar result followed on the reckoning with the servant to whom two talents had been entrusted. We mark that, although he could only speak of two talents gained, he met his Master with the same frankness as he who had made five. For he had been as faithful, and laboured as earnestly as he to whom more had been entrusted. And, what is more important, the former difference between the two servants, dependent on greater or less capacity for work, now ceased, and the second servant received precisely the same welcome and exactly the same reward, and in the same terms, as the first. And a yet deeper, and in some sense mysterious, truth comes to us in connection with the words : ' Thou hast been faithful over a few things, I will set thee over many things.' Surely, then, if not after death, yet in that other ' dispensation,' there must be work to do for Christ, for which the preparation is in this life by faithful application for Him of what He has entrusted to us—be it much or little. This gives quite a new and blessed meaning to the life that now is—as most truly and in all its aspects part of that into which it is to unfold.

It only remains to refer to the third servant, whose unfaithfulness and failure of service we already, in some measure, understand. Summoned to his account, he returned the talent entrusted to him, with this explanation, that, knowing his Master to be a hard man, reaping where he did not sow, and gathering (the corn) where he did not 'winnow,' he had been afraid of incurring responsibility, and hence hid in the earth the talent which he now restored. We recognise here those who, although His servants, yet, from self-indulgence and worldliness, will not do work for Christ with the one talent entrusted to them—that is, even though the responsibility and claim upon them be the smallest; and who deem it sufficient to hide it in the ground—not to lose it—or to preserve it, as they imagine, from being used for evil, without using it to trade for Christ. The falseness of the excuse, that he was afraid to do anything with it lest, peradventure, he might do more harm than good, was now fully exposed by the Master. Confessedly, it proceeded from a want of knowledge of Him, as if He were a hard, exacting Master, not One Who reckons even the least service as done to Himself; from misunderstanding also of what work for Christ is, in which nothing can ever fail or be lost; and, lastly, from want of sympathy with it. And so the Master put aside the pretext. Addressing him as a 'wicked and slothful servant,' He pointed out that, even on his own showing, if he had been afraid to incur responsibility, he might have 'cast' (a word intended to mark the absence of labour) the money to 'the bankers,' when, at His return, He would have received His own, 'with interest.' Thus he might, without incurring responsibility, or much labour, have been, at least in a limited sense, faithful to his duty and trust as a servant.

But as regards the punishment of the 'unprofitable' servant in the Parable, the well-known one of him that had come to the Marriage-Feast without the wedding-garment shall await him, while the talent, which he had failed to employ for his master, shall be entrusted to him who had shown himself most capable of working.

3. To these Parables, that of the King who on his return makes reckoning with his servants and his enemies may be regarded as supplemental. It is recorded only by St. Luke, and placed by him in somewhat loose connection

with the conversion of Zacchæus.[a] The most superficial
perusal will show such unmistakable similarity
with the Parable of 'The Talents,' that their
identity will naturally suggest itself to the reader. On
the other hand, there are remarkable divergences in detail,
some of which seem to imply a different standpoint from
which the same truth is viewed. We have also now the
additional feature of the message of hatred on the part of
the citizens, and their fate in consequence of it.

A brief analysis will suffice to point out the special
lessons of this Parable. It introduces 'a certain Nobleman,' who has claims to the throne, but has not yet received the formal appointment from the suzerain power.
As he is going away to receive it, he deals as yet only
with his servants. His object, apparently, is to try their
aptitude, devotion, and faithfulness; and so he hands—
not to each according to his capacity, but to all equally, a
sum, not large (such as talents), but small—to each a
'mina,' equal to about 3l. 5s. of our money. To trade
with so small a sum would, of course, be much more difficult, and success would imply greater ability, even as it
would require more constant labour. Here we have some
traits in which this differs from the Parable of the Talents.
The same small sum is supposed to have been entrusted
to all, in order to show which of them was most able and
most earnest, and hence who should be called to largest
employment, and with it to greatest honour in the Kingdom. While 'the Nobleman' was at the court of his
suzerain, a deputation of his fellow-citizens arrived to urge
this resolution of theirs : 'We will not that this one reign
over us.' It was simply an expression of hatred ; it stated
no reason, and only urged personal opposition, even if such
were in the face of the personal wish of the sovereign who
appointed him king.

In the last scene, the King, now duly appointed, has
returned to his country. He first reckons with his servants, when it is found that all but one have been faithful
to their trust, though with varying success (the *mina* of
the one having grown into ten ; that of another into five,

a St. Luke xix. 11–28

and so on). In strict accordance with that success is now
their further appointment to rule—work here corresponding
to rule there, which, however, as we know from the Parable
of the Talents, is also work for Christ : a rule that is work,
and work that is rule. At the same time, the acknowledgment is the same to all the faithful servants. Similarly,
the motives, the reasoning, and the fate of the unfaithful
servant are the same as in the Parable of the Talents. But
as regards His ' enemies,' that would not have Him reign
over them—manifestly, Jerusalem and the people of Israel
—who, even after He had gone to receive the Kingdom,
continued the personal hostility of their ' We will not that
this One shall reign over us '—the ashes of the Temple,
the ruins of the City, the blood of the fathers, and the
homeless wanderings of their children, attest that the
King has many ministers to execute that judgment which
obstinate rebellion must surely bring, if His Authority is
to be vindicated, and His Rule to secure submission.

CHAPTER LXXVIII.

THE FOURTH DAY IN PASSION-WEEK—THE BETRAYAL—
JUDAS : HIS CHARACTER, APOSTASY, AND END.

(St. Matt. xxvi. 1–5, 14–16 ; St. Mark xiv. 1, 2, 10, 11 ; St. Luke xxii. 1–6.)

THE three busy days of Passion-Week were past. Only
two days more, as the Jews reckoned them—that Wednesday and Thursday—and at its even the Paschal Supper.
And Jesus passed that day of rest and preparation in quiet
retirement with His disciples, speaking to them of His
Crucifixion on the near Passover. They sorely needed
His words; they, rather than He, needed to be prepared
for what was coming.

On that Wednesday it was impossible to misunderstand; it could scarcely have been possible to doubt what
Jesus said of His near Crucifixion. If illusions had still
existed, the last two days must have rudely dispelled them.

The triumphal Hosannas of His Entry into the City, and the acclamations in the Temple, had given place to the cavils of Pharisees, Sadducees, and Scribes, and with a 'Woe' upon it Jesus had taken His last departure from Israel's Sanctuary. And better far than those rulers, whom conscience made cowards, did the disciples know how little reliance could be placed on the adherence of the 'multitude.' And now the Master was telling it to them in plain words; was calmly contemplating it, and that not as in the dim future, but in the immediate present—at that very Passover, from which scarcely two days separated them. Much as we wonder at their brief scattering on His arrest and condemnation, those humble disciples must have loved Him much to sit around Him in mournful silence as He thus spake, and to follow Him unto His Dying.

But to one of them, in whose heart the darkness had long been gathering, this was the decisive moment. The prediction of Christ, which Judas as well as the others must have felt to be true, extinguished the last glimmering of such light of Christ as his soul had been capable of receiving. By the open door out of which he had thrust the dying Christ 'Satan entered into Judas.'[a] Yet, even so, not permanently.[b] It may indeed be doubted whether, since God is in Christ, such can ever be the case in any human soul, at least on this side eternity.

a St Luke xxii. 3
b St. John xiii. 2 and 27

It is a terrible study, that of Judas. We seem to tread our way over loose stones of hot molten lava, as we climb to the edge of the crater, and shudderingly look down into its depths. And yet there, near there, have stood not only St. Peter in the night of his denial, but mostly all of us, save they whose Angels have always looked up into the Face of our Father in heaven. There, near there, have we stood. But He prayed for us—and through the night came the Light of His Presence, and above the storm rose the Voice of Him Who has come to seek and to save that which was lost.

A terrible study this of Judas, and best to make it here, at once, from its beginning to its end.

We remember that ' Judas, the man of Kerioth,' was, so far as we know, the only disciple of Jesus from the province of Judæa. This circumstance; that he carried the bag, i.e. was treasurer and administrator of the small common stock of Christ and His disciples; and that he was both a hypocrite and a thief [a]—this is all that we know for certain of his history. From the circumstance that he was appointed to such office of trust in the Apostolic community, we infer that he must have been looked up to by the others as an able and prudent man, a good administrator. The question, why Jesus left him 'the bag' after He knew him to be a thief—which, as we believe, he was not at the beginning, and only became in the course of time and in the progress of disappointment—is best answered by this other : Why He originally allowed it to be entrusted to Judas? It was not only because he was best fitted for such work, but also in mercy to him, in view of his character. To engage in that for which a man is naturally fitted is the most likely means of keeping him from dissatisfaction, alienation, and eventual apostasy. On the other hand, it must be admitted that, as most of our life-temptations come to us from that for which we have most aptitude, when Judas was alienated and unfaithful in heart, this very thing became also his greatest temptation, and, indeed, hurried him to his ruin. But only after he had first failed inwardly.

This very gift of ' government' in Judas may also help us to understand how he may have been first attracted to Jesus, and through what process, when alienated, he came to end in that terrible sin which had cast its snare about him. Judas was drawn to Jesus as the *Jewish* Messiah, and he believed in Him as such ; but he expected that His would be the success, the result, and the triumphs of the Jewish Messiah, and he also expected to share in them. How deep-rooted were such feelings even in the purest, and most unselfish of Jesus' disciples, we gather from the request of the mother of John and James for her sons, and from Peter's question : ' What shall we have ? '

He had, from such conviction as we have described,

[a] St. John xii. 5, 6

joined the movement at its very commencement. Then, multitudes in Galilee followed His Footsteps, and watched for His every appearance. The Baptist, who had bowed before Him and testified to Him, was still lifting his voice to proclaim the near Kingdom. But the people had turned after Jesus, and He swayed them. And Judas also had been one of them who, on their early Mission, had temporarily had power given him, so that the very devils had been subject to them. But step by step had come the disappointment. John was beheaded, and not avenged; on the contrary, Jesus withdrew Himself. This constant withdrawing, whether from enemies or from success—almost amounting to flight—even when they would have made Him a King; this refusal to show Himself openly, either at Jerusalem, as His own brethren had taunted Him, or indeed, anywhere else; this uniform preaching of discouragement to them, when they came to Him elated and hopeful at some success; this gathering enmity of Israel's leaders, and His marked avoidance of, or, as some might have put it, His failure in taking up the repeated public challenge of the Pharisees to show a sign from heaven; last, and chief of all, this constant and growing reference to shame, disaster, and death—what did it all mean, if not disappointment of those hopes and expectations which had made Judas at the first a disciple of Jesus?

He that so knew Jesus, not only in His Words and Deeds, but in His inmost Thoughts, even to His night-long communing with God on the hill-side, could not have seriously believed in the coarse Pharisaic charge of Satanic agency as the explanation of all. Yet, from the then Jewish standpoint, he could scarcely have found it impossible to suggest some other explanation of His miraculous power. But, as increasingly the moral and spiritual aspect of Christ's Kingdom became apparent, the bitter disappointment of his Messianic thoughts and hopes must have gone on increasing in proportion as, side by side with it, the process of moral alienation, unavoidably connected with his resistance to such spiritual manifestations, continued and increased.

On that spring day, in the restfulness of Bethany, when the Master was taking His Farewell of friends and disciples, and told them what was to happen only two days later at the Passover, it was all settled in the soul of Judas. ' Satan entered ' it. Christ would be crucified ; this was quite certain. In the general cataclysm let Judas have at least something. And so he left them to seek speech of them that were gathered, not in their ordinary meeting-place, but in the High-Priest's Palace. Even this indicates that it was an informal meeting, consultative rather than judicial. For it was one of the principles of Jewish Law that, in criminal cases, sentence must be spoken in the regular meeting-place of the Sanhedrin. There had previously been a similar gathering and consultation, when the report of the raising of ^a St. John xi. Lazarus reached the authorities of Jerusalem.^a ^{47, 48} The practical resolution adopted at that meeting had apparently been, that a strict watch should henceforth be kept on Christ's movements, and that every one of them, as well as the names of His friends, and the places of His secret retirement, should be communicated ^b ver. 57 to the authorities, with the view to His arrest at the proper moment.^b

It was probably in professed obedience to this direction, that the traitor presented himself that afternoon in the Palace of the High-Priest Caiaphas. Those assembled there were the ' chiefs ' of the Priesthood—no doubt, the Temple-officials, heads of the courses of Priests, and connections of the High-Priestly family, who constituted what was designated as the Priestly Council. But in that meeting in the Palace of Caiaphas, besides these Priestly Chiefs, the leading Sanhedrists (' Scribes and Elders') were also gathered. They were deliberating how Jesus might be taken by subtilty and killed. Probably they had not yet fixed on any definite plan. Only at this conclusion had they arrived—perhaps in consequence of the popular acclamations at His Entry into Jerusalem, and of what had since happened—that nothing must be done during the Feast, for fear of some popular tumult. They knew only too well the character of Pilate, and how in any such tumult all parties—the leaders as well as the led—might experience summary vengeance.

It must have been intense relief when, in their perplexity, the traitor now presented himself before them with his proposals. Yet his reception was not such as he may have looked for. He probably expected to be hailed and treated as a most important ally. They were, indeed, ' glad, and covenanted to give him money,' as he promised to dog His steps, and watch for the opportunity which they sought. Yet, withal, they treated Judas not as an honoured associate, but as a common informer, and a contemptible betrayer. This was in the circumstances the wisest policy, alike in order to save their own dignity, and to keep most secure hold on the betrayer. And Judas had at last to speak it out barefacedly—so selling himself as well as the Master : ' What will ye give me ? ' It was in literal fulfilment of prophecy,[a] that they 'weighed out' to him from the very Temple-treasury those

ᵃ Zech. xi. 12

thirty pieces of silver (about 3*l.* 15*s.*) And yet it was surely as much in contempt of the seller as of Him Whom he sold, that they paid the legal price of a slave. Or did they mean some kind of legal fiction, such as to buy the Person of Jesus at the legal price of a slave, so as to hand it afterwards over to the secular authorities ?

Yet Satan must once more enter the heart of Judas at that Supper, before he can finally do the deed.[b] But, even so, we believe it was not for always— for he had still a conscience working in him. With this element he had not reckoned in his bargain in the High Priest's Palace. On the morrow of His condemnation would it exact a terrible account. That night in Gethsemane never more passed from his soul. In the thickening gloom all around, he must have ever seen only the torchlight glare as it fell on the pallid Face of the Divine Sufferer. In the stillness before the storm, he must have ever heard only these words : ' Betrayest thou the Son of Man with a kiss ? ' He did not hate Jesus then—he hated nothing; he hated everything. He was utterly

ᵇ St. John xiii. 27

desolate, as the storm of despair swept over his soul. No one in heaven or on earth to appeal to ; no one, Angel or man, to stand by him.   Not the Priests, who had paid him the price of blood, would have aught of him ; not even the thirty pieces of silver, the blood-money of his Master and of his own soul—even as the modern Synagogue, which approves of what has been done, but not of the deed, will have none of him !   With their ' See thou to it ! ' they sent him back into his darkness.   Not so could conscience be stilled.   And, louder than the ring of the thirty silver pieces as they fell on the marble pavement of the Temple, it rang in his soul : ' I have betrayed innocent blood ! '

Deeper—farther out into the night ! to its farthest bounds—where rises and falls the dark flood of death. The storm has lashed the waters into fury : they toss and break at his feet.   One narrow rift in the cloud-curtain overhead, and, in the pale, deathlike light lies the Figure of the Christ, calm and placid, untouched and unharmed, as It had been that night on the Lake of Galilee, when Judas had seen Him come to them over the surging billows, and then bid them be peace.   Peace !   What peace to him now—in earth, or heaven ?   It was the same Christ, but thorn-crowned, with nail-prints in His Hands and Feet.   And this Judas had done to the Master ! Only for one moment did it seem to lie there ; then it was sucked up by the dark waters beneath.   And again the cloud-curtain is drawn, only more closely ; the darkness is thicker, and the storm wilder than before.   Out into that darkness, with one wild plunge—there, where the Figure of the Dead Christ had lain.   And the waters have closed around him in eternal silence.

Can there be a store in the Eternal Compassion for the Betrayer of Christ ?

CHAPTER LXXIX.

THE FIFTH DAY IN PASSION-WEEK—'MAKE READY THE PASSOVER!'

(St. Matt. xxvi. 17–19; St. Mark xiv. 12–16; St. Luke xxii. 7–13; St. John xiii. 1.)

WHEN the traitor returned from Jerusalem on the Wednesday afternoon, the Passover, in the popular and canonical, though not in the Biblical sense, was close at hand. It began on the 14th Nisan, that is, from the appearance of the first three stars on Wednesday evening [the evening of what had been the 13th], and ended with the first three stars on Thursday evening [the evening of what had been the 14th day of Nisan]. The absence of the traitor so close upon the Feast would therefore be the less noticed by the others. Necessary preparations might have to be made, even though they were to be guests in some house—they knew not which. Those would, of course, devolve on Judas. Besides, from previous conversations they may also have judged that 'the man of Kerioth' would fain escape what the Lord had all that day been telling them about, and which was now filling their minds and hearts.

Everyone in Israel was thinking about the Feast. For the previous month it had been the subject of discussion in the Academies, and, for the last two Sabbaths at least, of discourse in the Synagogues. Everyone was going to Jerusalem, or had those near and dear to them there, or at least watched the festive processions to the Metropolis of Judaism. It was a gathering of universal Israel, that of the memorial of the birth-night of the nation, and of its Exodus, when friends from afar would meet, and new friends be made. National and religious feelings were alike stirred in what reached back to the first, and pointed forward to the final Deliverance. On that day a Jew might well glory in being a Jew. But we must try to follow the footsteps of Christ and His Disciples, and see or know only what on that day they saw and did.

M M 2

For ecclesiastical purposes Bethphage and Bethany seem to have been included in Jerusalem. But Jesus must keep the Feast in the City itself, although, if His purpose had not been interrupted, He would have spent the night outside its walls. The first preparations for the Feast would begin shortly after the return of the traitor. For on the evening [of the 13th] commenced the 14th of Nisan, when a solemn search was made with lighted candle throughout each house for any leaven that might be hidden or have fallen aside by accident. Such was put by in a safe place, and afterwards destroyed with the rest. In Galilee it was the usage to abstain wholly from work; in Judæa the day was divided, and actual work ceased only at noon, though nothing new was taken in hand even in the morning. This division of the day for festive purposes was a Rabbinic addition; and by way of a hedge round it, an hour before midday was fixed after which nothing leavened might be eaten. The more strict abstained from it even an hour earlier (at ten o'clock), lest the eleventh hour might insensibly run into the forbidden midday. But there could be little real danger of this, since, by way of public notification, two desecrated thankoffering cakes were laid on a bench in the Temple, the removal of one of which indicated that the time for eating what was leavened had passed; the removal of the other, that the time for destroying all leaven had come.

It was probably after the early meal, and when the eating of leaven had ceased, that Jesus sent Peter and John[a] with the view of preparing the ordinary Paschal Supper. For the first time we see them here joined together by the Lord, these two, who henceforth were to be so closely connected: he of deepest feeling with him of quickest action. The direction which the Lord gave, while once more evidencing to them the Divine fore-knowledge of Christ, had also its human meaning. Evidently neither the house where the Passover was to be kept, nor its owner, was to be named beforehand within hearing of Judas. The sign which Jesus gave the two Apostles reminds us of that by which Samuel of old had

a St. Luke xxii. 8

conveyed assurance and direction to Saul.[a] On their entrance into Jerusalem they would meet a man—
[a] 1 Sam. x. 3 manifestly a servant—carrying a pitcher of water.
Without accosting, they were to follow him, and when they
reached the house, to deliver to its owner this message:
'The Master saith, My time is at hand—with thee [i.e. in
thy house: the emphasis is on this] I hold the Passover
[b] St. Mat- with my disciples.[b] Where is My hostelry [or
thew 'hall'] where I shall eat the Passover with My
[c] St. Mark
and St. Luke disciples?'[c]

Two things here deserve marked attention. The disciples were not bidden ask for the chief or 'upper
chamber,' but for what we have rendered, for want of
better, by 'hostelry,' or 'hall'—the place in the house
where, as in an open Khân, the beasts of burden were un-
loaded, shoes and staff, or dusty garment and burdens put
down—if an apartment, at least a common one, certainly
not the best. Except in this place,[d] the word
[d] St. Mark only occurs as the designation of the 'inn' or
xiv. 14; St.
Luke xxii. 11 'hostelry' in Bethlehem, where the Virgin-
Mother brought forth her first-born Son, and laid Him in
[e] St. Luke a manger.[e] He Who was born in a 'hostelry'
ii. 7 was content to ask for His last meal in one.
Only, and this we mark secondly, it must be His own. It
was a common practice that more than one company partook of the Paschal Supper in the same apartment. In
the multitude of those who would sit down to the Paschal
Supper this was unavoidable, for all partook of it, includ-
ing women and children, only excepting those who were
Levitically unclean. And though each company might
not consist of less than ten, it was not to be larger than
that each should be able to partake of at least a small
portion of the Paschal Lamb—and we know how small
lambs are in the East. But while He only asked for His
last meal in some hall opening on the open court, Christ
would have it His own—to Himself, to eat the Passover
alone with His Apostles. Not even a company of disciples—such as the owner of the house unquestionably
was—nor yet, be it marked, even the Virgin-Mother,

might be present, witness what passed, hear what He said,
or be at the first Institution of His Holy Supper. To us
at least this also recalls the words of St. Paul: 'I have
^a 1 Cor. xi.   received of the Lord that which I also delivered
²³   unto you.' ^a

    There can be no reasonable doubt that the owner of
the house was a disciple, although at festive seasons un-
bounded hospitality was extended to strangers generally,
and no man in Jerusalem considered his house as strictly
his own, far less would let it out for hire. And this unnamed disciple would assign to Him, not the Hall, but
the best and chiefest, 'the upper chamber,' or *Aliyah*, at
the same time the most honourable and the most retired
place, where from the outside stairs entrance and departure
might be had without passing through the house. 'The
^b St. Mark   upper room' was 'large,' 'furnished and ready.' ^b
    From Jewish authorities we know that the
average dining-apartment was computed at fifteen feet
square ; the expression 'furnished,' no doubt, refers to the
arrangement of couches all round the Table, except at its
end, since it was a canon that the very poorest must partake of that Supper in a reclining attitude, to indicate
rest, safety, and liberty ; while the term 'ready' seems to
point to the ready provision of all that was required for
the Feast. In that case, all that the disciples would have
to 'make ready' would be 'the Paschal Lamb,' and
perhaps that first festive Sacrifice, which, if the Paschal
Lamb itself would not suffice for Supper, was added
to it. And here it must be remembered that it was
of religion to fast till the Paschal Supper—as the Jerusalem Talmud explains, in order the better to relish the
Supper.

    Perhaps it is not wise to attempt lifting the veil which
rests on the unnamed 'such an one,' whose was the privilege of being the last Host of the Lord and the first
Host of His Church, gathered within the new bond of the
fellowship of His Body and Blood. And yet to us at
least it seems most likely that it was the house of Mark's
father (then still alive)—a large one, as we gather from

Acts xii. 13. For the most obvious explanation of the
introduction by St. Mark alone of such an incident as
that about the young man who was accompanying Christ
as He was led away captive, is that he was none other
than St. Mark himself. If so, we can understand how
the traitor may have first brought the Temple-guards, who
had come to seize Christ, to the house of Mark's father,
where the Supper had been held, and that, finding Him
gone, they had followed to Gethsemane, for 'Judas knew
the place, for Jesus ofttimes resorted thither with His
disciples'[a]—and how Mark, startled from his
sleep by the appearance of the armed men,
would hastily cast about him his loose tunic and run after
them : then, after the flight of the disciples, accompany
Christ, but escape intended arrest by leaving his tunic in
the hands of his would-be captors.

    If the owner of the house had provided all that was
needed for the Supper, Peter and John would find there
the Wine for the four Cups, the cakes of unleavened Bread,
and probably also 'the bitter herbs.' Of the latter five
kinds are mentioned, which were to be dipped once in salt
water, or vinegar, and another time in a mixture made of
nuts, raisins, apples, almonds, &c. The wine was the ordinary one of the country, only red ; it was mixed with
water, generally in the proportion of one part to two of
water. The quantity for each of the four Cups is stated by
one authority at what may be roughly computed at half a
tumbler—of course mixed with water. The Paschal Cup
is described as two fingers long by two fingers broad, and
its height as a finger, half a finger, and one-third of a
finger. All things being, as we presume, ready in the
furnished upper room, it would only remain for Peter and
John to see to the Paschal Lamb and anything else required for the Supper, possibly also to what was to be
offered as festive sacrifice, and afterwards eaten at the
Supper. If the latter were to be brought, the disciples
would have to attend earlier in the Temple. The cost of
the Lamb, which had to be provided, was very small. So
low a sum as about threepence of our money is mentioned

[a] St. John xviii. 1, 2

for such a sacrifice. But we prefer the more reasonable computation of from 2*s*. 6*d*. to 7*s*. 6*d*. of our money.

If we mistake not, these purchases had, however, already been made on the previous afternoon by Judas. It is not likely that they would have been left to the last; nor that He Who had so lately condemned the traffic in the Courts of the Temple, would have sent His two disciples thither to purchase the Paschal Lamb, which would have been necessary to secure an animal that had passed Levitical inspection, since on the Passover-day there would have been no time to subject it to such scrutiny. On the other hand, if Judas had made this purchase, we perceive not only on what pretext he may have gone to Jerusalem on the previous afternoon, but also how, on his way from the Sheep-market to the Temple to have his lamb inspected, he may have learned that the Chief-Priests and Sanhedrists were just then in session in the Palace of the High-Priest close by.

On the supposition just made, the task of Peter and John would indeed have been simple. They left the house of Mark with wondering but saddened hearts. Once more had they had evidence how the Master's Divine glance searched the future in all its details. And now it would be time for the Evening Service and Sacrifice. Ordinarily this began about 2.30 P.M.—the daily Evening Sacrifice being actually offered up about an hour later; but on this occasion, on account of the Feast, the Service was an hour earlier. As at about half-past one of our time the two Apostles ascended the Temple-Mount, following a dense crowd of Pilgrims, they would find the Priests' Court filled with white-robed Priests and Levites—for on that day all the twenty-four Courses were on duty, and all their services would be called for, although only the Course for that week would that afternoon engage in the ordinary Service, which preceded that of the Feast. There must have been to them a mournful significance in the language of Ps. lxxxi., as the Levites chanted it that afternoon in three sections, broken three times by the threefold blast from the silver trumpets of the Priests.

Before the incense was burnt for the Evening Sacrifice, or yet the lamps in the Golden Candlestick were trimmed for the night, the Paschal Lambs were slain. The worshippers were admitted in three divisions within the Court of the Priests. When the first company had entered, the massive Nicanor Gates—which led from the Court of the Women to that of Israel—and the other side gates into the Court of the Priests were closed. A threefold blast from the Priests' trumpets intimated that the Lambs were being slain. This each Israelite did for himself. We can scarcely be mistaken in supposing that Peter and John would be in the first of the three companies into which the offerers were divided; for they must have been anxious to be gone, and to meet the Master and their brethren in that 'upper room.' Peter and John had slain the Lamb. In two rows the officiating Priests stood, up to the great Altar of Burnt-offering. As one caught up the blood from the dying Lamb in a golden bowl, he handed it to his colleague, receiving in return an empty bowl; and so the blood was passed on to the Great Altar, where it was jerked in one jet at the base of the Altar. While this was going on, the *Hallel*[a] was being chanted by the Levites. We remember that only the first line of every Psalm was repeated by the worshippers; while to every other line they responded by a *Halleluyah*, till Ps. cxviii. was reached, when, besides the first, these three lines were also repeated :—

> Save now, I beseech Thee, LORD ;
> O LORD, I beseech Thee, send now prosperity.
> Blessed be He that cometh in the Name of the LORD.

Little more remained to be done. The sacrifice was laid on staves which rested on the shoulders of Peter and John, flayed, cleansed, and the parts which were to be burnt on the Altar removed and prepared for burning. The Lamb would be roasted on a pomegranate spit that passed right through it from mouth to vent, special care being taken that, in roasting, the Lamb did not touch the oven. Everything else also would be made ready and placed on a table which could be carried in and moved at will; finally, the festive lamps would be prepared.

'It was probably as the sun was beginning to decline that Jesus and the other ten disciples descended once more over the Mount of Olives into the Holy City. . . . It was the last day-view which the Lord could take, free and unhindered, of the Holy City till His Resurrection. . . . He was going forward to accomplish His Death in Jerusalem; to fulfil type and prophecy, and to offer Himself up as the true Passover Lamb—"the Lamb of God, Which taketh away the sin of the world." They who followed Him were busy with many thoughts. They knew that terrible events awaited them, and they had only shortly before been told that these glorious Temple-buildings, to which, with a national pride not unnatural, they had directed the attention of their Master, were to become desolate, not one stone being left upon the other. Among them, revolving his dark plans, and goaded on by the great Enemy, moved the betrayer. And now they were within the City. Its Temple, its royal bridge, its splendid palaces, its busy marts, its streets filled with festive pilgrims, were well known to them, as they made their way to the house where the guest-chamber had been prepared. Meanwhile, the crowd came down from the Temple-Mount, each bearing on his shoulders the sacrificial Lamb, to make ready for the Paschal Supper.'[1]

[1] 'The Temple and its Services,' pp. 194, 195.

CHAPTER LXXX.

THE PASCHAL SUPPER—THE INSTITUTION OF THE LORD'S SUPPER.

(St. Matt. xxvi. 17-19; St. Mark xiv. 12-16; St. Luke xxii. 7-13; St. John xiii. 1; St. Matt. xxvi. 20; St. Mark xiv. 17; St. Luke xxii. 14-16; 24-30; 17, 18; St. John xiii. 2-20; St. Matt. xxvi. 21-24; St. Mark xiv. 18-21; St. Luke xxii. 21-23; St. John xiii. 21-26; St. Matt. xxvi. 25; St. John xiii. 26-38; St. Matt. xxvi. 26-29; St. Mark xiv. 22-25; St. Luke xxii. 19, 20.)

THE period designated as ' between the two even-ings,' [a] when the Paschal Lamb was to be slain, was past. The first three stars had become visible, and the threefold blast of the Silver Trumpets from the Temple-Mount rang out that the Pascha had once more commenced. In the festively-lit ' upper chamber' of St. Mark's house the Master and the Twelve were gathered.

[a] Ex. xii. 6; Lev. xxiii. 5; Numb. ix. 3, 5

So far as appears, or we have reason to infer, this Passover was the only sacrifice ever offered by Jesus Himself. If Christ were in Jerusalem at any Passover before His Public Ministry began, He would have been a guest at some table, not the Head of a Company (which must consist of at least ten persons). Hence, He would not have been the offerer of the Paschal Lamb. And of the three Passovers since His Public Ministry had begun, at the first His Twelve Apostles had not been gathered,[b] so that He could not have appeared as the Head of a Company; while at the second He was not in Jerusalem but in the utmost parts of Galilee, in the borderland of Tyre and Sidon, where no sacrifice could be brought.[c] What additional meaning does this give to the words which He spake to the Twelve as He sat down with them to the Supper: ' With desire have I desired to eat this Pascha with you before I suffer ! '

[b] St. John ii. 13

[c] St. Matt. xv. 21 &c.

A significant Jewish legend connected almost every great event and deliverance in Israel with the Night of the

Passover. The Pascha was indeed a Sacrifice distinct from all others. It was not of the Law, for it was instituted before the Law had been given or the Covenant ratified by blood ; nay, in a sense it was the cause and the foundation of all the Levitical Sacrifices and of the Covenant itself. Just as the Priesthood of Christ was real, yet not after the order of Aaron, so was the Sacrifice of Christ real, yet not after the order of Levitical sacrifices, but after that of the Passover.

It is difficult to decide how much, not only of the present ceremonial, but even of the rubric for the Paschal Supper as contained in the oldest Jewish documents, may have been obligatory at the time of Christ. We may take it that, as prescribed, all would appear at the Paschal Supper in festive array. We also know that, as the Jewish Law directed, they reclined on pillows around a low table, each resting on his left hand, so as to leave the right free. But ancient Jewish usage casts a strange light on the scene with which the Supper opened. The Supper began with ' a contention among them, which of them should be accounted to be greatest.' We can have no doubt that its occasion was the order in which they should occupy places at the table. We know that this was subject of contention among the Pharisees, and that they claimed to be seated according to their rank. Even if we had not further indications of it, we should instinctively associate such a strife in this instance with the presence of Judas.

Around a low Eastern table, oval or rather elongated, two parts covered with a cloth, and standing or else suspended, the single divans or pillows are ranged in the form of an elongated horseshoe, leaving free one end of the table, somewhat as in the accompanying woodcut. Here A represents the table, B B respectively the ends of the two rows of single divans on which each guest reclines on his left side, with his head (C) nearest the table, and his feet (D) stretching back towards the ground.

Christ reclined on the middle divan. We know from the Gospel-narrative that John occupied the place on His right, at that end of the divans—as we may call it—at the head of the table, otherwise he could not have leaned back upon His Bosom. But the chief place next to the Master would be that to His left, or above Him. In the strife of the disci-ples, which should be ac-counted the greatest, this had been claimed, and we believe it to have been actually occupied by Judas. This explains how, when Christ whispered to John by *a St. John* what sign to recog-*xiii. 26* nise the traitor,[a] none of the other disciples heard it. It also explains how Christ would first hand to Judas the sop, which formed

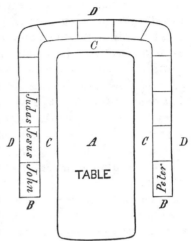

part of the Paschal ritual, beginning with him as the chief guest at the table, without thereby exciting special notice. Lastly, it accounts for the circumstance that when Judas, desirous of ascertaining whether his treachery was known, dared to ask whether it was he, and received the affirmative *b St. Matt.* answer,[b] no one at table knew what had passed. *xxvi. 25* But this could not have been the case, unless Judas had occupied the place next to Christ ; in this case, necessarily that at His left, or the post of chief honour. As regards Peter, we can quite understand how, when the Lord with such loving words rebuked their self-seeking and taught them of the greatness of Christian humility, he should, in his impetuosity of shame, have rushed to take the lowest place at the other end of the table. Finally, we can now understand how Peter could beckon to John, who sat at the opposite end of the table, over against him, and *c St. John* ask him across the table who the traitor was.[c] *xiii. 24* The rest of the disciples would occupy such places as were most convenient, or suited their fellowship with one another.

The words which the Master spoke as He appeased

their unseemly strife must, indeed, have touched them to the quick. First, He showed them the difference between worldly honour and distinction in the Church of Christ. In the world kingship lay in supremacy and lordship, and the title of Benefactor accompanied the sway of power. But in the Church the 'greater' would not exercise lordship, but become as the less and the younger [the latter referring to the circumstance that age, next to learning, was regarded among the Jews as a claim to distinction and the chief seats]; while instead of him that had authority being called Benefactor, the relationship would be reversed, and he that served would be chief.[a] Having thus shown them the character and title to that greatness in the Kingdom which was in prospect for them, He pointed them in this respect also to Himself as their example. The reference here is, of course, not to the act of symbolic foot-washing, but to the tenor of His whole Life and the object of His Mission, as of One Who served, not was served. Lastly, He woke them to the higher consciousness of their own calling. Assuredly, they would not lose their reward; but not here, nor yet now. They had shared, and would share His 'trials'—His being set at nought, despised, persecuted; but they would also share His glory. As the Father had 'covenanted' to Him, so He 'covenanted' and bequeathed to them a Kingdom, ' in order,' or ' so that,' in it they might have festive fellowship of rest and of joy with Him. What to them must have been ' temptations,' and in that respect also to Christ, they had endured: instead of Messianic glory, such as they may at first have thought of, they had witnessed only contradiction, denial, and shame—and they had ' continued ' with Him. But the Kingdom was also coming. When His glory was manifested, their acknowledgment would also come. Here Israel had rejected the King and His Messengers, but then would that same Israel be judged by their word. A Royal dignity this, indeed, but one of service; a full Royal acknowledgment, but one of work.

So speaking, the Lord commenced the Supper, which in itself was symbol and pledge of what He had just said

a St. Luke xxii. 25, 26

and promised. The Paschal Supper began, as always, by the Head of the Company taking the first cup, and speaking over it 'the thanksgiving.' The form presently in use consists really of two benedictions—the first over the wine, the second for the return of this Feastday with all that it implies, and for being preserved once more to witness it.[1] Turning to the Gospels, the words which follow the record

ᵃ St. Luke xxii. 17, 18 of the benediction on the part of Christ ᵃ seem to imply that Jesus had, at any rate, so far made use of the ordinary thanksgiving as to speak both these benedictions. That over the wine was quite simple: 'Blessed art Thou, Jehovah our God, Who hast created the fruit of the Vine!' We need not doubt that these were the very words spoken by our Lord. It is otherwise as regards the benediction 'over the day,' which contains words expressive of Israel's national pride and self-righteousness, such as we cannot think would have been uttered by our Lord. With this exception, however, they were no doubt identical in contents with the present formula. This we infer from what the Lord added, as He passed the cup round the circle of the disciples. No more, so He told them, would He speak the benediction over the fruit of the vine—not again utter the thanks 'over the day,' that they had been ' preserved alive, sustained, and brought to this season.' Another Wine, and at another Feast, now awaited Him—that in the future, when the Kingdom would come. It was to be the last of the old Paschas; the first, or rather the symbol and promise, of the new.

The cup in which, according to express Rabbinic testimony, the wine had been mixed with water before it was ' blessed,' had passed round. The next part of the ceremonial was for the Head of the Company to rise and ' wash

ᵇ St. John xiii. hands.' It is this part of the ritual of which St. John ᵇ records the adaptation and transformation on the part of Christ. The washing of the disciples' feet is evidently connected with the ritual of ' handwashing.' Now this was done twice during the Paschal Supper : the first time by the Head of the Company alone, immediately

---

[1] The whole formula is given in ' The Temple and its Services,' pp. 204, 205.

after the first cup; the second time by all present, at a much later part of the service, immediately before the actual meal (on the Lamb, &c.) If the footwashing had taken place on the latter occasion, it is natural to suppose that when the Lord rose all the disciples would have followed His example, and so the washing of their feet would have been impossible. Again, the footwashing, which was intended both as a lesson and as an example of humility and service,[a] was evidently connected with the dispute 'which of them should be accounted to be greatest.' If so, the symbolical act of our Lord must have followed close on the strife of the disciples, and on our Lord's teaching what in the Church constituted rule and greatness. Hence the act must have been connected with the first handwashing—that by the Head of the Company—immediately after the first cup, and not with that at a later period, when much else had intervened.

a St. John xiii. 12–16

All else fits in with this. For clearness' sake, the account given by St. John[b] may here be recapitulated. The opening words concerning the love of Christ to His own unto the end form the general introduction. Then follows the account of what happened 'during Supper'[c]—the Supper itself being left undescribed—beginning, by way of explanation of what is to be told about Judas, with this: 'The Devil having already cast into his (Judas') heart, that Judas Iscariot, the son of Simon, shall betray Him.' General as this notice is, it contains much that requires special attention. Thankfully we feel that the heart of man was not capable of originating the Betrayal of Christ; humanity had fallen, but not so low. It was the Devil who had 'cast' it into Judas' heart—with force and overwhelming power. Again we mark the full description of the name and parentage of the traitor. It reads like the wording of a formal indictment.

b St. John xiii.

c ver. 2

If what Satan had cast into the heart of Judas explains his conduct, so does the knowledge which Jesus possessed account for that He was about to do.[d] Many as are the thoughts suggested by the words,

d ver. 3

'Knowing that the Father had given all things into His Hands, and that He came forth from God, and goeth unto God'—yet, from their evident connection, they must in the first instance be applied to the footwashing, of which they are, so to speak, the logical antecedent. And so, 'during Supper,' which had begun with the first cup, 'He riseth from Supper.' The disciples would scarcely marvel except that He should conform to that practice of handwashing, which, as He had often explained, was, as a ceremonial observance, unavailing for those who were not inwardly clean, and needless and unmeaning in them whose heart and life had been purified. But they must have wondered as they saw Him put off His upper garment, gird Himself with a towel, and pour water into a basin, like a slave who was about to perform the meanest service.

From the position which, as we have shown, Peter occupied at the end of the table, it was natural that the Lord should begin with him the act of footwashing. Besides, had He first turned to others, Peter must either have remonstrated before, or else his later expostulation would have been tardy, and an act of self-righteousness or needless humility. As it was, the surprise with which he and the others had witnessed the preparation of the Lord, burst into characteristic language when Jesus approached him to wash his feet. 'Lord—Thou—of me washest the feet!' It was the utterance of deepest reverence for the Master, and yet of utter misunderstanding of the meaning of His action, perhaps even of His Work. Jesus was now but doing what before He had spoken.

But Peter had understood none of these things. He only felt the incongruousness of their relative positions. And so the Lord, partly also wishing thereby to lead his impetuosity to the absolute submission of faith, and partly to indicate the deeper truth he was to learn in the future, only told him that though he knew it not now, he would understand hereafter what the Lord was doing. Hereafter— when, after that night of terrible fall, he would learn by the Lake of Galilee what it really meant to feed the lambs and to tend the sheep of Christ; hereafter—when no longer,

N N

as when he had been young, he would gird himself and walk whither he would. But, even so, Peter could not content himself with the prediction that in the future he would understand and enter into what Christ was doing in washing their feet. Never, he declared, could he allow it. The same feelings, which had prompted him to attempt withdrawing the Lord from the path of humiliation and suffering,[a] now asserted themselves again. It was personal affection, indeed, but it was also unwillingness to submit to the humiliation of the Cross. And so the Lord told him that if He washed him not, he had no part with Him. Not that the bare act of washing gave him part in Christ, but that the refusal to submit to it would have deprived him of it; and that to share in this washing was, as it were, the way to have part in Christ's service of love, to enter into it, and to share it.

Still Peter did not understand. But as, on that morning by the Lake of Galilee, it appeared that when he had lost all else he had retained love, so did love to the Christ now give him the victory—and, once more with characteristic impetuosity, he would have tendered not only his feet to be washed, but his hands and head. Yet here also was there misunderstanding. There was deep symbolical meaning, not only in *that* Christ did it, but also in *what* He did. What He did, meant His work and service of love; the constant cleansing of our walk and life in the love of Christ, and in the service of that love. The action was symbolic, and meant that the disciple who was already bathed and made clean in heart and spirit, required only this—to wash his feet in spiritual consecration to the service of love which Christ had here shown forth in symbolic act. And so His Words referred not to the forgiveness of our daily sins—the introduction of which would have been abrupt and unconnected with the context—but, in contrast to all self-seeking, to the daily consecration of our life to the service of love after the example of Christ.

They were clean, these disciples, but not all. For He knew that there was among them he 'that was betraying Him.' He knew it, but not with the knowledge of an inevitable fate impending, far less of an absolute decree, but with that knowledge which would again and again speak out the warning, if by any means he might be saved.

The solemn service of Christ now went on in the silence

^a St. John xiii. 12-17 of reverent awe.[a] None dared question Him nor resist. It was ended, and He had resumed His upper garment, and again taken His place at the Table. It was His now by illustrative words to explain the practical application of what had just been done. They were wont to call Him by the two highest names of Teacher and Lord, and these designations were rightly His. For the first time He fully accepted and owned the highest homage. How much more, then, must His Service of love, Who was their Teacher and Lord, serve as example of what was due by each to his fellow-disciple and fellow-servant! No principle better known, almost proverbial in Israel, than that a servant was not to claim greater honour than his master, nor yet he that was sent than he who had sent him. They knew this, and now also the meaning of the symbolic act of footwashing; and if they acted it out, then theirs would be the promised 'Beatitude.'

This reference to what were familiar expressions among the Jews, leads us to supplement a few illustrative notes from the same source. The Greek word for 'the towel,' with which our Lord girded Himself, occurs also in Rabbinic writings, to denote the towel used in washing and at baths. Such girding was the common mark of a slave, by whom the service of footwashing was ordinarily performed. Again, the combination of these two designations, 'Rabbi and Lord,' or 'Rabbi, Father, and Lord,' was among those most common on the part of disciples. The idea that if a man knows (for example, the Law) and does not do it, it

^b Comp. ver. 17 were better for him not to have been created,[b] is not unfrequently expressed. But the most interesting reference is in regard to the relation between the sender and the sent, and a servant and his master. In regard to the former, it is proverbially said, that while he that is sent stands on the same footing as he who sent him, yet he must expect less honour. And as regards Christ's

N N 2

statement that ' the servant is not greater than his Master,' there is a passage in which we read, in connection with the sufferings of the Messiah : ' It is enough for the servant that he be like his Master.'

But to return. The footwashing on the part of Christ, in which Judas had shared, together with the explanatory words that followed, required this limitation : ' I speak not of you all.' For it would be a night of moral sifting to them all. We come here upon these words of deepest mysteriousness : ' I know those I chose ; but that the Scripture may be fulfilled, He that eateth My Bread lifteth up his heel against Me.[a] Jesus had, from the first, known the inmost thoughts of those He had chosen to be His Apostles ; but by this treachery of one of their number, the terrible prediction of the worst enmity, that of ingratitude, would receive its complete fulfilment. The word ' *that* ' does not mean ' in order that,' or ' for the purpose of ; ' it never means this in such a connection ; and it would be altogether irrational to suppose that an event happened in order that a special prediction might be fulfilled. Rather does it indicate the higher internal connection in the succession of events, when an event had taken place in the free determination of its agents, by which, all unknown to them and unthought of by others, that unexpectedly came to pass which had been Divinely foretold. Thus the word ' that ' marks not the connection between causation and effect, but between the Divine antecedent and the human subsequent.

a Ps. xli. 9

We know not whether Christ spoke all these things continuously, after He had sat down, having washed the disciples' feet. More probably it was at different parts of the meal. This would also account for the seeming abruptness of this concluding sentence : [b] ' He that receiveth whomsoever I send receiveth Me.' And yet the internal connection of thought seems clear. The apostasy and loss of one of the Apostles was known to Christ. His words conveyed an assurance that any such break would not be lasting, and that in this respect also ' the foundation of God standeth.'

b St. John xiii. 20

In the meantime the Paschal Supper was proceeding. According to the rubric, after the ' washing ' the dishes were immediately to be brought on the table. Then the Head of the Company would dip some of the bitter herbs into the salt-water or vinegar, speak a blessing, and partake of them, then hand them to each in the company. Next, he would break one of the unleavened cakes (according to the present ritual the middle of the three), of which half was put aside for after supper. This is called the *Aphiqomon*, or after-dish, and as we believe that ' the bread' of the Holy Eucharist was the *Aphiqomon*, some particulars may here be of interest. The dish in which the broken cake lies (not the *Aphiqomon*), is elevated, and these words are spoken : ' This is the bread of misery which our fathers ate in the land of Egypt. All that are hungry, come and eat ; all that are needy, come, keep the Pascha.' In the more modern ritual the words are added : ' This year here, next year in the land of Israel ; this year bondsmen, next year free ! ' On this the second cup is filled, and the youngest in the company is instructed to make formal inquiry as to the meaning of all the observances of that night, when the Liturgy proceeds to give full answers as regards the festival, its occasion, and ritual. We do not suppose that even the earlier ritual represents the exact observances at the time of Christ. But so much stress is laid in Jewish writings on the duty of fully rehearsing at the Paschal Supper the circumstances of the first Passover and the deliverance connected with it, that we can scarcely doubt that what the Mishnah declares as so essential, formed part of the services of that night. And as we think of our Lord's comment on the Passover and Israel's deliverance, the words spoken when the unleavened cake was broken come back to us, and with deeper meaning attaching to them.

After this the cup is elevated, and then the service proceeds somewhat lengthily, the cup being raised a second time and certain prayers spoken. This part of the service concludes with the two first Psalms in the series called 'The Hallel,'[a] when the cup is raised a third

[a] Ps. cxiii. to cxviii.

time, a prayer spoken, and the cup drunk. This ends
the first part of the service. And now the Paschal meal
begins by all washing their hands—a part of the ritual
which we scarcely think Christ observed. It was, we
believe, during this lengthened exposition and service
that the 'trouble in spirit' of which St. John speaks [a]
[a] St. John xiii. 21 passed over the soul of the God-Man. Almost
presumptuous as it seems to inquire into its
immediate cause, we can scarcely doubt that it concerned
not so much Himself as them. It was the beginning of
the hour of Christ's utmost loneliness, of which the climax
was reached in Gethsemane. And in the trouble of His
Spirit did He solemnly 'testify' to them of the near
Betrayal. We wonder not that they all became exceeding
sorrowful, and each asked, 'Lord, is it I?'

The answer of Christ left the special person undetermined, while it again repeated the awful prediction—shall
we not add, the most solemn warning?—that it was one
of those who took part in the Supper. It is at this point
[b] ver. 22 that St. John resumes the thread of the narrative.[b]
As he describes it, the disciples were looking one
on another, doubting of whom He spake. In this suspense
Peter beckoned from across the table to John, whose head,
instead of leaning on his hand, rested in the absolute
surrender of love and intimacy born of sorrow on the
bosom of the Master. Peter would have John ask of
whom Jesus spake. And to the whispered question of
John, 'leaning back as he was on Jesus' Breast,' the Lord
gave the sign, that it was he to whom He would give 'the
sop' when He had dipped it. Even this perhaps was not
clear to John, since each one in turn received 'the sop.'

We have direct testimony that, about the time of
Christ, 'the sop' which was handed round consisted of
these things wrapped together: flesh of the Paschal Lamb,
a piece of unleavened bread, and bitter herbs. This, we
believe, was 'the sop,' which Jesus, having dipped it for
him in the dish, handed first to Judas, as occupying the
first and chief place at Table. But before He did so,
probably while He dipped it in the dish, Judas, who could

not but fear that his purpose might be known, reclining
at Christ's left Hand, whispered into the Master's Ear, 'Is
it I, Rabbi?' It must have been whispered, for no one at
the Table could have heard either the question of Judas or
the affirmative answer of Christ.[a] It was the last
outgoing of the pitying love of Christ after the
traitor. It must have been in a paroxysm of mental mania,
when all feeling was turned to stone, and self-delusion was
combined with moral perversion, that Judas ' took ' from
the Hand of Jesus ' the sop.' That moment Satan entered
again into his heart. But the deed was virtually done;
and Jesus, longing for the quiet fellowship of His own with
all that was to follow, bade him do quickly that he did.

a St. John
xiii. 28

From the meal scarcely begun Judas rushed into the
night. None there knew why this strange haste, unless
from obedience to something that the Master had bidden
him. Even John could scarcely have understood the sign
which Christ had given of the traitor. Some of them
thought he had been directed by the words of Christ to
purchase what was needful for the feast; others, that he
was bidden go and give something to the poor. It must
have been specially necessary to make preparations for
the offering of the *Chagigah,* or festive sacrifice, when, as
in this instance, the first festive day, or 15th Nisan, was to
be followed by a Sabbath, on which no such work was permitted. It would be quite natural too that the poor, who
gathered around the Temple, might then seek to obtain
the help of the charitable.

The departure of the betrayer seemed to clear the
atmosphere. He was gone to do his work; but let it
not be thought that it was the necessity of that betrayal
which was the cause of Christ's suffering of soul. He
offered Himself willingly—and though it was brought
about through the treachery of Judas, yet it was Jesus
Himself Who freely brought Himself a Sacrifice, in fulfilment of the work which the Father had given Him.
All the more did He realise and express this on the
departure of Judas. And this voluntary sacrificial aspect is further clearly indicated by His selection of the

terms 'Son of Man' and 'God' instead of 'Son' and
'Father.'[a] 'Now is glorified the Son of Man, and
God is glorified in Him.   And God shall glorify
Him in Himself, and straightway shall He glorify Him.'
If the first of these sentences expressed the meaning of
what was about to take place, as exhibiting the utmost
glory of the Son of Man in the triumph of the obedience
of His Voluntary Sacrifice, the second sentence pointed
out its acknowledgment by God : the exaltation which
followed the humiliation—the Crown after the Cross.

   Thus far for one aspect of what was about to be enacted.   As for the other—that which concerned the disciples : only a little while would He still be with them.
Then would come the time of sad and sore perplexity—
when they would seek Him, but could not come whither
He had gone—during the terrible hours between His
Crucifixion and His manifested Resurrection.   With reference to that period especially, but in general to the
whole time of His Separation from the Church on earth,
the great commandment, the bond which alone would hold
them together, was that of love one to another, and such
love as that which He had shown towards them.[a]

   As recorded by St. John, the words of the Lord
were succeeded by a question of Peter, indicating perplexity
as to the primary and direct meaning of Christ's going away.
On this followed Christ's reply about the impossibility of
Peter's now sharing his Lord's way of Passion, and, in
answer to the disciple's impetuous assurance of his readiness to follow the Master not only into peril, but to lay
down his life for Him, the Lord's indication of Peter's
present unpreparedness and the prediction of his impending denial.   It may have been that all this occurred in
the Supper-Chamber and at the time indicated by St. John.
But it is also recorded by the Synoptists as on the way to
Gethsemane, and in what we may term a more natural
connection.   Its consideration will therefore be best reserved till we reach that stage of the history.

   We now approach the most solemn part of that night :
The Institution of the Lord's Supper.

[a] St. John

[a] St. John
xiii. 31–35

If we ask ourselves at what part of the Paschal Supper the new Institution was made, we cannot doubt that it a St. Matt. was before the Supper was completely ended.[a] xxvi. 26 ; We have seen that Judas had left the Table at St. Mark xiv. 22 the beginning of the Supper. The meal continued amidst such conversation as has already been noted. According to the Jewish ritual, the third cup was filled at b 1 Cor. x. 16 the close of the Supper. This was called, as by St. Paul,[b] 'the Cup of Blessing,' partly, because a special ' blessing ' was pronounced over it. It is described as one of the ten essential rites in the Paschal Supper. Next, ' grace after meat ' was spoken. On this we need not dwell, nor yet on ' the washing of hands ' that followed. But we can have little doubt that the Institution of the Cup was in connection with this third ' Cup of Blessing.' If we are asked what part of the Paschal Service corresponds to the ' Breaking of Bread,' we answer, that this being really the last Pascha, and the cessation of it, our Lord anticipated the later rite, introduced when, with the destruction of the Temple, the Paschal as all other Sacrifices ceased. While the Paschal Lamb was still offered, it was the Law that, after partaking of its' flesh, nothing else should be eaten. But since the Paschal Lamb has ceased, it is the custom after the meal to break and partake, as ' after-dish,' of that half of the unleavened cake, which, as will be remembered, had been broken and put aside at the beginning of the Supper. The Paschal Sacrifice having now really ceased, Christ anticipated this, and connected with the breaking of the Unleavened Cake at the close of the Meal the Institution of the breaking of Bread in the Holy Eucharist.

What did the Institution really mean, and what does it mean to us ? We cannot believe that it was intended as merely a sign for remembrance of His Death. Such remembrance is often equally vivid in ordinary acts of faith or prayer ; and it seems difficult, if no more than this had been intended, to account for the Institution of a special Sacrament, and that with such solemnity, and as the second great rite of the Church—that for its nourishment. Again, if it were a mere token of remembrance, why the Cup as well as the Bread? If we may venture an explanation, it would be that 'this,' received in the Holy Eucharist, conveys to the soul as regards the Body and Blood of the Lord, the same effect as the Bread and the Wine to the body—receiving of the Bread and the Cup in the Holy Communion is, really, though spiritually, to the Soul what the outward elements are to the Body: that they are both the symbol and the vehicle of true inward, spiritual feeding on the Very Body and Blood of Christ. So is this Cup which we bless fellowship of His Blood, and the Bread we break of His Body—fellowship with Him Who died for us, and in His dying; fellowship also in Him with one another, who are joined together in this, that for us this Body was given, and for the remission of our sins this precious Blood was shed.

Most mysterious words these, yet 'he who takes from us our mystery takes from us our Sacrament.'[1] And ever since has this blessed Institution been not only the seal of His Presence and its pledge, but also the promise of His Coming. 'For as often as we eat this Bread and drink this Cup, we do show forth the Death of the Lord'—for the life of the world, to be assuredly yet manifested—'till He come.' 'Even so, Lord Jesus, come quickly!'

CHAPTER LXXXI.

THE LAST DISCOURSES OF CHRIST—THE PRAYER OF CONSECRATION.

(St. John xiv.; xv.; xvi.; xvii.)

THE new Institution of the Lord's Supper did not finally close what passed at that Paschal Table. According to the Jewish ritual the Cup is filled a fourth time, and the remaining part of the *Hallel*[a] repeated. Then follow, besides Ps. cxxxvi., a number of prayers

[a] Ps. cxv.-cxviii.

[1] The words are a hitherto unprinted utterance on this subject by the late *Prof. J. Duncan*, of Edinburgh.

and hymns, of comparatively late origin. The same remark applies to what follows after the fourth Cup. But, so far as we can judge, the Institution of the Holy Supper was followed by the Discourse recorded in St. John xiv. Then

* St.Matt.
xxvi. 30;
St. Mark
xiv. 26
ᵇ St. John
xvii.
ᶜ St. John
xviii. 1

the concluding Psalms of the *Hallel* were sung,[a] after which the Master left the ' upper chamber.' The Discourse of Christ recorded in St. John xvi., and His prayer,[b] were certainly uttered after they had risen from the Supper, and before they crossed the brook Kidron.[c] In all probability they were, however, spoken before the Saviour left the house. We can scarcely imagine such a Discourse, and still less such a Prayer, to have been uttered while traversing the narrow streets of Jerusalem on the way to Kidron.

1. In any case there cannot be doubt that the first

ᵈ Recorded
in St. John
xiv.
ᵉ vv. 1-4
ᶠ vv. 5-14
ᵍ vv. 15-24
ʰ vv. 24-31

Discourse[d] was spoken while still at the Supper-Table. If so, it may be arranged under these four particulars : *explanatory and corrective ;* [e] *explanatory and teaching ;* [f] *hortatory and promissory ;* [g] *promissory and consolatory.* [h] Thus there is constant and connected progress, the two great elements in the discourse being teaching and comfort.

At the outset we ought, perhaps, to remember the very common Jewish idea, that those in glory occupied different abodes, corresponding to their ranks. If the words of Christ, about the place whither they could not follow Him, had awakened any such thoughts, the explanation which He now gave must effectually have dispelled them. Let not their hearts, then, be troubled at the prospect. As they believed in God, so let them also have trust in Him. It was His Father's House of which they were thinking, and although there were ' many mansions,' or rather ' stations,' in it—and the choice of this word may teach us something—yet they were all in that one House. Could they not trust Him in this ? Surely, if it had been otherwise, He would have told them, and not left them to be bitterly disappointed in the end. Indeed, the object of His going was the opposite of what they feared : it was to prepare by His Death and Resurrection a place for them.

Nor let them think that His going away would imply a permanent separation, because He had said that they could not follow Him thither. Rather did His going, not away, but to prepare a place for them, imply His coming again, primarily as regarded individuals at death, and secondarily as regarded the Church—that He might receive them unto Himself, there to be with Him. 'And whither I go, ye know the way.' [a]

* St John
xiv. 1-4

Jesus had referred to His going to the Father's House, and implied that they knew the way which would bring them thither also. But how could they find their way thither? If any Jewish ideas of the disappearance and the final manifestation of the Messiah lurked beneath the question of Thomas, the answer of the Lord placed the matter in the clearest light. He had spoken of the Father's House of many 'stations,' but only one road led thither. They must all know it: it was that of personal apprehension of Christ in the life, the mind, and the heart. Except through Him, no man could consciously come to the Father. Thomas had put his twofold question thus: What was the goal? and, what was the way to it? In His answer Christ significantly reversed this order, and told them first what was the way—Himself; and then what was the goal.

But once more appeared in the words of Philip that carnal literalising, which would take the words of Christ in only an external sense.[b] Sayings like these help us to perceive the absolute need of another Teacher, the Holy Spirit. Philip understood the words of Christ as if He held out the possibility of an actual sight of the Father; and this, as they imagined, would for ever have put an end to all their doubts and fears. In His reply Jesus once more returned to this truth, that the vision, which was that of faith alone, was spiritual, and in no way external; and that this manifestation had been, and was fully in Him. Or did Philip not believe that the Father was really manifested in Christ, because he did not actually behold Him? Those words which had drawn them and made them feel that heaven was so near, they were not His

^b ver. 8

own, but the message which He had brought them from the Father; those works which He had done, they were the manifestation of the Father's ' dwelling ' in Him. Let them then believe this vital union between the Father and Him—and, if their faith could not absolutely rise to that height, let it at least rest on the lower level of the evidence of His works. Yea, and if they were ever tempted to doubt His works, faith might have evidence of them in personal experience. Primarily, no doubt, the words [a] about the greater works which they who believed in Him would do, because He went to the Father, refer to the Apostolic preaching and working in its greater results after the outpouring of the Holy Spirit. To this also must primarily refer the promise of unlimited answer to prayer in His Name.[b] But in a secondary sense, both these promises have, ever since the Ascension of Christ, also applied both to the Church and to all individual Christians.

[a] St. John xiv. 12

[b] vv. 13, 14

And for such faith, which compasseth all things in the obedience of love to Christ, and can attain all by the prayer of faith in His Name, there will be a need of Divine Presence ever with them.[c] While He had been with them, they had had one *Paraclete*, or ' Advocate,' Who had pleaded with them the cause of God, explained and advocated the truth, and guarded and guided them. Now that His outward Presence was to be withdrawn from earth, and He was to be their Paraclete or Advocate in Heaven with the Father,[d] He would, as His first act of advocacy, pray the Father, Who would send them another Paraclete or Advocate, Who would continue with them for ever. To the guidance and pleadings of that Advocate they could implicitly trust themselves, for He was ' the Spirit of Truth.' The world, indeed, would not listen to His pleadings, nor accept Him as their Guide, for the only evidence by which they judged was that of outward sight and material results. But they would know the reality of His Existence and the truth of His pleadings by the continual presence with them as a body of this Paraclete, and by His dwelling in them individually.

[c] ver. 16

[d] 1 John ii. 1

In view of this promised Advent of the other Advocate, Christ could tell the disciples that He would not leave them ' orphans ' in this world. Nay, in this Advocate Christ Himself came to them. On that day of the Advent of His Holy Spirit would they have full knowledge, because experience, of the Christ's Return to the Father, and of their own being in Christ, and of His being in them. And, as regarded this threefold relationship, this must be ever kept in view : to be in Christ meant to love Him, and this was to have and to keep His commandments ; Christ's being in the Father implied that they who were in Christ or loved ᵃ St. John Him· would be loved also of His Father; and, xiv. 20, 21 lastly, Christ's being in them implied that He would love them and manifest Himself to them.ᵃ

One outstanding novel fact here arrested the attention of the disciples. It was contrary to all their Jewish ideas about the future manifestation of the Messiah, and it led to the question of one of their number, Judas—not Iscariot : ' Lord, what has happened, that to us Thou wilt manifest Thyself, and not to the world ? ' Again they thought of an outward, while He spoke of a spiritual and inward manifestation. It was of this coming of the Son and the Father for the purpose of making ' station ' with them that He spoke, of which the condition was love to Christ, manifested in the keeping of His Word, and which secured the love of the Father also. On the other hand, not to keep His Word was not to love Him, with all that it involved, not ᵇ vv. 22-24 only as regarded the Son, but also the Father, since the Word which they heard was the Father's.ᵇ

All this He could say to them now in the Father's Name—as the first Representative, Pleader, and ' Advocate ' or Paraclete. But what, when He was no longer present with them ? For that He had provided ' another Paraclete,' Advocate, or Pleader. This ' Paraclete, the Holy Spirit, Whom the Father will send in My Name, that same will teach you all things, and bring to your remembrance all things that I said to you.' Christ came in the Name of the Father, as the first Paraclete, as His Representative ; the Holy Spirit comes in the Name of Christ, as the second

Paraclete, the Representative of Christ, Who is in the Father.

And so at the end of this Discourse the Lord returned again, and now with fuller meaning, to its beginning. Then He had said : ' Let not your heart be troubled ; ye believe in God, believe also in Me.' Now, after the fuller communication of His purpose, and of their relation to Him, He could convey to them the assurance of peace, even His own peace, as His gift in the present, and His legacy for the future.[a] In their hearing, the fact of His going away, which had filled them with such sorrow and fear, had now been conjoined with that of His Coming to them. Therefore if, discarding thoughts of themselves, they had only given room to feelings of true love to Him, instead of mourning they would have rejoiced because He went to the Father, with all that this implied, not only of rest and triumph to Him, but of the perfecting of His Work—since this was the condition of that Mission of the Holy Ghost by the Father, Who sent both the Son and the Holy Spirit. And in this sense also should they have rejoiced, because, through the presence of the Holy Ghost in them, as sent by the Father in His ' greater ' work, they would, instead of the present selfish enjoyment of Christ's Personal Presence, have the more power of showing their love to Him in apprehending His Truth, obeying His Commandments, doing His Works, and participating in His Life. Not that Christ expected them to understand the full meaning of all these words. But afterwards, when it had all come to pass, they would believe.[b]

a St. John xiv. 27

b ver. 29

With the meaning and the issue of the great contest on which He was about to enter thus clearly before Him, did He now go forth to meet the last assault of the ' Prince of this World.'[c] But why that fierce struggle, since in Christ ' he hath nothing ' ? To exhibit to ' the world ' the perfect love which He had to the Father ; how even to the utmost of self-exinanition, obedience, submission, and suffering He was doing as the Father had given Him commandment, when He sent Him for the redemption

c ver. 30

of the world.   And so might the world be won from its
Prince by the full manifestation of Christ, in His infinite
obedience and righteousness, doing the Will of the Father

^a St. John
xiv. 31

and the Work which He had given Him, and in
His infinite love doing the work of our salvation.^a

2. The work of our salvation!   To this aspect of the
subject Christ now addressed Himself, as He rose from the
Supper-Table.   If in the Discourse recorded in the four-
teenth chapter of St. John's Gospel the Godward aspect of
Christ's impending departure was explained, in that of the
fifteenth chapter the new relation is set forth which was to
subsist between Him and His Church.   And this may be
summarised in these three words: Union, Communion,
Disunion.   The Union between Christ and His Church is
corporate, *vital*, and *effective*, alike as regards results and
blessings.^b   This Union issues in Communion—

^b xv. 1-8

of Christ with His disciples, of His disciples with
Him, and of His disciples among themselves.   Lastly, this
Union and Communion had for their necessary counterpart
Disunion, separation from the world.

As regards the relation of the Church to the Christ
Who is about to depart to the Father, and to come to them
in the Holy Ghost as His Representative, it is to be one of
Union—corporate, *vital*, and *effective*.   In the nature of it,
such a truth could only be set forth by illustration.   When
Christ said : ' I am the Vine, the true one, and My Father
is the Husbandman;' or again, ' Ye are the branches,' He
meant that He, the Father, and the disciples, stood in
exactly the same relationship as the Vine, the Husbandman,
and the branches.   Nor can we forget, in this connection,
that in the Old Testament, and partially in Jewish thought,
the Vine was the symbol of Israel, not in their national but
in their Church capacity.   There are many branches, yet
a grand unity in that Vine ; there is one Church of which
He is the Head, the Root, the Sustenance, the Life.

Yet, though it be one Vine, the Church must bear
fruit not only in her corporate capacity, but individually
in each of the branches.   The branches that bear not fruit
must refer to those who have by Baptism been inserted

into the Vine, but remain fruitless—since a merely outward profession of Christ could scarcely be described as 'a
branch in' Him.   On the other hand, every fruit-bearing
branch the Husbandman 'cleanseth'—in whatever manner
may be requisite—so that it may produce the largest
possible amount of fruit.   As for them, the process of
cleansing had 'already' been accomplished through, or
because of [the meaning is much the same], the Word
which He had spoken unto them.   The proper, normal
condition of every branch in that Vine was to bear much
fruit, of course, in proportion to its size and vigour.   But,
both figuratively and really, the condition of this was to
abide in Him, since 'apart' from Him they could do nothing.

And now as regarded the two alternatives: he that
abode not in Him was the branch 'cast outside' and
withering, which, when ready for it, men would cast into
the fire—with all of symbolic meaning as regards the
gatherers and the burning that the illustration implies.
On the other hand, if the corporate and vital union was
effective, if they abode in Him, and, in consequence, His
Words abode in them, then: 'Whatsoever ye will ye
shall ask, and it shall be done to you.'   It is very noteworthy that the unlimitedness of prayer is limited, or
rather conditioned, by our abiding in Christ and His
Words in us.   For it were the most dangerous fanaticism,
and entirely opposed to the teaching of Christ, to imagine
that the promise of Christ implies such absolute power—
as if prayer were magic—that a person might ask for anything, no matter what it was, in the assurance of obtaining
his request.   The believer may, indeed, ask for anything,
because he may always and absolutely go to God; but the
certainty of special answers to prayer is proportionate to
the degree of union and communion with Christ.

This union, being inward and moral, necessarily un-
folds into communion, of which the principle is love.
'Like as the Father loved Me, even so loved I you.   Abide
in My love.   If ye keep My commandments, ye shall
abide in the love that is Mine.'   This is connected, not
with sentiment nor even with faith, but with obedience.

In this, also, were they to have communion with Him:
communion in that joy which was His in consequence of
His perfect obedience. 'These things have I spoken to
you, in order that the joy *that is* Mine may be in you, and
your joy may be fulfilled [completed].'

But what of those commandments to which such importance attached ?   Clean as they now were through the
Words which He had spoken, one great commandment
stood forth as specially His own, consecrated by His
example and to be measured by His observance of it:
the love of the Father in sending His Son for man, the
work of the Son in seeking and saving the lost at the
price of His Own Life, and the new bond which in Christ
bound them all in the fellowship of a common calling,
common mission, and common interests and hopes—love
of the brethren was the one outstanding Farewell-Command

ª St. John   of Christ.ª   And to keep His commandments
xv. 12-14   was to be His friend.   And they were His
friends.   'No longer' did He call them servants, for the
servant knew not what his lord did.   He had now given
them a new name, and with good reason: 'You have I
called friends, because all things which I heard of My
Father I made known to you.'   'Not you did choose Me,
but I did choose you'—the object of His 'choosing' [that
to which they were 'appointed'] being that, as they went
forth into the world, they should bear fruit, that their
fruit should be permanent, and that they should possess
the full privilege of that unlimited power to pray

ᵇ ver. 16   of which He had previously spoken.ᵇ

But this very choice on His part, and their union of
love in Him and to one another, also implied not only

ᶜ ver. 18   separation from, but repudiation by, the world.ᶜ

For this they must be prepared.   It had come
to Him, and it would be evidence of their choice to discipleship.   For evil or for good, they must expect the
same treatment as their Master; and should they not also
remember that the ultimate ground of the world's hatred

ᵈ vv. 19-21   was ignorance of Him Who had sent Christ ?ᵈ

And yet, though this should banish all thoughts

of personal resentment, they who rejected Him were guilty, since : ' He that hateth Me, hateth My Father also.' For there was, besides the evidence of His Words, that of His Works.[a] If they could not apprehend the former, yet, in regard to the latter, they could see by comparison with the works of other men that they were unique. They saw it, but only hated Him and His Father, ascribing all to the power and agency of Beelzebul. And so the ancient prophecy had now been fulfilled : ' They hated Me gratuitously.'[b] But all was not yet at an end : neither His Work through the other Advocate, nor yet theirs in the world. ' When the Advocate is come, Whom I will send to you from the Father—the Spirit of the Truth—Who proceedeth from the Father [goeth forth on His Mission as sent by the Father], this Same will bear witness about Me. And ye also bear witness, because ye are with Me from the beginning.'

[a] St. John xv. 22-24

[b] Ps. xxxv. 19 ; lxix. 4

3. The last of the parting Discourses of Christ, in the sixteenth chapter of St. John, was interrupted by questions from the disciples. But these, being germane to the subject, carry it only forward.

The chapter appropriately opens by reflecting on the predicted enmity of the world.[c] Christ had so clearly foretold it, lest this should prove a stumbling-block to them.. Best to know distinctly that they would not only be put out of the Synagogue, but that everyone who killed them would deem it ' to offer a religious service to God.' Indeed, according to Jewish Law, ' a zealot' might have slain without formal trial those caught in flagrant rebellion against God—or in what might be regarded as such, and the Synagogue would have deemed the deed as meritorious as that of Phinehas. This spirit of enmity arose from ignorance of the Father and of Christ. Although they had in a general way been prepared for it before, yet He had not told it all so definitely and connectedly from the beginning, because He was still there.[d] But now that He was going away, it was absolutely necessary to do so. For

[c] St. John xvi.

[d] vv. 1-4

the very mention of it had thrown them into such confusion of personal sorrow, that the main point, whither
Christ was going, had not even emerged into their

a St. John
xvi. 5
view.[a]

But the Advent of the ' Advocate' would mark
b ver. 7
a new era, as regarded the Church [b] and the
world. It was their Mission to go forth into the
world and to preach Christ. That other Advocate, as the
Representative of Christ, would go into the world and convict on the three cardinal points on which their preaching
turned. These three points, on which all Missioning proceeds, are—Sin, Righteousness, and Judgment.

Quite other was that cause of Christ which, as His
Advocate, He would plead with the disciples, and quite
other in their case the effect of His advocacy. Not speaking from Himself, but speaking whatsoever He shall hear
—as it were, according to His heavenly ' brief'—He would
guide them into all truth. And here His first ' declaration' would be of ' the things that are coming.' As
Christ's Representative, the Holy Spirit would be with
them, not suffer them to go astray into error or wrong, but
be their ' wayleader' into all truth. Further, as the Son
glorified the Father, so would the Spirit glorify the Son,
and in analogous manner—because He shall take of His
and ' declare' it unto them. And this work of the Holy
Spirit, sent by the Father, in His declaration about Christ,
was explained by the circumstance of the union and communication between the Father and Christ.[c] And
c vv. 8-15
so—to sum up, in one brief Farewell, all that He
had said to them—there would be ' a little while' in which
they would not ' behold' Him, and again a little while and
they would ' see' Him, though in quite different
d ver. 16
manner, as even the wording shows.[d]

On that day of joy would He have them dwell in
thought during their present night of sorrow. That would
be, indeed, a day in which there would be no need of
e ver. 23,
comp. ver. 19
their making further inquiry of Him.[e] All would
then be clear in the new light of the Resurrection. A day this, when whatsoever they asked the Father

He would give it them in Christ's Name. Hitherto they had not yet asked in His Name; let them ask: they would receive, and so their joy be completed. Hitherto He had only been able to speak to them, as it were, in parables and allegory, but then would He ' declare' to them in all plainness about the Father. And as He would be able to speak to them directly and plainly about the Father, so would they then be able to speak directly to the Father— as the Epistle to the Hebrews expresses it, come with ' plainness' or ' directness' to the throne of grace. They would ask directly in the Name of Christ; and no longer would it be needful, as at present, first to come to Him that He may ' inquire' of the Father ' about' them. For God loved them as lovers of Christ, and as recognising that He had come forth from God. And so it was—He had come forth from out the Father when He came into the world, and now that He was leaving it, He was going to the Father.

The disciples imagined that they understood this. Christ had read their perplexed inquiry among themselves as to the meaning of the twofold 'little while,' and there was no need for anyone to put express questions.[a] He knew all things, and by this they believed—it afforded them evidence—that He came forth from God. But how little did they know their own hearts! The hour had even come when they would be scattered, every man to his own home, and leave Him alone—yet, truly, He would not be alone, because the Father would be with Him.[b] Even so, His thought, as before,[c] was of them; and through the night of scattering and of sorrow did He bid them look to the morning of joy. For the battle was not theirs, nor yet the victory doubtful : ' I [emphatically] have overcome [it is accomplished] the world.' [d]

We now enter most reverently what may be called the innermost Sanctuary.[e] For the first time we are allowed to listen to what was really 'the Lord's Prayer,' and, as we hear, we humbly worship. That prayer was the great preparation for His Agony, Cross, and Passion ; and also, the outlook on the Crown beyond.

a St. John xvi. 30
b ver. 32
c xiv. 1
d xvi. 33
e St. John xvii.

The first part of that prayer [a] is the consecration of
Himself by the Great High-Priest. The final
hour had come. In praying that the Father
would glorify the Son, He was not asking anything for
Himself, but that 'the Son' might 'glorify' the Father.
It was really in accordance ('even as') with the power or
authority which the Father gave Him over 'all flesh,' when
He put all things under His Feet as the Messiah—the
object of this Messianic Rule being, 'that the totality'
(the all) 'that Thou hast given Him, He should give to
them eternal life.' In what follows [b] we must
remember that, as regards the substance, we have
here Christ's own Prayer for eternal life for each of His
own people. And what constitutes 'the eternal life'? It
is the realisation of what Christ had told them in these
words : 'Ye believe in God, believe also in Me.' Returning from this explanation of 'the eternal life,' the Great
High-Priest first offered up to the Father that part of His
Work which was on earth and which He had completed.
And then, both as the consummation and the sequel of it,
He claimed what was at the end of His Mission : His
return to that fellowship of essential glory which He
possessed together with the Father before the
world was.[c]

And now again His thought was of them for whose
sake He had consecrated Himself. These He now solemnly
presented to the Father.[d] He introduced them
as those (the individuals) whom the Father had
specially given to Him out of the world. As such they
were really the Father's, and given over to Christ—and
He now brought them in prayer before God.[e]
He was interceding, not for the 'world' that was
His by right of His Messiahship, but for them whom the
Father had specially given Him. Therefore, although all
the world was the Son's, He prayed not now for it; and
although all in earth and heaven were in the Father's
Hand, He sought not now His blessing on them, but on
those whom, while He was in the world, He had shielded
and guided. They were to be left behind in a world of

marginal notes:

[a] St. John xvii. 1-5

[b] ver. 3

[c] vv. 4, 5

[d] vv. 6-10

[e] vv. 9-12

sin, evil, temptation, and sorrow, and He was going to the Father. And this was His Prayer : ' Holy Father, keep them in Thy Name which Thou hast given Me, that so (in order that) they may be one (a unity), as We are.' The peculiar address, ' Holy Father,' shows that the Saviour once more referred to the keeping in holiness, and, what is of equal importance, that ' the unity ' of the Church sought for was to be primarily one of spiritual character, and not a merely outward combination.

While He was ' with them,' He ' kept' them in the Father's Name. But ere He went to the Father, He prayed thus for them, that in this realised unity of holiness the joy that was His might be ' completed ' in them.[a] And there was the more need of this since they were left behind with nought but His Word, in a world that hated them, because, as Christ, so they also were not of it [' from ' it]. Nor yet did Christ ask with a view to their being taken out of the world, but with this, ' that ' [in order that] the Father should ' keep them [preserve] from the Evil One.' And the preservative which He sought for them was not outward but inward, the same in kind as while He had been with them,[b] only coming now directly from the Father. It was sanctification ' in the truth,' with this significant addition : ' The word that is Thine is truth.' [c]

In its last part this intercessory Prayer of the Great High-Priest bore on the work of the disciples and its fruits. As the Father had sent the Son, so did the Son send the disciples into the world—in the same manner, and on the same Mission. And for their sakes He now solemnly offered Himself, ' consecrated ' or ' sanctified ' Himself, that they might ' in truth ' be consecrated. And in view of this their work, to which they were consecrated, did Christ pray not for them alone, but also for those who through their word would believe in Him, ' in order,' or ' that so,' ' all may be one '—form a unity. Christ, as sent by the Father, gathered out the original ' unity ;' they, as sent by Him, and consecrated by His consecration, were to gather others, but all were to form

[a] St. John xvii. 13

[b] ver. 12

[c] vv. 12-17

one great unity, through the common spiritual communication. 'As Thou in Me, and I also in Thee, so that [in order that] they also may be in Us, so that [in order that] the world may believe that Thou didst send Me.' 'And the glory that Thou hast given Me'—referring to His Mission in the world, and His setting apart and authorisation for it—'I have given to them, so that [in order that] [in this respect also] they may be one, even as We are One [a unity]. I in them, and Thou in Me, so that they may be perfected into One'—the ideal unity and real character of the Church, this—'so that the world may know that Thou didst send Me, and lovedst them as Thou lovedst Me.'

After this sublime consecration of His Church, and communication to her of His glory as well as of His Work, we cannot marvel at what follows and concludes 'the ^{a St. John} Lord's Prayer.'^a 'That which Thou hast given ^{xvii. 24–26} Me, I will that, where I am, they also may be with Me—so that they may gaze [behold] on the glory that is Mine, which Thou hast given Me [be sharers in the Messianic glory]: because Thou lovedst Me before the foundation of the world.'

And we all would fain place ourselves in the shadow of this final consecration of Himself and of His Church by the Great High-Priest, which is alike final appeal, claim, and prayer : 'O Righteous Father, the world knew Thee not, but I know Thee, and these know that Thou sentest Me. And I made known unto them Thy Name, and will make it known, so that [in order that] the love wherewith Thou lovedst Me may be in them, and I in them.'

CHAPTER LXXXII.

GETHSEMANE.

(St. Matt. xxvi. 30–56 ; St. Mark xiv. 26–52 ; St. Luke xxii. 31–53 ;
St. John xviii. 1–11.)

WE turn once more to follow the steps of Christ, now among the last He trod upon earth. The 'hymn,' with which the Paschal Supper ended, had been sung.

Probably we are to understand this of the second portion
of the *Hallel*,[a] sung some time after the third
Cup, or else of Psalm cxxxvi., which, in the
present ritual, stands near the end of the service. The
last Discourses had been spoken, the last Prayer, that of
Consecration, had been offered, and Jesus prepared to go
forth out of the City, to the Mount of Olives.

Passing out by the gate north of the Temple, we
descend into a lonely part of the valley of black Kidron,
at that season swelled into a winter torrent. Crossing it
we turn somewhat to the left, where the road leads towards
Olivet. Not many steps farther (beyond, and on the
other side of the present Church of the Sepulchre of the
Virgin) we turn aside from the road to the right, and reach
what tradition has since earliest times—and probably
correctly—pointed out as ' Gethsemane,' the ' oil-press.'
It was a small property enclosed, ' a garden' in the Eastern
sense, where probably, amidst a variety of fruit trees and
flowering shrubs, was a quiet summer-retreat, connected
with, or near by, the ' olive-press.' The present Gethsemane is only some seventy steps square, and though its
old gnarled olives cannot be those (if such there were) of
the time of Jesus, since all trees in that valley—those also
which stretched their shadows over Jesus—were hewn
down in the Roman siege, they may have sprung from the
old roots, or from the old kernels. But we love to think
of this ' Garden' as the place where Jesus ' often'—not
merely on this occasion, but perhaps on previous visits to
Jerusalem—gathered with His disciples. And as such it
was known to Judas, and thither he led the armed band,
when they found the ' upper chamber' no longer occupied
by Jesus and His disciples.

It was, we imagine, after they had left the City behind
them, that the Lord addressed Himself first to the disciples
generally. We can scarcely call it either prediction or
warning. To them He would that night be even a
stumbling-block. And so had it been foretold of old,[b]
that the Shepherd would be smitten, and the
sheep scattered. Did this prophecy of His

[a] Ps. cxv. to cxviii.

[b] Zech. xiii. 7

suffering, in its grand outlines, fill the mind of the
Saviour as He went forth on His Passion? A peculiar
significance also attaches to His prediction that, after He
was risen, He would go before them into Galilee.[a]
For with their scattering upon His Death it
seems to us the Apostolic circle or College, as
such, was for a time broken up. They continued, indeed,
to meet together as individual disciples, but the Apostolic
bond was temporarily dissolved. This explains many
things: the absence of Thomas on the first, and his
peculiar position on the second Sunday; the uncertainty
of the disciples, as evidenced by the words of those on the
way to Emmaus; as well as the seemingly strange movements of the Apostles—all which are quite changed when
the Apostolic bond is restored. Similarly, we mark that
only seven of them seem to have been together by the
Lake of Galilee,[b] and that only afterwards the
Eleven met Him on the mountain to which He
had directed them.[c] It was here that the
Apostolic circle or College was once more re-
formed, and the Apostolic commission renewed,[d]
and thence they returned to Jerusalem, once more
sent forth from Galilee, to await the final events of His
Ascension, and the Coming of the Holy Ghost.

ª St. Matt. xxvi. 32; St. Mark xiv. 28

b St. John xxi. 2

c St. Matt. xxviii. 16

d vv. 18-20

But in that night they understood none of these things.
While all were staggering under the blow of their predicted
scattering, the Lord seems to have turned to Peter individually. What He said, and how He put it, equally demand
our attention: ' Simon, Simon'[e]—using his old
name when referring to the old man in him—
' Satan has obtained you, *for the purpose* of sifting like as
wheat. But I have made supplication for thee, that thy
faith fail not.'

e St. Luke xxii. 31

The words admit us into two mysteries of heaven.
This night seems to have been ' the power of darkness,'
when, left of God, Christ had to meet by Himself the
whole assault of hell and to conquer in His own strength
as Man's Substitute and Representative. The second
mystery of that night was Christ's supplication for Peter.

We dare not say, as the High-Priest—and we know not when and where it was offered. But the expression is very strong, as of one who has need of a thing. And that for which He made such supplication was, that Peter's faith should not fail. To these words of His Christ added this significant commission : ' And thou, when thou hast turned again, confirm thy brethren.' And how fully he did this, both in the Apostolic circle and in the Church, history has chronicled. This, then, is the first fulfilment of Christ's Prayer, that the Father would ' keep them from the Evil One.'^a Not by any process from without, but by the preservation of their faith.

ᵃ St. John xvii. 15

We can understand the vehement earnestness and sincerity with which Peter protested against the possibility of any failure on his part. We mostly deem those sins farthest which are nearest to us ; else, much of the power of their temptation would be gone, and temptation changed into conflict. And when, to enforce the warning, Christ predicted that before the repeated crowing of the cock ushered in the morning, Peter would thrice deny that he knew Him, Peter not only persisted in his asseverations, but was joined in them by the rest. Yet—and this seems the meaning and object of the words of Christ which follow —they were not aware how terribly changed the former relations had become, and what they would have to suffer in consequence.^b When formerly He had sent them forth, both without provision and defence, had they lacked anything ? No ! But now no helping hand would be extended to them ; nay, what seemingly they would need even more than anything else would be ' a sword '—defence against attacks, for at the close of His history He was reckoned with transgressors. But once more they only understood Him in a grossly realistic manner. These Galileans, after the custom of their countrymen, had provided themselves with short swords, which they concealed under their upper garment. Two of them—among them Peter—now produced swords. But this was not the time to reason with them, and our Lord simply put it aside. Events would only too soon teach them.

ᵇ St. Luke xxii. 35–38

They had now reached the entrance to Gethsemane. It may have been that it led through the building with the 'oil-press,' and that the eight Apostles, who were not to come nearer, were left there. Or they may have been taken within the entrance of the Garden, and left there, while, pointing forward with a gesture of the Hand, He went 'yonder' and prayed.[a] According to St. Luke, He added the parting warning to pray that they might not enter into temptation.

a St. Matt. xxvi. 36

Eight did He leave there. The other three—Peter, James, and John—companions before of His glory, both when He raised the daughter of Jairus[b] and on the Mount of Transfiguration[c]—He took with Him farther. If in that last contest His Human Soul craved for the presence of those who stood nearest Him and loved Him best, or if He would have them baptised with His Baptism, and drink of His Cup, these were the three of all others to be chosen. And now of a sudden the cold flood broke over Him. Within these few moments He had passed from the calm of assured victory into the anguish of the contest. Increasingly with every step forward, He became ' sorrowful,' full of sorrow, ' sore amazed,' and ' desolate.' He told them of the deep sorrow of His Soul, even unto death, and bade them tarry there to watch with Him. Himself went forward to enter the contest with prayer. Only the first attitude of the wrestling Saviour saw they, only the first words in that Hour of Agony did they hear. For, as in our present state not uncommonly in the deepest emotions of the soul, and as had been the case on the Mount of Transfiguration, irresistible sleep crept over their frame. But what, we may reverently ask, was the cause of this sorrow unto death of the Lord Jesus Christ? Not fear, either of bodily or mental suffering: but Death. Man's nature, created of God immortal, shrinks (by the law of its nature) from the dissolution of the bond that binds body to soul. Yet to fallen man Death is not by any means fully Death, for he is born with the taste of it in his soul. Not so Christ. It was the Unfallen Man dying; it was He, Who had no

b St. Mark v. 37
c St. Matt. xvii. 1

experience of it, tasting Death, and that not for Himself but for every man, emptying the cup to its bitter dregs. No one as He could know what Death was; no one could taste its bitterness as He. His going into Death was His final conflict with Satan for man, and on his behalf. By submitting to it He took away the power of Death; He disarmed Death by burying his shaft in His own Heart.

Alone, as in His first conflict with the Evil One in the Temptation in the wilderness, must the Saviour enter on the last contest. Alone—and yet even this being 'parted from them'[a] implied sorrow.[b] And now, 'on His knees,' prostrate on the ground, prostrate on His Face, began His Agony. His very address bears witness to it. It is the only time, so far as recorded in the Gospels, when He addressed God with the personal pronoun: 'My Father.'[c] The object of the prayer was that 'if it were possible, the hour might pass away from Him.'[d] The subject of the prayer (as recorded by the three Gospels) was that the Cup itself might pass away, yet always with the limitation, that not His Will but the Father's might be done. The petition of Christ, therefore, was subject not only to the Will of the Father, but to His own Will that the Father's Will might be done.

It was in this extreme Agony of Soul almost unto death, that the Angel appeared (as in the Temptation in the wilderness) to 'strengthen' and support His Body and Soul. And so the conflict went on, with increasing earnestness of prayer, all that terrible hour.[e] For the appearance of the Angel must have intimated to Him that the Cup could not pass away. And at the close of that hour His Sweat, mingled with Blood, fell in great drops on the ground. And when the Saviour with this mark of His Agony on His Brow returned to the three, He found that deep sleep held them. His words, primarily addressed to 'Simon,' roused them, yet not sufficiently to fully carry to their hearts either the loving reproach, the admonition to 'Watch and pray' in view of the coming

a St. Luke xxii. 41
b Comp. Acts xxi.
c St. Matt. xxvi. 39, 42
d St. Mark xiv. 36
e St. Matt. xxvi. 40

temptation, or the most seasonable warning about the weakness of the flesh, even where the spirit was willing, ready, and ardent.

The conflict had been virtually, though not finally, decided, when the Saviour went back to the three sleeping disciples. He now returned to complete it, though both the attitude in which He prayed (no longer prostrate) and the wording of His Prayer—only slightly altered as it was —indicate how near it was to perfect victory. And once more, on His return to them, He found that sleep had weighted their eyes, and they scarce knew what answer to make to Him. Yet a third time He left them to pray as before. And now He returned victorious. After three assaults had the Tempter left Him in the wilderness; after the threefold conflict in the Garden he was vanquished. Christ came forth triumphant. No longer did He bid His disciples watch. They might, nay they should, sleep and take rest, ere the near events of His Betrayal—for the hour had come when the Son of Man was to be betrayed into the hands of sinners.

A very brief period of rest this, soon broken by the call of Jesus to rise and go to where the other eight had been left, at the entrance of the Garden—to go forward and meet the band which was coming under the guidance of the Betrayer. And while He was speaking, the heavy tramp of many men and the light of lanterns and torches indicated the approach of Judas and his band. During the hours that had passed all had been prepared. When, according to arrangement, he appeared at the High-Priestly Palace, or more probably at that of Annas, who seems to have had the direction of affairs, the Jewish leaders first communicated with the Roman garrison. By their own admission they had no longer (for forty years before the destruction of Jerusalem) the power of pronouncing capital sentence. The Sanhedrin, not possessing the power of the sword, had, of course, neither soldiery, nor regularly armed band at command. The 'Temple-guard' under their officers served merely for purposes of police, and, indeed, were neither regularly armed nor trained. Nor would the Romans have tolerated a regular armed Jewish force in Jerusalem.

But in the fortress of Antonia, close to the Temple and connected with it by two stairs, lay the Roman garrison. During the Feast the Temple itself was guarded by an armed cohort, consisting of from 400 to 600 men, so as to prevent or quell any tumult among the numerous pilgrims. It was to the captain of this 'cohort' that the Chief Priests and leaders of the Pharisees would, in the first place, apply for an armed guard to effect the arrest of Jesus, on the ground that it might lead to some popular tumult. This, without necessarily having to state the charge that was to be brought against Him, which might have led to other complications. Although St. John speaks of 'the band' by a word which always designates a 'cohort,' yet there is no reason for believing that the whole cohort was sent. Still, its commander would scarcely have sent a strong detachment out of the Temple, and on what might lead to a riot, without having first referred to the Procurator, Pontius Pilate. And if further evidence were required, it would be in the fact that the band was led not ^{a St. John xviii. 12} by a Centurion, but by a Chiliarch,[a] who, as there were no intermediate grades in the Roman army, must represent one of the six tribunes attached to each legion. This also explains not only the apparent preparedness of Pilate to sit in judgment early next morning, but also how Pilate's wife may have been disposed for those dreams about Jesus which so affrighted her.

This Roman detachment, armed with swords and 'staves' —with the latter of which Pilate on other occasions also directed his soldiers to attack them who raised a tumult— was accompanied by servants from the High-Priest's Palace, and other Jewish officers, to direct the arrest of Jesus. They bore torches and lamps placed on the top of ^{b ver. 3} poles, so as to prevent any possible concealment.[b]

Having received this band, Judas proceeded on his errand. As we believe, their first move was to the house where the Supper had been celebrated. Learning that Jesus had left it with His disciples, perhaps two or three hours before, Judas next directed the band to the spot he knew so well: to Gethsemane. A signal by which to recognise Jesus seemed almost necessary with so large a band, and where escape or resistance might be apprehended. It was—terrible to say—none other than a kiss. As soon as he had so marked Him, the guard were to seize and lead Him safely away.

As the band reached the Garden, Judas went somewhat in advance of them,[a] and reached Jesus just as He had roused the three and was preparing to go and meet His captors. He saluted Him, ' Hail, Rabbi,' so as to be heard by the rest, and not only kissed but covered Him with kisses. The Saviour submitted to the indignity, not stopping, but only saying as He passed on : ' Friend, that for which thou art here;'[b] and then, perhaps in answer to his questioning gesture : ' Judas, with a kiss deliverest thou up the Son of Man ?'[c]

a St. Luke

b St. Matt.
xxvi. 49;
comp. St.
Mark xiv. 45

c St. Luke
xxii. 48

Then leaving the traitor, and ignoring the signal which he had given them, Jesus advanced to the band, and asked them : ' Whom seek ye ?' To the brief spoken, perhaps somewhat contemptuous, ' Jesus the Nazarene,' He replied with infinite calmness: ' I am (He).' The immediate effect of these words was, we will not say magical, but Divine. They had no doubt been prepared for quite other ; either compromise, fear, or resistance. But the appearance and majesty of that calm Christ were too overpowering in their effects on the untutored heathen soldiery, who perhaps cherished in their hearts secret misgivings of the work they had in hand. The foremost of them went backward, and they fell to the ground. But Christ's hour had come. And once more He now asked them the same question as before, and on repeating their former answer, He said : ' I told you that I am He ; if therefore ye seek Me, let these go their way,'—the Evangelist seeing in this watchful care over His own the initial fulfilment of the words which the Lord had previously spoken concerning their safe preservation,[d] not only in the sense of their outward preservation, but in that of their being guarded from

d St. John
xvii. 12

such temptations as, in their then state, they could not have endured.

The words of Christ about those that were with Him seem to have recalled the leaders of the guard to full consciousness—perhaps awakened in them fears of a possible rising at the incitement of His adherents. Accordingly,

^a St. Matt. xxvi. 50 *b*

^b St. Mark xiv. 46

^c St. John xviii. 11, 26

it is here that we insert the notice of St. Matthew,^a and of St. Mark,^b that they laid hands on Jesus and took Him. Then it was that Peter,^c seeing what was coming, drew the sword which he carried, and putting the question to Jesus, but without awaiting His answer, struck at Malchus, the servant of the High-Priest—perhaps the Jewish leader of the band— cutting off his ear. But Jesus immediately restrained all such violence; nay, with it all merely outward zeal, pointing to the fact how easily He might, as against this 'cohort,'

^d St. Matthew

^e St. John

^f St. Luke

have commanded Angelic legions.^d He had in wrestling Agony received from His Father that Cup to drink,^e and the Scriptures must in that wise be fulfilled. And so saying, He touched the ear of Malchus, and healed him.^f

But this faint appearance of resistance was enough for

^g St. John

the guard. Their leaders now bound Jesus.^g It was to this last, uncalled-for indignity that Jesus replied by asking them, why they had come against Him as against a robber—one of those wild, murderous Sicarii. Had He not been all that week daily in the Temple, teaching? Why not then seize Him? But this 'hour' of theirs that had come, and 'the power of darkness'—this also had been foretold in Scripture!

And as the ranks of the armed men now closed around the bound Christ, none dared to stay with Him, lest they also should be bound as resisting authority. So they all forsook Him and fled. But there was one there who joined not in the flight, but remained, a deeply interested onlooker. When the soldiers had come to seek Jesus in the upper chamber of his home, Mark, roused from sleep, had hastily cast about him the loose linen garment or wrapper that lay by his bedside, and followed the armed band to

P P

see what would come of it.   He now lingered in the rear, and followed as they led away Jesus, never imagining that they would attempt to lay hold on him, since he had not been with the disciples nor yet in the Garden.   But they, perhaps the Jewish servants of the High-Priest, had noticed him.   They attempted to lay hold on him; when, disengaging himself from their grasp, he left his upper garment in their hands and fled.

So ended the first scene in the terrible drama of that night.

CHAPTER LXXXIII.

THURSDAY NIGHT—BEFORE ANNAS AND CAIAPHAS— PETER AND JESUS.

(St. John xviii. 12–14; St. Matt. xxvi. 57, 58; St. Mark xiv. 53, 54; St. Luke xxii. 54 55; St. John xviii. 24, 15–18, 19–23; St. Matt. xxvi. 69, 70; St. Mark xiv. 66–68; St. Luke xxii. 56, 57; St. John xviii. 17, 18; St. Matt. xxvi. 71, 72; St. Mark xiv. 69, 70; St. Luke xxii. 58; St. John xviii. 25; St. Matt. xxvi. 59–68; St. Mark xiv. 55–65; St. Luke xxii. 67–71, 63–65; St. Matt. xxvi. 73–75; St. Mark xiv. 70–72; St. Luke xxii. 59–62; St. John xviii. 26, 27.)

IT was not a long way that they led the bound Christ. Probably through the same gate by which He had gone forth with His disciples after the Paschal Supper, up to where, on the slope between the Upper City and the Tyropœon, stood the well-known Palace of Annas.

If every incident in that night were not of such supreme interest, we might dismiss the question as almost idle, why they brought Jesus to the house of Annas, since he was not at that time the actual High-Priest.   That office now devolved on Caiaphas, his son-in-law, who, as * St. John   the Evangelist significantly reminds us,[a] had been xviii. 14   the first to enunciate in plain words what seemed to him the political necessity for the judicial murder of b xi. 50   Christ.[b]   He had spoken as the bold, unscrupulous, determined man that he was; Sadducee in heart rather than by conviction; a worthy son-in-law of Annas.

No figure is better known in contemporary Jewish history than that of Annas; no person deemed more fortunate or successful, but none also more generally execrated than the late High-Priest. He had held the Pontificate for only six or seven years; but it was filled by not fewer than five of his sons, by his son-in-law Caiaphas, and by a grandson. While these acted publicly, he really directed affairs, without either the responsibility or the restraints which the office imposed. His influence with the Romans he owed to the religious views which he professed, to his open partisanship of the foreigner, and to his enormous wealth. The Sadducean Annas was an eminently safe Churchman, not troubled with any special convictions nor with Jewish fanaticism, a pleasant and a useful man also, who was able to furnish his friends in the Prætorium with large sums of money. We have seen what immense revenues the family of Annas must have derived from the Temple-booths, and how nefarious and unpopular was the traffic. The names of those licentious, unscrupulous, degenerate sons of Aaron were spoken with whispered curses. Without referring to Christ's inter-ference with that Temple-traffic, which, if His authority had prevailed, would of course have been fatal to it, we can understand how antithetic in every respect a Messiah, and such a Messiah as Jesus, must have been to Annas. He was as resolutely bent on His Death as his son-in-law, though with his characteristic cunning and coolness, not in the hasty, bluff manner of Caiaphas. It was probably from a desire that Annas might have the conduct of the business, or from the active, leading part which Annas took in the matter; perhaps for even more prosaic practical reasons, such as that the Palace of Annas was nearer to the place of Jesus' capture, and that it was desirable to dismiss the Roman soldiery as quickly as possible—that Christ was first brought to Annas, and not to the actual High-Priest.

In any case, the Roman soldiers had evidently orders to bring Jesus to the late High-Priest.

We know absolutely nothing of what passed in the

house of Annas—if, indeed, anything passed—except that Annas sent Jesus bound to Caiaphas.

Of what occurred in the Palace of Caiaphas we have two accounts. That of St. John [a] seems to refer to a more private interview between the High-Priest and Christ, at which, apparently, only some personal attendants of Caiaphas were present, from one of whom the Apostle may have derived his information. The second account is that of the Synoptists, and refers to the examination of Jesus at dawn of day [b] by the leading Sanhedrists, who had been hastily summoned for the purpose.

a St. John xviii. 19-23

b St. Luke xxii. 66

The questions of Caiaphas bore on two points: the disciples of Jesus, and His teaching—the former to incriminate Christ's followers, the latter to incriminate the Master. To the first inquiry it was only natural that Jesus should not have condescended to return an answer. The reply to the second was characterised by that 'openness' which He claimed for all that He had said.[c] If Caiaphas really wanted information, there could be no difficulty in procuring witnesses to speak to His doctrine: all Jewry knew it. He always spoke 'in Synagogue and in the Temple, whither all the Jews gather together.' If the inquiry were a fair one, let the judge act judicially, and ask not Him, but those who had heard Him.

c St. John xviii. 20

It must be admitted that the answer sounds not like that of one accused, who seeks either to make apology, or even greatly cares to defend himself. It was this which emboldened one of those servile attendants, with the brutality of an Eastern in such circumstances, to strike the Christ. We are almost thankful that the text leaves it in doubt, whether it was with the palm of the hand, or the lesser indignity—with a rod. In pursuance of His Human submission, the Divine Sufferer, without murmuring or complaining, and without asserting His Divine Power, only answered in such tone of patient expostulation as must have convicted the man of his wrong, or at least have left him speechless.

2. The Apostle John was no stranger in the Palace of Caiaphas. We have already seen that, after the first panic of Christ's sudden capture and their own flight, two of the disciples at least, Peter and John, seem speedily to have rallied. Combining the notices [a] we derive the impression that Peter, so far true to his word, had been the first to stop in his flight, and to follow ' afar off.' If he reached the Palace of Annas in time, he certainly did not enter it, but probably waited outside during the brief space which preceded the transference of Jesus to Caiaphas. He had now been joined by John, and the two followed the melancholy procession which escorted Jesus to the High-Priest. John seems to have entered ' the court' along with the guard,[b] while Peter remained outside till his fellow-Apostle, who apparently was well known in the High-Priest's house, had spoken to the maid who kept the door—the male servants being probably all gathered in the court—and so procured his admission.

a St. Matt. xxvi. 58; St. Mark xiv. 54; St. Luke xxii. 54, 55

b St. John xviii. 15

It was a chill night when Peter, down ' beneath,' looked up to the lighted windows. There, among the serving-men in the court, he was in every sense ' without.' [d] He approached the group around the fire. He would hear what they had to say; besides, it was not safe to stand apart; he might be recognised as one of those who had only escaped capture in the Garden by hasty flight. And then it was cold—and not only to the body, the chill had struck to his soul. Was he right in having come there at all ?

c St. Mark xiv. 66
d St. Matt. xxvi. 69

Peter was very restless, and yet he must seem very quiet. He ' sat down ' among the servants,[e] then he stood up among them.[f] It was this restlessness of attempted indifference which attracted the attention of the maid who had at the first admitted him. As in the uncertain light she scanned the features of the mysterious stranger, she boldly charged him,[g] though still in a questioning tone, with being one of the disciples of the Man Who stood incriminated up there before the High-Priest. Peter vehemently

e The Synoptists
f St. John
g St. John

denied all knowledge of Him to Whom the woman referred—nay, of the very meaning of what she said. He
had said too much not to bring soon another charge upon
himself. We need not inquire which of the slightly varying reports in the Gospels represents the actual words of
the woman or the actual answer of Peter. Perhaps neither;
perhaps all; certainly she said all this, and certainly he
answered all that, though neither of them would confine
their words to the short sentences reported by each of the
Evangelists.

What had he to do there ? And why should he incriminate himself, or perhaps Christ, by a needless confession to those who had neither the moral nor the legal right
to exact it ? That was all he now remembered and thought;
nothing about any denial of Christ. And so, as they were
still chatting together, Peter withdrew. We cannot judge
how long time had passed, but this we gather, that the
words of the woman had either not made any impression
on those around the fire, or that the bold denial of Peter
had satisfied them. Presently, we find Peter walking away

^a St. Mat-   down 'the porch,'^a which ran round and opened
thew   into 'the outer court.'^b He was not thinking of
^b St. Mark   anything else now than how chilly it felt, and
how right he had been not to be entrapped by that
woman. And so he heeded it not, while his footfall sounded
along the marble-paved porch, that just at this moment ' a
cock crew.' But there was no sleep that night in the
High-Priest's Palace. As he walked down the porch towards the outer court, first one maid met him; and then,
as he returned from the outer court, he once more encountered his old accuser, the door-portress ; and as he crossed
the inner court to mingle again with the group around the
fire, where he had formerly found safety, he was first
accosted by one man, and then all those around the fire
turned upon him—and each and all had the same thing to
say, the same charge, that he was also one of the disciples
of Jesus of Nazareth. But Peter's resolve was taken ; he
was quite sure it was right ; and to each separately, and to
all together, he gave the same denial, more brief now, for

he was collected and determined, but more emphatic—even ᵃ St. Mat- thew with an oath.ᵃ And once more he silenced suspicion for a time. Or, perhaps, attention was now otherwise directed.

3. For, already, footsteps were heard along the porches and corridors. They were the leading Priests, Elders, and Sanhedrists, who had been hastily summoned to the High-Priest's Palace, and who were hurrying up just as the first faint streaks of grey light were lying on the sky.

Whatever view be taken, thus much at least is certain, that this was no formal, regular meeting of the Sanhedrin.

It is admitted on all hands, that forty years before the destruction of the Temple the Sanhedrin ceased to pronounce capital sentences. But besides, the trial and sentence of Jesus in the Palace of Caiaphas would have outraged every principle of Jewish criminal law and procedure. Such causes could only be tried, and capital sentence pronounced, in the regular meeting-place of the Sanhedrin, not, as here, in the High-Priest's Palace; no process, least of all such an one, might be begun in the night, not even in the afternoon, although if the discussion had gone on all day, sentence might be pronounced at night. Again, no process could take place on Sabbaths or Feast-days, or even on the eves of them. Lastly, in capital causes there was a very elaborate system of warning and cautioning witnesses, while it may safely be affirmed that at a regular trial Jewish Judges, however prejudiced, would not have acted as the Sanhedrists and Caiaphas did on this occasion.

But as we examine it more closely, we perceive that the Gospel-narratives do not speak of a formal trial and sentence by the Sanhedrin. Such references as to 'the Sanhedrin' ('council'), or to 'all the Sanhedrin,' must be taken in the wider sense, which will presently be explained. On the other hand, the four Gospels equally indicate that the whole proceedings of that night were carried on in the Palace of Caiaphas, and that during that night no formal sentence of death was pronounced. And when in the morning, in consequence of a fresh consultation, also in the Palace of Caiaphas, they led Jesus to the Prætorium, it was not as a prisoner condemned to death of whom they asked the execution,[a] but as one against whom they laid certain accusations worthy of death;[b] while, when Pilate bade them judge Jesus according to Jewish Law, they replied not that they had done so already, but that they had no competence to try capital causes.[c]

a St. John xviii. 29, 30
b St. Luke xxiii. 2;
St. Matt. xxvii. 12
c St. John xviii. 31

4. But although Christ was not tried and sentenced in a formal meeting of the Sanhedrin, there can be no question that His condemnation and Death were the work, if not of the Sanhedrin, yet of the Sanhedrists—of the whole body of them ('all the council'), in the sense of expressing what was the judgment and purpose of the Supreme Council and Leaders of Israel, with only very few exceptions. We bear in mind, that the resolution to sacrifice Christ had for some time been taken. Terrible as the proceedings of that night were, they even seem a sort of concession—as if the Sanhedrists would fain have found some legal and moral justification for what they had determined to do. They first sought 'witness,' or as St. Matthew rightly designates it, 'false witness' against Christ. But it was altogether too hasty and excited an assemblage, and the witnesses contradicted themselves so grossly, or their testimony so notoriously broke down, that for very shame such trumped-up charges had to be abandoned. And to this result the majestic calm of Christ's silence must have greatly contributed.

Abandoning this line of testimony, the Priests next brought forward probably some of their own order, who at the first Purgation of the Temple had been present when Jesus, in answer to the challenge for 'a sign' in evidence of His authority, had given them that mysterious 'sign' of the destruction and upraising of the Temple of His Body.[d] They had quite misunderstood it at the time, and its reproduction now as the ground of a criminal charge against Jesus must have been directly due to Caiaphas and Annas. We remember that this

d St. John ii. 18, 19

had been the first time that Jesus had come into collision, not only with the Temple authorities, but with the avarice of ' the family of Annas.' We can imagine how the incensed High-Priest would have challenged the conduct of the Temple-officials, and how, in reply, he would have been told what they had attempted, and how Jesus had met them. Perhaps it was the only real inquiry which a man like Caiaphas would care to institute about what Jesus said.

Dexterously manipulated, the testimony of these witnesses might lead up to two charges. It would show that Christ was a dangerous seducer of the people, Whose claims might have led those who believed them to lay violent hands on the Temple; while the supposed assertion, that He would [a] or was able [b] to build the Temple again within three days, might be made to imply Divine or magical pretensions. The purpose of the High-Priest was not to formulate a capital charge in Jewish Law, since the assembled Sanhedrists had no intention so to try Jesus, but to formulate a charge which would tell before the Roman Procurator. And here none other could be so effective as that of being a fanatical seducer of the ignorant populace, who might lead them on to wild tumultuous acts.

[a] St. Mark
[b] St. Matt.

But this charge of being a seducer of the people also broke down, through the disagreement of the two witnesses whom the Mosaic Law required,[c] and who, according to Rabbinic ordinance, had to be separately questioned. All this time Jesus preserved the same majestic silence as before, nor could the impatience of Caiaphas, who sprang from his seat to confront, and, if possible, browbeat his Prisoner, extract from Him any reply.

[c] Deut. xvii.
6

Only one thing now remained. Jesus knew it well, and so did Caiaphas. It was to put the question, which Jesus could not refuse to answer, and which, once answered, must lead either to His acknowledgment or to His condemnation. As we suppose, the simple question was first addressed to Jesus, whether He was the Messiah:

to which He replied by referring to the needlessness of such an inquiry, since they had predetermined not to credit His claims, nay, had only a few days before in the Temple refused [a] to discuss them.[b] It was upon this that the High-Priest, in the most solemn manner, adjured the True One by the Living God, Whose Son He was, to say whether He were the Messiah and Divine—the two being so joined together, not in Jewish belief, but to express the claims of Jesus. No doubt or hesitation could here exist. Solemn, emphatic, calm, majestic, as before had been His silence, was now His speech. And His assertion of what He was, was conjoined with that of what God would show Him to be, in His Resurrection and Sitting at the Right Hand of the Father, and of what they also would see, when He would come in those clouds of heaven that would break over their city and polity in the final storm of judgment.

marginal notes:
[a] St. Matt. xxii. 41-46
[b] St. Luke xxii. 67, 68; the clause 'nor let Me go' is spurious

They all heard it—and, as the Law directed when blasphemy was spoken, the High-Priest rent both his outer and inner garment, with a rent that might never be repaired. But the object was attained. Christ would neither explain, modify, nor retract His claims. They had all heard it; what use was there of witnesses, He had spoken 'blaspheming.' Then, turning to those assembled, he put to them the usual question which preceded the formal sentence of death. As given in the Rabbinic original, it is: 'What think ye, gentlemen? And they answered, if for life, "For life!" and if for death, "For death."' But the formal sentence of death, which, if it had been a regular meeting of the Sanhedrin, must now have been spoken by the President, was not pronounced.

5. After this meeting of the Sanhedrists had broken up, so far as recorded, not a word escaped His Lips. He was drinking, slowly, with the consciousness of willing self-surrender, the Cup which His Father had given Him.

When Caiaphas and the Sanhedrists quitted the audience-chamber, Jesus was left to the unrestrained licence of the attendants. Even the Jewish Law had it, that no 'prolonged death' might be inflicted, and that he who was condemned to death was not to be previously scourged. At last they were weary of insult and smiting, and the Sufferer was left alone, perhaps in the covered gallery, or at one of the windows that overlooked the court below.

About one hour had passed [a] since Peter's second denial had, so to speak, been interrupted by the arrival of the Sanhedrists. Since then the excitement of the mock-trial, with witnesses coming and going, and, no doubt, in Eastern fashion repeating what had passed to those gathered in the court around the fire; then the departure of the Sanhedrists, and again the insults and blows inflicted on the Sufferer, had diverted attention from Peter. Now it turned once more upon him; and, in the circumstances, naturally more intensely than before. The chattering of Peter, whom conscience and consciousness made nervously garrulous, betrayed him. This one also was with Jesus the Nazarene: truly, he was of them—for he was also a Galilean! So spake the bystanders; while, according to St. John, a fellow-servant and kinsman of that Malchus, whose ear Peter in his zeal had cut off in Gethsemane, asserted that he actually recognised him. To one and all these declarations Peter returned only a more vehement denial, accompanying it this time with oaths to God and imprecations on himself.

[a] St. Luke

The echo of his words had scarcely died out when loud and shrill the second cock-crowing was heard. There was that in its harsh persistence of sound that also wakened his memory. He looked up; and as he looked, he saw, how up there, just at that moment, the Lord turned round and looked upon him—yes, in all that assembly, upon Peter! His Eyes spake His Words; nay, much more; they searched dow·ı ɯ the innermost depths of Peter's heart. They had pierced through all self-delusion, false shame, and fear: they had reached the man, the disciple, the lover of Jesus. Forth they burst, the waters of conviction, of true shame, of heart-sorrow, of the agonies of self-condemnation; and bitterly weeping he rushed out into the night.

CHAPTER LXXXIV.

THE MORNING OF GOOD FRIDAY.

(St. Matt. xxvii. 1, 2, 11–14; St. Mark xv. 1–5; St. Luke xxiii. 1–5 ; St. John xviii. 28–38; St. Luke xxiii. 6–12; St. Matt. xxvii. 3–10; 15–18 ; St. Mark xv. 6–10; St. Luke xxiii. 13–17; St. John xviii. 39, 40; St. Matt. xxvii. 19; 20–31; St. Mark xv. 11–20; St. Luke xxiii. 18–25 ; St. John xix. 1–16.)

THE pale grey light had passed into that of early morning, when the Sanhedrists once more assembled in the Palace of Caiaphas. A comparison with the terms in which they who had formed the gathering of the previous night are described will convey the impression, that the number of those present was now increased, and that they who now came belonged to the wisest and most influential of the Council. It is not unreasonable to suppose, that some who would not take part in deliberations which were virtually a judicial murder might, once the resolution was taken, feel in Jewish casuistry absolved from guilt in advising how the informal sentence might best be carried into effect. It was this, and not the question of Christ's guilt, which formed the subject of deliberation on that early morning. The result of it was to 'bind' Jesus and hand Him over as a malefactor to Pilate, with the resolve, if possible, not to frame any definite charge;[a] but, if this became necessary, to lay all the emphasis on the purely political, not the religious aspect of the claims of Jesus.[b]

[a] St. John xviii. 29, 30
[b] St. Luke xxiii. 2

It is recorded that they who brought Him would not themselves enter the portals of the Palace of Herod, which it is probable that Pilate occupied when in Jerusalem with his wife, 'that they might not be defiled, but might eat the Passover.'

It is certain that entrance into a heathen house did Levitically render impure for that day—that is, till the evening. But to have so become 'impure' for the day, would not have disqualified for eating the Paschal Lamb, since that meal was partaken of after the evening, and

when a new day had begun. It follows, that these Sanhedrists could not have abstained from entering the Palace
of Pilate because by so doing they would have been disqualified for the Paschal Supper.

The point is of importance, because many have interpreted the expression 'the Passover' as referring to the
Paschal Supper, and have argued that, according to the
fourth Gospel, our Lord did not on the previous evening
partake of the Paschal Lamb, or else that in this respect
the account of the fourth Gospel does not accord with that of
the Synoptists. But as it is impossible to refer the expression 'Passover' to the Paschal Supper, we have only to
inquire whether the term is not also applied to other offerings. And here both the Old Testament[a] and
Jewish writings show that the term 'Passover'
was applied not only to the Paschal Lamb, but
to all the Passover sacrifices, especially to what was
called the *Chagigah*, or 'festive offering.' This was brought
on the first festive Paschal Day. We can therefore
quite understand that not on the eve of the Passover, but
on the first Paschal day, the Sanhedrists would avoid
incurring a defilement which, lasting till the evening,
would not only have involved them in the inconvenience
of Levitical defilement on the first festive day, but have
actually prevented their offering on that day the Passover,
festive sacrifice, or *Chagigah*. For we have these two express rules: that a person could not in Levitical defilement
offer the *Chagigah*; and that the *Chagigah* could not be
offered for a person by some one else who took his place.
These considerations and canons seem decisive as regards
the views above expressed. There would have been no
reason to fear 'defilement' on the morning of the Paschal
Sacrifice; but entrance into the *Prætorium* on the morning of the first Passover-day would have rendered it impossible for them to offer the *Chagigah*, which is also designated
by the term *Pesach*.

It may have been about seven in the morning, probably
even earlier, when Pilate went out to those who summoned
him to dispense justice. The first question of Pilate was

[a] Deut. xvi. 1–3; 2 Chron. xxxv. 1, 2, 6, 18

what accusation they brought against Jesus. The inquiry would come upon them the more unexpectedly, that Pilate must, on the previous evening, have given his consent to the employment of the Roman guard which effected the arrest of Jesus. Their answer displays humiliation, ill-humour, and an attempt at evasion. If He had not been 'a malefactor,' they would not have 'delivered' Him up. On this vague charge Pilate, in whom we mark throughout a strange reluctance, refused to proceed. He proposed that the Sanhedrists should try Jesus according to Jewish Law.   Under ordinary circumstances, Pilate would not have wished to hand over a person accused of setting up Messianic claims to the Jewish authorities, to try the case as a merely religious question.[a] Taking this in connection with the fact that on the previous evening the Governor had given a Roman guard for the arrest of the prisoner, and the dream and warning of Pilate's wife, a peculiar impression is conveyed to us. We can understand it all, if, on the previous evening, after the Roman guard had been granted, Pilate had spoken of it to his wife, whether because he knew her to be, or because she might be interested in the matter. Tradition has given her the name *Procula* ; an Apocryphal Gospel describes her as a convert to Judaism ; while the Greek Church has actually placed her in the catalogue of Saints. What if the truth lay between these statements, and Procula had not only been a proselyte, like the wife of a previous Roman Governor, but known about Jesus and spoken of Him to Pilate on that evening ? This would best explain his reluctance to condemn Jesus, as well as her dream of Him.

[a] Acts xxii. 30 ; xxiii. 28, 29 ; xxiv. 9, 18-20

As the Jewish authorities had to decline the Governor's offer to proceed against Jesus before their own tribunal, on the avowed ground that they had not power to pronounce capital sentence, it now behoved them to formulate a capital charge. This is recorded by St. Luke alone.[b] It was that Jesus had said He Himself was Christ a King. It will be noted, that in so saying they falsely imputed to Jesus their own political expectations

[b] St. Luke xxiii. 2, 3

concerning the Messiah. But even this is not all. They prefaced it by this, that He perverted the nation and forbade to give tribute to Cæsar. The latter charge was so grossly unfounded, that we can only regard it as in their mind a necessary inference from the premiss that He claimed to be King. And, as telling most against Him, they put this first and foremost, treating the inference as if it were a fact.

This charge of the Sanhedrists explains what passed within the Prætorium. We presume that Christ was within, probably in charge of some guards. Pilate now called Jesus and asked Him : ' Thou art the King of the Jews ? ' There is that mixture of contempt, cynicism, and awe in this question which we mark throughout in his bearing and words. It was as if two powers were contending for the mastery in his heart. Out of all that the Sanhedrists had said, Pilate took only this, that Jesus claimed to be a King. Christ, Who had not heard the charge of His accusers, now ignored it, in His desire to stretch out salvation even to a Pilate. He first put it to Pilate, whether the question was his own, or merely the repetition of what His Jewish accusers had told Pilate of Him. The Governor quickly disowned any personal inquiry. How could he raise any such question ? he was not a Jew, and the subject had no general interest. Jesus' own nation and its leaders had handed Him over as a criminal : what had He done ?

The answer of Pilate left nothing else for Him Who, even in that supreme hour, thought only of others, but to bring before the Roman directly that truth for which his words had given the opening. It was not, as Pilate had implied, a Jewish question : it was one of absolute truth ; it concerned all men. The Kingdom of Christ was not of this world at all, either Jewish or Gentile. Had it been otherwise, He would have led His followers to a contest for His claims and aims, and not have become a prisoner of the Jews. One word only in all this struck Pilate. ' So then a King art Thou ! ' He was incapable of apprehending the higher thought and truth. We mark in his words the same mixture of scoffing and misgiving. Pilate was now in no doubt as to the nature of the Kingdom; his exclamation and question applied to the Kingship. That fact Christ would now emphasise in the glory of His Humiliation. He accepted what Pilate said; He adopted his words. But He added to them an appeal, or rather an explanation of His claims, such as a heathen, and a Pilate, could understand. His Kingdom was not of this world, but of that other world which He had come to reveal, and to open to all believers. His Birth or Incarnation, as the Sent of the Father, and His own voluntary Coming into this ᵃ St. John world—for both are referred to in His words ᵃ— xviii. 37 had for their object to testify of the truth concerning that other world, of which was His Kingdom. This was no Jewish-Messianic Kingdom, but one that appealed to all men. And all who had moral affinity to ' the truth ' would listen to His testimony, and so come to own Him as ' King.'

It is not merely cynicism, but utter despair of all that is higher—a moral suicide—which now appears in Pilate's question : ' What is truth ? ' But even so his inquiry seems an admission, an implied homage to Christ. Assuredly, he would not have so opened his inner being to one of the priestly accusers of Jesus.

That Man was no rebel, no criminal! They who brought Him were moved by the lowest passions. And so he told them, as he went out, that he found no fault in Him. Then came from the assembled Sanhedrists a perfect hailstorm of accusations. As we picture it to ourselves, all this while the Christ stood near, perhaps behind Pilate, just within the portals of the Prætorium. And to this clamour of charges He made no reply. But as He stood in the calm silence of Majesty, Pilate greatly wondered. Did this Man not even fear death; was He so conscious of innocence, so infinitely superior to those around and against Him ?

Fain would he have withdrawn; not that he was moved for absolute truth or by the personal innocence of the Sufferer, but that there was that in the Christ which made him reluctant to be unrighteous and unjust. And so when, amidst these confused cries, he caught the name Galilee as the scene of Jesus' labours, he gladly seized on what offered the prospect of devolving the responsibility on another. Jesus was a Galilean, and therefore belonged to the jurisdiction of King Herod. To Herod, therefore, who had come for the Feast to Jerusalem, and there occupied the old Maccabean Palace close ^{a St. Luke} to that of the High-Priest, Jesus was now ^{xxiii. 6-12} sent.[a]

To St. Luke alone we owe the account of what passed there. The opportunity now offered was welcome to Herod. It was a mark of reconciliation (or might be viewed as such) between himself and the Roman, and in a manner flattering to himself, since the first step had been taken by the Governor, and that by an almost ostentatious acknowledgment of the rights of the Tetrarch, on which possibly their former feud may have turned. Besides, Herod had long wished to see Jesus, of whom he had ^{b St. Luke} heard so many things.[b] But in vain did he ply ^{ix. 7-9} Christ with questions. He was as silent to him as formerly against the virulent charges of the Sanhedrists. But a Christ Who would or could do no signs, nor even kindle into the same denunciations as the Baptist, was to Antipas only a helpless figure that might be insulted and scoffed at, as did the Tetrarch and his men of war. And so Jesus was once more sent back to the Prætorium.

It is in the interval during which Jesus was before Herod, or probably soon afterwards, that we place the last ^{c St. Matt.} weird scene in the life of Judas, recorded by St. ^{xxvii. 3-10} Matthew.[c]

Sufficient had already passed to convince Judas what the end would be. The words which Jesus had spoken to him in the Garden must have burnt into his soul. He was among the soldiery that fell back at Christ's look. Since then Jesus had been led bound to Annas, to Caiaphas, to the Prætorium, to Herod. Even if Judas had not been present at any of these occasions, and we do not suppose that his conscience had allowed this, all Jerusalem must

Q Q

by that time have been full of the report, probably in even exaggerated form. One thing he saw : that Jesus was condemned. Judas did not ' repent' in the Scriptural sense ; but ' a change of mind and feeling' came over him. Whether this might have passed into repentance ; whether, if he had cast himself at the Feet of Jesus, as undoubtedly he might have done, this would have been so, we need not here ask. The mind and feelings of Judas, as regarded the deed he had done, and as regarded Jesus, were now quite other. The road, the streets, the people's faces—all seemed now to bear witness against him and for Jesus. He read it everywhere ; he felt it always. What had been ; what was ; what would be ! Heaven and earth receded from him ; there were voices in the air, and pangs in the soul—and no escape, help, counsel, or hope anywhere.

It was despair, and his a desperate resolve. He must get rid of these thirty pieces of silver. Then at least his deed would have nothing of the selfish in it : only a terrible error, a mistake, to which he had been incited by these Sanhedrists. Back to them with the money, and let them have it again ! And so forward he pressed amidst the crowd, which would give way before the haggard face that crime had made old in those few hours, till he came upon the knot of priests and Sanhedrists, perhaps at that very moment speaking of it all. A most unwelcome sight and intrusion on them, this necessary but odious figure in the drama—belonging to its past, and who should rest in its obscurity. But he would be heard ; nay, his words would cast the burden on them to share it with him, as with hoarse cry he broke into this : ' I have sinned—in that I have betrayed—innocent blood !' They turned from him with impatience, in contempt, as so often the seducer turns from the seduced : ' What is that to us ? See thou to it !' And presently they were again deep in conversation or consultation. For a moment he stared before him, the very thirty pieces of silver that had been weighed to him, and which he had now brought back, and would fain have given them, still clutched in his hand. For a moment only, and then he rushed forward, towards the Sanctuary itself, probably to where the Court of Israel bounded on that of the Priests, where generally the penitents stood in waiting, while in the Priests' Court the sacrifice was offered for them. There bending forward, he hurled from him those thirty pieces of silver, so that each resounded as it fell on the marble pavement.

Out from the Temple, out of Jerusalem, 'into solitude.' Down into the horrible solitude of the Valley of Hinnom, the 'Tophet' of old, with its ghastly memories, the Gehenna of the future, with its ghostly associations. Across the Valley, and up the steep sides of the mountain. We are now on 'the potter's field' of Jeremiah—somewhat to the west above where the Kidron and Hinnom valleys merge. It is soft clayey soil, where the footsteps slip, or are held in clammy bonds. Here jagged rocks rise perpendicularly : perhaps there was some gnarled, bent, stunted tree. Up there he climbed to the top of that rock. Now slowly and deliberately he unwound the long girdle that held his garment. It was the girdle in which he had carried those thirty pieces of silver. He is now quite calm and collected. With that girdle he will hang himself on that tree close by, and when he has fastened it, he will throw himself off from that jagged rock.

It is done. But as he swung heavily on that branch, under the burden the girdle gave way, or perhaps the knot unloosed, and he fell heavily forward among the rocks beneath, and perished in the manner of which St. Peter reminded his fellow-disciples in the days before Pentecost.[a] But in the Temple the priests knew not what to do with these thirty pieces of money. Their unscrupulous scrupulosity came again upon them. It was not lawful to take into the Temple-treasury, for the purchase of sacred things, money that had been unlawfully gained. In such cases the Jewish Law provided that the money was to be restored to the donor, and, if he insisted on giving it, that he should be induced to spend it on something for the public weal By a fiction of law the money was still considered to be Judas', and to have been

[a] Acts i. 18, 19

applied by him [a] in the purchase of the well-known 'pot-

a Acts i. 18
b St. Matt.
xxvii. 7

ter's field,' for the charitable purpose of burying in it strangers.[b] But from henceforth the old name of 'potter's field' became popularly changed into that of 'field of blood.'

We are once more outside the Prætorium, to which Pilate had summoned from the Temple Sanhedrists and people. The crowd was momentarily increasing from the town. It was not only to see what was about to happen, but to witness another spectacle, that of the release of a prisoner. For it seems to have been the custom, that at the Passover the Roman Governor released to the Jewish populace some notorious prisoner who lay condemned to death. On the present occasion it might be more easy for the Sanhedrists to influence the people among whom they mingled, since Bar-Abbas belonged to that class, not uncommon at the time, which, under the colourable pretence of political aspirations, committed robbery and other crimes. These movements had deeply struck root in popular sympathy.

But when the Governor, hoping to enlist some popular sympathy, put this alternative to them—nay, urged it, on the ground that neither he nor yet Herod had found any crime in Jesus, and would even have appeased their thirst for vengeance by offering to submit Him to the cruel punishment of scourging, it was in vain. It was now that Pilate sat down on 'the judgment seat.' But ere he could proceed, came that message from his wife about her dream, and the warning entreaty to have nothing to do 'with that righteous man.' An omen such as a dream, and an appeal connected with it, especially in the circumstances of that trial, would powerfully impress a Roman. And for a few moments it seemed as if the appeal to popular feeling on

c St. Mark
xv. 11

behalf of Jesus might have been successful.[c] But once more the Sanhedrists prevailed. Apparently, all who had been followers of Jesus had been scattered. It was Bar-Abbas for whom, incited by the priesthood, the populace now clamoured with increasing vehemence. To the question—half bitter, half mocking—what they wished him to do with Him Whom their own leaders had in their accusation called ' King of the Jews,' surged back, louder and louder, the cry : ' Crucify Him ! ' In vain Pilate expostulated, reasoned, appealed. Popular frenzy only grew as it was opposed.

All reasoning having failed, Pilate had recourse to one more expedient, which, under ordinary circumstances, ^{a St. Matt.} would have been effective.[a] When a Judge, after ^{xxvii. 24, 25} having declared the innocence of the accused, actually rises from the judgment-seat, and by a symbolic act pronounces the execution of the accused a judicial murder, from all participation in which he wishes solemnly to clear himself, surely no jury would persist in demanding sentence of death. But in the present instance there was even more. Although we find allusions to some such custom among the heathen, that which here took place was an essentially Jewish rite, which must have appealed the more forcibly to the Jews that it was done by Pilate. And not only the rite, but the very words were Jewish. It does not affect the question, whether or not a judge could, especially in the circumstances recorded, free himself from guilt. Certainly, he could not. But such conduct on the part of Pilate appears so unusual, as, indeed, his whole bearing towards Christ, that we can only account for it by the deep impression which Jesus had made upon him. All the more terrible would be the guilt of Jewish resistance. There is something overawing in Pilate's ' See ye to it '—a reply to the Sanhedrists' ' See thou to it,' to Judas, and in the same words.

The Evangelists have passed as rapidly as possible over the last scenes of indignity and horror, and we are too thankful to follow their example. Bar-Abbas was at once released. Jesus was handed over to the soldiery to be scourged and crucified, although final and formal judgment ^{b St. John} had not yet been pronounced.[b] Indeed, Pilate ^{xix. 1, and} seems to have hoped that the horrors of the ^{following} ^{c ver. 4, and} scourging might still move the people to desist ^{following} from the ferocious cry for the Cross.[c] Without repeating the harrowing realism of a Cicero, scourging was the terrible introduction to crucifixion—'the intermediate death.' Stripped of His clothes, His hands tied and back bent, the Victim would be bound to a column or stake, in front of the Prætorium. The scourging ended, the soldiery would hastily cast upon Him His upper garments, and lead Him back into the Prætorium. Here they called the whole cohort together, and the silent, faint Sufferer became the object of their ribald jesting. From His bleeding Body they tore the clothes, and in mockery arrayed Him in scarlet or purple. For crown they wound together thorns, and for sceptre they placed in His Hand a reed. Then alternately, in mock proclamation they hailed Him King, or worshipped Him as God, and smote Him or heaped on Him other indignities.

Such a spectacle might well have disarmed enmity, and for ever allayed worldly fears. And so Pilate had hoped, when at his bidding Jesus came forth from the Prætorium, arrayed as a mock-king, and the Governor presented Him to the populace in words which the Church has ever since treasured: 'Behold the Man!' But so far from appeasing, the sight only incited to fury the 'chief priests' and their subordinates. This Man before them was the occasion, that on this Paschal Day a heathen dared in Jerusalem itself insult their deepest feelings, mock their most cherished Messianic hopes! 'Crucify!' 'Crucify!' resounded from all sides. Once more Pilate appealed to them, when, unwittingly and unwillingly, it elicited this from the people, that Jesus had claimed to be the Son of God.

If nothing else, what light it casts on the mode in which Jesus had borne Himself amidst those tortures and insults, that this statement of the Jews filled Pilate with fear, and led him to seek converse again with Jesus within the Prætorium. His first question to Jesus was, whence He was? And when, as was most fitting—since he could not have understood it—Jesus returned no answer, the feeling of the Roman became only the more intense. Would He not speak; did He not know that he had abso-lute power 'to release or to crucify' Him? Nay, not absolute power—all power came from above; but the guilt in the abuse of power was far greater on the part of apostate Israel and its leaders, who knew whence power came, and to Whom they were responsible for its exercise.

So spake not an impostor; so spake not an ordinary man—after such sufferings and in such circumstances—to one who, whencesoever derived, had the power of life or death over Him. And Pilate felt it—the more keenly, for his cynicism and disbelief of all that was higher. And the more earnestly did he now seek to release Jesus. But, proportionately, the louder and fiercer was the cry of the Jews for His Blood, till they threatened to implicate in the charge of rebellion against Cæsar the Governor himself, if he persisted in unwonted mercy.

Such danger a Pilate would never encounter. He sat down once more in the judgment-seat, outside the Prætorium, in the place called 'Pavement,' and, from its outlook over the City, 'Gabbatha,' 'the rounded height.' So solemn is the transaction that the Evangelist pauses to note once more the day—nay, the very hour, when the .process had commenced. It had been the Friday in Passover-week, and between six and seven of the morning. And at the close Pilate once more in mockery presented to them Jesus: 'Behold your King!' Once more they called for His Crucifixion—and, when again challenged, the chief priests burst into the cry, which preceded Pilate's final sentence, to be presently executed: 'We have no king but Cæsar!'

With this cry Judaism was, in the person of its representatives, guilty of denial of God, of blasphemy, of apostasy.

CHAPTER LXXXV.

' CRUCIFIED, DEAD, AND BURIED.'

(St. Matt. xxvii. 31–43 ; St. Mark xv. 20–32ᵃ ; St. Luke xxiii. 26–38 ; St. John xix. 16–24 ; St. Matt. xxviii. 44 ; St. Mark xv. 32ᵇ ; St. Luke xxiii. 39–43 ; St. John xix. 25–27 ; St. Matt. xxvii. 45–56 ; St. Mark xv. 33–41 ; St. Luke xxiii. 44–49 ; St. John xix. 28–30 ; 31–37 ; St. Matt. xxvii. 57–61 ; St. Mark xv. 42–47 ; St. Luke xxiii. 50–56 ; St. John xix. 38–42 ; St. Matt. xxvii. 62–66.)

IT matters little as regards their guilt, whether, pressing the language of St. John,ᵃ we are to understand that Pilate delivered Jesus to the Jews to be crucified, or, as we rather infer, to his own soldiers. This was the common practice, and it accords both with the Governor's former taunt to the Jews,ᵇ and with the after-notice of the Synoptists. They, to whom He was 'delivered,' ' led Him away to be crucified ; ' and they who so led Him forth 'compelled ' the Cyrenian Simon to bear the Cross.

ᵃ St. John xix. 16

ᵇ ver. 6

Once more was He unrobed and robed. The purple robe was torn from His wounded Body, the crown of thorns from His Brow. Arrayed again in His own, now blood-stained, garments, He was led forth to execution. Only about two hours and a half had passedᶜ since the time that He had first stood before Pilate (about half-past six),ᵈ when the melancholy procession reached Golgotha (at nine o'clock A.M.) In Rome an interval, ordinarily of two days, intervened between a sentence and its execution ; but the rule does not seem to have applied to the provinces, if, indeed, in this case the formal rules of Roman procedure were at all observed.

ᶜ St. Mark xv. 25

ᵈ St. John xix. 15

The preparations were soon made : the hammer, the nails, the Cross, the very food for the soldiers who were to watch under each Cross. Four soldiers would be detailed for each Cross, the whole being under the command of a centurion. As always, the Cross was borne to the place of execution by Him Who was to suffer on it—perhaps His Arms bound to it with cords. But there is happily no evidence—

rather, every indication to the contrary—that, according to ancient custom, the neck of the Sufferer was fastened within the *patibulum*, two horizontal pieces of wood placed at the end, to which the hands were bound. Ordinarily, the procession was headed by the centurion, or preceded by one who proclaimed the nature of the crime, and carried a white wooden board, on which it was written. Commonly, also, it took the longest road to the place of execution, and through the most crowded streets, so as to attract most public attention. But we would suggest that alike this long circuit and the proclamation of the herald were, in the present instance, dispensed with. They are not hinted at in the text, and seem incongruous to the festive season, and the other circumstances of the history.

Discarding all later legendary embellishments, we will try to realise the scene as described in the Gospels. Under the leadership of the centurion, Jesus came forth bearing His Cross. He was followed by two malefactors —'robbers'—probably of the class then so numerous, that covered its crimes by pretensions of political motives. These two, also, would bear each his cross, and probably be attended each by four soldiers. Crucifixion was not a Jewish mode of punishment, although the Maccabee King Jannæus had so far forgotten the claims of both humanity and religion as on one occasion to crucify not less than 800 persons in Jerusalem itself. But even Herod, with all his cruelty, did not resort to this mode of execution. Nor was it employed by the Romans till after the time of Cæsar, when, with the fast increasing cruelty of punishments, it became fearfully common in the provinces. Especially does it seem to characterise the domination of Rome in Judæa under every Governor. During the last siege of Jerusalem hundreds of crosses daily arose, till there seemed not sufficient room nor wood for them, and the soldiery diversified their horrible amusement by new modes of crucifixion.

As mostly all abominations of the ancient world, whether in religion or life, crucifixion was of Phœnician origin, although Rome adopted and improved on it. The modes of execution among the Jews were: strangulation, beheading, burning, and stoning. In all ordinary circumstances the Rabbis were most reluctant to pronounce sentence of death. The indignity of hanging—and this only after the criminal had been otherwise executed—was reserved for the crimes of idolatry and blasphemy.

Three kinds of Cross were in use : the so-called St. Andrew's Cross (×, the *Crux decussata*), the Cross in the form of a T (*Crux commissa*), and the ordinary Latin Cross (+, *Crux immissa*). We believe that Jesus bore the last of these. This would also most readily admit of affixing the board with the threefold inscription, which we know His Cross bore. This Cross, as St. John expressly states, Jesus Himself bore at the outset. And so the procession moved on towards Golgotha. Not only the location, but even the name of that which appeals so strongly to every Christian heart, is matter of controversy. The name cannot have been derived from the skulls which lay about, since such exposure would have been unlawful, and hence must have been due to the skull-like shape and appearance of the place.

Whether or not the 'tomb of the Herodian period in the rocky knoll to the west of Jeremiah's Grotto' was the most sacred spot upon earth — the ' Sepulchre in the Garden,' we dare not positively assert, though every probability attaches to it.

From the ancient Palace of Herod that procession descended, and probably passed through the gate in the first wall, and so into the busy quarter of Acra. As it proceeded, the numbers who followed from the Temple, from the dense business-quarter through which it moved, increased. Shops, bazaars, and markets were, indeed, closed on the holy feast-day. But a crowd of people would come out to line the streets and to follow; and especially women, leaving their festive preparations, raised loud laments, not in spiritual recognition of Christ's claims, but in pity and sympathy.[a] Since the Paschal Supper Jesus had not tasted either food or drink. After the deep emotion of that Feast, with all of holiest institution which it included; after the anticipated betrayal

[a] St. Luke

of Judas, and after the farewell to His disciples, He had passed into Gethsemane. There had He agonised in mortal conflict, till the great drops of blood forced themselves on His Brow. There had He been delivered up, while the disciples had fled. To Annas, to Caiaphas, to Pilate, to Herod, and again to Pilate ; from indignity to indignity, from torture to torture, had He been hurried all that livelong night, all that morning. Unrefreshed by food or sleep, while His pallid Face bore the blood-marks from the crown of thorns, His Body was unable to bear the weight of the Cross. No wonder that the pity of the women of Jerusalem was stirred.

Up to that last Gate which led from the ' Suburb ' towards the place of execution did Jesus bear His Cross. Then, as we infer, His strength gave way under it. A man was coming from the opposite direction, one from that large colony of Jews which, as we know, had settled in Cyrene. He would be specially noticed ; for few would at that hour, on the festive day, come ' out of the country,' although such was not contrary to the Law. He seems, besides, to have been well known, at least afterwards, in the Church—and his sons Alexander and Rufus even better than he.[a] On him the soldiery laid hold, and against his will forced him to bear the Cross after Christ. Yet another indication of the need of such help comes to us from St. Mark,[b] who uses an expression which conveys that the Saviour had to be supported to Golgotha from the place where they met Simon.

a St. Mark xv. 21

b ver. 22

Here we place the next incident in this history.[c] While the Cross was laid on Simon, the women who had followed with the populace closed around the Sufferer, raising their lamentations. At His Entrance into Jerusalem,[d] Jesus had wept over the daughters of Jerusalem ; as He left it for the last time they wept over Him. But far different were the reasons for His tears from theirs of mere pity. And, if proof were required of His Divine strength, even in the utmost depth of His Human weakness—how, conquered, He was Conqueror—it would surely be found in the words in which He

c St. Luke xxiii. 27-31

d as St. Luke also records

bade them turn their thoughts of pity where pity would be called for, even to themselves and their children in the near judgment upon Jerusalem.

It was nine of the clock when the procession reached Golgotha, and the preparations for the Crucifixion commenced. Avowedly, the punishment was invented to make death as painful and as lingering as the power of human endurance. First, the upright wood was planted in the ground. It was not high, and probably the Feet of the Sufferer were not above one or two feet from the ground. Thus could the communication described in the Gospels take place between Him and others; thus, also, might His sacred Lips be moistened with the sponge attached to a short stalk of hyssop. Next, the transverse wood was placed on the ground, and the Sufferer laid on it, when His Arms were extended, drawn up, and bound to it. Then (this not in Egypt, but in Carthage and in Rome), a strong, sharp nail was driven, first into the right, then into the left Hand. Next, the Sufferer was drawn up by means of ropes, perhaps ladders; the transverse either bound or nailed to the upright, and a rest or support for the Body fastened on it. Lastly, the Feet were extended, and either one nail hammered into each, or a larger piece of iron through the two. And so might the crucified hang for hours, even days, till consciousness at last failed.

It was a merciful Jewish practice to give to those led to execution a draught of strong wine mixed with myrrh, so as to deaden consciousness. This charitable office was performed at the cost of, if not by, an association of women in Jerusalem. That draught was offered to Jesus when He reached Golgotha. But having tasted it, and ascertained its character and object, He would not drink it. It was like His former refusal of the pity of the 'daughters of Jerusalem.' Nor would He suffer and die as if it had been a necessity, not a voluntary self-surrender. He would meet Death and conquer by submitting to the full.

And so was He nailed to His Cross, which was placed between, probably somewhat higher than, those of the two malefactors crucified with Him. One thing only still remained: to affix to His Cross the so-called 'title,' on which was inscribed the charge on which He had been condemned. As already stated, it was customary to carry this board before the prisoner, and there is no reason for supposing any exception in this respect. Indeed, it seems implied in the circumstance, that the 'title' had evidently been drawn up under the direction of Pilate. It was—as might have been expected, and yet most significantly—trilingual : in Latin, Greek, and Aramæan. We imagine that it was written in that order, and that the words were those recorded by the Evangelists (excepting St. Luke, who seems to give a modification of the original, or Aramæan, text). The inscription given by St. Matthew exactly corresponds with that which *Eusebius* records as the Latin title on the cross of one of the early martyrs. We therefore conclude that it represents the Latin words. Again, it seems only natural that the fullest, and to the Jews most offensive, description should have been in Aramæan, which all could read. This is given by St. John. It follows, that the inscription given by St. Mark must represent that in Greek. Although much less comprehensive, it had the same number of words, and precisely the same number of letters, as that in Aramæan.

It seems probable that the Sanhedrists had heard from some one, who had watched the procession on its way to Golgotha, of the inscription which Pilate had written— partly to avenge himself on, and partly to deride, the Jews. We suppose that, after the condemnation of Jesus, the Sanhedrists had gone from the Prætorium into the Temple, to take part in its services. When informed of the offensive tablet, they hastened once more to the Prætorium, to induce Pilate not to allow it to be put up. We imagine that they had originally no intention of doing anything so un-Jewish as not only to gaze at the sufferings of the Crucified, but to even deride Him in His Agony— that, in fact, they had not intended going to Golgotha at all. But when they found that Pilate would not yield to their remonstrances, some of them hastened to the place of Crucifixion, and, mingling with the crowd, sought to

incite their jeers, so as to prevent any deeper impression
which the significant words of the inscription might have
produced.

Before nailing Him to the Cross, the soldiers parted
among them the poor worldly inheritance of His raiment.
On this point there are slight seeming differences between
the notices of the Synoptists and the more detailed account
of the Fourth Gospel. Such differences, if real, would
afford only fresh evidence of the general trustworthiness
of the narrative. For we bear in mind that, of all the
disciples, only St. John witnessed the last scenes, and that
therefore the other accounts of it circulating in the early
Church must have been derived, so to speak, from second
sources. This explains, why the most detailed as well as
precise account of the closing hours in the Life of Christ
comes to us from St. John. In the present instance these
differences may be explained in the following manner.
There was, as St. John states, first a division into four
parts—one to each of the soldiers—of such garments of the
Lord as were of nearly the same value. The head-gear,
the outer cloak-like garment, the girdle, and the sandals,
would differ little in cost. But the question, which of
them was to belong to each of the soldiers, would naturally
be decided, as the Synoptists inform us, by lot.

But besides these four articles of dress, there was the
seamless woven inner garment, by far the most valuable
of all, and for which, as it could not be partitioned without
being destroyed, they would specially cast lots (as St. John
reports). To St. John, the loving and loved disciple,
greater contrast could scarcely exist than between this
rough partition by lot among the soldiery, and the character and claims of Him Whose garments they were thus
apportioning, as if He had been a helpless Victim in their
hands. Only one explanation could here suggest itself :
that there was a Divine meaning in the permission of such
an event—that it was in fulfilment of ancient prophecy.
• Ps. xxii. 18 As he gazed on the terrible scene, the words of
                the Psalm[a] which portrayed the desertion, the
sufferings, and the contempt even unto death of the Servant

of the Lord, flashed upon his mind—for the first time he understood them. That this quotation is made in the fourth Gospel alone, proves that its writer was an eye-witness; that it was made in the fourth Gospel at all, that he was a Jew, deeply imbued with Jewish modes of religious thinking.

It was when they thus nailed Him to the Cross, and parted His raiment, that He spake the first of the so-called ' Seven Words ' : ' Father, forgive them, for they know not what they do.' Even the reference in this prayer to 'what they do' points to the soldiers as the primary, though certainly not the sole object of the Saviour's prayer.[a] But higher thoughts also come to us. When Jesus is most human (in the moment of His being nailed to the Cross), then is He most Divine, in the utter discarding of the human elements of human instrumentality and of human suffering. Then also in the utter self-forgetfulness of the God-Man—which is one of the aspects of the Incarnation—does He only remember Divine mercy, and pray for them who crucify Him; and thus only does the Conquered truly conquer His conquerors by asking for them what their deed had forfeited.

[a] Comp. Acts iii. 17; 1 Cor. ii. 8

This was His first Utterance on the Cross—as regarded them; as regarded Himself; and as regarded God.

And now began the real agonies of the Cross—physical, mental, and spiritual. Before sitting down to their watch over the Crucified,[b] the soldiers would refresh themselves by draughts of the cheap wine of the country. As they quaffed it, they drank to Him, and mockingly came to Him, asking Him to pledge them in response. Their jests were, indeed, chiefly directed not against Jesus personally, but in His representative capacity, and so against the hated, despised Jews, whose King they now derisively challenged to save Himself.[c] Yet even so, it seems to us of deepest significance, that He was thus treated and derided in His representative capacity and as the King of the Jews. But what we find so difficult to understand is, that the leaders of Israel had the indescribable baseness of joining

[b] St. Matthew

[c] St. Luke

in the jeer at Israel's great hope, and of leading the popular chorus in it.

And did none of those who so reviled Him in all the chief aspects of His Work feel that, as Judas had sold the Master for nought and committed suicide, so they were doing in regard to their Messianic hope ? For their jeers cast contempt on the four great facts in the Life and Work of Jesus, which were also the underlying ideas of the Messianic Kingdom : the new relationship to Israel's religion and the Temple ('Thou that destroyest the Temple, and buildest it in three days ') ; the new relationship to the Father through the Messiah, the Son of God ('if Thou be the Son of God') ; the new all-sufficient help brought to body and soul in salvation ('He saved others') ; and, finally, the new relationship to Israel in the fulfilment and perfecting of its Mission through its King ('if He be the King of Israel '). On all these, the taunting challenge of the Sanhedrists, to come down from the Cross and save Himself, if He would claim the allegiance of their faith, cast what St. Matthew and St. Mark characterise as the 'blaspheming' of doubt.

There is a remarkable relationship between what St. Luke quotes as spoken by the soldiers : ' If Thou art the King of the Jews, save Thyself,' and the report of the words in St. Matthew :[a] ' He saved others— Himself He cannot save. He is the King of Israel ! Let Him now come down from the Cross, and we will believe on Him ! ' These are the words of the Sanhedrists, and they seem to respond to those of the soldiers, as reported by St. Luke, and to carry them further. The ' if ' of the soldiers : ' If Thou art the King of the Jews,' now becomes a direct blasphemous challenge. At the beginning of His Work, the Tempter had suggested that the Christ should achieve absolute victory by an act of presumptuous self-assertion ; and now, at the close of His Messianic Work, he suggested in the challenge of the Sanhedrists that Jesus had suffered absolute defeat, and that God had publicly disowned the trust which the Christ had put in Him. ' He trusteth in God : let Him

[a] St. Matt. xxvii. 42

deliver Him now, if He will have Him.' Here, as in the Temptation of the Wilderness, the words misapplied were those of Holy Scripture—in the present instance those of Ps. xxii. 8. And the quotation, as made by the Sanhedrists, is the more remarkable, that, contrary to what is generally asserted by writers, this Psalm[a] was Messianically applied by the ancient Synagogue.

a Ps. xxii.
b ver. 7

More especially was this verse,[b] which precedes the mocking quotation of the Sanhedrists, expressly applied to the sufferings and the derision which Messiah was to undergo from His enemies : ' All they that see Me laugh Me to scorn : they shoot out the lip, they shake the head.'

The derision of the Sanhedrists under the Cross had a special motive. The place of Crucifixion was close to the great road which led from the North to Jerusalem. On that Feast-day, when there was no law to limit locomotion to a ' Sabbath day's journey,' many would pass in and out of the City, and the crowd would naturally be arrested by the spectacle of the three Crosses. Equally naturally would they have been impressed by the title over the Cross of Christ. The words, describing the Sufferer as ' the King of the Jews,' might, when taken in connection with what was known of Jesus, have raised most dangerous questions. And this the presence of the Sanhedrists was intended to prevent, by turning the popular mind in a totally different direction.

St. Matthew and St. Mark merely remark in general that the derision of the Sanhedrists and people was joined in by the thieves on the Cross. But St. Luke records a vital difference between the two ' robbers.' The impenitent thief takes up the jeer of the Sanhedrists : ' Art Thou not the Christ ? Save Thyself and us!' The words are the more significant that—strange as it may sound—it is noted by historians, that those on the cross were wont to utter insults and imprecations on the onlookers, goaded nature perhaps seeking relief in such outbursts.

If a more close study of the words of the ' penitent thief' may seem to diminish the fulness of meaning which

R R

the traditional view attaches to them, they gain all the
more as we perceive their historic reality.   His first words
were of reproof to his comrade.   In that terrible hour,
amidst the tortures of a slow death, did not the fear of God
at least prevent his joining with those who insulted the
dying agonies of the Sufferer?   And this all the more, in
the peculiar circumstances.   They were all three sufferers;
but they two justly, while He Whom he insulted had done
nothing amiss.   From this basis of fact, the penitent rapidly
rose to the height of faith.

One thing stood out before his mind, who in that hour
did fear God.   Jesus had done nothing amiss.   And this
surrounded with a halo of moral glory the inscription on
the Cross, long before its words acquired a new meaning.
But how did this Innocent One bear Himself in suffering?
With what calm of endurance He had borne the insult and
jeers of those who, even to the spiritually unenlightened
eye, must have seemed so infinitely far beneath Him!
This man did feel the ' fear ' of God, who now learned the
new lesson in which the fear of God was truly the beginning of wisdom.   Rapidly he passed into the light, and
onwards and upwards : ' Lord, remember me, when Thou
comest in Thy Kingdom ! '

The familiar words of our Authorised Version—' When
Thou comest into Thy Kingdom '—convey the idea of
what we might call a more spiritual meaning of the petition.   But we can scarcely believe that at that moment
it implied either that Christ was then going into His Kingdom, or that the ' penitent thief ' looked to Christ for admission into the Heavenly Kingdom.   The words are true
to the Jewish point of vision of the man.   He recognised
and owned Jesus as the Messiah, and he did so, by a
wonderful forthgoing of faith, even in the utmost humiliation of Christ.   And this immediately passed beyond the
Jewish standpoint, for he expected Jesus soon to come
back in His Kingly might and power, when he asked to be
remembered by Him in mercy.   The answering assurance
of the Lord conveyed not only the comfort that his prayer
was answered, but the teaching of spiritual things which

he so much needed to know. The 'penitent' had spoken of the future, Christ spoke of 'to-day'; the penitent had prayed about that Messianic Kingdom which was to come, Christ assured him in regard to the state of the disembodied spirits, and conveyed to him the promise that he would be there in the abode of the blessed—'Paradise'—and that through means of Himself as the Messiah : 'Amen, I say unto thee—To-day, with Me shalt thou be in the Paradise.' Thus did Christ give him that spiritual knowledge which he did not yet possess—the teaching concerning the 'to-day,' the need of admission into Paradise, and that with and through Himself—in other words, concerning the forgiveness of sins and the opening of the Kingdom of Heaven to all believers. This, as the first and foundation-creed of the soul, was the first and foundation-fact concerning the Messiah.

Some hours—probably two—had passed since Jesus had been nailed to the Cross. We wonder how it came that St. John, who tells us some of the incidents with such exceeding particularity, and relates all with the vivid realisation of a most deeply interested eyewitness, should have been silent as to others—especially as to those hours of derision, as well as to the conversion of the penitent thief. His silence seems to us to have been due to absence from the scene. We part company with him after his de-
^{a St. John} tailed account of the last scene before Pilate.^a
^{xix. 2-16} The final sentence pronounced, we suppose him to have hurried into the City, and to have acquainted such of the disciples as he might find—but especially those faithful women and the Virgin-Mother—with what had passed since the previous evening. Thence he returned to Golgotha, just in time to witness the Crucifixion, which he again describes with peculiar fulness of details.^b
^{b vv. 17-24} When the Saviour was nailed to the Cross, St. John seems once more to have returned to the City—this time to bring back with him those women, in company of whom we now find him standing close to the Cross. Alone of all the disciples, he is there—not afraid to be near Christ, in the Palace of the High-Priest, before Pilate, and now under the Cross. And alone he renders to Christ this

tender service of bringing the women and Mary to the Cross, and to them the protection of his guidance and company. He loved Jesus best ; and it was fitting that to his manliness and affection should be entrusted Christ's dangerous inheritance.

ᵃ St. John xix. 25-27 The narrative ᵃ leaves the impression that with the beloved disciple these four women were standing close to the Cross : the Mother of Jesus, the sister of His Mother, Mary the wife of Clopas, and Mary of Magdala. ᵇ St. Matt. xxvii. 55 ᶜ St. Mark xv. 40, 41 A comparison with what is related by St. Matthew ᵇ and St. Mark ᶜ supplies further important particulars. We read there of only three women, the name of the Mother of our Lord being omitted. But then it must be remembered that this refers to a later period in the history of the Crucifixion. It seems as if John had fulfilled to the letter the Lord's command : ' Behold thy mother,' and literally ' from that very hour ' taken her to his own home. If we are right in this supposition, then, in the absence of St. John—who led away the Virgin-Mother from that scene of horror—the other three women would withdraw to a distance, where we find them at the end, not ' by the Cross,' as in St. John xix. 25, but ' beholding from afar,' and now joined by others also, who had loved and followed Christ.

We further notice that, the name of the Virgin-Mother being omitted, the other three are the same as mentioned by St. John ; only, Mary of Clopas is now described as ' the mother of James and Joses,' and Christ's ᵈ St. Mark ' Mother's sister ' as ' Salome ' ᵈ and ' the mother ᵉ St. Matthew of Zebedee's children.' ᵉ Thus Salome, the wife of Zebedee and St. John's mother, was the sister of the Virgin, and the beloved disciple the cousin (on the mother's side) of Jesus, and the nephew of the Virgin. This also helps to explain why the care of the Mother had been entrusted to him. Nor was Mary the wife of Clopas unconnected with Jesus. What we have every reason to regard as a trustworthy account describes Clopas as the brother of Joseph, the husband of the Virgin. Thus, not only Salome as the sister of the Virgin, but Mary also as the wife of Clopas, would, in a certain sense, have been His aunt, and her sons His cousins. And so we notice among the twelve Apostles five cousins of the Lord : the two sons of Salome and Zebedee, and the three sons of Alphæus or Clopas and Mary : James, Judas surnamed Lebbæus and Thaddæus, and Simon surnamed Zelotes or Cananæan.

For three hours had the Saviour hung on the Cross. It was midday. And now the sun was craped in darkness from the sixth to the ninth hour. It seems only in accordance with the Evangelic narrative to regard the occurrence of this event as supernatural, while the event itself might have been brought about by natural causes; and among these we must call special attention to the earthquake in a St. Matt. which this darkness terminated.[a] For it is a xxvii. 51 well-known phenomenon that such darkness not unfrequently precedes earthquakes.

The darkness was such not only to Nature; Jesus, also, entered into darkness: Body, Soul, and Spirit. It was now, not as before, a contest—but suffering. Into this, to us, fathomless depth of the mystery of His Sufferings, we dare not, as indeed we cannot, enter. It was of the Body ; yet not of the Body only, but of physical life. The increasing, nameless agonies of the Crucifixion were deepening into the bitterness of death. All nature shrinks from death, and there is a physical horror of the separation between body and soul which, as a purely natural phenomenon, is in every instance only overcome, and that only by a higher principle. And we conceive that, the purer the being, the greater the violence of the tearing asunder of the bond with which God Almighty originally bound together body and soul. In the Perfect Man this must have reached the highest degree. So, also, had in those dark hours the sense of man-forsakenness and of His own isolation from man; so, also, had the intense silence of God, the withdrawal of God, the sense of His God-forsakenness and absolute loneliness. The sacrificial, vicarious, expiatory, and redemptive character of His Death, if it does not explain to us, yet helps us to understand, Christ's sense of God-forsakenness in the supreme moment of the Cross.

It was the combination of the Old Testament idea of sacrifice, and of the Old Testament ideal of willing suffering as the Servant of Jehovah, now fulfilled in Christ, which found its fullest expression in the language of the twenty-second Psalm. It was fitting—rather, it was true—that the willing suffering of the true Sacrifice should now find vent in its opening words: ' My God, My God, why hast Thou forsaken Me ? '—*Eli, Eli, lema sabacthanei*? These words, cried with a loud voice at the close of the period of extreme agony, marked the climax and the end of this suffering of Christ, of which the utmost compass was the withdrawal of God and the felt loneliness of the Sufferer. But they that stood by the Cross, misinterpreting the meaning, and mistaking the opening words for the name *Elias*, imagined that the Sufferer had called for Elias. We can scarcely doubt that these were the soldiers who stood by the Cross. They were not necessarily Romans; on the contrary, as we have seen, these Legions were generally recruited from Provincials. On the other hand, no Jew would have mistaken *Eli* for the name of Elijah, nor yet misinterpreted a quotation of Psalm xxii. 1 as a call for that prophet.

It can scarcely have been a minute or two from the time that the cry from the twenty-second Psalm marked the high-point of His Agony, when the words ' I thirst ' [a] seem to indicate, by the prevalence of the merely human aspect of the suffering, that the other and more terrible aspect of sin-bearing and God-forsakenness was past. To us therefore this seems the beginning, if not of Victory, yet of Rest, of the End. St. John alone records this Utterance, prefacing it with this distinctive statement, that Jesus so surrendered Himself to the human feeling, seeking the bodily relief by expressing His thirst: ' knowing that all things were now finished, that the Scripture might be fulfilled.' In other words, the climax of Theanthropic Suffering in His feeling of God-forsakenness, which had led to the utterance of Psalm xxii. 1, was

[a] St. John xix. 28

now, to His consciousness, the end of all which in accordance with Scripture-prediction He had to bear.

One of the soldiers—may we not be allowed to believe, one who either had already learned from that Cross, or was about to learn, to own Him Lord—moved by sympathy, now ran to offer some slight refreshment to the Sufferer by filling a sponge with the rough wine of the soldiers and putting it to His Lips, having first fastened it to the stem ('reed') of the caper ('hyssop'), which is said to grow to the height of even two or three feet. But, even so, this act of humanity was not allowed to pass unchallenged by the others, who would bid him leave the relief of the Sufferer to the agency of Elijah, which in their opinion He had invoked. Nor should we perhaps wonder at the weakness of that soldier himself, who, though he would not be hindered in his good deed, yet averted the opposition of the others by apparently joining in their mockery. [a]

ª St. Matt. xxvii. 48, 49 ; St. Mark xv. 36

By accepting the physical refreshment offered Him, the Lord once more indicated the completion of the work of His Passion. For, as He would not enter on it with His senses and physical consciousness lulled by narcotised wine, so He would not pass out of it with senses and physical consciousness dulled by the absolute failure of life-power. And so He immediately passed on to 'taste death for every man.' For the two last 'sayings' of the Saviour now followed in rapid succession: first, that with a loud voice, which expressed it, that the work given Him to do, as far as concerned His Passion, was 'finished;' [b] and then, that in the words of Psalm xxxi. 5, in which He commended His Spirit into the Hands of the Father.[c] Attempts at comment could only weaken the solemn thoughts which the words awaken. Yet some points should be noted for our teaching. His last cry 'with a loud voice' was not like that of one dying. St. Mark notes that this made such deep impression on the Centurion.[d] Christ encountered Death, not as conquered, but as the Conqueror. And with this agrees the peculiar language of

ᵇ St. John

ᶜ St. Luke

ᵈ St. Mark xv. 39

St. John, that He 'bowed the Head, and gave up the Spirit.'

Nor should we fail to mark the peculiarities of His last Utterance. The ' My God' of the fourth Utterance had again passed into the 'Father' of conscious fellowship. That in dying—or rather meeting and overcoming Death —He chose and adapted these words, is matter for deepest thankfulness to the Church. They have been the last words of a Polycarp, a Bernard, Huss, Luther, and Melanchthon. And in 'the Spirit' which He had committed to God did He now descend into Hades, 'and preached unto the spirits in prison.'[a] But [a] 1 Pet. iii. 18, 19 behind this great mystery have closed the two-leaved gates of brass, which only the Hand of the Conqueror could burst open.

And now a shudder ran through Nature, as its Sun had set. We follow the rapid outlines of the Evangelic narrative. As the first token, it records the rending of the Temple-Veil in two from the top downward to the bottom; as the second, the quaking of the earth, the rending of the rocks and the opening of the graves. Although most writers have regarded this as indicating the strictly chronological succession, there is nothing in the text to bind us to such a conclusion. Thus, while the rending of the Veil is recorded first, as being the most significant token to Israel, it may have been connected with the earthquake, although this alone might scarcely account for the tearing of so heavy a Veil from the top to the bottom. Even the latter circumstance has its significance. That some great catastrophe, betokening the impending destruction of the Temple, had occurred in the Sanctuary about this very time, is confirmed by not less than four mutually independent testimonies: those of Tacitus, of Josephus, of the Talmud, and of earliest Christian tradition. The most important of these are, of course, the Talmud and Josephus. The latter speaks of the mysterious extinction of the middle and chief light in the Golden Candlestick, forty years before the destruction of the Temple ; and both he and the Talmud refer to a supernatural opening by themselves of the great Temple-gates that had been previously closed, which was regarded as a portent of the coming destruction of the Temple. We can scarcely doubt that some historical fact must underlie so widespread a tradition, and we cannot help feeling that it may be a distorted version of the occurrence of the rending of the Temple-Veil (or of its report) at the Crucifixion of Christ.

But even if the rending of the Temple-Veil had commenced with the earthquake, and, according to the Gospel to the Hebrews, with the breaking of the great lintel over the entrance, it could not be wholly accounted for in this manner. According to Jewish tradition, there were indeed two Veils before the entrance to the Most Holy Place. These were so heavy, that, in the exaggerated language of the time, it needed 300 priests to manipulate each. If the Veil was at all such as is described in the Talmud, it could not have been rent in twain by a mere earthquake or the fall of the lintel, although its composition in squares fastened together might explain how the rent might be as described in the Gospel.

As we compute, it may just have been the time when, at the Evening-Sacrifice, the officiating Priesthood entered the Holy Place, either to burn the incense or to do other sacred service there. To see before them the Veil of the Holy Place rent from top to bottom—that beyond it they could scarcely have seen—and hanging in two parts from its fastenings above and at the side, was indeed a terrible portent, which would soon become generally known, and must, in some form or other, have been preserved in tradition. And they all must have understood that it meant that God's Own Hand had rent the Veil, and for ever deserted and thrown open that Most Holy Place where He had so long dwelt in the mysterious gloom, only lit up once a year by the glow of the censer of him who made atonement for the sins of the people.

Other tokens were not wanting. In the earthquake the rocks were rent, and their tombs opened. This, as Christ descended into Hades. And when He ascended on the third day, it was with victorious saints who had left those open graves. To many in the Holy City on that ever-memorable first day, and in the week that followed, ap-peared the bodies of many of those saints who had fallen on sleep in the hope of that which had now become reality.

But on those who stood under the Cross, and near it, did all that was witnessed make the most lasting impres-sion. Among them we specially mark the Centurion under whose command the soldiers had been. Many a scene of horror must he have witnessed, but none like this. Only one conclusion could force itself on his mind. It was that which, we cannot doubt, had made its impression on his heart and conscience. Jesus was not what the Jews, His infuriated enemies, had described Him. He was what He professed to be, what His bearing on the Cross and His Death attested Him to be: 'righteous,' and hence, 'the Son of God.' From this there was only a step to personal allegiance to Him, and we may possibly owe to the Cen-turion some of those details which St. Luke alone has preserved.

The brief spring-day was verging towards the 'evening of the Sabbath.' In general, the law ordered that the body of a criminal should not be left hanging unburied over night.[a] Perhaps in ordinary circumstances

the Jews might not have appealed so confidently to Pilate as actually to ask him to shorten the sufferings of those on the Cross, since the punishment of crucifixion often lasted not only for hours but days, ere death ensued. But here was a special occasion. The Sabbath about to open was a 'high-day'—it was both a Sabbath and the second Paschal Day, which was regarded as in every respect equally sacred with the first—nay, more so, since the so-called Wavesheaf was then offered to the Lord. And what the Jews now proposed to Pilate was, indeed, a shortening, but not in any sense a mitigation, of the punishment. Sometimes there was added to the punishment of crucifixion that of breaking the bones (crurifragium) by means of a club or hammer. This would not itself bring death, but the breaking of the bones was always followed by a coup de grâce, by sword, lance, or stroke, which immediately put an end to what remained of life. Thus the 'breaking of the bones' was a sort of increase of punishment, by way of compensation for its shortening by the final stroke that followed.

St. John alone records how Pilate acceded to the Jewish demand, and gave directions for the *crurifragium*, and permission for the after-removal of the dead bodies, which otherwise might have been left to hang, till putrescence or birds of prey had destroyed them. But St. John also tells us what he evidently regards as so great a prodigy that he specially vouches for it, pledging his own veracity as an eyewitness, and grounding on it an appeal to the faith of those to whom his Gospel is addressed. It is, that certain 'things came to pass [not as in our A.V., 'were done'] that the Scripture should be fulfilled,' or, to put it otherwise, by which the Scripture was fulfilled. These things were two, to which a third phenomenon, not less remarkable, must be added. For, first, when the soldiers had broken the bones of the two malefactors, and then came to the Cross of Jesus, they found that He was dead already, and so 'a bone of Him' was 'not broken.' Had it been otherwise, the Scripture concerning the Paschal Lamb,[a] as well as that concerning the Righteous Suffering Servant of Jehovah,[b] would not have been accomplished. And this outward fact served as the finger to point to the predictions which were fulfilled in Him.

[a] Ex. xii. 46; Numb. ix. 12
[b] Ps. xxxiv. 20

Not less remarkable is the second fact. If, on the Cross of Christ, these two fundamental ideas in the prophetic description of the work of the Messiah had been set forth: the fulfilment of the Paschal Sacrifice, which, as that of the Covenant, underlay all sacrifices, and the fulfilment of the ideal of the Righteous Servant of God, suffering in a world that hated God, and yet proclaiming and realising His Kingdom, a third truth remained to be exhibited. This had been indicated in the prophecies of Zechariah,[c] which foretold how, in the day of Israel's final deliverance and national conversion, God would pour out the spirit of grace and of supplication, and as

[c] Zech. xii. 10

'they shall look on Him Whom they pierced,' the spirit of true repentance would be granted them, alike nationally and individually. The application of this to Christ is the more striking, that even the Talmud refers the prophecy to the Messiah. And as these two things really applied to Christ, alike in His rejection and in His future return,[a] so did the strange historical occurrence at His Crucifixion once more point to it as the fulfilment of Scripture prophecy. For although the soldiers, on finding Jesus dead, broke not one of His Bones, yet, as it was necessary to make sure of His Death, one of them with a lance 'pierced His Side,' with a wound so deep, that Thomas might afterwards have thrust his hand into His Side.[b]

a Rev. i. 7

b St. John xx. 27

And with these two, as fulfilling Holy Scripture, yet a third phenomenon was associated, symbolic of both. As the soldier pierced the Side of the Dead Christ, 'forthwith came thereout Blood and Water.' It has been thought by some, that there was physical cause for this—that Christ had literally died of a broken heart. In such case, the lesson would be that reproach had broken His Heart.[c] But we can scarcely believe that St. John could have wished to convey this without clearly setting it forth. We rather believe that to St. John, as to most of us, the significance of the fact lay in this, that out of the Body of One dead had flowed Blood and Water—that corruption had not fastened on Him. To the symbolic bearing of the flowing of Water and Blood from His pierced Side, on which the Evangelist dwells in his Epistle,[d] and to its eternal expression in the symbolism of the two Sacraments, we can only point the thoughtful Christian.

c Ps. lxix. 20

d 1 John v. 6

Yet one other scene remains to be recorded. Whether before, or, more probably, after the Jewish deputation to the Roman Governor, another and a strange application came to Pilate. It was from one apparently well known, a man not only of wealth and standing,[e] but who was known as a just and a good man.[f] Joseph of Arimathæa was a Sanhedrist, but he had not consented either to the counsel or the deed of his col-

e St. Matthew

f St. Luke

leagues. It must have been generally known that he was one of those 'which waited for the Kingdom of God.' But he had advanced beyond what that expression implies. Although secretly, for fear of the Jews,[a] he was a disciple of Jesus. It is in strange contrast to this 'fear,' that St. Mark tells us that, 'having dared,' 'he went in unto Pilate and asked for the Body of Jesus.' No longer a secret disciple, but bold in the avowal of his reverent love, he would show to the Dead Body of his Master all veneration. It was Friday afternoon, and the Sabbath was drawing near. No time therefore was to be lost, if due honour were to be paid to the Sacred Body. Pilate gave it to Joseph of Arimathæa. Such was within his power, and a favour not unfrequently accorded in like circumstances. But two things must have powerfully impressed the Roman Governor, and deepened his former thoughts about Jesus: first, that the death on the Cross had taken place so rapidly, a circumstance on which he personally questioned the Centurion,[b] and then the bold appearance and request of such a man as Joseph of Arimathæa. Or did the Centurion express to the Governor also some such feeling as that which had found utterance under the Cross in the words: 'Truly this Man was the Son of God'?

[a] St. John

[b] St. Mark

The proximity of the holy Sabbath, and the consequent need of haste, may have suggested or determined the proposal of Joseph to lay the Body of Jesus in his own new tomb, wherein no one had yet been laid.[c] These rock-hewn sepulchres, and the mode of laying the dead in them, have been already fully described in connection with the burying of Lazarus. We may therefore wholly surrender ourselves to the sacred thoughts that gather around us. The Cross was lowered and laid on the ground; the nails drawn out, and the ropes unloosed. Joseph, with those who attended him, 'wrapped' the Sacred Body 'in a clean linen cloth,' and rapidly carried It to the rock-hewn tomb in the garden close by. Such a tomb or cave had niches where the dead were laid. It will be remembered, that at the entrance to 'the

[c] St. Luke

tomb'—and within 'the rock'—there was 'a court,' nine
feet square, where ordinarily the bier was deposited, and
its bearers gathered to do the last offices for the Dead.
Thither we suppose Joseph to have carried the Sacred
Body, and then the last scene to have taken place. For
now another, kindred to Joseph in spirit, history, and
position, had come. We remember how at the first
Nicodemus had, from fear of detection, come to Jesus by
night, and with what bated breath he had pleaded with
his colleagues not so much the cause of Christ, as on His
behalf that of law and justice.[a] He now came,
bringing 'a roll' of myrrh and aloes, in the
fragrant mixture well known to the Jews for purposes of
anointing or burying.

a St. John
vii. 50

It was in 'the court' of the tomb that the hasty em-
balmment—if such it may be called—took place. None
of Christ's former disciples seem to have taken part in the
burying. Only a few faithful ones,[b] notably
among them Mary Magdalene and the other
Mary, the mother of Joses, stood over against the tomb,
watching at some distance where and how the Body of
Jesus was laid. It would scarcely have been in accordance
with Jewish manners, if these women had mingled more
closely with the two Sanhedrists and their attendants.
From where they stood they could only have had a dim
view of what passed within the court, and this may explain
how, on their return, they 'prepared spices and ointments'[c] for the more full honours which they
hoped to pay the Dead after the Sabbath was
past. For it is of the greatest importance to remember
that haste characterised all that was done. It seems as if
the 'clean linen cloth' in which the Body had been
wrapped, was now torn into 'cloths' or swathes, into
which the Body, limb by limb, was now 'bound,' no doubt
between layers of myrrh and aloes, the Head being wrapped
in a napkin. And so they laid Him to rest in the niche
of the rock-hewn new tomb. And as they went out, they
rolled, as was the custom, a 'great stone' to close the entrance to the tomb, probably leaning against it for support,

b St. Luke

c St. Luke

as was the practice, a smaller stone. It would be where the one stone was laid against the other, that on the next day, Sabbath though it was, the Jewish authorities would have affixed the seal, so that the slightest disturbance might become apparent.

. . . . . .

' It was probably about the same time, that a noisy throng prepared to follow delegates from the Sanhedrin to the ceremony of cutting the Passover-sheaf. The Law had it, " he shall bring a sheaf [literally, the Omer] with the first-fruits of your harvest, unto the priest ; and he shall wave the Omer before Jehovah, to be accepted for you." This Passover-sheaf was reaped in public the evening before it was offered, and it was to witness this ceremony that the crowd had gathered around the elders. . . . But as this festive procession started amidst loud demonstrations, a small band of mourners turned from having laid their dead Master in His resting-place. . . . And yet, not in the Temple, nor by the priest, but in the silence of that garden-tomb, was the first Omer of the new Paschal flour to be waved before the Lord.' [1]

. . . . .

' Now on the morrow, which is after the preparation [the Friday], the chief priests and the Pharisees were gathered together unto Pilate, saying, Sir, we remember that that deceiver said, while He was yet alive, After three days I rise again. Command, therefore, that the sepulchre be made sure until the third day, lest haply His disciples come and steal Him away, and say unto the people, He is risen from the dead : so the last error shall be worse than the first. Pilate said unto them, Take a guard, go your way, make it as sure as ye can. So they went, and made the sepulchre sure, sealing the stone, the guard being with them.'

[1] See ' The Temple and its Services,' pp. 221–224.

CHAPTER LXXXVI.

ON THE RESURRECTION OF CHRIST FROM THE DEAD.

THE history of the Life of Christ upon earth closes with a Miracle as great as that of its inception. It may be said that the one casts light upon the other. If He was what the Gospels represent Him, He must have been born of a pure Virgin, without sin, and He must have risen from the Dead. If the story of His Birth be true, we can believe that of His Resurrection; if that of His Resurrection be true, we can believe that of His Birth. In the nature of things, the latter was incapable of strict historical proofs; and in the nature of things, His Resurrection demanded and was capable of the fullest historical evidence. If such exists, the keystone is given to the arch; the miraculous Birth becomes almost a necessary postulate, and Jesus is the Christ in the full sense of the Gospels. And yet we mark, as another parallel point between the account of the miraculous Birth and that of the Resurrection, the utter absence of details as regards these events themselves. If this circumstance may be taken as indirect evidence that they were not legendary, it also imposes on us the duty of observing the reverent silence so well-befitting the case, and of not intruding beyond the path which the Evangelic narrative has opened to us.

What thoughts concerning the Dead Christ filled the minds of Joseph of Arimathæa, of Nicodemus, and of the other disciples of Jesus, as well as of the Apostles and of the pious women? They believed Him to be dead, and they did not expect Him to rise again from the dead—at least in our accepted sense of it. Of this there is abundant evidence from the moment of His Death: in the burial-spices brought by Nicodemus, in those prepared by the women (both of which were intended as against corruption), in the sorrow of the women at the empty tomb, in their supposition that the Body had been removed, in the perplexity and bearing of the Apostles, in the doubts of so many, and indeed in the express statement, 'For as yet they knew not the Scripture, that He must rise again from the dead.'[a] And the notice in St. Matthew's Gospel,[b] that the Sanhedrists had taken precautions against His Body being stolen, so as to give the appearance of fulfilment to His prediction that He would rise again after three days—that, therefore, they knew of such a prediction, and took it in the literal sense —would give only more emphasis to the opposite bearing of the disciples and their manifest non-expectancy of a literal Resurrection. What the disciples expected, perhaps wished, was not Christ's return in glorified corporeity, but His Second Coming in glory into His Kingdom.

But if they regarded Him as really dead and not to rise again in the literal sense, this had evidently no practical effect, not only on their former feelings towards Him, but even on their faith in Him as the promised Messiah. This appears from the conduct of Joseph and Nicodemus, from the language of the women, and from the whole bearing of the Apostles and disciples. All this must have been very different, if they had regarded the Death of Christ, even on the Cross, as having given the lie to His Messianic claims. The fact of the Resurrection itself would be quite foreign to Jewish ideas, which embraced the continuance of the soul after death and the final resurrection of the body, but not a state of spiritual corporeity, far less under conditions such as those described in the Gospels. Clearly, the Apostles had not learned the Resurrection of Christ either from the Scriptures—and this proves that the narrative of it was not intended as a fulfilment of previous expectancy —nor yet from the predictions of Christ to that effect; although without the one, and especially without the other, the empty grave would scarcely have wrought in them the assured conviction of the Resurrection.

Hence, the question to be faced is this: Considering their previous state of mind and the absence of any motive, how are we to account for the change of mind on the part of the disciples in regard to the Resurrection? There can at least be no question that they came to believe, and with

a St. John xx. 9
b St. Matt. xxvii. 62-66

the most absolute certitude, in the Resurrection as an historical fact; nor yet, that it formed the basis and substance of all their preaching of the Kingdom; nor yet, that St. Paul, up to his conversion a bitter enemy of Christ, was fully persuaded of it; nor—to go a step back —that Jesus Himself expected it. Indeed, the world would not have been converted to a dead Jewish Christ, however His intimate disciples might have continued to love His memory. But they preached everywhere, first and foremost, the Resurrection from the dead. In the language of St. Paul: 'If Christ hath not been raised, then is our preaching vain, your faith also is vain. Yea, and we are found false witnesses of God . . . ye are yet in your sins.'[a] We must here dismiss what probably underlies the chief objection to the Resurrection : its miraculous character. The objection to Miracles, as such, proceeds on that false Supranaturalism, which traces a miracle to the immediate *fiat* of the Almighty without any intervening links ; and, as already shown, it involves a vicious *petitio principii*. But, after all, the Miraculous is only the to us unprecedented and uncognisable—a very narrow basis on which to refuse historical investigation. And the historian has to account for the undoubted fact, that the Resurrection was the fundamental personal conviction of the Apostles and disciples, the basis of their preaching, and the final support of their martyrdom.

[a] 1 Cor. xv. 14, 15, 17

CHAPTER LXXXVII.

'ON THE THIRD DAY HE ROSE AGAIN FROM THE DEAD; HE ASCENDED INTO HEAVEN.'

(St. Matt. xxviii. 1–10; St. Mark xvi. 1–11; St. Luke xxiv. 1–12; St. John xx. 1–18; St. Matt. xxviii. 11–15; St. Mark xvi. 12, 13; St. Luke xxiv. 13–35; 1 Cor. xv. 5; St. Mark xvi. 14; St. Luke xxiv. 36–43; St. John xx. 19–25; 26–29; St. Matt. xxviii. 16; St. John xxi. 1–24; St. Matt. xxviii. 17–20; St. Mark xvi. 15–18; 1 Cor. xv. 6; St. Luke xxiv. 44–53; St. Mark xvi. 19, 20; Acts i. 3–12.)

GREY dawn was streaking the sky, when they who had so lovingly watched Him to His Burying were making their way to the rock-hewn Tomb in the Garden.

The difference, if such it may be called, in the recorded names of the women who at early morn went to the Tomb, scarcely requires elaborate discussion. It may have been that there were two parties, starting from different places to meet at the Tomb, and that this also accounts for the slight difference in the details of what they saw and heard at the Grave. At any rate, the mention of the two Maries [a St. Luke xxiv. 10] and Joanna is supplemented in St. Luke[a] by that of 'the other women with them,' while, if [b St. John xx. 1] St. John speaks only of Mary Magdalene,[b] her report to Peter and John: 'We know not where they have laid Him,' implies that she had not gone alone to the Tomb. It was the first day of the week—according to Jewish reckoning the third day from His Death. The narrative leaves the impression that the Sabbath's rest had delayed their visit to the Tomb; but it is at least a curious coincidence that the relatives and friends of the deceased were in the habit of going to the grave up to the third day (when presumably corruption was supposed to begin) so as to make sure that those laid there were really dead.

1. Whether or not there were two groups of women who started from different places to meet at the Tomb, the most prominent figure among them was Mary Magdalene—as prominent among the pious women as Peter was among the Apostles. She seems to have first reached the Grave,

and, seeing the great stone that had covered its entrance rolled away, hastily judged that the Body of the Lord had been removed. Without waiting for further inquiry, she ran back to inform Peter and John of the fact. The Evangelist here explains that there had been a great earthquake, and that the Angel of the Lord, to human sight as lightning and in brilliant white garment, had rolled back the stone and sat upon it, when the guard, affrighted by what they heard and saw, and especially by the look and attitude of heavenly power in the Angel, had been seized with mortal faintness. Remembering the events connected with the Crucifixion, which had no doubt been talked about among the soldiery, and bearing in mind the impression of such a sight on such minds, we could readily understand the effect on the two sentries who that long night had kept guard over the Tomb. The event itself (we mean: as regards the rolling away of the stone), we suppose to have taken place after the Resurrection of Christ, in the early dawn, while the holy women were on their way to the Tomb. The earthquake cannot have been one in the ordinary sense, but a shaking of the place, when the Lord of Life burst the gates of Hades to re-tenant His Glorified Body, and the lightning-like Angel descended from heaven to roll away the stone. But there is a sublime irony in the contrast between man's elaborate precautions and the ease with which the Divine Hand can sweep them aside, and which, as throughout the history of the Christ and of His Church, recalls the prophetic declaration: ' He that sitteth in the heavens shall laugh at them.'

While the Magdalene hastened, probably by another road, to the abode of Peter and John, the other women also had reached the Tomb, either in one party, or it may be, in two companies. They had wondered and feared how they could accomplish their pious purpose—for who would roll away the stone for them ? But, as so often, the difficulty apprehended no longer existed. Perhaps they thought that the now absent Mary Magdalene had obtained help for this. At any rate, they entered the vestibule of the Sepulchre. Here the appearance of the Angel filled them with fear. But the heavenly Messenger bade them dismiss apprehension; he told them that Christ was not there, nor yet any longer dead, but risen, as indeed He had foretold in Galilee to His disciples; finally, he bade them hasten with the announcement to the disciples, and with this message, that as Christ had directed them before they were to meet Him in Galilee.

The main reason, and that which explains the otherwise strange, almost exclusive, prominence given at such a moment to the direction to meet Christ in Galilee, has already been indicated in a previous chapter. With the scattering of the Eleven in Gethsemane on the night of Christ's betrayal, the Apostolic College was temporarily broken up. They continued, indeed, still to meet together as individual disciples, but the bond of the Apostolate was, for the moment, dissolved. And the Apostolic circle was to be re-formed, and the Apostolic Commission renewed and enlarged, in Galilee; not, indeed, by its Lake, where only seven of the Eleven seem to have been present,[a] but on the mountain where He had directed them to meet Him.[b] Thus was the end to be like the beginning. Where He had first called and directed them for their work, there would He again call them, give fullest directions, and bestow new and amplest powers. His appearances in Jerusalem were intended to prepare them for all this, to assure them completely of the fact of His Resurrection—the full teaching of which would be given in Galilee. And when the women, perplexed and scarcely conscious, obeyed the command to go in and examine for themselves the now empty niche in the Tomb, they saw two Angels—probably as the Magdalene afterwards saw them—one at the head, the other at the feet, where the Body of Jesus had lain. They waited no longer, but hastened, without speaking to any one, to carry to the disciples the tidings of which they could not even yet grasp the full import.

2. Whatever unclearness of detail may rest on the narratives of the Synoptists, owing to their great compression, all is distinct when we follow the steps of the

a St. John xxi. 2
b St. Matt. xxviii. 16

Magdalene, as these are traced in the fourth Gospel. Hastening from the Tomb, she ran to the lodging of Peter and to that of John—the repetition of the preposition ' to ' probably marking that the two occupied different, although perhaps closely adjoining, quarters. Her startling tidings induced them to go at once—' and they went towards the Sepulchre.' ' But they began to run, the two together '— probably so soon as they were outside the town and near ' the Garden.' John, as the younger, outran Peter. Reaching the Sepulchre first, and stooping down, ' he seeth ' the linen clothes, but, from his position, not the napkin which lay apart by itself. If reverence and awe prevented John from entering the Sepulchre, his impulsive companion, who arrived immediately after him, thought of nothing else than the immediate and full clearing up of the mystery. As he entered the Sepulchre, he ' steadfastly (intently) beholds ' in one place the linen swathes that had bound the Sacred Limbs, and in another the napkin that had been about His Head. There was no sign of haste, but all was orderly, leaving the impression of One Who had leisurely divested Himself of what no longer befitted Him. Soon ' the other disciple ' followed Peter. The effect of what he saw was that he now believed in his heart that the Master was risen—for till then they had not yet derived from Holy Scripture the knowledge that He must rise again. It was not the belief previously derived from Scripture, that the Christ was to rise from the Dead, which led to expectancy of it, but the evidence that He had risen which led them to the knowledge of what Scripture taught on the subject.

3. Yet whatever light had risen in the inmost sanctuary of John's heart, he spake not his thoughts to the Magdalene, whether she had reached the Sepulchre ere the two left it, or met them by the way. The two Apostles returned to their home, either feeling that nothing more could be learned at the Tomb, or to wait for further teaching and guidance. Or it might even have been partly due to a desire not to draw needless attention to the empty Tomb. But the love of the Magdalene could not rest satis-

fied, while doubt hung over the fate of His Sacred Body.
It must be remembered that she knew only of the empty
Tomb. For a time she gave way to the agony of her sorrow; then, as she wiped away her tears, she stooped to
take one more look into the Tomb, which she thought
empty, when, as she 'intently gazed,' the Tomb seemed no
longer empty. At the head and feet, where the Sacred
Body had lain, were seated two Angels in white. Their
question, so deeply true from their knowledge that Christ
had risen: 'Woman, why weepest thou?' seems to have
come upon the Magdalene with such overpowering suddenness, that, without being able to realise who it was that
had asked it, she spake, bent only on obtaining the information she sought: 'Because they have taken away my
Lord, and I know not where they have laid Him.'

But already, as she spake, she became conscious of
another Presence close to her. Quickly turning round,
'she gazed' on One Whom she recognised not, but regarded as the gardener, from His presence there and from
His question: 'Woman, why weepest thou? Whom
seekest thou?' The hope that she might now learn what
she sought, gave to her words intensity and pathos. If
the supposed gardener had borne to another place the
Sacred Body, she would take It away, if she only knew
where It was laid. This depth and agony of love, which
made the Magdalene forget even the restraints of a Jewish
woman's intercourse with a stranger, was the key that
opened the Lips of Jesus. A moment's pause, and He
spake her name in those well-remembered accents, that had
first unbound her from sevenfold demoniac power and
called her into a new life. It was as another unbinding,
another call into a new life. She had not known His
appearance, just as the others did not know Him at first,
so unlike, and yet so like, was the glorified Body to that
which they had known. But she could not mistake the
Voice when It spake her name.

Perhaps we may here be allowed to pause, and, from
the non-recognition of the Risen Lord till He spoke, ask
this question: With what body shall we rise? Like or

unlike the past? Assuredly, most like. Our bodies will then be true; for the soul will body itself forth according to its past history—not only impress itself, as now on the features, but express itself, so that a man may be known by what he is, and as what he is. And the Christ also must have borne in His glorified Body all that He was, all that even His most intimate disciples had not known or understood while He was with them, and which they even now failed at first to recognise, but knew at once when He spake to them.

It was precisely this which now prompted the action of the Magdalene—prompted also, and explains, the answer of the Lord. As in her name she recognised His Name, the rush of old feeling came over her, and with the familiar ' Rabboni !'—my Master—she would fain have grasped Him. Probably she was not at the moment distinctly conscious of the impulse which prompted her action. But whatever it may have been there was but one answer: ' Touch Me not, for I am not yet ascended to the Father.' Not the Jesus appearing from heaven—for He had not yet ascended to the Father ; not the former intercourse, not the former homage and worship. There was yet a future of completion before Him in the Ascension, of which Mary knew not. Let her rather go and tell His ' brethren' of the Ascension. So would she best and most truly tell them that she had seen Him ; so also would they best learn how the Resurrection linked the past of His Work of love for them to the future : ' I ascend unto My Father and, your Father, and to My God, and your God.'

4. Yet another scene on that Easter morning does St. Matthew relate, in explanation of how the well-known Jewish calumny had arisen that the disciples had stolen away the Body of Jesus. He tells how the guard had reported to the chief priests what had happened, and how they in turn had bribed the guard to spread this rumour, at the same time promising that, if the fictitious account of their having slept while the disciples robbed the Sepulchre should reach Pilate, they would intercede on their behalf. Whatever else may be said, we know that from the time

of *Justin Martyr* this has been the Jewish explanation. Of late, however, it has among thoughtful Jewish writers given place to the so-called ' Vision-hypothesis.'

5. It was the early afternoon of that spring-day, perhaps soon after the early meal, when two men from that circle of disciples left the City. Their narrative affords deeply interesting glimpses into the circle of the Church in those first days. The impression conveyed to us is of utter bewilderment, in which only some things stood out unshaken and firm: love to the Person of Jesus ; love among the brethren ; mutual confidence and fellowship ; together with a dim hope of something yet to come—if not Christ in His Kingdom, yet some manifestation of, or approach to it.

These two men had on that very day been in communication with Peter and John. ' The women ' had come to tell of the empty Tomb and of their vision of Angels, who said that He was alive. But as yet the Apostles had no explanation to offer. Peter and John had gone to see for themselves. They had brought back confirmation of the report that the Tomb was empty, but they had seen neither Angels nor Him Whom they were said to have declared alive. And, although the two had evidently left the circle of the disciples, if not Jerusalem, before the Magdalene came, yet we know that even her account did not
ᵃ St. Mark carry conviction to the minds of those that
xvi. 11 heard it.ᵃ

Of the two, who on that early spring afternoon left the City in company, we know that one bore the name of Cleopas. The other, unnamed, has for that very reason, and because the narrative of that work bears in its vividness the character of personal recollection, been identified with St. Luke himself. If so, then, as has been finely remarked,[1] each of the Gospels would, like a picture, bear in some dim corner the indication of its author : the first, that of 'the publican ;' that by St. Mark, that of the young man who in the night of the Betrayal had fled from his captors ; that of St. Luke, in the companion of

[1] By *Godet*.

Cleopas; and that of St. John, in the disciple whom Jesus loved. Uncertainty, almost equal to that about the second traveller to Emmaus, rests on the identification of that place. But such great probability attaches, if not to the exact spot, yet to the locality, or rather the valley, that we may in imagination follow the two companions on their road.

We leave the City by the Western Gate. A rapid progress for about twenty-five minutes, and we have reached the edge of the plateau. Other twenty-five or thirty minutes—passing here and there country-houses—and we pause to look back on the wide prospect far as Bethlehem. A short quarter of an hour more, and we have left the well-paved Roman road and are heading up a lovely valley. The path gently climbs in a north-westerly direction, with the height on which Emmaus stands prominently before us. About equidistant are, on the right Lifta, on the left Kolonieh. The roads from these two, describing almost a semicircle (the one to the north-west, the other to the north-east), meet about a quarter of a mile to the south of Emmaus. Along the course of the stream, which low in the valley is crossed by a bridge, are scented orange- and lemon-gardens, olive-groves, fruit trees, pleasant enclosures, bright dwellings, and on the height lovely Emmaus. A sweet spot to which to wander on that spring afternoon; a most suitable place where to meet such companionship, and to find such teaching, as on that Easter Day.

It may have been where the two roads from Lifta and Kolonieh meet, that the mysterious Stranger, Whom they knew not, their eyes being 'holden,' joined the two friends. Yet all these six or seven miles their converse had been of Him, and even now their faces bore the marks of sadness on account of those events of which they had been speaking—disappointed hopes, all the more bitter for the perplexing tidings about the empty Tomb and the absent Body of the Christ. To the question of the Stranger about the topics of a conversation which had so visibly affected them, they replied in language which shows that they were so absorbed by it themselves, as scarcely to understand how even a festive pilgrim and stranger in Jerusalem could have failed to know it, or to perceive its supreme importance. Yet, strangely unsympathetic as from His question He might seem, there was that in His Appearance which unlocked their inmost hearts. They told Him their thoughts about this Jesus; how He had showed Himself a Prophet mighty in deed and word before God and all the people; then, how their rulers had crucified Him; and lastly, how fresh perplexity had come to them from the tidings which the women had brought, and which Peter and John had so far confirmed, but were unable to explain. Their words were almost childlike in their simplicity, and with a craving for guidance and comfort that goes straight to the heart. To such souls it was that the Risen Saviour would give His first teaching. The very rebuke with which He opened it must have brought its comfort. Did not the Scriptures with one voice teach this twofold truth about the Messiah, that He was to suffer and to enter into His glory? Then why wonder—why not rather expect, that He had suffered, and that Angels had proclaimed Him alive again?

He spake it, and fresh hope sprang up in their hearts, new thoughts rose in their minds. Their eager gaze was fastened on Him as He now opened up, one by one, the Scriptures, from Moses and all the prophets, and in each well-remembered passage interpreted to them the things concerning Himself. All too quickly fled the moments. The brief space was traversed, and the Stranger seemed about to pass on from Emmaus—not feigning it, but really: for the Christ will only abide with us if our longing and loving constrain Him. But they could not part with Him. 'They constrained Him.' Love made them ingenious. It was toward evening; the day was far spent; He must even abide with them.

The Master allowed Himself to be constrained. He went in to be their guest, as they thought, for the night. The evening-meal was spread. He sat down with them to the frugal board. And now He was no longer the Stranger; He was the Master. No one asked or questioned, as He took the bread and spake the words of blessing, then breaking, gave it to them. But that moment it was as if an unfelt hand had been taken from their eyelids, as if suddenly the film had been cleared from their sight. And as they knew Him, He vanished from their view—for that which He had come to do had been done.

6. That same afternoon, in circumstances and manner to us unknown, the Lord had appeared to Peter.[a]

a 1 Cor. xv. 5

We may perhaps suggest that it was after His manifestation at Emmaus. This would complete the cycle of mercy: first, to the loving sorrow of the woman; next, to the loving perplexity of the disciples; then, to the anxious heart of the stricken Peter—last, in the circle of the Apostles, which was again drawing together around the assured fact of His Resurrection.

7. These two in Emmaus could not have kept the good tidings to themselves. Even if they had not remembered the sorrow and perplexity in which they had left their fellow-disciples in Jerusalem that forenoon, they could not have remained in Emmaus, but must have gone to their brethren in the City. So they left the uneaten meal, and hastened back the road they had travelled with the now well-known Stranger.

They knew well the trysting-place where to find 'the Twelve'—nay, not the Twelve now, but 'the Eleven,' and even thus their circle was not complete, for, as already stated, it was broken up, and at least Thomas was not with the others on that Easter-Evening of the first 'Lord's Day.' But, as St. Luke is careful to inform us,[b] with them were the others who then associated with them.

b St. Luke xxiv. 33

When the two from Emmaus arrived, they found the little band as sheep sheltering within the fold from the storm. Whether because they apprehended persecution simply as disciples, or because the tidings of the empty Tomb which had reached the authorities would stir the fears of the Sanhedrists, special precautions had been taken. The outer and inner doors were shut, alike to conceal their gathering and to prevent surprise. But those assembled were now sure of at least one thing : Christ was risen. And when they from Emmaus told their wondrous story, the others could reply by relating how He had appeared, not only to the Magdalene, but also to Peter. And still they seem not yet to have understood His Resurrection ; to have regarded it as rather an Ascension to Heaven, from which He had made manifestation, than as the reappearance of His real, though glorified Corporeity.

ᵃ St. Mark xvi. 14 They were sitting at meat ᵃ—if we may infer from the notice of St. Mark, and from what happened immediately afterwards, discussing, not without considerable doubt and misgiving, the real import of these appearances of Christ. That to the Magdalene seems to have been put aside—at least, it is not mentioned ; and even in regard to the others, they seem to have been considered, at any rate by some, rather as what we might call spectral appearances. But all at once He stood in the midst of them. The common salutation fell on their hearts at first with terror rather than joy. They had spoken of spectral appearances, and now they believed they were ' gazing' on ' a spirit.' This the Saviour first, and once for all, corrected, by the exhibition of the glorified marks of His Sacred Wounds, and by bidding them handle Him to convince themselves that His was a real Body, and what they saw not a disembodied spirit. The unbelief of doubt now gave place to the not daring to believe all that it meant for very gladness, and for wondering whether there could now be any longer fellowship or bond between this Risen Christ and them in their bodies. It was to remove this also, which was equally unbelief, that the Saviour now partook before them of their supper of broiled fish, thus holding with them true human fellowship as of old.

It was this lesson of His continuity—in the strictest sense—with the past, which was required in order that the Church might be, so to speak, reconstituted now in the Name, Power, and Spirit of the Risen One Who had lived and died. Once more He spake the ' Peace be unto you!'

and now it was to them not occasion of doubt or fear, but the well-known salutation of their old Lord and Master. It was followed by the re-gathering and constituting of the Church as that of Jesus Christ, the Risen One. ' As the Father has sent Me [in the past, for His Mission was completed], even so send I you [in the constant present, till His Coming again].' This marks the threefold relation of the Church to the Son, to the Father, and to the world, and her position in it. And so it was that He made it a very real commission when He breathed on them, not individually but as an assembly, and said : ' Take ye the Holy Ghost ; ' and this, manifestly not in the absolute sense, since the Holy Ghost was not yet given, but as the connecting link with, and the qualification for the authority bestowed on the Church.

It still remains to explain, so far as we can, these two points : in what this power of forgiving and retaining sins consists, and in what manner it resides in the Church. In regard to the former we must first inquire what idea it would convey to those to whom Christ spake the words. It has already been explained, that the power of ' loosing ' and ' binding ' referred to the legislative authority claimed by, and conceded to the Rabbinic College. In the true sense, therefore, this is rather administrative, disciplinary power, ' the power of the keys '—such as St. Paul would have had the Corinthian Church put in force—the power of admission and exclusion, of the authoritative declaration of the forgiveness of sins. And yet it is not, as is sometimes represented, ' absolution from sin,' which belongs only to God and to Christ as Head of the Church, but absolution of the sinner, which He has delegated to His Church : ' Whosoever sins ye forgive, they are forgiven.' These words also teach us that what the Rabbis claimed in virtue of their office, that the Lord bestowed on His Church in virtue of her receiving, and of the indwelling of the Holy Ghost.

In answering the second question proposed, we must bear in mind one important point. The power of ' binding ' and ' loosing ' had been primarily committed to the

Apostles,[a] and exercised by them in connection with the
Church.[b] On the other hand, that of forgiving
and retaining sins, in the sense explained, was
primarily bestowed on the Church, and exercised
by her through her representatives, the Apostles,
and those to whom they committed rule.[c] Although, therefore, the Lord on that night committed this power to His Church, it was in the person of
her representatives and rulers. The Apostles alone could
exercise legislative functions, but the Church has to the
end of time ' the power of the keys.'

[a] St. Matt.
xvi. 19;
xviii. 18
[b] Acts xv.
22, 23
[c] 1 Cor. v.
4, 5, 12, 13;
2 Cor. ii. 6, 10

8. There had been absent from the circle of disciples
on that Easter-Evening one of the Apostles, Thomas.
Even when told of the marvellous events at that gathering,
he refused to believe, unless he had personal and sensuous
evidence of the truth of the report. It can scarcely have
been that Thomas did not believe in the fact that Christ's
Body had quitted the Tomb, or that He had really appeared.
But he held fast by what we may term the spectral theory.

A quiet week had passed, during which—and this also
may be for our twofold learning—the Apostles excluded
not Thomas, nor yet Thomas withdrew from the Apostles.
Once more the day of days had come—the Octave of the
Feast. The disciples were again gathered, under circumstances precisely similar to those of Easter, but now
Thomas was also with them. Once more—and it is again
specially marked: ' the doors being shut '—the Risen
Saviour appeared in the midst of the disciples with the
well-known salutation. He now offered to Thomas the
demanded evidence; but it was no longer either needed or
sought. With a full rush of feeling he yielded himself to
the conviction, which, once formed, must immediately have
passed into act of adoration: ' My Lord and my God!'
We remember how, under similar circumstances, Nathanael
had been the first to utter fullest confession.[d]
We also remember the analogous reply of the
Saviour. As then, so now, He pointed to the higher: to
a faith which was not the outcome of sight, and therefore
limited and bounded by sight, whether of the senses or of

[d] St. John
i. 45-51

perception by the intellect. As one has remarked : 'This last and greatest of the Beatitudes is the peculiar heritage of the later Church'[1]—and thus most aptly comes as the consecration gift of that Church.

9. The next scene presented to us is once again by the Lake of Galilee. The manifestation to Thomas, and with it the restoration of unity in the Apostolic Circle, had originally concluded the Gospel of St. John.[a] But the report which had spread in the early Church, that the Disciple whom Jesus loved was not to die, led him to add to his Gospel, by way of Appendix, an account of the events with which this expectancy had connected itself.

a St. John xx. 30, 31

The history itself sparkles like a gem in its own peculiar setting. It is of green Galilee, and of the blue Lake, and recalls the early days and scenes of this history. As St. Matthew has it,[b] 'the eleven disciples went away into Galilee '—probably immediately after that Octave of the Easter. It can scarcely be doubted that they made known not only the fact of the Resurrection, but the trysting which the Risen One had given them— perhaps at that Mountain where He had spoken His first 'Sermon.' And so it was that 'some doubted,'[c] and that He afterwards appeared to the five hundred at once.[d] But on that morning there were by the Lake of Tiberias only seven of the disciples, and but five of them are named. They are those who most closely kept in company with Him—perhaps also they who lived nearest the Lake.

b St. Matt. xxviii. 16

c St. Matt. xxviii. 17

d 1 Cor. xv. 6

The scene is introduced by Peter's proposal to go a-fishing. It seems as if the old habits had come back to them with the old associations. Peter's companions naturally proposed to join him. All that still, clear night they were on the Lake, but caught nothing. Early morning was breaking when on the pebbly 'beach' there stood the Figure of One Whom they recognised not—nay, not even when He spake. Yet His Words were intended to bring them this knowledge. The direction to cast the net to the

[1] Canon *Westcott*.

right side of the ship brought them, as He had said, the haul for which they had toiled all night in vain. And more than this: such a multitude of fishes, that they were not able to draw up the net into the ship. This was enough for 'the disciple whom Jesus loved.' He whispered it to Peter: 'It is the Lord,' and Simon, only gathering about him his fisher's upper garment, cast himself into the sea. Yet even so, except to be sooner by the side of Christ, Peter seems to have gained nothing by his haste. The others, leaving the ship, and transferring themselves to a small boat, which must have been attached to it, followed, rowing the short distance of about one hundred yards, and dragging after them the net, weighted with the fishes.

They stepped on the beach, hallowed by His Presence, in silence, as if they had entered Church or Temple. They dared not even dispose of the netful of fishes which they had dragged on shore, until He directed them what to do. This only they noticed, that some unseen hand had prepared the morning-meal, which, when asked by the Master, they had admitted they had not of their own. And now Jesus directed them to bring the fish they had caught. When Peter dragged up the weighted net it was found full of great fishes, not less than a hundred and fifty-three in number. On the fire of coals there seems to have been only one fish, and beside it but one bread. To this meal He now bade them, for they seem still to have hung back in reverent awe, nor durst they ask Him Who He was, well knowing it was the Lord. This, as St. John notes, was the third appearance of Christ to the disciples as a body.

10. And still this morning of blessing was not ended. The simple meal was past, with all its significance of just sufficient provision for His Servants, and abundant supply in the unbroken net beside them. But some special teaching was needed, more even than that to Thomas, for him whose work was to be so prominent among the Apostles, whose love was so ardent, and yet in its very ardour so full of danger to himself. Had Peter not confessed, quite honestly, yet, as the event proved, mistakingly, that his

T T

love to Christ would endure even an ordeal that would disperse all the others ? ^a And had he not, almost immediately afterwards, and though prophetically warned of it, thrice denied his Lord ? Jesus had, indeed, since then appeared specially to Peter as the Risen One. But this threefold denial still stood, as it were, uncancelled before the other disciples, nay, before Peter himself. It was to this that the threefold question of the Risen Lord now referred. Turning to Peter, with pointed though most gentle allusion to the danger of self-confidence, He asked : 'Simon, son of Jona '—as it were with fullest reference to what he was naturally—' lovest thou Me more than these ? ' Peter understood it all. No longer with confidence in self, avoiding the former reference to the others, and even with marked choice of a different word to express his affection from that which the Saviour had used, he replied, appealing rather to his Lord's than to his own consciousness : ' Yea, Lord, Thou knowest that I love Thee.' And even here the answer of Christ is characteristic. It was to set him first the humblest work, that which needed most tender care and patience : ' Feed [provide with food] My Lambs.'

ª St. Matt. xxvi. 33 ; St. John xiii. 37

    Yet a second time came the same question, although now without the reference to the others, and with the same answer by Peter, the now varied and enlarged commission : ' Feed [shepherd] My Sheep.' Yet a third time did Jesus repeat the same question, now adopting in it the very word which Peter had used to express his affection. Peter was grieved at this threefold repetition. It recalled only too bitterly his threefold denial. And yet the Lord was not doubtful of Peter's love, for each time He followed up His question with a fresh Apostolic commission. But now that He put it for the third time, Peter would have the Lord send down the sounding-line quite into the lowest deep of his heart : ' Lord, Thou knowest all things—Thou perceivest that I love Thee ! ' And then the Saviour spake it : ' Feed [provide food for] My Sheep.' His Lambs, His Sheep, to be provided for, to be tended as such : only love can do such service.

Yes, and Peter did love the Lord Jesus. And Jesus saw it all—and how this love of the ardent temperament which had once made him rove at wild liberty, would give place to patient work of love, and be crowned with that martyrdom which, when the beloved disciple wrote, was already matter of the past. And the very manner of death by which he was to glorify God was indicated in the words of Jesus.

As He spake them, He joined the symbolic action to His ' Follow Me.' This command, and the encouragement of being in death literally made like Him—following Him— were Peter's best strength. He obeyed ; but as he turned to do so, he saw another following. As St. John himself puts it, it seems almost to convey that he had longed to share Peter's call, with all that it implied. For St. John speaks of himself as the disciple whom Jesus loved, and he reminds us that in that night of betrayal he had been specially a sharer with Peter, nay, had spoken what the other had silently asked of him. Was it impatience, was it a touch of the old Peter, or was it a simple inquiry of brotherly interest which prompted the question, as he pointed to John : ' Lord—and this man, what ? ' What- ever had been the motive, to him, as to us all, when, per- plexed about those who seem to follow Christ, we ask it— sometimes in bigoted narrowness, sometimes in ignorance, folly, or jealousy—is this the answer : ' What is that to thee ? follow thou Me.' For John also had his life-work for Christ. It was to ' tarry ' while He was coming—to tarry those many years in patient labour, while Christ was coming.

But what did it mean ? The saying went abroad among the brethren that John was not to die, but to tarry till Jesus came again to reign, when death would be swallowed up in victory. But Jesus had not so said, only : ' If I will that he tarry while I am coming.' What that ' Coming' was, Jesus had not said, and John knew not. So, then, there are things, and connected with His Coming, which Jesus means us not to know at present, and which we should be content to leave as He has left them.

11. Beyond this narrative we have only briefest notices:
by St. Paul, of Christ manifesting Himself to James, which
probably finally decided him for Christ, and of His manifestation to the five hundred at once; by St. Matthew, of
the Eleven meeting Him at the mountain, where He had
appointed them; by St. Luke, of the teaching in the
Scriptures during the forty days of communication between
the Risen Christ and the disciples.

But this twofold testimony comes to us from St.
Matthew and St. Mark, that then the worshipping disciples
were once more formed into the Apostolic Circle—Apostles
now of the Risen Christ. And this was the warrant of
their new commission: 'All power (authority) has been
given to Me in heaven and on earth.' And this was their
new commission: 'Go ye, therefore, and make disciples of
all the nations, baptising them into the Name of the Father,
and of the Son, and of the Holy Ghost.' And this was
their work: 'Teaching them to observe all things whatsoever I commanded you.' And this is His final and sure
promise: 'And lo, I am with you alway, even unto the
end of the world.'

12. We are once more in Jerusalem, whither He had
bidden them go to tarry for the fulfilment of the great
promise. The Pentecost was drawing nigh. And on that
last day—the day of His Ascension—He led them forth to
the well-remembered Bethany. From where He had made
His last triumphal Entry into Jerusalem before His Crucifixion, would He make His triumphal Entry visibly into
Heaven. Once more would they have asked Him about
that which seemed to them the final consummation—the
restoration of the Kingdom to Israel. But such questions
became them not. Theirs was to be work, not rest;
suffering, not triumph. The great promise before them
was of spiritual, not outward, power: of the Holy Ghost—
and their call not yet to reign with Him, but to bear
witness for Him. And as He so spake, He lifted His
Hands in blessing upon them, and, as He was visibly
taken up, a cloud received Him. And still they gazed,
with upturned faces, on that luminous cloud which had

received Him, and two Angels spake to them this last message from Him, that He should so come in like manner —as they had beheld Him going into Heaven.

Henceforth, neither doubting, ashamed, nor yet afraid, they 'were continually in the Temple, blessing God.' 'And they went forth and preached everywhere, the Lord working with them, and confirming the word by the signs that followed. Amen.'